Child ᴬⁿᵈ Adolescent
Psychopathology

SECOND
EDITION

Child and Adolescent Psychopathology

A CASEBOOK

Linda Wilmshurst

Elon University

Los Angeles | London | New Delhi
Singapore | Washington DC

For information:

 SAGE Publications, Inc.
2455 Teller Road
Thousand Oaks, California 91320
E-mail: order@sagepub.com

SAGE Publications Ltd.
1 Oliver's Yard
55 City Road
London EC1Y 1SP
United Kingdom

SAGE Publications India Pvt. Ltd.
B 1/I 1 Mohan Cooperative Industrial Area
Mathura Road, New Delhi 110 044
India

SAGE Publications Asia-Pacific Pte. Ltd.
33 Pekin Street #02-01
Far East Square
Singapore 048763

Printed in the United States of America.

Library of Congress Cataloging-in-Publication Data

Wilmshurst, Linda.
 Child and adolescent psychopathology : a casebook / Linda Wilmshurst. — 2nd ed.
    p. cm.
 Includes bibliographical references and index.
 ISBN 978-1-4129-8249-8 (pbk.)
   1. Child psychopathology—Case studies. 2. Adolescent psychopathology—Case studies. I. Title.
 RJ499.W46 2011

618.92'89—dc22   2010018742

This book is printed on acid-free paper.

10 11 12 13 14   10 9 8 7 6 5 4 3 2 1

Acquisitions Editor:	Christine Cardone
Editorial Assistant:	Sarita Sarak
Production Editor:	Karen Wiley
Copy Editor:	Brenda Weight
Typesetter:	C&M Digitals (P) Ltd.
Proofreader:	Penny Sippel
Indexer:	Jeanne Busemeyer
Cover Designer:	Gail Buschman
Marketing Manager:	Stephanie Adams

Contents

Preface

Tell me and I'll forget. Show me, and I may not remember. Involve me, and I'll understand.

—Native American Proverb

The major goal of this casebook is to provide the reader with an opportunity to gain deeper insight into the complexities of child and adolescent psychopathology.

A case study approach is used to *involve* the reader in the simulated practice of child psychopathology. As problems unfold, a dynamic illustration of a given child's problems can be observed during several different stages of development and from the perspective of different theoretical viewpoints. Within a developmental context, complex problems of child and adolescent adjustment become grounded in the realities of family and school experiences. Case studies presented in this text are especially relevant to the study of child and adolescent psychopathology, because all cases are based on actual clinical cases. Although the cases have been altered to maintain confidentiality, they continue to represent actual *living files,* and as such, provide a unique opportunity to capture the dynamics of child and adolescent psychopathology in virtual presentations of life as the children develop and their stories unfold before the reader's eyes.

Cases have been selected to include a breadth of childhood and adolescent psychopathology and are representative of the high rates of comorbidity demonstrated in this population. Each case presents an opportunity to practice and develop clinical skills in the assessment, diagnosis, and treatment of childhood disorders from a number of theoretical perspectives and at various levels of interest and expertise. The text is suitable for upper-level undergraduate students in its rich presentation of case materials that demonstrate applications of many of the core concepts in child psychopathology (e.g., how therapists from differing theoretical backgrounds would approach a given case). The text is suitable for graduate students in providing opportunities to practice and hone clinical skills across a breadth of clinical cases with opportunities for in-depth discussion and application in specialty areas of concentration: assessment, diagnosis, and treatment. The text can be a valuable resource for courses in child psychopathology, abnormal child psychology, developmental psychopathology, school psychology, behavior problems of childhood, child psychotherapy, child assessment, and case formulation in child psychopathology.

- Case studies provide diagnostic information at two levels. Case studies are presented to illustrate the dual nature of diagnosis in its emphasis on diagnosis as case formulation (an ongoing process of information gathering, problem solving, and hypothesis testing) and diagnosis as the formulation of an outcomes statement (the classification or conclusion).

- Case studies provide comprehensive assessment information. Case information is available from a variety of sources (case history, observations, psychometric assessment, raw data, clinical interviews) and developmental contexts (individual child, family, school, peers) to encourage students to develop skills in integrating information from diverse sources.
- Case studies provide opportunities to develop and practice skills in case formulation. A semistructured flexible format for case formulation is presented and demonstrated to emphasize how case formulation can apply to a wide variety of theoretical perspectives and developmental contexts.

Each case provides an opportunity to develop case formulations that address developmental issues relative to the case and to evaluate outcomes relative to expectations.

- Case studies provide information on current research findings and conceptual issues. Questions posed at the end of each case will challenge the reader to integrate information concerning conceptual issues and/or research findings with material presented in each case.
- Case studies provide information concerning evidence-based treatments. Each case is accompanied by a discussion of current *issues in treatment*.

However, advanced students can also have the challenging opportunity of forging new directions in integrating information from effectiveness studies in the development of individual intervention plans and a "case-based" pragmatic approach to treatment (Fishman, 2000).

- Case studies provide opportunities to discuss issues in classification from a variety of conceptual frameworks and different systems of service delivery.
- Case studies demonstrate unique issues in the classification of childhood disorders.

Research has demonstrated that insecure attachment and social skills deficits can have a profound impact on a child's mental health; however, for purposes of classification, neither of these maladaptive patterns is recognized by *DSM-IV-TR* (*Diagnostic and Statistical Manual of Mental Disorder;* APA, 2000) as a disorder. Other issues in classification include variations between classification systems (categorical, dimensional, developmental) and unique classification features within different systems of service delivery (mental health vs. education).

Although the case study can be seen to provide the materials necessary to develop and enhance clinical skills in all the areas listed previously, the reader should not lose sight of the fact that, ultimately, each case study in this text is a story about a lost child. In these "living files," the children have lost the path to normal development. Based on clues provided in the story, the reader's goals are to determine a child's current path relative to normal adjustment and redirect the child's course in the right direction. With these goals in mind, read their stories and develop your expertise so that you can be better prepared to help the next child who may find you.

About the Author

Linda Wilmshurst, PhD, ABPP, received her BA and MA in Psychology from the University of Windsor and her PhD from the University of Toronto. Linda is a Diplomate in Clinical Psychology (ABPP) and is a Licensed Psychologist and School Psychologist in North Carolina. Linda is an Associate Professor in the Psychology Department at Elon University, where she teaches courses in child and adult psychopathology, developmental psychology, psychology in the schools, and introductory psychology; supervises student internships; and mentors undergraduate research, primarily in areas related to resiliency, self-perceptions, and well-being in college students with attention-deficit/hyperactivity disorder. Linda has authored two textbooks: *Abnormal Child Psychology: A Developmental Perspective* and *Essentials of Child Psychopathology;* as well as coauthored two books with Alan W. Brue: *A Parent's Guide to Special Education* and *A Complete Guide to Special Education* (in press).

Introduction: Understanding the Complexities of Child and Adolescent Psychopathology

A fundamental challenge inherent in the study of child and adolescent psychopathology is distinguishing normal from atypical behavior. There are several reasons why this decision-making process is so complex and why the task is so difficult.

Determining "normal" from "abnormal" behavior requires an evaluation of the *frequency* of the behavior (e.g., does the behavior occur on a daily, hourly basis), the *duration* (is this a recent or ongoing problem), and whether the behavior is *pervasive* across all situations (or situation specific). With these factors in mind, we can now begin to probe whether the behavior is atypical within a developmental context. Ten of the most important questions that will need to be addressed are the following:

1. *Is the behavior atypical, given the child's developmental stage?* An understanding of normal developmental milestones provides the foundation for decisions regarding whether a behavior is atypical. For example, Grace is concerned because her 2-year-old is aggressive. Yesterday, he shoved another child off the swing because he wanted the swing. We know that aggression typically peaks around 2 years of age and then progressively declines, as children develop increased skills in self-control and emotion management. Furthermore, *instrumental aggression* (pushing the child to obtain an object, e.g., the swing) is a typical form of early aggression, which is less serious than *hostile aggression*, which is an intent to injure someone. As a result, we would be able to tell Grace with some measure of confidence that the aggressive behavior is not atypical, and will likely decline from this point onward.

2. *Is the behavior typical at one stage and not at another?* Some behaviors are more typical or atypical at various developmental stages. For example, toddlers often engage in oppositional behaviors (the "terrible twos") as they flex their newfound sense of independence. However, when introduced to the cases of Jeremy Jones (6 years old) and Scott Michaels (9 years old), we see "oppositional behavior" that is atypical for their ages. Both boys are defiant and refuse to comply with the most reasonable of requests. Unchecked, these behaviors can continue to escalate in severity, perhaps even developing into conduct disorder (CD), a more serious variant of the disruptive behavior disorders, which we see in the case of Jason Coleman.

3. *Is it possible for the same disorders to have different symptom presentations at different developmental stages?* Matthew Morgan and Jenny Sloan are case studies of bipolar disorder (BPD); however, while Matthew has child-onset BPD, Jenny has adolescent-onset BPD. Matthew's symptoms evidence high levels of aggression and rapid mood swings, typical of child-onset BPD, while Jenny's symptoms are closer to the adult version of the disorder, manifested in pressured speech, grandiosity, the need for little sleep, and eventually crashing into a depression and suicide attempt.

4. *Do symptoms of disorders appear the same in children and adults?* Many times, symptom presentations in children are different from adult versions of the disorders. The question is an important one because the *DSM-IV-TR* (APA, 2000) actually has very few disorders that specifically refer to children (disorders with onset in infancy, childhood, and adolescence). This has led to some dissatisfaction with the *DSM-IV-TR,* since symptoms for the majority of disorders (including anxiety and depression) are based on field trials with adults. The text revision in the latest *DSM-IV-TR* (the TR stands for text revision) added increased descriptions of child and adolescent criteria to the disorders, as well as associated developmental features. For example the "depressed/sad" features of adult depression may appear as "irritable mood" in a child. Child and adolescent symptoms for posttraumatic stress disorder (PTSD) differ from adults and across different developmental levels. While younger children (like Ericka White) will often reenact traumatic experiences through repetitive play, adolescents (like Jason Coleman and Juan Hernendez) may respond by engaging in high-risk behaviors (e.g., theft, fast driving, moving in with a girlfriend and leaving home, etc.). Compared to adults, children experience far higher rates of *comorbidity* (more than one disorder occurring at the same time). As a result, it is important to recognize that there are different patterns of comorbidity and that some disorders have a greater tendency to occur together than others. The next three questions (5, 6, and 7) refer to issues of comorbidity.

5. *What are internalizing behaviors, and do they have a tendency to be comorbid? Internalizing behaviors,* or overcontrolled behaviors, refer to syndromes that signify "problems within the self, such as anxiety, depression and somatic complaints that are without known medical cause and result in withdrawal from social contact" (Achenbach & Rescorla, 2001, p. 93). Comorbidity among internalizing disorders is frequent, since they share many common symptoms. Prior to adolescence, anxiety and depression may often appear somewhat undifferentiated as *negative affectivity* (Achenbach & Rescorla, 2001; Kronenberger & Meyer, 2000).

6. *What are externalizing behaviors and are they comorbid as well?* Externalizing, or *undercontrolled behaviors,* are referred to in the *DSM-IV-TR* as the *disruptive behavior disorders:* oppositional defiant disorder (ODD) and conduct disorder (CD). The hyperactive/impulsive and combined types of attention-deficit/hyperactivity disorder (ADHD) often are comorbid with ODD and CD. Scott Michaels and Jeremy Jones are case studies that exemplify comorbid ODD and ADHD (hyperactive-impulsive type).

7. *Can internalizing and externalizing disorders ever exist in the same child?* Children can have a number of different disorders at the same time (e.g., specific learning disability, ODD, and

ADHD). Having a multitude of comorbid disorders can result in symptoms of depression, due to the cumulative effect of these disorders on adjustment. The case of Jordan Coleman provides an illustration of how many of the internalizing and externalizing disorders can occur together in the same child.

Developmental trajectories are the outcome of interactions between *child characteristics* (intelligence, social competence, heritability, temperament, etc.) and *environmental characteristics* (family, school, teachers, peers, neighborhood, etc.). An investigation of situational or contextual variables can uncover the underlying dynamics that precipitate and maintain problem behaviors. Question 8 is related to environmental influences.

8. *What are some of the influences in the environment that can contribute to problem behaviors?* Problems may be more evident in one environment (home) than another (school) or pervasive across situations. The case study of Jeremy Jones reveals how a "well meaning" mom and grandma exacerbate his behavior problems through reinforcement (at times thinking his behaviors are "cute," and at other times giving in to his demands out of exhaustion). Jeremy is more controlled at school, due to the structure in the classroom. The case of Colby Tyler illustrates how conflict in the home can tip the scales. Even though he is trying to keep his world together, academically and emotionally, with his parents going through a difficult divorce, Colby's resources have been stretched to the limit.

Some factors can place children at increased risk for negative outcomes, while other factors can provide a protective buffer against harm. Risks and protective factors are addressed in Question 9.

9. *What are some important risk and protective factors?* There has been increased effort to uncover protective factors that can contribute to resilience despite hardship. Knowledge of risk factors can alert practitioners to warning signs, while knowledge of protective factors can provide the foundation for the development of preventive measures. A number of risk and protective factors will be discussed at the end of this chapter.

It is important to know that there are several possible pathways (developmental trajectories) that may produce the same outcome—*equifinality*—and that children who experience similar risks may have very different outcomes—*multifinality* (Cicchetti & Rogosch, 1996). The final question addresses these issues.

10. *What are equifinality and multifinality?* In the case studies to follow, you will meet Neesha Wilson and her brother, Tyrone Wilson: two African American siblings who have very different outcomes, despite living in the same home and being exposed to the some of the same risk factors. Neesha is 10 years of age and Tyrone is 15 years of age. However, while Neesha's story is one of resilience, her brother follows the path of least resistance, developing a substance-abuse problem and joining a street gang to support his habit. Neesha and Tyrone illustrate the concept of multifinality. Although they were exposed to similar circumstances growing up, Neesha is successful despite the odds. When you read these two cases, ask yourself what factors could have contributed to the very different outcomes for these two siblings.

Whereas adults often self-refer, children are most likely to be referred based on adult concerns. However, behaviors that may be concerning to parents (nightmares, aggression, overactivity) are often frequently reported in "normal" children. In addition, there may be wide variations in parent responsiveness to a child's given problems, based on extraneous circumstances at the time, such as tolerance level, and stressors, like financial difficulties or family conflict.

With an understanding of the complexities inherent in child and adolescent psychopathology, we can now turn our focus to a number of theoretical perspectives that have been developed to explain how problem behaviors develop and provide direction for treatment and intervention.

OVERVIEW OF THE CASEBOOK

Part I. Case Formulation, Theoretical Foundations, Risks, and Protective Factors

The casebook is designed to involve the child clinician in the process of developing case formulations for children and adolescents who demonstrate a wide variety of maladaptive thoughts, behaviors, and emotions. Beginning with the "Case of Terry Hogan" as a guide, this chapter will introduce readers to several fundamental concepts that will be important for understanding the cases to follow.

The Case Formulation: Initial discussions will evolve around developing a case formulation and the three stages that are involved in the process (problem identification, problem explanation, and treatment planning).

Five Theoretical Perspectives: Case formulations can be influenced and guided by assumptions that are derived from a variety of theoretical frameworks. There are a number of theoretical approaches available to assist our understanding of the nature of child and adolescent psychopathology (how disorders develop and why they persist) and inform us as to potential treatment alternatives. The theories that will be discussed in this casebook include biological, psychodynamic, behavioral, cognitive, and attachment and parenting (including family systems theories). Some of the basic principles of those theoretical foundations will be introduced and discussed.

A Transactional Bio-Psycho-Social Perspective: An Overarching Framework: This part of the chapter will focus on integrating the various theoretical perspectives using Bronfenbrenner's ecological-biological model. Within this model, Bronfenbrenner visualizes the child at the center of three concentric circles, each representing a level of influence, including the immediate environment (family, school, peers, neighborhood), the ecosystem (SES, extended family, access to resources), and the macrosystem (laws and culture).

Risks and Protective Factors: Finally, the chapter will conclude with a discussion of risk and protective factors that have been associated with the different levels of influence.

Part II. Case Studies in Child and Adolescent Psychopathology

Children and youth depicted in the 21 case studies in this section manifest symptoms of several comorbid disorders, as is often seen in real life. The cases are divided into three developmental periods, including four cases of children in the early years (5 to 6 years of age), eight cases of school-age children, and nine cases in the adolescent years. Two of the cases, Bradley Hunter (6 years of age) and Ericka White (10 years of age), are not yet diagnosed and provide an opportunity for readers to develop their own diagnoses for those cases. The case studies provide an in-depth look at the multiple pathways that can lead to maladaptive behaviors and how children can be buffered from harm or become increasingly more vulnerable based on individual and environmental factors. Each case study is presented in the same format and includes the following information:

- Overview
- Introduction
- Developmental History / Family Background
- Reason for Referral
- Assessment Results
- Issues, Trends, and Treatment Alternatives
- Post-Case Questions
- References

At the end of each case study, there is a discussion of relevant issues or trends and a review of the latest empirical findings regarding developmentally appropriate treatment programs. Finally, a number of post-case questions challenge the reader to apply theory and research to case-based practice.

Appendices. Additional Information and Resources

The Appendices contribute a wealth of additional information for advanced areas of study.

Appendix A: Supplemental Case Information

This appendix will be especially helpful for readers interested in increasing their understanding of the assessment process. Actual raw data are provided for four cases (Colby Tyler, Scott Michaels, Arthur Watson, and Shirley Yong), and readers are encouraged to use this information in practicing skills in developing case formulations and generating a written report. A sample psychological report and an exercise in differential diagnoses are provided for the case of Colby Tyler.

Appendix B: Systems of Classification

Appendix B provides an in-depth discussion of the educational classification system as it relates to four primary childhood disorders: specific learning disabilities, intellectual disabilities (previously, *mental retardation*), ADHD, and emotional disturbance. This information is a must for advising parents and for integrating assessment results within a school-based setting. The section includes recent updates of the Individuals With Disabilities Education Improvement Act (IDEA, 2004), and the Americans With Disabilities Act Amendments Act of 2008 (ADAAA), which impacts Section 504 of the Rehabilitation Act of 1973. This section will also address the *discrepancy criterion* and *response to intervention (RTI)* as they relate to criteria for determining whether a child meets criteria for designation as learning disabled.

Appendix C: Guidelines to the Interpretation of Test Scores and Assessment Information

In this section, readers will find a guide to interpreting standard scores and T scores, as well as descriptions of the specific assessment instruments used in the text.

Appendix D: The *DSM-IV-TR* (APA, 2000) Diagnostic Guidelines

This is an important section because it contains the *DSM-IV-TR* diagnostic criteria for the disorders presented in the case studies. Many of the post-case questions will ask readers to determine if there are sufficient symptoms evident in the case to warrant one or more diagnoses for the case. Readers will be able to refer to this appendix to assist them in the decision-making process.

PART I

Case Formulation:
The Case of Terry Hogan

Case of Terry Hogan

Terry's fourth-grade teacher is concerned due to progressively declining grades. Terry was in a bike accident in the third grade and was thrown from the bicycle, causing a separation of the cartilage from the rib cage. This very painful condition resulted in Terry missing several weeks of school and ultimately repeating the Grade 3 program. Terry was assessed 4 months ago and the psychological assessment revealed intellectual functioning to be in the average range (range 87–100), with academic functioning at a mid–Grade 3 level in all areas (standard score range 85–87). Terry did not qualify for special education assistance since the discrepancy between intellectual and academic scores was not significant. However, academic concerns have continued to escalate, and Terry is becoming more and more vocal about disliking school. There are frequent complaints of stomachaches, and there is often a refusal to eat lunch. In the past 5 months, Terry has been absent for 17 days and tardy on 16 occasions. The school is requesting further assessment to clarify the nature of the problems. During the follow-up assessment, Terry completed a number of self-report scales (depression, anxiety, personality), and scores indicate clinically significant elevations for all internalizing scales, including depression, anxiety, and somatization.

After reading the case of Terry Hogan, ask yourself the following question: Does Terry suffer from a significant mental illness? According to Shaffer and colleagues (1996), chances are approximately 1:5 that Terry does. However, unlike children who have disruptive behavior disorders, Terry's symptoms are not readily apparent. How can the clinician determine the nature and severity of Terry's problems? What are the essential questions that need to be addressed?

Kronenberger and Meyer (2001) present a framework for diagnosis, assessment, and treatment based on three essential questions that must be answered by the child clinician. The authors suggest that regardless of the presenting problem or the theoretical background of the therapist, the child clinician is usually faced with providing answers to three primary questions:

1. What are the primary characteristics of the child's problem?
2. How does the clinician conduct an in-depth evaluation of the problem?
3. How does the clinician decide which interventions are important?

The authors suggest that each of the questions addresses a specific issue or aspect of child psychopathology. Clinicians respond to the first question when they classify a child's problem relative to a *diagnostic category,* or provide a *provisional diagnosis* or a *case formulation* based on the presenting symptoms and characteristics. The second question involves the in-depth evaluation. Here, the assessment process requires knowledge of appropriate *interview and observational techniques,* as well as *broad assessment strategies* (e.g., cognitive, behavioral, and emotional functioning) and *syndrome-specific tests* (e.g., instruments to detect anxiety, depression, etc.). These assessment instruments can assist in confirming or ruling out potential diagnoses. The final question requires knowledge of developmentally appropriate evidence-based treatment methods that can be applied to modify the problem (Kronenberger & Meyer, 2001, pp. 1–2).

Although the questions can be answered by the majority of theoretical viewpoints, Held (1996) emphasizes the need for therapists to spend more time reconsidering the nature and composition of the theoretical system that guides their decision-making process, in what she calls the *three predetermined components* of therapy:

1. What constitutes problems or impediments to solutions?
2. What causes those problems or impediments to occur?
3. What methods can help clients to solve their problems, overcome their impediments, and obtain their goals? (p. 37)

Since a clinician's theoretical perspective can influence decisions, it is very important that clinicians are aware of their own theoretical biases in forming their opinions. Looking at a case through a set of theoretically colored lenses can affect all aspects of information processing, from hypothesis testing to treatment. The influence of theory on practice will become increasingly clear as case formulations are constructed from various theoretical viewpoints and applied to the case of Terry Hogan.

CASE FORMULATION AND CHILD AND ADOLESCENT PSYCHOPATHOLOGY

Weerasekera (1996) defines *case formulation* as a process conducted to provide a "hypothesis of how an individual comes to present with a certain disorder or circumstance at a particular point in time" (p. 5). Case formulations have been explored from a number of theoretical approaches, including *psychodynamic* (Eells, 1997; McWilliams, 1999; Shirk & Russell, 1996), *behavioral* (Barlow, 1986; Kazdin, 1983; Mash & Terdal, 1997; Turkat, 1985), *cognitive-behavioral* (Bruch & Bond, 1999; Persons, 1989), and *family systems* perspectives (Berman, 1997). Within the realm of child psychopathology, research linking child outcomes to *parenting styles* (Baumrind, 1991) and *attachment patterns* (Ainsworth, Blehar, Waters, & Wall, 1978) suggests that these areas could also provide rich materials for weaving into the fabric of case formulations. Case formulation can provide a framework for assessing and organizing information in a way that informs treatment planning, by going beyond symptom presentation to deriving hypotheses regarding how the behavior developed and why it is being maintained. Although the concept of case formulation has its origins in the psychodynamic approach, the approach is readily adaptable to a variety of theoretical perspectives and is gaining increased recognition across a wide variety of theoretical models regarding adult as well as child populations (Hersen & Porzelius, 2002; Shirk & Russell, 1996).

The *case formulation* approach is particularly well suited to clinical/developmental child concerns, because the approach

1. supports an understanding of underlying processes (cognitive, behavioral, and emotional);
2. readily allows for consideration of the impact of personal and environmental factors on past and present functioning at several levels: *individual, immediate, social* and *economic,* and *culture;*
3. provides an opportunity to address how risks and protective factors can impede or assist treatment;
4. provides a unique opportunity to place therapeutic interventions within an ecologically valid context; and
5. can accommodate behavioral (Weisz, Weiss, Han, Granger, & Morton, 1995) and cognitive-behavioral training programs that have been demonstrated to reduce anxiety (Kendall et al., 1992) and depression (Stark, Reynolds, & Kaslow, 1987; Stark, Swearer, Kurkowski, Sommer, & Bowen, 1996), disruptive behavior disorders (Spaccarelli, Cotler, & Penman, 1992) and, combined with pharmacology, symptoms of ADHD (Barkley, 1997).

THREE STAGES IN CASE FORMULATION: A CONCEPTUAL MODEL

As a construct, case formulation seeks to address the essential questions posed by Kronenberger and Meyer (2001) and Held (1996). When a diagnosis is made, a wealth of clinical knowledge about the disorder is readily available. The case formulation is a hypothesis about potential underlying influences that *precipitate* (cause) and *maintain* the behavior, including child and environmental (family, school, peers, community) factors. To this end, the case formulation provides a better understanding of

- Problem identification (What is the problem?)
- Precipitating factors (What caused the problem?)
- Maintaining factors (Why is the problem persisting?)

The case formulation presents a three-stage model that provides an organizational framework for discussing diagnosis and assessment. The three stages of the case formulation include

Stage 1: Problem identification (clarification and classification)

Stage 2: Problem interpretation/understanding

Stage 3: Treatment formulation

Stage 1: Problem Identification. Knowledge of normative expectations, awareness of the etiology of disorders, and familiarity with empirical research all add to our understanding of specific disorders. At this stage, a wide variety of assessment methods allow us to access information from multiple sources (parents, teachers, child). In some multiple-problem cases, there may be a need to prioritize among problem areas based on urgency and/or severity of problems. Sometimes, what was originally thought to be "the main problem" is actually secondary to a different concern. In these cases, hypotheses are reformulated. For example, although Terry's poor academic progress was the initial concern, a very different set of problems eventually unfolded that provided increased insight into the high rates of absenteeism and increasingly negative attitude toward school.

Stage 2: Problem Interpretation/Understanding. Developmental and family history can provide important information regarding potential genetic (family pathology) or event-based causes (family or school history, traumatic events, etc.). Knowledge of risks and protective factors can also assist in better understanding conditions that might exacerbate or moderate the problem. At this stage, theoretical assumptions can influence how the problem is conceptualized; however, the ability to integrate information from diverse theoretical perspectives can increase our understanding of the dynamics involved.

Stage 3: Treatment Formulation. Knowledge of evidence-based treatments that best apply to the unique aspects of the case will increase opportunities for success. Monitoring and evaluating treatment effectiveness are also important in order to validate the effectiveness of the treatment.

Box 1.1. Thinking Out Loud

Sections titled "Thinking Out Loud" will provide opportunities to consolidate information, identify areas for further exploration, and assist in working through the process of case formulation.

Although case formulation involves three stages, it is a dynamic and ongoing process that has a built-in capacity for flexible thinking and revision at all stages. In this way, case formulation can become case *reformulation,* allowing for ongoing refinement and evaluation of problem areas and treatment plans.

CASE FORMULATION: APPLICATIONS TO THE CASE OF TERRY HOGAN

With the first goal of case formulation in mind, return to the sidebar description of Terry Hogan and reread the scenario with the following questions in mind:

1. What are Terry's main problems?
2. What is Terry's primary problem? Why has the problem developed and what is causing the problem to persist?
3. What other information is needed to respond to the above questions? Is Terry a boy or girl? Read the scenario again to see if you can find the answer. Risk factors for males and females can be different, so Terry's gender may also be a factor in determining targets for intervention.

Box 1.2. Thinking Out Loud

Although Terry is struggling academically, initial assessment provided information that lack of success in school was not a function of *lack of ability* (intelligence was in the average range), but was more a *lack of performance* (production). Terry said that she disliked school. Could lack of performance be attributed to lack of motivation, interest, and effort?

Based on the information to date, pinpointing the problem is not an easy task. Understanding the problem requires sifting through the information and focusing on behavior patterns that are most likely to yield relevant insights into Terry's difficulties. Based on the latest assessment results, the psychologist records the following impressions:

During the follow-up assessment session, Terry seemed even more agitated than she had been previously. She appeared pale and had dark circles under her eyes. When asked about school, she said that things were worse than before (referring to 4 months ago). Her younger sister, Lilly, is now in the same grade and even though they are in different classrooms, her younger sister is a constant reminder of her failure. Terry said the family was living with her grandparents until last week. She said her grandfather gets "too angry" at her and yells a lot. Just before they moved out, her grandfather had taken the belt out to hit her and she ran out the front door and down the street. She said she didn't care if she was hit by a car, it was better than being hit by him. When asked about her absenteeism, she said that she felt sick a lot. She also mentioned that her back hurt, because she had been sleeping on a sofa bed that has a bar across the middle that digs into her back at night, and wakes her up. So she hasn't been sleeping very well.

Her mother is a waitress who works long hours some nights. Since they are no longer living with her grandparents, Terry and her sister now go to the restaurant to eat their dinner and then walk home with their mother when she is finished with work. She said that the restaurant can be noisy, so it is hard to do her homework. Terry's father is a truck driver and is often away. When asked about friends, Terry said she used to have some friends, but when she repeated the third grade, they wouldn't play with her anymore because she was only a third grader. Terry's favorite pastime is watching TV. She said that she liked to watch Disney movies because "they always have a happy ending, not like most things."

Terry's responses to the Revised Children's Manifest Anxiety Scale (RCMAS-2) indicated significant levels of Social Anxiety (feelings of isolation from peers, and feelings of inadequacy compared to other girls her age). On the Child Depression Index (CDI), scores for Total Depression, Negative Mood, Ineffectiveness, and Anhedonia were all in the clinically significant range. There were indications of suicidal ideation, although Terry stated that she "would not do it." Although responses to the Personality Inventory for Youth (PIY) revealed a valid profile (nondefensive), there were also indications of possibly an exaggerated response profile. Responses indicated little pleasure derived from academics and school-based activities, high scores for distractibility and concentration problems, and tendencies to be irritable and impatient. Terry admitted to having problems with compliance issues and following the rules. She endorsed many somatic complaints often associated with anxiety and depression (frequent headaches, stomachaches, dizziness, fatigue), placing her score on the somatic scale in the clinically significant range. Terry's profile suggests that when she is psychologically distressed, she reacts with physical responses, such as feeling ill, loss of appetite, and sleep disturbance. Responses to the family dysfunction scale revealed that she is unlikely to view her home as a source of satisfaction and instead sees home as conflicted and fragmented. Responses suggest a troubled relationship with her parents, who she describes as argumentative, frequently absent, and in disagreement with each other. Responses indicated that one or both of her parents may drink to excess or demonstrate other signs of less than stable emotional adjustment.

Terry's teacher completed the Behavioral Assessment System for Children (BASC-2), a rating scale of behavioral and emotional problems in children. Unfortunately, the parent version of the scale has not been returned to the school, despite several calls. Similar to Terry's responses, her teacher also confirmed clinically significant concerns on all internalizing scales, including Total Internalizing Problems, Depression, Anxiety, Somatization, Learning Problems, and Withdrawal (tendency to evade others and avoid social contact).

Based on the assessment results, the psychologist has a growing concern that Terry is experiencing many symptoms of depression, anxiety, and somatization. However, why these problems are occurring and seemingly escalating can only be speculated, until there is contact with Terry's family. Several weeks later, Mrs. Hogan agreed to meet with the school psychologist to discuss the assessment results. At that time, she gave notice that the family was relocating to Tennessee at the end of the week to live with her sister's family, which would place them closer to her husband's new truck route. When the assessment results were discussed, Mrs. Hogan became very defensive and stated that Terry was pretty good at pulling the wool over people's eyes, implying that Terry had the psychologist "fooled." She said that living with Terry has been difficult since the day she was born. Terry was an irritable baby who never slept well and was always a fussy eater. She was a clingy baby who cried every time her mother left her, so it was hard to find sitters that would look after her. She said that Terry was a selfish child who only thought about herself. She wished that Terry could be more like her sister, Lilly, who was easy to get along with and had many friends. On the other hand, Terry was moody, irritable, and difficult to please; she often walked around with a "chip on her shoulder." Mrs. Hogan said that unfortunately, Terry took after her father, who was the same way, especially when he was drinking. When asked about family history for depression, Mrs. Hogan said she suspected that her husband might be "down in the dumps" sometimes, especially when he would start drinking. However, with the truck driving job, drinking was no longer an option. Mrs. Hogan admitted to having financial problems and blamed Terry's willful and disobedient attitude for getting them "booted out" of Terry's grandfather's place. She explained that her father (Terry's grandfather) had always had problems controlling his temper and that Terry would "mouth off" at her grandfather, and that would cause him to lose his temper. She described Terry as a complainer who often said that she was not feeling well to get out of doing chores or helping around the house. As a result, her sister often had to carry twice the load.

The psychologist emphasized her concerns about Terry's emotional well-being and her symptoms of depression, and recommended that Mrs. Hogan find a counselor for Terry when they arrived in Tennessee. However, Mrs. Hogan stated that she felt that would just encourage Terry to feel sorry for herself and make it worse. The psychologist requested permission to send the reports to Terry's new school and Mrs. Hogan reluctantly agreed.

Box 1.3. Thinking Out Loud

Applying Theory to Case Formulations

The psychologist has now amassed information from several sources and can begin building hypotheses regarding Terry's internalizing problems (depression, anxiety, and somatization). The following case formulations will provide an increased understanding of how the problem can be conceptualized from a variety of theoretical perspectives.

CASE FORMULATION FROM FIVE DIFFERENT PERSPECTIVES

The following section is devoted to case formulations developed from five different theoretical frameworks: biological; behavioral; cognitive (social cognitive); psychodynamic; and attachment, parenting, and family systems.

Case Formulation Based on the Biological Perspective

Terry's family history may be positive for depression (father) and if so, then she would have an increased risk (20% to 45%) for developing depressive symptoms (Rutter, Silberg, O'Connor, & Simonoff, 1999). Imbalanced levels of serotonin, norepinephrine, and possibly dopamine and acetycholine have been associated with depression in adults (Thase, Jindal, & Howland, 2002). Abnormalities in the gene responsible for transporting the neurotransmitter serotonin (5-HTT gene) have been linked to increased risk for depressive disorder (Caspi et al., 2003; Hecimovic & Gilliam, 2006). Caspi and colleagues (2003) found that children who inherited the short allele of the serotonin transporter (5-HTT) were more likely to respond to stressful events with symptoms of depression and suicidal ideation than peers who did not inherit the short allele.

Cortisol is a hormone that is released by the hypothalamic-pituitary-adrenal system (HPA) in times of stress. High cortisol levels can result in heightened sensitivity to threat that have been linked to increased risk for depression (Pliszka, 2002).

Therapeutic Implications. Although medical management is common in the treatment of depression in adults, approximately 30% to 40% of children with depression do not respond to medical treatment (Emslie et al., 1997). Fluoxetine (Prozac) is the only medication that has been approved by the FDA for use with children 8 years of age and older. Results of a 6-year-long investigation with adolescents found that combined treatment using antidepressants and cognitive-behavioral therapy was superior to cognitive-behavioral therapy alone (Apter, Kronenberg, & Brent, 2005). However, in 2006, the FDA issued a *black box warning* (the highest level of caution) for antidepression medications potentially increasing depression and suicidal behaviors in youth and young adults up to 25 years of age.

Box 1.4. Thinking Out Loud

Does the benefit outweigh the risk?

   Based on results of their exhaustive review of clinical pediatric trials between 1988 and 2006, Bridge and colleagues (2007) conclude that not taking prescription medication for depression places children at greater risk than taking the medications.

Case Formulation Based on the Behavioral Perspective

According to Mash and Terdal (1997), the behavioral systems assessment (BSA) is a "functional/utilitarian approach" to the assessment of children and families that closely adheres to the broader meaning of diagnosis as "an analytic information-gathering process directed at understanding *the nature of a problem, its possible causes, treatment options* and *outcomes.*" In direct contrast to psychodynamic theories, "BSA is more often concerned with behaviors, cognitions and affects as *direct samples of the domains of interest*" rather than attempting to speculate about "*some underlying or remote causes*" (pp. 11–12; emphasis added). There has been increased focus on the use of BSA practices and strategies in the decision-making process (La Greca & Lemanek, 1996). For example, functional behavioral assessments (FBA) are routinely conducted in the schools with the goal of developing behavioral intervention plans (BIP), although unlike the case at hand (Terry's problem is one of depression), the majority of behavioral strategies focus on increasing "off task behaviors" (as in the case of children with ADHD) or increasing "compliance" (as in cases of oppositional and defiant children). It has been debated by some that FBA is a better approach to intervention planning than classification of disorders by either the dimensional or categorical systems (Cone, 1997; Haynes & O'Brien, 1990). An example of the FBA approach can be found in the case of Jeremy Jones, where issues of noncompliance are addressed in a program designed to increase compliance. Proponents of BSA/FBA argue that the problem-solving strategy inherent in this approach provides a flexible system of hypothesis testing that includes diagnosis, prognosis, treatment design, and treatment efficacy/evaluation (Mash & Terdal, 1997). The continuity between conducting the BSA/FBA and developing the BIP are emphasized by proponents of the system (Mash & Terdal, 1997; Wielkiewicz, 1995). The behavioral framework consists, at its basis, of a four-stage process to *identify the problem, analyze the problem, implement a plan,* and *evaluate the plan.*

From a behavioral perspective, principles of operant conditioning can be very helpful in understanding how Terry's symptoms of depression, often manifested in claims of "not feeling well," have become ingrained in a repetitive pattern of avoidance behaviors. When Terry initially stated that she was "not feeling well," it is likely that responses included increased attention from those around her (*positive reinforcement*) and an opportunity to escape from doing chores (*negative reinforcement*). Either way, "feeling sick" was reinforced with a positive outcome, thereby increasing the likelihood for the behavior to be repeated in the future. *Positive reinforcement* involves the addition of a reward (e.g., when you feel sick, I will comfort you and nourish you), while *negative reinforcement* involves the removal of a negative situation. *Negative reinforcement,* not to be confused with punishment, is rewarding because it involves the removal of a negative (e.g., if you are sick, you do not have to do chores, or go to school). Negative reinforcement has sometimes been called *escape* because it allows one to escape a negative consequence.

Coercion theory (Patterson, Capaldi, & Bank, 1991) can also help explain how Terry and her mother have established a negative cycle of interaction patterns. Parents who eventually yield to a child's escalating and demanding behaviors serve to *positively reinforce the child's misbehavior* (Terry's "feeling sick" has resulted in numerous absences from school) while, at the same time, provide themselves with *negative reinforcement for their own compliance* (if she is allowed to play the sick role, then she stops whining and complaining) because she doesn't have to go to school. Therefore, the parent learns that giving in will stop the demands, while the child learns that increased demands result in parent compliance. Since positive and negative reinforcement serve to strengthen behaviors, parent and child become "locked in" to an escalating and never-ending battle.

Therapeutic Implications. Based on behavioral analysis, the "pay off" for Terry "feeling ill" has been an ability to escape negative situations, such as doing chores around the house or having to attend school, where she is failing academically and socially. In developing a behavioral program, goals would be to increase her sense of academic and social competency at school in an attempt to reduce her need to escape from a negative situation. At home, reintroduction of chores should be done in a way that requires a sense of responsibility but is also inherently rewarding, for example, preparing dessert for the family. Terry and her sister should have a chore list that is negotiated between them in the presence of their parents, with a list of rewards (e.g., allowance, privileges) that can be earned and traded at the end of each week as compensation for completion of required tasks.

Through the use of behavioral tools such as knowledge of schedules of reinforcement and objective observation techniques, behavior intervention plans can be developed, monitored, and modified to assist with behavioral change. Rewarding obedience with attention and praise, issuing demands that are clear and age appropriate, and providing consistent follow-through would strengthen Terry's compliant behaviors while increasing her self-confidence and breaking the cycle of avoidance behaviors. Building on earlier successes has proven to be a source of motivation in increasing compliance with more difficult tasks later on (Ducharme & Popynick, 1993).

Box 1.5. Thinking Out Loud

Although Mash and Terdal (1997) argue against narrowly contrasting BSA with more traditional assessment approaches, they do suggest some fundamental conceptual differences between the two approaches. The BSA approach tends to focus on state (situation-specific patterns of behavior) versus trait (underlying personality dynamic) characteristics, and ideographic versus nomothetic comparisons, and places emphasis on stability and discontinuity over time versus consistency and stability of underlying causes.

Case Formulation Based on the Cognitive Perspective

Negative appraisals can be part of the maladaptive thought processes inherent in a bias to interpret situations and behaviors in a negative way (Beck, 1997, 2002). These negative attitudes produce errors in thinking, such as minimizing the positive and accentuating the negative, which can be automatic and reflexive. For Beck, the *"cognitive triad"* refers to thought processes involving feelings of *helplessness, hopelessness,* and *worthlessness.* One potential outcome of this type of thinking bias is the development of *learned helplessness,* a behavior pattern based on tendencies to give up in the face of adversity (Seligman, 1975). Cognitive theorists today believe that learned helplessness is caused by a range of negative attributions that can be global or specific, blame internal or external causes, and are seen as stable or unstable (Abramson et al., 2002). Attributions that are *global* ("Nobody loves me"), *internal* ("Nobody loves me because I am worthless"), and *stable* ("No one will ever love me") are the most likely combination to result in learned helplessness. Beck suggests that maladaptive and negative thought patterns often begin in childhood based on responses to negative treatment and evaluations within the context of their family. Although Mrs. Hogan does not admit to being depressed herself, she is very critical of her daughter. Research shows that compared to mothers who are not depressed, depressed mothers engage in less activity with their children, are more inconsistent in routines, and are more frustrated (irritable, controlling, and impatient) in dealing with child problems (Malphurs, Field, Larraine, Pickens, & Pelaez-Nogueras, 1996).

By the end of the preschool period, children have developed consistent expectations about their social worlds and act accordingly (Main, 1995; Main & Hesse, 1990). Studies have demonstrated that children's faulty reasoning about their social relationships can influence inappropriate behavior (Hartup & Laursen, 1993). For Terry, social exchanges with her mother have been very negative. The child's cognitive belief system can be reinforced by adult responses to child-behavior patterns, and research has demonstrated that adults respond with less-than-positive reactions to children who present as "difficult" to manage (Bugental, Blue, & Lewis, 1990). These adult responses can set the stage for a further extension of the child's belief system.

Terry's cognitive framework for social interaction places her at risk for social rejection (Dodge, Bates, & Pettit, 1990). If Terry is overly sensitive to rejection, then she is likely to misinterpret ambivalent social situations as hostile and rejecting, or what has come to be known as the *hostile attribution bias*. Recently, Beauchaine, Strassberg, Kees, and Drabick (2002) found that parents of children with poor relationship skills were especially deficient in providing solutions to issues of noncompliance, especially when required to do so under pressured conditions. The authors recommend the need for treatment plans to target the underlying processes of negative attribution bias and affect regulation, which they suggest are the pivotal factors that drive coercive parenting patterns. Mrs. Hogan's communication pattern with Terry is high on *expressed emotion*, a negative, critical, and disapproving interactive style. Such communication styles have been found to increase the risk for psychopathology in vulnerable family members (Nomura et al., 2005).

Therapeutic Implications. Cognitive-behavioral therapy (CBT) seeks to facilitate positive integration of thoughts and behaviors. For Terry, CBT would focus on how Terry's faulty belief system contributes to feelings of negative self-worth and avoidant behaviors. Social cognitive treatment might involve role-play in areas of social cue awareness and the underlying processes that contribute to the development of prosocial behavior, such as secure attachment, social perspective taking, empathy, and self-control. Parent training using CBT methods would focus on negative attributions, emotion regulation, and, ultimately, on increasing effective strategies for more positive communication.

In their recent meta-analyses, Weisz, Doss, and Hawley (2005, 2006) found that the most common treatment approaches included some form of behavior/learning approach, and that among these, CBT was the most frequent treatment for depression. In an earlier study, Weisz and colleagues (1995) found that an 8-session school-based group CBT program was effective in reducing symptoms of depression, relative to a wait-list control group. The program focused on activity scheduling and increasing the likelihood of positive reinforcement. A comprehensive CBT program developed by Stark and colleagues (1996) focused on ways to promote positive mood and decrease negative thought patterns using individual and group formats. Individual sessions provided an opportunity for children to discuss topics that may be too embarrassing to bring up in the group, while group sessions allowed for practice in developing social skills within a safe social context.

Box 1.6. Thinking Out Loud

Beauchaine and colleagues (2002) questioned whether parents using ineffective and harsh methods of discipline fail to generate alternative solutions due to (a) an *availability deficit* (limited repertoire) or (b) an *accessibility deficit* (processing deficit during times of stress). In order to enhance treatment efficacy, the authors stress the need to address both negative attributions and affect regulation in parent training programs. They suggest that negative parent attributions may undermine successful use of the skills taught.

Case Formulation Based on the Psychodynamic Perspective

On a psychodynamic level, Terry's internalizing problems would be represented as the internal manifestations of unconscious conflicts stemming from an imbalance in the underlying personality structure. In Terry's case, her mother's rejection represents a symbolic loss resulting in feelings of depression and feelings of guilt and self-blame for driving her mother away. Freud would interpret the loss within the context of unmet needs (lack of parental nourishing) during the oral stage. This pervasive sense of loss can result in feelings of emptiness and withdrawal from social contact, which can increase symptoms of depression. Individuals may remain overly dependent on others, feel unworthy of love, and have low self-esteem (Busch, Rudden, & Shapiro, 2004). In addition, Terry's somatic complaints represent tendencies to translate psychic pain into physical pain.

Ego psychologists might interpret Terry's insecurities as resulting from a lack of resolution of the "rapprochement phase" in the separation individuation process. In this phase, the toddler is faced with awareness of separation, separation anxiety, and conflicting desires to stay close to the mother. Normally, the process of gaining greater independence and self-identity is facilitated by the parent, who performs the dual role of remaining emotionally available while gently encouraging the push toward greater independence (Settlage, 1977). However, as Terry's mother was not emotionally available for her, theory would predict that conflicts between autonomy and dependence would be repeated throughout development, especially in vulnerable times (Kramer & Akhtar, 1989). Successful resolution of the conflict at this stage is achieved through the development of an internal representation or model of the parent-child relationship that can sustain separation due to the securely developed ego. To ego theorists, the focus is on consolidation of the ego, while for attachment theorists (to be discussed later), the focus is on the relationship (Fonagy, 1999).

Therapeutic Implications. Depending on the therapist's psychodynamic orientation, the therapeutic process might focus on the individual child (working through internal conflicts in play therapy), the parent (helping a parent resolve his or her own childhood conflicts and traumas), or the parent-child dyad (conjoint play therapy). In Terry's case, all three approaches would be appropriate—initially engaging Terry and her mother in individual therapy sessions and ultimately bringing them together in conjoint play therapy sessions. Psychodynamic developmental therapy for children (PDTC) is a relatively recent advancement in psychodynamic therapy developed by Fonagy and Target (1996). Although the approach is psychodynamic in origin, principles of social information processing (social cognition) are used to assist children in linking thoughts to feelings and behaviors (*reflective processes*). A PDTC therapist might provide *corrective experiences* through play therapy and the use of metaphor to assist Terry in replacing self-damaging feelings with increased positive views.

Box 1.7. Thinking Out Loud

The foundations of psychodynamic theory are rooted in uncovering the internal and often unconscious processes that drive an individual's behaviors and the internal working models responsible for a weakened sense of ego development. As such, the psychodynamic approach is not an easy fit with empirical research. While Messer (2000) has called for the development of databases for case-based research to remedy this problem, Fonagy, Target, Cottrell, Phillips, and Kurtz (2002) have provided empirical support for the PDTC approach, which has an 85% success rate for internalizing disorders.

Case Formulation Based on the Attachment, Parenting, and Family Systems Perspectives

Attachment and Parenting Style

Greenberg (1999) has embedded attachment theory in an ecological-developmental framework to explain psychopathology resulting from the interplay of factors evident in the child, parent, and environmental context. Drawing on principles of *equifinality* (different pathways may lead to the same disorder) and *multifinality* (similar disorders may produce multiple outcomes), Greenberg builds his model drawing on four underlying processes found in theoretical models of attachment: internal working models, neurophysiology of emotion regulation, observed behaviors, and functional-motivational processes.

Internal Working Models. The degree of security/insecurity inherent in primary attachment relationships provides *internal working models* or templates for all future relationships (Ainsworth et al., 1978; Belsky, 1988; Bowlby, 1969/1982). While secure attachments can be a protective factor, insecure attachments may place the child at increased risk for developing problems. Terry's avoidant behaviors may be the result of internal working models (IWMs) based on an early *avoidant attachment pattern*. It is likely that Terry's mother was, at times, withdrawn and emotionally unavailable, and at other times harsh, emotionally charged, and highly punitive (negative and highly critical). This *authoritarian parenting style* is a controlling and harsh style of interacting that is lacking in warmth and often predictive of *avoidant attachment patterns* (Rubin, Hymel, Mills, & Rose-Krasnor, 1991). Baumrind (1991) found four different parenting styles, based on the amount of structure and warmth parents provided. In most situations, the *authoritative parenting* approach (high structure and high warmth) is the desired practice and yields the best child outcomes. The authoritarian parenting style, although high on structure, is very low on warmth, and children raised in this type of household may become aggressive and uncooperative. Parents who are *uninvolved* provide little structure or warmth, and children are prone to develop a number of negative traits, including truancy. *Permissive parenting* provides warmth but minimal structure. Based on an avoidant attachment pattern and authoritarian parenting practices, Terry's IWM is likely to evolve around avoidance and withdrawal to shield her from fears of rejection. Within this framework, parent-child dyads can be thrust into a hostile/helpless pattern, with one member of the dyad being the hostile aggressor and the other member becoming the passive, helpless, and overwhelmed recipient (Lyons-Ruth, Bronfman, & Atwood, 1999).

Neurophysiology of Emotion Regulation. Neurological findings suggest that humans require positive experiences of resolving fearful situations to allow for a build-up of brain structures that help to regulate responses to anxiety and fear-producing situations (Siegel, 1999). In dysfunctional attachment relationships, caregivers are not a source of assistance in the regulation of emotion and can become a source of threat. Deficits in the acquisition of mechanisms to regulate emotions result in an inability to self-soothe when upset, thereby reducing the ability to cope in stressful situations.

Results of a recent neuroimaging study have found that the anterior cingulate cortex (ACC), which is activated during physical pain, is also activated in response to distress caused by social exclusion and rejection (Eisenberger, Lieberman, & Williams, 2003). The researchers suggest that these neural connections may be part of the social attachment survival system to promote the goal of social connectedness. Results help explain Terry's feelings of physical pain in response to her emotional loss and rejection.

Observed Behaviors. Avoidance behaviors may serve an instrumental role in the attachment process by acting to control and regulate caregiver proximity and attentiveness. Through the use of avoidant techniques, Terry can shield her sensitivity to her mother's harsh and rejecting responses. It has been suggested that these maladaptive behaviors may fit with the overall schema of family dysfunction (Marvin & Stewart, 1990).

Motivational Processes. Maladaptive attachment patterns can influence social orientation and subsequent prosocial competencies. Terry's lack of social reciprocity and withdrawal from social contact preclude strong social motivation at this point in her life. For Terry, the social world is a hostile territory that she would rather escape from than attempt to cope with. On the other hand, there is evidence that children with early secure attachments are more socially oriented and compliant and have better-developed abilities to regulate their emotions (Ainsworth et al., 1978; Greenberg, 1999).

Insecure attachments can develop for a variety of reasons, including child characteristics (e.g., difficult temperament) and characteristics in the immediate environment, such as parenting style (Belsky, 1999). In Terry's case, there is strong evidence to suggest that both factors are highly interrelated. Greenberg, Speltz, DeKlyen, and Endriga (1993) incorporate four factors in their risk model for behavioral disorders, all of which are evident in the case study of Terry: *insecure attachment, atypical child characteristics, ineffective parenting,* and *family environment.* Although quality of attachment can be seen as a risk or protective factor in its own right, living in an environment that contains multiple risk factors (low SES, family stress, parent maladjustment, etc.) also increases the likelihood of developing an insecure attachment (Belsky, 1997).

Therapeutic Implications. Therapeutic attempts to improve the attachment relationship have remained largely rooted in a psychodynamic approach and have focused primarily on infant-parent psychotherapy (see Lieberman & Zeanah, 1999, for review). Many of the programs are lengthy due to the emphasis on building a therapeutic working alliance with the therapist and the need for extensive ongoing assessments of child-parent or child-caregiver (foster care) interactions and family circumstances. Observations and discussions of joint play provide opportunities for insight-oriented dialogue designed to assist parents in acquiring more appropriate perceptions of their child and developing interactional patterns that have greater empathic attunement with the child's needs. Based on the belief that obstacles to attachment can occur on several levels (infant, parent, environment), therapeutic goals in these programs are to determine the nature of the obstacles blocking attachment (individual differences) and to design treatment to address these specific areas (Zeanah et al., 1997).

The Seattle Program, developed by Speltz and colleagues (Greenberg & Speltz, 1988; Speltz, 1990) is a parent training program to assist families of children with insecure attachment that melds attachment theory with a cognitive-behavioral approach. The program focuses on communication breakdown in the parent-child dyad and emphasizes the need for better "negotiation skills." The four-phase intervention program includes components of parent education, reframing of the child's behaviors within a developmental framework, limit setting and problem prioritizing, and communication/negotiation skills.

Box 1.8. Thinking Out Loud

Secure attachments can lead to better understanding rather than avoidance of negative emotions (Laible & Thompson, 1998). Terry demonstrates very few coping skills to effectively deal with negative emotions or negative information. Thompson (1999) suggests that "lessons learned" in attachment relationships may be instrumental in defining expectations in such areas as how others react when the child is experiencing difficulties coping with stress, anxiety, or fears.

Family Systems Theoretical Perspective

Family systems theory represents a variety of approaches that emphasize the family unit as the focus of assessment and intervention. The family unit is composed of many subsystems: parent-child, marriage partners, siblings, extended family, and so on. Within families, behaviors are often directed toward maintaining or changing *boundaries, alignment,* and *power.* Often, a family's degree of dysfunction can be defined by boundaries that are poorly or inconsistently defined, or those that are too extreme (too loose or too rigid).

Salvador Minuchin (1985), a proponent of structural family therapy, described several family patterns that can contribute to dysfunction. In enmeshed families, boundaries between family members are often vague, resulting in family members being overly involved in each other's lives. According to Minuchin, enmeshed families (lacking in boundaries) may see a child's need to individuate as a threat to the family unit. Triangular relationships that serve to shift the balance of power include *the parent-child coalition, triangulation* (mother and Terry's sister versus Terry), and *detouring* (maintaining Terry as the focus of the problem to avoid acknowledging other family problems, such as marital conflict).

Treatment Implications. Within the family systems approach, the family therapist would create an alliance by joining the family and observing family interactional patterns from the inside out. Once the problem has been formulated, the therapist works with the family to restructure the family interactions toward positive growth and change. In Terry's case, the therapist would likely focus on repositioning the balance of power and on improved problem solving and communication.

INTEGRATING THEORETICAL PERSPECTIVES: A TRANSACTIONAL ECOLOGICAL BIO-PSYCHO-SOCIAL FRAMEWORK

Bronfenbrenner and the Contexts of Influence

Bronfenbrenner's (1979, 1998) *ecological systems theory* was developed to explain the importance of contextual influences on human development and provides an excellent framework for the integration of numerous theoretical perspectives. Bronfenbrenner depicts the child at the center of a series of concentric circles, each circle representing a level of influence. Interactions between the child and the environment are ongoing and transactional, such that changes at one level can influence changes at other levels. For example, in the interaction between the child and his parent, responses have a reciprocal influence and both can be altered in the process. More recently, Bronfenbrenner and Morris (1998) have suggested that the model might more appropriately be referred to as a *bioecological model* to emphasize biological characteristics in the dynamic and ongoing interplay between the *child's characteristics* (biological and genetic) and the *environmental characteristics* (proximal and distal factors).

The ecological-transactional model (Bronfenbrenner, 1979; Cicchetti & Lynch, 1993) can provide an overarching framework for discussing ecological contexts "consisting of a number of nested levels with varying degrees of proximity to the individual" (Lynch & Cicchetti, 1998, p. 235). There are three levels of environmental influence: the *microsystem,* the *exosystem,* and the *macrosystem.* The microsystem represents the immediate environment and includes influences of family (caregivers and siblings), teachers, peers, the neighborhood, and school settings. Next is the exosystem, which incorporates influences from more distal factors, such as parents' employment and social economic status. The macrosystem is the outer rim that represents influences resulting from cultural beliefs and societal laws. Bronfenbrenner refers to the communication among factors within the microsystem as the *mesosystem,* which can be a very potent influence in the child's ongoing success.

Box 1.9. Thinking Out Loud

Mesosystem Effects: If parents and teachers communicate regularly and share the same goals for the child, the potential for academic success will increase significantly. Conversely, poor communication between home and school has been associated with increased risk for academic difficulties. Similarly, if both parents share the same goals in their communications with the child, the child will benefit from the consistency in the message.

Risks and Protective Factors

Bronfenbrenner's (1979) model also provides an excellent framework for a discussion of risks and protective factors that can influence development from a number of different levels. While children who experience risks in their immediate environment (microsystem) are prone to develop externalizing problems, disturbances at the exosystem level, for example, family hardship, can increase the risk for internalizing problems (Atzaba-Poria, Pike & Deater-Deckard, 2004). We also know that the number of risks experienced can add significantly to the overall risk. For example, the combined effect of social maladjustment *and* poor academic achievement can result in a *multiplier effect* that can have a fourfold increase in the risk for long-term adjustment problems relative to the presence of only one risk factor (Burchinal, Vernon-Feagans, & Cox, 2008; Sameroff & Fiese, 2000). Child characteristics that can increase the risk for negative outcomes include male gender (Rutter, 1979), physical handicaps (Werner & Smith, 1992), and having a difficult temperament (Bates, Pettit, Dodge, & Ridge, 1998). Protective factors at this level include good intelligence, having a positive self-concept, and having an outgoing style of social engagement (Masten & Coatsworth, 1998; Williams, Anderson, McGee, & Silva, 1990). Egeland and Sroufe (1981) found that within the immediate environment (microsystem), having an anxious and insecure attachment pattern can place a child at risk for maltreatment (anxious attachment), while an avoidant attachment pattern can increase the risk of physical abuse or having a parent that is emotionally unavailable.

Risk and protective factors can be conceptualized along a continuum where a factor can be considered a risk if it is at one end of the spectrum, and a protective factor at the opposite end (Masten & Powell, 2003). For example, while having a positive self-concept can serve as a protective factor and buffer a child from harm, having a poor self-concept can increase the risk for negative outcomes. Durlak (1998) conducted a meta-analysis of over 1,000 prevention outcome studies and found the following breakdown of risks and protective factors within the context of Bronfenbrenner's ecological model. The risk and protective factors from that study are summarized in Table 1.1.

Table 1.1	Summary of Risks and Protective Factors	
Environmental Context	*Risk Factor*	*Protective Factor*
Child Characteristics	Early onset problems Difficult temperament	Social competence Self-efficacy
Microsystem	*Family:* Harsh or punitive discipline Marital problems Family psychopathology *School:* Poor-quality schools *Peers:* Negative peer influence Negative role models *Neighborhood:* Poor resources Violence	*Family:* Positive parent-child relationship *School:* Good-quality schools *Peers:* Positive peer influence Positive role models *Neighborhood:* Adequate resources Safe
Exosystem	Poverty	Lack of financial hardship
Macrosystem	Poorly administered schools Cultural conflict	Effective school policies Cultural acceptance

While social difficulties can increase the risk for negative outcomes, such as school dropout and delinquency (Blum et al., 2000), gender can make a difference in the nature of these risks. Girls who feel isolated and are without friends are twice as likely to engage in suicidal ideation than girls who belong to a social circle. While girls are protected from suicide by a supportive and cohesive support network, for males sharing activities with friends was a protective factor (Bearman & Moody, 2004).

THE CASE OF TERRY HOGAN: A BRIEF SUMMATION

Our case formulations for Terry Hogan have provided increased awareness of how different theoretical perspectives can contribute to an overall understanding of the nature and seriousness of her depressive symptoms. For Terry, risk factors evident on several levels have added to the severity of her problems. At the individual level, Terry's difficult temperament was a poor fit for her mother's impatient, inherently negative, and hostile approach to parenting (authoritarian parenting style). At a biological level, it is possible that Terry inherited a genetic vulnerability to depression. Terry's poor relationship with her mother and isolation from her peers have added to her feelings of being ineffectual, culminating in a sense of learned helplessness. Her tendencies to use withdrawal and avoidance, likely patterned after an avoidant attachment relationship, have successfully allowed her to escape from situations of discomfort (school and chores) by claiming to be feeling ill, which has resulted in these patterns being negatively reinforced, thereby increasing and strengthening this avoidant behavior pattern. Her mother has focused on Terry as the "problem child," allowing her to ignore major problems in the marital relationship. In addition to these underlying dynamics, Terry is at increased risk for major depression and possibly a suicide attempt because of the presence of a multitude of risk factors. It is unknown whether her recent move to Tennessee will provide a more stable environment with increased support from her aunt's family, or begin a spiral that leads to increased symptoms of depression and increased risk for suicide.

REFERENCES

Abramson, L. Y., Alloy, L. B., Hankin, B. L., Haeffel, G. J., MacCoon, D. G., & Gibb, B. E. (2002). Cognitive vulnerability: Stress models of depression in a self-regulatory and psychological context. In I. H. Gotlib & C. L. Hammen (Eds.), *Handbook of depression* (pp. 268–294). New York: Guilford.

Ainsworth, M. D. S., Blehar, M. C., Waters, E., & Wall, S. (1978). *Patterns of attachment.* Hillsdale. NJ: Lawrence Erlbaum.

American Psychiatric Association (APA). (2000). *Diagnostic and statistical manual of mental disorders* (4th ed., text rev.). Washington, DC: Author.

Apter, A., Kronenberg, S., & Brent, D. (2005). Turning darkness into light: A new landmark study on the treatment of adolescent depression. Comments on the TADS study. *European Child and Adolescent Psychiatry, 14,* 113–116.

Atzaba-Poria, N., Pike, A., & Deater-Deckard, K. (2004). Do risk factors for problem behaviour act in a cumulative manner? An examination of ethnic minority and majority children through an ecological perspective. *Journal of Child Psychology and Psychiatry, 45,* 707–718.

Barkley, R. A. (1997). *Attention deficit hyperactivity disorder.* New York: Guilford.

Barlow, D. H. (1986). In defense of panic disorder with agoraphobia in the behavioral treatment of panic: A comment on Kleiner. *The Behavior Therapist, 9,* 99–100.

Bates, J. E., Pettit, G. S., Dodge, K. A., & Ridge, B. (1998). The interaction of temperamental resistance to control and parental discipline in the prediction of children's externalizing problems. *Developmental Psychology, 34,* 982–995.

Baumrind, D. (1991). The influences of parenting style on adolescent competence and substance use. *Journal of Early Adolescence, 11,* 56–95.

Bearman, P. S., & Moody, J. (2004). Suicide and friendships among American adolescents. *American Journal of Public Health, 94,* 89–95.

Beauchaine, T. P., Strassberg, Z., Kees, M. R., & Drabick, D. A. G. (2002). Cognitive response repertoires to child noncompliance by mothers of aggressive boys. *Journal of Abnormal Child Psychology, 30,* 89–101.

Beck, A. T. (1997). Cognitive therapy: Reflections. In J. K. Zeig (Ed.), *The evolution of psychotherapy: The third conference.* New York: Brunner/Mazel.

Beck, A. T. (2002). Cognitive models of depression. In R. L. Leahy & E. T. Dowd (Eds.), *Clinical advances in cognitive psychotherapy: Theory and application* (pp. 29–61). New York: Springer.

Belsky, J. (1988). Child maltreatment and the emergent family system. In K. Browne, C. Davies, & P. Strattan (Eds.), *Early prediction and prevention of child abuse* (pp. 291–302). New York: John Wiley.

Belsky, J. (1997). Variation in susceptibility to environmental influence: An evolutionary argument. *Psychological Inquiry, 8,* 82–186.

Belsky, J. (1999). Patterns of attachment in modern evolutionary perspective. In J. Cassidy & P. R. Shaver (Eds.), *Handook of attachment* (pp. 141–161). New York: Guilford.

Berman, P. S. (1997). *Case conceptualization and treatment planning: Exercises for integrating theory and clinical practice.* Thousand Oaks, CA: Sage.

Blum, R. W., Beuhring, T., Shew, M. L., Bearinger, L. H., Sieving, R. E., & Resnick, M. D. (2000). The effects of race/ethnicity, income and family structure on adolescent risk behaviors. *American Journal of Public Health, 90,* 1885–1891.

Bowlby, J. (1982). *Attachment and loss: Vol. 1. Attachment* (2nd ed.). New York: Basic Books. (Original work published 1969)

Brestan, E. V., & Eyberg, S. M. (1998). Effective psychosocial treatments of conduct disordered children and adolescents: 29 years, 82 studies, and 5, 272 kids. *Journal of Clinical Child Psychology, 27,* 180–189.

Bridge, J. A., Iyengar, S., Salary, C. B., Barbe, R. P., Birmaher, B., Pincus, H. A., et al. (2007). Clinical response and risk for reported suicidal ideation and suicide attempts in pediatric antidepressant treatment: A meta-analysis of randomized controlled trials. *Journal of the American Medical Association, 297,* 1683–1696.

Bronfenbrenner, U. (1979). *The ecology of human development.* Cambridge, MA: Harvard University Press.

Bronfenbrenner, U. (1989). Ecological systems theory. *Annals of Child Development, 6,* 187–249.

Bronfenbrenner, U., & Morris, P. A. (1998). The ecology of developmental processs. In R. M. Lerner (Ed.), *Handbook of chld psychology: Vol 1. Theoretical models of human development* (5th ed., pp. 535–584). New York: John Wiley.

Bruch, M., & Bond, F. W. (1999). *Beyond diagnosis: Case formulation approaches in CBT.* New York: John Wiley.

Bugental, D. B., Blue, J., & Lewis, J. (1990). Caregiver beliefs and dysphoric affect directed to difficult children. *Developmental Psychology, 26,* 631–638.

Burchinal, M., Vernon-Feagans, L., & Cox, M. (2008). Cumulative social risk, parenting, and infant development in rural low-income communities. *Parenting: Science and Practice, 8,* 41–69.

Busch, F. N., Rudden, M. G., & Shapiro, T. (2004) *Psychodynamic treatment of depression.* Washington, DC: American Psychiatric Publishing.

Caspi, A., Sugden, K., Moffit, T. E., Taylor, A., Craig, I., Harrington, H., et al. (2003). Influence of life stress on depression moderation by a polymorphism in the 5-HTT gene. *Science, 18,* 386–389.

Cicchetti, D., & Lynch, M. (1993). Toward an ecological/transactional model of community violence and child maltreatment: Consequences for children's development. *Psychiatry, 56,* 96–118.

Cicchetti, D., & Rogosch, F. A. (1996). Editorial: Equifinality and multifinality in developmental psychopathology. *Developmental Psychopathology, 8,* 597–600.

Cone, J. D. (1997). Issues in functional analysis in behavioral assessment. *Behavior Research and Therapy, 35,* 259–275.

Dodge, K., Bates, J., & Pettit, G. (1990). Mechanisms in the cycle of violence. *Science, 250,* 1678–1683.

Ducharme, J. M., & Popynick, M. (1993). Errorless compliance to parental requests: Treatment effects and generalization. *Behavior Therapy, 24,* 209–226.

Durlak, J. (1998). Common risk and protective factors in successful prevention programs. *American Journal of Orthopsychiatry, 68,* 512–520.

Eells, D. (Ed.). (1997). *Handbook of psychotherapy case formulation.* New York: Guilford.

Egeland, B., & Sroufe, L. A. (1981). Developmental sequelae of maltreatment in infancy. In D. Cicchetti & R. Rizley (Eds.), *New directions in child development: Developmental approaches to child maltreatment.* San Francisco: Jossey-Bass.

Eisenberger, N. I., Lieberman, M. D., & Williams, K. D. (2003). Does rejection hurt? An fMRI study of social exclusion, *Science, 302,* 290–292.

Emslie, G. J., Rush, A. J., Weinberg, W. A., Kowatch, R. A., Hughes, C., Carmody, T., et al. (1997). A double-blind, randomized, placebo-controlled trial of fluoxetine in children and adolescents with depression. *Archives of General Psychiatry, 54,* 1031–1037.

Fonagy, P. (1999). Psychoanalytic theory from the viewpoint of attachment theory and research. In J. Cassidy & P. Shaver (Eds.), *Handbook of attachment: Theory, research and clinical applications* (pp. 595–624). New York: Guilford.

Fonagy, P., & Target, M. (1996). A contemporary psychoanalytical perspective: Psychodynamic developmental therapy. In E. D. Hibbs & P. S. Jensen (Eds.), *Psychosocial treatments for child and adolescent disorders: Empirically based strategies from clinical practice* (pp. 619–638). Washington, DC: American Psychological Association.

Fonagy, P., Target, M., Cottrell, D., Phillips, J., & Kurtz, Z. (2002). *What works for whom? A critical review of treatments for children and adolescents.* New York: Guilford.

Greenberg, M. T. (1999). Attachment and psychopathology in childhood. In J. Cassidy & P. Shaver (Eds.), *Handbook of attachment: Theory, research and clinical applications* (pp. 469–496). New York: Guilford.

Greenberg, M. T., & Speltz, M. L. (1988). Contributions of attachment theory to the understanding of conduct problems during the preschool years. In J. Belsky & T. Nezworski (Eds.), *Clinical implications of attachment* (pp. 177–218). Hillsdale, NJ: Lawrence Erlbaum.

Greenberg, M. T., Speltz, M. L., DeKlyen, M., & Endriga, M. C. (1993). The role of attachment in early development of disruptive behavior problems. *Development and Psychopathology, 5,* 191–213.

Hartup, W., & Laursen, B. (1993). Conflict and context in peer relations. In C. Hart (Ed.), *Children on playgrounds: Research perspectives and applications.* Ithaca: State University of New York Press.

Haynes, S. N., & O'Brien, W. H. (1990). Functional analysis in behavior therapy. *Clinical Psychology Review, 10,* 649–668.

Hecimovic, H., & Gilliam, F. G. (2006). Neurobiology of depression and new opportunities for treatment. In F. Gilliam, A. M. Kanner, & Y. I. Sheline (Eds.), *Depression and brain dysfunction* (pp. 51–84). New York: Taylor & Francis.

Held, B. (1996). Solution-focused therapy and the postmodern. In S. D. Miller, M. R. Hubble, & B. Duncan (Eds.), *Handbook of solution-focused brief therapy* (pp. 27–43). San Francisco: Jossey-Bass.

Hersen, M., & Porzelius, L. K. (Eds.). (2002). *Diagnosis, conceptualization and treatment planning for adults: A step-by-step guide.* Mahwah, NJ: Lawrence Erlbaum.

Kazdin, A. E. (1983). Psychiatric diagnosis, dimensions of dysfunction and child behavior therapy. *Behavior Therapy, 14,* 73–99.

Kendall, P. C., Chansky, T. E., Kane, M., Kim, R., Kortlander, E., Roana, K., et al. (1992). *Anxiety disorders in youth: Cognitive-behavioral interventions.* Needham Heights, MA: Allyn & Bacon.

Kramer, S., & Akhtar, S. (1989). The developmental context of internalized preoedipal object relations: Clinical applications of Mahler's theory of symbiosis and separations-individuation. *Psychoanalytic Quarterly, 57,* 547–576.

Kronenberger, W. G., & Meyer, R. G. (2001). *The child clinician's handbook* (2nd ed.). Needham Heights, MA: Allyn & Bacon.

La Greca, A. M., & Lemanek, K. L. (1996). Editorial: Assessment as a process in pediatric psychology. *Journal of Pediatric Psychology, 21,* 137–151.

Laible, D. J., & Thompson R. A. (1998). Attachment and emotional understanding in preschool children. *Developmental Psychology, 34,* 1038–1045.

Lieberman, A. F., & Zeanah, C. H. (1999). Contributions of attachment theory to infant-parent psychotherapy and other interventions with infants and young children. In J. Cassidy & P. Shaver (Eds.), *Handbook of attachment: Theory, research and clinical applications* (pp. 555–574). New York: Guilford.

Lynch, M., & Cicchetti, D. (1998). An ecological-transactional analysis of children and contexts: The longitudinal interplay among child maltreatment, community violence, and children's symptomatology. *Development and Psychopathology, 10,* 235–257.

Lyons-Ruth, K., Bronfman, E., & Atwood, G. (1999). A relational diathesis model of hostile-helpless states of mind: Expressions in mother-infant interaction. In J. Solomon & C. George (Eds.), *Attachment disorganization* (pp. 33–70). New York: Guilford.

Main, M. (1995). Recent studies in attachment: Overview, with selected implications for clinical work. In S. Goldberg, R. Muir, & J. Kerr (Eds.), *Attachment theory: Social, developmental and clinical perspectives* (pp. 407–474). Hillsdale, NJ: Analytic Press.

Main, M., & Hesse, E. (1990). Parents' unresolved traumatic experiences are related to infant disorganized attachment status: Is frightened and/or frightening parental behavior the linking mechanism? In M. T. Greenberg, D. Cicchetti, & E. M. Cummings (Eds.), *Attachment in the preschool years: Theory, research, and intervention* (pp. 161–184). Chicago: University of Chicago Press.

Malphurs, J., Field, T., Larraine, C., Pickens J., & Pelaez-Nogueras, M. (1996). Altering withdrawn and intrusive interaction behaviors of depressed mothers. *Infant Mental Health Journal, 17,* 152–160.

Marvin, R. S., & Stewart, R. B. (1990). A family systems framework for the study of attachment. In M. T. Greenberg, D. Cicchetti, & E. M. Cummings (Eds.), *Attachment in the preschool years: Theory, research, and intervention* (pp. 51–86). Chicago: University of Chicago Press.

Mash, E. J., & Terdal, L. G. (1997). *Assessment of childhood disorders* (3rd ed.). New York: Guilford.

Masten, A. S., & Coatsworth, J. D. (1998). The development of competence in favorable and unfavorable environments: Lessons from research on successful children. *American Psychologist, 53205–53220.

Masten, A. S., & Powell, J. L. (2003). A resilience framework for research, policy and practice. In S. S. Luthar (Ed.), *Resiliency and vulnerability: Adaption in the context of childhood adversities* (pp. 1–28). Cambridge, UK: Cambridge University Press.

McWilliams, N. (1999). *Psychoanalytic case formulation.* New York: Guilford.

Messer, S. (2000). A psychodynamic clinician responds to Fishman's case study proposal. *Prevention & Treatment, 3*(1). Retrieved October 31, 2009, from http://search.ebscohost.com, doi:10.1037/1522-3736.3.1.39c

Minuchin, P. (1985). Families and individual development: Provocations from the field of family therapy. *Child Development, 56,* 289–302.

Nomura, H., Inoue, S., Kamimura, N., Shimodera, S., Mino, Y., Gregg, L., et al. (2005). A cross-cultural study on expressed emotion in careers of people with dementia and schizophrenia: Japan and England. *Social Psychiatry and Psychiatric Epidemiology, 40*(7), 564–570.

Patterson, G. R., Capaldi, D., & Bank, L. (1991). An early starter model for predicting delinquency. In D. Pepler & K. H. Rubin (Eds.), *The development and treatment of childhood aggression* (pp. 139–168). Hillsdale, NJ: Lawrence Erlbaum.

Persons, J. B. (1989). *Cognitive therapy in practice: A case formulation approach.* New York: W. W. Norton.

Pliszka, S. R. (2002). *Neuroscience for the mental health clinician.* New York: Guilford.

Rubin, K. H., Hymel, S., Mills, S. L., & Rose-Krasnor, L. (1991). Conceptualizing different developmental pathways to and from social isolation in children. In D. Cicchetti & S. L. Toth (Eds.), *Rochester Symposium on Developmental Psychopathology: Vol. 2. Internalizing and externalizing expressions of dysfunction* (pp. 91–122). Hillsdale, NJ: Lawrence Erlbaum.

Rutter, M. (1979). Protective factors in children's responses to stress and disadvantage. In M. Whalen & J. E. Rolf (Eds.), *Primary prevention of psychopathology: Vol. 3. Social competence in children* (pp. 49–79). Hanover, NH: University Press of New England.

Rutter, M., Silberg, J., O'Connor, T., & Simonoff, E. (1999). Genetics and child psychiatry II: Empirical research findings. *Journal of Child Psychology and Psychiatry and Allied Disciplines, 40,* 19–55.

Sameroff, A. J., & Fiese, B. H. (2000). Transactional regulation: The developmental ecology of early intervention. In J. P. Shonkoff & S. J. Meisels (Eds.), *Handbook of early childhood intervention* (2nd ed., pp. 135–159). New York: Cambridge University Press.

Seligman, M. E. P. (1975). *Helplessness*. San Francisco: W. H. Freeman.

Settlage, C. F. (1977). The psychodynamic understanding of narcissistic and borderline personality disorders. Advances in developmental theory. *Journal of the American Psychoanalytic Association, 25,* 805–833.

Shaffer, D., Fisher, P., Dulcan, M. K., Davies, M., Piacentini, J., Schwab-Stone, M. E., et al. (1996). The NIMH Diagnostic Interview Schedule for Children Version 2.3 (DISC- 2.3): Description, acceptability, prevalence rates and performance in the MECA study. Methods for the Epidemiology of Child and Adolescent Mental Disorders Study. *Journal of the American Academy of Child and Adolescent Psychiatry, 35,* 865–877.

Shirk, S. R., & Russell, R. L. (1996). *Change processes in child psychotherapy.* New York: Guilford.

Siegel, D. (1999). *The developing mind: Toward a neurobiology of interpersonal experience.* New York: Guilford.

Spaccarelli, S., Cotler, S., & Penman, D. (1992). Problem-solving skills training as a supplement to behavioral parent training. *Cognitive Therapy and Research, 27,* 171–186.

Speltz, M. (1990). The treatment of preschool conduct problems: An integration of behavioral and attachment concepts. In M. T. Greenberg, D. Cicchetti, & M. Cummings (Eds.), *Attachment in the preschool years: Theory, research, and intervention* (pp. 399–426). Chicago: University of Chicago Press.

Stark, K., Reynolds, W., & Kaslow, N. (1987). A comparison of the relative efficacy of self-control therapy and behavioral problem-solving therapy for depression in children. *Journal of Abnormal Child Psychology, 15,* 91–113.

Stark, K. D., Swearer, S., Kurkowski, C., Sommer, D., & Bowen, B. (1996). Targeting the child and family: A holistic approach to treating child and adolescent depressive disorders. In E. D. Hibbs & P. S. Jensen (Eds.), *Psychosocial treatments for child and adolescent disorders: Empirically based strategies for clinical practice* (pp. 207–238). Washington, DC: APA.

Thase, M. E., Jindal, R., & Howland, R. H. (2002). Biological aspects of depression. In I. H. Gotlib & C. L. Hammen (Eds.), *Handbook of depression* (pp. 192–218). New York: Guilford.

Thompson, R. A. (1999). Early attachment and later development. In J. Cassidy & P. Shaver (Eds.), *Handbook of attachment: Theory, research and clinical applications* (pp. 265–286). New York: Guilford.

Turkat, I. D. (1985). *Behavioral case formulation*. New York: Kluwer Academic/Plenum.

Weerasekera, P. (1996). *Multi-perspective case formulation: A step towards treatment integration.* Malabar, FL: Krieger.

Weisz, J. R., Doss, A. J., & Hawley, K. M. (2005). Youth psychotherapy outcome research: A review and critique of the evidence base. *Annual Review of Psychology, 56*(1), pp. 337–363.

Weisz, J. R., Doss, A. J., & Hawley, K. M. (2005). Evidence-based youth psychotherapies versus usual clinical care: A meta-analysis of direct comparisons. (2006*). American Psychologist, l 61*(7), pp. 671–689.

Weisz, J. R., Weiss, B. B., Han, S. S., Granger, D. A., & Morton, E. (1995). Effects of psychotherapy with children and adolescents revisited: A meta-analysis of treatment outcome studies. *Psychological Bulletin, 117,* 450–468.

Werner, E., & Smith, R. (1992*). Overcoming the odds.* New York: Cornell University Press.

Wielkiewicz, R. M. (1995). *Behavior management in the schools: Principles and procedures* (2nd ed.). Needham Heights, MA: Allyn & Bacon.

Williams, S., Anderson, J., McGee, R., & Silva, P. A. (1990). Risk factors for behavioral and emotional disorder in preadolescent children. *Journal of the American Academy of Child and Adolescent Psychiatry, 29,* 413–419.

Zeanah, C., Boris, N. W., Heller, S. S., Hinshaw-Fuselier, S., Larrieu, J., Lewis, M., et al. (1997). Relationship assessment in infant mental health. *Infant Mental Health Journal, 18,* 182–197.

Part II

Case Studies

The Early Years

Jeremy Jones

Mommy and Me and Grandma Makes Three

Jeremy is a 6-year-old Caucasian boy who came to the clinic accompanied by his mother, Debbie, and his maternal grandmother, Blanche. Jeremy was referred for assessment by his pediatrician. Despite trials of numerous medications and doses, Jeremy has continued to demonstrate problem behaviors that are hyperactive, impulsive, and noncompliant. Jeremy currently takes Adderol twice daily (morning and noon) and Resperdol three times daily (morning, noon, and evening). Jeremy has been taking Adderol for 2 years and Resperdol for the past year. Although Jeremy appears to be a very bright boy, he is currently repeating the kindergarten program, since he was considered "too immature" to progress to Grade 1.

DEVELOPMENTAL HISTORY/FAMILY BACKGROUND

Jeremy's mother provided the following background information. Jeremy weighed 7 pounds 6 ounces at birth. Although the pregnancy, labor, and delivery were all normal, Jeremy was severely jaundiced at birth. As a result, he remained hospitalized for 5 days while he was placed under special lights called bili lights to alleviate the jaundice. Neonatal jaundice was the result of G6PD deficiency (an inherited human enzyme deficiency), a condition that causes an allergic reaction to fava beans, which can induce a severe anemic response. A similar response could develop if Jeremy developed viral hepatitis or pneumonia. He is monitored by his pediatrician, and all medication trials have been closely supervised. Jeremy has had no adverse reactions to the Adderol or the Resperdol.

Jeremy's milestones were advanced: walking at 8 months and speaking in simple phrases at 7 months. However, Jeremy continues to exhibit articulation problems, which his mother attributes to constant bouts of recurring ear infections. Mother and grandmother reported that by 2½ years of age, Jeremy was using words such as *humiliation* and *victimization* in his conversation and would have long conversations about experiments he was conducting in his "*laboratory*." Currently, Jeremy is receiving assistance for articulation from the speech pathologist at the school.

Shortly after his second birthday, Jeremy began to say "No" to everything, and power struggles have been ongoing ever since. According to grandmother, "Jeremy is as stubborn as a mule!" However, as much as Jeremy will say "No" or "I amn't gonna' do it," he will not take "No" for an answer. Jeremy coined the word amn't as a short version of "am not" when he was about 2 years of age, and his mother and grandmother continue to find it very amusing and repeatedly taunt him with it, saying they "amn't gonna' do it either." Apparently, Jeremy will argue about anything and everything and will "throw a fit" if he does not get his way. Although he likes to be challenged by doing difficult tasks (multipiece puzzles), he is very quickly frustrated and easily upset when he can't solve something. His mother believes Jeremy's stubbornness and strong desire to be first have caused problems at school, since Jeremy will push others out of the way in order to be first, and many of the other children avoid him. Reportedly, Jeremy loves to go to school, but adjusting to formal school routines and expectations has been difficult for him. His impulsive and willful behaviors get him into trouble, and his tendencies to carry boisterous and loud activities from the schoolyard into the classroom are disruptive. Jeremy was retained in kindergarten due to issues of immaturity, problems relating to peers, and lack of productivity regarding academic schoolwork. His teacher was unable to estimate Jeremy's current levels of functioning due to issues of noncompliance and failure to complete assigned work.

Jeremy was described as a very active and curious toddler. He was generally a good sleeper (mother said that he just wore himself out) and had a good appetite. When asked about any health issues, mother stated that Jeremy has been in good health. He has not had an ear infection in the past 2 years. He is vulnerable to skin rashes and seasonal allergies. They believe that Jeremy inherited both of these conditions from his grandmother, who has significant bouts of psoriasis and allergies to pollens and grasses. During the interviews, Grandma's psoriasis was very noticeable, as patches covered her exposed arms.

According to his mother, Jeremy has always had his "good days and bad days." He can be fun and playful, but then again, he can be very difficult and demanding. There were some difficulties with "potty training" and once again, parents suggested this might be due to Jeremy's stubborn nature. Grandmother was quite proud of the fact that her "potty training" methods made the difference in Jeremy finally becoming trained. Grandmother said that eventually he was trained by 3 years of age; however, she attributes successful training to monetary rewards. At one point, grandmother was rewarding successful potty episodes at $5.00 each.

There is a history of mental instability in the maternal family. Jeremy's mother and grandmother are currently on medication for depression (Prozac), and Jeremy's mother, Debbie, said that she has suffered from episodes of depression "on and off" for years. She did not do well in school and also wonders whether she has a learning disability or attentional problems. Mother is 25 years of age, is unemployed, and is currently taking one course at the local college. Grandmother is 55 years of age and is on a small disability pension. Grandmother reports that she is a highly anxious individual, as well as depressed, and "worries" about most things. Blanche said that most people in the family have "some mental problem or another" and added that her sister (Jeremy's great aunt) will not leave the house (agoraphobic?) and has panic attacks. Apparently, the maternal grandfather is an alcoholic and is also subject to violent outbursts and depression (bipolar?); his inability to tolerate medication made him "impossible to live with." Shortly after Jeremy's birth, Blanche moved in with her daughter and Jeremy to help with child rearing, since Debbie suffered an episode of postpartum depression lasting about 3 months. During this period, Debbie spent much of her time in bed sleeping, while Blanche cared for Jeremy. She said that she was "very anxious," since she had not cared for a baby in 20 years, and was fearful that she might do something wrong. Debbie reported that Jeremy's birth father told her he was "clinically classified as insane" and that he often engaged in reckless, dangerous behaviors and had been in trouble with the law. Jeremy has had no contact with his birth father or grandfather since his birth.

Debbie was in a car wreck 9 months ago, when her car was sideswiped by a truck. Although she was not hospitalized, she did sustain major bruising and continues to receive chiropractic treatment twice a week. Apparently, a teacher at Jeremy's school showed Jeremy a picture of the car, which had appeared in the newspaper, and Jeremy was so upset that he did not want to separate from his mother to go to school for the next 6 weeks. This has been a very difficult time for the family because of the stress of the accident and Jeremy's behaviors. School attendance has been sporadic, since some days, Blanche doesn't have the energy to "drag" Jeremy to school while Debbie is recuperating from her injuries.

REASON FOR REFERRAL

When asked the primary reason for having Jeremy assessed, the immediate response was that the pediatrician recommended it. When pressed further, both stated that they were very interested in knowing what Jeremy's IQ was. There was no mention of possibly finding a solution to managing his behavior problems.

ASSESSMENT RESULTS

Descriptions of the test instruments used in this assessment and guidelines for interpretation of standard scores and T scores are available in Appendix C.

Jeremy literally exploded into the clinician's office, abruptly letting go of his mother's hand and immediately trying to pry open the test kit on the table. The psychologist was able to halt further efforts to dismantle the test kit with a firm, "Not yet, Jeremy," while providing drawing paper and markers for his immediate attention. Despite his whirlwind arrival, his mother did confirm that Jeremy had taken his medication prior to coming. Mother left immediately after introducing Jeremy to the psychologist, and Jeremy evidenced no noticeable reaction to being left with a stranger or to his mother's departure. Although the psychologist attempted to engage Jeremy in conversation, Jeremy's poor articulation skills made conversation difficult.

Jeremy was far more interested in getting to the test materials, which were undoubtedly the "good stuff" of the assessment for him. Test behaviors and learning style revealed a youngster who was highly active and very fidgety and restless throughout the assessment sessions. Although he was responsive, he did have some difficulty staying on task when required and in complying with specific requests. Jeremy had trouble remaining seated and took turns sitting, standing, kneeling, rocking, and walking around the room. Attention span and compliance with task demands varied considerably across tasks. Tasks requiring manipulation of materials and hands-on activity were responded to with far more enthusiasm and focus than verbal tasks. Questions that required oral responses and provided minimal visual input were responded to poorly, if at all. During the vocabulary test, rather than provide oral answers in response to word definitions, Jeremy delighted in giving clues to the psychologist in visual form in a game-playing type of format. When asked to spell the word *cat* on the test protocol, Jeremy jumped out of his chair and drew a large picture of a cat on the blackboard. When asked to describe what a "clock" was, Jeremy made an arrow on the blackboard in the room pointing to the clock above it. When asked for a definition for the word *hat,* Jeremy again ran to the blackboard and added a hat to his drawing of the cat.

On tasks that were maximally engaging (blocks, puzzles, working with pictures), it was often necessary to curb Jeremy's enthusiasm. On these tasks, Jeremy often attempted to grab test materials before they were introduced and ignored instructions to wait until materials were presented. Jeremy was very intent on pursuing his own agenda, and there were frequent compliance issues. Redirection to task was frequently required throughout the assessment. There were two 35-minute assessment sessions, one week apart. At the completion of the first session, Jeremy heard the elevator and immediately ran out of the room and down the hall toward the top of a long staircase. The psychologist was concerned regarding safety issues, since Jeremy could easily have fallen down the stairs. Mother and grandmother took the opportunity to scold Jeremy for his behavior and, as a consequence, they were no longer going to stop at a restaurant on the way home.

When engaged in a task he enjoyed doing, Jeremy was able to attend to the stimulus materials adequately and problem solve without impulsive responding. He did evidence frustration on occasion, when he was unable to obtain an adequate solution, and appeared fatigued after working unsuccessfully on a block design for 1½ minutes. However, he was able to regroup and was more successful on the next two designs attempted. His speech evidenced many sound substitution errors ("wabbit" for "rabbit" and "ewebwoddy" for "everybody") and cluttering of words resulting in indistinct utterances. However, Jeremy readily repeated phrases when asked for clarification.

Responses to the Wechsler Intelligence Test for Children (WISC-IV) revealed that Jeremy's Verbal Comprehension Index (VCI) was within the average to high average range at approximately the 66th percentile (VCI range 99–112). Jeremy's Perceptual Reasoning Index (PRI) was within the superior range, at approximately the 98th percentile (PRI range 121–137). There was a 26-point discrepancy between his VCI and his PRI, which is highly significant and occurs in less than 10% of the population at Jeremy's age. Given the magnitude of this discrepancy, the full scale IQ was not calculated, since it would merely represent the numerical average of two very discrepant scores (Kaufman & Lichtenberger, 2000). Caution should be used in interpretation of the VCI score as a valid indicator of Jeremy's verbal skills, since his motivation and cooperation were questionable during the administration of the verbal items. Given Jeremy's attention span and interest level, it was not possible to administer tasks for the Working Memory Index (WMI), including digit recall and number-letter sequence. He did, however, complete the coding and symbol search tasks of the Processing Speed Index (PSI) well above average (scale score of 16 for the coding test and scale score of 13 for symbol search). Scores for visual reasoning were more consistent and revealed very strong performance overall. Relative strengths were noted in picture reasoning, matrix reasoning, and block designs, all of which were at the 98th percentile. Academically, Jeremy's responses to the Wide Range Achievement Test (WRAT-3) revealed inconclusive information, since Jeremy completed only those questions he wanted to try. When asked to draw a boy, Jeremy stated that he would draw a man instead. The drawing was very immature in areas of line juncture and body proportion. Jeremy participated in providing responses to the

Joseph Pre-School and Primary Self-Concept Screening Test. Jeremy's responses indicated that his Global Self-Esteem was within the high positive range.

During the clinical intake interview, Jeremy's mother completed several checklists derived from criteria outlined in the *Diagnostic and Statistical Manual of Mental Disorders* (*DSM-IV-TR;* APA, 2000). Mother endorsed the following items from the ADHD scale as occurring often or always: *fidgets with hands or feet (squirmy); has problems awaiting his turn; problems playing quietly; problems sustaining attention in tasks; does not listen; problems organizing tasks; problems remaining seated; easily distracted; forgetful; loses necessary items; runs about and climbs incessantly; often on the go, driven; blurts out answers before questions are asked;* and *avoids tasks that require sustained mental effort.* On informal scales for problem behaviors, Jeremy's mother noted that he is very often "noncompliant" and "defiant" and that he can, at times, be very difficult to deal with. Particular behaviors that occurred frequently included *loss of temper; blames others for his mistakes; argues with adults; touchy, easily annoyed;* and *actively defies or refuses to comply with adult requests.*

As well as informal, diagnostic scales, Jeremy's mother also completed the Conners Parent Rating Scale (CPRS-R:L) and the Child Behavior Checklist (CBCL). According to ratings on the CPRS-R:L, Jeremy demonstrates clinically significant symptoms of attention-deficit hyperactivity disorder, predominantly the impulsive/hyperactive type. In addition, oppositional behaviors and perfectionistic tendencies were also in the clinical range. There were indications that Jeremy complains of physical symptoms more than the average child and that he can be prone to anxiety. Symptoms of distractibility and tendencies to perseverate on ideas were evident on the CBCL. As part of the intake information, mother also completed the Parenting Stress Index (PSI; Abidin, 1995) where she rated Jeremy at or above the 99th percentile for distractibility/hyperactivity, inability to adjust to changes in environment, and demandingness. Elevations on these scales are typical for parents of children with ADHD, with demandingness often the peak scale (Abidin, 1995). With respect to family stresses, mother endorsed only concerns about her health as a significant stressor. Grandmother declined to complete any forms, saying that "Debbie is the mother."

Jeremy's teacher completed the Conners Teacher Rating Scale (CTRS-R:L) and the Teacher Report Form (TRF: Achenbach). Although the teacher ratings were less elevated than Jeremy's mother's ratings in all areas, his teacher also noted some concerns regarding perfectionistic tendencies. According to the TRF, hyperactive-impulsive behaviors were at the 95th percentile, indicating significant difficulties in this area. In addition, thought persistence was also noted as problematic.

Based on assessment results, intake information, and clinical observations, the psychologist produced the following preliminary summary and diagnostic impression:

Summary of Jeremy's Formal Assessment

Jeremy is a 6-year-old boy who is currently repeating kindergarten at J.J.B. Elementary School. Jeremy is a bright and engaging child; however, he is experiencing difficulties at home and at school as a result of hyperactive and impulsive behaviors and tendencies to be noncompliant in situations where he is not in control and where he is expected to follow directions that may or may not be to his liking.

Although Jeremy scored in the superior range on tasks of visual reasoning, his scores on verbal reasoning tasks were less impressive due to several factors, including Jeremy's lack of interest and motivation to respond to verbal tasks. It is suspected that his weaker performance on verbal tasks reflects his lack of task engagement rather than his learning potential. Despite his excellent reasoning ability, Jeremy may continue to experience difficulties due to poor ability to regulate activity levels relative to task demands; Jeremy was either *understimulated* (task was not interesting to him), or *overstimulated* (task was very exciting). In the former case, Jeremy revealed poor attention span and distractibility, while in the latter case he showed poor restraint and impulsivity. Problems with compliance were also noted throughout, suggesting that Jeremy has developed a strong repertoire of manipulative strategies that may be more resistant to correction than if he were not so high functioning. Another way in which his superior intelligence may be a risk factor is that Jeremy's lack of success academically may be even more frustrating for him. The significant discrepancy between VCI and PRI may also indicate a specific learning disability, which might complicate academic progress. Certainly at this point, Jeremy's academic skill levels are virtually nonexistent. Whether academic difficulties result from a specific learning disability or an inability to apply himself to the task at hand remains to be seen.

Mother and grandmother jointly completed the Home Situations Questionnaire (Barkley, 1997) to provide increased understanding of the nature of Jeremy's noncompliant behaviors and how they were being managed within the home. The Home Situations Questionnaire classifies compliance problems in three areas within the home: instructions, commands, or rules. Results revealed four primary problematic situations: when parents are talking on the telephone, when parents are watching television, when Jeremy is asked to do chores (cleaning the room), and when Jeremy is asked to do homework. Problem areas were discussed at length, and parents engaged in role-play to demonstrate how each would interact with Jeremy under problem conditions. Based on the dialogue and role-play, two areas of compliance difficulty were targeted for further investigation. The parents selected problems with chores (specifically, when Jeremy is asked to clean up his room, pick up his toys, etc.) and talking on the telephone (Jeremy's intrusiveness when mother or grandmother is occupied) as the two problem areas of most concern.

1. Compliance with requests to clean his room: Parents agreed that when asked to clean his room, Jeremy typically engages in argumentative behaviors (why he shouldn't have to do it), delay tactics (says he will do it later), manipulations (asks for help), or refusals (says he can't or won't do it). There was also agreement about the methods used by each parent, saying that they had figured out the "good cop, bad cop" routine wasn't working, nor was mother's response to count to three. Jeremy had pretty well figured out that most times there wasn't going to be anything happening after the three count, so this was not very effective. Mom's response to Jeremy not cleaning his room usually involved yelling and screaming. She proudly related a scenario that had recently happened, where Jeremy yelled back at her "as loud as possible," but mother retaliated as loud as she could, just to show him that she could out-scream him. He tried but he couldn't do it; as a result, mother said that he had learned his lesson that she screams the loudest. While mother screams, grandmother basically gives in and will clean the room for him to avoid any further problems. A functional behavioral assessment and behavioral intervention plan to increase compliant behaviors will be discussed as a treatment alternative later in the chapter.

2. Interruptions while trying to talk on the telephone. Specifically, "Jeremy will stand in your face and talk at you, so you can't hear the person on the telephone; he won't wait until the call is finished." Mother's typical response to the above problem was to take the phone outside (if the weather was nice) or to yell at Jeremy. Grandmother reported getting very upset with him and hanging up the phone as a result.

ISSUES, TRENDS, AND TREATMENT ALTERNATIVES

Jeremy has a long history of family psychopathology (Cicchetti & Toth, 1998), including attention problems (mother and possibly father); mood disorders (mother, maternal grandmother, possibly maternal grandfather); anxiety disorders (grandmother, potentially maternal aunt); substance abuse (maternal grandfather); and antisocial personality disorder (father). Studies reveal that 50% of parents with ADHD have a child who is also ADHD (Biederman et al., 1995). Genetic transmission for depression is estimated to be between 20% and 45% (Rutter, Silberg, O'Connor, & Simonoff, 1999), with almost half developing bipolar disorder; odds for bipolar increase if there is a family history for the disorder (Geller et al., 2002). General anxiety disorder, panic attacks, or obsessive thoughts and behaviors result from malfunctions of GABA (gamma-amniobutyric acid), which normally inhibits arousal, resulting in heightened levels of stimulation (Lloyd, Fletcher, & Minuchin, 1992). Heritability of GABA malfunction can be as high as 30 to 40% (Eley, 1999). If antisocial personality disorder is present in the immediate family, there is an increased risk for aggressive and disruptive behavior disorders (*DSM-IV-TR;* APA, 2000). Studies have found that individuals with disorders of impulse control, such as antisocial personality disorder, react to stressful circumstances in a dysregulated and destructive manner, often directing their destructive actions toward violation of rights of others. In these cases, individuals who inherit the short allele (5HTT) of the serotonin neurotransmitter react with heightened activation of the amygdale and cortical systems (Barr et al., 2003; Hairiri, 2002). During these stressful episodes, aggressive behaviors (destructive impulses toward others) become more probable (Stanley, Molcho, & Stanley, 2000). Lyons-Ruth and colleagues (2007) found that the short form of the 5HTT was linked to an increased risk for antisocial symptoms; individuals who had inherited the short form of the serotonin transporter allele were twice as likely to express impulse disorder symptoms, while those who inherited two of the short alleles were at four times the risk of developing impulse disorders.

Child temperament can be another biological marker influencing a child's response to his or her environment. Rydell, Berlin, and Bohlin (2001) studied children who were high on *emotionality* (intensity of emotional arousal) and low on *social adaptation* (respond to emotionally charged situations in either a "flight" [withdrawal and avoidance] or "fight" [anger and .aggression] pattern). They found that children with this combination were poorly equipped to manage their emotional responses to environmental demands. Although previous research has demonstrate that maladaptive responses occur in response to highly negative conditions (e.g., internalizing children would withdraw and avoid social contact, while externalizing children would aggress and break rules), Rydell and colleagues (2001) found that children with externalizing problems escalated out of control in highly positive charged situations, as well (e.g., the child cannot manage negative or positive emotions).

Although above-average intelligence is usually thought of as a protective factor (Luthar & Zigler, 1992), in Jeremy's case, superior intelligence may place him at greater risk for maladaptive behaviors, if he uses his intellectual capacity to "outwit and outsmart" his caregivers by developing manipulative strategies and engaging them in power struggles.

Environmental factors can interact with biological traits and vulnerabilities in a way that exacerbates existing conditions. Barkley (1997) suggests a four-factor model to explain factors that can maintain and increase noncompliant behavior. According to this model, predisposing characteristics include

1. the temperament of the child (temperamental, high emotional reactivity, impulsive, active, inattentive),

2. the temperament of the parents (immature, temperamental, and impulsive),

3. child management patterns (inconsistent, harsh, indiscriminate, and coercive parenting, and poor monitoring of child activities), and

4. distressed family environment (financial, health, and personal stressors).

The model is well suited as a framework for developing case formulations that can integrate information across theoretical models.

Disruptive behaviors can be enduring, with patterns of persistent oppositional and aggressive behaviors beginning in the preschool years and persisting across development (Owens & Shaw, 2003). Jeremy has several risk factors for the development of disruptive behavior patterns. Historically, Jeremy's temperament has been problematic in areas of adaptation to change and emotional reactivity, resulting in difficulties with emotion regulation (Bridges & Grolnick, 1995). When we place this temperament pattern within the context of the underlying dynamics inherent in this mother-grandmother-parented family that often seems to shift roles as to who is the parent and who is the child, the problems increase in intensity. Other environmental risk factors for disruptive behavior disorders include insecure attachment (Rutter, 1995; Sroufe, 1997), cycles of maternal depression and rejection (postpartum depression), child aggression and impulsivity (Owens & Shaw, 2003), poor school adjustment, and lack of positive peer relationships (Blum et al., 2000). Maternal depression with features of irritability, criticism, and lack of positive affect can also increase the risk of disruptive behaviors in children (Aguilar, Sroufe, Egeland, & Carlson, 2000).

Parenting, Attachment, and Family Systems

Insecure attachment may pave the way for Jeremy to develop separation anxiety in response to his mother's recent car accident, resulting in excessive need for proximity and heightened fears of possible loss. When placed in fearful situations, being soothed by the parent can assist the infant in building brain structures that can help regulate responses to fearful situations in the future. However, in dysfunctional attachment relationships, caregivers do not provide assistance in the regulation of emotions, such as fear, and actually can become a fear-provoking agent. In these circumstances, infants do not learn how to self-soothe in stress-producing situations. Lyons-Ruth and colleagues (2007) found that early child care problems resulted in negative outcomes several years later. As a result, Lyons-Ruth (2008) suggests that "disruptions in early mother-infant communication are clearly important to long-term prediction of some forms of psychopathology" (p. 209). Since early attachment patterns provide the schema for later relationships, Lyons-Ruth goes on to suggest that contradictory cues may disable an individual's ability to develop an appropriate working model for relationships. Pertinent to Jeremy's case, research has also found transgeneration effects that explain how the controlling pattern of hostile, punitive, or rejecting behaviors of mothers with insecurely attached boys with oppositional defiant disorder mimic their own backgrounds of insecure attachment patterns (DeKlyen, Speltz, & Greenberg, 1996). Disruptive behaviors may play an instrumental role in the attachment process by acting to control and regulate caregiver proximity and attentiveness. Through the use of negative attention-seeking behaviors, such as noncompliance, the child can "lock in" attachment figures based on the use of negative attachment behaviors. It has been suggested that these maladaptive behaviors may fit with the overall schema of family dysfunction (Marvin & Stewart, 1990).

Family systems theory would recognize several problems inherent in this family triad that has few limits and very loosely defined boundaries. Mother, grandmother, and Jeremy seem to be enmeshed in each other's lives (Minuchin, 1985) and, as a result, Jeremy is often privy to information that is well beyond his years. It is also likely that triangulation can occur, with the balance of power and status shifting among the family members, depending on which two members are aligned together.

Today, many grandparents fill the role of *surrogate parent* for their grandchildren (Edwards, 2003). Within the past 20 years, the number of grandparents who assume an active role in caring for their grandchildren has increased dramatically (Cox, 2000; Goodman & Silverstein, 2005). Currently, approximately 4.5 million children are living in grandparent-headed households (AARP, 2007), with the average age of grandparents in this situation between 55 and 64 (Smith & Dannison, 2002).

Within this situation, family members are often placed in a non-normative relational context that can place grandparents in a conflicted relationship (Cox, 2000), and many grandparents have revealed feelings of being "torn" between tending to their grandchildren's needs and the needs of their own adult children (Musil, Schrader, & Mutikani, 2000). According to Cox (2000), this ambiguous role often leaves grandparents confused regarding how to define their position in the family, while at the same time feeling "responsible for shaping and giving meaning to this new identity, defining it according to their own personalities, resources, and values" (p. 6). In their research, Williamson, Softas-Nall, and Miller (2003) identified a number of positive feelings that grandparents associated with their surrogate role, including the emotional feeling of *grandmothering* and being able to contribute; however, a number of negative experiences were also revealed, including depression, financial worries, abuse and neglect of grandchildren, and problems with disciplining the children.

Erbert and Alemán (2008) investigated the dialectical tensions inherent in the grandparenting experience, and identified three contradictory processes that occurred in their sample: *connection versus separation* (a feeling of greater connectedness with their family is offset by the loss of their own retirement activities and fears about their inabilities to care for grandchildren), *stability versus change* (becoming reinvolved in the raising of children at a time when the intergenerational gap has widened, e.g., an inability to relate to their social world in the face of fears of increasing gang violence), and *protection versus expression* (fears of being unable to protect the children from threats that are so different from when they raised their children, e.g., gangs, kidnapping, molestation, etc.).

Grandparents raising children are twice as likely to be diagnosed with depression than their peers who are not in a caregiver role (Fuller-Thompson, Minkler, & Driver, 2000) and experience lower levels of psychological well-being (Baker & Silverstein, 2008). Grandparent-headed households reveal a significantly higher rate for poverty level than parent-headed households, while children in these families are twice as likely to receive public assistance (Fuller-Thompson et al., 2000).

Social Cognitive Perspective

Parents of aggressive children may be unsuccessful in de-escalating conflict due to a *negative attribution bias* regarding their aggressive children, blaming the defiant behavior on the child's personality trait (e.g., stubbornness), which is beyond the parent's control (Dix & Lochman, 1990; Strassberg, 1995). Especially in ambivalent situations, or when compliance is not immediate, some parents may anticipate more defiance and resistance and act accordingly (Bargh, Lombardi, & Higgins, 1988). The coercion model describes the processes involved in the parent-child exchange that serve to precipitate and maintain aggressive and defiant behaviors (Campbell, Pierce, Moore, Marakovitz, & Newby, 1996; Patterson, Capaldi, & Bank, 1991; Snyder, Schrepferman, & St. Peter, 1997). Within this paradigm, parents' negative schema drive coercive parenting practices that escalate and maintain aggressive child responses, in a pattern of increasing arousal that becomes negatively reinforced (Snyder, Edwards, McGraw, Kilgore, & Holton, 1994). Observational studies of parent-child attempts at conflict resolution have determined that while mothers of nonaggressive boys are successful in decreasing conflict, mothers of aggressive boys tend to escalate conflict (Snyder et al., 1994).

Parents of aggressive children generate fewer cognitive strategies for noncompliance, (Azar, Robinson, Hekimian, & Twentyman, 1984). Parent strategies are weakest when required to perform under pressured conditions, and tend to dissipate over the course of several trials (Beauchaine, Strassberg, Kees, & Drabick, 2002). The authors recommend the need for treatment plans to target the underlying processes of negative attribution bias and affect regulation, which they suggest are the pivotal factors that drive coercive parenting patterns.

Behavioral Perspective

Mash and Terdal (1997) suggest that behavioral assessments provide a form of data collection that naturally lends itself to an increased understanding of the nature of a problem, the precipitating causes, treatment options, and potential outcomes. By maintaining a focus on the "observable," the behavioral approach to case formulation distinguishes itself from other theoretical approaches that target underlying process.

Based on results of the Home Situations Questionnaire, behavioral analysis revealed two situations that were especially problematic for Jeremy and his parents:

1. problems with chores (noncompliance when asked to clean up his room); and
2. interruptions while trying to talk on the telephone (Jeremy's demands for attention when parents are otherwise engaged, e.g., talking on the telephone).

In the next section (treatment alternatives), a functional behavioral assessment will be conducted and, based on the prevailing assessment information, a behavior management program will be developed for implementation in the home. The exercise will demonstrate how behavioral assessment can be applied to this and future case studies.

Treatment Alternatives

Cognitive-Behavioral Treatment

The cognitive-behavioral approach seeks to understand the link between thinking and behaving. Therefore, the cognitive-behavioral therapist would focus on how Jeremy's faulty belief system might contribute to aggressive behavior. Social cognitive treatment might involve role-play in such areas as social perspective taking, empathy, and self-control. Parent training using cognitive-behavioral methods would focus on negative attributions, emotion regulation, and, ultimately, on increasing effective strategies for behavior management.

In their investigation of maternal responses to child noncompliance, Beauchaine and colleagues (2002) investigated whether parents using ineffective and harsh methods of discipline fail to generate alternative solutions due to an availability deficit (limited repertoire) or an accessibility deficit (processing deficit during times of stress). The authors contend that research support for the accessibility bias has important implications for parent training programs devoted to teaching parents alternate methods of child management, since parent attributions may undermine successful use of the skills taught. The authors emphasize the need to address negative attributions and adding an affect-regulation component to parent training programs in order to enhance treatment effectiveness.

Functional Behavioral Assessment and the Behavioral Intervention Plan

Functional Behavioral Assessment. The behavioral framework consists of a four-stage process designed to

- identify the problem,
- analyze the problem,
- implement a plan, and
- evaluate the plan.

Jeremy's noncompliant behavior can be identified as a *behavioral deficit* (low levels of obedience) or a *behavioral excess* (high levels of noncompliance). Placing Jeremy's behaviors within a functional behavior assessment paradigm (see Text Box 1.1), the goal is to identify the problem as it relates to precipitating conditions, consequences, and results.

One of his parents' presenting complaints is Jeremy's lack of compliance when asked to clean his room. In this case, the *precipitating conditions* would represent the requests initiated by the parents that would begin the behavioral sequence of events. When faced with these requests, Jeremy demonstrates the following repertoire of *behaviors* (argues, delays, manipulates, refuses). When faced with these behaviors, parents respond with a number of reactions or consequences ranging from doing the task themselves (in whole or part) to escalating battles that may end in either abandoning the request or in harsh punishment.

Text Box 1.1	Behavior Assessment Paradigm		

Precipitating Conditions	*Behaviors*	*Consequences*	*Results (Rewards)*
Requests to clean room (e.g., pick up paper on the floor or put away toys)	Says "It's not fair" *(argues)*	Engagement in conflict	Negative attention; Escape/avoid task
	Says he will "do it later" *(delays)*	Repeated requests	Escape/avoid task
	Asks for help *(manipulation)*	Assistance provided	Punishment; Physical or verbal aggression; Escape/avoid task
	Says "No!" *(refuses)*	Power struggles and escalation of conflict	
		Abandonment of request	

Behavioral Intervention Plan. In developing a behavioral plan, it is preferable to concentrate on increasing a deficit behavior rather than on reducing an excessive behavior. In this case, it is preferable to increase obedient behavior rather than to attempt to reduce noncompliant behavior, since increasing a positive behavior can be inherently rewarding in itself. At this time, the positive reinforcement that Jeremy is receiving due to his noncompliance far outweighs the occasional and inconsistent punishment he may receive. The behavior plan would be to shift the positive reinforcement to obedience rather than reduce noncompliance.

Principles of operant conditioning predict that there are two options available for increasing or maintaining obedient behavior: *positive reinforcement* or *negative reinforcement.* Reinforcements are acts that have a positive outcome and, as such, will be rewarding, thereby increasing the likelihood that a behavior will be repeated. *Positive reinforcement* involves the addition of a reward (e.g., clean your room and you will get a sticker book). *Positive reinforcement,* however, is not always what it appears to be, and in Jeremy's case his parents unknowingly reinforce many of his negative behaviors in various ways: humor (suggesting acceptance), boasting (suggesting pride), and providing increased attention. In this case, Jeremy is rewarded by *negative attention,* which to Jeremy might be better than no attention at all. *Negative reinforcement,* not to be confused with punishment, is also rewarding because it involves the removal of a negative (e.g., if you clean your room, you will not have to take out the trash). Negative reinforcement has sometimes been called *escape* because it allows one to escape a negative consequence. Jeremy's argumentativeness and noncompliance are often negatively reinforcing because they allow him to escape having to do a task. Principles of learning also provide a set of assumptions for reducing or eliminating behavior: *punishment* that involves adding a negative consequence and/or *penalty,* removing a positive. Complete withholding of any reinforcement will eventually result in elimination of the behavior, or what the behaviorists refer to as *extinction.*

Although coercion theory from a cognitive framework attends to the underlying processes of negative attribution and emotion regulation, a behaviorist might use the theory to describe the antecedents and consequences of noncompliance. Parents who eventually yield to a child's escalating and demanding behaviors serve to *positively reinforce the child's misbehavior* (child eventually gets what child wants) and at the same time give *negative reinforcement for their own compliance* (cessation of whining and complaining). Therefore, the parent learns that giving in will stop the demands, while the child learns that increased demands result in parent compliance. Since positive and negative reinforcement serve to strengthen behaviors, parent and child become "locked in" to an escalating and never-ending battle.

The importance of developing early treatment interventions to reduce noncompliant behaviors is evident in the repeated associations of defiant behavior and later maladjustment in adolescence and adulthood. In their meta-analysis of psychosocial treatments for children and youth with oppositional defiant disorder and conduct disorder, Brestan and Eyberg (1998) revealed behavioral parent training programs to be a successful method for reducing deviant behavior in young children.

Home-based, parent-delivered interventions often are the result of programs directed toward *parent management training* (PMT), and research has demonstrated that between one-third and two-thirds of children show clinically significant improvement (Barkley, 1997; Kazdin, 1996). The rationale for PMT is based on the premise that coercive parent-child interchanges and environmental contingencies are predisposing factors in the development and maintenance of oppositional, defiant, and noncompliant behaviors. Given the dynamics involved in this family and the issues of compliance, the goal was to develop a home-based behavioral intervention plan. Barkley (1997) suggests a number of components that are helpful in organizing a behavior intervention plan, including assessment and establishment of a baseline, operationalizing treatment goals, psychoeducation for parents concerning issues of behavior management, monitoring, contingency management, generalization to other settings, maintenance and relapse prevention, and follow-up.

A behavioral intervention program was developed for Jeremy for use in the home, based on behaviors targeted by mother and grandmother on the Home Situations Questionnaire. A written copy of "Jeremy's Star Chart Program" was provided, outlining agreed-upon consequences for rule infractions, such as loss of stars, as well as other possible strategies (time out, logical consequences, loss of privilege). A general description of possible rewards was discussed; however, it was urged that Jeremy also be involved in selecting some of the rewards to increase incentive and participation in the program. Goals of the behavior program were to assist with increasing compliant behaviors and applying a consistent approach to consequencing Jeremy for noncompliance. The program involved posting of house rules on the fridge and dealing with rule infractions through the use of (a) time out, (b) logical consequences, and (c) a Response Cost Coupon Program. The *Response Cost Coupon Program*, called Jeremy's Star Chart, was illustrated in a booklet with rules outlined for loss of stars, regaining of lost stars, and adding up of star gains to trade for rewards on the Star Chart menu. The program was monitored by weekly telephone contact. An example of the Star Chart is shown in Text Box 1.2.

Another powerful source of learning is observation. Bandura's (1977) understanding of the social aspects of learning has been instrumental in increasing our awareness of the possible implications of observing the behavior of others. Children's observation and subsequent modeling of adult behavior can have positive (nurturing and empathic caring behaviors) or negative (aggressive responses, e.g., witness of domestic violence) consequences. These responses can be immediately observable or can be evident in a delayed response.

Text Box 1.2	Jeremy's Daily Star Chart			
Morning	*Afternoon*	*Evening*	*Bedtime*	*Total Stars*
☆☆☆	☆☆☆	☆☆☆	☆☆☆	

All-Star Rules:

1. Rule-breaking or misbehavior = 1 lost star
2. At the end of each day, stars are added up .
3. Jeremy can trade his stars for the following rewards:

    5 ☆ = _____   10 ☆ = _____   15 ☆ = _____

    20 ☆ = _____   25 ☆ = _____   30 ☆ = _____

Research has repeatedly demonstrated that the nature of parent-child interactions is a strong predictor of childhood noncompliant, defiant, and aggressive behavior patterns. Poor management practices due to ineffective, inconsistent, and indiscriminate parental controls often result in overly harsh but inconsistent discipline and inadequate monitoring of activities. As a result, child noncompliance becomes an effective means of avoidance or escape from doing undesirable tasks such as picking up toys or cleaning a bedroom. Mother and grandmother are often at odds over setting limits and often present Jeremy with contradictory messages. Grandmother is particularly reinforcing of Jeremy's manipulations and often gives in, allowing his successful escape or avoidance of unpleasant tasks. Jeremy's mother often responds with escalating and coercive responses ("screaming as loud as possible"), likely due to their occasional success ("he couldn't scream as loud, even though he tried, so I won that time"). In this context, Jeremy has learned how to successfully avoid unpleasant tasks on the one hand, and learned to model negative behaviors on the other.

Post-Case Questions

1. Jeremy presents with symptoms of ADHD and ODD. Using the *DSM-IV-TR* (APA, 2000) guidelines available in Appendix D, describe how Jeremy's symptoms match criteria as outlined in the *DSM-IV-TR*. Based on what you have found, would Jeremy meet criteria for either disorder, and if so, which disorder(s) and why?

2. Jeremy's parents indicated two areas on the Home Situations Questionnaire that were in need of behavior management. One problem, compliance with chores, was selected to demonstrate how a functional behavioral assessment and behavior intervention plan were developed to assist in increasing compliant behaviors. What was the second problem that his parents identified? Conduct a functional behavioral assessment and develop a behavioral intervention plan to assist his parents with the second problem.

3. According to Bronfenbrenner (1989), the *mesosystem* predicts the degree to which a system remains healthy, functional, and in balance. Given the information you know about Jeremy's family and the school system, describe what you believe the current status to be and how you would attempt to maximize the mesosystem between these two environmental contexts.

4. Using coercion theory as the overarching dimension, describe power struggles in the family from the viewpoint of cognitive, behavioral, and family systems theories.

REFERENCES

Abidin, R. R. (1995). *Parenting Stress Index: PSI* (3rd ed.). Odessa, FL: Psychological Assessment Resources.

Aguilar, B., Sroufe, L. A., Egeland, B., & Carlson, E. (2000). Distinguishing the early-onset/persistent and adolescent-onset antisocial behavior types. From birth to 16 years. *Development and Psychopathology, 12,* 109–132.

American Association of Retired Persons (AARP). (2007). *Grandparents and other relatives raising children* [State fact sheets]. Retrieved October 2009 from http://www.grandfactsheets.org/state_fact_sheets.cfm

American Psychiatric Association (APA). (2000). *Diagnostic and statistical manual of mental disorders* (4th ed., text rev.). Washington, DC: Author.

Azar, S. T., Robinson, D., Hekimian, D., & Twentyman, C. T. (1984). Unrealistic expectations and problem-solving ability in maltreating and comparison mothers. *Journal of Consulting and Clinical Psychology, 52,* 687–691.

Baker, L. A., & Silverstein. M. (2008). Depressive symptoms among grandparents raising grandchildren: The impact of participation in multiple roles. *Journal of Intergenerational Relationships, 6*(3), 285–304.

Bandura, A. (1977). *Social learning theory*. Englewood Cliffs, NJ: Prentice Hall.

Bargh, J. A., Lombardi, W. J., & Higgins, E. T. (1988). Automaticity of chronically accessible constructs in person by situation effects on person perception: It's just a matter of time. *Journal of Personality and Social Psychology, 55,* 599–605.

Barkley, R. A. (1997). *Defiant children, 2nd ed.: A clinician's manual for assessment and parent training*. New York: Guilford.

Barr, C. S., Newman, T. K., Shannon, C., Parker, C., Dvoskin, R. L., & Becker, M. L. (2003). Rearing condition and rh5-HTTLPR interact to influence limbic–hypothalamic–pituitary–adrenal axis response to stress in infant macaques. *Biological Psychiatry, 55,* 733–738.

Beauchaine, T., Strassberg, Z., Kees, M. R., & Drabick, D.G. (2002). Cognitive response repertoires to child noncompliance by mothers of aggressive boys. *Journal of Abnormal Child Psychology, 30,* 89–101.

Biederman, J., Wozniak, J., Kiely, K., Ablon, S., Faraone, S., Mick, E., et al. (1995). CBCL clinical scales discriminate prepubertal children with structured-interview-derived diagnosis of mania from those with ADHD. *Journal of the American Academy of Child and Adolescent Psychiatry, 34,* 464–471.

Blum, R. W., Beuhring, T., Shew, M., Bearinger, L., Sieving, R., & Resnick, T. (2000). The effects of race/ethnicity, income and family structure on adolescent risk behaviors. *American Journal of Public Health, 90,* 1885–1891.

Brestan, E. V., & Eyberg, S. M. (1998). Effective psychosocial treatments of conduct-disordered children and adolescents: 29 Years, 82 Studies and 5,272 Kids. *Journal of Clinical Child Psychology, Vol. 27,* 180–189.

Bridges, L., & Grolnick, W. (1995). The development of emotional self-regulation in infancy and early childhood. In N. Eisenberg (Ed.), *Social development: Review of child development research* (pp. 185–211). Thousand Oaks, CA: Sage.

Bronfenbrenner, U. (1989). Ecological systems theory. *Annals of Child Development, 6,* 187–249.

Campbell, S. B., Pierce, E. W., Moore, G., Marakovitz, S., & Newby, K. (1996). Boys' externalizing problems at elementary school: Pathways from early behavior problems, maternal control, and family stress. *Development and Psychopathology, 8,* 836–851.

Cicchetti, D., & Toth, S. L. (1998). The development of depression in children and adolescents. *American Psychologist, 53,* 221–241.

Cox, C. B. (2000). Why grandchildren are going to and staying at Grandmother's house and what happens when they get there. In C. B. Cox (Ed.), *To Grandmother's house we go and stay: Perspectives on custodial grandparents* (pp. 3–19). New York: Springer.

DeKlyen, M., Speltz, M. L., & Greenberg, M. T. (1996, January). *Predicting early starting behavior disorders: A clinical sample of preschool oppositional defiant boys.* Paper presented at the International Society for Research in Child and Adolescent Psychopathology, Santa Monica, CA.

Dix, T., & Lochman, J. E. (1990). Social cognition and negative reactions to children: A comparison of mothers of aggressive and nonaggressive boys. *Journal of Social and Clinical Psychology, 9,* 418–438.

Edwards, O. W. (2003). Living with grandma: A grandfamily study. *School Psychology International, 24,* 204–217.

Eley, T. C. (1999). Behavioral genetics as a tool for developmental psychology: Anxiety and depression in children and adolescents. *Clinical Child and Family Psychology Review, 2,* 21–36.

Erbert, L. A., & Alemán, M. W. (2008). Taking the grand out of grandparent: Dialectical tensions in grandparent perceptions of surrogate parenting. *Journal of Social and Personal Relationships, 25,* 671–695.

Fuller-Thompson, E. F., Minkler, M., & Driver, D. (2000). American's grandparent caregivers: Who are they? In B. Hayslip, Jr., & R. Goldberg-Glen (Eds.), *Grandparents raising grandchildren: Theoretical, empirical and clinical perspectives* (pp. 3–21). New York: Springer.

Geller, B., Zimerman, B., Williams, M., DelBello, R., Bolhofner, J., Craney, J., et al. (2002). *DSM–IV* mania symptoms in a prepubertal and early adolescent bipolar disorder phenotype compared to attention-deficit hyperactive and normal controls. *Journal of Child and Adolescent Psychopharmacology, 12,* 11–25.

Goodman, C. C., & Silverstein, M. (2005). Grandmothers who parent their grandchildren. *Journal of Family Issues, 22,* 557–578.

Hairiri, A. (2002). Serotonin transporter genetic variation and the response of the human amygdala. *Science, 297,* 400–403.

Kaufman, A. S., & Lichtenberger, E. (2000). Essentials of WISC-III and WPPSI-R assessment. New York: John Wiley.

Kazdin, A. E. (1996). Problem solving and parent management in treating aggressive and antisocial behavior. In E. D. Hibbs & P. S. Jensen (Eds.), *Psychosocial treatments for child and adolescent disorders* (pp. 377–408). Washington, DC: American Psychological Association.

Lloyd, G. K., Fletcher, A., & Minuchin, M. C. W. (1992). GABA agonists as potential anxiolytics. In C. D. Burows, S. M. Roth, & R. Noyes, Jr., *Handbook of anxiety* (Vol. 5). Oxford, UK: Elsever.

Luthar, S. S., & Zigler, E. (1992). Intelligence and social competence among high-risk adolescents. *Development and Psychopathology, 4,* 287–299.

Lyons-Ruth, K. (2008). Contributions of the mother-infant relationship to dissociative, borderline and conduct symptoms in young adulthood. *Infant Mental Health Journal, 29,* 203–218.

Lyons-Ruth, K., Holmes, B., Sasvari-Szekely, M., Ronai, Z., Nemoda, Z., & Pauls, D. (2007). Serotonin transporter polymorphism and borderline or antisocial traits among low-income young adults. *Psychiatric Genetics, 17,* 339–343.

Marvin, R. S., & Stewart, R. R. (1990). A family systems framework for the study of attachment. In M. T. Greenberg, D. Cicchetti, & E. M. Cummings (Eds.), *Attachment in the preschool years: Theory, research, and intervention* (pp. 51–86). Chicago: University of Chicago Press.

Mash, E. J., & Terdal, L. G. (1997). *Assessment of childhood disorders.* New York: Guilford.

Minuchin, P. (1985). Families and individual development: Provocations from the field of family therapy. *Child Development, 56,* 289–302.

Musil, C. M., Schrader, S., & Mutikani, J. (2000). Social support, stress, and special coping tasks of grandmother caregivers. In C. B. Cox (Ed.), *To grandmother's house we go and stay: Perspectives on custodial grandparents* (pp. 56–70). New York: Springer.

Owens, E. B., & Shaw, D. S. (2003). Predicting growth curves of externalizing behavior across the preschool years. *Journal of Abnormal Child Psychology, 31*(6), 575–590.

Patterson, G. R., Capaldi, D., & Bank, L. (1991). An early starter model for predicting delinquency. In D. Pepler & K. H. Rubin (Eds.), *The development and treatment of childhood aggression* (pp. 139–168). Hillsdale, NJ: Erlbaum.

Rutter, M. (1995). Clinical implications of attachment concepts: Retrospect and prospect. *Journal of Child Psychology and Psychiatry, 36,* 549–571.

Rutter, M., Silberg, J., O'Connor, T., & Simonoff, E. (1999). Genetics and child psychiatry II: Empirical research findings. *Journal of Child Psychology and Psychiatry and Allied Disciplines, 40,* 19–55.

Rydell, A., Berlin, L., & Bohlin, G. (2001). Emotionality, emotion regulation and adaptation among 5- to 8-year-old children. *Emotion, 3,* 30–47.

Smith, A., & Dannison, L. (2002). Educating educators: Programming to support grandparent-headed families. *Contemporary Education, 72*(2), 47–51.

Snyder, J., Edwards, P., McGraw, K., Kilgore, K., & Holton, A. (1994). Escalation and reinforcement in mother-child conflict: Social processes associated with the development of physical aggression. *Development and Psychopathology, 6,* 305–321.

Snyder, J., Schrepferman, L., & St. Peter, C. (1997). Origins of antisocial behavior: Negative reinforcement and affect dysregulation of behavior as socialization mechanisms in family interaction. *Behavior Modification, 21,* 187–215.

Sroufe, L. A. (1997). Psychopathology as an outcome of development. *Development and Psychopathology, 9,* 251–268.

Stanley, B., Molcho, A., & Stanley, M. (2000). Association of aggressive behavior with altered serotonergic function in patients who are not suicidal. *American Journal of Psychiatry, 157,* 609–614.

Strassberg, Z. (1995). Social information processing in compliance situations by mothers of behavior-problem boys. *Child Development, 66,* 376–389.

Williamson, J., Softas-Nall, B., & Miller, J. (2003). Grandmothers raising grandchildren: An exploration of their experiences and emotions. *The Family Journal, 11,* 23–32.

Winnie Kent

Silence Is Not Golden

W innie, a 5½-year-old girl, was referred for assessment by her pediatrician. Winnie was accompanied by her mother, Isabel. Despite being a seemingly normal and talkative youngster at home, Winnie had always been rather shy and reticent in larger group settings. Although her mother had anticipated some early reservations on Winnie's part regarding her initial school placement, Isabel was totally unequipped to deal with the current situation, which had developed over the past 6 months of enrollment in the kindergarten program.

DEVELOPMENTAL HISTORY/FAMILY BACKGROUND

Isabel Kent and her husband Frank were both in their early forties. They met and married while attending graduate school. Frank is an engineer, and Isabel is currently a stay-at-home mom. Prior to Winnie's birth, Isabel was a research assistant for a pharmaceutical company. Isabel stated that there was no serious mental illness on either side of the family, although she described herself as "high-strung" and a bit of a loner. She felt that her husband was a workaholic, since he spent the majority of his time either working or thinking about working. She described their marriage "as successful as most enduring marriages."

Isabel stated that although Winnie is an only child, it was not by choice. The pregnancy was planned and it was decided that when the baby was born, Isabel would quit her job and devote her time to child rearing. Although the plan was to have two or three children, Isabel suffered a miscarriage when Winnie was about 14 months old, and then a second miscarriage about 5 months later. Isabel described herself as depressed during this period with frequent bouts of crying and fatigue. Her physician suggested a trial of Prozac; however, Isabel developed headaches and nervousness/agitation as side effects. A trial of Paxil produced fewer side effects and eventually, with the help of Paxil, Isabel was coping much better. Because of the risk of complications in pregnancy, given Isabel's age, and fear of the depression returning if she had another miscarriage, the Kents decided to abandon any further attempts to conceive a child.

Winnie weighed 5 pounds 6 ounces at birth, and although pregnancy and delivery were normal, complications developed later on. Immediately after the birth, an attempt to intubate a blocked nasal passage resulted in swelling. Winnie was fed intravenously and required an artificial airway until the swelling subsided and surgery could finally be performed to remove the membrane that was blocking the nasal passage. During this time, Winnie experienced what her mother described as "blue spells," a term she used to describe the color of Winnie's face and body resulting from lack of oxygen. Isabel said that this was a very emotionally draining time for her. Isabel was very fearful and anxious concerning Winnie's health, even though the medical staff assured her that Winnie would be fine. Winnie remained in the neonatal intensive care unit for 3 weeks before Isabel could take her home from the hospital.

As an infant, Winnie had bouts of being fretful and colicky, and she had some difficulties keeping her food down. Mrs. Kent recalled that at least twice a week, if not more, Winnie would lose almost half her intake in rather severe episodes of projectile vomiting. Mrs. Kent was concerned and asked the pediatrician about it, but his response was that it was likely due to a sensitive and immature digestive system. He suggested they change the baby formula; that helped somewhat, but the matter never really resolved itself until Winnie was totally on solid food. Mrs. Kent stated that even today, Winnie is a picky eater, and if she is upset, she tends to eat very little because her stomach is easily upset.

Motor milestones were slightly advanced developmentally, and Winnie was sitting independently at 4 months, standing at 7–8 months, and walking at 10 months of age. Language development lagged behind motor skills. Winnie did not say her first word until about 15 months, and simple sentences weren't produced until about 2½ years of age. Winnie had some articulation problems and substituted a few sounds, the most prominent of which were "w" for "r" (wabbit for rabbit) and "l" for "y" (lellow for yellow). The articulation errors stopped about a year ago. Currently, Isabel believes that Winnie's speech is normal for her age, based on conversations between Winnie and her best friend Kate's daughter, Molly, who is almost the same age as Winnie. At home, she described Winnie as very chatty and quite the conversationalist, with speech far more adultlike than childlike.

Isabel described herself as somewhat aloof and not one to initiate a lot of social contact. She was fortunate that Kate lived across the street, since Winnie and Molly were about the same age and played very well together. Kate was more outgoing than Isabel and was often responsible for organizing activities for the foursome, such as outings to the park, or attending movies or concerts. Isabel and her husband Frank rarely went out in the evenings, due to Frank's long work hours, but when they did, Winnie would just go over and spend the night at Kate's house with Molly. Similarly, Molly would spend the night with them whenever Kate and Brian went out for an evening. People often mistook Winnie and Molly for twins, since they were about the same age and looked somewhat alike. Unfortunately, about 9 months ago, Brian was suddenly transferred and the family moved out of state. Isabel said that until the separation, she never really realized how much time the four of them had spent together. Isabel said that she really misses Kate's company and she is sure that Winnie must really miss Molly, too, although she doesn't talk about Molly very much. Isabel wondered if she were grieving in silence or just didn't feel as strongly as an adult might.

About 2 months after Kate and Molly left, Isabel decided to enroll in a Tuesday morning art class at the local gallery and enroll Winnie in a once-weekly preschool program for that morning. Isabel thought that this would be good for both herself and Winnie. However, when she tried to drop Winnie off at the preschool center, Winnie had a severe temper tantrum, attached herself to her mother's leg, and began sobbing uncontrollably. Isabel was in shock since she had never seen such behavior from Winnie before. Isabel stayed with Winnie for the next half hour hoping that Winnie would calm down. Eventually, sobs dissipated into heaving sighs and Isabel decided to make another attempt to leave. On cue, Winnie's sobs began again, this time even more violently and accompanied by screaming and begging her mother not to go. The preschool staff encouraged Isabel not to give in to Winnie at this point, since it would only make matters worse. Isabel left, without looking back, afraid if she saw Winnie, she would not be able to carry on. When Isabel returned 3 hours later, Winnie looked as though she was totally drained. She was engaged in subdued solitary play in the corner, rocking her doll. Her eyes were red and swollen from crying. The preschool staff said that she continued with her sobbing for quite some time after Isabel had left. That night, Winnie was like Velcro and refused to sleep alone. The whole ordeal was far more than Isabel had bargained for. The next night, had it not been for Frank's insistence that Winnie sleep in her own bed, the nightly ritual probably would have continued. As it was, Winnie started calling out at night, and often Isabel would have to go into Winnie's bedroom to comfort her. Isabel ended up sleeping in Winnie's room the next night because Winnie had a nightmare that her mom had gone away. Isabel started leaving the light on in Winnie's bedroom so she would not be afraid of the dark.

The following Tuesday, Winnie started crying when Isabel began to prepare to leave. Winnie started to complain that her stomach was hurting and held on tightly to her stomach saying, "It hurts, it hurts." Although Isabel could not be definite, she was pretty sure that Winnie was saying she was sick and wanted to stay home. Rather than give in, she picked Winnie up and carried her to the car, with Winnie sobbing and complaining about her aching stomach. The tears, the sobbing, the protests, and the aches and pains continued every Tuesday for the next 3 months. Eventually, Winnie would comply, but began to sit beside the preschool window waiting and watching for signs of her mother's return. When they were home, Winnie was constantly in need of reassurance that her mother was all right and that everything was okay.

Despite the difficulties, Isabel persisted in taking Winnie to preschool because kindergarten would be starting shortly, and Isabel knew Winnie had to become more prepared. Winnie was having considerable difficulty adjusting to preschool, which was only one day a week. How would she cope with kindergarten on a daily basis? She also needed more practice socially. She seemed so withdrawn at the preschool and didn't seem to interact with the other children. Her teachers said that she was very cooperative, but she didn't seem comfortable talking to anyone.

Isabel was thrilled when a new family moved in a few doors down the road because they had a daughter Winnie's age. Isabel really pushed herself to be more social and extended an invitation to the new mother and daughter to come over for afternoon tea. Winnie seemed to get along well with her new friend and soon they were playing together, much like she and Molly had. After a few months, Winnie was invited to a sleepover at Becky's. Although the girls had planned the event for some time, Winnie began to get anxious just before it was time to leave. She asked an endless series of questions about what her mother would be doing in her absence. Isabel continued to reassure her that she was just going to take a bath and watch television. Winnie immediately became concerned that her mother might slip in the bathtub and if nobody else was home, she could drown. Isabel continued to attempt to calm Winnie's fears. Finally, Becky and her mother came to pick up Winnie for the sleepover. Winnie's goodbye hug was more like a desperate attempt to carry her mother along with her. Two hours later, Winnie was standing at the door, sleeping bag in tow, complaining that she had to come home because she didn't feel well.

Kindergarten finally started and after much struggle and distress, Isabel finally got Winnie to walk to school with her friend Becky. Winnie would walk beside Becky with her head bent down, constantly looking sideways to see if her mother was still watching from the outside steps. The school was only a block away, and Winnie told herself that if she looked really hard, she could probably see her house between the trees. At school, Winnie just seemed to go through the motions until it was home time. On the playground, she was always peering through the fence, trying to see her house. Her teachers were very patient and encouraging, and Winnie was cooperative, but she would not participate verbally in any activities that were going on. For the first month, her teachers thought it was just a case of reluctance to talk in the new environment. After all, Winnie did appear to be very shy, and her mother had cautioned the kindergarten teachers that Winnie was slow to warm up. They anticipated that it might take a while for her to feel comfortable talking to the teachers and the other children. However, 4 months had gone by and Winnie had not said a word. When asked a question, Winnie would nod her head in the affirmative or shake her head to signal "no," but no words accompanied the gestures. Winnie would talk only to Becky at school, and then only in whispers, until they got far enough away from the schoolyard that no one could hear. Then she would talk to Becky as if they were at home.

REASON FOR REFERRAL

Isabel finally brought Winnie to the pediatrician for help, not understanding why her daughter was giving the school situation the silent treatment. The pediatrician suggested that Isabel take Winnie to see a child psychologist, who could evaluate the causes of Winnie's silent behaviors and suggest ways to best deal with this behavior in the school.

ASSESSMENT RESULTS

When Isabel contacted the psychologist at the clinic, prior to seeing Winnie in the clinic, the psychologist requested permission to observe Winnie in the classroom. Isabel was very much in agreement. After observing Winnie for a morning and interviewing her teachers, the psychologist sat beside Winnie and asked her to draw a picture for her. Winnie drew a picture of a little girl skipping. The psychologist found it interesting that the skipping rope surrounded the little girl's head, as if her head were in a space capsule. The drawing was sophisticated enough, however, to suggest that Winnie was likely, at least, of average intelligence. The psychologist contacted Isabel and suggested she bring Winnie to the clinic for a comprehensive assessment.

Isabel brought Winnie to the clinic the following week. Winnie would not go into the assessment room unless her mother came with her. Throughout the assessment, Winnie would not speak directly to the psychologist or answer any questions verbally. On occasion, Winnie would bend over toward her mother and whisper something into her mother's ear. But even on these occasions, she would cup her hand around her mouth, blocking the psychologist from any entry into her verbal world.

Winnie's drawing of a person (Draw-A-Person) and Bender Visual Motor Gestalt designs were all within the average range. Scores on the Peabody Picture Vocabulary Test (PPVT-III) also revealed an understanding of vocabulary that was above the expected level for her age (SS = 110). The psychologist asked Winnie's teacher and mother to complete the Behavioral Assessment System for Children (BASC2) Preschool Scales. Based on Winnie's responses to the school setting, Mrs. Kent rated Winnie in the clinical range for Adaptability; however, all other ratings were within the norm. Winnie's teacher rated clinical elevations for Anxiety, Atypicality, Adaptability, and Social Skills.

ISSUES, TRENDS, AND TREATMENT ALTERNATIVES

Separation Anxiety Disorder

Anxiety disorders can result from a combination of genetic factors (heredity, inhibited temperament) and environmental factors, such as cumulative risks, exposure to traumatic events/repeated exposure to negative outcomes, and overprotective parenting practices (Ollendick, Vasey, & King, 2001; Vasey & Dadds, 2001). Although most infants go through normal anxieties related to separation from caregivers, which usually decline after 2 years of age, for some children, separation anxiety may intensify and persist well into early childhood (Kearney, Sims, Pursell, & Tillotson, 2003). Separation anxiety disorder (SAD) is an intense emotional response resulting from excessive worry surrounding the possibility of separation from the caregiver. The *DSM-IV-TR* (APA, 2000) lists a number of possible symptoms of the disorder resulting from excessive distress, fears of harm coming to the caregiver, and fears of being alone (see Appendix D for the complete list of criteria). Because it is so painful for the child to separate from the caregiver, young children will often refuse to participate in activities that remove them from their caregiver. As a result, approximately 75% of children with SAD will demonstrate school refusal when it is time to begin school, or refuse to return to school, following an absence due to illness or a school move (Black & Uhde, 1995; Kearney & Albano, 2004).

While some research has linked SAD to problematic or chaotic home environments (Egger, Costello, & Angold, 2003; Kearney et al., 2003), other findings have suggested that children are at increased risk for SAD if their mothers were diagnosed with an anxiety or major depressive disorder (Biederman et al., 2001). Deiner and Kim (2004) found that mothers who reported feelings of separation anxiety, themselves, were significantly more likely to have children who evidenced social withdrawal and problems with self-regulation. In their study, Dallaire and Weinraub (2005) reported that children who were classified as insecurely attached at 15 months of age demonstrated significantly higher levels of separation anxiety at 6 years of age compared to securely attached peers.

Selective Mutism

Although initially thought to be a rare disorder (e.g., fewer than 1%, according to the *DSM-IV-TR*), in their study out of California, Bergman, Piacentini, and McCracken (2002), recently found as many as 7 children in every 1,000 in kindergarten through second grade had the disorder. As it is currently conceptualized by the *DSM-IV-TR*, selective mutism is one of the five disorders listed under the category of "Other disorders of infancy, childhood or adolescence": separation anxiety disorder; reactive attachment disorder; stereotypic movement disorder; and disorder of infancy, childhood, or adolescence NOS.

Black and Uhde (1992) have suggested that since the onset of the disorder often coincides with initial school entrance for the majority of children, an underlying feature of the disorder may be school refusal. Issues regarding how the disorder should be conceptualized have affected research, diagnosis, assessment, and treatment. There has been significant debate regarding whether selective mutism should best be conceptualized as an early precursor to social phobia (Krysanski, 2003). However, while elective mutism has onset most likely in the 4- to 7-year range, social phobia is most likely to have onset in adolescence, which makes this line of reasoning difficult to support.

There have been a number of suggestions regarding how to best classify variants of the disorder. Although initially called elective mutism (*DSM-III;* APA, 1980), current emphasis is on the "selective" nature of those that the child will speak to. As such, Cunninghan, McHolm, and Boyle (2006) suggest that one possibility for classifying groups with selective mutism is to use the same system of categorization used for social phobia: *generalized* (for those whose symptoms are demonstrated across a variety of situations) and *specific* (for those whose symptoms are restricted to speaking in classrooms at school). Cunningham and colleagues (2006) found that children with the generalized variant of selective mutism experienced more symptoms of obsessive thinking, somatic complaints, and depression and were less proficient socially than controls, leading the authors to suggest that the generalized variant was the more severe form of selective mutism. Another form of categorizing for the disorder has suggested division along the dimension of passive, shy, fearful, and insecure behaviors versus noncompliant and resistant types of responders (Lesser-Katz, 1988). However, more recent research suggests that the vast majority (90%) of children with selective mutism will conform to the anxious-compliant type (Black & Uhde, 1995; Drummit et al., 1997). Finally, Beidel and colleagues (Beidel, Turner, & Morris, 1999) outline several areas of social anxiety in children that might be seen to overlap with selective mutism, such as fears of reading aloud in class, joining in on conversations, speaking to adults, and starting conversations.

Treatment for Separation Anxiety Disorder and Selective Mutism

Separation Anxiety Disorder. Treatments that have been successful for children's phobic disorders have also been successful for treating separation anxiety disorder (Werry & Wollersheim, 1991). In their extensive review of treatments for childhood phobic disorders, Ollendick and King (1998) found one well-established method (contingency management) and a number of probably efficacious treatments (systematic desensitization, modeling, cognitive behavioral). Contingency management relies on principles of operant conditioning and differs fundamentally from the other approaches discussed. Conceptually, while systematic desensitization, modeling, and cognitive-behavioral methods share a belief that reducing the fear is a necessary precursor to increasing the desired behaviors, contingency management focuses directly on increasing the desired behavior through rewarded practice. Using contingency management methodology, a child afraid of the dark would be rewarded for spending time in the dark, resulting in increased dark tolerance (Leitenberg & Callahan, 1973). Applying these methods to separation anxiety disorder (SAD), children would be rewarded for spending time away from their caregiver and for developing greater tolerance for separation. Using cognitive-behavioral methods to reduce fear of the dark might involve modeling and verbal rehearsal to assist children to generate positive self-statements. Graziano and Mooney (1980, 1982) combined parent reward for "brave statements" with "brave" self-statement training, relaxation training, and imagined positive scenes to successfully reduce fear of the dark in young children. Ollendick and King (1998) reviewed several modeling techniques and concluded that although modeling is generally successful, participant modeling (actual engagement with the feared object, in conjunction with observation of the model) is the superior method.

Systematic desensitization (Wolpe, 1958) was a procedure designed to incorporate two inherent assumptions: (a) fears are conditioned responses (learned behaviors) and can be de-conditioned (unlearned), and (b) fear/anxiety and relaxation are two competing and incompatible responses. Although there are variations on the method, at its basis, systematic desensitization involves the following steps:

a. lessons in deep muscle relaxation;

b. creation of a fear hierarchy (least to most fearful); and

c. graduated pairings of the feared thought with deep muscle relaxation.

Feared thoughts can involve actual behaviors ("in vivo") or "mental images." An interesting variation that has been used successfully with children is emotive imagery (Cornwall, Spence, & Schotte, 1997; Lazarus & Abramowitz, 1962). In this variation, emphasis is placed on conquering the fear, rather than on pairing the feared responses with relaxation, and "child mastery" becomes the antidote to fear. Children participate in creating exciting stories, and as their heroes defeat the elements of the fear hierarchy, a new sense of control and mastery develops to replace the anxiety and fear.

In a recent study of cognitive-behavioral therapy (CBT) for youth (7 to 14 years of age) with a principal diagnosis of separation anxiety disorder (47), generalized anxiety disorder (88), or social phobia (63), Suveg and colleagues (2009) found comparable results for individual child-focused CBT and child-focused family CBT in decreasing symptoms and improving adaptive functioning. Furthermore, a family-based education support and attention approach (a 16-session treatment featuring education about youth anxiety and providing attention and support, but not including any training in how to manage anxious responses or exposure tasks) also proved to be equally effective.

Selective Mutism. Graduated behavioral exposure treatments (systematic desensitization) can also be very helpful in the treatment of selective mutism (McHolm, Cunningham, & Vanier, 2005; Stone, Kratochwill, Sladeczek, & Serlin, 2002).

Currently, given the research findings, selective mutism is considered by most to be a form of anxiety disorder (Anstending, 1999). It is not surprising, then, that CBT, which have been so successful in treating childhood anxiety disorders (Kendall, 1994), are under current investigation regarding their potential role in the treatment of selective mutism. Given the high rates of comorbidity with social phobia, behavior therapies often used in the treatment of phobias have also been adapted for use in treating selective mutism. A third avenue of treatment for the disorder is a pharmacological approach.

Various theories about selective mutism have been advanced, including psychodynamic (fixation at the anal stage), family systems (enmeshment and overprotection), behavioral (avoidance), and cognitive (maladaptive thinking). Success has been minimal for the psychodynamically oriented therapies, such as play therapy or family therapy (Dow, Sonies, Scheib, Moss, & Leonard, 1995).

Behaviorally based treatments that combine multimodal techniques have been the most successful (Sluckin, Foreman, & Herbert, 1991). Kehle, Hintze, and DuPaul (1997) outline several behavioral interventions that have been successfully integrated into treatment programs, including contingency management (rewarding speech and ignoring silence); shaping and fading (e.g., reward speech in school in the presence of mother; gradually remove mother's presence); minimizing escape and avoidance, by ignoring attempts to escape/avoid and rewarding any efforts to approach/engage; and self-modeling of videotaped presentations of desired behaviors (Kehle et al., 1997). Blum and colleagues (1998) investigated the potential use of audiotape recordings as a self-modeling technique. Results were very encouraging, suggesting that this easy-to-use and brief technique can provide a successful intervention approach for use in school settings. Fung (2002) recently adapted a CBT program for children (*Coping Bear Workbook;* Mendlowitz et al., 1999) into a web-based Internet program for selective mutism and reports success in alleviating symptoms of selective mutism in a 7-year-old child. In cases where behavioral interventions are not successful, selective serotonin reuptake inhibitors (SSRIs) have met with success, especially if anxiety is a comorbid feature (Black & Uhde, 1994; Dow et al., 1995).

Post-Case Questions

1. Does Winnie meet the *DSM-IV-TR* criteria for separation anxiety disorder (SAD) and selective mutism? If so what symptoms are evident. If not, why not? The *DSM-IV-TR* criteria are available in Appendix D.

2. There are several models that can be advanced to explain the sequential development of internalizing disorders, such as anxiety disorders, and the factors that might be responsible for variable outcomes. From the perspective of the diathesis-stress model, an inherited genetic vulnerability to anxiety may remain dormant until environmental conditions are adverse (peer rejection; family conflict; parent psychopathology, e.g., depression), causing the disorder to become overt (Kazdin & Weisz, 1998). In addition, temperamental factors such as behavioral inhibition may also account for why one child may be more vulnerable to stressful or unfamiliar surroundings than another child (Kagan & Snidman, 1991). Discuss how Winnie's separation anxiety might be explained using the diathesis-stress model.

3. There are a number of possible theories that can be suggested to account for the etiology or development and onset of separation anxiety disorder (SAD). There is some support to suggest that children with SAD come from families that share a greater prevalence for anxiety and mood disorders (Black & Uhde, 1995). Attachment theory might predict that an anxiously attached infant might be more prone to develop SAD than a securely attached or resistant infant. Discuss the onset and development of Winnie's SAD as a psychologist from each of the following perspectives: behavioral, cognitive, and psychodynamic. Suggest possible treatment alternatives that might be developed for each of these perspectives relative to probable cause.

4. Discuss how selective mutism might be influenced by the various contexts of development, using Bronfenbrenner's model: individual characteristics, immediate environment, social and economic factors, and cultural factors.

5. Develop a case formulation for Winnie, based on factors discussed in Part I, from the perspectives of the family systems and attachment theories.

REFERENCES

American Psychiatric Association (APA). (1980). *Diagnostic and statistical manual of mental disorders* (3rd. ed.). Washington, DC: APA.

American Psychiatric Association (APA). (2000). *Diagnostic and statistical manual of mental disorders* (4th ed., text rev.). Washington, DC: APA.

Anstending, K. D. (1999). Is selective mutism an anxiety disorder? Rethinking *DSM-IV* classification. *Journal of Anxiety Disorders, 13,* 417–434.

Beidel, D. C., Turner, S. M., & Morris, T. L. (1999). Psychopathology of childhood social phobia. *Journal of the American Academy of Child and Adolescent Psychiatry, 38,* 643–650.

Bergman, R. L., Piacentini, J., & McCracken, J. T. (2002). Prevalence and description of selective mutism in a school-based population. *Journal of the American Academy of Child and Adolescent Psychiatry, 41,* 938–946.

Biederman, J., Faraone, S. V., Hirshfeld-Becker, D. R., Friedman, D., Robin, J. A., & Rosenbaum, J. F. (2001). Patterns of psychopathology and dysfunction in high-risk children of parents with panic disorder and major depression. *American Journal of Psychiatry, 158,* 49–57.

Black, B., & Uhde, T. W. (1992). Treatment of elective mutism as a variant of school phobia. *Journal of the American Academy of Child and Adolescent Psychiatry, 31,* 1090–1094.

Black, B., & Uhde, T. W. (1994). Treatment of elective mutism with fluoxetine: A doubleblind, placebo-controlled study. *Journal of the American Academy of Child and Adolescent Psychiatry, 33,* 1000–1006.

Black, B., & Uhde, T. W. (1995). Psychiatric characteristics of children with selective mutism: A pilot study. *Journal of the American Academy of Child and Adolescent Psychiatry, 32,* 847–856.

Blum, N. J., Kell, R. S., Star, H. L., Lender, W. L., Bradley-Klug, K. L., Osborne, M., L., et al. (1998). Case study: Audio feedforward treatment of selective mutism. *Journal of the American Academy of Child and Adolescent Psychiatry, 37,* 40–43.

Cornwall, E., Spence, S. H., & Schotte, D. (1997). The effectiveness of emotive imagery in the treatment of darkness phobia in children. *Behavior Change, 13,* 223–229.

Cunninghan, C. E., McHolm, A. E., & Boyle, M. H. (2006). Social phobia, anxiety, oppositional behavior, social skills, and self-concept in children with specific selective mutism, generalized selective mutism, and community controls. *European Child and Adolescent Psychiatry, 15,* 245–255.

Dallaire, D. H., & Weinraub, M. (2005). Predicting children's separation anxiety at age 6: The contributions of infant–mother attachment security, maternal sensitivity, and maternal separation anxiety. *Attachment & Human Development, 7*(4): 393–408.

Deiner, M., & Kim, D. (2004). Maternal and child predictors of preschool children's social competence. *Applied Developmental Psychology, 25,* 3–24.

Dow, S. P., Sonies, B. C., Scheib, D., Moss, S. E., & Leonard, H. L. (1995). Practical guidelines for the assessment and treatment of selective mutism. *Journal of the American Academy of Child and Adolescent Psychiatry, 34,* 836–846.

Drummit, E. S., Klein, R. G., Tancer, N. K., Asche, B., Martin, J., & Fairbanks, J. A. (1997). Systematic assessment of 50 children with selective mutism. *Journal of the American Academy of Child and Adolescent Psychiatry, 36,* 653–660.

Egger, E. L., Costello, J., & Angold, A. (2003). School refusal and psychiatric disorders: A community study. *Journal of the American Academy of Child and Adolescent Psychiatry, 42,* 797–807.

Fung, D. S. (2002, February). Web-based CBT for selective mutism [Letter to the editor]. *Journal of the American Academy of Child and Adolescent Psychiatry.*

Graziano, A. M., & Mooney, K. C. (1980). Family self-control instruction for children's nighttime fear reduction. *Journal of Consulting and Clinical Psychology, 48,* 206–213.

Graziano, A. M., & Mooney, K. C. (1982). Behavioral treatment of "nightfears" in children: Maintenance of improvement at 2½ to 3 year follow-up. *Journal of Consulting and Clinical Psychology, 50,* 598–599.

Kagan, J., & Snidman, N. (1991). Temperamental factors in human development. *American Psychologist, 46,* 856–862.

Kazdin, A. E., & Weisz, J. R. (1998). Identifying and developing empirically supported child and adolescent treatments. *Journal of Consulting Clinical Psychologist, 66,* 19–36.

Kearney, C. A., & Albano, A. M. (2004). The functional profiles of school refusal behavior: Diagnostic aspects. *Behavioral Modification, 28,* 147–161.

Kearney, C. A., Sims, K. E., Pursell, C. R., & Tillotson, C. A. (2003). Separation anxiety disorder in young children: A longitudinal and family analysis. *Journal of Clinical Child and Adolescent Psychology, 32,* 593–598.

Kehle, T., Hintze, J. M., & DuPaul, G. J. (1997). Selective mutism. In G. Bear, K. Minke, & A. Thomas (Eds.), *Children's needs II. Development, problems and alternatives* (pp. 329–386). Bethesda, MD: NASP.

Kendall, P. C. (1994). Treating anxiety disorders in children: Results of a randomized clinical trial. *Journal of Consulting and Clinical Psychology, 64,* 724–730.

Krysanski, V. L. (2003). A brief review of selective mutism literature. *Journal of Psychology: Interdisciplinary and Applied, 137*(1), 29–40.

Lazarus, A. A., & Abramowitz, A. (1962). The use of "emotive imagery" in the treatment of children's phobias. *Journal of Mental Science, 108,* 191–195.

Leitenberg, H., & Callahan, E. J. (1973). Reinforced practice and reduction of different kinds of fears in adults and children. *Behavior Research and Therapy, 11,* 19–30.

Lesser-Katz, M. (1988). The treatment of elective mutism as stranger reaction. *Psychotherapy, 25,* 305–313.

McHolm, E. A., Cunninghan, A. E., & Vanier, K. M. (2005). *Helping your child with selective mutism: Practice steps to overcome a fear of speaking.* Oakland, CA: New Harbinger Publications.

Mendlowitz, S., Manassis, K., Bradley, S., Scapiliato, D., Miezitis, S., & Shaw, B. F. (1999). Cognitive-behavioral group treatments in childhood anxiety disorders. *Journal of the American Academy of Child and Adolescent Psychiatry, 38,* 1223–1229.

Ollendick, T. H., & King, N. J. (1998). Empirically supported treatments for children with phobic and anxiety disorders: Current status. *Journal of Clinical Child Psychology, 27,* 156–167.

Ollendick, T. H., Vasey, M. W., & King, N. J. (2001). Operant conditioning influences in childhood anxiety. In M. W. Vasey & M. R. Dadds (Eds.), *The developmental psychopathology of anxiety* (pp. 231–252). New York: Oxford University Press.

Sluckin, A., Foreman, N., & Herbert, M. (1991). Behavioral treatment programs and selectivity of speaking at follow-up in a sample of 25 selective mutes. *Psychologist, 26,* 132–137.

Stone, B. P., Kratochwill, T. R., Sladeczek, J., & Serlin, R. C. (2002). Treatment of selective mutism: A best-evidence synthesis. *School Psychology Quarterly, 17,* 168–190.

Suveg, C., Hudson J. N., Brewer, G., Flannery-Schroeder, E., Gosch, E., & Kendall, P. C. (2009). Cognitive-behavioral therapy for anxiety-disordered youth: Secondary outcomes from a randomized clinical trial evaluating child and family modalities. *Journal of Anxiety Disorders, 23,* 341–349.

Vasey, M. W., & Dadds, M. R. (2001). *The developmental psychopathology of anxiety.* New York: Oxford University Press.

Werry, J. S., & Wollersheim, J. P. (1991). Behavior therapy with children and adolescents: A twenty-year overview. In S. Chess & M. E. Hertzig (Eds.), *Annual progress in child psychiatry and child development, 1990* (pp. 413–447). New York: Brunner/Mazel.

Wolpe, J. (1958). *Psychotherapy by reciprocal inhibition.* Stanford, CA: Stanford University Press.

Dylan Bach

The World According to Dylan

Dylan's behavior was discussed at a school intervention meeting shortly after Dylan enrolled in the kindergarten program at Cyprus Springs Elementary School. His teacher was concerned because Dylan displayed very "odd" behaviors and despite being very verbal seemed to be in "his own world." Dylan's speech was indistinct, and although he seemed to chatter a lot, it was very difficult to comprehend what he was saying. Often he would talk to himself, in a singsong refrain, reciting entire monologues. Dylan was a spontaneous reader, and he would take great pleasure in reading everything from book titles to footnotes. He could also spell his name. However, Dylan preferred solitary activities and it was very difficult to engage Dylan in the normal classroom routines and group activities. Dylan could be very resistant. Not only did the teacher have problems engaging Dylan in regular classroom activities, it was equally difficult trying to disengage Dylan from an activity that he was involved in. When asked to participate in activities not to his liking, Dylan had thrown a number of temper tantrums. On these occasions, he would scream a very loud and persistent "No!!!!"

Dylan was awkward and poorly coordinated and often seemed to walk into things. Dylan seemed to be in constant motion and was very fidgety. During quiet times, like story or circle time, Dylan's constant motion (rocking, squirming, fidgeting) was often disturbing to the other children. This, coupled with Dylan's poor coordination, would often result in his falling into other children or tripping over things in the classroom.

DEVELOPMENTAL HISTORY/FAMILY BACKGROUND

The school social worker met with Dylan's mother, Celeste Bach, to discuss the school's concerns and to obtain a social history. Celeste and her husband Arnold were both 23 years old when Dylan was born. They had been married for 2 years. The Bachs owned an art studio and made their living through the sale of their own creative art pieces. Celeste was an oil painter and Arnold was a sculptor. They supplemented their income from the sale of their artwork by giving art lessons and selling art supplies. Celeste described a difficult and unpleasant pregnancy. She was nauseated through most of the pregnancy and also developed toxemia midway through the pregnancy. Dylan was born 2 weeks ahead of schedule after a very long labor (40 hours) and weighed almost 9 pounds (8 lbs. 10 oz.). The delivery was uneventful.

Celeste described Dylan as cheerful, affectionate, and sociable during his first year. He had a good appetite but was difficult to put on a schedule. He experienced many colicky bouts, and sleep was often disrupted. When he woke, it was difficult to get him back to sleep. Milestones were achieved within the norm, and Dylan was walking and saying his first words by 1 year of age. Mrs. Bach admitted to difficulties with toilet training, and at almost 5 years of age, Dylan continued to exhibit occasional bed-wetting incidents. Accidental soiling stopped about a year ago. Health was described as good, with the exception of vulnerability to ear infections and food allergies (dairy products). Dylan is rarely ill; however, when he does get ill, he tends to develop a fever and requires monitoring.

Family history notes a paternal uncle with cerebral palsy and mental retardation. There is a history of bipolar disorder with obsessive-compulsive disorder in the family (maternal grandmother), as well as anxiety (paternal aunt). Celeste stated that Dylan's pediatrician felt that Dylan might be autistic; however, no further assessment was conducted. She added that Dylan can be stubborn at home, but that he will comply when necessary. Dylan gets along well with their adult neighbors, who have all been very impressed with Dylan's reading and writing abilities. Celeste added that they currently live in an area that has no children Dylan's age and that he has had very little practice socializing with peers.

Toward the end of the kindergarten program (Dylan was 5 years 6 months of age), a brief assessment was conducted by the school psychologist to obtain information regarding Dylan's cognitive functioning. The Differential Ability Scales (DAS) were administered and revealed a Verbal Cluster standard score of 56, and a Nonverbal Cluster score of 86. The school psychologist noted that rapport was very difficult to establish and cautioned interpretation of the assessment results due to Dylan's immaturity, lack of compliance, low frustration tolerance, and insistence on doing things his own way.

The school convened a staffing meeting to determine eligibility for special education programming and decided on the following course of action. Due to difficulties establishing whether the results of the assessment were valid, based on Dylan's test behavior, Dylan was given a temporary designation as Developmentally Delayed, which would lapse on his sixth birthday, the age established by the Local Educational Authority (LEA) for discontinuation of services under the category of developmental delay. (See Appendix B for an explanation of the classification of developmental delay under IDEA, 2004.) The decision allowed for an additional 6-month period in which a more valid and in-depth evaluation of Dylan's ability levels could be conducted. Dylan would be provided with services from occupational therapy, speech and language therapy, and the special-programs teacher, while awaiting his reevaluation.

Unfortunately, Dylan's parents moved over the summer holidays, and Dylan began attending Lawton Elementary School for the next academic year. Meetings were convened prior to the start of school to determine how to best accommodate Dylan's special needs within the new school environment. At this time, the decision was made to have Dylan attend the kindergarten program for a half day and receive specialized services in a class for children with varying exceptionalities (VE Program) for the remainder of the day. Speech therapy was provided on a daily basis by the school speech pathologist, and occupational therapy was programmed for a once-weekly visit. Dylan had always experienced problems with adjusting to new routines, and it was not surprising that the move to a new school was very difficult for Dylan.

The first struggle began when he did not want to get on the bus and threw himself on the ground kicking and screaming. However, his parents were persistent and eventually his resistance mellowed. After about 3 weeks, Dylan began to settle into his new routines. Recently, he has begun to reexperience difficulties, and resistance to riding on the school bus has resurfaced. Just prior to his formal reassessment, Dylan was observed throwing himself to the ground and refusing to get on the school bus. School officials were currently investigating potential reasons for the resurgence of Dylan's refusals to board the school bus.

REASON FOR REFERRAL

A referral for reevaluation was initiated by Dylan's new school to remove his temporary designation as developmentally delayed. A full assessment was requested to update intellectual estimates of Dylan's abilities and to determine how to best meet Dylan's academic, social, and emotional needs within the current school system.

ASSESSMENT

Knowing the difficulties that the previous school psychologist had encountered in attempting to conduct a comprehensive assessment, the school psychologist took several precautions to obtain a valid assessment of Dylan's functioning on several levels. Several observations of Dylan's behaviors were obtained by classroom observations of Dylan's behaviors in different classroom environments, and more formal psychometric tasks were administered in environments that were within Dylan's comfort zone and within his tolerance for removal from normal classroom routines.

Classroom Observations

The school psychologist began a series of observations of Dylan in the two classroom settings. Observation of Dylan in the kindergarten program revealed a number of interesting behaviors. On one occasion, Dylan was observed while his teacher read a story to the class. The children were sitting on the floor, gathered around the teacher's chair. Although Dylan seemed attentive initially, he soon began a series of excessive movements (fidgeting, rocking, sprawling on the floor, hanging upside down) that were distracting to the other children. He spontaneously got up and walked to the back of the classroom in search of paper and crayons. For the next 15 minutes, the teacher would make comments to redirect Dylan back to the circle and Dylan would comply momentarily, then get up and return to the back of the classroom. At one point he was very insistent on leaving the circle, saying, "I want to do my work!" The teacher responded by saying, "You *will* sit and listen to the story!" Dylan responded, "I *won't* sit and listen to the story!" At this point, the teacher reminded him of good and bad choices and the consequence of losing a star for bad choices. If he did not do as he was told, he would lose a "star." (The star chart was a classroom behavior merit program. Children earned stars for good behavior and lost stars for poor behavior. Stars could be traded in for activities and small prizes at the end of the day.) Dylan immediately complied and remained on the floor. However, his constant motion eventually resulted in his kicking another child (by accident), resulting in the child breaking into tears. Dylan seemed oblivious to his role in the event and clearly did not understand the teacher's request to apologize to the other child for the infraction. Within the kindergarten program, the teacher's goals and expectations for Dylan were the same as for all children in her classroom. Within this environment, Dylan struggled with the lack of flexibility and did not understand the need to be involved in activities that held little interest for him.

For Dylan, the Varying Exceptionalities (VE) Program had several advantages: fewer children, older children (7–9 years of age), and a teacher trained in special education. In this environment, Dylan seemed to enjoy the freedom of being allowed to work on a task at his own pace. Dylan worked very quickly and seemed to thoroughly enjoy coloring in pictures, drawing animated cartoons, and writing captions beside the drawings. He was highly productive and was not distracted by the grouped activities that were going on around him. Since the children were of varying levels of ability (slow learners, learning disabled), the children were often grouped for instructional purposes. Due to Dylan's uniqueness, his teacher provided instruction on a 1:1 basis and then provided opportunities for independent learning (computer access) or individual seatwork. While he worked, Dylan was observed to be singing to himself, mimicking lyrics from various audio computer programs (e.g., "Rock and Roll," "ABC's"). Dylan often repeated refrains over and over in a singsong fashion while he worked. Although reluctant to disengage from a task when requested to do so, he did comply and brought his work to the teacher for her remarks. He followed routines relatively well and enjoyed his times when called on to read to the teacher, which he did flawlessly. He was rewarded for following routines and completing seatwork with individual computer time. During individual computer time, Dylan quickly became totally absorbed in the computer programs, repeating the monologue as if he were narrating the program himself.

Comments on Classroom Observations. The school psychologist noted that many behaviors demonstrated by Dylan fit descriptions in the literature on Asperger's disorder: idiosyncratic areas of interest, odd and peculiar behaviors, intense interest in specific areas, poor coordination, and lack of social reciprocity. Having the opportunity to watch Dylan's behavior in the two different classroom settings provided considerable insight. While Dylan constantly resisted attempts to engage him in group-oriented activities in the regular kindergarten program, he welcomed an opportunity provided by the special education setting to work within the confines of his own little world, without attempts to draw him into any group activities.

Individual Assessment Sessions

In addition to observational assessments, Dylan was seen for three individual assessment sessions. The psychologist decided to conduct Dylan's assessment in a small resource room off the VE classroom. Dylan was familiar with the room because he received his language and occupational therapy in the same room; also, he could readily see his teacher through the glass windows. By this time, Dylan was also familiar with the school psychologist and willingly accompanied her into the room. Since Dylan seemed to enjoy artwork, as an introductory task, Dylan was asked to draw a person. Dylan responded by saying that he would draw a pig, which he did. The pig had a big sign on its neck: "Babe." Apparently, Dylan had been watching the movie *Babe* (a story about a pig) over and over and was very interested in pigs at this time. He did comply with a request to copy Bender Designs and completed the Bender design drawings in a short period of time. Dylan used a whole-hand pencil grip for all drawing and printing.

Throughout the assessment sessions, Dylan's enthusiasm waxed and waned, and his compliance shifted relative to his interest in the task at hand. Dylan was very excited about doing the Picture Completion subtest of the WISC-IV (a supplementary test that was included due to the suspected level of interest that the task would have for Dylan). He loved to find out what was missing in the picture and repeated the phrase "What is missing!" over and over again. He wanted to draw in the missing parts in the Picture Completion booklet and the examiner had to confiscate writing materials to ensure this did not happen. Dylan's enthusiasm for visual materials far outweighed his interest in responding to verbal questions, and assessment results reflect this disparity. Despite a predominance of fidgety and tense behaviors, Dylan became very focused, deliberate, and methodical working with block designs. He carefully moved each block with precision, checking and rechecking with the stimulus card to ensure accuracy. Dylan also made humorous comments, and when the 11th block design was revealed, he said, "Scary!" and laughed. Then he added, "You will have to help me on this one." Throughout the assessment, when one subtest was completed, Dylan repeatedly asked if he could play "What is missing?" (the picture completion task from the WISC-IV) again. Eventually, the examiner had to remove the stimulus book from the room, since Dylan kept trying to find it, to play the picture completion task.

Williams (1995) discusses the impact of sensory overload on children with Asperger's disorder, stating that these children can be overwhelmed by very little change and that sensory overload can throw these children off balance. During the course of this first session, Dylan fell off his chair three times. A combination of poor coordination and becoming overly stimulated served to throw him off balance, literally and figuratively.

When the examiner arrived in the classroom for the second session, Dylan jumped up from his seat (almost falling into the desk) and greeted her with an enthusiastic and announced, "You're back! You're back!" He spontaneously took her hand and led her to the assessment room. The Woodcock Johnson Test of Achievement (WJ-III) was introduced and Dylan completed the Letter Word Identification subtest with ease. The Passage Comprehension subtest was next, and it was anticipated that this would be another area of high interest for Dylan. However, what transpired was not expected. The Passage Comprehension subtest requires that the students read a passage and then orally fill in the blank to complete the sentence in the stimulus book. For example, a statement that "Children often like to play on swings in the park," is followed by a statement to test comprehension, such as: "Children like to play on ____ in the park." When this task was introduced, Dylan was insistent on filling in the blanks by writing the answer in the stimulus book. Although the school psychologist made several attempts to explain why Dylan could not write in the book, it was not possible to console him. He became visibly upset and started to shake, was on the verge of tears, and repeatedly stated, "You must fill in the blank with the missing word! . . . You must fill in the blank with the missing word!" Dylan was extremely distraught. At this point, the examiner removed the book from the room and brought in sheets of paper and crayons, allowing Dylan to draw and color his favorite cartoons. Drawing seemed to be an activity that served to soothe Dylan in times of stress; this discovery could play an important role in the development of a treatment plan.

After Dylan calmed down, the examiner accompanied Dylan to the kindergarten room, where he was supposed to go after lunch. However, when they arrived, the other students had already left for physical education (PE) and the examiner began to walk Dylan over to the playground to join his class. Given Dylan's poor coordination and reluctance to engage in group activities, it is not surprising that PE is his least favorite subject. He became very upset about going to PE and began clinging to the examiner's arm, refusing to let go. The examiner talked to him about all the good choices he had made that day and added that he might earn a star for joining his class, because this was a very good choice indeed. Reluctantly, he separated and joined his class in session. The psychologist then talked to his teacher to ensure that he did receive a star for compliance, to provide support for his difficult choice.

In order to complete the academic assessment the following day, the examiner photocopied the Passage Comprehension and Applied Problems subtests of the WJ-III. The plan was to provide Dylan with worksheets that would allow him to fill in the blanks on the actual pages rather than respond orally. Although this technique was not part of the standardized procedure, the psychologist wanted to avoid unduly upsetting Dylan, who was "locked into" a "filling in the blanks" mode of operation. The psychologist considered the deviation in protocol a minimal concession, and it avoided the risk of another emotional upset for Dylan. In addition, the task actually became more difficult, since Dylan now had to spell the words to complete the sentences, rather than just provide the answers orally. When presented with the sheets, Dylan proceeded to fill in a large number of blanks correctly, and also spelled the words appropriately. He was rewarded by being allowed to color in the pictures and then draw another series of cartoon animals. As he was drawing, Dylan recited, verbatim, an entire dialogue from a computer program that he had previously heard: "This CD program is a Random House Production. As a special bonus feature, be sure to try our newsletter and programs for kids. . . . Each issue is packed with behind-the-scenes action and fun-filled games for kids. Your first issue is free. . . . To obtain your free issue send the enclosed postcard to Random House Productions, P.O. Box 1478, Chicago, Illinois, Postal Code 68374. So don't miss an issue. Send your postcard in today!"

Dylan's drawings were quite remarkable and very well done. He titled his drawing of animated characters as the "Wakabe Rabbit Collection." Dylan also drew another picture, this time of the Windows 2000 logo, complete with copyright. Ultimately, Dylan completed the academic assessment, although it required considerable redirection to task. Dylan fell out of his chair again during this assessment session.

Dylan was able to engage with the examiner socially, albeit within a restricted range. Although eye contact was established, at times he would actually open his eyes wide with a penetrating stare, but at other times visual distance and lack of eye contact was far more comforting. Dylan displayed a sense of humor and could be very engaging; however, laughter would often escalate quickly out of control. Dylan preferred to engage the examiner on his own terms, and could become totally absorbed in paper-and-pencil tasks or verbal monologues that effectively excluded social contact. Dylan was able to request help when needed for a cognitive problem-solving task (puzzles, blocks); however, he experienced difficulty eliciting assistance when emotionally upset, due to a very high level of anxiety and distress. On these occasions, Dylan seemed to respond either by clinging or by attempting to escape (tantrums).

ASSESSMENT RESULTS

Information regarding specific assessment instruments and guidance in the interpretation of standard scores and T scores can be found in Appendix C.

Dylan's responses to the Wechsler Intelligence Scale for Children—Fourth Edition (WISC-IV) revealed a Verbal Comprehension Index (VCI = 92; range 86–99) in the average range and a Perceptual Reasoning Index (PSI = 115; range 106–122) in the high average range. Both scores were considered to be an underestimate of global cognitive reasoning, yet likely an adequate picture of day-to-day functioning. Verbal tasks were responded to poorly, and despite an excellent base vocabulary, Dylan's responses to verbal tasks were lower than anticipated, but in the predicted direction for Asperger's disorder. A relative strength was noted in Vocabulary (12), while weaknesses were noted in Comprehension (4) and Similarities (5). On tasks of perceptual reasoning (Perceptual Reasoning Index: PRI), significant strengths were evident on Block Design (16) and Picture Reasoning (14) with a weakness noted in Picture Completion (8). Dylan's WISC-IV profile of superior visual to verbal ability was not in the predicted direction (Klin, Sparrow, Volkmar, Cicchetti, & Rourke, 2001); however, Dylan was also more compliant on visual tasks, which may have served to alter overall scores. Despite this fact, subtest scatter actually did conform to suggested patterns in the literature on Asperger's disorder: Vocabulary much higher than Comprehension (Klin, Volkmar, Sparrow, Cicchetti, & Rourke, 1995). Dylan received an error score of 9 for his reproductions of Bender Designs, which was within the expected range for his age. His substitution of lines for dots in designs 2, 3, and 5 is often associated with brain dysfunction.

Standard scores for academic performance on the Woodcock Johnson Achievement Test (WJIII) revealed a score for Broad Reading equivalent to a standard score of 150, which is in the highly gifted range. The Broad Reading score is a composite based on performance from three reading tasks: Letter Word Identification (SS = 135), Reading Fluency (SS = 119), and Passage Comprehension (SS = 128). Scores for written expression revealed Spelling (SS = 148) and Writing Samples (SS = 140) to also be within the gifted range. Scores for Math Calculation (SS = 94) and Applied Problems (SS = 84) were Dylan's weakest areas of performance.

Dylan's mother completed the Vineland Adaptive Behavior Scale, the Gilliam Autism Rating Scale (GARS), and the Asperger Syndrome Diagnostic Scale (ASDS). Mrs. Bach's ratings placed Dylan within the normal range of behaviors on the GARS (SS = 87), which would suggest below average indicators for autism. Ratings on the ASDS indicated an overall Asperger's Syndrome Quotient of 105, suggesting a likely diagnosis of Asperger's disorder. A significant elevation was noted for the Social Behavior scale on the ASDS. According to Dylan's mother, overall adaptive behavior on the Vineland was within the expected range for his age level.

Dylan's teachers also completed the GARS and the ASDS. Since Dylan was observed to behave very differently in the two classroom settings, it was not surprising that the kindergarten teacher and the special programs teacher (VE teacher) rated Dylan's behaviors quite differently. On the GARS, the kindergarten teacher rated Dylan as having an average probability of autism (SS = 91), with only Communication slightly elevated. The VE teacher rated Dylan much higher on the Autism scale (SS = 126), suggesting a "high" probability of autism with significant elevations on the Communication scale (scale score = 14) and Social Interaction scale (SS = 19). Teachers reported better agreement on the ASDS, with his kindergarten teacher suggesting a likely (SS = 97) probability of Asperger's syndrome and his VE teacher ratings indicating a very likely (SS = 111) probability of Asperger's syndrome. According to the ASDS, the kindergarten teacher noted significant escalation on the Cognitive scale (SS = 13), while the VE teacher noted significant elevations on the Social (SS = 13) and Sensorimotor scales (SS = 13).

ISSUES, TRENDS, AND TREATMENT ALTERNATIVES

Prior to the fourth edition of the *DSM-IV* (APA, 1994), Asperger's disorder was not a recognized Axis I disorder. Currently, Asperger's disorder is listed under the category of pervasive developmental disorders (PDDs), which are characterized by severe and lifelong impairments in a number of areas. The term *autistic spectrum disorders* has been used to refer to disorders that have autistic-like features. There is much confusion in the area because many disorders have overlapping features, and given the relative newness of Asperger's disorder as an official category, considerable research on treatment planning is needed. Unlike autism, Asperger's disorder is often accompanied by a well-developed vocabulary basis with the deficit in communication evident at the level of social-pragmatic speech. Associated features can include relative strengths in verbal areas and weaknesses in visual-motor or visual-spatial skills. Motor clumsiness may also be evident. While autism is often diagnosed around 3 to 4 years of age, Asperger's disorder may not be fully recognized until the child is enrolled in a peer group setting, such as preschool or kindergarten (*DSM-IV-TR;* APA, 2000).

Asperger's disorder involves a severe impairment in the area of reciprocal social interaction skills, and two broad criteria are required for diagnosis, namely (a) severe, sustained impairment in social interaction; and (b) the demonstration of restricted and repetitive, stereotypical behavior patterns. Two additional criteria are listed for differential diagnosis relative to autism: Asperger's disorder is ruled out if there is indication of a significant language delay or significant cognitive or adaptive delays (other than social). The severe social impairment noted in Asperger's disorder is described similarly for autism, but is often manifested in a different manner. With Asperger's disorder, lack of reciprocity often takes the form of a self-sustained monologue in an area of self-interest and preoccupation, regardless of the interest or positive response from others. Often there is an intense preoccupation with specific areas of interest.

The *DSM-IV-TR* (APA, 2000) criteria for Asperger's disorder rule out language delay, suggesting that children with the disorder will have normal language development, producing single words by 2 years and phrases by 3 years of age. While those with autism often perseverate on parts of objects (spinning a wheel), the child with Asperger's disorder will often become preoccupied and perseverate on themes or topics of interest. As a result, these children can become very knowledgeable in a given area (e.g., dinosaurs, cars), sometimes referred to as *savant skills* (Klin & Volkmar, 1997). Some children can become preoccupied with numbers or letters and demonstrate an ability to decode almost anything (*hyperlexic*) at a very early age. Children with Asperger's disorder are able to form attachments to family members; however, their ability to relate to others is often not evident outside the family circle, and the skills do not transfer to peers. Attempts to carry on a meaningful reciprocal conversation with children who have Asperger's disorder is often derailed by their tendencies to produce pedantic monologues on topics of interest to them and their lack of understanding of the give and take necessary in areas of social pragmatics (Attwood, 1998).

The ability to form and maintain social relationships and friendships are often at the core of normal emotional development and can provide children with feelings of belongingness, emotional security, and self-worth (Rubin et al., 2004). In normally developing adolescents, friendships provide the basis for gaining increased social-cognitive awareness through disclosures evident in intimate relationships, such as sharing information with close friends (Allen, Porter, McFarland, Marsh, & McElhaney, 2005). Although it was once thought that children with Asperger's disorder preferred to be alone, more recent investigations have found that although adolescents with the disorder demonstrate less participation in social activities (Orsmond, Krauss, & Seltzer, 2004), lack of social relationships may not be related to lack of desire, but to difficulties they encounter with social understanding due to such deficits as theory of mind (Kaland et al., 2002). As a result, adolescents with Asperger's disorder can become very lonely and isolated at a time when they want to join peer groups (Klin & Volkmar, 1997; Whitehouse, Durkin, Jaquet, & Ziatas, 2009). Since individuals with Asperger's disorder are at increased risk for depression and anxiety disorders, relative to the population at large (Sofronoff, Attwood, & Hinton, 2005), Whitehouse and colleagues (2009) investigated the relationship between depression and quality of friendship in youth with Asperger's disorder. Results revealed that relative to their peers, youth with Asperger's disorder demonstrated less intrinsic motivation to engage in friendships, and experienced poorer quality of friendships and elevated levels of loneliness and depression. The researchers suggest that intervention to improve social competence in adolescents with Asperger's disorder (possibly through the use of story modeling techniques; Carrington, Papinczak, & Templeton, 2003) might have significant implications for enhanced mental health.

Rourke and colleagues (2002) note two areas where diagnostic confusions exist: distinguishing Asperger's disorder from "high-functioning autism" (HFA), and distinguishing Asperger's disorder from nonverbal learning disabilities.

Asperger's Disorder and High-Functoning Autism (HFA)

HFA is an informal subcategory of autism for approximately 25% of children with autism who score above the mentally retarded range (who have an IQ greater than 70). Although individuals with Asperger's disorder share more similarities with individuals with HFA, compared to those with more severe autism, Macintosh and Dissanayake (2004) report that results of their meta-analysis revealed unique differences in language development and cognitive/neurological functioning that distinguish Asperger's disorder from individuals with HFA. Although many of the language differences that distinguish HFA from Asperger's disorder are somewhat resolved by adolescence, qualitative differences remain (Siegel, 1998). Individuals with Asperger's disorder are far more likely to attempt conversations with others (although usually one-sided in nature) than those with HFA. Ghaziuddin (2008) suggests that in social interactions, while those with HFA tend to be more aloof and passive, individuals with Asperger's disorder tend to appear more active, but odd.

Although individuals with HFA and Asperger's disorder score higher on IQ tests than those with autism, those with HFA usually perform better on tasks of perceptual reasoning, while those with Asperger's disorder perform better on verbal tasks (Ehlers et al., 1997). Sahyoun, Soulieres, Belliveau, Mottron, and Mody (2009) found that while individuals with HFA used visuospatial processing during a pictorial reasoning task, those with Asperger's disorder used linguistic mediation to solve the same tasks.

Asperger's Disorder and Nonverbal Learning Disabilities (NLD):

The distinction between children with Asperger's disorder and children with an NLD (NLD: See Case of Sandy for a comparison) is also difficult because both share similar features of a social disability due to poor understanding of the pragmatics of social communication, inability to read social cues, and poor understanding of nonverbal social indicators. Klin and colleagues (1995) suggest that it is most likely that these disorders represent different perspectives on a heterogeneous set of disorders that share some overlapping features.

Rourke and colleagues (2002) found more similarities in processing between youth with NLDs and Asperger's disorder than between youth with HFA and Asperger's. Youth with Asperger's disorder and youth with NLD shared strengths in processing left-hemisphere functions (e.g., verbal ability) and deficits in right-hemisphere processing (weaknesses in social interaction, complex reasoning, and nonverbal communication). Although they note that little research has been published regarding interventions for Asperger's, Klin and colleagues (1995) suggest that interventions developed to address NLDs might also be helpful for this population.

Communication and Social-Pragmatic Speech

Woodbury-Smith, Klin, and Volkmar (2002) suggest that although the *DSM-IV-TR* (APA, 2000) rules out language delay as a criterion for Asperger's disorder, it is important to recognize that individuals with Asperger's disorder process social information and communicate in a different way from those with autism. Although both disorders share impairments in social relationships, the social disability is unique to each disorder with their own unique patterns of behaviors and communication deficits. Individuals with Asperger's disorder do have communication abnormalities (pragmatic communication impairments) that "interfere with the ability to initiate and sustain a conversation," even though deficits are "fundamentally different from the type of language and communication impairments described in autism in which the language is delayed, ecolalic idiosyncratic and repetitive" (p. 238).

Treatment/Intervention

Far more research evidence is available for the treatment of individuals with autism than for those with Asperger's disorder. Given the wide variations in intellectual functioning between these two populations, severity of problems exhibited, and the range of areas targeted for improvement, it becomes difficult to generalize results from these studies of autism readily to an Asperger's population.

The Asperger Syndrome Diagnostic Scale (Myles, Bock, & Simpson, 2001) is a recent advancement toward providing a more reliable method of assessing the degree to which observed behaviors match criteria for Asperger's disorder as defined in the *DSM-IV* and *International Classification of Diseases and Related Health Problems—Tenth Edition* (ICD-10; World Health Organization, 1992). The scale provides an Asperger Syndrome Quotient derived from observer ratings for 50 behaviors distributed over five behavioral indexes: language, social, maladaptive, cognitive, and sensorimotor behaviors. The potential value of this scale in providing direction for future research and outcomes for treatment planning is yet to be determined.

Since the typical age for diagnosis of Asperger's disorder (11 years) is much later than for autism (usually 5½ years; Howlin & Asgharian, 1999), early treatment and intervention can be challenging. Approaches most often used for children with autism include applied behavioral analysis and approaches that draw on a variety of behavioral, developmental, and social-pragmatic resources (Tsatsanis, Foley, & Donehower, 2004). For the most part, treatment has focused on increasing social and emotional awareness and improving social exchange. Techniques that have been developed to assist social competence include direct instruction in role playing, social skills groups, practicing of skills with peers, and the use of social stories.

Social stories can provide a framework for teaching lessons about appropriate social behavior, the sequencing of social events, and the interpretation of social cues. Scripts can provide a template for social exchange and increase the child's understanding of what is likely to happen and how to respond. Since the story can include different characters, the child with Asperger's disorder can also learn how to take the perspective of another person, a skill that is often difficult for individuals with Asperger's disorder (Attwood, 2000). Sansosti and Powell-Smith (2006) introduced children with Asperger's disorder to emotions within themselves and others through the use of social stories. Despite a small sample and lack of long-term effects, the procedure is a promising avenue for further investigation, especially if stories are infused with highly visual supports (Kana, Keller, Cherkassky, Minshew, & Just, 2006).

Results from neurological research have revealed that when children with autism and Asperger's are presented with tasks that involve decoding facial expressions and vocal tone, their brains are activated in areas used to identify objects in normal populations (Schultz et al., 2000). Lindner and Rosen (2006) suggest that children with Asperger's focus too heavily on the verbal message and ignore relevant signals in facial cues and tone. LaCava, Golan, Baron-Cohen, and Myles (2007) used a computer-generated program to teach children with Asperger's disorder to recognize emotional expressions and complex emotional voice patterns.

Marriage, Gordon, and Brand (1995) developed a social skills intervention program for Asperger's children, targeting skill deficiencies peculiar to the Asperger's population. The program of eight weekly 2-hour sessions was followed by six weekly 1-hour reinforcement sessions. Multimodal techniques (role-play, videotaping, games, show and tell) were practiced during the sessions, and homework was assigned to provide carry-over into the home. To assist skill generalization, sessions were varied across a number of different settings within the clinic. Parents met for an informal discussion group while the children attended the sessions. Although results did not reveal significant positive outcomes, the authors suggest that lack of positive outcomes may have been an artifact of the measurement process, since anecdotal comments and observation pointed to overall social gains. The authors' recommended future studies include increased generalization of the program within an actual school setting.

On a more practical note, Williams (1995) suggests several guidelines for teachers of students with Asperger's disorder. A number of school-based programming suggestions are provided that target seven defining characteristics of Asperger's disorder: insistence on sameness, impairment in social interaction, restricted range of interests, poor concentration, poor motor coordination, academic difficulties, and emotional vulnerability. Describing children with Asperger's as "easily stressed, and emotionally vulnerable" (p. 9), Williams states that although there are no precise recipes for success due to the diverse nature of the disorder, broad strategies can be adapted to meet the needs of the individual child. For example, insistence on sameness can be counteracted by giving the student sufficient warning or pretraining regarding pending changes, incorporating consistent routines, minimizing transitions, and providing a safe and predictable environment. Issues of emotional vulnerability can be addressed by skill-building exercises to reduce stressful responding. The introduction of step-by-step problem-solving exercises can be very helpful in providing a structured plan to adopt in times of stress.

Post-Case Questions

1. Discuss how some of Dylan's symptoms conform to a diagnosis of Asperger's disorder and how some symptoms and behaviors are not in the predicted direction.

2. In terms of differential diagnosis, how do Dylan's behaviors fit with an Asperger profile relative to that of high-functioning autism or nonverbal learning disability? Use illustrations from Sandy's case (Case of Sandy Smith) and Dylan's case presentation to compare and contrast the most salient features.

3. Provide some possible explanations for the wide discrepancies in ratings between the three raters (two teachers and parent). Discuss these potential differences relative to various levels of influence, or developmental contexts, suggested by Bronfenbrenner's model. Design an intervention program drawing on the strengths of both classroom programs.

REFERENCES

American Psychiatric Association (APA). (1994). *The diagnostic and statistical manual of mental disorders* (4th ed.). Washington, DC: American Psychiatric Press.

American Psychiatric Association (APA). (2000). *The diagnostic and statistical manual of mental disorders (4th ed., text rev.).* Washington, DC: American Psychiatric Press.

Allen, J. P., Porter, M. R., McFarland, F. C., Marsh, P., & McElhaney, K. B. (2005). The two faces of adolescents' success with peers: Adolescent popularity, social adaptation, and deviant behavior. *Child Development, 76,* 747–760.

Attwood, T. (1998). *Asperger's syndrome: A guide for parents and professionals.* London, UK: Jessica Kingsley.

Attwood, T. (2000). Strategies for improving the social integration of children with Asperger syndrome. *Autism, 4,* 85–100.

Carrington, S., Papinczak, T., & Templeton, E. (2003). A phenomenological study: The social world of five adolescents who have Asperger's syndrome. *Australian Journal of Learning Disabilities, 8,* 15–21.

Ehlers, S., Nyden, A., Gillberg, C., Dahlgren, S. A., Dahlgren, S. O., Hjelmquist, E., et al. (1997). Asperger syndrome, autism and attention disorders: A comparative study of the cognitive profiles of 120 children. *Journal of Child Psychology and Psychiatry, 38,* 207–217.

Ghaziuddin, M. (2008). Defining the behavioral phenotype of Asperger syndrome. *Journal of Autism and Developmental Disorders, 38,* 138–142.

Howlin, P., & Asgharian, A. (1999). The diagnosis of autism and Asperger syndrome: Findings from a survey of 770 families. *Development and Medical Child Neurology, 41,* 834–839.

Kaland, N., Moller-Nielsen, A., Callesen, K., Mortensen, E. L., Gottlieb, D., & Smith, L. (2002). A new "advanced" test of theory of mind: Evidence from children and adolescents with Asperger syndrome. *Journal of Child Psychology and Psychiatry, 43,* 517–528.

Kana, R., Keller, T., Cherkassky, V., Minshew, N., & Just, M. (2006). Sentence comprehension in autism: Thinking in pictures with decreased functional connectivity. *Brain, 129,* 2484–2493.

Klin, A., Sparrow, S. S., Volkmar, F. R., Cicchetti, D. V., & Rourke, B. P. (1995). Asperger syndrome. In B. P. Rourke (Ed.), *Syndrome of nonverbal learning disabilities: Neurodevelopmental manifestations.* New York: Guilford.

Klin, A., & Volkmar, F. R. (1997). Asperger's syndrome. In D. Cohen & F. R. Volkmar (Eds.), *Handbook of autism and pervasive developmental disorders* (2nd ed., pp. 94–122). New York: John Wiley.

LaCava, P. G., Golan, O., Baron-Cohen, S., & Myles, B. S. (2007). Using assistive technology to teach emotion recognition to students with Asperger syndrome: A pilot study. *Remedial and Special Education, 28,* 174–181.

Lindner, J. L., & Rosen, L. A. (2006). Decoding of emotion through facial expression, prosody and verbal content in children and adolescents with Asperger's syndrome. *Journal of Autism and Developmental Disorders, 36,* 769–777.

Macintosh, K. E., & Dissanayake, C. (2004). Annotation: The similarities and differences between autistic disorder and Asperger's disorder: A review of the empirical evidence. *Journal of Child Psychology and Psychiatry, 45*(3), 421–434.

Marriage, K. J., Gordon, V., & Brand, L. (1995). A social skills group for boys with Asperger's syndrome. *Australian and New Zealand Journal of Psychiatry, 29,* 58–62.

Myles, B. S., Bock, S. J., & Simpson, R. (2001). *Asperger Syndrome Diagnostic Scale.* Austin, TX: PRO-ED.

Orsmond, G., Krauss, I., & Seltzer, M. M. (2004*). Journal of autism and developmental disorders, 34*(3), 245–256.

Rourke, B. P., Ahmad, S., Collins, D., Jayman-Abello, B., Hayman-Abello, S., & Warriner, E. M. (2002). Child clinical/pediatric neuropsychology: Some recent advances. *Annual Review of Psychology, 53,* 309–339.

Rubin, K. H., Dwyer, K. M., Booth-LaForce, C., Kim, A. H., Burgess, K. B., & Rose-Krasnor, L. (2004). Attachment, friendship, and psychosocial functioning in early adolescence. *Journal of Early Adolescence, 24,* 326–356.

Sahyoun, C. P., Soulieres, I., Belliveau, J. W., Motton, L., & Mody, M. (2009). Cognitive differences in pictorial reasoning between high-functioning autism and Asperger's syndrome. *Journal of Autism and Developmental Disorders, 39,* 1014–1023.

Sansosti, F. J., & Powell-Smith, K. A. (2006). Using social stories to improve the social behaviour of children with Asperger syndrome. *Journal of Positive Behavior Interventions, 8,* 43–57.

Schultz, R. T., Gauthier, I., Klin, A., Fulbright, R. K., Anderson, A.W., & Volkmar, F. (2000). Abnormal ventral temporal cortical activity during face discrimination among individuals with autism and Asperger syndrome. *Archives of General Psychiatry, 57*(4), 331–340.

Siegel, D. J. (1998). Evaluation of high-functioning autism. In G. Goldstein, P. D. Nussbaum, & S. R. Beers (Eds.), *Neuropsychology* (pp. 107–134). New York: Plenum Press.

Sofronoff, K., Attwood, T., & Hinton, S. (2005). A randomised controlled trial of a CBT intervention for anxiety in children with Asperger syndrome. *Journal of Child Psychology and Psychiatry, 46,* 1152–1160.

Tsatsanis, K. D., Foley, C., & Donehower, C. (2004). Contemporary outcome research and programming guidelines for Asperger syndrome and high-functioning autism. *Topics in Language Disorders, 24,* 249–259.

Whitehouse, A. J., Durkin, K., Jaquet, E., & Ziatas, K. (2009). Friendship, loneliness and depression in adolescents with Asperger's syndrome. *Journal of Adolescence, 32,* 309–322.

Williams, K. (1995). Understanding the student with Asperger syndrome: Guidelines for teachers. *Focus on Autistic Behavior, 10,* 9–16.

Woodbury-Smith, M., Klin, A., & Volkmar, F. (2002). Asperger's syndrome: A comparison of clinical diagnoses and those made according to the ICD-10 and *DSM-IV. Journal of Autism and Developmental Disorders, 35,* 235–240.

World Health Organization. (1992). *ICD-10 Guide for Mental Retardation.* Geneva, Switzerland: WHO.

CASE 4

Bradley Hunter

Not Yet Diagnosed

Bradley is an African American male who is 5 years 5 months of age and enrolled in the kindergarten program at John Williams Elementary School. He is currently receiving services from the special education resource teacher under the category of developmental delay. He also receives speech and language, as well as occupational therapy as related services. Reevaluation was requested to determine the extent of his delays currently, and the nature of his learning problems.

DEVELOPMENTAL HISTORY/FAMILY BACKGROUND

Bradley is at risk for neurodevelopmental difficulties due to a history of prematurity and its complications. Bradley's mother provided the following information regarding his developmental history. Mother was 22 when she was pregnant with Bradley and reported that she did not smoke or drink during the pregnancy. She was, however, involved in a car accident when she was 25 weeks pregnant and was admitted to emergency due to vaginal bleeding. Throughout the remainder of the pregnancy, there were several incidents of vaginal discharge. Bradley weighed 3 pounds at birth and was born at 28 weeks gestation. Apgar was 6 at 1 minute and 7 at 5 minutes. Bradley was placed on a ventilator for two and a half weeks after birth because he suffered from respiratory distress syndrome.

A tracheotomy was performed due to upper airway obstruction as Bradley was not getting enough oxygen. He remained in the hospital until he was discharged, 120 days after his birth. While hospitalized, he developed pneumonia several times. Two years ago, he returned to the hospital, where he had a laryngoscopy and adenoidectomy in preparation for having the tracheotomy tube removed 2 months later.

Bradley's motor and speech and language milestones have all been delayed, and Bradley did not begin walking until he was 19 months of age. When he was 26 months old, he was seen at the Infant Care Clinic for physical therapy and speech and language assessments. At that time, his expressive and receptive language score was 18 months, while global language was 16 months. Physical therapy evaluation at that time revealed that motor skills ranged from 14 months for stationary skills to 17 months for locomotion to 19 months for object manipulation.

Due to the severity of his problems and pervasive delays, Bradley was seen in the Child Developmental Clinic when he was 34 months of age. At that time, the Bayley Infant Scales (Bayley-2) were administered and Bradley scored an age equivalent of 22 months, with a Mental Development Index (MDI) of 54. Mother was interviewed and the Vineland Adaptive Behavior Scales were administered. Bradley scored in the following ranges: Communication SS = 64 (16 months), Daily Living SS = 67 (19 months), Socialization Skills SS = 83 (24 months), Motor Skills SS = 70 (23 months), and the Adaptive Behavior Composite SS = 65 (21 months). At 34 months of age, Bradley was in the process of being toilet trained; however, nocturnal eneuresis was occurring on a nightly basis. The examiner noted that although Bradley was almost 3 years old, his mother reported that he was not yet able to drink from a cup or use a fork. He was, however, able to use a spoon and drink from a sippy cup. During the interview with the psychologist at the clinic, Bradley's mother described him as being a highly active youngster who was impulsive and easily distracted. She also noted that he can be very stubborn and aggressive, especially with his brother, whom he often fights with. He is difficult to manage and is prone to throw temper tantrums when he cannot have his way.

Mother is now 27 and father is 30, and they both have some community college education. Mother said that neither she nor Bradley's father had any learning problems in school. Bradley has an older brother who is 8 years old who has significant developmental delays and receives special education services. Mother and father are no longer living together, and Bradley lives with his mother, the maternal grandmother, an uncle, and his older brother. Bradley has not had any contact with his biological father since his birth. Several paternal cousins have behavior problems and ADHD. A paternal aunt has an intellectual disability.

REASON FOR REFERRAL

It has been approximately 2 years since Bradley has had an assessment of intellectual and adaptive functioning. Having the benefit of having scores from his previous assessments will be helpful in understanding how Bradley's skills have developed since that time. There was a question as to whether Bradley might have symptoms of a pervasive developmental disorder, so a comprehensive assessment was conducted to provide as much information as possible to assist with future planning.

ASSESSMENT RESULTS

Bradley was initially observed in the regular kindergarten classroom for a 30-minute observation period. At the time, the class was engaged in determining the sequential pattern of a series of interlocking colored blocks (independent seatwork), followed by a small-group interactive activity about community helpers.

During the first part of this observation period, Bradley dropped a block and he bent down to pick it up until the teacher came over to see why he was not working. He then told the teacher that he could not work because the block fell on the floor. The teacher instructed him to pick up the block and continue with the sequencing task. This delay set him behind his classmates in completing the task. While he worked, he talked out loud to himself in order to guide his selections (e.g., "blue, blue, black . . .) but then shortened the scheme ("blue/black . . . blue/black) which resulted in completing the task incorrectly. He seemed excited about completing the task ("I did it!") and was not discouraged when the teacher noted that it was incorrect, and he set out to fix it.

Bradley seemed to be very aware of the class routines and followed the other children as they participated in snack time and tidying up. Although he did not interact with the other children, he did seem to be observing them, and then would follow along and imitate what they were doing. After snack time, Bradley went to the play mat and was joined by a couple of other children. He then made some strange guttural noises and faces, which the other two boys repeated, until the teacher told the boys to stop imitating him. The final activity was matching community uniforms to community/employment roles. Bradley was the only one in the group to recognize the word "astronaut" and was very pleased to be able to dress the cut-out appropriately in the correct uniform. Although Bradley demonstrated an ability to follow predictable routines, he also revealed an inability to adapt if something unpredictable happened, such as dropping the block. Adaptive behavior deficits seemed to be most pronounced in areas of social and pragmatic concerns.

The psychologist administered the Differential Ability Scales (DAS-2) and Bradley obtained the following standard scores, placing his ability in the low average range: Nonverbal Reasoning Ability, SS = 87; Verbal Ability, SS = 85; and Spatial Ability, SS = 83. Overall, General Conceptual Ability was a standard score of 81, at the 10th percentile. Academically, his scores on the Young Children's Achievement Test (Y-CAT), revealed standard scores above his ability level in all areas except Spoken Language (SS = 79). Other academic scores included General Information, SS = 90; Reading, SS = 100; Mathematics, SS = 91; and Writing, SS = 109. Compared to his previous assessment results, Bradley had made excellent gains in his ability and academic skills.

Bradley's mother and teacher completed the rating scales for the Adaptive Behavior Assessment System (ABAS II). There was a significant difference between scores obtained on the mother's ratings when compared to the teacher's ratings. Scaled scores can range between 1 (very inferior) to 19 (very superior). While his mother rated him extremely low (all scores were scaled scores of 1 or 2), the teacher's ratings were significantly higher. However, both mother and teacher rated Bradley a scale score of 1 for communication. According to his teacher, his functional academics were within the average range (scale score of 11), which is consistent with Bradley's scores on the YCAT. However, even though his teacher rated him significantly higher than his mother, his adaptive scores were much lower than would be predicted, given his scores on the DAS-2. According to the teacher, his adaptive scores for Social were SS = 70, and Practical SS = 75, with an Overall General Adaptive Composite of SS = 70. According to his mother, these scores were significantly lower: Social, SS = 54, Practical, SS = 40, and Overall General Adaptive Composite, SS = 41.

The parent and teacher completed an informal screening questionnaire concerning symptoms often associated with pervasive developmental disorders. The following list of descriptions was endorsed as occurring sometimes or frequently, both at home and at school:

Social Interaction:

- Requires specific instructions to begin task
- Lacks subtlety in expression of emotion
- Has difficulty cooperating in a group
- Has difficulty playing with other children
- Does certain things repetitively or ritualistically
- Has difficulty understanding when being teased
- Fails to predict consequences in social events

Communication:

- Repeats or echoes words or phrases
- Speaks with flat affect
- Fails to initiate conversations
- Inappropriately answers questions
- Uses pronouns inappropriately

Stereotypical Behavior:

- Flaps hands or fingers
- Eats specific foods, a fussy eater
- Rocks back and forth while seated or standing
- Flaps hand or fingers in front of his face
- Demonstrates eccentric forms of behaviors
- Has abnormal focus, preoccupied with specific objects
- Requires extensive direction from others
- Is clumsy or uncoordinated

Cognitive Patterns:

- Talks about single subjects excessively
- Displays superior knowledge or skill in a specific area
- Has difficulty understanding jokes, humor, sarcasm
- Shows excellent memory

Pragmatic Skills:

- Has difficulty understanding slang
- Has difficulty understanding when being teased

- Has difficulty understanding when ridiculed or made fun of
- Has difficulty understanding what causes others to dislike him
- Fails to predict probable consequences to social events

Mother and teacher agreed that Bradley has a love of reciting the alphabet, and that he has the same two books that he wants to read on a daily basis. At home, when Bradley wants something, he repeats it over and over again, if the answer is no.

Mother and teacher also completed the Devereux Scales of Mental Disorders (DSMD). Results revealed a number of areas of concern. There is a consistent agreement between raters regarding externalizing problems, especially in areas of conduct problems. Although attentional problems are very evident at school, in the home situation, these are less pronounced. Teacher and parent agreed that the following attention problems occur at school and in the home, at least occasionally, in the form of the following behaviors: he fidgets or acts restless, becomes easily distracted, and fails to pay attention. During classroom activities, Bradley is easily distracted, preoccupied, has trouble concentrating, and fails to follow through on assignments.

Other areas that have some overlap between the home and school environments include behaviors that are atypical (e.g., autism). According to parent and teacher ratings, there was a consensus that Bradley frequently or very frequently makes odd movements, facial grimaces, and noises that can be disruptive in the classroom.

Post-Case Questions

1. Based on the referral information and the assessment results, what are your impressions of Bradley? Does he meet criteria for any of the *DSM-IV-TR* diagnoses that you are familiar with? If so, which diagnoses?

2. If you were assessing Bradley, what other information might be valuable in developing a case formulation? What other assessments could you conduct, or what other interview information might be relevant?

3. What would you recommend to assist Bradley in better meeting his educational and adaptive goals?

Middle Childhood

Scott Michaels

Boys Will Be Boys?

Scott came to the intake interview accompanied by his mother, Ruth. Scott is 9 years old and is currently in Grade 4 at Second Street School, which he has attended since his earliest enrollment in kindergarten. According to Ruth, the presenting concerns are twofold: academic problems at school and behavior problems at home.

DEVELOPMENTAL HISTORY/FAMILY BACKGROUND

Ruth described the birth history as uneventful. Scott was born 2 days early and weighed 8 pounds 4 ounces. Developmental milestones were mildly delayed, and Scott walked at 15 months. Scott was slow to speak and did not use simple phrases at 3 years. Speech problems continued, and Scott received assistance for problems with articulation and speech production in prekindergarten and kindergarten.

Scott was described as an active infant who was not content to take long naps. Sleeping was not a problem, however, since he seemed to need his rest after all the activity. There was a problem with bed-wetting until Scott was 6 years old. The problem was resolved when they stopped allowing Scott to have apple juice before bedtime. As a toddler, Scott seemed to be more demanding than all of Ruth's other children put together. Scott was not content to stay in the playpen like his other siblings. He would often scream and have tantrums until Ruth took him out of the playpen. However, when he was out of the playpen, he seemed to be into everything. Scott was very easily frustrated and difficult to calm down, especially if he couldn't have his way. At first, Ruth said she could distract him by offering something else, but that usually didn't last very long. Ruth added that for Scott the "terrible twos" never went away, but just got worse with each passing year.

Ruth recalled one incident that occurred shortly after Scott's sixth birthday. On this occasion, Ruth had asked Scott to help her pick up some toys that his brother Brian (age 4) and sister Tia (age 2) had scattered. All of a sudden, Scott started grabbing toys out of their hands and throwing them at Tia and Brian. Then he went over to his toy box and dumped the entire toy box all over the floor. The event made such a lasting impression on Ruth that since that time she has not asked Scott to help her with cleaning up.

Scott's academic difficulties became evident early in his schooling, and Ruth was contacted by the teacher diagnostician, who recommended that Scott have his vision and hearing tested to rule out any physical reasons for Scott's learning problems. Although Scott's vision was normal, testing of central auditory processing (CAP) revealed a selective attention deficit in the left ear, problems tuning in to auditory information, and likely difficulties with visual tracking. Recommendations from the CAP assessment were to present information to the dominant right ear, cue prior to presenting information, and provide assistance in copying information from the board. Ruth stated that she had asked her family physician for a referral to have Scott tested for learning problems; however, when she took Scott to the appointment (about a year ago), she was told that testing was not necessary because Scott did not have any "developmental" problems. Ruth could not elaborate further on the nature of the therapist's expertise.

Ruth outlined the following family history during the course of the intake interview. There is a history of depression (maternal grandmother) and alcohol abuse (maternal grandfather) in Ruth's family. Ruth's father was incarcerated several times for assault resulting from fights in local bars. Ruth's only brother, Jacob, was bright but did poorly in school. Jacob seemed to fall in with the wrong crowd and dropped out in Grade 9. He spent some time in juvenile detention for breaking and entering, but eventually got back on track when he joined the armed forces, where he received training as a mechanic.

Ruth's husband Eric knows very little about his own family history, since he was adopted as an infant. Eric's adoptive parents were killed in a car accident shortly after Ruth and Eric were married. Eric has no known siblings. Ruth liked school and graduated from high school prior to getting married to Eric. Eric did not do well in school, and he did not complete high school. He currently works at a local box-making factory. Ruth worked as a grocery clerk at the local supermarket after graduation, until the birth of her daughter when she was 20. Ruth has not returned to work since that time. Ruth admitted that they have had financial problems recently, since the money from her husband's inheritance has been exhausted.

Although she was never diagnosed with depression, Ruth does admit to feeling overwhelmed and exhausted much of the time, especially since the birth of Tia. Ruth is considering returning to work now that Tia is in school, but she is afraid of what the consequences will be for Scott's behavior. Ruth recalled recently going to a shower for a neighborhood friend and returning home to find the kitchen an absolute mess. Apparently, Scott had deliberately messed up the kitchen in her absence because he was upset that she was not there to make his lunch. When asked why he had messed up the kitchen, Scott said that it was his mother's fault. If she had been home, it wouldn't have happened. When asked how he would feel about his mom returning to work, Scott said that it would be unfair, and that moms should be home for their kids.

Ruth described Scott's relationship with his siblings in the following way. Scott gets along with his youngest sister, Tia (5 years), the best, while his relationship with his older sister, Christine (11 years), is the most problematic. She added that Scott often responds to Christine in the same way he responds to his mother. When asked to clarify what she meant, Ruth replied that whenever Christine wants Scott to help her with dinner or the dishes, he starts a huge argument. It always ends the same way, with Scott saying that "it's unfair" and that he has to do all the work, or it's not his turn. Finally, Christine ends up just doing it herself, rather than argue with Scott. His relationship with his younger brother Brian (7 years) is less predictable. When Scott wants to play with Brian and Brian goes along with him, they have a great time. However, when Brian does not want to follow Scott's lead, Scott loses his temper very quickly.

REASON FOR REFERRAL

When asked what brought her and Scott to the clinic at this time, Ruth stated that Scott had become progressively more difficult to manage. He walks around with a "chip on his shoulder" and responds to even the smallest requests with an inflated emotional response. The outbursts have increased in frequency and intensity. Ruth admitted that she is beginning to "lose it" more frequently, herself. According to Scott, his mother is always picking on him and asking him to do things, like chores, that his brother and sisters should be doing. He added that he only gets mad when his mother is "not fair." Scott's school reports have noted increasing difficulties, especially in reading comprehension. Scott struggles with retaining the sequential order of information and has problems recalling information he has read. He is slow to copy information from the board and his notes are not only messy, but often incomplete.

Scott is receiving approximately 30 minutes daily of resource help to focus on reading, spelling, and written work. His teacher is very supportive of an assessment for Scott to provide specific information to assist with programming. The teacher noted that although behavioral problems are not significant at school, Scott does have some difficulty accepting criticism and waiting his turn. The teacher has also noted, on more than one occasion, that Scott will complain that the teacher has not been fair. Homework assignments are often incomplete or not returned, despite attempts to set up a home-school communication system. Socially, he is not well liked by peers, because he tends to want to be in control and often interrupts or intrudes on others. Problems waiting his turn are also evident on the playground, and Scott has to constantly be reminded to give others a chance to talk.

Scott was asked to comment on his feelings about school. Scott said that the kids were all right, but that some of the teachers were not so great. When asked what he liked best about school, Scott rolled his eyes back and said "Recess." Scott became defensive when questioned about academics and said that he could do better if the teacher didn't pick on him. He also said that the teacher is always busy with other students and doesn't have the time to answer his questions. He says he has to sit and wait until the teacher finally gets around to his question and that's why he doesn't get his work done. According to Scott, the resource room teacher is also too busy with other kids to help him. Scott added that if the teacher would explain schoolwork better, he would be able to understand it better. He described his teacher as unfair in the amount of work she expected students to do. Outside of school, Scott said he really likes playing hockey and that he probably would drive race cars, like NASCAR, when he was older. He said he wouldn't go to school if he didn't have to.

Ruth began to describe the current home situation by saying that Scott is a good-natured boy when things are going his way. However, he can be very difficult to manage when asked to comply with any requests that interfere with his own agenda. Ruth has tried various incentive programs (such as using the purchase of a new bike as a reward for completing his homework for a week); however, after receiving his incentive, Scott loses all motivation and things go right back to where they began. She described it as a tug of war to get him to do anything. Attempts to set up a communication system with the school have been undermined by Scott's forgetfulness to bring messages home. At times, when asked to do something, Scott will be very touchy, talk back to her, and begin yelling and complaining that it is unfair and comparing himself to his sister who he says has no responsibilities around the house. At the worst of times, tantrums will escalate into a shouting match that involves throwing things and yelling. During these times, Ruth admits to "losing it" and producing numerous threats and ultimatums. More often than not, these scenarios end with Ruth completing the tasks herself, just to stop the battle. At the best of times, Scott will not be confrontational, though he will still avoid doing tasks by either passively ignoring the requests or trying to buy time, saying he will do it later (when a TV program is finished, or when he finishes what he is working on, etc.). Ruth stated that sometimes it just seems easier to do it herself than to nag and hound Scott. Scott seems to be in constant motion, and he has a hard time even sitting down for dinner. He becomes very restless and squirmy when he is asked to remain seated, and often his leg is in motion while he is sitting down.

Scott's relationship with his older sister is very poor, since Scott is often jealous and resentful of any attention that she receives. Yesterday, when Christine asked him to turn down the volume on the television because she was on the telephone, Scott deliberately turned the volume up to the absolutely loudest notch. Ruth seemed notably depressed in her admission that it is getting to the point that everyone at home is afraid to ask Scott to do anything for fear of retaliation.

When asked about her husband Eric's role in the management of Scott's behaviors, Ruth stated that her husband often works the 4:00–11:00 p.m. shift and is not home when Scott has his behavioral outbursts. Although Eric tries to be supportive of her, he has said that he thinks Ruth is making too much out of Scott's behavior. He says that he was like Scott when he was a kid. After all, he says, "Boys will be boys." When Eric and Scott do things together, like fishing, there are rarely any outbursts.

Ruth is very hopeful that the assessment will not only provide help for her to manage Scott's behavior at home, but perhaps also help convince her husband that Scott is in need of some kind of management program. Right now, Eric is of the opinion that Scott will just grow out of it.

At the completion of the intake interview, Ruth admitted in confidence to the psychologist that she was feeling increasingly overwhelmed, distraught, and alone. Her husband seemed to be withdrawing from the family and was coming home from work later and later, often stopping in at the local sports bar before returning home. There were many arguments about money and Ruth's desire to return to work, since her husband was not in favor of her working. Ruth was feeling less and less capable of managing Scott's escalating problems. At Ruth's request, a referral was provided to a therapist for her to obtain supportive therapy.

ASSESSMENT RESULTS

The actual raw scores for Scott's assessment are available in Appendix A. The following is a summary of those findings. Guidelines to the interpretation of standard scores and T scores, as well as information regarding specific assessment instruments used in this text and other assessment resources can be found in Appendix C.

Examiner comments noted frequent requests for repetition throughout the assessment, word-finding problems, and tendencies toward word substitutions (e.g., using "found" instead of "lost"). Overall intellectual functioning on the Weschler Intelligence Scale for Children (WISC-IV) was within the low average to average range (IQ = 88; range 83–93), with no significant discrepancy between scores for the Verbal Comprehension Index (VCI), low average range (index score = 83; range 77–91) and Perceptual Reasoning Index (PRI), average range (PSI = 93; range 85–100). The Working Memory Index (WMI) was an area of relative weakness (WMI = 80; range 74–89), and Scott experienced significant difficulties understanding the instructions to the letter number sequence task, which tied for his lowest subtest score (scale score of 6), along with comprehension, which also was a scale score of 6. On the comprehension subtest, as the questions became more complex, Scott asked for several repetitions of the questions and asked for further explanations, which are not permitted, according to the manual.

Academically, according to the Wide Range Achievement Test (WRAT 4) and the Woodcock-Johnson Achievement Test (WJIII-R Ach), Scott was functioning commensurate with his intellectual level in most areas assessed (standard scores ranged from highs of 103 for math computation and 95 in spelling (WRAT-4) to lows of 79 for reading comprehension (WJIII-R Ach) and 80 for sentence comprehension (WRAT-4). Although the two lowest scores were below his full scale IQ of 88, the discrepancy of 9 points (88–79) was not significant. (In Scott's school district, a discrepancy between IQ and achievement must be in excess of one and a half standard deviations, which requires a discrepancy of at least 22 points. For further information on applications of the discrepancy criteria, please see Appendix B: Learning Disabilities and the Discrepancy Model.) Analysis of cognitive processing revealed that academic difficulties are largely due to problems in cognitive fluency (SS = 67). Scott required more than the anticipated time to label common objects and to perform tasks that required him to recall names for "as many"----- (friends, foods, etc.) that he could name in one minute. In this task, after naming two or three objects, or names, Scott would either go blank or repeat names he had already given.

Response to parent ratings scales (ASEBA) revealed borderline clinical elevations on Withdrawn/Depressed and Total Internalizing Behaviors, and significant clinical elevations on Attention Problems, Aggressive Behavior, Total Externalizing, and Total Problems. Teacher ratings noted clinical elevations for Social Problems and Attention Problems. While his mother's comments pertained to aggressive behaviors in the home (e.g., argues, brags, is mean, is stubborn, disobeys, etc.), his teacher noted many problems in the classroom (e.g., acts young, fails to finish, poor schoolwork, doesn't listen, etc.) and with classmates (doesn't get along, is not well liked, prefers younger kids). On the Conners scales, Scott's mother rated Scott's Hyperactivity/Impulsivity (*DSM-IV* scales) as in the borderline clinical range. Oppositional behaviors and the emotional lability scale of the Global Index were both within the clinically significant range. Scott's teacher rated him as borderline clinical for Social Problems, and in the clinically significant range for Cognitive Problems/Inattention, Inattentive scale (*DSM-IV*), Hyperactive-Impulsive scale (*DSM-IV*), and the *DSM-IV* Total scale.

Scott endorsed items at the borderline clinical level on the Beck Youth Inventory (BYI-2) for Disruptive Behaviors (SS = 68; 94th percentile) and in the highly significant clinical range for the Anger Inventory (SS = 86; 99th percentile).

CURRENT ISSUES, TRENDS, AND TREATMENT ALTERNATIVES

Oppositional defiant disorder (ODD) is one of the most stable disorders of childhood; the prognosis is therefore often poor (Rey, 1993). The transition from normal behavior demonstrated in what has been called the "terrible twos" to ODD behavior is evident in the frequency and intensity of noncompliant behaviors that continue to persist well beyond the toddler period (Gabel, 1997). Results of a recent longitudinal investigation suggest that by 25 years of age, ODD was persistent in 16.6% of the ODD group (Biederman et al., 2008), although Harpold and colleagues (2007) found that of referred adults with ADHD who had ODD in childhood, 30% continued to demonstrate symptoms of ODD into adulthood. Risk factors that have been associated with ODD include attachment problems noted in insecure attachment (DeKlyen, 1996) and anxious avoidant attachment patterns (Erickson, Sroufe, & Egeland, 1985); difficult temperament (Rey, 1993); and parenting style and level of parental involvement (Frick et al., 1993; Griest, Wells, & McMahon, 1980). One of the difficulties with isolating risk factors specific to ODD is that many studies have examined "behavior disorders" or "disruptive behavior disorders," which combine populations of children and youth with oppositional defiant disorder (ODD) and conduct disorder (CD). As a result, far less is known about the specific risks for children with ODD or long-term prognosis for children who demonstrate both ODD and ADHD, despite comorbid rates as high as 65% for youth exhibiting both disorders (Biederman et al., 1996; Kadesjo & Gillberg, 2001; Petty et al., 2009). A more recent investigation has suggested that comorbid ADHD and ODD may represent a distinct familial subtype, and, furthermore, that antisocial, mood, anxiety, and addictive disorders found in relatives were related to risk for CD and not ODD when the two groups are separated out. Based on these findings, Petty and colleagues (2009) suggest further support for considering ODD and CD as separate and distinct entities (Biederman et al., 1996; Greene et al., 2002), which they hope will deter "lumping" CD and ODD together in future clinical studies.

Biederman and colleagues (2008) investigated the long-term outcomes for children who are diagnosed with comorbid ODD and ADHD. Their results suggest that youth with comorbid ADHD and ODD demonstrated higher scores on the CBCL "Aggressive Behavior" scale compared to those with ADHD alone. Youth with ODD at 10-year follow-up were at increased risk for major depressive disorder compared to controls. Longitudinally, the majority of youth with comorbid ODD and ADHD demonstrate a decline in ODD symptoms with age (Biederman et al., 2008; Whittinger, Langley, Fowler, Thomas, & Thapar, 2007). Although some youth with ODD will later progress to CD (Rowe, Maughan, Pickles, Costello, & Angold,

2002; Whittinger et al., 2007), results suggest that the majority of subjects with ADHD and comorbid ODD will not develop CD (Biederman et al., 1996, 2008).

One of the difficulties in locating evidence-based treatments specifically for ODD is that despite evidence of the existence of ODD and conduct disorder (CD) as two distinct disorders (Biederman et al., 2008; Frick et al., 1993), treatments are often discussed relative to the broader category of "disruptive behavior disorders," which include both ODD and CD. Brestan and Eyberg (1998) reviewed psychosocial treatments for disruptive behavior disorders (ODD or CD) in 82 studies involving more than 5,000 youths. The authors then evaluated the treatment programs relative to criteria suggested by the APA Task Force. Results revealed two models of intervention, both involving parent training, that met with the more stringent criteria established for "well established psychosocial interventions":

1. A parent training program involving videotaped modeling (Webster-Stratton, 1984) has been successful in reducing deviant behaviors in children and increasing parent competencies in the management of behavior problems (Spaccarelli, Colter, & Penman, 1992; Webster-Stratton, 1984, 1994). In this model of intervention, parents receive training in therapist-led groups.

2. Behavioral parent training programs (Alexander & Parsons, 1973; Bernal, Klinnert, & Shultz, 1980; Firestone, Kelly, & Fike, 1980) based on a manual called *Living With Children,* developed by Patterson and Gullion (1968), have also demonstrated success across several controlled studies. Lessons obtained from the manual *Living With Children* have been successfully incorporated into behavioral treatment programs designed to teach parents how to implement behavioral change by targeting problem behaviors, rewarding incompatible behaviors, and ignoring or punishing undesirable behaviors.

Other treatments for school-aged children that are cited as "probably efficacious treatments" (Brestan & Eyberg, 1998) include problem-solving skills training (Kazdin, Esveldt-Dawson, French, & Unis, 1987; Kazdin, Siegel, & Bass, 1992) and anger control therapy (Lochman, Burch, Curry, & Lampron, 1984; Lochman, Lampron, Gemmer, & Harris, 1989).

Problem-Solving Skills Training (PSST; Kazdin, 1996)

A typical problem-solving intervention would teach children how to approach a problem in a logical and predictable fashion, using a six-step procedure (Kazdin et al., 1987; Kendall, 1988).

1. Define the problem
2. Identify the goal
3. Generate options
4. Evaluate options
5. Choose the best option
6. Evaluate the outcome

Children are taught how to apply this approach to social problems in a number of ways, including role playing, social reinforcement, and therapeutic games. The PSST procedure is administered individually over 20 sessions, each lasting approximately 45 minutes.

Coping Power (Larson & Lochman, 2002)

This anger-control program has evolved from an original 12-session school-based program called Anger Coping (Lochman, Lampron, Gemmer, & Harris, 1987), to a 33-session program called Coping Power (Lochman & Wells, 1996), with sessions for a parent group recently added. Children develop skills in anger management through in vivo practice sessions (weekly groups of six children) using problem-solving techniques to address specific goals and objectives in social situations. Children are also taught to be aware of feelings and physiological states associated with anger arousal.

In their research review, Brestan and Eyberg (1998) found that the majority of interventions involved direct contact with the child and/or the child's parent (usually mother) and usually were based on cognitive-behavioral techniques. In their summation, the authors conclude that age may be the overarching variable that determines the effectiveness of the outcome of treatment: parent training programs would be more effective for younger children, while cognitive-behavioral methods may be more applicable for older, school-aged populations. There is evidence to suggest, however, that for some groups (Kazdin et al., 1992), combining PSST and parent training may be more effective than either treatment alone.

Collaborative Problem Solving (Greene et al. 2001, 2003, 2004)

Since many children with ODD also experience ADHD, Greene (2001) and colleagues (Greene, Ablon, & Goring, 2003; Greene, Ablon, Goring, Fazio, & Morse, 2004) have developed a program that focuses on deficits in cognitive skills involved in "executive functions" such as *working memory, self-regulation* (emotion regulation, frustration tolerance, and regulation of arousal to engage in goal-directed activity), *shifting of cognitive set* (flexibility and transfer of rules and expectations from one situation to another), and *problem solving* (organization of information and generating a plan of action). The program, Collaborative Problem Solving (CPS; Greene, 2001; Greene et al., 2004) focuses on parent education (underlying parent/child dynamics) and interventions aimed at deficits in executive functions.

Many children diagnosed with mood disorders (Geller & Luby, 1997) and anxiety disorders (Greene et al., 2002) also have comorbid ODD. In one study, 70% of youth with major depressive disorder (MDD), 85% of those with bipolar disorder, and 45% of those with an anxiety disorder had comorbid ODD (Greene et al., 2002). In addition, language processing problems are also prevalent, with over 20% of youth diagnosed with ODD also demonstrating processing problems that can compromise problem solving in academic as well as social situations. Previous research by Dodge and colleagues (Dodge & Coie, 1987; Dodge, Price, Bachorowski, & Newman, 1990) demonstrated that some children act aggressively when they misread social cues based on *cognitive distortions* such as the *hostile attribution bias* (e.g., child interprets an ambivalent facial expression or provocation as hostile and responds aggressively as a result). In order to address these processing issues, Green and colleagues incorporate tasks of social cognitive processing in their program to assist children in developing increased ability to analyze social situations, develop alternative responses, and monitor outcomes. The program also focuses on parent-child compatibility by helping parents understand the processing difficulties, the need for providing consistent patterns of discipline, and the need for increased monitoring and feedback. The program has been very successful.

Academic Interventions

An empirical review of specific programming remediation for difficulties in reading and written expression reveals the following information. The importance of developing phonological awareness for reading acquisition and spelling has been demonstrated by several researchers (see Rathvon, 1999, for a review). Therefore, strategies that focus on improving phonics (e.g., Fernald Keller approach) can be helpful in assisting Scott in developing greater phonetic awareness. Given Scott's learning profile, the following specific strategies may be helpful. A *repeated readings* approach (O'Shea & O'Shea, 1988) is suggested to target difficulties in decoding (sight word vocabulary, fluency) and comprehension, and to enhance Scott's attention to task as well as independent work habits. Cognitive approaches to spelling, such as the *12 plus 1* strategies for remediation of misspellings (Montgomery, 1990), would also be very helpful in emphasizing the phonetic as well as rule-based aspects of spelling.

The focus is on improving homework submission and reducing home conflict regarding homework completion. A homework management program would be helpful to increase productivity (percentage of homework completed) and accuracy (percentage completed correctly) of homework, using a combination of home-note, self-monitoring, and group-contingency approaches based on the *Good Behavior Game Plus Merit* approach developed by Darveaux (1984).

Post-Case Questions

1. Using situational and contextual factors, explain why Scott's behaviors were described as more oppositional at home than at school. Is this a common finding?

2. Barkley (1997a) has developed a theoretical model for ADHD that places "behavioral inhibition" as the focal point of the model. According to this model, the ability to delay or inhibit a given response allows for the necessary time required for executive information processing to occur. Included within these executive processes are abilities to manipulate information mentally (working memory), self-regulation (emotional control, motivation/drive), self-reflection (inner speech, problem solving), and reconstitution (analysis and synthesis). Furthermore, the ability to maintain the delay is also required to block possible interference factors (see Barkley, 1997b, for a complete description of this model of hyperactivity and impulsivity).

   How might the concept of "behavioral inhibition" be used to help explain Scott's behaviors? At a minimum, Scott demonstrates at least two comorbid disorders. What are the two disorders? How often do they occur together in clinical populations? Using Barkley's model of behavioral inhibition, explain the underlying dynamics in these two comorbid disorders.

3. The role of parenting practices in the maintenance and management of disruptive behavior disorders has been well documented (Barkley, 1997a; Chamberlain & Reid, 1991, 1998; Patterson, Reid, & Dishion, 1992). Various theoretical perspectives have focused on different aspects of parent-child interactions in maintaining maladaptive behaviors—for example, coercion theory (Patterson et al., 1992) and conflicting goals of connectiveness versus individuation (Mahler, Pine, & Bergman, 1975). Develop case formulations to explain how Scott's interactions with his family members serve to sustain his disruptive behavior from the following perspectives: behavioral, cognitive, family systems, and parenting style/attachment.

4. Although most children who have ODD do not progress to CD, some are more at risk than others. Taking into consideration what research suggests are risk factors for ODD developing into CD, and looking at Scott's individual assessment results (Appendix A), do you think that Scott is at risk for developing CD? If so, why? If not, why not?

5. Using information from the case study itself and the supplementary assessment data found in Appendix A and D, identify as many symptoms as you can find of ODD and ADHD that meet criteria for the *DSM-IV-TR*. Remember to specify the predominant type of ADHD that Scott's symptoms match.

REFERENCES

Alexander, J. F., & Parsons, B. V. (1973). Short-term behavioral intervention with delinquent families: Impact on family process and recidivism. *Journal of Abnormal Psychology, 81,* 219–225.

Barkley, R. A. (1997a). Attention deficit hyperactivity disorder. In E. J. Mash & L. G. Terdal (Eds.), *Assessment of childhood disorders* (pp. 71–129). New York: Guilford.

Barkley, R. A. (1997b). Behavior inhibition, sustained attention and executive function. *Psychological Bulletin, 121,* 65–94.

Bernal, M. E., Klinnert, M. D., & Schultz, L. A. (1980). Outcome evaluation of behavioral parent training and client-centered parent counseling for children with conduct problems. *Journal of Applied Behavior Analysis, 13,* 677–691.

Biederman, J., Faraone S. V., Milberger, S., Garcia Jetton, J., Chen, L., Mick, E., et al. (1996). Is childhood oppositional defiant disorder a precursor to adolescent conduct disorder? Findings from a four-year follow-up study of children with ADHD. *Journal of the American Academy of Child and Adolescent Psychiatry, 35,* 1193–1204.

Biederman, J., Petty, C. R., Dolan, C., Hughes, S., Mick, E., Monuteaux, M. C., et al. (2008). The long-term longitudinal course of oppositional defiant disorder and conduct disorder in ADHD boys: Findings from a controlled 10-year prospective longitudinal follow-up study. *Psychological Medicine, 38,* 1027–1036.

Brestan, E. V., & Eyberg, S. M. (1998). Effective psychosocial treatments of conduct disordered children and adolescents: 29 years, 82 studies and 5,272 kids. *Journal of Clinical Child Psychology, 27,* 180–189.

Chamberlain, P., & Reid, J. (1991). Using a specialized foster care community treatment model for children and adolescents leaving the state mental hospital. *Journal of Community Psychology, 19,* 266–276.

Chamberlain, P., & Reid, J. (1998). Comparison of two community alternatives to incarceration for chronic juvenile offenders. *Journal of Consulting and Clinical Psychology, 66,* 624–633.

Darveaux, D. X. (1984). The Good Behavior Game Plus Merit: Controlling disruptive behavior and improving student motivation. *School Psychology Review, 13,* 510–514.

DeKlyen, M. (1996). Disruptive behavior disorder and intergenerational attachment patterns: A comparison of clinic-referred and normally functioning preschoolers and their mothers. *Journal of Consulting and Clinical Psychology, 64,* 357–365.

Dodge, K. A., & Coie, J. D. (1987). Social-information-processing factors in reactive and proactive aggression in children's peer groups. *Journal of Personality and Social Psychology, 53,* 1146–1158.

Dodge, K. A., Price, J. M., Bachorowski, J., & Newman, J. P. (1990). Hostile attributional biases in severely aggressive adolescents. *Journal of Abnormal Psychology, 99,* 385–392.

Erickson, M. F., Sroufe, L. A., & Egeland, B. (1985). The relationship between quality of attachment and behavior problems in preschool in a high-risk sample. In I. Betherton & E. Waters (Eds.), *Growing points of attachment theory and research.* Monographs of the Society for Research in Child Development, 50(1–2, Series No. 209), 147–166.

Firestone, P., Kelly, M. J., & Fike, S. (1980). Are fathers necessary in parent training groups? *Journal of Clinical Child Psychology, 9,* 44–47.

Frick, P. J., Lahey, B. B., Loeber, R., Tannenbaum, L., Van Horn, Y., Christ, M. A., et al. (1993). Oppositional defiant disorder and conduct disorder: A meta-analytic review of factor analyses and cross-validation in a clinic sample. *Clinical Psychology Review, 13,* 319–340.

Gabel, S. (1997). Oppositional defiant disorder. In J. D. Noshpitz (Ed.), *Child and adolescent psychiatry* (Vol. 2, pp. 351–359). New York: John Wiley.

Geller, B., & Luby, J. (1997). Child and adolescent biopolar disorder: A review of the past 10 years. *Journal of the American Academy of Child and Adolescent Psychiatry, 36,* 1168–1176.

Greene, R. W. (2001). *The explosive child: Understanding and parenting easily frustrated, chronically inflexible children.* New York: HarperCollins.

Greene, R. W., Ablon, J. S., & Goring, J. C. (2003). A transactional model of oppositional behavior: Underpinnings of the collaborative problem solving approach. *Journal of Psychosomatic Research, 55,* 67–75.

Greene, R. W., Ablon, J. S., Goring, J. C., Fazio, V., & Morse, L. R. (2004). Treatment of oppositional defiant disorder in children and adolescents. In P. M. Barrett & T. H. Ollendick (Eds.), *Handbook of interventions that work with children and adolescents* (pp. 369–393). Chichester, UK: John Wiley.

Greene, R. W., Biederman, J., Zerwas, S., Monuteaux, M. C., Goring, J. C., & Faraone, S. V. (2002). Psychiatric comorbidity, family dysfunction, and social impairment in referred youth with oppositional defiant disorder. *American Journal of Psychiatry, 159,* 1214–1224.

Griest, D., Wells, K. C., & McMahon, R. J. (1980). An examination of differences between nonclinic and behavior problem clinic referred children and their mothers. *Journal of Abnormal Psychology, 89,* 497–500.

Harpold, T., Biederman, J., Gignac, M., Hammerness, P., Surman, C., Potter, A., et al. (2007). Is oppositional defiant disorder a meaningful diagnosis in adults? Results from a large sample of adults with ADHD. *Journal of Nervous and Mental Disease 195,* 601–605.

Kadesjo, B., & Gillberg, C. (2001). The comorbidity of ADHD in the general population of Swedish school-age children. *Journal of Child Psychology and Psychiatry, 42,* 487–492.

Kazdin, A. E. (1996). Problem solving and parent management in treating aggressive and antisocial behavior. In E. S. Hibbs & P. S. Jensen (Eds.), *Psychosocial treatments for child and adolescent disorders: Empirically based strategies for clinical practice* (pp. 377–408). Washington, DC: American Psychological Association.

Kazdin, A. E., Esveldt-Dawson, K., French, N. H., & Unis, A. S. (1987). Problem solving skills training and relationship therapy in treatment of antisocial child behavior. *Journal of Consulting and Clinical Psychology, 55,* 76–85.

Kazdin, A. E., Siegel, T. C., & Bass, D. (1992). Cognitive problem-solving skills training and parent management training in the treatment of antisocial behavior in children. *Journal of Consulting and Clinical Psychology, 60,* 733–747.

Kendall, P. C. (1988). *Stop and think workbook* (2nd ed.). Ardmore, PA: Workbook.

Larson, J., & Lochman, J. E. (2002). *Helping school children cope with anger: A cognitive-behavioral intervention.* New York: Guilford.

Lochman, J. E., Burch, P. R., Curry, J. F., & Lampron, L. B. (1984). Treatment and generalization effects of cognitive-behavioral and goal-setting interventions with aggressive boys. *Journal of Consulting and Clinical Psychology, 52,* 915–916.

Lochman, J. E., Lampron, L. B., Gemmer, T. C., & Harris, S. R. (1987). Teacher consultation and cognitive-behavioral intervention with aggressive boys. *Psychology in the Schools, 26,* 915–916.

Lochman, J. E., Lampron, L. B., Gemmer, T. C., & Harris, S. R. (1989). Teacher consultation and cognitive behavioral interventions with aggressive boys. *Psychology in the Schools, 26,* 179–188.

Lochman, J. E., & Wells, K. C. (1996). A social cognitive intervention with aggressive children: Prevention effects and contextual implementation issues. In R. D. Peters & R. J. McMahon (Eds.), *Preventing childhood disorders, substance abuse and delinquency* (pp. 111–143). Thousand Oaks, CA: Sage.

Mahler, M. S., Pine, F., & Bergman, A. (1975). *The psychological birth of the human infant.* New York: Basic Books.

Montgomery, D. (1990). *Children with learning difficulties.* New York: Nicholas Publishing.

O'Shea, L., & O'Shea, D. (1988). Using repeated reading. *Teaching Exceptional Children, 1,* 26–30.

Patterson, G. R., & Gullion, M. E. (1968). *Living with children: New methods for parents and teachers.* Champaign, IL: Research Press.

Patterson, G. R., Reid, J. B., & Dishion, T. J. (1992). *Antisocial boys.* Eugene, OR: Castalia.

Petty, C. R., Monteaux, M. C., Mick, E., Hughes, S., Small, J., Faraone, S. V., et al. (2009). Parsing the familiality of oppositional defiant disorder from that of conduct disorder: A familial risk analysis. *Journal of Psychiatric Research, 43,* 345–352.

Rathvon, N. (1999). *Effective school interventions: Strategies for enhancing academic achievement and social competence.* New York: Guilford.

Rey, J. M. (1993). Oppositional defiant disorder. *American Journal of Psychiatry, 150,* 1769–1777.

Rowe, R., Maughan, B., Pickles, A., Costello, E. J., & Angold, A. (2002). The relationship between *DSM-IV* oppositional defiant disorder and conduct disorder: Findings from the Great Smoky Mountains Study. *Journal of Child Psychology and Psychiatry, 43,* 365–373.

Spaccarelli, S., Cotler, S., & Penman, D. (1992). Problem-solving skills training as a supplement to behavioral parent training. *Cognitive Therapy and Research, 16,* 1–18.

Webster-Stratton, C. (1984). Randomized trial of two parent-training programs for families with conduct-disordered children. *Journal of Consulting and Clinical Psychology, 52,* 666–678.

Webster-Stratton, C. (1994). Advancing videotape parent training: A comparison study. *Journal of Consulting and Clinical Psychology, 62,* 583–593.

Whittinger, N. S., Langley, K., Fowler T. A., Thomas, H. V., & Thapar, A. (2007). Clinical precursors of adolescent conduct disorder in children with attention-deficit/hyperactivity disorder. *Journal of the American Academy of Child and Adolescent Psychiatry, 46,* 179–187.

Sandy Smith

Marching to the Tune of a Different Drummer

When Eileen opened the clinic door, it was as if she were facing her worst fears head on. Sandy's pleas and verbal exchanges could be heard by the office staff all the way from the elevator at the other end of the building. Although Sandy was physically petite for her 8 years, her stiff posture almost anchored her mother's arm to the ground. Eileen was embarrassed by Sandy's behavior, but Sandy's reaction only served to confirm her resolve to finally seek professional help. As Eileen approached the receptionist's desk, Sandy bumped into the desk and slid onto the couch awkwardly beside her mother, with her legs entwined around each other like a pretzel. In the waiting room, Eileen tried to collect her thoughts about her daughter's development in anticipation of the many interview questions that might be asked.

DEVELOPMENTAL HISTORY/FAMILY BACKGROUND

Eileen had hoped for a daughter her entire pregnancy, even though Tom's family lineage had produced predominantly males. Against the odds, Eileen's hopes were answered and miraculously Sandy was born 8 years ago. The pregnancy and delivery were uneventful. Sandy was a beautiful baby, and Tom was proud to be the father of a baby girl. Sandy was also adored by her two older brothers, Jason, 6 years, and Sean, 4 years of age. Everything seemed to be going well. There were some minor stresses initially when Eileen had to give up attempts to nurse Sandy. Eileen had no problem nursing her other two infants, but due to Sandy's erratic sleep habits and irritability, her doctor recommended switching to the bottle. This switch proved difficult; Sandy's poor coordination meant that propping the bottle wouldn't work, since she often lost the bottle if her mother was not holding it. Sandy was a very active baby and she seemed to require little sleep. Eileen reasoned that perhaps the fact that the baby needed less sleep was a sign of curiosity and intelligence. Eileen placed a brightly colored mobile over the bed and added the crib activity center that her infant sons had enjoyed so much. However, Sandy had no interest in the mobile or in exploring the activity center. Sandy actually became very agitated with the crib additions, and Eileen responded by removing everything from the crib, which seemed to calm Sandy down. Through trial and error, Eileen eventually found that the sound of a wind-up merry-go-round on the dresser could be helpful in soothing Sandy. To this day, Sandy listens to music to help calm her down when she is anxious.

Despite her difficulties adjusting to any changes in her environment or schedule, Sandy did demonstrate one extremely advanced area of development. She was a very early talker and had amassed an amazing vocabulary by the time she was 2. At 2½ years of age, Sandy was sounding more like a miniature adult than a child and would repeat her grandmother's phrases "verbatim." Sandy would surprise onlookers in the grocery store with her pseudo-adult comments on the quality of the fruits and vegetables. By 3 years of age, Sandy could repeat stories from taped texts, word for word, and Sandy often recited these stories riding in the car, during dinner, or when playing by herself.

Sandy's strong verbal skills were in sharp contrast to her slower-developing motor skills. Sandy was a highly verbal but very awkward toddler. Initially, Eileen worried about her muscle coordination, since Sandy was slow to sit and would fall over if not securely propped with a pillow. When Sandy began to walk, she looked as though she was drunk, swaying to the left and with an off-balance gait. Sandy's legs were black and blue from falling down and bumping into things. At first, Eileen thought that Sandy was so preoccupied with talking that she wasn't looking where she was going. She eventually had Sandy's vision checked, but results came back negative. Sandy's poor coordination also seemed to influence her choices of play activities. Unlike the boys, Sandy had little interest in Legos, blocks, or puzzles. Sandy was definitely much more interested in chatting than doing. Eileen tried to enroll Sandy in a preschool gymnastics program to improve her coordination. However, this strategy backfired, since Sandy was extremely frustrated and unable to reproduce many of the tumbling movements; she could not touch her toes to her head, and repeatedly fell off the balance beam. The other children were soon making fun of Sandy, imitating her awkward movements, and Eileen removed her from the program. Eileen was becoming concerned about Sandy's fears of going anywhere new and her increasingly clingy behavior. Sandy was soon going to be kindergarten age, and Eileen worried about the transition. She enrolled Sandy in a morning preschool program 2 days a week. Each day was torture, getting Sandy into the car and over to the day-care center. Sandy did not want to go and would scream, hide, and run away (often running into something) in a frenzied panic. Eileen was determined to persist, however, knowing that it would only be worse if she were to give in.

Sandy's preschool experience was not very successful. As long as she could sit and read by herself or play on the flannel board, spelling words with preformed letters, Sandy was quite content. However, other children did not seem to want to play with Sandy and during free playtime, Sandy was often left alone. On the few occasions that Sandy tried to enter a group activity, her awkward sense of timing and poor social skills usually resulted in a negative experience, and Sandy would withdraw once again. She did not seem to profit from experiences, either. The following day, Sandy would approach the same child in the same way, setting herself up for another rejection and subsequent retreat. When Sandy was enrolled in the kindergarten program, her social struggles continued on a regular basis.

Social skills were very immature and Sandy did not seem to take nonverbal communication (facial expressions, conversational tone) into consideration at any time. Her sense of social-personal space was also poor, and Sandy would often stand too close and encroach on other children's sense comfort zone. Eventually, Sandy preferred to shadow the teacher instead of interacting with the other children. She gained her rewards when she could read aloud to the class and write words on the board in big letters. However, a lot of kindergarten activities were very difficult for Sandy: cutting and pasting, tracing, drawing, painting, and the big shoe with the lace to be tied and untied. Sandy often cried at home, asking if she could please stay home from school.

Sandy continued to experience problems with coordination. At 8 years of age, Sandy had yet to learn how to ride a two-wheeler. She never made the transition from training wheels, and even with the training wheels on, Sandy continued to lose her balance and fall over. Had it not been for the bicycle helmet, Eileen was sure that Sandy might have also had a head injury to deal with. Luckily, to Eileen's knowledge, Sandy never injured her head in any of the falls, although she did sustain many bruises on her arms and legs. Recently, Sandy's teacher had contacted Eileen concerning Sandy's reluctance to participate in the gym class and the many excuses that she gave to avoid engaging in the ongoing activities. Sandy had begged her mother to write a note to the teacher to get her out of gym class, but Eileen refused. Sandy's lack of coordination and clumsiness also seemed to permeate her total appearance. Despite her mother's extensive efforts at home to coordinate and organize Sandy's outfits for the next day, Sandy always looked somewhat disheveled and thrown together: buttons would not match the right button holes; shoelaces were dangling from her feet. Eileen eventually refurbished Sandy's wardrobe, removing button-up shirts and replacing lace-up shoes with Velcro-strap shoes. Sandy's lack of organization and messiness was pervasive. If Sandy wanted to remove an object from her dresser drawer, half the drawer often spilled over onto the floor. It was the same with her desk at school, which was jammed with papers crumpled and rolled into little balls.

Although Sandy's messiness and disorganization were annoying, they were not the reasons that brought Eileen to the clinic. Eileen was frustrated and confused. Sandy was a real puzzle to her and Eileen was now very motivated to find out what could possibly explain how her daughter's abilities could be so extreme: seemingly so very bright in some areas, yet totally lost in others. Sandy had an excellent vocabulary and wonderful memory for words. As a result, she could read beautifully and spell most words she had seen, without error. However, despite Sandy's excellent vocabulary, spelling, and reading skills, she was having increasing problems with reading comprehension. Sandy could recall a passage verbatim, but she seemed to have real problems answering any questions that required an inference going beyond information presented in the passage. Eileen recalled last night's homework assignment involving a reading passage that described a family eating breakfast together. Sandy had to answer a number of comprehension questions about the story. Sandy had no idea how to answer one question, which asked, "What time of day is it?" Even with Eileen's help and questions directed at passage clues, Sandy was unable to answer the question, saying: "I read it over and over. It doesn't tell you the time of day!" Eileen wondered if Sandy's problems telling time could somehow be related to her difficulties with comprehension. Sandy was still unable to tell time on an analogue clock. Even if she could tell you the time on a digital clock, she seemed oblivious to how time related to activities. Eileen recalled an incident where Sandy wanted to have some ice cream for breakfast. When Eileen told Sandy, "You don't have ice cream for breakfast," Sandy's response was: "Fine. Then I'll have dinner, now!" Initially, she thought Sandy was joking, but she was completely serious. There were other situations as well, where Sandy's odd thinking caught Eileen completely off guard. Sandy seemed to take things very literally, all the time. Sandy could be very gullible, and Eileen had to monitor her brothers carefully so they would stop playing tricks on Sandy. Eileen remembered one time that Sean told Sandy if she ate her ice cream cone from the bottom of the cone, she would get more ice cream. Eileen came in to find Sandy trying to eat the ice cream cone upside down with it melting all over the place. Eileen recalled another incident when they were watching a TV movie about an odd character and Tom mentioned that, "He certainly marches to the tune of a different drummer." Sandy looked up and said, "Where's the parade?" Tom tried to explain the expression, but Sandy just didn't get it and continued to ask about the drummer in the parade. She was very upset that she missed the parade. She eventually went to bed that evening upset, talking about the parade and how drummers march. At school, Sandy's literal interpretations often were not appreciated by her teacher, who thought that Sandy was just being smart.

Mathematics was another area of real difficulty for Sandy. It was as if mathematics involved a foreign language. Homework was an endless struggle involving hours and hours of explanations and discussions. Sandy didn't seem to be able to perform the same task twice in a row without having it all explained over and over again. The next day, it was as if she had never heard the explanation. Academic problems were compounded by Sandy's poor handwriting. Numbers as well as letters were often scrawled across the page without attention to writing between the lines, spacing, or direction. Often, her writing was impossible to decipher. As a result of her problems with math, comprehension, and writing, Sandy was falling farther and farther behind. At a recent school conference, Eileen was informed that the school was recommending that Sandy repeat the third grade.

Socially, Sandy seemed to have few friends at school. At the parent-teacher conference, Eileen asked Sandy's teacher what was keeping Sandy from forming more friendships with the other children. According to Sandy's teacher, it was Sandy's poor sense of timing that often turned the other kids off. Sandy often made comments at inappropriate times or out of context, and the other girls seemed to respond by ignoring and excluding her. Sandy also talked nonstop and didn't give the other girls a chance to get a word in. Eileen was very disappointed last week by the poor showing of classmates at Sandy's birthday party. After Sandy struggled for hours making invitations to her birthday party (cutting, coloring, and pasting were never Sandy's strengths), only one child showed up. Ann, a 5-year-old who lives next door, was the only one who attended the party. Although initially upset, Sandy soon became absorbed in playing a new audiotape she received as a gift and totally ignored Ann for the rest of the party. When Ann finally left, Sandy seemed to have no idea as to where she went or why she might have left.

REASON FOR REFERRAL

Eileen had talked to Sandy's pediatrician, hoping to gain insight into Sandy's "odd" ways of thinking and marginal school progress. Eileen had always thought that Sandy would outgrow her awkward ways, but she was now beginning to fear that her daughter's difficulties were more permanent. Her concerns were also escalating because of the lack of social contacts in her daughter's life and how this might impact negatively on her social development later on. Finally, Eileen decided that "knowing" was better than "not knowing," and she brought Sandy to the clinic with the hope that she could find some answers to her questions.

ASSESSMENT RESULTS

Information regarding specific assessment instruments and guidance in the interpretation of standard scores and T scores can be found in Appendix C.

The psychologist administered the Wechsler Intelligence Scale for Children (WISC-IV) and noted the following test behaviors. Sandy was very verbal throughout the assessment, and comments often resulted in digressions away from the target task. Sandy often had to be redirected to the task at hand. When verbal responses were required, such as on the Vocabulary and the Comprehension subtests, Sandy tended to overelaborate, giving verbose responses far in excess of what was required. When nonverbal tasks were presented, Sandy used self-talk to work her way through the task. Sandy frequently requested feedback regarding her performance and seemed to become somewhat agitated when informed by the examiner that he was unable to tell her how she was doing. Sandy seemed to be somewhat comforted, however, when the examiner expressed comments of encouragement and praised her effort in general.

Visual tasks were very difficult for Sandy. She was able to reproduce the initial block designs by placing the blocks on top of the designs in the model booklet, itself. However, as the designs increased in complexity and external cues were reduced, Sandy became visibly upset. She wanted to know where the lines went in the sixth design: "There are supposed to be lines to tell you where the blocks go!" She also reproduced two of the designs correctly, but in a rotated manner, not recognizing the need to match the orientation as well as the colors of the blocks. Although able to complete the initial items on the Picture Concepts task, when a third row of pictures was added, which increased the complexity and demands for abstract reasoning, Sandy began to respond in a random manner. Sandy was extremely frustrated by the Matrix Reasoning task, which requires the child to select the correct solution to complete a pattern from five possible alternatives.

Responses to the WISC-IV revealed a significant, 29-point discrepancy between her Verbal Comprehension Index (VCI = 112; range 103–119), which was in the high average range, and her Perceptual Reasoning Index (PSI = 83; range 80–98), which was in the low average range. Less than 1% of the population would have had a discrepancy of this extent between these two components. Scores for the Working Memory Index (WMI = 94; range 87–102) and the Processing Speed Index (PSI = 88; range 80–98) were in the upper low average to average range. On the VCI, Sandy revealed a significant strength in Vocabulary (SS = 14), while scores on the PRI were very weak overall: Block Design (SS = 7), Picture Concepts (SS = 7), and Matrix Reasoning (SS = 6). Sandy's full scale IQ was 91 (range 83–101), which places her functioning in the average range.

Academically, Sandy's scores for language arts subjects on the Woodcock Johnson Achievement Tests (WJIII) revealed average to low average scores for Basic Reading (SS = 102; 55th percentile), Reading Comprehension (SS = 88; 20th percentile), and Written Expression (SS = 86; 18th percentile). Scores for Math Calculation (SS = 75; 5th percentile) and Math

Reasoning (SS = 73; 4th percentile) were significantly below what would be anticipated given her overall intellectual ability and represent a discrepancy of more than one standard deviation (e.g., greater than 15 points) between her full scale IQ of 91 and her Math Calculation score (IQ 91 – 75 = 16) and Math Reasoning score (IQ 91 – 73 = 18). Math was at an early Grade 2 level with difficulties noted in computation, word problems, and math reasoning. Sandy demonstrated some letter and number reversals, especially on the fluency tests, which were timed tests. Handwriting was very poor.

Sandy's response to the Bender Gestalt test revealed a visual motor perception score to be equivalent to a child of 5 years 5 months, two standard deviations below her expected age level. Sandy's drawings were extremely immature, despite taking excessive time to complete the task (in excess of 15 minutes). Although Sandy counted and recounted dots, and often traced designs with her finger before execution, the resulting reproductions were poor due to problems with rotations, design integration, substitution of circles for dots, and tendencies to run designs into each other. When asked to "draw a person," Sandy seemed to take forever to produce the finished product, and after many erasures, the resulting image was very immature. Somewhat embarrassed by the lack of results, and partially as an evasive tactic, Sandy eventually produced a stick figure. She compensated for her poor motor skills, however, by creating an elaborate story about what the stick figure was doing and how he came from the "land of stick people." Parent responses to the Achenbach, Child Behavior Checklist (CBCL) revealed significant elevations on Withdrawn, Social Problems, Thought Problems, and Attention Problems, while Conners Scale responses (CPRS-R:L) noted elevations for Cognitive Problems/Inattention, Anxious/Shy, and *DSM-IV* Inattentive scale. Teacher responses to the Achenbach, Teacher Report Form (TRF) revealed significant concerns in Social Problems, Thought Problems, and Attention, while responses to the Conners Scale (CTRS-R:L) revealed significant elevations on scales measuring Opposition, Cognitive Problems/Inattention, and Social Problems.

Sandy's responses to the Revised Child Manifest Anxiety Scales (RCMAS-2) revealed significant elevations in areas of Worry/Oversensitivity, and Attention/Social Concerns. There were no significant elevations on the Child Depression Index (CDI).

ISSUES, TRENDS, AND TREATMENT ALTERNATIVES

Children who experience specific learning disabilities (SLD) differ from children with general learning problems or intellectual and developmental disabilities (IDD) in that those with IDD will demonstrate generalized problems across a wide variety of adaptive areas commensurate with impaired intellectual functioning (e.g., cognitive ability, functional academics, life skills, communication, etc.), while those with SLD will experience difficulties in a specific domain (such as reading, written expression, or mathematics) despite having average intelligence. Between 2% to 10% of children will be diagnosed with SLD (*DSM-IV-TR*, APA, 2000). The most prevalent type of SLD (80%) is dyslexia, a reading disability often evident in poor oral reading, fluency problems, and faulty reading comprehension. Disorders of written expression are often detected in errors of punctuation, grammar, organization, spelling, and poor handwriting. Mathematics disorders are relatively rare and seen in approximately 1% of the population. Many children who experience SLD in reading and/or written expression will be significantly stronger on tasks of visual/perceptual reasoning (PRI) than those that measure verbal reasoning (VCI).

The criteria for identifying children with SLD differ depending on the classification system used. While the *DSM-IV-TR* (APA, 2000) refers to *learning disorders* (reading disorder, mathematics disorder, disorders of written expression), and provides criteria for diagnosis, the educational system (IDEA, 2004) refers to *specific learning disabilities* (SLD) and provides guidelines for determining whether children meet criteria for special education services based on the extent and nature of their learning disability. An in-depth discussion of the criteria used by the different systems of classification and additional insight into current issues in the identification process can be found in Appendix B. Children who suffer from reading disorders (dyslexia) experience problems decoding words due to basic phonological processing deficits; however, they are usually able to perform adequately in math. However, children with nonverbal learning disability (NLD) experience just the opposite pattern: they are able to fluently decode words but encounter significant problems with mathematics (Rourke, 1999; Rourke, Hayman-Abello, & Collins, 2003). Although not all children with NLD will experience math problems (Pennington, 1991; Semrud-Clikeman & Hynd, 1990), Rourke (2000) suggests that based on extensive research, he has found that 72% of children with NLD will experience deficits in math reasoning, and in some cases, math skills may be limited to achievement levels equivalent to the fifth grade (Rourke, 1995).

The syndrome of NLD, which has also been referred to as nonverbal learning disorder, or developmental right hemisphere syndrome (DRHS), has been described in a number of sources over the past 10 to 15 years (Gross-Tsur, Shalev, Manor, & Amir, 1995; Harnadek & Rourke, 1994; Palombo, 2006; Rourke, 1989; Strang & Casey, 1994). Information processing and motor impairments are evident in three broad areas: motor skills (coordination), analysis and synthesis of visual information (visuospatial integration), and social/pragmatic awareness and development.

The core symptom presentation includes social problems due to interpersonal skill deficits, motor slowness, weak visual-perceptual organization, difficulties with nonverbal problem solving, and especially weak arithmetic ability. Soft neurological signs can also be evident on the left side of the body (Gross-Tsur et al., 1995). Often symptoms of ADHD are comorbid with the disorder. Results of a recent investigation by Garcia-Sanchez, Estevez-Gonzalez, Suarez-Romero, and Junque (1997) suggest that visuospatial deficits associated with right hemisphere dysfunction are more pronounced in those youth who had attention-deficit disorder without hyperactivity, compared to youth with ADHD hyperactive-impulsive type. Recent studies have increased our understanding of the role of visuospatial processing problems in children with NLD to the extent that Cornoldi, Venneri, Marconato, Molin, and Montinari (2003) suggest calling the disorder a *visuospatial learning disability*. In one study, Liddell and Rasmussen (2005) found that despite average ability to recall verbal information, children with NLD demonstrated significant deficits in the recall of visual information. Of special note was the very poor performance of these children on a task of immediate recall for faces, even though their scores improved on the delayed facial recall task. The researchers suggest that right hemisphere processing deficits (right temporal lobe) may contribute to the problem, while the need for additional time to consolidate information may explain the better performance on the delayed task. Rourke and colleagues (2002) have also addressed deficits in the right cerebral hemisphere of individuals with NLD, suggesting potential damage to white matter (myelinated fibers) evident in mild abnormalities to the right hemisphere in brain scans of those with NLD (Rourke, 1995).

In a recent investigation of the clinical characteristics associated with NLD or DRHS, Gross-Tsur and colleagues (1995) found the following characteristics that were shared by children in their sample: 65% demonstrated left-sided soft neurological signs; the mean Verbal IQ was approximately 20 scale score points higher than the mean Performance IQ of 85; the lowest Verbal scale score was Arithmetic, followed by Comprehension; the lowest Performance scale score was for Coding; 94% had at least one specific learning disability, and 67% had dyscalculia (math disability). In this particular sample, 90% demonstrated graphomotor impairment evidenced by weak performance on Coding and the Bender Visual Motor Gestalt Test, and 80% were referred for slow cognitive and motor performance.

Descriptions of slow cognitive and motor output were noted in an inability to complete schoolwork, sluggish response to activity, and slowness to initiate and complete routine tasks. All children demonstrated poor social skills, often evident in inadequate or inappropriate facial expression, eye contact, weak pragmatic language, and poor comprehension of social rules. Children with NLD display considerable difficulties in nonverbal problem solving. According to Harnadek and Rourke (1994), deficits in concept formation and hypothesis testing result in poor ability to profit from environmental reinforcers that normally shape our behavior. These children do not readily establish a cause-and-effect relationship, which brings structure and contextual meaning to our experiences. They fare poorly in complex or novel situations and can appear scripted and inappropriate in their responses.

Rourke and colleagues (2002) compared the syndrome of NLD to other pediatric neurological disorders and ranked the disorders from high to low on the basis of symptom overlap. They found the closest sharing of similar features was for Asperger's syndrome (impairment in motor skills, social pragmatics, and pragmatic communication, and visuospatial deficits). Individuals with Williams syndrome shared similar features of deficits in visuospatial processing and the pragmatics of communication, although obvious differences were also evident in overall cognitive ability and hypersociability.

Interventions and Treatment

Empirically supported interventions for NLD continue to remain a high-need area for research. Despite the lack of empirically supported programs for NLD, a number of recommendations have been suggested as clinically effective in remediating neuropsychological deficits (visual-perceptual organization, psychomotor and concept-formation skills) responsible for problems in areas of social skills, mathematical abilities, and responses to novel problem-solving situations (Rourke, 1993). Treatment suggestions involve direct instruction and guided practice. The following list summarizes some of the suggested directions for treatment (Foss, 1991; Rourke, 1995):

- Teach the child in a predictable, step-by-step, rote manner.
- Ensure that language concepts are clarified.
- Enhance verbal reasoning.

- Encourage the application of problem-solving strategies and their transfer to new situations.
- Teach a problem-solving format, or template, that the child can use to structure the situation (e.g., **STOP**: Stop and see what is happening; Think about what I am going to do now; Observe how others are responding to me; Practice and improve).
- Enhance social cognition through the use of direct instruction to teach appropriate verbal social responses and how to read verbal cues.
- Provide many opportunities for practicing these new skills and applying them to new situations until the responses become more fluid and automatic.
- Teach the child to link visual information (facial expression, body posture) with auditory information—not only what is said, but how (tone, inflection) it is said.
- Teach visual-organizational skills.
- Teach comprehension directly.
- Enhance self-esteem and feelings of self-efficacy.

As is evident in these guidelines, direct instruction is crucial to assisting children with NLD to make connections that they may miss due to subtleties in the language, interpreting information literally, or not attending to nonverbal communication (facial expressions and body language). Since children and youth with NLD often take things literally, one of the major difficulties with problem solving is generalizing from one situation to another or interpreting statements in a more generic manner (Marti, 2004). As a result, directions need to be as specific as possible, for example, the statement "I want you to clean up your room," could lead to an array of probable uncertainties *(Does cleaning mean washing my room? How do I do that? What part of the room do I clean? How long do I have to do that for? When do I know I am done?* And so on.) that could be circumvented through proper elaboration.

Despite increasing awareness of NLD, Thompson (1997) suggests that many school districts have not recognized NLD because the syndrome does not conform to the more traditional concept of a language-based learning disability. In these cases, students may not receive appropriate CAMS (compensations, accommodations, modifications, and strategies). Furthermore, if students with NLD fall into the minority of those with the disability that do not have significant problems in math, they will likely not qualify for special education assistance, despite encountering many problems in the regular classroom (Semrud-Clikeman & Glass (2008). The dangers and risks of not detecting or providing early intervention can be found in retrospective studies of adults with NLD. These retrospective studies (Ellison & Semrud-Clikeman, 2007; Rourke, Young, & Leenaars, 1989; Rourke, Young, Strang, & Russell, 1986) suggest that undetected children with NLD demonstrate a greater degree of developing internalizing disorders, such as depression; are at greater risk for suicidal behaviors; and report a greater incidence of loneliness and social isolation as adults. Palombo (2006) suggests a wide variety of therapeutic approaches that might be applied to strengthen functioning in two important areas: enhanced self-efficacy and increased awareness of the nature of their problems and how to navigate stressful and challenging situations, academically and socially.

In a case study investigation, Brodeur (2006) demonstrated that direct instruction techniques were highly beneficial for a 15-year-old female with NLD who participated in a class to increase awareness of social pragmatics. After attending the classes, the student demonstrated significant gains on all measures of adaptive, social, and leadership skills (self ratings, teacher ratings, and parent ratings). Recommendations for future research included a focus on forming and maintaining friendships for older students, and instruction focusing on maintaining eye contact and turn taking for younger children with NLD.

Post-Case Questions

1. Children who demonstrate a nonverbal learning disability (NLD) may pose a particular problem for diagnosis and intervention since their symptoms do not conform to the traditional concept of a language-based learning disability.

   Discuss some of the difficulties of diagnosis of NLD with respect to how learning disabilities are defined by (a) the *DSM-IV-TR* (APA, 2000), (b) Education (IDEA, 2004), and (c) National Joint Committee on Learning Disabilities (NJCLD; see Appendix B).

2. Discuss the similarities and differences between a nonverbal learning disability (NLD) and Asperger's syndrome (Dylan's case) or Williams syndrome (Williams's case).

3. Discuss case formulations from the following theoretical frameworks: biomedical, psychodynamic, behavioral, cognitive, family systems, and attachment/parenting style.

4. Social skills are often an area of weakness for children with NLD. Using a social information processing model, develop a case formulation for Sandy's social skills deficits and explain how you would target specific areas for treatment.

REFERENCES

American Psychiatric Association (APA). (2000). *Diagnostic and statistical manual of mental disorders* (4th ed., text rev.). Washington, DC: American Psychiatric Press.

Brodeur, C. (2006). Building social competence in children with nonverbal learning disabilities: A preliminary study. *Dissertation Abstracts International: B. The Sciences and Engineering, 67,* 531.

Cornoldi, C., Venneri, A., Marconato, R., Molin, A., & Montinari, C. (2003). A rapid screening measure for the identification of visuospatial learning disability in schools. *Journal of Learning Disabilities, 36,* 299–306.

Ellison, P. A., & Semrud-Clikeman, M. (2007). *Child neuropsychology.* New York: Springer.

Foss, J. M. (1991). Nonverbal learning disabilities and remedial interventions. *Annals of Dyslexia, 41,* 128–140.

Garcia-Sanchez, C., Estevez-Gonzalez, A., Suarez-Romero, E., & Junque, C. (1997). Right hemisphere dysfunction in subjects with attention-deficit disorder with and without hyperactivity. *Journal of Child Neurology, 12,* 107–115.

Gross-Tsur, V., Shalev, R. S., Manor, O., & Amir, N. (1995). Developmental right hemisphere syndrome: Clinical spectrum of the nonverbal learning disability. *Journal of Learning Disabilities, 28,* 80–86.

Harnadek, M. C. S., & Rourke, B. P. (1994). Principal identifying features of the syndrome of nonverbal learning disabilities in children. *Journal of Learning Disabilities, 27,* 144–153.

IDEA. (2004). Retrieved December 2009 from www.ed.gov/offices/OSERS/IDEA/index.html

Liddell, G., & Rasmussen, C. (2005). Memory profile of children with nonverbal learning disability. *Learning Disabilities Research & Practice, 20,* 137–141.

Marti, L. (2004). Helping children with nonverbal learning disability: What I have learned from living with nonverbal learning disability. *Journal of Child Neurology, 19,* 830–836.

Palombo, J. (2006). *Nonverbal learning disabilities: A clinical perspective.* New York: Norton.

Pennington, B. (1991). *Diagnosing learning disorders: A neuropsychological framework.* New York: Guilford.

Rourke, B. P. (1989). *Nonverbal learning disabilities: The syndrome and the model.* New York: Guilford.

Rourke, B. P. (1993). Arithmetic disabilities, specified and otherwise: A neuropychological perspective. *Journal of Learning Disabilities, 26,* 214–226.

Rourke, B. P. (1995). Treatment program for the child with NLD. In B. P. Rourke (Ed.), *Syndrome of nonverbal learning disabilities: Neurodevelopmental manifestations.* New York: Guilford.

Rourke, B. P. (2000). Neuropsychological and psycho-social subtyping: A review of investigations within the University of Windsor laboratory. *Canadian Psychology, 41,* 34–51.

Rourke, B. P., Ahmad, S., Collins, D., Jayman-Abello, B., Hayman-Abello, S., & Warriner, E. M. (2002). Child clinical/pediatric neuropsychology: Some recent advances. *Annual Review of Psychology, 53,* 309–339.

Rourke, B. P., Hayman-Abello, B. A., & Collins, D. W. (2003). Learning disabilities: A neuropsychological perspective. In B. S. Fogel, R. B. Schiffer, & S. M. Rao (Eds.), *Neuropsychiatry* (2nd ed., pp. 630–659). New York: Lippincott, Williams, & Wilkins.

Rourke, B. P., Young, G. C., & Leenaars, A. A. (1989). A childhood learning disability that predisposes those afflicted to adolescent and adult depression and suicide risk. *Journal of Learning Disabilities, 22,* 169–175.

Rourke, B. P., Young, G. P., Strang, J. D., & Russell, D. L. (1986). Adult outcomes of childhood central processing deficiencies. In I. Grant & K. M. Adams (Eds.), *Neuropsychological assessment of neuropsychiatric disorders* (pp. 244–267). New York: Oxford University Press.

Semrud-Clikeman, M., & Glass, K. (2008). Comprehension of humor in children with nonverbal learning disabilities, reading disabilities, and without learning disabilities. *Annual of Dyslexia, 58,* 163–180.

Semrud-Clikeman, M., & Hynd, G. W. (1990). Right hemisphere dysfunction in nonverbal learning disabilities: Social, academic, and adaptive functioning in adults and children. *Psychological Bulletin, 107,* 196–209.

Strang, J. D., & Casey, J. E. (1994). The psychological impact of learning disabilities: A developmental neurological perspective. In L. F. Koziol & E. E. Scott (Eds.), *The neuropsychology of mental disorders: A practical guide* (pp. 171–186). Springfield, IL: Charles C Thomas.

Thompson, S. (1997). Nonverbal learning disorders revisited in 1997. Retrieved September 17, 2002, from http://www.nldline.com/nld.htm

Brian Williams

My Name Is Williams, Too

Brian came to the clinic accompanied by his grandmother. At 9 years 7 months of age, Brian was a walking paradox. On the one hand he was a highly sociable youngster and showed a maturity in caring and empathy for others. His welcoming and friendly demeanor should have set the stage for a host of social relationships. However, he experienced extreme problems with social functioning. Despite a keen love of people, and a strong desire to have friends, Brian could also appear anxious, experience numerous peer difficulties, and then withdraw socially. Brian's original assessment results from testing conducted when he was 4 years old and again when he was 6½ have revealed wide variations in patterns of strengths and weaknesses for intellectual and adaptive functioning. An update was requested to evaluate interim gains and to reexamine his profile of strengths and weaknesses, especially in the social arena, and to provide intervention strategies to assist with social functioning. Academically, Brian continues to struggle, especially with very basic math concepts, while language-based functions are an area of relative strength. A reevaluation was requested to better identify the nature of his difficulties to assist with recommendations for interventions in the future.

DEVELOPMENTAL HISTORY/FAMILY BACKGROUND

Brian's paternal grandmother accompanied him to the clinic and provided the information for the family background and developmental history for this African American family. Brian's mother gave birth to Brian when she was only 17. The delivery was by cesarean section due to fetal distress. Brian was a full-term baby, born at approximately 41 weeks gestation, and weighing 7 pounds 11 ounces. The Apgar score was 9 for entries recorded at 1 and 5 minutes. Brian's biological father was 20 years old at the time of his birth. Brian currently lives with his father and paternal grandparents and has visitation with his mother two or three times monthly. Currently, his father works as a machine operator and his mother is a cashier.

Motor milestones were achieved on schedule and he was able to roll over at 3 months, sit at 6 months, and walk at 11 months. Despite achieving these gross motor milestones, fine motor skills have always been problematic, and he has experienced problems with writing, buttoning his clothes, and tying his shoes. Although speech was initially delayed, not saying his first word until his first birthday, once he began to combine words and produce two-word utterances, his language skills seemed to improve dramatically. Currently, language is an area of strength for Brian, while fine motor skills continue to be an area of significant weakness.

When discussing his general health and outlook, his grandmother said that Brian started out as a very fussy and colicky baby who had a lot of problems swallowing and keeping his food down, and falling asleep and staying asleep. However, when he outgrew that stage, he developed into a very agreeable and happy youngster. In fact, he was so overly social that she was afraid he would go away with anyone. He seemed to be totally focused on people, their faces, and their voices, from the time he could walk, and teaching him about "stranger danger" continues to be a worry. However, even though he is drawn to people, he is also anxious enough that she believes he would not really go away with anyone. He has many fears and often can be clingy. He can also worry about the strangest things. Grandmother recalled that after hearing a story about sink holes on the news, Brian was worried that he would be swallowed up if a sink hole happened in his yard, or the school yard. Once he starts worrying about something, she said, it takes considerable patience to have him stop dwelling on it. There are times, she admitted, when he can be oppositional at home, but his teachers really do not see that behavior at school. For the most part, his teachers describe him as a pleasant child who tries to be accommodating. However, grandmother and teachers have been puzzled about why there is such a disconnect between his social desires and the outcomes of his relationships, and to this point, no one seems to be able to shed any light on the subject. His health has been good; however, he was diagnosed with a heart murmur last fall, which is being monitored. In view of this, the pediatrician has recommended that he lose weight, although his grandmother does not think he needs to. He was prescribed glasses this spring for strabismus and unlike most kids who balk at wearing glasses, he was delighted because the preacher wears glasses.

When asked about his personality and strengths he might have, his grandmother responded with a huge smile and said, "That boy is gonna be a preacher some day!" She said church is one of his favorite activities and he loves to sing the hymns, which he has committed to memory. He is also able to recite the sermon when they get home and often she finds Brian standing in front of the mirror preaching the sermon that they have just heard and using the exact emphasis on the words, sounding just like the preacher. The choir master has said that Brian has "absolute pitch," a rare gift, especially in one so young, without any formal training. She was very proud of Brian's performance in church last Sunday when he sang a duet in front of the congregation that was flawless, and he had absolutely no sense of stage fright. Grandmother also mentioned that despite his gift and love for music, he has very sensitive hearing and will sometimes overreact to sounds (especially high-frequency sounds) by covering up his ears. Brian did have a middle-ear infection (otitis media) a few years ago, but it has not happened since. She had mentioned this overreactivity to sound on the last visit to the pediatrician, who has scheduled an appointment with a hearing specialist. Grandmother wondered why Brian has such a short attention span for school subjects (he is very distractible at school) but he can listen to music for a long time and doesn't miss a musical note.

She said that she has tried to get him to slow down on the sermons, but he seems to be obsessed and often just goes on whether she likes it or not. Although he has tried to bring this behavior into the classroom, it was quickly discouraged, as disruptive, and he has complied with his teachers' requests.

Brian has been assessed twice in the past, and results have been inconclusive, with little explanation of why his profile is so extreme or to help explain his problems in the social area. The following is a summary of those findings.

Brian was seen by the child development center prior to his entrance into the kindergarten program, just before his fifth birthday. At that time, scores on the Differential Abilities Scale (DAS) revealed the following standard scores: Verbal Cluster of 70 (range 70–87) and Nonverbal Cluster of 67 (range 61–72). General Conceptual Ability was a standard score of 65. The Spatial Cluster was not reported. Scores on the Bracken Basic Concept Scale (BBCS-R) revealed significant delays in conceptual development, with an overall standard score of 63 (1st percentile), equivalent to an age score of 2 years 6 months at a chronological age of 4 years 10 months. The evaluator noted, however, that there was significant variability in his conceptual skills, with significant weaknesses noted for conceptual skills in areas of Direction/Position and significant strengths noted in concepts related to Self/Social Awareness. Grandmother completed the Vineland Adaptive Behavior Scales, which resulted in an overall Adaptive Behavior Concept of 69 (3 years 4 months). Strengths were noted in areas of Socialization (SS = 76; 3 years 0 months), Communication (SS = 76; 3 years 3 months), and Daily Living (SS = 86; 4 years 1 month). A significant weakness was evident in Motor Skill Development (SS = 61; 3 years 1 month).

Brian was again seen in the child development clinic when he was 6 years 6 months of age. At that time, the Standford Binet 5 was administered. His overall full-scale score was 67 (range 60–75), with a standard score for Verbal Reasoning of 72 and Nonverbal Reasoning of 66. Overall Visual Spatial Reasoning was a significant weakness (SS = 59), while Working Memory for auditory information was a relative strength (SS = 12). Academically, according to the Woodcock Johnson Test of Achievement (WJIII), he was functioning at the following levels: Broad Reading (SS = 86), Broad Math (SS = 69), and Broad Written Expression (SS= 85). As a result of his assessment, it was recommended that physical therapy be added to his services for "awkward gait" and fine motor problems. Brian was already receiving occupational therapy.

REASON FOR REFERRAL

When asked what one thing she would like to find out about Brian from the current assessment, his grandmother said, "To finish the puzzle." She explained that although he had been assessed twice before, no one could provide any "name" for his condition or explain why he behaves the way he does and how to help him. She said that he is becoming increasingly frustrated socially, and she is afraid that he will begin to withdraw into his fantasy world about being a preacher. She just wanted him to have fun with friends and wanted to know how to help.

ASSESSMENT RESULTS

When Brian entered the room, he presented as a child who looked much younger than his 9½ years. He had a short stature, and his facial features were distinct with pronounced eyes, puffiness around the eyes, a short nose with a broad tip, and large ear lobes. His cheeks were full and filled with a wide smile. Yet his features seemed almost top heavy, with a broad forehead and a jaw that was very narrow and slight. Although Brian was very interested in meeting the psychologist, he was somewhat apprehensive and anxious, so his grandmother sat with them for the first 5 minutes and then Brian was fine. Although he was cooperative initially, he was very easily distracted and had a hard time remaining seated. He preferred to stand during parts of the assessment, and often shifted his weight from side to side. When asked about his likes and dislikes, Brian said music and "preaching" were his favorite things. As for dislikes, Brian said that he hated broccoli, because it tasted like "sand and rocks," and he also didn't like surprises because they were scary. When asked what else was "scary," Brian said loud noises, especially fire alarms, and that it was scary when another teacher was in his class because his teacher was sick.

Responses to the Differential Abilities Scale (DAS:2) revealed an overall General Conceptual Ability Level (GCA) of 70 (range 66–77), placing his functioning in the borderline range, at the 2nd percentile. However, as had been found on previous assessments, there was a significant discrepancy between ability levels in different areas. While he scored within the low average range for Verbal Reasoning (SS = 84), he scored within the extremely low range for Spatial Reasoning (SS = 64). Nonverbal Reasoning was approximately midway between (SS = 72). Brian encountered extreme difficulty with both spatial tasks: recall of designs and pattern construction. He encountered significant problems with design recall because of his very poor fine motor skills and his inability to recall how the design parts fit together or their orientation in space. He could reproduce some parts, but there was no relationship between them. Brian did not seem to be frustrated by the pattern construction task; he just placed his blocks down on the desk and would then look at the psychologist to indicate that he was done. He did not seem to understand that the blocks had to be turned to match the direction of the picture or that there was a pattern that was to be constructed. This behavior pattern was in sharp contrast to his skills on the verbal reasoning tasks, where he was able to provide very good definitions for words and made good attempts at the verbal similarities; however, this task was more difficult for him due to the abstract nature of the task.

Academically, scores on the Woodcock Johnson Achievement Tests (WJIII) revealed the following standard scores and grade-level equivalents: Basic Reading (SS = 76; grade equivalent of 2.2), Reading Comprehension (SS = 60; grade equivalent of 1.7), Math Reasoning (SS = 54; grade equivalent of K.8), and Written Expression (SS = 63; grade equivalent of 1.5). Given these results, Brian is achieving above the level expected, given his GCA (70) in Basic Reading; however, all other scores are below the expected level. Math Reasoning is significantly (16 points) below his anticipated level of functioning.

Brian's teacher and grandmother completed the Adaptive Behavior Assessment System (ABAS II), and the discrepancy between scores obtained on this adaptive measure for the various areas were even more extreme than had been obtained in early administrations. Despite having an ability level for cognitive functioning that places his reasoning ability within the borderline range (GCA 70), ratings for Total Social Adaptation were well in excess of this level and in the average range, as rated by his teacher (SS = 95) and grandmother (SS = 107). Also, in terms of the Practical Adaptive score (measuring community use, home/school living, health and safety, and self-care), Brian scored in the average range (SS = 101) according to his grandmother, and just below the average range (SS = 89) according to his teacher. However, in the area of Total Concepts (including communication, functional academics, and self-direction), Brian was well below the range expected, given his GCA. On this area, his grandmother rated him in the extremely low range with a standard score of 55, and his teacher rated him with a standard score of 61. As can be seen, although his Overall General Adaptive Composite for grandmother's rating (SS = 80) and teacher's rating (SS = 84) is a score that reflects overall functioning in the low average range, it is based on a profile of abilities that are widely spaced apart.

Finally, the Conners parent and teacher rating scales were completed by Brian's grandmother and teacher. Although his teacher rated him as clinically significant in the area of inattention and in the at-risk range for hyperactivity, his grandmother did not rate his behaviors on this scale as significant and did not feel there were significant concerns regarding the possibility of Brian having symptoms of ADHD.

Grandmother and teacher completed the Devereux Scales of Mental Disorders (DSMD), which revealed significant attention problems, only on the teacher ratings. However, grandmother and teacher ratings did agree on the existence of significant symptoms of anxiety, especially endorsing fearfulness in many areas, and endorsed several items relating to social intrusiveness (annoys others, talks too much, interacts with strangers inappropriately, etc.).

Summary of the Psychologist's Findings/Impressions

Brian is a 9½-year-old boy who demonstrates a wide discrepancy between and within his intellectual, adaptive, and functional skills. Intellectually, although his overall functioning is within the borderline range, this represents a composite score of three very different ability levels: a significant strength in Verbal Reasoning (low average); a significant weakness in Spatial Analysis (extremely low); and a Nonverbal Reasoning Ability (borderline) that is midway between these two levels. From an adaptive perspective, while he has obvious strengths in social adaptation and a desire to make friends, he is currently not successful in maintaining any long-term friendships. He has some obvious and possible "savant skills" in the areas of musical ability (pitch, tone, and recall for lyrics and melodies), and can sustain attention for musical activities over a long period of time. On the other hand, academically, his attention span is short and he is highly distractible and fidgety when required to focus on academics in the classroom (or in the assessment situation). During the assessment session, he was very restless and moved about constantly. He has acquired a good ability to decode and read; however, this is likely due to his good memory for phonetic information. His reading comprehension and written expression lag behind, likely due to cognitive deficits in dealing with more abstract applications of language functions. Mathematical skills that can benefit from visual-spatial abilities are an obvious area of weakness for Brian.

Brian's physical features, including his short stature, distinctive facial features (broad forehead; wide eyes with puffiness around the eyes; a short nose with a broad tip; full lips; wide smile; full cheeks; and small, receding chin), his intellectual and adaptive profile, his musical ability, and his intense interest and desire for social connectivity all suggest the possibility of a diagnosis of Williams syndrome (WS). Individuals with WS often present as a paradox because they are drawn to social contact, and on the surface, due to strengths in verbal skills, seem that they should be among the most popular children. However, deficits in processing cognitive information may result in their inability to interpret the subtle nuances of social situations or to understand the more complex social dynamics evident in visual-spatial processing (e.g., appreciating social space), and they are likely to be rejected by peers as a result. Because of their empathy and sensitivity, however, this may result in their becoming more apprehensive and anxious in social situations, and they may withdraw from social contact. Since they are drawn to social contact, though, they may place themselves in this situation in a repetitive basis, which may result in increased anxiety and depression in adulthood. Since the majority of individuals with WS have cardiovascular problems, and especially in light of a heart murmur being recently diagnosed, it is recommended that Brian receive a complete cardiology work-up. Also, since individuals with Williams share many symptoms of ADHD, and given his behavior in the classroom and assessment setting, further consultation with the family physician is recommended. Brain also has many fears and anxieties that can be overwhelming for him at times, especially loud unexpected noises, like fire alarms. He also has a tendency to dwell on things that cause him to be fearful, and it takes much convincing to calm him down.

ISSUES, TRENDS, AND TREATMENT ALTERNATIVES

In the introduction to their book about WS, Semel & Rosner (2003) pose the question, "How is it possible to conceptualize a group of children who test as though retarded, speak as though gifted, behave sometimes as though emotionally disturbed, and function like the learning disabled?" (p. 1). In essence, this summarizes some of the puzzling aspects of individuals with WS, a genetic neurodevelopmental disorder occurring in approximately 1 in 7,500 births. While the disorder is most commonly referred to as Williams syndrome in the United States, in Europe the disorder is often referred to as Williams-Beuren syndrome (Morris, 2006a). There is a deletion on chromosome 7 (part of the chromosome is missing), and although it occurs as a random genetic mutation, individuals with WS have a 50% chance of passing the gene on to their children (Bellugi et al., 2007). The deletion involves the elastin gene (ELN), which is a major component of connective tissues, such as ligaments, lungs, heart valves, and arteries, allowing them to expand and contract (Gosline et al., 2002). Approximately 80% of those with WS will have some cardiovascular anomaly, while 95% will have developmental delay (Morris, 2006b). Individuals with WS often exhibit early cardiovascular problems that may result in premature death (average life span of 50 years). Some of the more common cardiovascular difficulties include narrowing of the arteries, hypertension, and strokes (Kaplan, 2006). In one study of individuals with WS, 75% were diagnosed with a heart murmur at some point in their lives (Jones & Smith, 1975). Problems with ears and hearing include middle-ear infections (otitis media experienced by 60% of children with WS) and ear pain or hyperacusis (Klein et al., 1990), often associated with heightened sensitivities to certain sounds, often high-frequency sounds (Dykens, 2003; Einfeld, Tonge, & Florio, 1997; Van Borsel, Curfs, & Fryns, 1997). By late childhood, some children with WS will develop sensorineural hearing loss for high-frequency sounds in one ear (Johnson, Comeau, & Clarke, 2001). There are also vision problems associated with WS, such as hypopia, which occurs in 68% of those with WS (Winter, Pankau, Amm, Gosch, & Wessel, 1996), and strabismus, which is likely in between 27% and 78% of the population (Olitsky, Sadler, & Reynolds, 1997). Infants with WS are often described as fussy and colicky, although the majority outgrow this in the first year and become much more content and happy as toddlers (Levine & Wharton, 2000). However, many children with WS have difficulty falling asleep and maintaining sleep (Einfeld et al., 1997), and they are more likely to experience "restless leg syndrome," periodic limb movements during sleep, than peers without the disorder (Arens et al., 1998).

While many with WS will exhibit developmental delays, there is a wide range of IQ scores possible within the WS population, from low average intelligence to severe mental retardation. Mean IQ scores have been reported in the 55 to 60 range (Mervis, Morris, Bertrand, &

Robinson, 1999a; Udwin et al., 1996). There are excellent strengths in verbal short-term memory (Udwin & Yule, 1991), and linguistic skills are far superior to those with Down syndrome (Bellugi, Lichtenberger, Jones, Lai, & St. George, 2000); however, Singer Harris, Bellugi, Bates, Jones, and Rossen (1997) found that the superiority of skills in those with WS did not surface until after the initial accumulation of approximately 50 words. As children and adults, despite overall limitations, intellectually they demonstrate remarkable skills in expressive vocabulary, syntax, and semantics (Bellugi, Wang, & Jernigan, 1994; Udwin & Yule 1990). However, in individuals with WS, there are significant deficits in the visuospatial area, including tasks of visual motor integration evident in difficulty with fine motor tasks such as handwriting and copying (Mervis, Robinson, & Pani, 1999b). According to Rourke and colleagues (2002), individuals with WS evidence processing deficits similar to those of individuals with nonverbal learning disabilities (NLD). This is especially true for strengths in verbal skills (yet obvious weaknesses in the subtle nuances of social pragmatics) and deficits in visual-spatial and visual motor integration. Often there is evidence of remarkable musical ability both in the ability to produce absolute and relative pitch (Lenhoff, 2006) and in memory for tone and lyrics, which may be related to their strong phonological memory skills (Peretz & Coltheart, 2003).

In their study of social competence in individuals with WS, Rosner, Hodapp, Fidler, Sagun, and Dykens (2004) found that compared to peers diagnosed with Down syndrome or Prader Willi syndrome, in a situation of free choice activities, those with WS tended to gravitate toward activities that included musical instruments, while they tended to avoid activities like puzzles that required visual-spatial skills. Occupational problems that have been associated with adolescents and adults with WS include job interference due to distractibility, social disinhibition and overfriendliness, and anxiety (Davies, Howlin, & Udwin, 1997). In addition, deficits in visual motor skills required in many chores, such as bed making, and entry-level jobs, such as assembly-line work, have also been identified as barriers to success (Dykens, Hodapp, & Finucane, 2000).

Individuals with WS are characteristically overly friendly and often can be socially inappropriate and somewhat intrusive due to their trait of "social disinhibition" (Wang, 2006). Bellugi and colleagues (2007) describe those with WS as demonstrating a "hypersociability, including overfriendliness and heightened approachability toward others, combined with anxiety relating to new situations and objects and a difficulty forming and maintaining friendships with peers" (p. 99). The researchers suggest that although they do not see social situations as threatening, per se, their overly anxious nature may undermine their ability to successfully connect their social perceptions with their social expression, resulting in an inability to successfully engage in social encounters. Also, they seem to lack social pragmatics, such as the recognition of social group membership, which can place them at a serious disadvantage and even risk, since they enthusiastically will approach strangers and family members in the same manner. They are also prone to repetitive greetings, unaware of social conventions, and may engage in incessant greeting behavior or use forms of address that are overly familiar when greeting virtual strangers (Semel & Rosner, 2003).

Although children with WS can be anxious by nature, they do not respond to threatening faces like other children do, as a result of unusually low activation levels in the amygdala, which is responsible for regulating the fear response (Meyer-Lindenberg et al., 2005). Fifty percent of individuals with WS are diagnosed with ADHD, and generalized anxiety, while about 50% have specific phobias, especially fear of loud noises (Doyle, Bellugi, Korenberg, & Graham, 2004; Klein-Tasman & Mervis, 2003).

Semel and Rosner (2003) identify six types of behavior problems that commonly occur in individuals with WS, including "fears and anxieties, distractibility and attentional problems, impulsivity, poor adaptability, low frustration tolerance, and atypical activity" (p. 295), evident in such behavior patterns as restlessness, fidgeting and stereotyped movements (squirmy or engaging in repetitive motor routines), wandering, overactivity, and hyperactivity. Individuals with WS also experience problems in regulating their emotions, which can result in heightened responses and inflated emotional reactions to unexpected sights, sounds, or tactile stimulation. Semel and Rosner (2003) suggest that inherent to their behavior problems are tendencies toward high reactivity in the presence of low self-regulation.

Intervention Programs

Medical management is an important component of planning and programming for children with WS. Kaplan (2006) suggests that "optimal medical, educational and community support can help the child with WS lead a fulfilling life" (p. 83). Physicians can consult the guidelines for managing WS produced by the American Academy of Pediatrics (2001), while parents can also consult specialists in multidisciplinary clinics that have been established throughout the United States for the treatment of WS. The multidisciplinary team servicing the WS clinic would have personnel with expertise in such areas as cardiology, genetics, developmental pediatrics, behavioral pediatrics, psychiatry, pediatric psychology, and neurology, as well as access to physical, occupational, and speech therapies. According to Kaplan (2006), children should be reevaluated in the clinic every 3 years.

Special education and related services would be an important aspect of the child's programming on a day-to-day basis. Because most of the children will require assistance with academics, special education programming would be required, especially in areas that are more dependent on visual-spatial analysis such as mathematics, and for assistance in understanding subject material that requires higher-order processing, such as reading comprehension, solving word problems, and written expression.

Related Services: Physical and occupational therapy should be provided, if needed, for possible areas of support such as awkward gait, handwriting, and fine motor skills.

Social skills training programs may be helpful to increase the ability to integrate social perceptions and social expression, and to provide an opportunity to practice skills in an environment that minimizes anxiety.

A successful cognitive-behavioral intervention for reducing anxiety in children is the Coping Cat Program (Kendall, 1994). The program is suited to children 7 to 16 years of age and has been used to treat several forms of anxiety, including separation anxiety disorder, generalized anxiety disorder, and social anxiety disorder. The program can be administered individually or in group settings (Flannery-Schroeder & Kendall, 2000) and focuses on the development of coping skills (first eight to nine lessons) and then on practicing those skills in either imagined or in vivo (actual) conditions (last eight to nine sessions). An acronym developed for the program acts as a memory aid for highlighting the four key steps in the process:

Feel frightened (recognition of physical symptoms that accompany anxiety)?

Expect the worse (recognition of negative self-talk)?

Attitude/Actions that can help (replace negative self-talk with positive coping comments).

Results and Rewards (self-monitoring, evaluation, and self-reward).

For adolescents and young adults with WS, concerns about completing chores and doing many entry-level jobs such as assembly-line work that rely on visual-spatial skills can be assisted with the ongoing support of job coaches (Dykens et al., 2000).

Semel and Rosner (2003) suggest a number of interventions that can assist the behavioral problems of those with WS. They suggest that techniques that draw on strengths of individuals with WS (e.g., verbal mediation, stress reduction, environmental control) would all potentially benefit those with WS. The following is a summary of some of the techniques that have been addressed by Semel and Rosner.

Fears and Anxieties. In addition to methods already suggested (e.g., Kendall's Coping Cat Program), Semel and Rosner (2003) suggest teaching verbal mediation strategies and providing reassurance, role-play, explanations, and self-instruction (self-statements to calm in times of stress) can all assist in reducing fears and anxieties. In addition, providing a structured and predictable environment and minimizing alterations to schedules can also assist in reducing anxiety. Teaching relaxation techniques for use in the presence of behavioral methods such as systematic desensitization and imagined or in vivo practice to overcome feared situations in a step-by-step manner can also be beneficial.

Learning and Distractibility. Using direct instruction to focus on the task at hand and ensuring that instructions are repeated to check for errors can assist with day-to-day performance in a number of areas, academically and socially.

Classroom Seating. Seating close to the board and where the child can have eye contact with the teacher will assist focused performance and reduce distractibility. Seating away from major traffic routes in the classroom can also improve chances of success.

Medication. To date, few studies have investigated psychopharmacology alternatives for individuals with WS for such problems as anxiety, depression, and ADHD.

Post-Case Questions

1. Individuals with Williams syndrome (WS) often meet criteria for mental retardation/intellectual disability. Given Brian's assessment results and symptoms as presented in the case study, would Brian meet criteria for mental retardation according to the *DSM-IV-TR* (APA, 2000)? Would he qualify under IDEA, 2004? Support your answer with specific references to the criteria and Brian's assessment results.

2. There are several similarities and differences between individuals with WS and individuals with nonverbal learning disabilities. Compare information from Brian's case with that of Sandy Smith. What are the similarities and what are the differences in these two cases?

3. Children with WS are often seen as the opposite of those with autism/Asperger's disorder. What are the similarities and differences between the case studies of Brian and Dylan Bach?

4. As Brian's therapist, how would you help him deal with his fear of loud noises? Develop a program that can be used in the home and in the school.

5. Using Brian's strengths, develop a program to help him feel more successful socially.

REFERENCES

American Academy of Pediatrics Committtee on Genetics. (2001). Health care supervision for children with Williams-Beuren syndrome. *Pediatrics, 107,* 1192–1204.

American Psychiatric Association (APA). (2000). *Diagnostic and statistical manual of mental disorders* (4th ed., text revision). Washington, DC: Author.

Arens, R., Wright, B., Elliott, J., Zhao, H., Wang, P. P., Brown, L. W., et al. (1998). Periodic limb movements in sleep in children with Williams syndrome. *Journal of Pediatrics, 133,* 670–674.

Bellugi, U., Jarvinen-Pasley, A., Doyle, T., Reilly, J., Reiss, A., & Korenberg, J. (2007). Affect, social behavior and the brain in Williams syndrome. *Current Directions in Psychological Science, 10,* 99–104.

Belllugi, U., Lichtenberger, L., Jones, W., Lai, Z., & St. George, M. (2000). The neurocognitive profile of Williams syndrome: A complex pattern of strengths and weaknesses. *Journal of Cognitive Neuroscience, 12*(suppl. 1), 7–29.

Bellugi, U., Wang, P., & Jernigan, T. L. (1994). Williams syndrome: An unusual neuropsychological profile. In S. H. Browman & J. Grafram (Eds.), *Atypical cognitive deficits in developmental disorders* (pp. 23–56). Hillsdale, NJ: Erlbaum.

Davies, M., Howlin, P., & Udwin, O. (1997). Independence and adaptive behavior in adults with Williams syndrome. *American Journal of Medical Genetics, 70,* 188–195.

Doyle, T. F., Bellugi, U., Korenberg, J. R., & Graham, J. (2004). "Everyone in the world is my friend": Hypersociability in young children with Williams syndrome. *American Journal of Medical Genetics, 124A,* 263–273.

Dykens, E. M. (2003) Anxiety, fears, and phobias in persons with Williams syndrome. *Developmental Neuropsychopathology, 23,* 291–316.

Dykens, E. M., Hodapp, R. M., & Finucane, B. M. (2000). *Genetics and mental retardation syndromes: A new look at behavior and interventions.* Baltimore, MD: Paul H. Brookes.

Einfeld, S. L., Tonge, B. J., & Florio, T. (1997). Behavioral and emotional disturbance in individuals with Williams-Beuren syndrome. *American Journal of Mental Retardation, 102,* 45–53.

Flannery-Schroeder, E., & Kendall, P. C. (2000). Group and individual cognitive-behavioral treatments for youth with anxiety disorders: A randomized clinical trial. *Cognitive Therapy and Research, 24,* 251–278.

Gosline, J., Lillie, M., Carrington, E., Guerette, P., Ortlepp, C., & Savage, K. (2002). Elastic proteins: Biological roles and mechanical properties. *Philosophical Transactions of the Royal Society of London, Series, B, Biological Science, 357,* 121–132.

Johnson, L. B., Comeau, M., & Clarke, K. D. (2001). Hyperacusis in Williams-Beuren syndrome. *Journal of Otolaryngology, 30,* 90–92.

Jones, K. L., & Smith, D. W. (1975). The Williams elfin faces syndrome. *Journal of Pediatrics, 86,* 718–723.

Kaplan, P. (2006). The medical management of children with Williams-Beuren syndrome. In C. A. Morris, H. M. Lenhoff, & P. P. Wang (Eds.), *Williams-Beuren Syndrome: Research, evaluation and treatment* (pp. 83–106). Baltimore: Johns Hopkins University Press.

Kendall, P. C. (1994). Treating anxiety disorders in children: Results of a randomized clinical trial. *Journal of Consulting and Clinical Psychology, 62,* 100–110.

Klein, A. J., Armstrong, B., Greer, M. K., & Brown, F. R. (1990). Hyperacusis and otitis media in individuals with Williams syndrome. *Journal of Speech & Hearing Disorders, 55*(2), 339–344.

Klein-Tasman, B. P., & Mervis, C. B. (2003). Distinctive personality characteristics of 8-, 9-, and 10-year-olds with Williams syndrome. *Developmental Neuropsychology, 23,* 269–290.

Lenhoff, H. M. (2006). Absolute pitch and neuroplasticity in Williams-Beuren syndrome. In C. A. Morris, H. M. Lenhoff, & P. P. Wang (Eds.), *Williams-Beuren syndrome: Research, evaluation and treatment* (pp. 325–342). Baltimore: Johns Hopkins University Press.

Levine, K., & Wharton, R. (2000). Williams syndrome and happiness. *American Journal of Mental Retardation, 105,* 363–371.

Mervis, C. B., Morris, C. A., Bertrand, J., & Robinson, B. F. (1999a). Williams syndrome: Findings from an integrated program of research. In H. Tager-Flushberg (Ed.), *Neurodevelopmental disorders: Contributions to a new framework from the cognitive neurosciences* (pp. 65–110). Cambridge: MIT Press.

Mervis, C. B., Robinson, B. F., & Pani, J. R. (1999b). Visuospatial construction. *American Journal of Human Genetics, 65,* 1222–1229.

Meyer-Lindenberg, A., Hariri, A., Munoz, K., Mervin, C., Mattay, V., Morris, C. A., et al. (2005). Neural correlates of genetically abnormal social cognition in Williams syndrome. *Nature Neuroscience, 8,* 991–993.

Morris, C. A. (2006a). The dysmorphology, genetics, and natural history of Williams-Beuren syndrome. In C. A. Morris, H. M. Lenhoff, & P. P. Wang (Eds.), *Williams-Beuren syndrome: Research, evaluation and treatment* (pp. 3–17). Baltimore: Johns Hopkins University Press.

Morris, C. A. (2006b). Genotype-phenotype correlations in Williams-Beuren syndrome. In C. A. Morris, H. M. Lenhoff, & P. P. Wang (Eds.), *Williams-Beuren Syndrome: Research, evaluation and treatment* (pp. 59–82). Baltimore: Johns Hopkins University Press.

Olitsky, S. D., Sadler, L. S., & Reynolds, J. D. (1997). Subnormal binocular vision in the Williams syndrome. *Journal of Pediatric Opthalmology and Strabismus, 34,* 478–481.

Peretz, I., & Coltheart, M. (2003). Modularity of music processing. *Nature Neuroscience, 6,* 674–681.

Rosner, B. A., Hodapp, R. M., Fidler, D. J., Sagun, J. N., & Dykens, E. M. (2004). Social competence in persons with Prader-Willi, Williams and Down's syndromes. *Journal of Applied Research in Intellectual Disabilities, 17,* 209–217.

Rourke, B. P., Ahmad, S., Collins, D., Jayman-Abello, B., Hayman-Abello, S., & Warriner, E. M. (2002). Child clinical/pediatric neuropsychology: Some recent advances. *Annual Review of Psychology, 53,* 309–339.

Semel, E., &. Rosner, S. R. (2003). *Understanding Williams syndrome: Behavioral patterns and interventions.* Mahwah, NJ: Lawrence Erlbaum.

Singer Harris, N. G., Bellugi, U., Bates, E., Jones, W., & Rossen, M. (1997). Contrasting profiles of language development in children with Williams and Down syndromes. *Developmental Neuropsychology, 13,* 345–370.

Udwin, O., Davies, M., & Howlin, P. (1996). A longitudinal study of cognitive abilities and educational attainment in Williams syndrome. *Developmental Medicine & Child Neurology, 38*(11), 1020–1029.

Udwin O., & Yule, W. (1990). Expressive language of children with Williams syndrome. *American Journal of Medical Genetics, 6,* 108–114.

Udwin, O., & Yule, W. (1991). A cognitive and behavioral phenotype in Williams syndrome. *Journal of Clinical and Experimental Neuropsychology, 13,* 232–244.

Van Borsel, J., Curfs, L. M., & Fryns, J. P. (1997). Hyperacusis in Williams-Beuren syndrome: A sample survey study. *Genetic Counseling, 8,* 121–126.

Wang, P. P. (2006). The behavioral neuroscience of Williams-Beuren syndrome: An overview. In C. A. Morris, H. M. Lenhoff, & P. P. Wang (Eds.), *Williams-Beuren syndrome: Research, evaluation and treatment* (pp. 147–158). Baltimore: Johns Hopkins University Press.

Winter, M., Pankau, R., Amm, M., Gosch, A., & Wessel, A. (1996). The spectrum of ocular features in the Williams-Beuren syndrome. *Clinical Genetics, 49,* 28–31.

Jordan Neeson

Let Me Count the Ways

Jordan appeared agitated and upset as he walked into the clinic accompanied by his mother, Sally Neeson. The last thing Jordan wanted to do this morning was get dressed and go to a clinic. After all, he was on his summer vacation. Mrs. Neeson brought Jordan to the clinic because the school had recommended he be retained in the Grade 3 program due to academic difficulties and problems with attention and concentration. Work was rarely handed in or completed, and Jordan was beginning to really hate school.

DEVELOPMENTAL HISTORY/FAMILY BACKGROUND

Sally Neeson completed the intake survey and was available for a telephone intake conversation prior to bringing Jordan in for his assessment session. In recalling Jordan's birth history, Sally stated that the pregnancy was very hard on her. She had considerable nausea in the first 3 months and was very fatigued throughout the majority of her pregnancy. The delivery was also difficult, and Jordan had a lowered Apgar score because of birth complications. During the delivery, there were knots in the umbilical cord that cut off or reduced the oxygen supply. It seemed to take forever, but he was finally breathing on his own. Jordan seemed to rebound, and Sally was able to bring Jordan home with her when she left the hospital. Sally reported that appetite and sleep habits were normal for the first year.

At one point in the rather lengthy telephone conversation, Sally seemed particularly agitated and wanted to know why the interviewer was asking her personal questions about her marriage and relatives. After all, she just wanted to have Jordan tested for school; there was absolutely nothing wrong with his behavior and he didn't have any "mental" problems. Sally described Jordan as a sensitive boy who was very aware of his academic difficulties. Sally was definitive in stating that Jordan did not have any behavior problems. Sally also was very sure that there was no mental illness in either her family or her husband's. However, Sally did recall an aunt, Bertha, who wouldn't leave her house. She remembered family members talking about Bertha at family functions, because she would never attend. They said she was afraid to go outside and that she even had to have groceries delivered to her door. Sally could not recall any more about Bertha, who died about 10 years ago. Sally described herself as a bit of a worrier and said that her husband, Ralph, was pretty easygoing and just liked to watch sports on TV when he finished work at the office. Ralph sold insurance and Sally was a full-time homemaker. Jordan has a sister, Susy, who is 2 years older than Jordan, but she is very mature for her age. Sally said that Susy is 11 years old, going on 20, while Jordan is 9 years old, going on 5. When asked how they get along, Sally said that there are times when Susy, who really is a very patient person, just loses it when Jordan goes into what she calls his "weirdness." Sally explained that Jordan can be very fussy about particular things, such as having his food all separate on the plate with nothing touching (peas separate from potatoes and chicken). If the foods touch each other, then he does not want to eat it. Susy also is very annoyed when she has to take Jordan to school, since he takes forever to get ready in the morning, and bathroom rituals, such as hand washing or teeth brushing, seem to take a very long time. In the evening, Sally said that these bathroom routines are a normal part of his getting ready for bed, and she is fine with it because, unlike some kids, Jordan really likes being clean, and she never has to remind him to wash up or brush his teeth at bedtime.

Sally stated that Jordan's milestones were achieved on time and he walked at about 14 months and talked a bit later. Sally admitted that she was not a very good historian about dates and times. Jordan had some ear infections and had tubes inserted for drainage when he was about 3 years old. Sally described Jordan as a bit of a "mama's boy." She said that they were like "two peas in a pod," and when Jordan was a toddler, Sally took him everywhere with her. Jordan never went to preschool and Sally chose to homeschool him rather than send him to kindergarten. Jordan was not eager to go to first grade. Most mornings, his sister Susy had to hold his hand all the way to school so that he would not try to run the other way. Jordan was finally starting to settle into Grade 1 by December, when the family had an opportunity to purchase a home in a better neighborhood across town. As a result, Jordan had to change schools in January. Jordan started to resist going to school all over again, and Susy was once again forced to drag him with her. One good thing about the relocation was that the house was within eyesight of the school. Jordan's mother told him that if he missed her, he could just look across the street and know that she was thinking about him. This seemed to comfort Jordan somewhat.

One day shortly after the move, Jordan's mother had an appendicitis attack and had to be rushed to the hospital. Unfortunately, shortly after the ambulance arrived, Jordan's class was let outside for recess. Jordan was terrified when he saw the ambulance in his driveway, and he ran across the street just as the ambulance pulled away. Jordan ran down the street, yelling and crying, until he was retrieved by the school principal. For the next 5 months, Jordan was very fearful of leaving the house. He was afraid that something might happen to his mother if he left. Often he would ask to stay home, saying that he wasn't feeling very well. Sally said that she felt she was to blame because she had scared him with her appendicitis attack. Often she felt sorry for him and would let him stay home. By the end of first grade, Jordan's teachers were becoming concerned. He had missed quite a bit of school (21 days) and did not have a firm grasp of the fundamentals. His handwriting was very poor and most of his letters and numbers were reversed or upside down.

The following year, Sally tried to keep Jordan's absences in check by making promises that they would do things together after class. Jordan went to school, but his midyear report was very poor. Jordan was falling further and further behind. Sally tried reading with him at home, but Jordan seemed to have a very poor memory for the words, and each day it was like he had not seen the word before. Recently, the school recommended that Jordan repeat Grade 3. Sally finally decided to have him assessed.

Sally noted that Jordan's health had been good except for frequent complaints of headaches and stomachaches. Vision and hearing had been recently tested and were within the normal range. Although the intake supervisor sent behavior rating scales to Mrs. Neeson (Behavior Assessment Scale for Children [BASC2] and the Conners Parent Rating Scale [CPRS-R: L]) to be completed prior to his first assessment session, Sally forgot to complete them ahead of time and brought them with her to the first assessment session. As a result, it was not possible to score these results until after Jordan's first assessment session. In hindsight, having this information beforehand would have provided significant insight into Jordan's emotional profile. On a positive note, Sally was able to locate Jordan's Grade 3 teacher, who volunteered to complete the teacher forms during her summer break.

REASON FOR REFERRAL

Sally brought Jordan to the clinic because she wanted to know why he was having academic problems and whether Jordan had this "attention deficit" problem his teacher had mentioned. It was important to Mrs. Neeson that an assessment be completed before the new school year because she was very concerned about his success in the Grade 4 program and Jordan's growing reluctance to continue attending school.

ASSESSMENT RESULTS

Information regarding the specific assessment instruments used in this assessment and guidance in the interpretation of standard scores and T scores can be found in Appendix C.

The examiner found Jordan to be a very cautious participant in the assessment process. Jordan took a long time to respond to open-ended questions, and it was often difficult to determine whether he was formulating a response to a question, not comprehending the question, or lost in his own thoughts. During the first assessment session, Jordan participated in a semistructured clinical interview, and completed the WISC-IV and Bender Gestalt.

Jordan obtained a full scale IQ within the average range (IQ = 91; range 85–98), with a minimal, 2-point discrepancy between his Verbal Comprehension Index and Perceptual Reasoning Index. Jordan's profile indicated a number of strengths and weakness. Strengths were noted in vocabulary knowledge, picture concepts, and matrix reasoning (SS in the 11–13 range), while relative weaknesses were evident in comprehension (SS = 7), block design (SS = 6), digit span (SS = 6), and coding (SS = 6). The Working Memory Index (WMI) was at the 8th percentile (WMI = 79; range 73–88).

Jordan became very anxious when the stopwatch was introduced for the block design, coding, and symbol search tasks and was visibly upset. He said he was afraid that he would not be able to do his work on time. At this point, the examiner explained that he would have plenty of time to compete the tasks, and encouraged Jordan to continue, which he did. Throughout the assessment, Jordan was hesitant and tentatively approached each task in an approach-retreat style. Requests for question repetition were frequent, and Jordan also evidenced word-finding problems throughout. On a supplementary task of mental arithmetic, Jordan was observed tapping on his leg with his index finger, three times, before he would verbalize a response. When he saw that the examiner had noticed this, he pulled himself farther under the desk to conceal his legs from view. Other mannerisms were noted, such as touching his shoe before lifting his pencil and touching his ear before writing. However, Jordan was very subtle and secretive in performing these touching and counting compulsions, and it is likely that these rituals had escaped detection in most situations.

In addition to these behaviors, Jordan also demonstrated perfectionistic tendencies on many tasks. For example, he spent considerable time and effort carefully aligning his blocks to ensure that the edges were straight, a procedure that resulted in the loss of any possible bonus points he may have earned on the task. Similarly, repeated erasures to make the symbols "just so" resulted in reducing his score on the coding subtest. At Jordan's age level, it is considered to be significant if the Bender Gestalt designs are not completed within 7 minutes. Jordan required 20 minutes to complete the task. Jordan requested a ruler prior to starting the Bender Gestalt so that his lines could be straight and the paper could be partitioned. However, he was told that this was a task to see how well he could reproduce the designs himself, without a ruler. At this point, Jordan folded the paper to make eight sections and proceeded to draw each design in one of the folded squares. Despite all the attempts to structure his responses, the designs were very poorly executed, due to his weak visual motor integration skills. He spent a great deal of time checking and rechecking the number of dots on the cards, rather than actually executing the designs. Jordan would count the dots and start to draw, then recount to make sure that he had remembered the number correctly. On one design, Jordan recounted the dots 15 times before he completed the drawing. His responses were delayed even further by a ritualistic tendency to punctuate each drawing by the touching and tapping compulsions noted previously. Furthermore, although Jordan achieved above average scores on the untimed tasks of picture concepts and matrix reasoning (WISC-IV), he required excessive time to complete these tasks (twice the amount of time that normally would be required).

Jordan's response to the Woodcock Johnson-III Test of Achievement was also enlightening. It took an entire assessment session (almost 2 hours) to complete this instrument, which usually takes about 40 minutes. Prior to starting tasks, Jordan had a series of questions he asked to make sure that he understood what was required. On the spelling dictation test, Jordan spent several minutes erasing and rewriting words to improve the quality of his writing. Each mathematical calculation had a pizza drawn beside it (he called them "pizza faces"), with pepperoni slices indicating the number. For example, in order to perform the calculation 5 + 6, Jordan drew two pizzas: one with five slices of pepperoni and one with six slices of pepperoni. He then added up the pepperoni slices to obtain the final answer. Reading was also performed very hesitantly, with much doubting as to the correct pronunciation. Jordan continually requested feedback about his performance. On tasks that were not timed, Jordan demonstrated functioning about 2 years behind his grade level in all areas. Timed tasks resulted in even more pronounced academic lags, with very poor scores for academic fluency across all areas. Jordan continued to demonstrate the touching and tapping rituals noted during his previous assessment session.

After Jordan's first assessment session, it became evident from clinical observations that Jordan was experiencing many symptoms of obsessive-compulsive disorder (OCD), and that these ritualistic compulsions were likely causing significant problems at school and at home. Subsequent assessment sessions and behavioral reports would confirm the extent to which Jordan's secret world would be revealed.

Mrs. Neeson completed three behavioral rating scales: the Achenbach CBCL, BASC-2, and Conners scales. Clinical elevations were noted on the Thought Problems and Anxious/Depressed scales of the Child Behavior Checklist (CBCL); the Atypicality scale (BASC-2), and the Perfectionistic scale (Conners). Teacher reports noted elevations on the Attention and Thought Problems scales (Achenbach TRF); and on Atypicality, Adaptability, Learning Problems, Social Problems, and Attention Problems (BASC-2; Conners).

Further clinical interviews with Mrs. Neeson confirmed several other OCD behaviors and possible family history for the disorder. Mrs. Neeson said that Jordan could be superstitious, much like her mother, who seemed to have a superstitious saying for everything. Her mother was also what she called a "clean freak" and "checking perfectionist." Often they would make several attempts to get out of the driveway because her mother would constantly get out of the car and return to the house to make sure that the stove and coffee maker were turned off, or the door was locked securely. Although Sally did not consider these behaviors to be mental health problems, she did say it was very annoying to try to do anything with her mother. During the course of the conversation, Sally began to discover several likenesses between Jordan and his grandmother.

Sally was aware that Jordan did have some superstitions, like counting or touching rituals; however, she did not know the extent to which Jordan engaged in these behaviors. Sally became aware of these rituals when she caught him on occasion and questioned his repetitive behaviors. Jordan explained that it was about "threes." Apparently, he had some system worked out that if he repeated an action three times or tapped three times, then it would prevent something from happening. Sometimes, he had to do more than one count of "threes," for example, count to 3 two or three times in a row before he was satisfied. Further conversation revealed that Jordan also hoarded useless items under his bed and had other peculiar habits involving arranging and placement of certain items in very specific places. At the dinner table, the family had just accepted the fact that Jordan's fork and knife had to be perfectly aligned on the stripe of the place mat before he would begin eating. They were also accustomed to his odd mannerism of eating his food starting at the outside of the plate and working toward the center. Sally had just accepted these behaviors as "Jordanisms" and reasoned to herself that he would eventually outgrow the habits, or they would later develop into other orderly and beneficial ways of organizing his world.

Although Jordan's bathroom routines in the morning could be a source of annoyance when trying to get Jordan to school, Mrs. Neeson never thought that these behaviors would signal any cause for concern. Sally said that personal cleanliness was a strength of Jordan's, and she surely did not want to discourage his excellent hygiene.

Jordan completed the BASC-2 but had considerable difficulty with the yes/no response format. He had trouble making up his mind and was very uncomfortable not being able to use "sort of" as a response. On the Personality Inventory for Youth (PIY), the Feelings of Alienation scale was somewhat elevated due to Jordan's endorsement of items referring to repetitive and distressing thoughts and behaviors. Jordan did not endorse significant symptoms on the Child Depression Inventory (CDI), which was in the normal range for his age. Jordan did, however, admit to having a significant number of symptoms that were indicative of Worry/Attentional Concerns and Physiological Indicators on the Revised Child Manifest Anxiety Scale (RCMAS-2).

Based on clinical interviews, observations, and assessment results, increasing confirmation and support were obtained to suggest that Jordan suffered from an OCD. Jordan evidenced a number of compulsions: repeating, touching, counting, arranging, cleaning, and hoarding. Obsessive thoughts that seemed to drive these compulsions included concerns regarding doubts, lack of symmetry, contamination, and danger. Upon completion of the Children's Yale Brown Obsessive-Compulsive Scale (CY-BOCS), the examiner felt that Jordan's compulsions were time-consuming (likely involving more than 1 hour a day) and were interfering significantly with his schoolwork and social relationships. Furthermore, Jordan seemed to have very little control over his obsessions, nor was he able to resist performing the compulsive acts.

ISSUES, TRENDS, AND TREATMENT ALTERNATIVES

Although initially thought to be uncommon among children, current prevalence rates (between .5% and 2%) for OCD are similar for children and adults (Heyman et al., 2003); however, OCD in children often goes undiagnosed (Valleni-Basile et al., 1994). Because the disorder involves distressing and often unpleasant thoughts (obsessions) that drive unwanted acts or behaviors (compulsions) that can often appear embarrassing to children, OCD may be hidden by young children and adolescents, who secretly suffer in silence. OCD is characterized by obsessive thoughts that cause individuals to feel anxious and distressed, unless they engage in compulsive behaviors that serve to reduce the anxious state. Though OCD was once thought to have a primarily psychological basis, many who suffer from it show evidence of a biological basis for the disorder. Two areas of research have investigated biological explanations for the disorder: one explanation involves relating OCD behaviors to low levels of the neurotransmitter serotonin; the other explanation looks to malfunctioning in a key area of the brain.

Support for the serotonin theory has come from clinical trials that have established SSRIs such as fluoxetine (which serve to increase serotonin levels) as a successful treatment approach for OCD in adults and children/adolescents (Riddle et al., 1992; Rosenberg, Russell, & Fougere, 2005). Other biological theorists suggest that regions of the brain that convert sensory information into thoughts and actions (orbital region of the frontal cortex and caudate nuclei) may be overactive in people with OCD. Because the system malfunctions, impulses that should be filtered pass on to the thalamus and the person becomes driven to perform the acts (Peterson et al., 1998; Saxena & Rauch, 2000). Although the

DSM-IV-TR (APA, 2000) currently considers OCD as one of several anxiety disorders, results from several recent investigations have led researchers to question whether OCD should be conceptualized apart from the other anxiety disorders, as a distinct disorder based on unique physiological and neurological dysfunctional patterns (Bartz & Hollander, 2006; MacMaster et al., 2006).

Implications of the basal ganglia in OCD have also been suggested due to the high rates of comorbidity between OCD and Tourette's syndrome (King, Leonard, & March, 1998). Recently, research has amassed increasing support for some children who develop acute OCD symptoms resulting after a strep infection. These children, who demonstrate OCD symptoms from an autoimmune response to streptococcal infection (PANDAS), may require a very different method of treatment. Murphy and Pichichero (2002) monitored 12 cases of OCD with new-onset PANDAS and found that antibiotic treatment was effective in alleviating symptoms of OCD in all the children on first trial, and readministration successfully resulted in symptom remission for the 7 children who suffered a future relapse. The PANDAS-related OCD symptoms included hand-washing behaviors and preoccupation with germs, and are thought to result from an inflammation of specific regions of the brain.

According to Leonard, Swedo, and Rappaport (1991), some indicators that OCD behaviors may be occurring in children and adolescents include hoarding of useless objects, repeated touching of objects, taking an inordinate amount of time to complete tasks, and constant erasures or reworking of homework assignments. The long-term consequences of OCD have long been established, and the disorder is also often associated with other comorbid disorders (Bolton, Luckie, & Steinberg, 1995). Research evidence supports the importance of early intervention in childhood and adolescence in reducing the long-term severity of OCD (Leonard et al., 1993). Some of the most frequently occurring compulsions in child and adolescent populations include hand washing, checking, counting, touching, rearranging, and hoarding. The following obsessions have also been identified as occurring most frequently in child and adolescent populations: doubts, danger, contamination, aggression, and sexual impulses (King et al., 1998; Leonard et al., 1991).

Piacentini, Bergman, Keller, and McCracken (2003) studied functional impairment in 151 children and youth with OCD and report that almost 50% indicated OCD-related problems were evident in all three major domains: home, school, and social relationships. At school, concentration and homework surfaced as the two most critical areas of difficulty. Within the home, 60% of families of children with OCD report detrimental effects of the OCD behaviors on siblings and marital discord due to increased distress and feelings of manipulation (children attempting to engage family members in the OCD behavioral rituals; Cooper, 1996). Perfectionistic tendencies have also been significantly associated with OCD, and many cognitive theorists see perfectionism and responsibility (self-blame) as two of the core features of cognitive models of OCD (Obsessive Compulsive Cognitions Working Group; OCCWG, 2001, 2005). In their study of perfectionism and OCD, Wu and Cortesi (2009) found that perfectionism was most strongly associated with checking rituals related to ordering, arranging, symmetry, and grooming, and more weakly associated with contamination obsessions and washing compulsions, a finding that supported results of an earlier study by Julien, O'Connor, Aardema, and Todorov (2006). Wu and Cortesi (2009) suggest that this finding provides an important contribution for targeting cognitive restructuring in those with checking rituals.

Treatment for OCD

Historically, theoretical explanations for OCD have focused on the maintenance of fear and anxiety due to negative reinforcement, for example, performing the compulsion serves to reduce the anxiety caused by the obsession (behavioral theories); and the faulty appraisals (excessive self-doubt and self-blame, and feeling overly responsible for the obsessive thoughts), which tend to lock individuals into the obsessive and compulsive rituals (cognitive theoretical perspective). As a result, the majority of treatments have focused on behavioral techniques, such as exposure and response prevention (ERP) and cognitive-behavioral therapy techniques (CBT) for reframing maladaptive thinking (e.g., self-blame, self-doubt) into more positive thought patterns. From a neurobiological perspective, unlike the other anxiety disorders that respond to a wide range of medications (benzodiazepines and norepinephrine reuptake inhibitors), antidepressant medication (serotonin reuptake inhibitors: SRI, such as fluoxetine) has been the only category of medication that has been successful in alleviating symptoms of OCD in adults and assisting some children in reducing symptoms of OCD (Geller et al., 2001; Riddle et al., 1992).

Barrett, Farrell, Pina, Peris, and Piacentini (2009) conducted a meta-analysis of evidence-based treatments for children and youth with OCD, based on 21 studies conducted since 1994 that adhered to Type 1, 2, or 3 criteria as set out by Nathan and Gorman (2002). The two treatments that maintained the highest quality of empirical rigor (Type 1: randomized, controlled studies) were studies conducted by Barrett, Healy-Farrell, and March (2004) and the POTS Team (2004). Barrett and colleagues (2004) compared family-focused individual therapy (ICBT) and family-focused group therapy (GCBT) using a manualized family component "Freedom From Obsessions and Compulsions Using Cognitive-Behavioral Strategies" (FOCUS: Barrett, 2007), which was adapted from an earlier version of the individual treatment program established by March and Mulle (1998). The FOCUS program included sessions devoted to education, cognitive training, exposure and response prevention, and parent sessions. Follow-up 12 and 18 months after the completion of the program revealed that 70 % of those in the ICBT program and 84 % from the GCBT program remained symptom free (Barrett, Farrell, Dadds, & Boulter, 2005). The POTS study (POTS Team, 2004) compared treatment groups of youth with OCD (7–17 years of age) who were randomly assigned to one of four conditions: ICBT alone, sertraline (SRI medication) alone, combined ICBT and sertraline, or placebo pill. The CBT protocol was based on the program developed by March and Mulle (1998) and included 14 sessions over a 12-week period. Results revealed that all three treatments were superior to placebo, but that combined CBT and sertraline was superior to either treatment alone, although both of the CBT conditions (with and without sertraline) were superior to the sertraline alone condition, suggesting that CBT alone or in conjunction with SRI is an effective treatment for OCD in children and youth. Another study, conducted by Asbahr and colleagues (2005) and also using the GCBT format prescribed by March and Mulle (1998), found that youth who received CBT in the group condition demonstrated significantly lower rates of symptoms compared to youth who were treated with sertraline.

In another recent research program designed to compare the effects of combined treatments, Neziroglu, Yaryura-Tobias, Walz, and McKay (2000) found that children who received a combination of fluvoxamine and exposure and response prevention demonstrated more immediate improvement and continued improvement 2 years later, than those receiving either treatment in isolation. However, Sabine (2001) argues that CBT may be at least as effective and a less stressful alternative than ERP for children and adolescents with OCD. Techniques commonly used in CBT programs include cognitive restructuring, psychoeducation (to dispel irrational fears of contamination, etc.), distraction, and relaxation.

Post-Case Questions

1. It is possible to explain obsessive-compulsive disorder (OCD) from a number of theoretical positions. Develop a case formulation to explain the development of obsessions and compulsions based on the following theoretical perspectives, in light of Jordan's history: biomedical, behavioral, psychodynamic, cognitive, and family systems. Provide the specific treatment implications for Jordan's OCD based on each of the case formulations derived.

2. Behavioral Interventions for OCD often include exposure techniques designed to elicit the anxiety (either gradually or completely) by either direct exposure (in vivo) or in an imagined state. Graduated levels of anxiety can be predetermined by the construction of an anxiety hierarchy (from least to most stressful situation). Anxiety can be reduced by pairing increasing levels of anxiety-provoking situations with a relaxation response (muscle relaxation exercises).

Another intervention for OCD involves exposure followed by response prevention. In this technique, the child would be limited in performing the compulsion (e.g., checking, counting) when he or she has an obsessive thought. The child would agree to limit the response and would be rewarded for following through.

Design a behavioral intervention plan for Jordan's use in the classroom, using exposure and response prevention.

3. Discuss the relationship between separation anxiety and OCD in Jordan's developmental history.

4. Based on the *DSM-IV-TR* (APA, 2000) criteria for OCD (see Appendix D), what symptoms of OCD does Jordan demonstrate, and does he qualify for a diagnosis of OCD according to the *DSM?*

REFERENCES

American Psychiatric Association (APA). (2000). *Diagnostic and statistical manual of mental disorders* (4th ed., text revision). Washington, DC: Author.

Asbahr, F. R., Castillo, A. R., Ito, L. M., Latorre, M. R. D. O., Moriera, M. N., & Lotufo-Neto, F. (2005). Group cognitive-behavioral therapy versus sertraline for the treatment of children and adolescents with obsessive-compulsive disorder. *Journal of the American Academy of Child & Adolescent Psychiatry, 44,* 1128–1136.

Barrett, P. M. (2007). *FOCUS: Freedom from obsessions and compulsions using skills (therapist manual and workbooks)*. Brisbane, Australia: Pathways Health and Research Centre.

Barrett, P. M., Farrell, L. J., Dadds, M., & Boulter, N. (2005). Cognitive-behavioral family treatment of childhood obsessive-compulsive disorder: Long-term follow-up and predictors of outcome. *Journal of the American Academy of Child and Adolescent Psychiatry, 44,* 1005–1014.

Barrett, P. M., Farrell, L., Pina, A. A., Peris, T. S., & Piacentini, J. (2009). Evidence-based psychosocial treatments for child and adolescent obsessive-compulsive disorder. *Adolescent Psychology, 37,* 131–155.

Barrett, P. M., Healy-Farrell, L. J., & March, J. S. (2004). Cognitive-behavioral family treatment of childhood obsessive-compulsive disorder: A controlled trial. *Journal of the American Academy of Child and Adolescent Psychiatry, 43,* 46–62.

Bartz, J. A., & Hollander, E. (2006). Is obsessive-compulsive disorder an anxiety disorder? *Progress in Neuro-Psychopharmacological & Biological Psychiatry, 30,* 338–352.

Bolton, D., Luckie, M., & Steinberg, D. (1995). Long-term course of obsessive compulsive disorder treated in adolescence. *Journal of the American Academy of Child and Adolescent Psychiatry, 34,* 1441–1450.

Cooper, M. (1996). Obsessive compulsive disorder: Effects on family members. *American Journal of Orthopsychiatry, 66,* 296–304.

Geller, D. A., Hogg, S., Heiligenstein, J., Ricardi, R., Tamura, R., Kluszynski, S., et al. (2001). Fluoxetine treatment of obsessive-compulsive disorder in children and adolescents: A placebo-controlled clinical trial. *Journal of the American Academy of Child and Adolescent Psychiatry, 40,* 773–779.

Heyman, I., Fombonne, E., Simmons, H., Ford, T., Meltzer, H., & Goodman, R. (2003). Prevalence of obsessive-compulsive disorder in the British nationwide survey of child mental health. *International Review of Psychiatry, 15,* 178–184.

Julien, D., O'Connor, K. P., Aardema, F., & Todorov, C. (2006). The specificity of belief domains in obsessive-compulsive symptom subtypes. *Personality and Individual Differences, 41,* 1205–1216.

King, R. A., Leonard, H., & March, J. (1998). Practice parameters for the assessment and treatment of children and adolescents with obsessive-compulsive disorder. *Journal of the American Academy of Child and Adolescent Psychiatry, 37,* 27–45.

Leonard, H. L., Swedo, S. E., Lenane, M. C., Rettew, D. C., Hamburger, S. D., & Bartko, J. J. (1993). A 2- to 7-year follow-up study of 54 obsessive-compulsive children and adolescents. *Archives of General Psychiatry, 50,* 429–439.

Leonard, H. L., Swedo, S. E., & Rappaport, J. L. (1991). Diagnosis and treatment of obsessive compulsive disorder in children and adolescents. In M. T. Pato & J. Zohar (Eds.), *Current treatments of obsessive compulsive disorder* (pp. 87–102). Washington, DC: APA Press.

MacMaster, F. P., Russell, A., Mirza, Y. K., Keshavan, M. S., Banerjee, S. P., & Bhandari, R. (2006). Pituitary volume in pediatric obsessive compulsive disorder. *Biological Psychiatry, 59,* 252–257.

March, J. S., & Mulle, K. (1998). *OCD in children and adolescents: A cognitive behavioral treatment manual.* New York: Guilford.

Murphy, M. L., & Pichichero, M. E. (2002). Prospective identification and treatment of children with pediatric autoimmune neuropsychiatric disorder associated with Group A streptococcal infection (PANDAS). *Archives of Pediatric and Adolescent Medicine, 156,* 356–361.

Nathan, P. E., & Gorman, J. M. (2002). *A guide to treatments that work* (2nd ed.). New York: Oxford University Press.

Neziroglu, F., Yaryura-Tobias, J., Walz, J., & McKay, D. (2000). The effect of fluvoxamine and behavior therapy on children and adolescents with obsessive-compulsive disorder. *Journal of the American Academy of Child and Adolescent Psychiatry, 10,* 295–306.

Obsessive Compulsive Cognition Working Group. (2001). Development and initial validation of the Obsessive Beliefs Questionnaire and the Interpretation of Intrusions Inventory. *Behaviour Research and Therapy, 39,* 987–1006.

Obsessive Compulsive Cognition Working Group. (2005). Psychometric validation of the Obsessive Beliefs Questionnaire and Interpretation of Intrusions Inventory. Part 2: Factor analyses and testing of a brief version. *Behaviour Research and Therapy, 43,* 1527–1542.

Pediatric OCD Treatment Study Team: POTS. (2004). Cognitive-behavior therapy, sertraline, and their combination for children and adolescents with obsessive-compulsive disorder. *Journal of the American Medical Association, 292,* 1969–1976.

Peterson, B. S., Leckman, J. F., Arnsten, A., Anderson, G. M., Staib, L. H., Gore, J. C., et al. (1998). Neuroanatomical circuitry. In J. F. Leckman, D. J. Cohen, et al. (Eds.), *Tourette's syndrome: Tics, obsessions, compulsions: Developmental psychopathology and clinical care.* New York: John Wiley.

Piacentini, J., Bergman, R. L., Keller, M., & McCracken, J. (2003). Functional impairment in children and adolescents with obsessive-compulsive disorder. *Journal of Child and Adolescent Psychopharmacology, 13,* 61–69.

Riddle, M. A., Scahill, L., King, R. A., Hardin, M. T., Anderson, G. M., & Ort, S. I. (1992). Double-blind, crossover trial of fluoxetine and placebo in children and adolescents with obsessive-compulsive disorder. *Journal of the American Academy of Child and Adolescent Psychiatry, 31,* 1062–1069.

Rosenberg, D. R., Russell, A., & Fougere, A. (2005). Neuropsychiatric models of OCD. In J. S. Abramowitz & A. C. Houts (Eds.), Concepts and controversies in obsessive-compulsive disorder: Series in anxiety and related disorders. New York: Springer Science and Business Media.

Sabine, W. (2001). Obsessive compulsive disorder. In W. Lyddon & J. V. Jones, Jr. (Eds.), *Empirically supported cognitive therapies: Current and future applications* (pp. 118–133). New York: Springer.

Saxena, S., & Rauch, S. L. (2000). Functional neuroimaging and the neuroanatomy of obsessive-compulsive disorder. *Psychiatric Clinics of North America, 23,* 563–586.

Valleni-Basile, L. A., Garrison, C. Z., Jackson, K. L., Waller, J. L., McKeown, R. E., & Addy, C. L. (1994). Frequency of obsessive-compulsive disorder in a community sample of young adolescents. *Journal of the American Academy of Child and Adolescent Psychiatry, 33,* 782–791.

Wu, K. D., & Cortesi, G. G. (2009). Relations between perfectionism and obsessive-compulsive symptoms: Examination of specificity among the dimensions. *Journal of Anxiety Disorders, 123,* 393–400.

Shirley Yong

Worried to Perfection

Shirley was referred to the clinic by her family physician, Dr. Long, to evaluate her emotional status. For the past 6 months Shirley has been suffering from alopecia (hair loss), which has resulted in a prominent bald spot on the side of her head. Shirley was wearing a hat when she came to the interview accompanied by her mother, Lilly. Shirley presented as a serious young girl who looked more mature than her age of 11 years. Shirley was currently attending Heartfield Middle School in the regular Grade 6 program. Shirley has one younger sibling, a brother, David, who is 4 years of age. Lilly Yong is a nurse and her husband, David, is a computer programmer. The Yongs came to the United States from China when David was offered a position as a senior computer programmer with an American-based firm. The move occurred approximately 4 years prior to Shirley's birth. Lilly began working soon after their arrival in the United States. With a background in nursing, Lilly was able to obtain a position very quickly, due to a nursing shortage.

DEVELOPMENTAL HISTORY/FAMILY BACKGROUND

Shirley weighed 7 pounds 5.5 ounces at birth. Shirley's mother described the pregnancy as difficult and the labor as lengthy (12 hours). Although the delivery was normal, there were minor complications due to meconium aspiration, and Shirley stayed overnight in the pediatric critical care unit. Lilly said that to her knowledge, Shirley was relatively easy to manage as an infant, and for the most part slept well and had a good appetite. Mrs. Yong admitted, however, that Shirley's early years were spent primarily under the care of her mother, Shirley's grandmother.

Shortly after Shirley was born, Lilly's widowed mother came from China to live with the Yong family. This situation provided Lilly with a full-time caregiver for Shirley and, as a result, Lilly was able to return to work at the hospital almost immediately. The situation was also helpful for Lilly's mother, who was grieving the loss of her husband. When asked about other extended family, Lilly was not eager to discuss the extended family, saying that she had lost contact with most of her relatives. Lilly stated that to her knowledge there were no known mental or physical difficulties for any of the extended family members. With the exception of her mother, all other extended family continued to reside in China.

Although Lilly could not recall much information about Shirley's early development, she did believe that developmental milestones were generally achieved within the norm. There were some difficulties with speech, however, and Shirley did not say her first word until 18 months of age. Lilly remembered this vividly, since a colleague at work had an infant boy who was already saying words at 13 months, and Lilly felt that Shirley should have been talking by then as well. She had read that, generally, girls begin to speak earlier than boys and felt that the delay was unusual. The concern actually resulted in a fight between Lilly and her own mother, since Lilly began to blame her mother for Shirley's speech delay. Lilly was worried that Shirley's language delay may have resulted from the use of both Chinese and English in the home. Despite Lilly's protests, her mother continued to speak to Shirley exclusively in Chinese, while Lilly communicated with Shirley only in English.

Although Shirley was described as a relatively timid and passive toddler, Lilly admitted that there were times when Shirley could become quite irritable or fussy. On these occasions, Shirley would experience problems falling or staying asleep. Lilly recalled these incidents because they were very annoying and disruptive to her schedule. Being a nurse, Lilly needed her sleep to survive the lengthy shifts at the hospital. When Shirley had those fretful and irritable nights, it was impossible to get any sleep or to soothe Shirley.

Shirley remained very close to her grandmother, who was her primary caregiver, until the grandmother's death 7 years ago. Shirley's grandmother passed away in her sleep of natural causes when Shirley was 4 years of age. When asked how Shirley responded to her grandmother's death, Lilly said that the whole family was very distraught. Not only had they suffered a great personal loss, but now they had to face child care problems as well. Shirley could not adjust to the new babysitters and would cry endlessly when her mother left for work, only to refuse being comforted upon her return. Fretfulness, eating difficulties, and sleeping problems were prominent during this period. After an endless parade of babysitters, Lilly eventually had to quit work and stay home to care for Shirley. Lilly readily admitted that this was not an easy time for both of them. Shirley's demands for consoling were exhausting and frustrating, and Lilly longed for the days when she could return to work at the hospital.

Lilly enrolled Shirley in a half-day Montessori program, but Shirley would often say she felt sick and begged her mother to let her stay home. Often, Lilly would give in to Shirley's demands in order to stop the nagging; however, she began to resent the loss of personal time and space. Lilly welcomed Shirley's sixth birthday, since this signaled mandatory schooling and some relief from parenting demands. Shirley was able to find work as a nurse in a physician's office, which meant that she did not have to contend with shift work in the evenings. For the next year, Lilly tolerated Shirley's complaints about her school, the teacher, and her classmates, although she often felt a sense of relief after she dropped Shirley off at school and went to work. However, after a year of working, Lilly found out that she was pregnant, and 7 months later, Lilly was again homebound with her new son, David Jr.

Shirley, who was now 7 years old, did not adjust well to having a baby brother who was able to stay home with her mother while she was forced to go to school. Mornings were often disruptive and chaotic. Shirley would compete with David's cries for food with her own complaints of stomachaches or headaches and asking to stay home from school. Shortly after the birth of David Jr., Lilly was diagnosed with postpartum depression, which manifested in fatigue, loss of pleasure in activities, overwhelming bouts of sadness, and self-blame. During this time, Lilly increasingly relied on Shirley to help out with the baby and to assist with household chores. Often, Lilly would give in to Shirley's requests to stay home from school, especially when Lilly did not have the energy to engage in yet another battle or tend to the household chores. Lilly would often take naps while the baby slept. On these occasions, Shirley felt good about helping her mother and took her job of housecleaning very seriously.

Lilly says that all the cleaning Shirley did as a child may have backfired somewhat, because Shirley can now be "a real neat freak" to the extent that others find it annoying. Shirley will often become very upset at David Jr. for playing with toys in an area that she has cleaned. She is always at him to clean up and put his toys away before he has even had a chance to play with them. Shirley's own bedroom is arranged to perfection, with a place for everything and everything in its place. Shirley has asked for a lock for her door to make sure David Jr. does not go into her room or touch her things.

REASON FOR REFERRAL

Shirley was reticent throughout the initial part of the interview and did not volunteer any information spontaneously. Lilly said that she was concerned most recently because Shirley was demonstrating more tension and mood swings than she had seen before. The hair loss was particularly upsetting for both mother and daughter. She described her daughter as being more moody and short-tempered in the past few months. She also thought that her daughter was starting to be more secretive and not sharing information about what she was doing at school. Shirley would often come straight home after school and go right up to her room, where she locked the door. A call from Shirley's teacher last week revealed that Shirley was not handing in her assignments and that she was falling behind the class, especially in her journal writing.

When Lilly confronted Shirley about the missing assignments, Shirley stomped into her room and slammed the door. Lilly said that this was totally unacceptable behavior from her daughter. She also complained that Shirley was spending more and more time in her room and less time with the family. When asked what she was doing in her room, Shirley would say that she was working on her homework.

When asked about stress in her life, Shirley looked at her mother and then responded to the interviewer in a disgruntled manner. Attempts to engage Shirley in a conversation about her school life also met with minimal response. However, when asked how she was feeling, physically, Shirley said that she was not feeling very well and complained of headaches, stomachaches, and feeling very tired. Lilly interjected that Shirley was probably feeling tired because she wasn't sleeping much. Lilly added that she was not sleeping well herself; she had been awakened again last night by Shirley's making herself a snack at midnight. Lilly said that this seemed to be becoming a nightly ritual. (Although it was not addressed in the interview due to Shirley's guarded nature, Lilly had mentioned when making the appointment that Shirley was putting on much weight recently and had gained about 10 pounds in the past 2 months.) Shirley was obviously upset by her mother's comments and responded defensively, saying, "Well, I was hungry because I didn't like the tofu stuff you made for dinner. It was awful . . . like eating chalk." When asked if she could change one thing in her life, Shirley's eyes filled with tears and she said, "Everything."

With encouragement and patience, Shirley began to outline some of her worries about herself and her school situation. Shirley said that reading had become harder and harder because she couldn't concentrate. She would read a page and then not remember what she had read. She wanted to make her work very neat, and so she would print out all her assignments. Often she would work long hours making sure that the printing was perfect. Many times, she would have erased so many words that she would have to start all over again from the beginning on a fresh piece of paper. It took so long to print her work that she had problems finishing the assignments. Shirley said that she received only a "C" on the last assignment she handed in because it was incomplete. Shirley said she didn't tell her mother about the paper because she was embarrassed about her grade and felt guilty that her mother would be ashamed of her.

When asked about social life at school, Shirley admitted that she was miserable socially. Shirley said that she had no friends and the girls at school teased her. They were calling her names and laughing at her bald spot, saying that she was going to be a "bald old fat man." She had also found a note hidden in her desk from someone, with a drawing of a fat, bald person with the label "Shirley" written across the top. One girl had started a rumor that Shirley was contagious and that if you touched her, your hair would fall out too. Now no one would even stand beside her in line. Shirley was so upset the other day that she just hid in the restroom during recess so she wouldn't have to go outside. When asked if she knew why her hair had fallen out, Shirley denied that she had anything to do with it. Her mother seemed incredulous that the interviewer would ask Shirley if she had been pulling out her own hair.

When asked if she was a worrier, Shirley looked concerned and said that she couldn't stop worrying and added, "I worry about doing poorly at school; I worry about being late for school; and I worry about making mistakes in my work. I worry so much that I keep waking up because I think I forgot to do something, or I am afraid I might sleep in and be late for school. I can't sleep so I straighten and clean my room or go to the kitchen and eat something. But then I can't remember if I have cleaned the kitchen, so I go back and check on it. Sometimes, I have to keep checking because I don't remember seeing it clean enough." In response to Shirley's list of concerns, Lilly shook her head and said, "Kids today, what can you do about them." She then looked at Shirley and in an attempt to minimize her difficulties, stated that Shirley was exaggerating her problems. In China, she said, we did what we were told and worked hard at our schoolwork. That was our job. We didn't have time to complain about all these things. In our culture, we value emotional restraint, not self-indulgence.

ASSESSMENT RESULTS

The actual raw scores for Shirley's assessment can be found in Appendix A. The following is a summary of those findings. Information regarding specific assessment instruments and the interpretation of standard scores and T scores is available in Appendix C.

Shirley's responses to the WISC-IV were notable. The examiner reported that Shirley lost bonus points due to slow task completion resulting from tendencies to waste time lining up edges to meet perfectly on the block designs. Multiple responses to verbal items were also observed, as if Shirley were unsure when to stop giving information. Requests for feedback were also frequent.

Shirley's full-scale IQ was in the lower average range (IQ = 85; range 81–91) with a significant strength in Verbal Comprehension (VCI) with an index score of 100, (range 93–107), which was in the average range. Generally, weaknesses were evident in Perceptual Reasoning (PRI), with an index score of 84 (range 79–93); Working Memory (WMI), with an index score of 83 (range 77–92); and Processing Speed (PSI), with an index score of 83 (range 76–94). Academically, Shirley was functioning at grade level in language arts (Grade 5 level on both decoding and comprehension), but she was approximately one year behind grade placement in math computation. Shirley's mother's response to CBCL noted significant elevations on all Internalizing scales: Withdrawn/Depressed (T score = 68; borderline clinical range) and Anxious/ Depressed (T = 73) and Somatic Complaints (T = 74) were all in the clinical range. In addition, Thought Problems (T = 73) were in the clinical range due to many obsessions and repetition of acts, while Attention Problems (T = 70) were also in the clinical range, evident in problems of concentration and frequent confusion. On the CPRS-R:L, Mrs. Yong also endorsed clinical levels for Inattention, Anxious-Shy, Perfectionism, Social Problems, and Psychosomatic concerns. Shirley's teacher responded to the TRF with clinical elevations on scales for Anxious-Depressed Mood (T = 72), and Thought Problems (T = 70) noted in obsessions and repetitive behaviors. On the CTRS-R:L, Shirley's teacher indicated significant concerns in areas of Inattention, Anxious-Shy, Perfectionism, and Social Problems. According to the YSR, Shirley self-reported significant concerns for all Internalizing scales: Withdrawn/Depressed, Somatic Complaints, and Anxious/Depressed symptoms, as well as Social Problems and Thought Problems. Other problems noted by Shirley included many fears, nightmares, nail biting, sleep problems, and concerns regarding being overweight.

On the Beck Youth Inventories of Social and Emotional Impairment, Shirley endorsed significantly low levels for Self-Concept (below the 4th percentile) and significantly high levels of anxiety (98th percentile) and Depression (95th percentile). Clinical levels of depression were also noted on the Child Depression Inventory (CDI; Kovacs, 1992), with significant concern in areas of Ineffectiveness, Anhedonia, and Negative Self-Esteem. On the CDI, Shirley admitted that *she thinks about killing herself, but would not do it.* Shirley scored just below the threshold for high hopelessness on the Hopelessness scale (Kazdin, Rodgers, & Colbus, 1986).

ISSUES, TRENDS, AND TREATMENT ALTERNATIVES

Anxiety disorders represent one of the highest prevalence rates for disorders occurring in childhood and adolescence, with a rate of up to 13% for one-year prevalence (Costello et al., 1996). Although the *DSM-IV-TR* (APA, 2000) lists separation anxiety disorder as the only anxiety disorder in the category "first diagnosed in infancy, childhood or adolescence," young children and adolescents can and do display many types of anxiety disorders. According to the *DSM-IV-TR,* when considering a diagnosis of general anxiety disorder (GAD) in children, "a thorough evaluation for the presence of other childhood anxiety disorders should be done to determine whether the worries may be better explained by . . . separation anxiety disorder, social phobia and obsessive compulsive disorder" (p. 474). There is also a likelihood that GAD symptoms of "restlessness" and "concentration problems" may be mistaken as symptoms of ADHD. In addition to the various forms of anxiety disorders, diagnosis in childhood is further complicated by some disorders appearing early and others manifesting at later developmental stages. One study reported an increase in prevalence rate for anxiety disorders from 7% at 11 years of age to almost 20% in early adulthood (Kovacs & Devlin, 1998). In addition, high rates of comorbidity are evident within the anxiety disorders, and studies report between 65% and 95% of the population demonstrating more than one anxiety or affective disorder (Last, Perrin, Jersen, & Kazdin, 1992). Many adults with anxiety and depressive disorders report that these problems had their onset in childhood, indicating that anxiety disorders can represent a stable construct across the life span (Ollendick & King, 1994).

Perfectionism can be conceptualized as an individual's tendency to set goals or expectations that are overly rigid, excessively high, and subject to self-criticism when the exceptionally high standards are not met (Frost, Marten, Lehart, & Rosenblate, 1990). Pushed to the extreme, perfectionistic tendencies can place individuals at increased risk for a number of mental health issues, including depression (Enns & Cox, 2005; Rice & Aldea, 2006) and worry (Change et al., 2007; Santanello & Gardner, 2007).

In childhood, rates for comorbidity of anxiety and depression have been reported to be as high as 60–70% (Kovacs & Devlin, 1998), which has led some theorists to speculate that in childhood "negative affectivity" may be a more accurate reflection of variations of the same syndrome (Laurent et al., 1999), rather than two unique disorders. There is support for this line of reasoning, based on high rates of comorbidity in childhood and the fact that developmentally, the onset of anxiety is earlier than the onset for depression (Kovacs & Devlin, 1998). In the past decade, research has focused on investigating the role of temperamental influences on increasing the risk for both disorders in children (Compas, Connor-Smith, & Jaser, 2004). Studies have demonstrated that children with high levels of negative affectivity (NA) are at increased risk for the development of anxiety and depression (Lonigan, Vasey, Phillips, & Hazen, 2004). With respect to anxiety, it has been demonstrated that an attentional bias toward threat can be an important factor in precipitating and maintaining anxiety problems (Dandeneau, Baldwin, Baccus, Sakellaropoulo, & Pruessner, 2007). Muris and Ollendick (2005) suggest that children who have a high tendency to react emotionally (high reactivity) and poor effortful control (EC) suffer from an inability to defer their attention from the bias to threat, resulting in increased fear (negative affectivity) and social withdrawal (internalizing problems). Other children who are also highly reactive, emotionally, but who have poor behavioral control may react aggressively (externalizing problems). Furthermore, Lonigan and Vasey (2008) suggest that while high NA is a necessary condition for anxiety, it is not a sufficient condition, and that low effortful control (EC) is also a required ingredient. Studies have found that these patterns (high NA, low EC) predicted internalizing problems in children (Muris, Meesters, & Bliglevens, 2007), and that fearfulness at age 10 predicted the development of internalizing symptoms 2–3 years later.

Longitudinal studies have demonstrated that children who experience the combined effect of anxiety and depression have more severe and persistent problems, as well as present with a more serious history of risk factors (Moffit et al., 2007). In addition to temperamental factors, such as NA and EC, contextual influences have also been related to the development of anxiety and depression in children. Some of the pathways that have been linked to anxiety and depression include family adversities and maternal distress (Essex et al., 2006; Rutter, Moffit, & Caspi, 2006), which can be moderated by the availability or lack of social support (Leech, Larkby, Day, & Day, 2006). In a recent study of the potential pathways and predictors of anxiety and depression, Karevold, Roysamb, Ystrom, and Mathiesen (2009) identified two main pathways: temperament (emotionality), and early family adversity in support of the concept of "equifinality" (Cicchetti & Toth, 1998), namely, that different pathways might lead to the same outcome. Leve, Kim, and Pears (2005) found that the combination of child shyness at 5 years of age and maternal distress predicted an increased trajectory for internalizing problems for girls in early, middle, and late childhood, through adolescence, while Essex, Klein, Cho, and Kraemer (2003) found that exposure to maternal depression, family conflict, or divorce from the preschool years forward increased the risk for internalizing problems in girls. Furthermore, Eaves, Silberg, and Erkani (2003) found that genes specific to depression can lead to an increased sensitivity to the impact of adverse life events, increasing the risk through genetic vulnerability in children of distressed mothers. Other factors in the family environment that have been associated with increased anxiety in children, include overprotective or overly controlling parents, overinvolvement, encouragement of avoidant/anxious responses, parental rejection, parental criticism, and lack of parental warmth (Hudson & Rapee, 2002; Micco & Ehrenreich, 2008).

Trichotillomania (TTM)

In addition to symptoms of anxiety and depression, Shirley also suffers from symptoms of TTM, which manifests in persistent and excessive pulling out of one's own hair, resulting in noticeable hair loss or alopecia. The most common areas affected include the scalp, eyebrows, and eyelashes. Since the dermatologist had already ruled out any medical cause for the hair loss, it was believed that Shirley was responsible for pulling out her own hair, although she and her mother adamantly denied this possibility.

According to the *DSM-IV-TR* (APA, 2000), TTM is one of the impulse-control disorders (e.g., pyromania, kleptomania, and pathologic gambling). The impulse disorders all share an increase in tension, prior to the impulse, in this case hair pulling, and a sense of pleasure or relief once the act (hair pulling) is completed. It has been suggested that individuals with the disorder often deny their hair-pulling behavior and try to conceal the results. Children may not meet criteria for the disorder because they may not be aware of the tension/release cycle. Nail biting is often also evident, as are symptoms of other disorders, such as the mood and anxiety disorders (especially obsessive compulsive disorder), and eating disorders (*DSM-IV-TR;* APA, 2000, pp. 674–676). It has been suggested (Kaplan, 1992) that TTM might better be included among the anxiety disorders, especially because of its association with obsessive-compulsive features. Onset is typically between 9 and 13 years, and children typically pull their hair when alone and in a relaxed situation: on the phone, watching television, reading, or falling asleep (Tay, Levy, & Metry, 2004).

The *DSM-IV-TR* suggests that hair pulling may represent a temporary "habit" in childhood, devoid of symptoms of tension and relief, and should not be diagnosed as trichotillomania unless it has persisted over several months. TTM can be triggered by a number of situations, including separation from an attachment figure, problems with school performance, birth of a young sibling, or sibling rivalry (Tay et al., 2004). Children with TTM also have more perfectionistic tendencies and low feelings of self-worth (Soriano et al., 1996).

Treatments of Anxiety Disorders in Children

Cognitive-Behavioral Methods. In their review of empirically supported treatments for children with phobic and anxiety disorders, Ollendick and King (1998) found several treatments to be effective in reducing fears and phobias. However, with respect to anxiety disorders, the authors found only one treatment method, cognitive-behavioral procedures, with or without family inclusion, that met criteria for the probably efficacious treatment category.

Despite the high rate of prevalence for anxiety disorders, until recently there have been relatively few studies regarding the treatment of childhood anxiety disorders. Cognitive-behavioral treatment (CBT) for childhood anxiety disorders has received increasing empirical support, with Ollendick and King (1998) citing several studies conducted by separate research teams in the United States and Australia. Kendall and colleagues (1992) have developed several treatment strategies, based on CBT methods, including a treatment manual called *Coping Cat,* for children with generalized anxiety disorder, which has been demonstrated effective in several studies. The CBT program focuses on four components: (a) training children to recognize feelings and physiological responses associated with anxiety, (b) helping them become aware of self-defeating negative attributions/expectations, (c) reframing negative thoughts into positive constructive thoughts, and (d) evaluating successful coping. Children are taught behavioral strategies over 16 sessions and increase their ability to manage anxious responses through the use of role-play, modeling, in vivo exposure, and relaxation training (Kane & Kendall, 1989; Kendall et al., 1992; Kendall & Treadwell, 1996). In Australia, researchers investigated the combined effect of CBT for children and a family component (FAM). The FAM included a parallel 12-week program for parents to learn skills in areas such as supportive praise for courageous behavior and planned ignoring for excessive anxious responses. Results revealed that the Australian children treated with a 12-week CBT + FAM performed significantly better than children treated by CBT alone (Bartlett, Dadds, & Rapee, 1996). More recently, Wood, Piacentini, Southam-Gerow, Chu, and Signam (2006) demonstrated that children who received CBT treatment for anxiety disorders with their families (family-focused CBT) had better outcomes than children who received child-focused CBT, with minimal parent involvement.

Medical Management of Anxiety Disorders. The selective serotonin reuptake inhibitors (SSRIs) have been found to successfully alleviate symptoms of obsessive-compulsive disorder (OCD) in adolescents and children (Riddle, Subramaniam, & Walkup, 1998). Other treatments that are currently under increased investigation include exposure with response prevention and cognitive-behavioral therapy. Exposure procedures such as desensitization or flooding can bring the child into increased contact with the anxiety-provoking stimulus either in reality (in vivo) or through guided imagery or pictures. The child is taught a form of muscle relaxation that is incompatible with heightened anxiety in an attempt to link the object or situation that evokes anxiety with a lower level of arousal (relaxed state).

Neziroglu, Yaryura-Tobias, Walz, and McKay (2000) found that combining an SSRI (fluvoxamine) with behavior therapy of exposure and response prevention was superior to medication alone and that children and adolescents in the study continued to show improvement 2 years later. March and Mulle (1998) have developed a cognitive-behavioral treatment manual for children and adolescents with OCD that provides a session-by-session guide for clinicians through the four stages of treatment: psychoeducational, cognitive training, mapping OCD, and graded exposure and response prevention. Initial studies of the effectiveness of the manualized program with adolescents are encouraging (Thieneman, Martin, Creggar, Thompson, & Dyer-Friedman, 2001).

Treatment of Trichotillomania (TTM) in Childhood

Treatment for TTM in children and youth can be challenging, since they often deny that they are pulling out their own hair. Nonpharmacologic treatments such as cognitive and cognitive-behavioral therapy should be considered initially, especially if the psychosocial trigger(s) can be identified (e.g., sibling rivalry, birth of a new sibling). Golomb and Vavrichek (2000) have developed a workbook for children and adolescents (10 to 16 years of age) to assist them in developing the means for "How to solve the trichotillomania puzzle" by developing strategies to help manage their behavior. Parents can adapt the workbook for use with younger children. Other behavioral methods that can be used with children include

- habit reversal (methods to increase awareness, develop competing replacement behaviors, practice stress/anxiety reduction, and increase parental support and encouragement);
- self-monitoring (charting behavior and responses); and
- teaching replacement behaviors (this can be used alone to develop socially appropriate behaviors that can be used as alternatives to hair pulling; Ellis & Roberts, 2006).

Post-Case Questions

1. The co-occurrence of depression and anxiety in childhood is not unusual.

   In younger children, this co-occurrence is frequently associated with a depressive-anxious syndrome (see CBCL: Achenbach). The features of this syndrome have also been referred to as *negative affectivity*. Research has demonstrated that while children in the sixth grade can demonstrate the separate syndromes for all three presentations of these disorders (anxiety, depression, and negative affectivity), children in the third grade are better represented by the combined syndrome of negative affectivity alone (Cole, Truglio, & Peeke, 1997). It has been suggested that developmentally, negative affectivity represents a less differentiated form of a syndrome primarily dominated by negative emotions. Developmentally, differentiation into anxious responses (physiological arousal) and depressed mood (deflated mood) would occur at a later date.

Given the information in the previous paragraph, describe how Shirley's anxious and depressed symptoms can be conceptualized with respect to negative affectivity.

2. According to the *DSM-IV-TR* (APA, 2000), Shirley might meet criteria for one of the anxiety disorders. Given the symptoms noted in the case and your understanding of the different anxiety disorders (see *DSM-IV-TR* criteria in Appendix D), which anxiety disorder does Shirley most likely exhibit? What are the symptoms that meet the *DSM-IV-TR* criteria?

3. Gibbs and Huang (2001) outline three broad ways in which ethnicity can influence mental health in children and adolescents. First, ethnicity can shape beliefs about what constitutes mental illness at a general and specific level. Next, cultures may also influence the manifestation of the symptoms (internalizing, through physical somatic symptoms, externalizing), as well as reactive patterns and defensive styles. Ultimately, ethnicity can also be highly influential in determining whether it is acceptable to seek assistance for mental health issues outside of the family, and who should be consulted for assistance (family elder, priest, minister, herbalist, etc.). Some high-risk factors related to cultural context include high risk for suicide in native populations and dropout rates for ethnic minorities.

Huang and Ying (2001) discuss a number of potential stressors and conflicts that may face the bicultural child who is attempting to incorporate values from both the Chinese and the American cultures. While expression of feelings is often encouraged in Western cultures, the Chinese culture values emotional restraint, especially for negative emotions. The authors also suggest that although many children develop somatic complaints in response to stress, this particular form of symptom expression is often accompanied by sleep and appetite disturbances, followed by declines in academic performance in children of traditional Chinese American families. A major barrier to effective treatment for these children is that mental health service is highly underutilized by the Chinese American population. For those few families who seek treatment, drop out after the initial sessions is highly probable.

Discuss the potential impact of cultural contexts on Shirley's emotional status.

4. Children of depressed mothers are twice as likely to become depressed themselves (Peterson, Compas, Brooks-Gunn, Ey, & Grant, 1993). Possible suggestions for this linkage include lack of adequate models for emotion regulation; excessive use of controlling, irritable, and impatient parenting (Cicchetti & Toth, 1998); and lack of emotional availability (Malphurs et al., 1996). Girls seem to be at much higher levels of risk for transmission of depression than boys (Hops, 1992). Based on this information, discuss Shirley's depressive features relative to her mother's.

5. While boys are more likely to use bullying tactics, which rely on physical aggression, girls have been found to engage in forms of *relational aggression,* such as causing hurt to others through the propagation of rumors, ridicule, exclusion from a peer group, or withdrawal of

friendship and support (Crick & Grotpeter, 1995). Research has demonstrated that girls are more relationally aggressive than males, and that relational aggression is associated with peer rejection and feelings of loneliness and isolation (Crick, Casas, & Mosher, 1997; Crick & Grotpeter, 1995).

Explain how relational aggression had an impact on Shirley's socialization. What could be done at a school level to counteract this behavior in peers?

REFERENCES

Bartlett, P. M., Dadds, M. R., & Rapee, R. M. (1996). Family treatment of childhood anxiety: A controlled trial. *Journal of Consulting and Clinical Psychology, 64,* 333–342.

Chang, E. C., Zumberg, K. M., Sanna, L. J., Girz, L. P., Kade, A. M., Shair, S. R., et al. (2007). Relationship between perfectionism and domains of worry in a college student population: Considering the role of BIS/BAS motives. *Personality and Individual Differences, 43,* 925–936.

Cicchetti, D., & Toth, S. L. (1998). The development of depression in children and adolescents. *American Psychologist, 53,* 221–241.

Cole, D. A., Truglio, R., & Peeke, L. (1997). Relation between symptoms of anxiety and depression in children: A multitrait-multimethod-multigroup assessment. *Journal of Consulting and Clinical Psychology, 65,* 110–119.

Compas, B. E., Connor-Smith, J., & Jaser, S. S. (2004). Temperament, stress reactivity, and coping, implications for depression in childhood and adolescence. *Journal of Clinical Child and Adolescent Psychology, 33,* 21–31.

Costello, E. J., Angold, A. A., Burns, B. J., Stangl, D. K., Tweed, D. L., Erkanli, A., et al. (1996). The Great Smoky Mountains study of youth. Goals, design, methods, and, the prevalence of *DSM-III-R* disorders. *Archives of General Psychiatry, 53,* 1129–1136.

Crick, N. R., Casas, J. F., & Mosher, M. (1997). Relational and overt aggression in preschool. *Developmental Psychology, 33,* 579–588.

Crick, N. R., & Grotpeter, J. K. (1995). Relational aggression, gender and social psychological adjustment. *Child Development, 66,* 710–722.

Dandeneau, D. D., Baldwin, M. W., Baccus, J. R., Sakellaropoulo, M., & Pruessner, J. C. (2007). Cutting stress off at the pass: Reducing vigilance and responsiveness to social threat by manipulating attention. *Journal of Personality and Social Psychology, 93,* 651–666.

Eaves, L., Silberg, J., & Erkani, A. (2003). Resolving multiple epigenetic pathways to adolescent depression. *Journal of Child Psychology and Psychiatry, 44,* 1006–1014.

Ellis, C. R., & Roberts, J. J. (2006). Anxiety disorder: Trichotillomania. *EMedicine Specialties*. Retrieved May 16, 2010, from http://emedicine.medscape.com/article/915057 (The article can be accessed once the reader registers to creates a free account.)

Enns, M. W., & Cox, B. J. (2005). Perfectionism, stressful life events, and the 1-year outcome of depression. *Cognitive Therapy and Research, 29,* 541–553.

Essex, M. J., Klein, M. H., Cho, E., & Kraemer, J. C. (2003). Exposure to maternal depression and marital conflict: Gender differences in children's later mental health symptoms. *Journal of the American Academy of Child and Adolescent Psychiatry 42,* 728–737.

Essex, M. J., Kraemer, J. C., Armstrong, J. M., Boyce, T., Goldsmith, H. H., Klein, K. M. H., et al. (2006). Exploring risk factors for the emergence of children's mental health problems. *Archives of General Psychiatry, 63,* 1246–1256.

Frost, R. O., Marten, P., Lahart, C., & Rosenblate, R. (1990). The dimensions of perfectionism. *Cognitive Therapy and Research, 14,* 449–468.

Gibbs, J. T., & Huang, L. N. (Eds.). (2001). *Children of color.* San Francisco: Jossey- Bass.

Golomb, R. G., & Vavrichek, S. M. (2000). *The hair pulling "habit" and "you": How to solve the trichotillomania puzzle.* Silver Springs, MD: Writers' Cooperative of Greater Washington.

Hops, H. (1992). Parental depression and child behavior problems: Implications for behavioral family intervention. *Behavior Change, 9,* 126–138.

Huang, L. N., & Ying, Y. W. (2001). Chinese American children and adolescents. In J. T. Gibbs, N. L. Huang, et al. (Eds.), *Children of color.* San Francisco: Jossey-Bass.

Hudson, J. L., & Rapee, R. M. (2002). Parent-child interactions and anxiety disorders: An observational study. *Journal of Clinical Child and Adolescent Psychology, 31,* 548–555.

Kane, M., & Kendall, P. C. (1989). Anxiety disorders in children: A multiple baseline evaluation of a cognitive-behavioral treatment. *Behavior Therapy, 20,* 499–508.

Kaplan, A. (2006). Trichotillomania: U.S. prevalence at 2%, experts report at national conference. *PsychiatricTimes, 9*(12), 33–34.

Karevold, E., Roysamb, E., Ystrom, E., & Mathiesen, K. S. (2009). Predictors and pathways from infancy to symptoms of anxiety and depression in early adolescence. *Developmental Psychology, 45,* 1051–1060.

Kazdin, A. E., Rodgers, A., & Colbus, D. (1986). The Hopelessness Scale for Children: Psychometric characteristics and concurrent validity. *Journal of Consulting and Clinical Psychology, 54,* 241–245.

Kendall, P. C., Chansky, T. E., Kane, M. T., Kim, R. S., Kortlander, E., Ronan, K. R., et al. (1992). *Anxiety disorders in youth: Cognitive behavioral interventions.* Needham Heights, MA: Allyn & Bacon.

Kendall, P. C., & Treadwell, K. R. H. (1996). Cognitive behavioral treatment for childhood anxiety disorders. In E. D. Hibbs & P. S. Jensen (Eds.), *Psychosocial treatments for child and adolescent disorders: Empirically-based strategies for clinical practice.* Washington, DC: American Psychological Association.

Kovacs, M. (1992). *Children's Depression Inventory manual.* Toronto: Multi-Health Systems.

Kovacs, M., & Devlin, B. (1998). Internalizing disorders in childhood. *Journal of Child Psychology and Psychiatry and Allied Disciplines, 39,* 47–63.

Last, C. G., Perrin, S., Jersen, M., & Kazdin, A. E. (1992). *DSM III-R* anxiety disorders in children: Sociodemographic and clinical characteristics. *Journal of the American Academy of Child and Adolescent Psychiatry, 31,* 1070–1075.

Laurent, J., Catanzaro, S. J., Joiner, T. E., Rudolph, K. D., Potter, K. I., Lambert, S., et al. (1999). A measure of positive and negative affect for children: Scale development and preliminary validation. *Psychological Assessment, 11*(3), 326–338.

Leech, S. L., Larkby, C. A., Day, R., & Day, N. L. (2006). Predictors and correlates of high levels of depression and anxiety symptoms among children at age 10. *Journal of the American Academy of Child and Adolescent Psychiatry, 45,* 223–230.

Leve, L. D., Kim, H. K., & Pears, K. C. (2005). Childhood temperament and family environment as predictors of internalizing and externalizing trajectories from ages 5 to 17. *Journal of the American Academy of Child and Adolescent Psychiatry, 45,* 223–230.

Lonigan, C. J., & Vasey, M. W. (2009). Negative affectivity, effortful control and attention to threat-relevant stimuli. *Journal of Abnormal Child Psychology, 37,* 387–399.

Lonigan, C. J., Vasey, M. W., Phillips, B., & Hazen, R. A. (2004). Temperament, anxiety, and the processing of threat-relevant stimuli. *Journal of Clinical Child and Adolescent Psychology, 33,* 8–20.

Malphurs, J. E., Field, T. M., Larraine, C., Pickens, J., Lelaez-Nogueras, M., Yando, R., et al. (1996). Altering withdrawn and intrusive interaction behaviors of depressed mothers. *Infant Mental Health Journal, 17,* 152–160.

March, J. S., & Mulle, K. (1998). *OCD in children and adolescents: A cognitive behavioral treatment manual*. New York: Guilford.

Micco, J. A., & Ehrenreich, J. T. (2008). Children's interpretation and avoidant response biases in response to non-salient and salient situations: Relationships with mothers' threat perception and coping expectations. *Journal of Anxiety Disorders, 22*, 371–385.

Moffit, T. E., Harrington, J., Caspi, A., Kim-Cohen, J., Goldberg, D., Gregory, A. M. et al. (2007). Depression and generalized anxiety disorder: Cumulative and sequential comorbidity in a birth cohort followed prospectively to age 32 years. *Archives of General Psychiatry, 64*, 651–660.

Muris, P., Meesters, C., & Blijlevens, P. (2007). Self reported reactive and regulative temperament in early adolescence: Relations to internalizing and externalizing problem behavior and "Big Three" personality factors. *Journal of Adolescence, 30*, 1035–1049.

Muris, P., & Ollendick, T. H. (2005). The role of temperament in the etiology of child psychopathology. *Clinical Child and Family Psychology Review, 8*, 271–289.

Neziroglu, F., Yaryura-Tobias, J. A., Walz, J., & McKay, D. (2000). The effects of fluvoxamine and behavior therapy on children and adolescents with obsessive compulsive disorder. *Journal of Child & Adolescent Psychopharmacology, 10*, 295–306.

Ollendick, T. H., & King, N. J. (1994). Diagnosis, assessment and treatment of internalizing problems in children: The role of longitudinal data. *Journal of Consulting and Clinical Psychology, 62*, 919–927.

Ollendick, T. H., & King, N. J. (1998). Empirically supported treatments for children with phobic and anxiety disorders: Current status. *Journal of Clinical Child Psychology, 27*, 156–167.

Peterson, A. C., Compas, B., Brooks-Gunn, J., Ey, S., & Grant, K. E. (1993). Depression in adolescence. *American Psychologist, 48*(2), 155–168.

Rice, K. G., & Aldea, M. A. (2006). State dependence and trait stability of perfectionism: A short-term longitudinal study. *Journal of Counseling Psychology, 53*, 205–213.

Riddle, M. A., Subramaniam, G., & Walkup, J. T. (1998). Efficacy of psychiatric medications in children and adolescents: A review of controlled studies. *Psychiatric Clinics of North America: Annual of Drug Therapy, 5*, 269–285.

Rutter, M., Moffit, T. E., & Caspi, A. (2006). Gene-environment interplay and psychopathology: Multiple varieties but real effects. *Journal of Child Psychology and Psychiatry, 47*, 226–261.

Santanello, A. W., & Gardner, F. L. (2007). The role of experiential avoidance in the relationship between maladaptive perfectionism and worry. *Cognitive Therapy and Research, 30*, 319–332.

Soriano, J. L., O'Sullivan, R. L., Baer, L., Phillips, K. A., McNally, R. J., & Jenike, M. A. (1996). Trichotillomania and self esteem: A survey of 62 hair pullers. *Journal of Clinical Psychiatry, 199*, 77–82.

Thieneman, M., Martin, J., Creggar, B., Thompson, H., & Dyer-Friedman, J. (2001). Manual-driven group cognitive-behavioral therapy for adolescents with obsessive compulsive disorder: A pilot study. *Journal of the American Academy of Child & Adolescent Psychiatry, 40*, 1254–1260.

Tay, Y.-K., Levy, M. L., & Metry, D. W. (2004). Trichotillomania in childhood: Case series and review. *Pediatrics, 113*, 494–498.

Wood, J. J., Piacentini, J. C., Southam-Gerow, M., Chu, B., & Sigman, M. (2006). Family cognitive behavioral therapy for child anxiety disorders. *Journal of the American Academy of Child and Adolescent Psychiatry, 45*, 314–321.

Matthew Morgan

Out of Control and In Control

Since Matthew's mother left, when he was only 1 year old, Tom has struggled continually to meet his son's escalating needs. Being a single father was a very difficult task, especially with all of Matthew's problems. In fact, Tom couldn't believe that Matthew would be celebrating his ninth birthday soon. For Tom, Matthew's childhood was just a blur, like watching a roller coaster speed down the track at 100 miles an hour. The highs and the lows were beginning to run into each other more and more. There were days when Matthew seemed to be able to handle things, and then he would just fall apart, crying and saying he hated himself.

DEVELOPMENTAL HISTORY/FAMILY BACKGROUND

Matthew had always been difficult, even as a baby. As an infant, he seemed to spit up more food than went down and then he would wake up crying in the middle of the night because he was hungry. Then he would overeat and cry again, his little stomach distended with gas. Matthew's mother would have had problems handling the best of babies; with Matthew, she didn't have a chance. Tom worked nights and would often arrive early in the morning after the night shift to hear Matthew screaming in the crib and his wife sleeping through it on the couch.

Eventually, she left, saying that she just wasn't cut out for motherhood. In the first 3 years, Tom struggled with Matthew's mother going in and out of his life. Matthew would wait patiently for her visits, and then she would either not show up or come over in one of her "moods." Her erratic behavior and mood swings were what caused the marriage break-up in the first place. Ultimately, she stopped coming for visits altogether, and it had now been 4 years since Matthew had seen his mother. In the beginning, Matthew talked about his mother incessantly, asking why she would not see him. Often he would cry himself to sleep at night. Although Matthew finally seemed to accept the fact that his mother would not return, Tom felt that Matthew never really understood why.

Matthew did not get along with his stepsister, Emily. Emily was 14 years old and Tom's daughter from his first marriage. Matthew and Emily were like night and day. While Matthew was extremely temperamental and hard to get along with, Emily was sweet, soft-spoken, and eager to please. Emily did well in school and had many friends. Often Matthew would deliberately set out to annoy Emily, as if he were angry that she seemed so happy. When Tom started dating again, Matthew went ballistic. One night when Emily was baby-sitting, Matthew went totally out of control. He started smashing things in Tom's room. Emily called her father on his cell phone and he came home immediately, but not before Matthew had made a complete mess of his room. Drawers were dumped on the floor and the lamp was smashed against the wall. Tom tried to restrain Matthew, who was flailing his arms and behaving like a human tornado. After this frenzied burst of activity, Matthew collapsed on the floor and began sobbing. He told his father he was sorry and felt very bad about the damage he had done. The pattern repeated itself again and again. Angry outbursts would be followed by remorse and guilt. Matthew seemed to have little control over his emotions in either direction. On days when he was having a good time, his exuberance would also spiral out of control. Tom remembered the day Matthew got his new bike. He went right out into the traffic and was almost hit by a truck. Matthew also had few friends because he always seemed to overreact and either get in fights with other kids or blame them if things were not going well. His behavior was often unpredictable and bossy. He would often come home from the playground in tears.

Although Matthew's behaviors made it difficult for Tom to have a social life, Tom eventually met Eileen, and despite Matthew's efforts to come between them, Eileen moved in. The next 2 years were horrible for everyone in the house. Matthew was very easily upset and seemed to have a continual chip on his shoulder. Eileen initially thought that Matthew would warm up to her in time; however, any time she attempted to get close to him, Matthew would do something to draw the line. Matthew's irritable disposition also made it difficult for anyone to get close to him. Discipline was very problematic because Matthew was unable to handle criticism at any level. Any time Eileen would reprimand Matthew, he would break into tears, yelling at her that she was not his mother and had no right to act as if she were. In time, Matthew's behavior became the focal point for arguments between Tom and Eileen. Matthew was also spending an inordinate amount of time in the garage working on his go-cart. On several nights in succession, Eileen found Matthew in the garage painting and putting decals on the cart well after bedtime. He was getting up at all hours of the night, seemingly obsessed with these late-night activities as well as seemingly not needing to sleep. Eileen and Tom incessantly argued about how to deal with the problem and could not agree on a resolution, so nothing was done. Homework assignments were not handed in and homework became another battleground for Matthew and Eileen. Finally, Eileen refused to get involved with Matthew's schoolwork and the job fell to Tom, who was often very tired after working a long day at the trucking firm. Matthew began to complain of headaches and stomachaches and wanted to stay home from school. While doing his homework, Matthew would make self-deprecating comments, calling himself stupid and a dummy. He complained frequently of feeling ill, and he was not eating or sleeping very well.

Eileen eventually left, saying that she could no longer tolerate the family situation. She said that Matthew was spoiled and that Tom did nothing to control his behavior. Their constant fights about Matthew had finally taken their toll. Matthew said that he was happy the "witch" was gone. Tom wondered, however, if Matthew felt that he had just lost another mother, or worse yet, that he had caused another mother to leave.

Matthew was also beginning to get into more trouble at school. His teacher had called Tom twice in the past week, and Tom was asked to come in for a parent-teacher conference. At the school's suggestion, Tom agreed to have the school psychologist observe Matthew in the classroom and conduct a full assessment to determine if Matthew might also be having learning problems that were adding to his difficulties.

When the school psychologist observed Matthew in the classroom, it was readily apparent which child she was there to observe. Matthew was sitting at his desk, slouched down with his arms folded around himself in one enormous pout. Apparently, his teacher had reprimanded Matthew on the way back from lunch because he was running in the hall. Matthew continued to glare at the teacher with his eyes bearing down on her and his lips pursed tightly. The teacher asked the class to break into small groups of six for the next activity, which was a math game. Matthew quickly got out of the chair and gleefully joined his group, hopping and bouncing up and down.

In the groups, children rotated the leadership role by selecting the next child to take the math lead. For a brief time, Matthew seemed to be doing well and getting along with the others in his group, until it was his time to pick another child to be the group leader. Instead of picking another child, Matthew began teasing the others in the group, pretending to pick someone and then changing his mind, pointing at them with his chalk and then retracting it. Finally, Matthew's group began to ignore him and selected another leader. At this point, Matthew threw the chalk on the floor, sulked, stomped his feet, and returned to his chair and resumed his position of master pouter. Matthew's teacher intervened, once again, and directed Matthew back to his group. At this point, Matthew returned to the group but threw himself down on the floor in the middle of the group, which was ignoring him. He managed to get the chalk away from the leader and would not give it back. At this point, the group was becoming very upset with Matthew and asked the teacher to intervene. This time, the teacher walked Matthew back to his seat, and Matthew sat quietly while the other children returned to their seats as well. When the teacher asked for volunteers to write their group's response on the board, Matthew's hand shot up and he started yelling, "Me, pick me!!" When he was not picked, Matthew threw his book on the floor and resumed the pout position.

Prior to the outburst that landed Matthew in the alternate school placement, Matthew started repeatedly asking if he could see his mother again. He was very disturbed that no one seemed to know where she was. Matthew was obsessed with finding her and would spend long hours at night searching for her on the Internet. At school, Matthew was getting into trouble on a regular basis. He was not sleeping well and was now irritable most of the time. He was having problems concentrating on schoolwork, and he seemed unable to cope with other children or school demands. Matthew would frequently burst into tears and had to be removed from the classroom on several occasions.

Socially, other children would either tease him or ignore him. Matthew's responses were very unpredictable: volatile and aggressive at one moment; at another time, crying and saying that he wished he were dead. Tom attended another school conference, and the school psychologist shared concerns regarding her observations of Matthew in class and around the school on her regular visits. After discussing Matthew's family history, the psychologist asked if Matthew's mother had ever had a psychiatric assessment, or if anyone in the family had a psychiatric disorder. Tom mentioned that his ex-wife had been diagnosed with bipolar disorder, but would not take the prescribed medication, saying it made her feel lousy. He added that her extreme mood swings made their marriage very difficult. The school psychologist said she wondered if Matthew might also have bipolar disorder. Tom scheduled a psychiatric appointment for Matthew; however, the earliest date he could get was in 2 months' time. In the interim, Tom agreed to take Matthew to his family physician for his medical opinion.

REASON FOR REFERRAL

On Friday morning, Tom took Matthew to his family physician. Tom did not tell the physician that the school psychologist mentioned the possibility of bipolar disorder, since he wanted the doctor to have an unbiased opinion. The physician said that given Matthew's problems with concentration, attention, and hyperactivity/impulsivity, Matthew was likely demonstrating symptoms of attention-deficit/hyperactivity disorder (ADHD), which could explain why he tended to be so impulsive and demonstrate such poor behavioral controls. The physician prescribed a trial of Ritalin and asked Tom to have the teacher rate his behavior on the rating scale when he dropped Matthew off at school and then again on Monday when the Ritalin would be started. The physician was hopeful that the Ritalin would reduce Matthew's impulsivity and attention problems. Two days after he began taking the Ritalin, when a peer started teasing him, Matthew ran out in front of the school bus and narrowly avoided being struck by the bus. When the teachers retrieved him and tried to get him back into the classroom, he began kicking and screaming. Matthew grabbed a chair and threw it at one of the teachers. Matthew was removed from the school and placed in an alternative school placement for the next 45 days. While in the alternative setting, the Ritalin was discontinued, since there were major concerns that the medication might have escalated his behaviors. While in the alternate setting, his behavior was charted on an hourly basis to see what, if any, patterns might be evident in his moods, and also to determine if certain triggers were likely to set him off. Tom was also asked to keep a similar record of Matthew's behaviors in the home. A pattern began to emerge, which seemed to repeat every 24 hours.

Results of the observations revealed mixed hypomania evident in *ultradian cycling* (brief manic episodes, lasting from minutes to hours, occurring on a daily basis) that became evident in the late afternoon and progressed onward until about 2:00 to 3:00 in the morning. Matthew would come to school in a very irritable mood, tired, sleepy, and very grumpy, since he had been up until very late the night before. This irritable mood, in which he was very "touchy," distractible, easily upset, and difficult to communicate with, began to wear off in the late afternoon, gradually being replaced by increased physical movement, agitation, and excessive need to talk about anything and everything. At home, shortly after dinner, around 7 o'clock in the evening, Matthew's behaviors would begin to escalate in a more rapid and consuming fashion; this was evident in giddy and silly behaviors (laughing, dancing, singing), with increased energy and insomnia until the early hours of the morning (around 2:00 to 3:00 a.m.), when he would literally crash into a deep sleep. It was nearly impossible to get him up for school in the morning, and Matthew would begin each day irritable, grumpy, and half asleep. The consulting psychiatrist diagnosed Matthew with pediatric bipolar disorder (bipolar II, mixed), and a trial of Risperdal proved relatively successful in reducing the depressive episodes and emotional volatility.

Matthew was referred for assessment to determine intellectual potential, academic progress, and emotional status.

ASSESSMENT RESULTS

Guidelines to the interpretation of standard scores and T scores, as well as information regarding specific assessment instruments used in this case can be found in Appendix C.

While in the alternate school placement, Matthew was assessed by the psychologist, who found that Matthew's intelligence on the Wechsler Intelligence Scale for Children (WISC-IV) was in the high average range overall, at the 79th percentile (IQ = 112, range 106–117). There was minimal discrepancy between Verbal Comprehension and Perceptual Reasoning abilities and no indication of problems with Working Memory or Processing Speed, which were within the average range. Academically, although reading and math were at grade level, written expression was about a year behind and in need of remediation. Matthew demonstrated problems with grammar and organizing his ideas.

During his clinical interview, Matthew talked at length about his real mother and said that he was having problems because she left. He said that he was sure he would be better if she would return. On the Achenbach System of Empirically Based Assessment (ASEBA; Achenbach & Rescorla, 2001), Matthew's father's ratings on the CBCL placed Matthew in the clinical range for Anxious/Depressed (T = 72), Attention Problems (T = 78), and Aggression (T = 74). His father endorsed the following items as very true (occurring often) for the three significant scales: Anxious/Depressed scale (*worries, talks of suicide, nervous, feels worthless, feels unloved, cries a lot*), Attention Problems scale (*acts young, problems sitting still, impulsive, poor schoolwork*), and Aggression scale (*argues a lot, mean, demands attention, destroys own things, destroys others' things, disobedient at home, screams a lot, mood changes, sulks, temper, threatens others*). Other items that were endorsed significantly included *brags, shows off, talks too much*.

Matthew's teacher did not endorse significant problems for the Anxious/Depressed scale (T = 64); however, she did see significant difficulties with Attention (T = 78) and Aggression (T = 72). Social Problems were in the high-risk range (T = 66). Similar to his father, items endorsed by his teacher for the Attention Problems scale suggested high rates of hyperactivity and impulsivity (*acts young, noisy, brags, fidgets, disturbs, impulsive, talks out, disrupts discussions, irresponsible, shows off, talks too much*). Aggressive behaviors that were significant included *argues, is mean, demands attention, destroys own things, attacks, screams, explosive, sulks, temper*.

On the Beck Youth Inventories (BYI-2), Matthew rated himself as significantly depressed (T = 70), aggressive (T = 82), and with low self-concept (T = 40). His score for anxiety was in the at-risk range (T = 66). During the course of the assessment sessions, Matthew's moods vacillated abruptly. He could be very cooperative and engaging, but in the next moment he could become difficult to engage and irritable. During one of his more expansive moods, Matthew stated that he hated the school he was attending and that he could teach better than the teachers in "this dump." He also said he believed that he was going to be very successful when he grew up and was intending to be a rock star or a movie star. When asked if he played an instrument or was ever involved in a school play, he immediately changed the subject.

ISSUES, TRENDS, AND TREATMENT ALTERNATIVES

The *DSM-IV-TR* (APA, 2000) defines mood disorders as consisting of two possible mood episodes: *major depressive episodes* and *bipolar episodes,* of which there are three types: manic, mixed, or hypomanic. Individuals who suffer from unipolar depression will experience a pervasive mood of sadness, or loss of pleasure that can appear as irritability in children. However, those who have bipolar disorder (BP) will not only experience the lows of depression, they will also experience mania.

In this case and the case of Jenny Sloan, bipolar disorder will be discussed as it relates to the manic part of the episode and will provide an opportunity for readers to compare how these manic and hypomanic states can appear in childhood and adolescence. For an in-depth discussion of a major depressive episode, readers are directed to the case of David Steele.

The *DSM-IV-TR* (APA, 2000) lists criteria for several types of BP, also referred to as the bipolar spectrum disorders, based on the nature of the manic episodes: bipolar I, mixed episode, bipolar II, cyclothymic disorder, rapid cycling, and bipolar disorder not otherwise specified (BP NOS). The *DSM-IV-TR* criteria for the bipolar spectrum disorders can be found in Appendix D. Individuals who are diagnosed with BP will meet criteria of having three out of a possible seven symptoms, and have a full manic episode (or mixed episodes, which vary between depression and mania) lasting for at least 1 week, or hypomanic episodes (less severe than full mania) lasting for at least 4 days. Cyclothymic disorder involves hypomanic episodes plus depressive episodes that do not meet criteria for major depressive disorder. Rapid cycling is said to occur if four or more episodes occur within a single year. BP NOS is a category that is reserved for those cases that do not meet the criteria for the other bipolar categories.

In addition to the previous categories of BP from the *DSM-IV-TR,* Geller and colleagues (2000) have identified two other cycling patterns that can occur in young children with BP:

- *Ultrarapid cycling:* manic episodes that are brief and recurrent (hours to days) but do not meet criteria for hypomania, since they do not last for 4 days; and
- *Ultradian cycling:* manic episodes that are brief (minutes to hours), occurring on a daily basis.

Although later-adolescent-onset BP will more closely resemble the adult version (see the case of Jenny Sloan), in younger children, symptoms are atypical and do not often resemble the adult version of the disorder. Although BP was once thought to be rare in children (Carlson, 2005), prevalence rates have shown dramatic increases. In their recent study of discharge rates for children with BP, Blader and Carlson (2007) found that the primary diagnosis of BP had increased from 10% in 1996 to 34% in 2004. Until the late 1990s, there was considerable debate as to whether bipolar disorder existed in children, or if the symptoms represented a more severe variant of ADHD. More recently, the emphasis has shifted from debates on whether the disorder exists to more productive discussions of how to best identify and treat the disorder in children (Wozniak, 2003).

Dilsaver, Benazzi, and Akiskal (2005) found that 82% of their sample of youth with depression evidenced mixed states, while in a later sample, Dilsaver and Akiskal (2009) found that 85% of their sample with depression had mixed moods states. Based on their findings, Dilsaver and colleagues (2005, 2009) suggest that "mixed hypomania" may be a common syndrome of those with juvenile bipolar disorder, who vacillate from depression early in the day to spikes of hypomania in the evening, with transitions between the two mood states occurring in the mid- to late afternoon. Furthermore, youth who demonstrate "mixed hypomania" (bipolar II, mixed) demonstrate a 24-hour cycle that begins with "depressed mood, quietness, lethargy and cognitive slowing" in the morning, with "rising afternoon and early evening mood" with evidence of pressured speech, racing thoughts, flight of ideas, and psychomotor agitation (increased goal directedness, energy, and lack of need for sleep), which often peaks between 11:00 p.m. and 3:00 a.m. (Dilsaver & Akiskal, 2009, p. 15).

Early diagnosis of BP in childhood is important for several reasons. It has been suggested that a prior episode of mania or depression can sensitize the child and increase the risk for more frequent episodes in the future, a theory that Post (2004) refers to as the "kindling hypothesis." Furthermore, research has documented the disruptive effect that BP can have on early childhood development by negatively affecting the child's relationships with parents and peers and undermining school success (Birmaher & Axelson, 2006; Pavuluri, O'Connor, Harral, Moss, & Sweeney, 2006; Schenkel, West, Harral, Patel, & Pavuluri, 2008). Furthermore, delays in diagnosis and identification can not only result in delayed treatment, but more important, can potentially result in "iatrogenic and exacerbatory effects of pharmacotherapy applied without consideration of an underlying bipolar diagnosis, e.g., psychostimulants or antidepressants [that are] not paired with a mood stabilizer" (Fields & Fristad, 2009, p. 167).

In younger children, symptoms can present with rapid fluctuations in mood and behavior that is often associated with comorbid ADHD and the disruptive behavior disorders, which can increase the complexity of diagnosing the disorder (AACAP, 2007). Manic states in very young children (preschoolers) can appear as "giddy, goofy, drunk-like" or severely irritable moods with temper outbursts (Wilens et al., 2003, p. 497), emotional states that vary widely from the euphoric states evident in adult versions of the disorder. Biederman and colleagues (2004) found that children with BP often can present with mixed episodes that are primarily evident as irritability and explosiveness, while Wozniak and colleagues (2004) have found that when both anger and dysphoria are evident, children are more likely to also have comorbid problems of conduct and anxiety, compared to those who demonstrate unipolar depression only.

Symptoms of BP in children often differ considerably from the cyclical patterns of depression and mania found in adults. Children's symptoms are atypical relative to adult symptoms and commonly are evident in mood lability (volatility), reckless behavior, irritability, and aggression, while the duration of mood shifts can involve hours or days, rather than the more stable and enduring pattern found in adults (Geller et al., 2000, 2004). Using the criteria of *grandiosity* and *elation* as symptoms of a manic phase in children, Geller and colleagues (2000, 2002, 2004) found that 10% of their sample met criteria for *ultrarapid cycling,* while 77% met criteria for *ultradian cycling.* Average age of onset for BP in their study was approximately 7 years of age, while the average number of cycles per day was approximately 3.7 cycles (Geller et al., 2004).

There is significant controversy about the appropriateness of the current *DSM-IV-TR* (APA, 2000) criteria for the diagnosis of BP in children. The National Institute of Mental Health (NIMH) Roundtable on Prepubertal Bipolar Disorder (2001) made a recommendation that one of two classifications be applied to children who manifest symptoms of juvenile bipolar disorder: a *"narrow" phenotype* for those who meet the *DSM-IV-TR* criteria for adult BP, including euphoria, grandiosity, and other classic manic symptoms (Geller, Tillman, Badner, & Cook, 2005; Leibenluft, Charney, Towbin, Bhangoo, & Pine, 2003); and a *"broad"* phenotype for those who do not meet adult criteria but evidence prominent symptoms of irritability and labile mood shifts (Wozniak et al., 2005). It has been argued by some that children with pediatric BP are basically *nosologic orphans,* since symptoms of the disorder in young children do not match the current *DSM-IV-TR* (APA, 2000) criteria (Carlson, Pine, Nottelmann, & Leibenluft, 2004).

Others have suggested using a non-*DSM* alternative, namely the Child Behavior Checklist Juvenile Bipolar Disorder Phenotype as an alternative (Biederman et al., 1995; Giles, DelBello, Stanford, & Strakowski, 2007). Based on their meta-analysis of seven studies, Mick and colleagues (2003) found a distinct CBCL profile associated with BP in children and youth, namely elevations on the subscales for attention problems, aggression, and anxious/depressed behaviors. These are the same three scales that Faraone, Althoff, Hudziak, Monuteaux, and Biederman (2005) identified as the CBCL pediatric bipolar profile (CBCL-PBD) in their study of BP in children. However, more recently, researchers have suggested that this profile may be a better indicator of functional impairment, severity of psychopathology, and comorbidity in general, rather than an identifier of bipolar disorder in particular (Meyer et al., 2009; Volk & Todd, 2007). Research has been consistent in associating elevations on these three scales (attention problems, aggression, anxiety/depression) with increased suicidal behaviors; greater impairment (Volk & Todd, 2007); and placing children at increased risk for developing bipolar disorder, anxiety, ADHD, or cluster-B personality disorders later on (Meyer et al., 2009).

The American Academy of Child and Adolescent Psychiatry (AACAP, 2007) Practice Parameters for the assessment and treatment of BP in children and adolescents have suggested several guidelines and cautions regarding the diagnosis of BP in very young children. The AACAP recognizes that the disorder can vary widely from adult forms of BP and include changes in "mood, energy levels, and behavior" marked by "labile and erratic" mood shifts rather than persistent moods, where "irritability, belligerence, and mixed manic-depressive features" are far more common than euphoria (AACAP, 2007, p. 111). However, the AACAP cautions that irritable mania may be difficult to distinguish from common anger problems in young children and that "hallmark manic symptoms of grandiosity, psychomotor agitation and reckless behavior must be differentiated from . . . more common childhood disorders such as hyperactivity, irritability, dangerous play, and inappropriate sexualized activity, as well as from normal childhood phenomena of boasting imaginary play, overactivity and youthful indiscretions" (AACP, 2007, p. 113). Increased prevalence rates for BP in very young children have been reported in research.

For example, Wilens and colleagues (2003), state that 26% of preschool children with ADHD have comorbid BP, while a survey conducted by the Child and Adolescent Bipolar Foundation (Hellander, 2002) reports that 24% of those diagnosed in the survey were between the ages of 1 and 8 years of age. As a result, the AACAP (2007) recommends adhering to the *DSM-IV-TR* (APA, 2000) criteria and advises extreme caution when considering a diagnosis of BP before the age of 6. The AACAP emphasizes that the validity of a diagnosis of BP in preschool children has not yet been established, and cautions against the aggressive use of pharmacotherapy in the prescription of mood stabilizers and atypical antipsychotics to children in this age group (Biederman et al., 2005a; Tumuluru, Weller, Fristad, & Weller, 2003). The AACAP (2007) endorses the use of the *DSM-IV-TR* (APA, 2000) criteria (symptoms and duration) for diagnosis of mania and hypomania in children, with the proviso that those who do not meet the criteria for duration (less than 4 days) be classified as bipolar disorder not otherwise specified (BP NOS). The AACAP document concludes with a list of several recommendations for the assessment and treatment of BP in children.

In their evaluation of current assessment practices for BP in children, Youngstrom, Findling, Youngstrom, and Calabrese (2005) suggest that although the child will often be referred for assessment due to explosive rages, resulting from aggressive and irritable behaviors, these behaviors in and of themselves do not constitute a diagnosis of BP. They recommend that in addition to a comprehensive clinical work-up, including family history, assessment should also include *handle symptoms* (symptoms that can assist the clinician to get a better "handle" on what the primary issue is), a history and evidence of the nature of cycling patterns and distinct changes in mood functioning, and multisession interviews to obtain sufficient information. The authors agree with Geller (2001) that an important part of the diagnosis should focus on differentiating BP from other disorders by emphasizing those symptoms that are most often associated with mania, such as elevated mood, grandiosity, hypersexuality, pressured speech, and racing thoughts.

In their study of the earliest symptoms that distinguished BP from non-BP children, Fergus and colleagues (2003) found that an "irritability/dyscontrol" factor including poor frustration tolerance, increased aggression, and temper tantrums could distinguish the two groups at ages 1 through 6. Further investigation focused on a bipolar cohort with onset prior to 9 years of age, which they labeled juvenile onset bipolar disorder (JO-BP). In this study, Luckenbaugh, Findling, Leverich, Pizzarello, and Post (2009) compared children with a diagnosis of ADHD (n = 22) to groups of JO-BP with or without comorbid ADHD (n = 27) and a control group (n = 26; no diagnosis). The researchers were able to demonstrate that brief and extended periods of elevated mood were present in the bipolar group as early as 3 years of age with the difference in magnitude increasing with age over the 10-year rating period. Three symptoms that distinguished the JO-BP group from those with ADHD (non-JO-BP) at the earlier ages were more severe irritability, decreased need for sleep, and inappropriate sexual behavior, while more periods of sadness, change in appetite, and suicidal ideation became significant discriminators after 7 years of age. Children in the JO-BP group also reported significantly more night terrors and bedwetting than those in the ADHD group. Classic symptoms of ADHD (hyperactivity, impulsivity, and decreased attention span) did not distinguish between groups, likely because the symptoms are similar for JO-BP, and the fact that 79% of those with JO-BP in the study had comorbid ADHD.

Treatment Approaches

The AACAP (2007) recommends a multimodal treatment plan combining medications and psychotherapeutic interventions that include

- *psychoeducational therapy* (informing parents and family about BP, its nature and course, and available treatment alternatives),
- *relapse prevention* (advising parents and family of the importance of compliance with medication regimes, and the need to monitor sleep patterns and outside stressors),
- *individual psychotherapy* (skill building in younger children),
- *social and family functioning* (enhance family and social relationships through improved communication and problem-solving skills),
- *academic skills and occupational functioning* (the need to monitor educational progress, special programs, and individual educational plans and any related services), and
- *community consultations* (treatment plans should include communication with any community agencies that may also be involved, e.g., social welfare, juvenile justice).

Because young children with BP experience difficulties with behavioral and emotional control, many behavioral programs can also be applied to assist parents in managing the child's behaviors. Functional behavioral analysis (FBA) can be helpful in isolating environmental triggers in the home and school that can exacerbate emotional reactivity and outbursts. Increased structure and predictability of routines can also serve to reduce stress and provide a framework for increased self-control.

Collaboration with school personnel is also an essential component of the treatment process for school-aged children (Kronenberger & Meyer, 2001). In *The Bipolar Child*, Papolos and Papolos (2000) present a mock-up IEP (individual education plan) for a hypothetical bipolar student, Elan. The plan is a practical example of how interventions can address children's needs across developmental contexts, such as the school environment. Elan's IEP is developed to incorporate six goals in his school programming aimed at learning and applying strategies to divert inappropriate thoughts, reduce anxiety, increase on-task behaviors, increase communication skills, increase academic competence, and reduce explosive outbursts. The plan is written in behavioral terms that allow Elan to earn points for meeting goals on a daily basis.

Medication and Medication Management. It is very important to monitor medications of children who have BP. If a child with BP is given an antidepressant without a mood stabilizer, the antidepressant can trigger a manic episode. Furthermore, if a child with BP is given stimulant medication (for ADHD-related symptoms), this can also exacerbate manic symptoms (Fields & Fristad, 2009). Atypical antipsychotics, such as Risperidone and Olanzapine, have also been effective in the treatment of severe mania in children as young as 6 years of age (Biederman et al., 2005b). In August 2007, the FDA approved Risperdal (an antipsychotic medication) for the treatment of BP in children and adolescents from 10 to 17 years of age.

Post-Case Questions

1. Using the framework for a functional behavioral assessment (FBA; Table 1.2), develop a case formulation outlining the precipitating and maintaining variables regarding Matthew's behavior. Working from this assessment information, develop a behavioral intervention plan for use in Matthew's school to assist in monitoring his behaviors.

2. Develop a case formulation from the perspective of an attachment theorist. What treatment plan would best accommodate Matthew's needs using this approach?

3. Develop a case formulation from the perspective of a family systems therapist. How would you attempt to restore the balance of power in this family?

4. Develop a case formulation for Matthew, relating his behaviors to developmental theory and contexts (Bronfenbrenner's model), using the framework of risks and protective factors.

5. The IDEA definition of emotional disturbance is highly controversial (see Appendix B: Systems of Classification). Based on the IDEA, would Matthew qualify for an exceptional designation as an emotionally disturbed or seriously emotionally disturbed child? If not, why not?

REFERENCES

American Academy of Child and Adolescent Psychiatry (AACAP). (2007). Practice parameter for the assessment and treatment of children and adolescents with bipolar disorder. *Journal of the American Academy of Child and Adolescent Psychiatry, 46,* 107–125.

American Psychiatric Association (APA). (2000). *Diagnostic and statistical manual of mental disorders* (4th ed., text revision). Washington, DC: Author.

Biederman, J., Faraone, S. V., Wozniak, J., Mick, E., Kwon, A., & Aleardi, M. (2004). Further evidence of unique developmental phenotypic correlates of pediatric bipolar disorder: Findings from a large sample of clinically referred preadolescent children assessed over the last 7 years. *Journal of Affective Disorders, 82,* S45–S58.

Biederman, J., McDonnell, M. A., Wozniak, J., Spencer, T., Aleardi, M., Falzone, R., et al. (2005a). Aripiprazole in the treatment of pediatric bipolar disorder: A systematic chart review. *CNS Spectrums, 10,* 141–148.

Biederman, J., Mick, E., Hammerness, P., Haarpold, T., Aleardi, M., Dougherty, M., & Wozniak, J. (2005b). Open-label, 8-week trial of olanzapine and risperidone for the treatment of bipolar disorder in preschool-age children. *Biological Psychiatry, 58,* 589–594.

Biederman, J., Wozniak, J., Kiely, K., Ablon, S. Faraone, S. V., Mick, E., et al. (1995). CBCL clinical scales discriminate prepubertal children with structured interview-derived diagnosis of mania from those with ADHD. *Journal of the American Academy of Child and Adolescent Psychology, 34*(4), 464–471.

Birmaher, B., & Axelson, D. (2006). Course and outcome of bipolar spectrum disorder in children and adolescents: A review of the existing literature. *Development and Psychopathology, 18*(4), 1023–1035.

Blader, J. C., & Carlson, G. A. (2007). Increased rates of bipolar disorder diagnoses among U.S. child, adolescent, and adult inpatients, 1996–2004. *Biological Psychiatry, 62*(2), 107–114.

Carlson, G. A. (2005). Early onset bipolar disorder: clinical and research considerations. *Journal of Clinical Child and Adolescent Psycholology, 34,* 333–443.

Carlson, G., Pine, D., Nottelmann, J., & Leibenluft, E. (2004). Defining subtypes of childhood bipolar illness. *Journal of the American Academy of Child and Adolescent Psychiatry, 43,* 3–4.

Dilsaver, S. C., & Akiskal, H. S. (2009). "Mixed hypomania" in children and adolescents: Is it a pediatric bipolar phenotype with extreme diurnal variation between depression and hypomania? *Journal of Affective Disorders, 116,* 12–17.

Dilsaver, S. C., Benazzi, F., & Akiskal, H. D. (2005). Mixed states: The most common presentation of bipolar depressed adolescents? *Psychopathology, 38,* 268–272.

Faraone, S. V., Althoff, R. R., Hudziak, J. J., Monuteaux, M., & Biederman, J. (2005). The CBCL predicts *DSM* bipolar disorder in children: A receiver operating characteristic curve analysis. *Bipolar Disorder, 7,* 518–524.

Fergus E. L., Miller, R. B., Luckenbaugh, D. A., Leverich, G. S., Findling, R. L., Speer, M. A., et al. (2003). Is there progression from irritability/dyscontrol to major depressive and manic symptoms? A retrospective community survey of parents of bipolar children. *Journal of Affective Disorders, 77,* 71–78.

Fields, B. W., & Fristad, M. A. (2009). Assessment of childhood bipolar disorder. *Clinical Psychology and Scientific Practice, 16,* 166–181.

Geller, B. (2001). A prepubertal and early adolescent bipolar disorder phenotype has poor one-year outcome. *The Brown University Child and Adolescent Psychopharmacology Update, 3,* 1–5.

Geller, B., Tillman, R., Badner, J., & Cook, E. (2005). Are the arginine vasopressin V1a receptor cirosatellites related to hypersexuality in children with prepubertal and early adolescent bipolar disorder phenotype? *Bipolar Disorders, 7,* 610–616.

Geller, B., Tillman, R., Craney, J. L., & Bolhofner, K. (2004). Four-year prospective outcome and natural history of mania in children with a prepubertal and early adolescent bipolar disorder phenotype. *Archives of General Psychiatry 61,* 459–467.

Geller, B., Zimerman, B., Williams, M., Bolhofner, K., Craney, J. L., Delbello, M. P., et al. (2000). Diagnostic characteristics of 93 cases of a prepubertal and early adolescent bipolar disorder phenotype by gender, puberty and comorbid attention deficit hyperactivity disorder. *Journal of Child and Adolescent Psychopharmacology, 10,* 157–164.

Geller, B., Zimerman, B., Williams, M., Delbello, M. P., Frazier, J., & Beringer, L. (2002). Phenomenology of prepubertal and early adolescent bipolar disorder: Examples of elated mood, grandiose behaviors, decreased need for sleep, racing thoughts and hypersexuality. *Journal of Child and Adolescent Psychopharmacology, 12,* 3–9.

Giles, L. L., DelBello, M. P., Stanford, K. E., & Strakowski, S. M. (2007). Child Behavior Checklist profiles of children and adolescents with and at high risk for developing bipolar disorder. *Child Psychiatry and Human Development, 38,* 47–55.

Hellander, I. (2002), A review of data on the health sector of the United States, January 2002. *International Journal of Health Services, 32,* 579–599.

Kronenberger, W. G., & Meyer, R. G. (2001). *The child clinician's handbook* (2nd ed.). Boston: Allyn and Bacon.

Leibenluft, E., Charney, D. S., Towbin, K. E., Bhangoo, R. K., & Pine, D. S. (2003). Defining clinical phenotypes of juvenile mania. *American Journal of Psychiatry, 160,* 430–437.

Luckenbaugh, D. A., Findling, R. L., Leverich, G. S., Pizzarello, S. M., & Post, R. M. (2009). Earliest symptoms discriminating juvenile-onset bipolar illness from ADHD. *Bipolar Disorders, 11,* 441–451.

Meyer, S. E., Carlson, G. A., Youngstrom, E., Ronsaville, D. S., Martinez, P. E., Gold, P. W., et al. (2009). Long-term outcomes of youth who manifested the CBCL-pediatric bipolar disorder phenotype during childhood and/or adolescence. *Journal of Affective Disorders, 113,* 227–235.

Mick, E., Biederman, J., Pandina, G., & Faraone, S. V. (2003). A preliminary meta-analysis of the Child Behavior Checklist in pediatric bipolar disorder. *Biological Psychiatry, 53,* 1021–1027.

Papolos, D., & Papolos, J. (2000). School: A child's world beyond home. Hypothetical baseline information and draft IEP for a bipolar student. In D. Papolos & J. Papolos, *The bipolar child* (pp. 280–284). New York: Broadway Books.

Pavuluri, M. N., O'Connor, M. M., Harral, E. M., Moss, M., & Sweeney, J. A. (2006). Impact of neurocognitive function on academic difficulties in pediatric bipolar disorder: A clinical translation. *Biological Psychiatry, 60*(9), 951–956.

Post, R. M. (2004). The status of the sensitization/kindling hypothesis of bipolar disorder. *Current Psychosis and Therapeutics Reports, 2*(4), 135–141.

Schenkel, L. S., West, A. E., Harral, E. M., Patel, N. B., & Pavuluri, M. N. (2008). Parent-child interactions in pediatric bipolar disorder. *Journal of Clinical Psychology, 64*(4), 422–437.

Tumuluru, R. V., Weller, E. B., Fristad, M. A., & Weller, R. A. (2003). Mania in six preschool children. *Journal of Child and Adolescent Psychopharmacology, 13,* 489–494.

Volk, H. E., & Todd, R. D. (2007). Does the Child Behavior Checklist juvenile bipolar disorder phenotype identify bipolar disorder? *Biological Psychiatry, 62,* 115–120.

Wilens, T., Biederman, J., Forkner, P., Ditterline, J., Morris, M., Moore, H., et al. (2003). Patterns of comorbidity and dysfunction in clinically referred preschool and school-age children with bipolar disorder. *Journal of Child and Adolescent Psychopharmacology, 13,* 495–505.

Wozniak, J. (2003). Pediatric bipolar disorder: The new perspective on severe mood dysfunction in children. *Journal of Child and Adolescent Psychopharmacology, 13,* 449–451.

Wozniak, J., Biederman, J., Kwon, A., Mick, E., Faraone, S., Orlovsky, K., et al. (2005). How cardinal are cardinal symptoms in pediatric bipolar disorder? An examination of clinical correlates. *Biological Psychiatry, 58,* 583–588.

Wozniak, J., Spencer, T., Biederman, J., Kwon, A., Monuteaux, M., Rettew, J., et al. (2004). The clinical characteristics of unipolar vs. bipolar major depression in ADHD youth. *Journal of Affective Disorders, 82,* S59–S69.

Youngstrom, E. A., Findling, R., Youngstrom, J. K., & Calabrese, J. R. (2005). Toward an evidence-based assessment of pediatric bipolar disorder. *Journal of Clinical Child and Adolescent Psychology, 34,* 433–448.

Neesha Wilson

Phoenix Rising

Neesha Wilson, a 10-year-old African American girl, was referred for assessment to the school psychologist as a result of a child study team meeting held at the school in May. Presenting problems included poor school progress and escalating behavioral concerns. It was the school's impression that Neesha might qualify for special education assistance as a child with an emotional disorder. Currently, Neesha has an older brother, Tyrone, who is attending an alternate school program for children and youth with severe emotional disturbance.

DEVELOPMENTAL HISTORY/FAMILY BACKGROUND

The school social worker completed Neesha's initial work-up just prior to the end of the academic term; intake information is summarized as follows:

Neesha lives with her 15-year-old brother, Tyrone, and her mother in a two-bedroom apartment. The social worker described the apartment as tiny but very well kept. Neesha has her own bedroom, and Tyrone sleeps on the couch, which folds out into a bed. The social worker noted that it was difficult to book an appointment with Mrs. Wilson, who was reportedly working two jobs: cleaning offices and working as a hairstylist. Mrs. Wilson graduated from hairstylist classes last year. Although her career as a hairstylist has a lot of potential, she is only beginning to develop clientele. She also works part time cleaning offices. Despite the lack of financial resources, the children were clean, well dressed, and did not miss any meals. The children were on the free-lunch program at the schools. According to Mrs. Wilson, Neesha's early history was unremarkable and motor and language milestones developed on schedule.

An immediate concern of the social worker's centered on who cared for the children when their mother, Tanya, had to work evenings cleaning offices. Tanya stated that it was not a problem for her because she would either send the children to her sister's apartment a few blocks away, or have a cousin who lived in the building check in on the kids. Also, Tyrone was 15, so he was capable of watching his sister, although she preferred to have an adult nearby, given Tyrone's behavior problems.

Neesha's mother described her as an easy baby and said that she never really had any problems with her. She added that it was Tyrone who was giving her all the problems, not Neesha. The family had struggled since her husband, Walt, left the family about 3 years ago, when Neesha was in Grade 1. In the past two years, Walt has virtually had no contact with the children. He moved in with his girlfriend and their one-year-old baby, and recently moved to another state. Neesha was very upset with the marriage breakdown and misses her father very much. Neesha visited with her dad and his new family, initially, but was very disappointed that the visits were neither consistent nor more frequent. Neesha did not like Walt's girlfriend and felt that her father was more interested in the new baby than her. According to Tanya, Neesha often talks about wanting to visit her father and continues to set herself up for disappointment. Tanya blames Walt's lack of involvement with the children for Tyrone's problems, which became more severe after Walt left.

When Walt moved out, Tanya could no longer afford to live in the apartment they were living in. Tanya described the previous 2 years as very difficult for her and the kids. As Tanya spoke, the social worker noted in the file that the mother's affect was very flat. She also seemed preoccupied with her financial situation and said, at times, she just wasn't sure how she would make the rent. They have struggled to survive financially, and Tanya often gets depressed, and when she isn't working evenings either goes to bed early or cries herself to sleep. On these occasions, Neesha is very quiet and tries to comfort her mother. Tanya said that when she woke up the other morning, Neesha had placed a handmade card on her pillow. The card was decorated with hearts and bows and huge letters: "I love you, Mom. Neesha." Tanya said she didn't understand why Neesha was doing so poorly in school, because she seemed to love to "play school" on the weekends and in the evening. When asked whether Neesha has demonstrated any behavior problems at home, Tanya said she is more like a little mother than a kid and has no behavior problems at all. Her brother is the problem; Neesha is more like a little adult. She described Neesha as a sweet and loving child who always tries to please.

The social worker expressed her concern to Tanya about her own symptoms of depression and fatigue, and wondered if Tanya might see her physician for a referral to talk to a counselor. The social worker stated that she was concerned because Tanya seemed overwhelmed by all the financial stresses the family faced that seemed to be taking their toll on her, emotionally. However, Tanya was quick to say that the extended family was very supportive and that her two sisters were always there for her to talk to when she needed it. She also said that her church was a continued source of comfort and support for herself and the children. In addition to information obtained from the clinical interview, the social worker also had Tanya complete the Behavioral Assessment System for Children (BASC-2).

In August, at the beginning of the new term, the school psychologist completed a review of Neesha's cumulative school record and obtained teacher ratings (BASC-2) from her previous years' teachers, which were on file in the guidance office. Neesha's school record contained the following additional information. Neesha began her formal schooling at Franklin Elementary School but transferred schools midway through the Grade 1 program. She completed Grade 1 and Grade 2 at Vista Springs Elementary. She has been attending Heartfield Elementary since her enrollment in the Grade 3 program. Neesha is currently repeating the fourth grade. Neesha's records reveal that her Grade 3 teacher was concerned because Neesha was repeatedly falling asleep in class. Because Neesha seemed overly fatigued, her mother took Neesha to the family physician to check out any possible physical reasons for Neesha being so tired; however, no medical reason was evident to explain her fatigue. Last year, Neesha was absent 15 days. On the days she attended school, Neesha was late more than one third of the time (51 days). The school counselor had written a summary report based on her observations of Neesha in the classroom, toward the end of the Grade 4 program, when the paperwork was being collected for her assessment in the fall. The notes indicated that Neesha was off task (*daydreaming; looking out the window; staring out into space*) for the majority of time that she was observed. The observation supported teacher comments that often Neesha did not complete her seatwork, and assignments were often handed in unfinished. During another observation session, the counselor recorded that during a 25-minute seatwork session, Neesha completed only two out of eight comprehension questions for the story read to them in class. Her teacher also reported that, at times, Neesha's lack of attention to task could also result in class-disturbing behaviors such as humming, playing with articles on her desk, and socializing.

As part of the referral process, in addition to notes on classroom observations, the teacher also was asked to record what interventions were attempted and to comment on the success of these attempts. Interventions included sending a daily agenda regarding Neesha's behavior for home signature, providing extra time for task completion, and seating proximity to the teacher's desk. However, the daily agenda often was returned unsigned, since her mother was sleeping, and providing extra time had not increased her productivity. In all, the interventions generally were not successful. Ultimately, the decision was made to have Neesha repeat the Grade 4 program, since she had not completed any assigned tasks during her Grade 4 year, and to place her on high priority for a comprehensive assessment early in the fall term.

The school psychologist saw Neesha for an initial assessment session, early in the fall term. Neesha was very well groomed, with matching accessories and her hair stylishly braided in a way that must have taken hours to complete. When asked about her hair, Neesha was very proud to say that her mother had done it for her, and that her mother was a very good hairdresser. Neesha was very polite and cooperative. Neesha's responses and demeanor suggested a precocious maturity for her 10 years. The psychologist felt that Neesha tried her best on all tasks presented, but questioned the validity of overall intellectual scores.

REASON FOR REFERRAL

The school was requesting assessment due to Neesha's escalating academic difficulties, and increased behavioral problems (irritability, moodiness, and beginning to strike out at other children). There were concerns that Neesha might warrant placement in a program for children with emotional problems.

ASSESSMENT RESULTS

Information concerning specific assessment instruments and the interpretation of standard scores and T scores can be found in Appendix C.

Responses to the Wechsler Intelligence Scale for Children (WISC-IV) revealed Neesha's overall intellectual score of 92, which was within the average range (IQ range 87–98). However, there were several indicators to suggest that this score was likely an underestimate of her "true potential." Neesha's mature conversational tone, insight, and academic levels obtained on standardized testing suggested intellectual functioning more appropriately suited to the upper average to high average range. Based on her overall obtained score, Neesha performed in the average range of ability at the 30th percentile when compared with children her age. A 5-point difference between the Verbal Comprehension Index (VCI = 90) and Perceptual Reasoning Index (PRI = 95) was not significant. Based on these scores, it would be anticipated that Neesha should be performing approximately at grade level, academically. An analysis of the individual pattern of test results indicated that Neesha had relative strengths in the areas of the Working Memory Index (WMI = 100), which involves the manipulation of mental information and short-term working memory, and Processing Speed Index (PSI = 103), which measures speed of copying and scanning information. An analysis of the individual pattern of subtest scores indicated that Neesha had relative strengths in the area of visual analysis and reasoning (picture concepts) and recall for letter and number sequences. Weaknesses were noted in vocabulary development, social judgment, and part-to-whole visual organization (block design).

Academically, according to the Woodcock Johnson III Test of Achievement, Neesha's current functioning levels were far in excess of her current grade placement and also exceeded predicted levels according to the WISC-IV (which was considered as an underestimate of her intellectual potential). Overall, Neesha was performing at a Grade 7.2 level in Broad Reading (age score of 12.7), Grade 5.8 level in Broad Math (age score 11.4), and Grade 7.9 level in Broad Written Expression (age score 13.2). Overall, Neesha was achieving in the high average range when scores were compared with those of other children her age who would be enrolled in a regular Grade 5 program. When compared with other children enrolled in a regular Grade 4 program (which Neesha was currently repeating), her scores represented functioning in the superior range.

Neesha was cooperative during the clinical interview, and provided thoughtful and conscientious responses to the interviewer's questions. When asked what types of things or situations made her feel happy, sad, angry, or frightened, Neesha provided the following information. Neesha stated that "compliments, surprises, and visits with her Dad" were all things that could make her "happy." She said she felt "sad" when kids threaten her or people say bad things about her or her family. She also stated that she gets very sad when her mother cries, because she doesn't know how to make it better.

Neesha looked sad as she spoke about her mother, and her voice trailed off as she swallowed hard. Neesha admitted to feeling angry and upset when her older brother (15 years of age) hits her, and she is "frightened" when she visits her aunt's neighborhood, because the kids are loud and scary. In response to what worries her presently, Neesha said that she is worried that she won't be able to advance to the fifth grade this year. She said that she asked her mother to talk to the principal because she is working very hard and wants to go to Grade 5. She said she did not want to be in Grade 4 again, and she is very afraid that the kids will start being mean again, and call her names like they did last year. She said she did not want to get into trouble this year, like she did last year.

When asked why she was falling asleep in class, Neesha said that in the past she had lots of problems falling asleep, but added that was 2 years ago and things were different then. She said that at that time she would come home from school very tired and fall asleep after dinner. Then she would wake up at night and not be able to go to sleep again. She said that she has stopped taking naps in the afternoon and now she doesn't wake up at night anymore. Neesha volunteered that she also worried a lot about things and that sometimes when she worries she has a hard time falling asleep. Not so much now, but it was bad then because she missed her dad and wanted him to come home. She said that last year she got in trouble for being late so many times, but it was hard to wake up. Neesha said that she was tired and had trouble getting herself ready for school. Her mom was sleeping late because she was working more nights cleaning the offices. Neesha said it was a very hard year. She was tired and cranky and just couldn't seem to concentrate on her work. She said she would read a page and then not remember what she read. Neesha said she got so far behind that she just gave up. She was also having problems with the other girls in the class, who were starting to tease her about sleeping in class and not doing her work. She said they called her names like "Sleepy" and "Dummy." She said that at first it made her very sad, and then it made her very mad. That's when she started to hit them to make them stop. When I asked what made the difference this year, Neesha said, for one, she now has an alarm clock. She sets the clock and lets her mom sleep in. The school bus picks the kids up on the corner, so she just goes and waits with the other kids who live in the apartment building. When asked about schoolwork, Neesha stated that she was very proud of her reading ability and said that she is now concentrating on finishing her work and that keeps her going.

Neesha completed several self-report inventories. Overall response to the Revised Children's Manifest Anxiety Scale (RCMAS-2) revealed total anxiety to be within normal limits. However, there was a significant elevation on the Physiological Indicator scale, and Neesha endorsed several items indicating a generalized heightened state of arousal often associated with stressful conditions, such as trouble getting her breath, feeling sick to her stomach, and hands feeling sweaty. She also admitted to worrying a lot of the time and having problems falling asleep. An elevated validity scale (the Lie scale on the RCMAS) was suggestive of Neesha's tendency to try to project a good image and suggesting that perhaps her anxiety was more of an issue than Neesha was letting on.

Neesha's responses to the Children's Depression Inventory (CDI) revealed overall depression level to be within the norm when compared to girls of a similar age. However, the elevation on the Negative Mood scale was significant, indicating problems with sleeping, fatigue, and worry about aches and pains. Neesha also completed the Personality Inventory for Youth (PIY), a 270-item questionnaire that assesses emotional and behavioral adjustment and family characteristics and interactions, as well as school adjustment. The instrument also includes validity scales that identify a respondent's level of consistency and/or defensiveness. Neesha's scores on the validity scales suggested that her profile was an honest attempt to reflect her current emotional and behavioral concerns. Scores indicated normal concerns typical of girls her age in most areas. However, consistent with the RCMAS, Neesha endorsed a significant number of items indicating somatic concern (T = 73). Scores in this range suggest a large and varied number of somatic symptoms and health concerns, such as fatigue, headache, stomachache, back pain, dizzy spells, trouble breathing, and the like. Results of this kind are often seen in children who worry about and are preoccupied with illness and may become emotionally upset when they are sick. Often these symptoms represent the physical aspects of anxiety and tension. Neesha's particular pattern of endorsement suggests that symptoms are likely connected to feelings of psychological distress within the home.

Projective assessment was also conducted using the Robert's Apperception Test, a series of pictures that are used as prompts for children's stories. The characters in Neesha's stories revealed difficulties in the following areas: conflicts with siblings, fear of being punished for doing something wrong, fear of being ill, and concerns regarding school performance. Family matters included a mother having a new baby and a young girl being a bridesmaid for her parents' wedding. Neesha's drawings for the House-Tree-Person indicated a positive openness to communication and were generally free of suggested pathology.

Two of Neesha's teachers from the fourth grade last year, her current teacher, and her mother completed the Behavioral Assessment System for Children (BASC-2). It should be noted that although the BASC-2 suggests that rating be conducted by individuals who have known the child for at least 6 months, the desire to have a current behavioral rating for comparison violated this suggestion since her current teacher has known Neesha only since the beginning of August (less than 2 months). Therefore, results should be interpreted with caution. The BASC-2 is a comprehensive measurement of common behavioral and emotional problems in children. Ratings of children are interpreted to indicate behavioral concerns that are normal, at risk, or clinical. Behaviors falling within the at-risk range represent an emerging problem area that needs attention but does not warrant a formal diagnosis, while behaviors within the clinical range are problems that warrant attention and intervention.

Ratings are based on the observations of informants in different situations, and it is not unusual for children to behave differently in various situations. Therefore, inconsistencies between informants are not unusual. According to Neesha's teachers last year, there was agreement in several areas on the BASC-2 ratings. The two teachers rated her behaviors as clinically significant in the following areas: Aggression (physical and verbal), Conduct Problems (rule-breaking behaviors), and overall Externalizing Problems. They also agreed that the following behaviors were at risk: Attention Problems, Leadership, Social Skills, and Study Skills. At-risk or clinically significant elevations were also noted for Composite Adaptive Skills (Adaptability, Social Skills, Leadership, Study Skills). Neesha's current teacher and Neesha's mother have indicated all behaviors currently to be within the normal range.

In the final assessment session, Neesha appeared very positive about her school successes this year and said that she was working very hard to go to the next grade level. When asked if she would like to meet with the school psychologist once in a while, just to talk about her worries, Neesha said that she would like that very much. As she left the office, she turned and thanked the psychologist for working with her, and added, "You know, sometimes, it's hard being a kid." When Neesha's mother came to talk to the school psychologist about the test results, the psychologist mirrored the social worker's earlier concerns about the mother being depressed and preoccupied. Affect was very flat despite the excellent news she was receiving regarding her daughter's academic skills and behavioral turnaround. Her mother reported that what Neesha had accomplished, she had done on her own. She stated that Neesha had received no help from her. Mother appeared preoccupied with the interview making her late for work and asked if she could please leave quickly.

Postscript

Three weeks later, at 10:00 a.m., the school principal received a call from Neesha's mother, who asked that her daughter not be sent home from school because she was going to kill herself. As she spoke on the telephone, she explained that she was holding a loaded gun to her head and that she had to do it, because she was not going to make this month's rent. She could not take it any longer, but she did not want Neesha to come home and find her dead.

While the guidance counselor continued to keep the mother talking, the school contacted the police, who apprehended mom while she was talking on her cell phone from her car in the driveway of the apartment building. The loaded gun was on her lap. Mother was Baker Acted (taken into custody due to fears regarding danger to self) and taken to the local psychiatric facility. Currently, mother is on medication for depression.

ISSUES, TRENDS, AND TREATMENT ALTERNATIVES

Considering Neesha's case within the framework of developmental contexts and environmental influences, there are several risk factors that are affecting her development that are not within Neesha's immediate control, including poverty, her mother's mental illness, and living with a sibling who has severe emotional disturbance.

Several researchers have focused on the role of protective factors in buffering some children living in high-risk environments. Emphasis has shifted from focusing on risks to determining environmental resources and adaptive strengths in children who do not show early signs of deviance (Richters & Weintraub, 1990). Rutter (1987) noted several years ago that instead of searching for broadly defined protective factors, emphasis needs to be placed on better understanding "why and how some individuals manage to maintain high self-esteem and self-efficacy in spite of facing the same adversities that lead other people to give up and lose hope" (p. 317). Further, Rutter (1990) suggests that we go beyond listing risk factors to looking at the underlying processes or mechanisms that are instrumental in producing the buffering effect. Rutter defines these processes as reducing risk impact, reducing negative chain reactions, increasing factors that promote self-esteem, and opening opportunities. The role of timing (life events) in changing the trajectory away from vulnerability is also discussed. In their discussion of risk and resilience, Werner and Smith (2001) concluded that certain environmental factors, such as positive emotional support from caregivers and mentors, could provide protection from negative outcomes, despite living in adverse conditions. Although resilience was once thought of as a trait, currently, resilience is thought of as "a process or phenomenon reflecting positive child adjustment despite conditions of risk" (Luthar & Zelazo, 2003, p. 510).

Durlak (1998) reviewed 1,200 outcome studies concerning prevention programs for children and identified several common risk and protective factors across seven major outcome areas: behavior problems, school failure, poor physical health, physical injury, pregnancy, drug use, and AIDS. Analysis of risk and protective factors linked each factor with the appropriate developmental context, including individual, immediate (family, school, peers), and community. Durlak found multiple factors playing a protective role for more than one outcome. For example, attending a "high quality school" protected against behavior problems, school failure, early pregnancy, drug use, and AIDS, and having "positive peer models" also protected across the same five areas. Having a good parent-child relationship and good personal and social skills protected across all seven major outcomes. High-risk factors included living in an impoverished neighborhood, low family SES, parental psychopathology, marital discord, and punitive parenting. Stress was considered to be a risk factor that crossed all levels of development, while social support was a protective factor that crossed all developmental levels.

When discussing risk and protective factors, the risks of being in an ethnic minority have rarely been addressed. Gibbs and Huang (2001) emphasize that when ethnic identity is combined with membership in a minority race, children are faced with a dual challenge. The authors also note that ethnic minority status has often been associated with restricted range of opportunities, and children growing up in minority families may be exposed to circumstances and experiences very different from the majority of the community. In addition, there is often an interaction among factors of ethnicity, race, and social class (SES), with higher status typically perceived for white, Anglo-Saxon, middle-class families, and lower status associated with nonwhite, ethnic minority, and lower-class families (Hacker, 1992). In their study of child poverty rates, Lichtner, Quian, and Crowley (2005) found that while 9% of white children were living below the poverty line, one third of all black children and 27% of Hispanic children were living at this level. According to the 1994 census, approximately 43% of African American youth under 18 years of age live below the poverty line (U.S. Bureau of the Census, 1996). Within this context, the role of the family has assumed a position of strength and resilience. One central value that is cultivated by African American families is the importance of being "independent" and the value of independence. In this manner, the family unit is sustained by members who are self-reliant. Other strong family values often include obedience, respect for elders, and emphasis on obtaining a good education. However, culture clash may be evident in the way in which family members or children whose sense of time is fluid and event oriented interact with largely white establishments where time is determined by the clock, calendar, or school agenda (Lynch & Hanson, 1998).

A growing body of research has revealed that maternal depression and depressive symptoms place children and adolescents at increased risk for negative social and emotional outcomes (Goodman & Gotlib, 2002). Recent studies have found that by adolescence, children and youth exposed to maternal depression demonstrate higher levels of internalizing and externalizing problems relative to peers whose mothers are not depressed (Foster, Garber, & Durlak, 2008; Nelson, Hammen, Brennan, & Ullman, 2003). Campbell, Morgan-Lopez, Cox, and McLoyd (2009) found that adolescents whose mothers reported chronic depressed symptoms across their childhood, evidenced more symptoms of depression, dysphoria, and loneliness compared to peers whose mothers were without a history of depression. It has also been found that children living in stressful conditions surrounding maternal depression (parent-child conflict, less parental monitoring and supervision) are likely to engage in more risk taking and externalizing behaviors (Wiesner & Kim, 2006). Research has also demonstrated that boys and girls may respond differently to maternal distress, with boys being more inclined to react with externalizing problems, while with increasing age, girls are more likely to develop internalizing problems (Angold, Erklani, Silberg, Eaves, & Costello, 2002). In addition to trajectories that might be predicted by gender, the principles of *equifinality* and *mulifinality* provide different mechanisms to assist our understanding of the nature of different outcomes (Cicchetti & Rogosch, 1996). The principle of equifinality is used to explain how similar symptoms (depression) can result from different sources (e.g., two children may both suffer from depression; however, one child may be reacting to a parental divorce, and another child may be depressed because of peer rejection). The second principle of mulifinality is important in understanding how individuals who experience similar circumstances may be on different paths that will predict very different outcomes. For example, although Neesha shows many signs of distress due to her stressful living conditions, she also demonstrates qualities that suggest resilience in the face of adversity.

However, her brother Tyrone, whom we will meet in greater depth in the case study of Tyrone Wilson, has moved further and further along a path of self-destructive behaviors, leading to his recent entry into the juvenile justice system. Therefore, despite living in the same stressful conditions, their outcomes are very different. Children who grow up in less-than-ideal conditions may accept these conditions as part of the "normalcy" of their life and learn to cope with what they have. Others may develop a sense of positive self-esteem and independence that may serve to buffer them from more negative outcomes (Cicchetti & Rogosch, 1997). Yet others, like Tyrone, will follow a path of aggression and retaliation and join others who are on a similar self-destructive trajectory.

Post-Case Questions

1. In discussing the plight of resilient children, Luthar (1993) contrasts earlier concepts of the invulnerable child with present concepts of the resilient child. Luthar observed that children who survived difficult circumstances without developing maladaptive outcomes often presented with more subtle internalizing problems. In Luthar's study, 85% of the resilient children had clinically significant symptoms of anxiety and depression. Similarly, longitudinal data from studies by Werner and Smith (1992) also noted that resilient children in adulthood were plagued with somatic complaints (headaches, backaches) and feelings of dissatisfaction. Discuss Neesha's current clinical profile in light of the information provided by these studies on resilience.

2. In a study of developmental response patterns to maternal depression, Solantaus-Simula (2002) found four response patterns: active empathy, emotional overinvolvement, indifference, and avoidance. Of the four types, children in the emotional overinvolvement and avoidance groups demonstrated the most internalizing and externalizing symptoms, independent of mother's level of depression. Furthermore, children in the active empathy group fared best. They did not feel guilty about their parent's depression and were able to discriminate their experiences from those of the depressed parent, supporting Beardslee's theory (1989) of the protective function of self-understanding. The most common response to maternal depression in the active group was to make some effort to cheer up the parent. Discuss these findings in relation to Neesha's case.

3. The way in which a child responds to distress can be strongly influenced by the cultural context in which the circumstance is embedded. Discuss this comment with respect to Neesha's case.

4. After reading the case of Neesha's brother, Tyrone Wilson, discuss the concepts of mulitfinality and equifinality as they related to the two case studies.

REFERENCES

Angold, A., Erklani, A., Silberg, J., Eaves, L., & Costello, E. J. (2002). Depression scale scores in 8–17-year-olds: Effects of age and gender. *Journal of Child Psychology and Psychiatry, 43,* 1052–1063.

Beardslee, W. R. (1989). The role of self-understanding in resilient individuals: The development of a perspective. *American Journal of Orthopsychiatry, 59,* 266–278.

Campbell, S. D., Morgan-Lopez, A. A., Cox, M. J., & McLoyd, V. C. (2009). A latent class analysis of maternal depression symptoms over 12 years and offspring adjustment in adolescence. *Journal of Abnormal Psychology, 118,* 479–493.

Cicchetti, D., & Rogosh, F. A. (1996). Editorial: Equifinality and multifinality in developmental psychopathology. *Development and Psychopathology, 8,* 597–600.

Cicchetti, D., & Rogosch, F. A. (1997). The role of self-organization in the promotion of resilience in maltreated children. *Development and Psychopathology, 9,* 797–815.

Durlak, J. A. (1998). Common risk and protective factors in successful prevention programs. *American Journal of Orthopsychiatry, 68,* 512–520.

Foster, C. J. E., Garber, J., & Durlak, J. (2008). Current and past maternal depression, maternal interaction behaviors, and children's externalizing and internalizing symptoms. *Journal of Abnormal Child Psychology, 36,* 527–537.

Gibbs, J. T., & Huang, L. N. (2001). Framework for the psychological assessment and treatment of minority youth. In J. T. Gibbs & L. N. Huang (Eds.), *Children of color* (pp. 112–142). San Francisco: Jossey-Bass.

Goodman, S., & Gotlib, I. (2002). *Children of depressed parents: Mechanisms of risk and implications for treatment.* Washington, DC: American Psychological Association.

Hacker, A. (1992). *Two nations: Black & white, separate, hostile, unequal.* New York: Scribner.

Lichtner, D., Quian, Z., & Crowley, M. (2005). Child poverty among racial minorities and immigrants: Explaining trends and differentials. *Social Science Quarterly, Special Issue, 86*(5), 1037–1059.

Luthar, S. S. (1993). Annotation: Methodological and conceptual issues in research on childhood resilience. *Journal of Child Psychology and Psychiatry, 34,* 441–453.

Luthar, S. S., & Zelazo, L. B. (2003). Research on resilience: An integrative review. In S. S. Luthar (Ed.), *Resilience and vulnerability: Adaptation in the context of childhood adversities* (pp. 511–549). Cambridge, UK: Cambridge University Press.

Lynch, E. W., & Hanson, M. J. (1998). *Developing cross-cultural competence* (2nd ed.). Baltimore, MD: Brooks.

Nelson, D. R., Hammen, C., Brennan, P. A., & Ullman, J. B. (2003). The impact of maternal depression on adolescent adjustment: The role of expressed emotion. *Journal of Consulting and Clinical Psychology, 71,* 935–944.

Richters, K., & Weintraub, S. (1990). Beyond diathesis: Toward an understanding of high-risk environments. In J. Rolf, A. Masten, D. Cicchetti, K. Nuechterlein, & S. Weintraub (Eds.), *Risk and protective factors in the development of psychopathology* (pp. 67–96). New York: Cambridge University Press.

Rutter, M. (1987). Psychosocial resilience and protective mechanisms. *American Journal of Orthopsychiatry, 57,* 316–330.

Rutter, M. (1990). Psychosocial resilience and protective mechanisms. In J. Rolf, A. Masten, D. Cicchetti, K. Nuechterlein, & S. Weintraub (Eds.), *Risk and protective factors in the development of psychopathology* (pp. 181–214). New York: Cambridge University Press.

Solantaus-Simula, T. (2002). Children's responses to low parental mood: Balancing between active empathy, overinvolvement, indifference, and avoidance. *Journal of American Academy of Child and Adolescent Psychiatry, 41,* 278–286.

U.S. Bureau of the Census. (1996). *Statistical abstract of the United States, 1996* (116th ed.). Washington, DC: U.S. Department of Commerce.

Werner, E. E., & Smith, R. S. (1982). *Vulnerable but invincible: A study of resilient children.* New York: McGraw-Hill.

Werner, E. E., & Smith, R. S. (1992). *Overcoming the odds: High risk children from birth to adulthood.* Ithaca, NY: Cornell University Press.

Werner, E. E., & Smith, R. S. (2001). *Journeys from childhood to midlife: Risk, resilience and recovery.* Ithica, NY: Cornell University Press.

Wiesner, M., & Kim, H. K. (2006). Co-occurring delinquency and depressive symptoms of adolescent girls and boys: A dual trajectory modeling approach. *Developmental Psychology, 42,* 1220–1235.

Ericka White

Not Yet Diagnosed

Ericka came to the Children's Center accompanied by her grandmother, who is the legal guardian. Although Ericka turned 10 years old 2 months ago, her appearance and her behavior suggest a child several years younger. Ericka has a history of severe emotional and behavioral problems that have interfered with her ability to be successful at school and with peers. She has two siblings who are also encountering some difficulties, but not to the extent that Ericka is. Her grandmother has decided to bring her to the Children's Center to obtain any guidance and direction that she can get about trying to manage Ericka's behaviors. As Ericka is getting older, the behaviors are becoming more and more difficult to control.

DEVELOPMENTAL HISTORY/FAMILY BACKGROUND

Ericka was placed with her grandmother by the Department of Social Services (DSS) when she was 5½ years old. Her two sisters, Cindy (7 years) and Debbie (2 years), were also placed at the same time. The grandmother was not sure of her milestones, but said that she was not totally bowel or bladder trained until she was 5 years old. Although there were no medical problems that the grandmother was aware of, she did not start talking clearly until she was 3 years old. Ericka has been described as tactile defensive, and she can create a huge fuss if she can feel the labels or seams of her clothing. She is noted to have an unusual gait (with a shuffle) and can resort to regressive behaviors (rocking, thumb sucking, tantrums) when she is stressed. Prior to her placement at her grandmother's home, there was a history of neglect and suspicions of sexual abuse by individuals who provided day care in their home. However, the suspicions were never substantiated and papers were never filed. Initially, Ericka was having unsupervised visits with her mother and monthly visits with her father; however, visits were then changed to supervised, since Ericka was soiling herself when she visited her mother. Currently, Ericka has not seen her father for the past 2 years, and maternal visits occur two or three times a year.

When Ericka was initially placed, there was an attempt to conduct an intellectual evaluation; however, Ericka was noncompliant and it was not possible to obtain a valid score. Ericka responded to the vocabulary subtest in very concrete answers with much pointing to objects in the room, rather than providing a definition. She also rarely responded to the initial request, and it would take several repetitions for her to engage in the tasks at hand. Ericka's drawing of a person and house were more typical of scribbles that would be produced by a 2- or 3-year-old, representing a person as a bodyless head that looked more like a "smiley" face.

The psychologist noted that Ericka's speech was difficult to understand, and that her interaction was similar to that of a 3- or 4-year-old. Although she seemed to be friendly, there were a lot of giddy and hyperactive behaviors that suggested underlying anxiety. Moods and behaviors vacillated during the assessment, including regressive behaviors (withdrawing, becoming absorbed into play activity to the exclusion of others, rocking, climbing under the testing table); hyperactive, impulsive, and restless behaviors when she became somewhat more comfortable; and noncompliant behaviors when she felt challenged. At times, Ericka would deliberately give an incorrect response and then laugh. The psychologist also noted that Ericka had an inappropriate sense of boundaries, at times wanting to hold hands, and at other times crossing her arms, pouting, and calling the psychologist a "retard." The psychologist also described her as a "hypervigilent child" who may be readily overwhelmed and overstimulated by her environment, since she tends to hyperfocus on details. Often, this intense focus on details results in her losing the overall concept of what is happening. Based on the interview information, the psychologist also believed that Ericka would need to stick to her routines in order to feel some sense of control in her environment that had been so chaotic. Currently, her only means of obtaining attention is to act out, test the limits, and provoke a response to her behavior.

Ericka is currently registered as a special education student at Forest Hills Elementary School, as a student with behavioral and emotional problems. Two years ago, Ericka was reassessed by the school psychologist. At that time, her full scale IQ score on the WISC-IV was 77 (range 73–83). Scores ranged from a strength on the Working Memory Index of 86, to a weakness on the Verbal Comprehension Index of 77. Academically, Ericka was functioning about at a mid–Grade 1 level. The school psychologist noted that results were of questionable validity due to issues of noncompliance during the assessment.

REASON FOR REFERRAL

Ericka's grandmother continues to experience extreme difficulties managing Ericka's behavior at home, and teachers are having similar problems at school. The problems have been increasing over the past year. Her grandmother has heard of children with autism who exhibit bizarre behaviors and wonders if Ericka might be autistic. A comprehensive assessment was recommended by the school to address grandmother's concerns and to obtain any additional information that might assist the home and school in better managing Ericka's behaviors. Currently, Ericka is often refusing to attend school, or if she gets to school, then she refuses to cooperate with teachers in the regular class or to complete any work that she is assigned. Behaviors have escalated to the point that she has threatened to kill students, her teacher, and anyone that gets in her way. She has also begun to tell the other students that God will punish them because they are bad.

When behaviors are not threatening, they are aimed at gaining attention (burping out loud, or yelling out inappropriate comments during class: "I am getting a training bra!").

Her teacher notes that Ericka is becoming increasingly preoccupied with boys and has made many in the class uncomfortable by asking to kiss them. She also tends to dwell on things that have upset her, and will relive the experience over and over, becoming increasingly upset even if the situation happened days ago. At times, she can be very affectionate and offers to help the teacher or tries to make others like her by giving them her possessions (pencils, books, stickers). According to her grandmother, the major complaints are Ericka's oppositional behaviors and her tendencies to obsess over things to an extreme (she says she is in love with her female teacher from last year).

ASSESSMENT RESULTS

Ericka was seen over the course of two assessment sessions. During the initial assessment period, the Wechsler Intelligence Scale for Children (WISC-IV) was administered. The Woodcock Johnson Tests of Achievement (WJIII) was administered during the second assessment session. Ericka was moderately cooperative; however, despite her attempts to comply, she often quickly tired of the task and wanted to discontinue, especially if the task was difficult. The Block Design task was discontinued, since Ericka was becoming notably frustrated with the task, which she clearly did not understand. Instead, the Picture Completion task was substituted, and she was able to have a much better understanding of the task demands. Effort was inconsistent throughout, with better attention and effort on "liked" versus "nonliked" tasks. Problems with attention span were notable, especially when asked to perform complex tasks, such as orally repeating a series of letter–number combinations. Her desire to socialize also interfered with task completion. This was especially notable during the second session, when she was asked to perform some academic tasks. As a result, the academic evaluation took considerable time, since work periods were interspersed with chats, coloring, and other more "fun" activities. Due to the wide range of effort expended among individual tasks and problems remaining focused on the task at hand, validity is suspect and caution is recommended in the interpretation of test scores.

Although the full scale score on the WISC-IV was 73 (range 69–79), there was a significant discrepancy between her Verbal Comprehension Index (VCI) score of 83 (range 77–91) and her index score for Processing Speed of 75 (range 69–87). When such unusual discrepancies exist, it can often be preferable to compute the General Ability Index (GAI) as the best estimate of overall cognitive ability, based on the scores obtained for the VCI and the Perceptual Reasoning Index (PRI), which was 79 (range 73–88). The overall GAI was 81 (range 76–87), placing her functioning just within the low average range at the 10th percentile. Scale scores between 8 and 12 are considered to be within the broad normal range. Ericka's scores range from a relative strength in verbal concept formation (scale score = 8) to a significant weakness in letter–number recall (scale score = 4).

Academically, although Ericka demonstrated good basic reading skills (standard score = 95; grade equivalent 3.7), she experienced significant difficulties with math reasoning (standard score = 66; grade equivalent 1.4). Written expression (standard score = 70; grade equivalent 2.0), reading comprehension (standard score = 84, grade equivalent 2.6), and math calculation skills (standard score = 77; grade equivalent 2.6) were within the expected ranges, given her intellectual level.

A number of different scales were administered to provide a better understanding of emotional and behavioral concerns at school and at home. Her grandmother and teacher both completed the Behavioral Assessment of Children (BASC-2), Devereaux Scales of Mental Disorders (DSMD), and an informal Autism Evaluation Form.

According to the BASC-2, grandparent and teacher agreement for clinical significance was noted on all composite scales, including Externalizing Problems, Internalizing Problems, the Behavioral Symptoms Index, and Adaptive Functioning. Individual scales that were significant for both raters (T score above 67) included aggression, depression, somatization, atypicality, attention problems, adaptability, social skills, and leadership.

On the DSMD, both grandmother and teacher endorsed significant concerns (T scores in excess of 67) for all composite scales, including Eternalizing, Internalizing, and Critical Pathology.

Problem areas noted by the teacher that included 100% endorsement of all items on the scale included moodiness/sullenness (*becomes easily upset, refuses to speak, holds a grudge, appears angry, irritable*), obsessions and compulsions (*insists on doing things one way, obsessed or preoccupied, insistence on same routine, shows no interest in more than one activity*), emotional lability (*temper tantrums, sudden mood swings, unpredictable, can't control anger, easily upset, irritable, angry when frustrated, overexcited, overreacts to change, reactive to mistakes*), somatic complaints (*problems sleeping, tired, complains of physical problems*), and inattention (*problems following rules, jumps from one thing to another, preoccupied, easily distracted, fails to pay attention, trouble concentrating, fails to complete assignments*). Problem areas noted by the grandmother that included 100% endorsement of all items on the scale included verbal aggression (*tells lies, swears or curses, argues with adults*).

In addition to these areas, other areas were also endorsed as showing 80% agreement and included hyperactivity, fearfulness (*distressed when separated from parent, unreasonable fear of strangers, easily startled or acts jumpy*), noncompliance (*refuses to go to school, refuses to eat, argues with adults, problems following rules, appears angry, refuses to speak*), social isolation (*avoids physical contact, withdraws, fails to participate*), and anger dyscontrol (*picks fights, tantrums, easily upset*).

The Autism Evaluation was also completed by Ericka's teacher and grandmother. According to her teacher, communication problems seen frequently included inappropriate responses to simple commands, while stereotypical behaviors were making high-pitched noises and preoccupations with objects and people. Her teacher saw her primarily as having a significant number of difficulties in the domain of social interactions, such as problems cooperating in a group; problems playing with others; inappropriate laughs or giggles; tantrums; repetition of certain acts; needs excessive amounts of reassurance; lacks subtle emotions, won't initiate tasks; lack of understanding as to why she is not liked. According to her grandmother, communication problems were evident in avoiding eye contact, repeating phrases, and responding to questions inappropriately. Stereotypical behaviors were noted in walks on tiptoes; slaps, hits, or bites self; requires extensive redirection; and shows obsessive interests. Difficulties with social interactions noted by the grandmother included avoids eye contact; problems with groups; laughs, giggles inappropriately; repetitive acts; and needs excessive reassurance.

In addition to test behaviors already described, the psychologist noted that Ericka was capable of many mood swings within a short period of time. When the psychologist was first introduced to Ericka, she seemed very startled and agitated, and did not want to make eye contact. She seemed to be very fearful and defensive and required considerable reassurance that she had not done anything wrong, and that they were just going to do some work together to see how she was doing in school. It took a while for rapport to be established, but Ericka seemed to like to draw and color, so extra materials were gathered and she sat for the first time while trying to draw a picture of a butterfly, like the one on the book cover that was on the desk. Eventually, after several erasures, she decided to trace the picture by placing her paper on top of the book. She was pleased with the result of her efforts.

Once she seemed more comfortable, the psychologist attempted to bring out some of the WISC-IV materials, beginning with the block design; however, since this was a very difficult task for Ericka to understand, she quickly became frustrated and started banging the blocks together to make a noise and then singing loudly. The psychologist suggested they do a different task (Picture Completion), which met with a more cooperative response, since she was able to understand the task demands "find what is missing in the picture." As Ericka became more familiar, she began to get more hyperactive and restless, squirming in her chair, and asking if they could go outside and play. The psychologist said she could take a break, and that she could do a few exercises by the desk to stretch. Again, Ericka began to push the boundaries, jumping up and down and wiggling her hips, singing, and asking if there was a radio to play music that she could dance to. When the psychologist said there wasn't, she immediately sat down in the chair, folded her arms, and pouted. These mood variations were ongoing throughout the majority of the assessment session.

When she arrived for the second session, she was overly familiar and wanted to hold the psychologist's hand as they walked down the hall from the classroom to the office. But soon she was swinging the psychologist's arm and became very hyper and asked if they could go out to play. When this was declined, she again became sullen and withdrew her hand and said that she didn't want to work today. She then asked the psychologist if she would come to her house after school to play. These types of inappropriate interactions were ongoing and occurred throughout the second session, with her demanding attention at one point and then withdrawing from contact when she did not get the response she wanted. As was noted many years ago in her initial assessment, Ericka continues to test limits with adults, and pushes boundaries. She is very needy of attention, but has little ability to control her emotional responses, or understand why she is not more successful socially. She seems to be challenged by significant problems that had their onset very early in her young life, and which she continues to struggle with years later.

Post-Case Questions

1. Ericka has many difficulties and a number of emotional and behavioral problems. Does Ericka qualify for any *DSM-IV* diagnosis, based on the information that is available from her history, the interviews, assessments, and her behaviors during the assessment? If so, what symptoms does she exhibit that meet criteria for a *DSM-IV* diagnosis or diagnoses?

2. Ericka's grandmother wondered if she had autism. Based on the assessment results, is there any support for her concerns? Are there any symptoms that might fall within the autistic spectrum, and if so, which ones?

3. What types of treatment would you recommend for Ericka given her intellectual challenges?

Adolescence

Colby Tyler

Attentional Problems or Distracted by Life?

Colby, a 14-year-old teenager in the ninth grade, came to the clinic accompanied by his mother, Tina. The appointment had finally been booked after Tina found Colby's midterm report card crumpled in the garbage can.

Not only was he failing one course, he was performing miserably across all subjects. When confronted, Colby lashed out at her, saying it was her fault, and ran out of the house. Tina admitted to running down the street after him, yelling like a "maniac." It was at this point that she realized that things had gotten out of control and that she needed help with Colby. His academic performance and temper outbursts were getting worse and worse. Tina explained that she also felt less able to cope with circumstances lately, due to her recent separation from her husband, Josh. Colby and his 7-year-old sister, Susy, continued to visit with their father every Wednesday and every second weekend.

Colby's parents both have university degrees. Tina works as an advertising account executive and Josh is an entrepreneur.

DEVELOPMENTAL HISTORY/FAMILY BACKGROUND

Despite a normal and full-term pregnancy, Tina stated that the labor was lengthy (12 hours) and ended with a forceps delivery. Tina reported that she was under a lot of stress during her pregnancy due to marital conflicts, and admitted to smoking and having an occasional drink during the pregnancy. Colby weighed 6 pounds 2 ounces, and although somewhat underweight, he seemed to be in good health at birth. The first 3 months were very difficult for Tina and Colby due to Colby's sensitive digestive system. After eating, Colby would often have bouts of projectile vomiting, diarrhea, and colicky behavior. Although Tina tried to nurse Colby, he was constantly hungry (feeding every 2 hours), and after 6 weeks, the doctor felt that Colby and mom would both be better off if he went on formula. Eventually, Colby settled into a better routine, although digestive problems and poor sleep patterns continue to be areas of difficulty for him, especially when under stress. On occasion, Colby will complain of stomachaches and ask to stay home from school. He also has difficulty both falling asleep and staying asleep. On many nights, Colby is still awake when Tina goes to bed, which is around midnight.

Developmental milestones were achieved within normative expectations, with the exception that Colby started to read spontaneously at 2 years of age. His first sight word was "Sears"; he pointed to the catalog after seeing a commercial on TV. After that, he started recognizing labels and logos on billboards and on the television. He was able to read printed words on paper by about 2½ years of age. Language skills also developed rapidly, and Colby's conversational skills were very well advanced by the time he entered nursery school.

Although Colby's health has been generally good, he had a severe outbreak of hives at 5 years of age (source never detected) and was placed on an elimination diet for 1 month during which time his food was restricted to rice and lamb broth. Colby has never been hospitalized, although he does have a tendency to be accident prone and has experienced cuts, scrapes, and bruises from falls and bike accidents. Colby's hearing and vision have both been assessed. Hearing is within normal limits, and glasses have been prescribed for distance vision.

When asked about family history, Tina noted that Colby's maternal grandmother has always been an anxious woman who has many fears and who has been on medication for depression. Colby's maternal grandfather was a heavy drinker and often became aggressive and physically abusive to his wife and eldest son. Colby's maternal grandfather also had Parkinson's disease and eventually died after a lengthy battle with Alzheimer's. Tina feels that her mother also likely suffers from posttraumatic stress disorder, due to the violence in the home. Although Tina's parents lived some distance away, Colby has maintained contact with his grandmother through her biyearly visits. Tina is herself an anxious woman who was a witness to domestic violence. Colby's paternal grandmother and grandfather are deceased and, according to Tina, there was no known pathology. There is a paternal uncle who has problems with alcohol and is also believed to have some psychotic features (hallucinations and delusions). He is unable to support himself, is currently on assistance, and is basically estranged from Tina's husband.

Tina described her marriage of 15 years as very turbulent. There was a previous marital separation due to Josh's infidelities, about 8 years earlier; however, Tina discovered that she was pregnant with Susy and they reconciled the marriage. Tina was never able to reestablish a sense of trust in Josh, and their relationship continued to slide. During the past year, the children had been exposed to many arguments and verbal accusations that centered on Josh's denial of any infidelities. Although Tina and her husband Josh had been living in the same house for the past year, they slept in separate rooms. Six months ago the house finally sold, and they moved into separate quarters. Tina has been seeing a counselor for the past year.

REASON FOR REFERRAL

Colby presented as an articulate and well-mannered adolescent. According to Colby, his mother really got very upset and angry when she found his report card. He wasn't eager to share it with her because she got very angry at him after the parent-teacher conference in January. He described the parent-teacher conference as embarrassing and frustrating.

First of all, both his mom and dad were present, and were throwing cold stares at each other across the room. All his teachers were in the room at the same time, and he felt like he was on trial. Only one teacher, his English teacher, Mr. Brighton, had anything good to say about him. The other teachers made him angry by saying that he wasn't trying, wasn't motivated, and didn't care about his schoolwork. Mrs. Fischer said that most times Colby wasn't prepared for class and didn't even bring his text with him. All accused him of wasting his potential. After all, Colby had been identified as a "gifted" student as part of the Grade 4 screening for the Gifted Program.

Colby's IQ was 147. However, in spite of all this intelligence, Colby had never really been a shining academic. In elementary school, Colby managed to get by with the little amount of effort he put in. However, Colby began to really slide academically when he entered Grade 9. Currently, Colby's grades are well below what would be expected, and he may not pass Chemistry at all.

Colby is up most nights until very late, and he can't get up in the morning. He has been late many times, and the school counselor has called Tina often to complain about Colby's tardiness.

Historically, Colby has always had problems sleeping. As a consequence, getting ready for school in the mornings had been problematic, with one exception. One day a week, when Colby attended the Gifted Program, he would have no difficulty getting up or being on time. The Gifted Program was Colby's favorite day of the week, and Colby was noticeably distressed upon learning that the gifted program would not extend into the secondary school level.

The level of Colby's intelligence was evident in his articulate conversational style and the depth of his knowledge in areas of interest, like computers. He was an engaging youth who was very captivating. However, as the conversation turned toward academics, Colby's entire demeanor changed, and he became very quiet. Tina addressed the issue of homework, which was a constant source of frustration for both of them. Colby seemed to have tremendous difficulty staying on task; everything was a potential distraction. Little things, like the telephone ringing or a noise outside, would be enough to break Colby's concentration, and once off-task it was very difficult to get him back on track. However, when Colby was playing computer games, he was riveted to the screen, and it would become very difficult to disengage Colby from the task. Tina could not understand how Colby could be so intensely focused when interested in something and so distractible when interest level was low. Like Colby's teachers, Tina thought it was a question of motivation. Tina described how Colby would begin each academic year all motivated and excited about school: new binders, pencils, and so on. Within a matter of weeks, however, old patterns would return and Colby would begin sleeping in, assignments would remain incomplete, and pencils would be lost or misplaced. According to Tina, Colby was the master of good intentions. Although Colby would often start projects with great enthusiasm, he had considerable difficulty sustaining this effort over the long haul. The Gifted Program was the only place where Colby really seemed to do well.

When asked what was so special about the Gifted Program, Colby said the teacher was fantastic, most of the kids were great, and they did a lot of computer work and mind-bender logic games. Tina interjected that she had talked at length with the teacher of the Gifted Program, who described Colby as a great kid and a wonderfully creative and divergent thinker. The teacher of the Gifted Program thought that one of Colby's difficulties might be that he had so many ideas that it was very hard for him to put things down on paper. He had, as she described it, "an explosive mind for brainstorming." Colby said that outside of the Gifted Program, it was difficult to concentrate and focus. When asked what helped to clear his head and give him a better ability to stick with something, he immediately said, "walking or riding my bike in the park." Colby explained that sometimes he had the clearest thoughts just walking by himself on the golf course. He wished he could bring that kind of focus into the classroom.

When asked about temper outbursts, Tina said that at times Colby seems incredibly patient, and she saw this behavior at its best when he was tutoring younger children in a reading program and giving golf lessons. However, at other times, Colby could be highly reactive and respond with a short fuse. At these times, Colby would be more prone to take things personally, be less responsive to logical reasoning, and be in a highly aroused state. When in this aroused stated it is not possible to reason logically with Colby until he settles down, which can take a while.

According to Colby's mother, behavioral outbursts had increased since the marital breakup. Tina stated that Colby has never adapted well to change and that the emotional split and physical move have likely added to the intensity of Colby's reactions. Having to shift between two households was not easy for Colby, especially in light of his problems with losing things and misplacing his notes. Colby now seemed even more disorganized than before. Tina also wondered whether Colby at some level somehow blames himself for the split.

When asked about the separation, Colby said very little. He said that his little sister was upset because he got to choose where he wanted to live and she didn't. He said she doesn't understand. It's awful to have to choose. Colby said his dad asked him why he chose to be with his mom and he said "because she is closer to school." Colby said that his dad called him "shallow." According to Tina, Colby has a tense relationship with his father because Josh tries to compete with Colby instead of supporting him. Tina said she is afraid that unless there are some answers to what is going on with Colby at this stage, Colby may end up having real problems. As it is, he can get very angry and flare up in a second, and this is really beginning to worry her. In response to that comment, Colby just looked at his mother and said, "I have been living in a house that is like the movie *The War of the Roses* . . . and you wonder why I get angry."

ASSESSMENT RESULTS

Guidelines for the interpretation of standard scores and T scores are available in Appendix C, as are descriptions of the assessment instruments used in the current assessment, as well as other resources. Colby's case serves as the prototypical case for this book, and with this goal in mind, actual test scores for each assessment measure and anecdotal examiner comments are available in Appendix A, along with scores for the assessments of three other children (Scott Michaels, Shirley Yong, and Arthur Watson). In addition, there is an in-depth discussion in Appendix A concerning how the clinician arrived at the case formulation for Colby based on differential diagnosis: evidence in support of a diagnosis of ADHD primarily inattentive type, and the rationale for ruling out other comorbid or competing diagnoses. There is also a written report wherein the clinical psychologist reports and shares her clinical and diagnostic impressions of Colby based on the assessment results. Since there is significant supplemental information for this particular case in Appendix A, the summary of assessment results in this chapter will be relatively brief.

Responses to the Wechsler Intelligence Scale for Children (WISC-IV) confirmed overall intellectual functioning within the very superior range (full scale IQ 147; range 141–151), with minimal difference noted between standard scores for the Verbal Comprehension Index (VCI 155; range 145–158) and Perceptual Reasoning Index (PRI 149; range 137–153). Colby's overall IQ score places him within the top .1% of the population (99.9th percentile). However, his scores were not evenly distributed among the different aspects of the IQ profile. As might be anticipated, although within the superior range, Colby's score of 129 on the Working Memory Index (WMI; range 119–134) was significantly below his VCI and PRI scores, while his score of 103 for Processing Speed (PSI; range 94–112) was severely impaired, relative to all his intellectual scores. Slow speed of psychomotor responses noted on paper-and-pencil tasks was accompanied by fatigue, awkward writing style, and ease of distraction. Despite adequate core academic skills (reading, spelling, math calculations), Colby had significant problems organizing his ideas when asked to write a short paragraph. Colby had difficulty getting started on the task, changed his topic many times, and after approximately 10 minutes, ultimately produced a very short but well-written passage of two lines.

Colby's mother completed the Conners Parent Rating Scale (CPRS-R:L) and the Achenbach Child Behavior Checklist (CBCL). Significant elevations were noted on scales of Somatic Complaints, Anxious-Depressed Mood, and Attention Problems. Teacher responses on the Teacher Report Form (TRF) also noted significant Somatic Complaints, and significant problems with Inattention and low frustration tolerance (Emotional Lability) were noted on the Conners (CTPS-R:L). Colby's self-ratings on the Youth Self-Report (YSF), Conners-Wells Adolescent Self-Report Scale (CASS:L), and Beck Youth Inventories (BYI-2) revealed significant elevations for Internalizing, Inattentive Behaviors, and Low Self-Concept, and significant elevation of Depressed and Anxious Moods. Further assessment with the Children's Depression Inventory (CDI) ruled out significant depression or suicidal ideation.

ISSUES, TRENDS, AND ALTERNATIVE TREATMENT METHODS

Attention-deficit/hyperactivity disorder (ADHD) is a commonly diagnosed mental health problem with between 3% to 5% of school-age children meeting criteria for the disorder (Barkley, 1998). Although once thought of as a childhood disorder, it is now estimated that between one third and two thirds of children with ADHD will continue to exhibit symptoms of the disorder throughout their lifetime (Wender, Wolf, & Wasserstein, 2001). Although hyperactivity and impulsivity decline with age, inattention and distractibility are likely to persist (Larsson, Lichtenstein, & Larsson, 2006) at a time when the educational setting is becoming more demanding (increased workload and expectations) and complex (multiple teachers), and requires more self-discipline and organization (Barkley, 1998).

Adolescents with ADHD are at increased risk for academic problems, difficult interpersonal relationships, low self-esteem, and car accidents, and have a higher incidence of psychiatric disorders, substance-use disorders, and antisocial behavior (Grenwald-Mayes, 2002; Thompson, Molina, Pelham, & Gnagy, 2007). Mannuzza and Klein (2000) found that children who demonstrate deficits in social skills and self-esteem continue to experience difficulties in these areas throughout adolescence and adulthood. Although there have been significant research and theoretical emphasis devoted to the primarily hyperactive-impulsive type of ADHD (Barkley, 1997), less is known about the predominantly inattentive type of ADHD, which has been in existence as a separate type of disorder only since the *DSM-III* (APA, 1980).

Medication as a Treatment

From a neurobiological perspective, ADHD has been associated with low levels of the *catecholamines* (dopamine, norepinephrine, epinephrine), neurotransmitters that impact attention and motor activity. Dopamine is especially important since pathways usually rich in dopamine, such as the prefrontal cortex, are underactive in brains of individuals with ADHD (Barkley, 1998). The most widely researched treatment for ADHD is the use of stimulant medication. The most commonly prescribed medications for ADHD are methylphenidate (Ritalin), dextroamphetamine (Dexedrine), and pemoline (Cylert), which act to increase the number of catecholamines in the brain. Each of these medications has been demonstrated to be effective in reducing the symptoms of ADHD in numerous clinically controlled trials (Greenhill, 1998; Spencer et al., 1995). Recently, a nonstimulant medication, atomoxetine (Strattera), a selective norepinephrine reuptake inhibitor, has met with FDA approval for ADHD.

Although some parents are concerned that giving their child medication for ADHD can result in a gateway phenomenon, leading to abuse of other types of substances later on, most research supports the opposite conclusion. Adults with ADHD who were not treated are more likely to abuse substances later in life compared to those whose ADHD was managed medically in their youth (Biederman, Wilens, Mick, Spencer, and Faraone, 1999). Wilens (2001) found youth with ADHD who took medication had lower rates of substance use (marijuana, cocaine, alcohol) compared with controls. However, Molina & Pelham (2003) conducted an 8-year follow-up of children and youth with ADHD and found higher levels of substance use across all substances (alcohol, tobacco, illicit drugs) compared to peers without ADHD. Surprisingly, the greatest substance use was related to the severity of attention problems, not impulsivity-hyperactivity, as had been noted previously (Barkley, DuPaul, & McMurray, 1990). However, in their longitudinal study of drug use outcomes for youth, August and colleagues (2006) found that youth with ADHD who also demonstrated externalizing problems had significantly worse drug outcomes (frequency of use and substance disorders) than those with ADHD-only or community controls, suggesting that ADHD without externalizing problems is not an increased risk for drug problems.

Although medication has been proven effective in reducing symptoms of inattention, impulsivity, and hyperactivity, effects have not consistently been demonstrated to carry over to other areas such as social relationships or academic achievement (Pelham, Wheeler, & Chronis, 1998). There has been significant controversy regarding the overuse of stimulant medication for children with ADHD (Diller, 1996). Although research has supported the use of methylphenidate (Ritalin) as a performance enhancer for children and adults with ADHD, it has been estimated that the use of stimulant medication has increased as much as 300% since 1990 (Hancock, 1996; Robison, Sclar, Skaer, & Galin, 1999). Although a recent study of prevalence rates for primarily inattentive, primarily hyperactive, and combined subtypes of ADHD conducted in Tennessee (Wolraich, Hannah, Pinnock, Baumgaerrel, & Brown, 1996) revealed 4.7%, 3.4%, and 4.4%, respectively, as many as 10% to 12% of all boys in the United States are currently taking Ritalin for ADHD (Leutwyler, 1996).

In part, the tendencies to overprescribe medication may result from the fact that the core symptoms of *inattention, restlessness,* and *impulsivity* found in ADHD also occur in other disorders, such as anxiety, learning disabilities, childhood depression, bipolar disorder, and posttraumatic stress disorder. There is also evidence that only one third to one half of children diagnosed with ADHD by their pediatrician have had any type of psychological or educational assessment to support the diagnosis (Leutwyler, 1996). More recently, Reich, Huang, and Todd (2006) studied treatment patterns for a large sample (1,555) of twins diagnosed with ADHD and found that 60% of boys and 45% of girls who met full diagnosis for ADHD were on stimulant medication, while 35% of the sample was receiving stimulant medication but did not meet *DSM-IV-TR* criteria for ADHD.

Multimodal and Alternative Treatment Methods

Some children may be unable to tolerate the side effects of medications for ADHD, or some parents may opt for alternative methods to treat the disorder. For these reasons, and the wide range of possible negative outcomes for children and youth with ADHD, the management of ADHD will often require a multimodal approach, combining psychosocial approaches in lieu of or conjoint with medical interventions. Other forms of treatment that have been used to treat children and youth with ADHD include behavior modification and contingency management in the classroom, cognitive behavior modification (CBM), parent training, and a variety of coaching techniques (Goldstein, 2005; Hallowell, 1995; Pelham et al., 1998).

There are many examples in the research literature of attempts to justify the use of CBM for children with ADHD, in programs designed to increase verbal self-instruction, problem-solving strategies, cognitive modeling, and self-monitoring. The underlying premise in these approaches is that training in problem solving will assist children with ADHD to manage behavioral self-control better (Hinshaw & Erhardt, 1991). However, while initial results of CBM were encouraging, more recent evidence suggests that CBM in isolation does not enhance outcomes for children with ADHD (Pelham et al., 1998).

In collaboration with the National Institute of Mental Health (NIMH), the MTA (multimodal treatment study of ADHD) investigated treatment alternatives for ADHD in six independent research centers. The investigators compared medical management alone (MEDMGT), behavioral modification (BEH), combined treatment (COMB), and a community comparison (CC). The BEH and CC groups did not receive medication. At the completion of the study, only the MEDMGT and COMB groups demonstrated symptom reductions (Swanson et al., 2001). However, follow-up at 14 months revealed that the effect size was reduced by 50%, while follow-up at 24 months revealed further deterioration. Within-group analysis revealed the greatest deterioration was for those who took medication as part of the study but discontinued after the study was completed, while the greatest long-term reduction in symptoms was for those children who were not medicated during the study, but who began taking medication once the study was completed (MTA Cooperative Group, 2004). One important side effect for the group who took medication the longest (throughout the study and remained on medication throughout the follow-up periods) was after the first 2 years; they demonstrated a 20% reduction in stimulant-related height gain (approximately 2 cm.) compared to peers who never took the medication. Although a rebound was expected in the third year, it never occurred, although no further reduction was evident; researchers continue to monitor the effects over 10- and 12-year periods for height and weight concerns and other long-term functional and symptomatic outcomes (Swanson et al., 2008).

Psychiatrist Ned Hallowell (1995) introduced the concept of "coaching" as a therapeutic measure for assisting adults with ADHD to manage life's challenges, and expressed his frustration at being unable to provide such support on a daily basis. In practice, the technique, which seems to make clinical sense, has gained momentum; however, there has been very little effort to empirically measure the effectiveness of this intervention (Goldstein, 2005). Although Jaksa and Ratey (1999) attempt to define coaching as a set of goal-driven and practical strategies that are developed by a coach and client to facilitate meeting the challenges of everyday life, they do not address how the strategies are developed, which strategies are most successful, and how success should be objectively measured and monitored. Recently, the Edge Foundation (2009) has funded a 27-month national study to document the effectiveness of coaching for college students with ADHD, which will examine the effects of coaching on 250 randomly selected students with ADHD, relative to peers who do not receive coaching, for such outcomes as grade point average, study skills, sense of well-being, and social adjustment. If the technique is successful, with the advent of technology, it is possible that coaching may be readily available and monitored electronically in the future.

When Colby mentioned that he could think more clearly after riding his bike or walking in the park or on the golf course, he had intuitively discovered a method of increasing his focus and attention in a way that has only recently been investigated empirically. Taylor and Kuo (2009) studied the attention and concentration abilities of 17 children diagnosed with ADHD (7 to 12 years of age) after taking a 20-minute walk in three different environments: downtown, in a neighborhood, or in the park. Children in the study concentrated significantly better after the walk in the park, relative to walks in the other two environments. The researchers suggest that "doses of nature" might be a "new tool in the tool kit for managing ADHD symptoms" (p. 402).

Post-Case Questions

1. According to Russell Barkley (1997), sustained attention comes in two different forms: *contingency-shaped attention* and *goal-directed persistence*.

   Factors that can be instrumental in increasing or decreasing contingent attention include task novelty, intrinsic interest, reinforcing properties inherent in the task, fatigue state of the participant, and presence or absence of adult supervision. According to Barkley, this form of sustained attention is often not problematic for ADHD children. However, goal-directed persistence requires sustained persistence of attention and effort in the absence of highly reinforcing task properties, which is extremely problematic for children with ADHD.

    a. Based on Barkley's descriptions of the two forms of sustained attention, prepare a response for Colby's mother that would address her questions regarding why Colby can stay focused for long periods of time playing video games but is extremely distracted while attempting his homework assignments.

    b. Given your understanding of sustained attention, how might Colby's "gifted" intelligence serve to further exacerbate his problems?

2. Based on the information presented in the case study, would Colby's symptoms match criteria in the *DSM* for attention-deficit/hyperactivity disorder (ADHD)? If so, which type of ADHD does Colby exhibit?

3. Develop a case formulation for Colby from two theoretical perspectives (e.g., family/parenting/attachment, cognitive-behavioral, or biological). How would these formulations affect different treatment outcomes?

4. Colby was identified as "gifted" when he was in the fourth grade. Do you believe that Colby's gifted label was ultimately a positive factor or a negative factor in his development? Explain.

REFERENCES

American Psychiatric Association (APA). (1980). *Diagnostic and statistical manual of mental disorders* (3rd ed.). Washington, DC: American Psychiatric Press.

August, G. J., Winters, K., Realmuto, G. M., Fahnhorst, T., Botzet, A., & Lee, S. (2006). Prospective study of adolescent drug use among community samples of ADHD and non-ADHD participants. *Journal of the American Academy of Child and Adolescent Psychiatry, 45,* 824–832.

Barkley, R. A. (1997). Attention deficit hyperactivity disorder. In E. J. Mash & L. G. Terdal (Eds.), *Assessment of childhood disorders* (pp. 71–129). New York: Guilford.

Barkley, R. A. (1998). *Attention deficit hyperactivity disorder: A handbook for diagnosis and treatment* (2nd ed.). New York: Guilford.

Barkley, R. A., DuPaul, G. J., & McMurray, M. D. (1990). A comprehensive evaluation of attention deficit disorder with and without hyperactivity. *Journal of Consulting and Clinical Psychology, 58*(6), 775–789.

Biederman, J., Wilens, T., Mick, E., Spencer, T., & Faraone, S. V. (1999). Pharmacotherapy of attention-deficit/hyperactivity disorder reduces risk for substance use disorder. *Pediatrics, 104,* e20.

Diller, L. H. (1996). The run on Ritalin: Attention deficit disorder and stimulant treatment in the 1990s. *Hastings Center Report, 26,* 12–18.

Edge Foundation (EDGE). (2009). *First national study of personal coaching's effectiveness for college students.* Retrieved June 22, 2009 from http://www.edgefoundation.org/press/press-releases/adhd-research-program/

Goldstein, S. (2005). Coaching as a treatment for ADHD. *Journal of Attention Disorders, 9,* 379–381.

Greenhill, L. (1998). Attention-deficit/hyperactivity disorder. In B. T. Walsh (Ed.), *Child psychopharmacology* (pp. 91–109). Washington, DC: American Psychiatric Association.

Grenwald-Mayes, G. (2002). Relationship between current quality of life and family of origin dynamics for college students with attention-deficit/hyperactivity disorder. *Journal of Attention Disorders, 5,* 211–222.

Hallowell, E. M. (1995). Coaching: An adjunct of the treatment of ADHD. *The ADHD Report, 3,* 7–9.

Hancock, L. N. (1996, March 18). Mother's little helper. *Newsweek,* pp. 51–56.

Hinshaw, S. P., & Erhardt, D. (1991). Attention-deficit hyperactivity disorder. In P. Kendall (Ed.), *Child and adolescent therapy: Cognitive-behavioral procedures* (pp. 98–128). New York: Guilford.

Jaksa, P., & Ratey, N. (1999). Therapy and ADD coaching: Similarities, differences, and collaboration. *Focus, 6,* 3–11.

Larsson, H. L., Lichtenstein, P., & Larsson, J. O. (2006). Genetic contribution to the development of ADHD subtypes from childhood to adolescence. *Journal of the American Academy of Child and Adolescent Psychiatry, 45,* 973–981.

Leutwyler, K. (1996). Paying attention: The controversy over ADHD and the drug Ritalin is obscuring a real look at the disorder and its underpinnings. *Scientific American, 272*(2), 12–13.

Mannuzza, S., & Klein. R. G. (2000). Long-term prognosis in attention-deficit/ hyperactivity disorder. *Child and Adolescent Psychiatric Clinics of North America, 9,* 711–726.

Molina, B., & Pelham, W. E. (2003). Childhood predictors of adolescent substance use in a longitudinal study of children with ADHD. *Journal of Abnormal Psychology, 112,* 497–507.

MTA Cooperative Group. (2004). National Institute of Mental Health Treatment Study of ADHD (NIMH; MTA) follow-up: 24-month outcomes of treatment strategies for attention-deficit/hyperactivity disorder. *Pediatrics, 113,* 754–761.

Pelham, W. E., Jr., Wheeler, T., & Chronis, A. (1998). Empirically supported psychosocial treatments for attention deficit hyperactivity disorder. *Journal of Clinical Child Psychology, 27,* 190–205.

Robison, L. M., Sclar, D. A., Skaer, T. L., & Galin, R. S. (1999). National trends in the prevalence of attention-deficit/hyperactivity disorder and the prescribing of methylphenidate among school children: 1990–1995. *Clinical Pediatrics, 38*(4), 209–217.

Reich, W., Huang, H., & Todd, R. D. (2006). ADHD medication use in a population-based sample of twins. *Journal of the American Academy of Child and Adolescent Psychiatry, 45,* 801–807.

Robison, L. M., Sclar, D. A., Skaer, T. L., & Galin, R. S. (1999). National trends in the prevalence of attention-deficit/hyperactivity disorder and the prescribing of methylphenidate among school children: 1990–1995. *Clinical Pediatrics, 38*(4), 209–217.

Spencer, T., Wilens, T., Biderman, J., Faraone, S. V., Ablon, J. S., & Lapey, K. (1995). A double-blind, crossover comparison of methylphenidate and placebo in adults with childhood-onset attention deficit hyperactivity disorder. *Archives of General Psychiatry, 52,* 434–443.

Swanson, J., Arnold, L. E., Kraemer, H., Hechtman, L., Molina, B., Hinshaw, S., et al. (2008). Evidence, interpretation, and qualification from multiple reports of long-term outcomes in the multimodal treatment study of children with ADHD (MTA): Part II: Supporting details. *Journal of Attention Disorders, 12,* 15–43.

Swanson, J. M., Kraemer, H. C., Hinshaw, S. P., Arnold, L. E., Conners, C. K., Abikoff, H. B., et al. (2001). Clinical relevance of the primary findings of the MTA: Success rates based on severity of ADHD and ODD symptoms at the end of treatment. *Journal of the American Academy of Child and Adolescent Psychiatry, 40*(2), 168–179.

Taylor, A. F., & Kuo, F. E. (2009). Children with attention deficits concentrate better after walk in the park. *Journal of Attention Disorders, 12,* 402–409.

Thompson, A., Molina, B., Pelham, W., & Gnagy, E. (2007). Risky driving in adolescents and young adults with childhood ADHD. *Journal of Pediatric Psychology, 32*(7), 745–759.

Wender, P. H., Wolf, L. E., & Wasserstein, J. (2001). Adults with ADHD: An overview. In P. J. Wassermen, L. Wolf, & F. F LeFever (Eds.), *Adult attention deficit disorder: Brain mechanisms and life outcomes* (pp. 1–16). New York: New York Academy of Sciences.

Wilens, T. E. (2001). ADHD and alcohol or drug abuse. Program and abstracts of the 154th Annual Meeting of the American Psychiatric Association, New Orleans.

Wolraich, M. L., Hannah, I. N., Pinnock, T. Y., Baumgaerrel A., & Brown, J. (1996). Comparison of diagnostic criteria for attention-deficit hyperactivity disorder in a county-wide sample. *Journal of American Academy of Child and Adolescent Psychiatry, 35,* 319–324.

Arthur Watson

Won't or Can't; a Case of Mistaken Identity

Arthur, who was 15 years and 5 months of age, came to the interview accompanied by his mother and father. Mr. and Mrs. Watson were requesting a psychological assessment of their son Arthur to determine whether Arthur might have a learning disability. The parents were concerned that weak academic progress and lack of behavior controls might be the result of frustration resulting from learning problems.

DEVELOPMENTAL HISTORY/FAMILY BACKGROUND

Arthur was delivered by cesarean section, 2 weeks post due date, weighing 8 pounds 3 ounces. The pregnancy was reportedly normal with the exception of fluid retention, which was monitored over the course of five ultrasound assessments as well as pelvic X-rays. Arthur was jaundiced at birth; however, this was treated and he was released from the hospital within the normal time frame.

Developmental motor milestones were delayed: sitting at 8 to 9 months, walking at 16 months. Language skills were also reported as delayed, and although he did say his first word at about 1 year, he reportedly did not speak much in his initial years. Descriptions of infant behaviors revealed that Arthur was not temperamental, nor was he overly active or colicky. Arthur experienced febrile convulsions, and he had a history of earaches, ear infections, and impacted ears due to wax build-up. There were difficulties with bed-wetting until Arthur was 11 years of age.

Family history reveals that Arthur is the oldest child in a family of three, having a younger sister (11 years) and brother (8 years). Arthur's siblings appear to be well adjusted both emotionally and academically. There is no known history of psychopathology in the families of either parent. Arthur's parents, Celia and Paul Watson, met at university and have been in a stable marital relationship for almost 20 years. Celia works as a counselor in a women's shelter, and Paul works as a financial consultant for the government.

Previous Assessment Results/School History

Arthur has had an extensive history of previous assessments, and his initial investigation was conducted by a developmental pediatrician when he was 3 years 8 months of age. At that time, Arthur presented with articulation problems and developmental delays. An EEG was conducted and results were normal. The recommendation was for enrollment in a nursery school program, and Arthur began attending a Montessori program the next year. However, progress continued to be difficult and problems with aggression, overactivity, and difficulty following directions made the transition to kindergarten problematic. Arthur's behaviors continued to be a concern with a high level of overactivity, aggressive responding, and poor ability to follow directions. Arthur was reassessed by the developmental pediatrician at 5½ years of age. On this occasion, Arthur presented with "silly" behaviors and appeared distractible and agitated, although he was able to score in the lower average range on a picture vocabulary test. The recommendation was for a classroom with reduced pupil-teacher ratio and a trial of stimulant medication. However, the placement broke down and Arthur's parents were asked to remove Arthur from the kindergarten program midway through the academic year. Apparently, Arthur's behavior could not be maintained within the kindergarten program and administrative staff felt that Arthur required more supervision than could be provided in the regular program.

Mr. and Mrs. Watson were becoming increasingly frustrated with the public education system and took Arthur to a private psychologist for an assessment when he was 5 years 9 months old. Results of the Wechsler Preschool and Primary Intelligence Test (WPPSI-R) revealed verbal functioning to be within the lower limits of the lower average range, while performance skills were within the borderline range. Results from the picture vocabulary test were identical to those obtained 6 months earlier by the developmental pediatrician, indicating receptive vocabulary to be within the lower average range. The recommendations were in support of a trial medication period, future assessment of central auditory processing, and the need for a structured behavioral management program. History repeated itself, however, and Arthur's continued behavioral outbursts resulted in his eventual removal from the regular class program in the public school. As a result, the school board recommendation was for future placement in a behavioral program. Parents appealed the decision, stating that Arthur had attention-deficit/hyperactivity disorder (ADHD) and that his needs would be better served in a program that addressed his learning needs. However, Arthur's parents were unable to produce a clear diagnostic statement to confirm that Arthur had ADHD, and Arthur had not responded favorably to stimulant medication. Ultimately, the school board decision to place Arthur in a special program was upheld; however, the designation of exceptionality was changed from "Emotionally and Behaviorally Disordered" (EBD) to "Learning Disabled" (LD).

Over the course of the next 4 years, Arthur attended programs in several schools with limited success. At 7 years of age, he enrolled in a day treatment program affiliated with a local children's mental health center. While at the center, assessment of intellectual level was attempted; it was only partially completed, however, due to lack of compliance on Arthur's part. Although results of that intellectual assessment were inconclusive, it was reported that subtest scores ranged from average (general information, block design) to very delayed (oral math, visual sequencing). Arthur scored at the 8th percentile on a readministration of the picture vocabulary test, which was well below previous scores. It was suggested that Arthur's outbursts might be attempts to avoid academic difficulties and were likely developmental in nature. The following year, Arthur was discharged from day treatment and placed in a primary learning disability program in a community school. However, Arthur's transition to the program was not successful and parents ultimately removed Arthur from school; he was homeschooled the following year.

Parents enrolled Arthur in a local private school when he was 9 years of age; progress was minimal and the school was forced to shut down due to financial reasons. For the next 2 years, Arthur returned to the public school system and was placed in a Junior Special Learning Class. Despite continued problems with attention and concentration, Arthur demonstrated improved work habits, and aggressive acting out was replaced with a newly developed sense of humor. Arthur seemed to relate to his teacher in a very positive manner. However, the following year, when Arthur was moved to a Senior Special Learning Class, previous difficulties with aggression resurfaced and Arthur was removed once again and homeschooled. Parents hired a tutor to assist Arthur during this period, and assessments conducted by the tutor revealed core academics to be at the first percentile (kindergarten/Grade 1 level). Reassessment on the picture vocabulary test revealed receptive language to be below the first percentile, and at 14 years of age, Arthur had a vocabulary that was approximately equivalent to a child half his age (7 years 9 months).

Arthur was now becoming a teenager, and aggressive outbursts were becoming more threatening to his parents and younger siblings. Out of desperation, parents sent Arthur to a private boarding school in upstate New York. They were hopeful that the school would be able to provide the structure and behavior management that Arthur required and that he would return from the school with many positive changes. A review of reports suggests, however, that the facility was more of a prep school than one geared to special needs and was highly inappropriate for Arthur. Parents have had little understanding of what transpired over the year, since Arthur has refused to share any information about his school experience with his parents. When Arthur returned home after 1 year in the program, he was more angry and resentful than ever. Behaviors continued to escalate, and Arthur was beginning to use threatening gestures toward his parents and physically and verbally abusive behaviors toward his siblings (kicking, swearing, hitting, pushing).

As a result of a recent violent outburst (Arthur chased his sister around the house with an electrical cord, saying he was going to get her), parents sought temporary placement for Arthur in a residential facility for youth with emotional and behavioral problems. At the time of the current interview, Arthur was being slowly integrated back into his home on weekends.

REASON FOR REFERRAL

Arthur's parents were desperate for any information that would help them with Arthur. They were requesting a formal assessment to clarify the nature of cognitive functioning, academic levels, and any other information that might assist in better understanding Arthur's social/emotional and behavioral difficulties. According to Mr. and Mrs. Watson, despite a number of previous attempts to assess Arthur's functioning, to their knowledge Arthur had not had a complete formal psychological assessment in the past.

During the interview, Arthur appeared highly agitated. He shifted his position in the chair continuously, slouching down with his long legs dangling across the floor. At approximately 5 feet 10 inches tall, Arthur towered over his parents when he stood up. Throughout the interview, Arthur would make grimacing faces, mimic his parents' comments, interrupt often, and correct his parents, especially his mother, in a loud and mocking voice. When asked about the private school he had attended in New York, Arthur said that he hated the school and he hated the kids at the school. In response to specific questions, Arthur was difficult to understand, partially due to poor articulation and sound substitutions ("s" for "t"), but mostly because he tended to be very tangential in his responses. Cluttered speech, a tendency to trail off at the ends of sentences, and a propensity to make "silly voices" also rendered communication difficult to understand.

When asked if he knew why he was at the clinic, Arthur said that he was "too violent" sometimes and added that lately he was "more bad than good." He did seem remorseful, however, and said that he wanted to be better. When asked if he might agree to take medication to help control his behavior and do better at school, Arthur responded that he was prepared to try, if it would work. He added that things were very difficult now, and he was getting into trouble a lot because of his temper. He said that he was also having trouble sleeping and falling asleep. In response to a question about what concerned him most, Arthur said that sometimes he did stuff that he wished he hadn't but then it was too late. He spontaneously added that he did not have any friends and that he hated his "zits" and wanted them to go away so he could get a girlfriend. He worried that he would not be able to get rich and find a wife when he got older.

Arthur was seen for three assessment sessions. Behavior varied across sessions, with Arthur becoming more vocal and volunteering more personal information as time progressed. However, Arthur was quite agitated when he arrived for the third session, and muttered an obscenity as his father dropped him off at the office. When asked if he wanted to talk, he said that he just wanted to do his work with the psychologist for the day, but then spontaneously began to discuss what had occurred. Arthur was of the impression that he would not be able to go back to school because it cost too much money and that he would have to stay home and do jobs all day. When he was reassured that parents and psychologist were working together to find out which school he would be happiest at, he seemed to be very relieved and was eager to get back to the assessment. A fourth assessment session was scheduled; however, further assessment was preempted when Arthur's behavior again escalated at home, resulting in admission to the crisis unit at the regional children's hospital. On that occasion, Arthur had threatened harm to his parents, sister, and eventually himself and was admitted to the hospital for one month to allow for medication trials, observation, and behavioral stabilization.

While in the hospital, Arthur responded well to a combination of sertraline and thioridazine, his behavior stabilized, and he was discharged back to his home at the end of the month. A discharge planning meeting was held prior to Arthur's release from the hospital, and parents again voiced their frustrations with the "system," complaining that they had been given very little direction regarding future placements for Arthur. Parents returned to the clinic to complete Arthur's assessment and for assistance regarding future planning.

ASSESSMENT RESULTS

Arthur's scores for all the assessment instruments that he completed and the scales completed by his parents are available in Appendix A. The following is a summary of those findings. Information regarding specific assessment instruments and guidelines for the interpretation of standard scores and T scores are available in Appendix C.

The Wechsler Intelligence Scale for Children (WISC-IV) was administered over three sessions to allow for sufficient rapport building and to accommodate Arthur's tangential response style. Spontaneous digressions were frequent throughout the assessment session. Arthur's effort was considered optimum, and although anxiety and low frustration tolerance were evident, results were considered to be a valid index of functioning levels. Although Arthur's overall score of 69 on the Perceptual Reasoning Index (PRI; range 65–76) was superior to his score of 55 for the Verbal Comprehension Index (VCI; range 51–62), the discrepancy was not significant. Therefore, Arthur's full scale IQ of 57 (range 53–64) is considered to be a good index of composite intellectual functioning. Scores for the Processing Speed Index (PSI) of 54 (range 49–61) and Working Memory Index (WMI) of 55 (range 51–62) were similar to scores for VCI. Overall intelligence was within the mentally deficient range below the 1st percentile. Arthur is cognitively challenged and his abilities range from the mentally deficient range to the level of mild mental retardation. Developmentally, cognitive skills are similar to a child several years his junior, at approximately 8 to 8 ½ years of age. Results suggest a global and pervasive cognitive deficit rather than any specific learning disability. Arthur is a concrete thinker, and transferring information between different environments is challenging for him. Verbal expression is weak and vocabulary knowledge, limited. Arthur often uses words inappropriately, familiar with the word but not completely grasping the meaning. His comprehension improves if visual aids (pictures) are added.

Academically, according to the Wide Range Achievement Test (WRAT-4), Arthur's academic performance was commensurate with his intellectual functioning, and Arthur scored consistently at the Grade 1 level across the core academic areas. He demonstrated a relative weakness in math calculation and a relative strength in spelling.

Parents completed the Adaptive Behavior Scale (ABS-S:2) and Vineland Adaptive Inventory. According to the ABS-S:2, Arthur was rated at age level in all areas of Personal and Personal-Social Responsibility. Similarly, parents also rated Trustworthiness and Social Engagement within the norm. Language Development, Hyperactive Behaviors, and Disturbing Interpersonal Behaviors were rated as minor problems. Ratings on the Vineland Interview were consistent with the ABS-S:2 and placed Daily Living Skills and Socialization within the normal range for his age and Communication Skills at a low average level. Caution was advised in interpreting overall adaptive functioning using the scores from the parental assessments, which evaluated his behavior in an environment of high familiarity (home, high predictability, highly structured), and offered situations with few external distracters. It was suggested that adaptive functioning would deteriorate considerably when he was in situations that were novel and unexpected, offered many distracters, were unstructured, and offered a wide variety of academic and social pressures.

According to parent ratings on the Conners Scales (CPL) and Achenbach (CBCL), Arthur demonstrated significant problems in areas of Conduct (T = 96), Learning (T = 71), Impulsivity (T = 68), and Anxiety (T = 68).

Further Assessment: Psychiatric Consult. A psychiatric referral was initiated to assist in the monitoring of Arthur's medication following his release from the hospital. Resulting from the psychiatric consult, the possibility of Tourette's disorder was also raised due to evidence of some complex motor and vocal tics with associated mimicry. During his interview with the psychiatrist, Arthur admitted that although he sometimes would engage in swearing, facial grimaces, silly voices, and mimicry on his own accord, at other times, he had difficulty controlling these behaviors. As a result, the psychiatrist suggested that Tourette's disorder might also be a possibility.

Although recent evidence of depression with aggressive behavior patterns had responded to a combination of sertraline and thioridazine, the psychiatrist recommended that the family slowly wean Arthur off the thioridazine, which was causing excessive sedation. The psychiatrist indicated that future pharmacological treatment might include an SSRI (sertraline or Prozac) in combination with stimulant medication. Other areas to be addressed would include possible risperidone for the motor tic disorder and/or lithium to reduce aggressive behavior.

ISSUES, TRENDS, AND TREATMENT ALTERNATIVES

The concept of mental retardation (MR) has evolved over the course of history. Seguin, the founding father of the American Association on Mental Retardation (AAMR), established the association in 1876 to advocate for the rights of individuals who had mental deficiencies resulting from arrested development. By the late 1950s, there was growing discontent with the practice of determining MR on the sole basis of intelligence testing (IQ below 85; one standard deviation below the mean), and criteria were expanded to include the need to establish accompanying deficits in adaptive functioning, in addition to onset in childhood (initially before age 16). Twenty years later, criteria were further narrowed to include an IQ level which was two standard deviations below the mean (IQ 70), and in 1992 the AAMR increased the age of onset to include onset prior to age 18 (AAMR, 1992), which is also the age of onset in the *DSM-IV-TR* (APA, 2000).

There are currently three different systems involved in the classification of intellectual and developmental disabilities (IDD) in North America: the *DSM-IV-TR* (APA, 2000), AAMR (2002), and the educational system (IDEA, 2004). A more detailed discussion of the similarities and differences between these systems regarding the classification of IDD is available in Appendix B. In addition to revealing impairment in intellectual functioning, deficits in adaptive functioning have also been a critical component of a determination of IDD for all three systems, although the systems vary in how they define adaptive behaviors. According to the *DSM-IV-TR* (APA, 2000), deficits should occur in at least two areas, including communication skills, self-care, home living, social/interpersonal skills, use of community resources, self-direction, functional academic skills, work, leisure, and health and safety.

In January 2007, the AAMR changed its name to the American Association on Intellectual and Developmental Disabilities (AAIDD) to address concerns with the use of the label *mental retardation* for individuals with intellectual disabilities (*AAMR News,* November 2006). The switch from mental retardation to *intellectual and developmental disability* was instituted to better conform to terminology used in Canada and Europe and to focus on the mission of AAIDD, which is to assist and advocate for those with developmental disabilities, such as autism, which often coexist with IDD.

Regarding the case of Arthur, in addition to deficits in mental capacity and adaptive behavior problems, there was also concern that Arthur might demonstrate symptoms of Tourette's disorder. According to the *DSM-IV-TR* (APA, 2000), Tourette's disorder is a developmental disorder that is characterized by uncontrollable tics (rapid, nonrhythmic movements or vocalizations) that are evident in multiple motor and at least one vocal tic. The course of the disorder is unpredictable, with many youth outgrowing the disorder in adulthood.

Behavioral Interventions and Treatments

Treatments and interventions for children and adolescents with mental impairments often focus on two broad areas:

1. intellectual-adaptive deficits, and
2. associated behavioral-emotional problems (Kronenberger & Meyer, 2001).

Evidence-based treatment for associated behavioral difficulties will be discussed first, followed by a discussion of the efficacy of educational treatments.

The Behavior Management of Behavioral and Emotional Problems

The prevalence of challenging behaviors among children and youth with intellectual disabilities has been estimated at approximately 7% (Kiernan & Qureshi, 1993), although rates for children attending special schools has been reported to be as high as 22% (Kiernan & Kiernan, 1994). Negative outcomes for youth with impaired cognitive functioning and challenging behaviors include physical risk to the youth or peers and increased risk of isolation, abuse, and other forms of inappropriate interactions with peers (Emerson, 2001), which increases the long-term risk of developing serious psychological difficulties (Deater-Deckard, 2001; LaFontana & Cillessen, 2002). Furthermore, in their study of child and adolescent impressions of those with challenging behaviors, Byrne and Hennessy (2009) found that similar to their average-functioning peers, children and adolescents with intellectual disabilities are less willing to engage in shared activities with peers who display challenging behaviors.

Treatment programs developed to assist with behavioral and emotional problems in populations with IDD have largely used methods of functional analysis based on *applied behavior analysis (ABA)*. ABA has been defined as "the extension of experimental methods to applied settings" (Kazdin, 1994, p. 25). Behavior management programs can be simplistic (using praise to increase or ignoring to decrease behaviors) or very complex (contingency-based programs). Behavior management techniques are based on sound empirical support that has been documented in countless studies (for review, see Lipsey & Wilson, 1993) and journals devoted specifically to behavioral research: *Behavior Modification, Journal of Applied Behavior Analysis, Behavior Therapy,* and others. However, successful behavior management programs require more than a knowledge of the mechanisms of behavioral change. They also require an understanding of how the child's different situational contexts contribute to the problem behaviors (Phares, Compas, & Howell, 1989).

Behavioral treatment programs can be developed to either increase deficit behaviors or decrease behavioral excess. Although it is always preferable to increase deficit behaviors, such as targeting increased compliance through the use of positive reinforcement or negative reinforcement, there are times when it is necessary to focus on reducing a behavioral excess (e.g., highly aggressive behavior) through the use of punishment or extinction. Behavioral principles of schedules of reinforcement, shaping behavior and behavior chaining, secondary rewards, and token economies have all been demonstrated as effective methods for managing behavioral change. Empirical studies have emphasized the need to assess baseline behavior rates and to monitor the effectiveness of programs (Jensen, 1988) and time-out techniques (Solnick, Rincover, & Peterson, 1977).

Behavioral programs can benefit from the use of an empirical approach to select target behaviors (Weist, Ollendick, & Finney, 1991). For example, research has investigated how to create a reinforcer hierarchy (Christian, 1983); the selection of reinforcers for specific populations, such as adolescent populations (Reynolds, Salend, & Beahan, 1989, 1992); and techniques to promote generalization of outcomes across situations (Rutherford & Nelson, 1988; Stokes & Baer, 1977). The efficacy of using contingency management systems or token economies to improve behavior in children and adolescents has been demonstrated across many settings (Wielkiewicz, 1995). Children can be motivated to increase desirable behaviors by earning tokens or coupons to be traded in for concrete reinforcers. Contingency programs to increase deficit behaviors can be used in the regular classroom (Brantley & Webster, 1993), special classroom (Kratochwill, Elliott, & Rotto, 1990), and home (Clark, 1985). Contingency programs can also be developed to reduce excess behaviors. Programs that target reducing behaviors function on a response cost basis, where children lose tokens, coupons, and the like when they demonstrate the undesirable behavior.

Response cost programs can also be effectively introduced in the regular class (Rapport, Murphy, & Bailey, 1982), the special class (Proctor & Morgan, 1991), and the home (Little & Kelley, 1989). Other approaches to improving behavior in populations with IDD have included the use of relaxation training (Cautela & Groden, 1978; McPhail & Chamove, 1989) and functional equivalence training or teaching of replacement behaviors (Horner & Day, 1991), while behavior reduction can involve techniques such as performing restitution or undoing/overcorrection (Azrin & Besalel, 1980). Behavior programs for training in adaptive skills and social behaviors have also demonstrated successful positive change (Embregts, 2000).

Parent training programs have also been demonstrated to be an effective component for treatment of children with IDD and other disabilities (Handen, 1998), and inclusion of parent treatment components can be superior to treatments conducted in clinics alone (Koegel, Schreibman, Britten, Burke, & O'Neill, 1982). Parent training programs have been proven effective whether administered in groups (Harris, 1983) or individually (Clark & Baker, 1983). Parent training programs can also be helpful in increasing compliant behaviors in the home (Forehand & McMahon, 1981).

Positive behavior support (PBS) is a theoretical framework for understanding problem behaviors that was primarily derived from ABA. The PBS approach emerged in the mid-1980s amid increasing concerns regarding the use of aversive techniques to control behavior (Will, 1999) with the goal of extending programs from the laboratory and clinics into the broader community at large (Horner et al., 1990).

Currently, PBS interventions encompass social, behavioral, educational, and biomedical science drawing on evidence-based practices conducted in naturalistic settings (Clarke & Dunlap, 2008; Gable, Hendrickson, & Van Acker, 2001; Scott et al., 2005) to improve quality of life and reduce problem behaviors (Carr et al., 2002). PBS has attempted to integrate the ABA framework of instrumental/operant learning (evident in principles of reinforcement, contingency management, stimulus control, shaping, fading, prompting, functional equivalence, generalization, and maintenance) with information available from other disciplines (Cooper, Heron, & Heward, 2007). As a result, PBS creates a cross-discipline view of behavior that encompasses pharmacological, genetic, neurodevelopmental, and psychological approaches that can assist in the development of a more comprehensive view of the range of factors that can influence the development of challenging behaviors and the interventions that can help alleviate them (Carr & Owen-DeSchryver, 2007; Eisenberg et al., 2005).

PBS has moved away from the tendency to emphasize immediate environmental contingencies in favor of a broader look at systems-level factors that may be influencing behaviors and potential outcomes (e.g., the classroom, the family). There has also been increased focus on strategies for prevention, intervention, and the importance of developing positive replacement behaviors to accompany the reduction of problem behaviors (Dunlap, Carr, Horner, Zarcone, & Schwartz, 2008). In a recent meta-analysis of interventions for challenging behaviors, Harvey, Boer, Meyer, and Evans (2009) found that behavioral interventions, especially when developed through functional behavioral analysis, significantly reduced challenging behaviors, and that teaching replacement skills for problem behaviors was highly effective.

Educational Programs: Academic Achievement and Intellectual-Adaptive Deficits

Fundamental to IDEA (Individuals with Disabilities Education Act, 2004) is the assurance that all children with disabilities in the United States receive a free and appropriate public education (FAPE) in the least restrictive environment. The IDEA also outlines procedures that should be followed by special education personnel, including obtaining informed written consent of the parents prior to assessment and the need to develop an individualized education program (IEP) for each disabled child. The IEP serves as the child's educational plan and outlines needs for meeting the child's educational goals through assessment, intervention, and monitoring of progress during annual reviews (see Appendix B for a more detailed discussion of IDEA, 2004). Controversy concerning the validity of special education placements evolves around two important questions:

1. Does placement in special education programs benefit students with special needs?

2. Should placements be categorical (separate placements for different disabilities) or noncategorical, for example, all children with special needs can benefit from the same resources?

With regard to issues of placement, IDEA (2004) focuses on providing education for children with disabilities in the least restrictive environment such that special education programs are complemented by *mainstreaming* (the integration of disabled children into the regular class program) for as much time as possible. Students who qualify for special education also are provided with *related services* (speech language, occupational therapy, etc.) if these are needed. Most recently, the Regular Education Initiative has taken the position that *full inclusion,* rather than mainstreaming, would be the best solution and that the needs of children with disabilities would be best served by full-time placement in the regular or general education program. Proponents of mainstreaming and inclusion frequently cite results from the Carlberg and Kavale (1980) meta-analysis comparing general with special education. Results of this analysis suggested that students with mild intellectual disabilities (MID) generally obtained better outcomes in regular programs. It has further been argued that placing students with MID in contained special classrooms can actually place them at a disadvantage, isolating them from normative role models (Ysseldyke, Thurlow, Christenson, & Muyskens, 1991).

More recently, Hocutt (1996) reviewed more than 100 studies conducted over the last 25 years and suggests that claims of the efficacy of special education placement versus regular placement are difficult to substantiate, since much of the research is flawed methodologically and/or outdated with respect to today's classification systems. On a more positive note, Hocutt (1996) suggests that it is the intervention program (intensive individualized instruction and monitoring of progress) rather than the placement that predicts success for students with MID. The question remains, however, whether adequate monitoring and intervention are more likely to occur in a class with smaller enrollment.

In response to the second question, regarding whether different disabilities warrant separate types of special education programming, early reports by Hallahan and Kauffman (1977) suggested that research did not support separate special education services for the major high-incidence disabilities: specific learning disabilities (SLD), mild intellectual disabilities (MID), or emotional and behavioral disabilities (E/BD). Further support for noncategorical special education was indicated by later research (Reschly, Tilly, & Grimes, 1999; Ysseldyke & Marston, 1999) published at a time when the need for cost-saving endeavors was increasing. More recently, Sabornie, Cullinan, Osborne, and Brock (2005) conducted a meta-analysis of 58 studies to determine whether separation of students into high-incidence categories (SLD, MID, E/BD) was meaningful based on research examining three dependent variables that are necessary for eligibility for special education placements, including intelligence (IQ), academic achievement, and behavior. Results of their study support the retention of different disability categories, especially for students with MID, based on significant differences between students with MID and the other two groups in areas of IQ; academic achievement; and the need for specific emphasis on functional and life skills, personal care skills, communication ability, social skills, and transition-oriented planning in their educational programming (p. 55).

Mortweet (1997) studied the effect of classwide peer tutoring of MID students within the regular program; results revealed positive gains academically and socially, although social interaction did not generalize to other settings outside the programmed instruction. However, Gottlieb, Alter, and Gottlieb (1991) found that mainstreaming did not have a positive impact on the academic achievement of children with MID, while Taylor (1986) cautioned that mainstreaming students with MID without attention to direct training in areas such as social skills can have detrimental effects. A comparison of 34 mainstreamed EMR students with a sample of 34 non-impaired peers, matched for sex, race, and grade level (Grades 3 through 6) revealed that children with MID reported feeling more lonely and dissatisfied with their social relationships in school than their non-MID peers. Lack of social awareness and inappropriate social behaviors may result in students with disabilities not only having fewer friends, but being actively rejected by peers (Farmer & Rodkin, 1996; Nabasoku & Smith, 1993). Furthermore, there is some evidence that students with MID who are mainstreamed may be stigmatized, avoided, and marginalized in that setting (Dovidio, Major, & Crocker, 2000), while students in segregated settings may be protected from being stigmatized (Todd, 2000). However, the potential negative impact of living within such a protective environment might be that they have more limited awareness of their potential, since their only comparables are other students with intellectual disabilities (Finlay & Lyons, 2000; Todd, 2000). In summary, comparing oneself to similar peers may be protective of self-esteem, while comparing oneself to nondisabled peers may lower one's self-esteem (Crabtree & Rutland, 2001).

Cooney, Jahoda, Gumley, and Knott (2006) studied 28 students attending mainstream schools and 32 who attended a segregated school (mean age 15.6 years; mean IQ = 62). While both groups of students reported similar levels of stigmatization beyond school (in the community), the students who were mainstreamed also reported stigmatization at school by their nondisabled peers and perceived problems with support from teachers and staff who they felt were not sympathetic to their learning needs. There was no difference between the two groups with respect to future goals and the likelihood of meeting these goals.

Although there has been attention paid to the possible positive and negative social implications of integration within the regular class program, there has been less attention paid to the longer-term and vocational implications of educational preparation for youth with MID. Polloway and his colleagues (Polloway, Patten, Smith, & Roderique, 1991) contend that the educational curriculum for the population with MID should focus on community integration, starting as early as elementary school. The Hawaii Transition Project (Patton, Beirne-Smith, & Payne, 1990) provides an example of such a program geared to providing a bridge from school to community functioning. The National Longitudinal Transition Study-2 (Wagner, Newman, Cameto, Garza, & Levine, 2005) revealed that students with MID demonstrate persistent underemployment, with only 52% of postgraduates with MID engaged in postgraduate activities, such as employment, training, or further schooling (Wagner, Newman, Cameto, Levine, & Garza, 2006). Hartman (2009) outlines a step-by-step approach to creating a community-based treatment program for students with intellectual disabilities that is focused on the integration of resources in schools, business partnerships, and training in self-determination and advocacy issues.

Post-Case Questions

1. Would Arthur's profile warrant a diagnosis of mental retardation (MR)/intellectual developmental disability (IDD)? Discuss this question from the perspective of each of the following classification systems: *DS-IV-TR* (APA, 2000), AAMR/AAIDD (American Association on Mental Retardation), and the educational system (IDEA, 2004). Information available in Appendix B will provide the framework for answering this question.

2. Lalli, Kates, and Casey (1999) investigated the rates of problem behavior relative to academic demands in two boys with MID. Results revealed that aggression was highest during spelling instruction, and that problem behavior was driven by negative reinforcement. Changes in instructional format produced a reduction in negative behaviors.

   a. Explain how these findings might be relevant to Arthur's case. How might a functional behavioral assessment of Arthur's behaviors have helped with programming? Based on information in the case presentation, develop a likely functional behavioral assessment for Arthur's disruptive classroom behaviors outlining *possible behaviors* (suggest possible examples of disruptive behaviors), *precipitating conditions* (situations that trigger the behavior), *consequences of behavior* (situations/events that follow the behavior), and *functions of behavior* (underlying processes/motivations that sustain the behavior).

   b. Show how you would conduct a similar assessment to determine the extent to which behaviors were also occurring in other contexts: playground, after-school program, home.

REFERENCES

American Association on Mental Retardation (AAMR). (1992). *Mental retardation: Definition, classification and systems of support* (9th ed.). Washington, DC: Author.

American Association on Mental Retardation (AAMR). (2002). *Mental retardation: Definition, classification and systems of support* (10th ed.). Washington, DC: Author.

American Association on Mental Retardation (AAMR). (November 29, 2006). *World's oldest organization on intellectual disability has a progressive new name* [Press release]. Retrieved May 2010 from http://msaaidd.org/PR1-20061129.htm

American Psychiatric Association (APA). (2000). *Diagnostic and statistical manual of mental disorders* (4th ed., text rev.), Washington, DC: American Psychiatric Press.

Azrin, N. H., & Besalel, V. A. (1980). *How to use overcorrection.* Lawrence, KS: H & H Enterprises.

Brantley, D. C., & Webster, R. E. (1993). Use of an independent group contingency management system in a regular classroom setting. *Psychology in the Schools, 30,* 60–66.

Byrne, A., & Hennessy, E. (2009). Understanding challenging behaviour: Perspectives of children and adolescents with a moderate intellectual disability. *Journal of Applied Research in Intellectual Disabilities, 22,* 317–325.

Carlberg, C., & Kavale, K. (1980). The efficacy of special versus regular class placement for exceptional children: A meta-analysis. *The Journal of Special Education, 14,* 295–308.

Carr, E. G., Dunlap, G., Horner, R. H., Koegel, R. L., Turnbull, A. P., Sailor, W., et al. (2002). Positive behavior support: Evolution of an applied science. *Journal of Positive Behavior Interventions, 4,* 4–16.

Carr, E. G., & Owen-DeSchryver, J. S. (2007). Physical illness, pain, and problem behavior in minimally verbal people with developmental disabilities. *Journal of Autism and Developmental Disorders, 37,* 413–424.

Cautela, J. R., & Groden, J. (1978). *Relaxation: A comprehensive manual for adults, children, and children with special needs.* Champaign, IL: Research Review.

Christian, B. (1983). A practical reinforcement hierarchy for classroom behavior modification. *Psychology in the Schools, 20,* 83–84.

Clark, D. B., & Baker, B. L. (1983). Predicting outcome in parent training. *Journal of Consulting and Clinical Psychology, 51,* 309–311.

Clark, L. (1985). *SOS! Help for parents.* Bowling Green, KY: Parents Press.

Clarke, S., & Dunlap, G. (2008). A descriptive analysis of intervention research published in the *Journal of Positive Behavior Interventions:* 1999–2005. *Journal of Positive Behavior Interventions, 10,* 67–71.

Cooney, G., Jahoda, A., Gumley, A., & Knott, F. (2006). Young people with intellectual disabilities attending mainstream and segregated schooling: Perceived stigma, social comparison and future aspirations. *Journal of Intellectual Disability Research, 50,* 432–444.

Cooper, J. O., Heron, T. E., & Heward, W. L. (2007). *Applied behavior analysis.* Upper Saddle River, NJ: Pearson Merrill Prentice Hall.

Crabtree, J., & Rutland, A. (2001). Self-evaluation and social comparison amongst adolescents with intellectual difficulties. *Journal of Community and Applied Social Psychology, 11,* 347–359.

Deater-Deckard, K. (2001). Recent research examining the role of peer relationships in the development of psychopathology. *Journal of Child Psychology and Psychiatry, 42,* 565–579.

Dovidio, J. F., Major, B., & Crocker, J. (2000). Stigma: Introduction and overview. In T. F. Heatherton, R. E. Kleck, M. R. Hebl, & J. G. Hull (Eds.), *The social psychology of stigma* (pp. 1–28). Hove, East Sussex, UK: Guilford.

Dunlap, G., Carr, E. G., Horner, R. H., Zarcone, J. R., & Schwartz, I. (2008). Positive behavior support and applied behavior analysis: A familial alliance. *Behavior Modification, 32*(5), 682–698.

Eisenberg, N., Sadovsky, A., Spinrad, T. L., Fabes, R. A., Losoya, S. H., Valiente, C., et al. (2005). The relations of problem behavior status to children's negative emotionality, effortful control, and impulsivity: Concurrent relations and prediction of change. *Developmental Psychology, 41,* 193–211.

Embregts, P. J. C. (2000). Effectiveness of video feedback and self-management on inappropriate social behavior of youth with mild mental retardation. *Research in Developmental Disabilities, 21,* 409–423.

Emerson, E. (2001). *Challenging behaviour: Analysis and intervention in people with severe intellectual disabilities.* Cambridge, UK: Cambridge University Press.

Farmer, T. W., & Rodkin, A. C. (1996). Antisocial and prosocial correlates of classroom social position: The social network centrality perspective. *Social Development, 5,* 174–178.

Finlay, W. M. L., & Lyons, E. (2000). Social categorizations, social comparisons and stigma: Presentations of self in people with intellectual difficulties. *British Journal of Social Psychology, 39,* 129–146.

Forehand, R., & McMahon, R. (1981). *Helping the noncompliant child: A clinician's guide to parent training.* New York: Guilford.

Gable, R. A., Hendrickson, J. M., & Van Acker, R. (2001). Maintaining the integrity of FBA based interventions in schools. *Education and Treatment of Children, 24,* 248–260.

Gottlieb, J., Alter, M., & Gottlieb, B. W. (1991). Mainstreaming mentally retarded children. In J. L. Matson & J. A. Mulick (Eds.), *Handbook of mental retardation* (pp. 63–73). New York: Pergamon.

Hallahan, D. P., & Kauffman, J. M. (1977). Labels, categories, behaviors: ED, LD, and EMR reconsidered. *Journal of Special Education, 11,* 139–149.

Handen, B. L. (1998). Mental retardation. In E. J. Mash & L. G. Terdal (Eds.), *Treatment of childhood disorders.* New York: Guilford.

Harris, S. L. (1983). *Families of the developmentally disabled: A guide to behavioral intervention.* New York: Pergamon.

Hartman, M. A. (2009). Step by step: Creating a community-based transition program for students with intellectual disabilities. *Teaching Exceptional Children, 41,* 6–11.

Harvey, S. T., Boer, D., Meyer, L. H., & Evans, I. M. (2009). Updating a meta-analysis of intervention research with challenging behaviour: Treatment validity and standards of practice. *Journal of Intellectual and Developmental Disability, 34,* 67–80.

Hocutt, A. M. (1996). Effectiveness of special education: Is placement the critical factor? *Future of Children, 6,* 77–102.

Horner, R. H., & Day, H. M. (1991). The effects of response efficiency on functionally equivalent competing behaviors. *Journal of Applied Behavior Analysis, 24,* 719–732.

Horner, R. H., Dunlap, G., Koegel, R. L., Carr, E. G., Sailor, W., Anderson, J., et al. (1990). Toward a technology of "non-aversive" behavioral support. *Journal of the Association for Persons With Severe Handicaps, 15,* 125–132.

Individuals With Disabilities Education Improvement Act (2004). Retrieved May 2010 from http://idea.ed.gov

Jensen, M. (1988). An unexpected effect: Restitution maintains object throwing. *Education and Treatment of Children, 2,* 252–256.

Kazdin, A. E. (1994). *Behavior modification in applied settings* (5th ed.). Pacific Grove, CA: Brooks/Cole.

Kiernan, C., & Kiernan, D. (1994). Challenging behaviour in schools for pupils with severe learning difficulties. *Mental Handicap Research, 7,* 117–201.

Kiernan, C., & Qureshi, H. (1993). Challenging behaviour. In C. Kiernan (Ed.), *Research to practice? Implications of research on the challenging behaviour of people with learning disabilities* (pp. 53–87). British Institute of Learning Disabilities: Kidderminster.

Koegel, R. L., Schreibman, L., Britten, K., Burke, J., & O'Neill, R. (1982). A comparison of parent training to direct child treatment. In R. L. Koegel, A. Rincover, & A. L. Ege (Eds.), *Educating and understanding autistic children* (pp. 260–279). San Diego, CA: College-Hill Press.

Kratochwill, T. R., Elliott, S. N., & Rotto, P. C. (1990). Best practices in behavioral consultation. In A. Thomas & J. Grimes (Eds.), *Best practices in school psychology-II* (pp. 147–170). Silver Spring, MD: National Association of School Psychologists.

Kronenberger, W. G., & Meyer, R. G. (2001). *The child clinician's handbook* (2nd ed.). Boston: Allyn & Bacon.

LaFontana, K. M., & Cillessen A. H. N. (2002). Children's perceptions of popular and unpopular peers: A multimethod assessment. *Developmental Psychology, 38,* 635–647.

Lalli, J. S., Kates, K., & Casey, S. D. (1999). Response covariation: The relationship between correct academic responding and problem behavior. *Behavior Modification, 23,* 339–357.

Lipsey, M. W., & Wilson, D. B. (1993). The efficacy of psychological, educational and behavioral treatment: Confirmation from meta-analysis. *American Psychologist, 48,* 1181–1209.

Little, L. M., & Kelley, M. L. (1989). The efficacy of response cost procedures for reducing children's noncompliance to parental instructions. *Behavior Therapy, 20,* 525–534.

McPhail, C. H., & Chamove, A. S. (1989). Relaxation reduces disruption in mentally handicapped adults. *Journal of Mental Deficiency Research, 33,* 399–406.

Mortweet, S. (1997). The academic and social effects of a class-wide peer tutoring for students with educable mental retardation and their typical peers in an inclusive classroom (doctoral dissertation, University of Kansas, 1997). *Dissertation Abstracts International: Section B: The Sciences & Engineering, 58,* 1515.

Nabasoku, D., & Smith, P. K. (1993). Sociometric status and social behavior of children with and without language difficulties. *Journal of Child Psychology and Psychiatry and Allied Disciplines, 34,* 1435–1448.

Patton, J. R., Beirne-Smith, M., & Payne, J. S. (1990). *Mental retardation.* New York: Macmillan.

Phares, V., Compas, B. E., & Howell, D. C. (1989). Perspectives on child behavior problems: Comparisons of children's self reports with parent and teacher reports. *Psychological Assessment, 1,* 68–71.

Polloway, E. A., Patten, J. R., Smith, J. D., & Roderique, T. W. (1991). Issues in program design for elementary students with mild retardation: Emphasis on curriculum development. *Education and Training in Mental Retardation, 26,* 144–150.

Proctor, M. A., & Morgan, D. (1991). Effectiveness of a response cost raffle procedure on the disruptive classroom behavior of adolescents with behavior problems. *School Psychology Review, 20,* 97–109.

Rapport, M. D., Murphy, H. A., & Bailey, J. S. (1982). Ritalin vs. response cost in the control of hyperactive children: A within-subject comparison. *Journal of Applied Behavior Analysis, 15,* 205–216.

Reschly, D. J., Tilly, W. D., & Grimes, J. (Eds.). (1999). *Special education in transition: Functional assessment and noncategorical programming.* Longmont, CO: Soptis West.

Reynolds, C. J., Salend, S. J., & Beahan, C. L. (1989). Motivating secondary school students: Bringing in the reinforcements. *Academic Therapy, 25,* 81–90.

Reynolds, C. J., Salend, S. J., & Beahan, C. L. (1992). Reinforcer preferences of secondary school students with disabilities. *International Journal of Disability, Development and Education, 39,* 77–86.

Rutherford, R. B., Jr., & Nelson, C. M. (1988). Generalization of treatment effects. In J. C. Witt, S. N. Elliott, & F. M. Gresham (Eds.), *Handbook of behavior therapy in education.* New York: Plenum.

Sabornie, E. J., Cullinan, D., Osborne, S. S., & Brock, L. B. (2005). Intellectual academic and behavioral functioning of students with high-incidence disabilities: A cross-categorical meta-analysis. *Exceptional Children, 72,* 47–63.

Scott, T. M., McIntyre, J., Liaupsin, C., Nelson, C. M., Conroy, M., & Payne, L. D. (2005). An examination of the relation between functional behavior assessment and selected intervention strategies with school-based teams. *Journal of Positive Behavior Interventions, 7,* 205–215.

Solnick, J. V., Rincover, A., & Peterson, C. R. (1977). Some determinants of the reinforcing and punishing effects of timeout. *Journal of Applied Behavior Analysis, 10,* 415–424.

Stokes, T. F., & Baer, D. M. (1977). An implicit technology of generalization. *Journal of Applied Behavior Analysis, 10,* 349–368.

Taylor, A. (1986, April). *Loneliness, goal orientation and sociometric status: Mildly retarded children's adaptation to the mainstream classroom.* Paper presented at the annual meeting of the American Educational Research Association, San Francisco.

Todd, S. (2000). Working in the public and private domains: Staff management of community activities for and the identities of people with intellectual disability. *Journal of Intellectual Disability Research, 44,* 600–620.

Wagner, M., Newman, L., Cameto, R., Garza, N., & Levine, P. (2005). *After high school: A first look at the post-school experiences of youth with disabilities.* Menlo Park, CA: SRI International.

Wagner, M., Newman, L., Cameto, R., Levine. P., & Garza, N. (2006). *An overview of findings from wave 2 of the national longitudinal transition study-2 (NLTS2).* (NGSER 2006–3004). Menlo Park, CA: SRI International.

Weist, M. D., Ollendick, T. H., & Finney, J. W. (1991). Toward the empirical validation of treatment targets in children. *Clinical Psychology Review, 2,* 515–538.

Wielkiewicz, R. M. (1995). *Behavior management in the schools* (2nd ed.). Boston: Allyn & Bacon.

Will, M. (1999). Foreward. In E. G. Carr, R. H. Horner, A. P. Turnbull, J. G. Marquis, D. M. McLaughlin, M. L. McAtee, et al. *Positive behavior support for people with developmental disabilities* (pp. 15–16). Washington, DC: American Association on Mental Retardation.

Ysseldyke, J., & Marston, D. (1999). Origins of categorical special education services in schools and a rationale for changing them. In D. J. Reschly, W. D. Tilly, & J. P. Grimes (Eds.), *Special education in transition: Functional assessment and noncategorical programming* (pp. 1–18). Longmont, CO: Sopris West.

Ysseldyke, J. E., Thurlow, M. L., Christenson, S. L., & Muyskens, P. (1991). Classroom and home learning differences between students labeled as educable mentally retarded and their peers. *Education and Training in Mental Retardation, 26,* 3–17.

Jenny Sloan

The All-American Girl

Jenny, a strikingly attractive 16-year-old, arrived at the clinic with her mother, Stella. Jenny was recently released from the hospital after an unsuccessful suicide attempt. Jenny's mother had found her on the bathroom floor, unconscious, amid empty bottles of nonprescription drugs: Advil, Tylenol, Sudafed. Fortunately, the ambulance arrived in time. What scared Stella the most was that there were no warning signs of depression and suicide. Or were there?

DEVELOPMENTAL HISTORY/FAMILY BACKGROUND

Jenny was a beautiful baby—bright, alert, and very easy to manage. Stella and Carl, both in their mid-thirties, were very proud of their baby girl and were especially thankful that they were able to conceive a child after so many years of trying. Although Carl was a successful banker, he kept his priorities in check and was often more interested in family life than corporate life. Stella did a lot of volunteer work in the community and the local school. They had a strong marriage and were well suited to each other. Stella, who was an avid reader, had purchased several books on child rearing and charted Jenny's milestones diligently in her daughter's journal. Jenny developed perfectly in tune with what the books would say. She began walking on her first birthday and actually was saying words before she was walking.

As a preschooler, Jenny was very social and loved attending school and playing with the other children. It seemed that the other children were drawn to Jenny by her infectious laughter, something that would continue throughout her school years. Jenny was very well coordinated, and Stella enrolled her in kinder-gym, dance, and swimming. Jenny embraced each new activity with vigor and enthusiasm and was an excellent gymnast, dancer, and swimmer.

In elementary school, Jenny won awards for track and field and was voted most popular girl in her Grade 5 class. She continued dance lessons and gymnastics and competed in several regional meets with relative success. Jenny seemed to be a born leader, and her popularity with the other children was readily apparent. It seemed as though there was no stopping her.

When Stella thought back, there may have been early warning signs that all was not well. Middle school seemed to launch Jenny into early adolescence, and her responses to change or adjustments in her life started to trigger more intense and extreme reactions. Stella recalled when Jenny's class schedule was changed by the guidance counselor, Jenny came home extremely irritated and agitated, complaining that the counselor had no right to do this to her. She demanded that her parents go to the school and have the schedule changed. Stella and Carl tried to reason with Jenny after they talked to the guidance counselor on the telephone. However, Jenny said they were all in on the conspiracy against her. She was up most of the night on the telephone with classmates, trying to organize a protest. The next day, she was very agitated and angry at her friends for not supporting her in the protest. Were it not for the fact that Jenny was so popular, Stella was sure that these behaviors would have cut off all her social contacts. However, Jenny continued to be very popular with her peers. She was a formidable leader, beautiful, full of life, and assertive. Many of her classmates may have cowered in her wake, but they secretly desired to be just like her.

Stella and Carl were concerned about Jenny's escalating behaviors; however, Stella had read several books on adolescence and convinced Carl that Jenny was probably just being a difficult adolescent and flexing her increased independence. When it came to parent-teacher conferences, some of Jenny's teachers were not pleased with her confrontational nature, but others seemed to admire her perseverance. Jenny's grades were good, and she excelled in extracurricular activities. She was beautiful, bright, and motivated. These were qualities to be admired. She was the "all-American girl." These comments left Stella and Carl uncertain about how to deal with Jenny's behaviors, and they wondered if they were over-reacting or maybe doing something wrong at home. They discussed whether they should take Jenny to a child psychiatrist or psychologist, but other parents convinced them that Jenny was just being a teenager, and that many parents would readily change places with them. How great it must be to have a teenager as motivated as Jenny.

Jenny seemed to embrace the transition to high school at a time when others were thrown off balance by the increased number of students and having so many different teachers. Jenny signed up for a number of school clubs, such as the Girls Athletic Club and the Glee Club, and although few would have had the courage to attempt it, she even tried out for the Junior Cheerleading Squad. She did not make the team, which was devastating for her, but she vowed that the following year she would come back with a vengeance. During her freshman year, Jenny continued to be actively involved in sports and school clubs and told herself that she would rather play on the girl's volleyball team than be a cheerleader anyway, since they got to travel to conferences. Jenny and her parents continued to have disagreements throughout the year, with Jenny wanting to stay out later and go on dates that her parents did not approve of. That summer, Jenny got a job as a camp counselor and spent the summer at camp away from her parents. When she returned in the fall, it was as if the break had restored all harmony, and her parents felt as if they had finally gotten their daughter back.

In the fall, Jenny tried out again for the Junior Cheerleading Squad, and this time she made it. Jenny was elated about being selected for the team and was eager to show off her new cheers and routines for her parents at home. However, shortly thereafter, things began to go noticeably out of control. Socially, Jenny began pushing the limits with her parents and dressing very provocatively despite their protests. Jenny's behavior became more erratic.

One day, Jenny decided that the cheerleading uniforms needed to be revamped: the skirts were too long and the design on the front of the sweater was outdated. For the next week, Jenny was relentless. She became obsessed with getting the uniforms changed. She rarely slept, and instead was consumed with ideas on how to improve the cheerleading outfits. She talked nonstop about cheerleading outfits, to the point that her parents asked her to please stop. Jenny would run home from school each day and search the Internet for costume designs. She spoke on the phone most of the night. Jenny's mother picked up the extension by mistake one time, and couldn't believe Jenny's rambling on about buying material and sewing patterns, pantsuits, designs, European fashion trends, and megaphones. Much of what Jenny was rambling on about seemed to make no sense. Of course, when her mother questioned her about the conversation, Jenny was furious at her mother for picking up the extension and eavesdropping on her. Eventually, Jenny's friends stopped calling. Jenny was now spending more and more time on the Internet at night when she was supposed to be doing her homework. She told her parents that she was doing "research"; what she didn't reveal was that her research was focused on trying to locate a uniform designer that the school could hire to redesign the uniforms. Ultimately, she began drawing her own designs and spending hours at night cutting out patterns and trying new designs. She was convinced that she had the talent to become a world-famous uniform designer and ran up expensive phone bills trying to contact clothing manufacturers across the United States who might support her line of uniforms: Jeunesse by Jenny. She got the name from the French word for "youth." She felt totally empowered; it was as if she were wearing magical senses: Colors were more intense, sounds were more reverberating, and touch was more penetrating. No one could possibly understand how euphoric her life had become.

During that week, Jenny amassed hundreds of dollars in international phone calls. Her parents were furious and Jenny was upset, saying that they didn't support her. Maybe they would believe her when she became famous. The problem intensified the night her mother found yards and yards of new fabric stuffed in a box in the basement, along with dozens of pictures of cheerleading uniforms. Some of the cloth had been cut into patches and sewn together to make patterns. That's when her mother found out that Jenny had also run up a sizable bill on her mother's account at the department store where she purchased all the fabric and patterns.

No one seemed to understand how intense Jenny could be. Her parents were the only windows on her all-night vigils, extensive phone bills and fabric bills, and constant diatribes at home. Yet her parents somehow felt powerless to intervene because they were constantly being reminded by parents of other teenagers that Jenny was "the all-American girl" and that they were fortunate to have such a talented and motivated daughter. Finally, after all the glitter and sparkle, came the crash . . . the awful crash. The mood swing was devastating.

In the hospital, Jenny admitted to her parents that she was beginning to feel out of control about a week before the suicide attempt. Jenny had been on the phone for hours frenetically attempting to organize a party that would be the biggest and best party ever, where she was going to launch her new "Jeunesse" line of cheerleading uniforms, but by the time the party was to begin, her mood had spiraled into a deep depression. It was as if someone had pulled the floor out from under her. Jenny felt riveted to the bed, immobile, as if her feet were stuck in buckets of poured concrete, and she was being sucked into the horrible pain of a black hole. It was as if someone had vacuumed out her very soul. The emptiness and the pain were unbearable. She felt as if she were worthless and would never amount to anything. On that night, the pain hurt so much, she woke up in a panic, ran to the bathroom, and devoured bottles of painkillers, anything she could find to end the pain once and for all.

A review of the intake information showed a history of bipolar disorder in Jenny's paternal grandmother, and alcohol abuse in the maternal grandfather. There were also several cousins with a history of depression and suicidal behavior.

REASON FOR REFERRAL

When Jenny was in the hospital, a comprehensive clinical assessment was conducted to determine her functioning on several levels, including intellectual, academic, and social/emotional status.

ASSESSMENT RESULTS

Information regarding specific assessment instruments and guidelines to the interpretation of standard scores and T scores can be found in Appendix C.

When Jenny arrived at the clinic, she brought with her the results of the assessment conducted in the hospital. Results of the WISC-IV revealed average intellectual ability, although scores may have been somewhat depressed, given her mood state at the time. Low scores were noted on the Working Memory Index, and it was noted that Jenny complained of having problems concentrating, likely resulting from her depressed state. Academically, Jenny scored at grade level, with the exception of arithmetic, which was approximately 2 years below grade level. Her mother's responses to the CBCL revealed clinical elevations for Attention, Anxious-Depressed, and Thought Problems. Scores for Delinquent Behaviors and Aggression were elevated but not significant. Jenny completed the Revised Child Manifest Anxiety Scale (RCMAS-2), the Youth Self Report (YSR), and the Beck Inventories for Youth (BYI-2). Jenny's responses indicated extreme elevations on the Physiological Indicators of Anxiety scale on the RCMAS-2, clinically significant elevations on the Anxiety-Depression and Thought Disorder scales (YSR), and significant problems with Self Concept and Depression (BYI-2). The semistructured diagnostic interview (K-SADS) revealed positive endorsement of manic and depressive symptoms.

ISSUES, TRENDS, AND TREATMENT ALTERNATIVES

In this case and the case of Matthew Morgan, bipolar disorder will be discussed as it relates to the manic part of the episode and will provide an opportunity for readers to compare how these manic and hypomanic states can appear in childhood and adolescence. For an in-depth discussion of a major depressive episode, readers are directed to the case of David Steele.

Compared to unipolar depression, which is a pervasive sad or irritable mood state accompanied by a loss of pleasure, disorders within the bipolar spectrum evidence mood states that vacillate between the lows of depression and euphoric, expansive, or irritable manic states that can be accompanied by inflated self-esteem, or grandiosity; pressured speech; reduced need for sleep; flight of ideas, or racing thoughts; distractibility; increase in goal-directed activities (psychomotor agitation); and engaging in activities that are at high risk for negative outcomes, such as spending sprees, fast driving, and sexual promiscuity (*DSM-IV-TR;* APA, 2000). Although historically there had been a tendency to not identify BP in children (Scott & Meyer, 2007), more recently, children are increasingly being diagnosed with BP (Youngstrom, Meyers, Youngstrom, Calabrese, & Findling, 2006), and as a result, there has been a growing body of research investigating how BP manifests in cases of childhood and adolescent onset (Biffin et al., 2009; Goldstein & Levitt, 2006; Goldstein et al., 2009). For a discussion of issues, trends, and treatment connected to childhood-onset BP, readers are referred to the case of Matthew Morgan. Matthew experienced very-early-onset BP, and although symptoms share some similarities to those experienced by adolescents, a comparison of the two cases will reveal significant differences in how BP can be experienced at the different stages of development. The following discussion focuses primarily on symptoms and risks associate with adolescent-onset BP.

There are different subtypes of BP based on the nature of the manic and depressive episodes. Bipolar I disorder involves either full manic or mixed manic episodes (lasting for at least 7 days) alternating with episodes of major depressive disorder. Bipolar II is a less severe form of the disorder with mood swings vacillating between hypomanic episodes (lasting at least 4 days) and episodes of major depressive disorder. Bipolar disorder not otherwise specified (BP NOS) is a category reserved for cases that meet some but not all criteria for BP I or BP II. Cyclothymia relates to mood shifts between hypomania and depression, although in this case depression does not meet criteria for a major depressive disorder. Individuals are considered to be in a state of rapid cycling if there is evidence of four episodes within a given year. Diagnostic criteria from the *DSM-IV-TR* (APA, 2000) for the various subtypes of BP can be found in Appendix D.

Responses to the national epidemiologic survey on alcohol and related conditions from over 1,400 respondents with a diagnosis of BP revealed that almost one fourth (24%) reported onset of the disorder in adolescence, compared to 8% who reported onset (Goldstein & Levitt, 2006). Studies have shown that individuals with adolescent onset are most likely to show depression as the initial affective episode (Biffin et al., 2009; Bowden, 2001; Lish, Dime-Meenan, Whybrow, Price, & Hirschfeld, 1994). However, adolescents who experience mania may also frequently experience psychotic symptoms, labile moods, and mixed manic and depressive characteristics (Pavuluri et al., 2004, 2005). Compared to younger children, those with later-adolescent-onset BP tend to have a cyclical course that is more similar to that found in adults (McClellan, McCurry, Snell, & DuBose, 1999) and manifest more classic BP symptoms of "mania" such as euphoria or grandiosity, and depression (Egeland, 2000). Steiner and colleagues (Steiner, 2000; Steiner, Saxena, & Chang, 2003) discuss displays of affective, reactive, and defensive aggression in adolescents with BP. Aggression can also be seen as escalating or intermittent, with adolescents tending to demonstrate more of the escalating types of aggression than younger children with the disorder. In older children, differential diagnosis between BP and conduct disorder may be difficult in the case of a youth who impulsively shoplifts, is sexually promiscuous, and engages in risky behavior. However, differential diagnosis would recognize that in the bipolar adolescent, these behaviors represent high-risk and stimulation-seeking behaviors devoid of the vindictive and antisocial elements noted in conduct disorder (Bowring & Kovacs, 1992). Similarly, delusions of grandeur, paranoia, irritability, and flight of ideas might be difficult to distinguish from schizophrenia. Geller and colleagues (1995) studied 26 children (13 were between 7 and 13 years of age; 13 were adolescents) with BP. Results revealed that 80% of the sample had rapid cycling patterns (100% of the younger group and 70% of the adolescent group). The authors also found a prevalence of hallucinations in the older group (hearing voices), delusions (grandeur, persecutory, somatic), and ideas of reference that may lead to misdiagnosis of this group as schizophrenic. Whether these patterns that resemble BP II are an age-specific and developmental antecedent to BP I in adulthood remains to be seen (Geller, Fox, & Clark, 1994).

One of the core symptoms of BP is sleep disturbance, which can relate to a reduced need for sleep during a manic or hypermanic episode, or insomnia or hypersomnia during a depressive episode (*DSM-IV-TR;* APA, 2000). Sleep disturbance has also been reported as a common feature of BP in youth, and a number of studies have reported high rates of insomnia or parasomnias (disorders causing arousal during REM or partial arousal from non-REM sleep, such as nightmares, night terrors, sleepwalking, etc). Studies have found that youth with BP report reduced REM sleep, lower sleep efficiency, and longer slow-wave sleep, relative to youth without BP (Faedda & Teicher, 2005; Mehl et al., 2006). Sleep disturbances have consistently been reported by half of parents of youth who later go on to develop BP, suggesting that sleep disturbances may be one of the earliest symptoms (Duffy, Alda, Crawford, Milin, & Grof, 2007; Faedda, Baldessarini, Glovinsky, & Austin, 2004). In their study of prodromes of episodes (early symptoms or warning signs), Jackson, Cavanagh, and Scott (2003) found that sleep disturbance was the most common prodrome reported by those with BP and the sixth most common prodrome reported by those with depression. In their review of studies concerning sleep disturbance and BP, Harvey, Talbot, and Gershon (2009) suggest that sleep disturbance can have far-reaching consequences on affect regulation, cognitive functioning, risk for substance use, impulsivity, and risk taking. Swann, Steinberg, Lijffijt, and Moeller (2008) found that different aspects of impulsivity coincided with different phases of bipolar illness: attentional impulsivity (lack of cognitive persistence) was most likely to be associated with depression and mania, motor impulsivity was associated with mania, and nonplanning impulsivity was associated with depression. Given the impact of sleep disturbance on emotion regulation, it is possible that sleep deprivation may be instrumental in triggering a manic episode.

Onset in adolescence may also result in a significant deterioration in academic functioning, especially in mathematics and interpersonal relationships. Of those with the disorder in adolescence, 42% will not graduate from high school on schedule (Kutcher, 2005). Increased stress in family or relationships can cause increased mood deterioration in youth who develop BP in adolescence (Kim, Miklowitz, Biukians, & Mullen, 2007). In studies comparing psychosocial functioning among bipolar youth of various ages, greater functional impairment was found in adolescence, regardless of the age of onset of BP (Biederman et al., 2005; Goldstein et al., 2009). It has been suggested that adolescents are more severely impaired relative to younger children because of the increased psychosocial demands occurring at a time when their illness prevents them from meeting these challenges (Goldstein et al., 2009). The authors suggest that increased impairment in adolescence may also result from increased social stresses, leading to further deterioration (Hammen's [1991] stress generation model), or increased vulnerability for future episodes based on past episodes (Post's [1994] kindling theory).

In one study of adolescents with BP, DelBello, Hanseman, Adler, Fleck, and Strakowski (2007) found that only 39% of adolescents who were hospitalized for an initial manic or mixed episode managed to achieve functional recovery one year later, despite demonstrating a reduction in severity and symptoms. Furthermore, Rademacher, DelBello, Adler, Stanford, and Strakowski (2007) reported that adolescents with BP scored below the national averages for the majority of domains measuring quality of life, with only marginal increases in functioning noted when they were reassessed after treatment. On a more positive note, results from at least two studies suggest that while impairment may exist in many domains, leisure activities and recreation (e.g., computer games) remain relatively unaffected domains even for BP youth who are in-episode (Goldstein et al., 2009; Rademacher et al., 2007).

Onset of BP in later adolescence was predictive of the disorder continuing at 24 years of age (Lewinsohn, Klein, & Seeley, 2000); however, although those who were diagnosed with BP NOS were at greater risk for psychopathology and negative outcomes as adults, the NOS category did not predict BP in adulthood. Goldstein and colleagues (2009) found that impaired functioning levels did not differ between subtypes of BP (e.g., BP I, B PII, BP-NOS) in their sample, which supports results reported for adults with BP who demonstrated similar levels of risk for impairment across the BP spectrum (Judd, Akiskal, Schettler, & Endicott, 2007). However, similar to findings with BP adults, youth with BP show more significant impairments in functioning during depressive episodes compared to manic or mixed cycling episodes (Goldstein et al., 2009). Adolescents who have BP are at increased risk of suicide attempts (Strober, 1992; Strober, Morrell, Lampert, & Burrough, 1990). Substance-use/abuse rates are also high in adolescents with BP (Findling et al., 2001; Wilens et al., 2004).

Bipolar is a highly heritable disorder with estimates in the range of 20 to 40% (Green et al., 2005; Rutter, Silberg, O'Connor, & Simonoff, 1999). Studies of potential abnormalities in brain structure and function have found that while adults with BP evidence both increased and decreased volume of the amygdala (Altshuler et al., 2000), there have been consistent reports of amygdala volume deficits in the brains of adolescents with BP (Blumberg et al., 2003; Chang et al., 2005; Dickstein et al., 2005). As a result, it is possible that adolescent BP may represent a separate phenotype of the disorder, or that amygdala volume development is compromised by the episodes themselves (Blumberg, 2007).

Treatment Alternatives

Medication Management. Adult treatment for BP typically includes lithium, valproate, and atypical antipsychotic medications such as risperidone and olanzapine. While mood stabilizers and antipsychotic medications have been proven effective for some adolescents with BP, stimulant medications and antidepressants are not effective (Biederman et al., 1999). However, youth with BP who have comorbid behavior disorders or ADHD seem to be less responsive to the medical management of BP (Masi et al., 2004; State et al., 2004). Lithium is a mood stabilizer that is well tolerated by youth with BP (Tueth, Murphy, & Evans, 1998), and it has been approved for the treatment of acute mania in youth with BP from age 12 and up. The main problem with lithium is that unpleasant side effects can occur (stomach upset, nausea, weight gain, tremors, enuresis, and acne), and frequent monitoring of blood levels is required, which may result in issues of compliance, especially in adolescents. Strober, Lampert, and Burrough (1990) studied adolescents with BP over an 18-month period and found that 12 out of the 13 cases who were noncompliant relapsed (greater than 90%), while approximately one third (37.5%) of those who were compliant relapsed as well. Based on the results of recent medication trials, it has been suggested that maintenance therapy should take place over a 12- to 24-month period to decrease the risk of relapse (Findling et al., 2001; Strober et al., 1990), while for some more severe cases, therapy maintenance may be required over the course of their lifetime. Frazier and colleagues (1999) noted that the atypical antipsychotic medication risperidone (Risperdal) was effective in 82% of the 28 adolescent cases surveyed in a retrospective chart review. Kowatch and colleagues (2000) investigated the effectiveness of three different mood stabilizers for the treatment of BP in children and adolescents: lithium, valproic acid, and carbamazepine. Results revealed positive responses (34 to 50%) with no statistical difference between the different medications.

Therapy. The practice parameters for the assessment and treatment of children and adolescents with BP (AACAP, 2007) outline a number of suggestions for therapeutic interventions, which are available in the discussion of treatment alternatives for the case of Matthew Morgan.

In their review of psychosocial interventions as an adjunct to pharmacological interventions, Lam, Burbeck, Wright, and Pilling (2009) found that therapy specifically designed for BP patients (e.g., cognitive-behavioral therapy [CBT], psychoeducation, focused family therapy [FFT]) can reduce the risk of or delay a possible relapse. Although the majority of studies reviewed included adult populations, the range of therapeutic options they explored provides an overview of the types of therapeutic approaches available for individuals who have BP. Disorder-specific therapies were found to include such components as "use of diathesis-stress model, psychoeducation, promoting medication adherence, self-monitoring and moderating behavior, promoting routine and structure, problem solving and active relapse prevention measures" (Lam et al., 2009, p. 474).

In the treatment of adults with BP, Miklowitz, George, Richards, Simoneau, and Suddath (2003) report that a family-focused intervention program targeting family members (spouses, parents, and siblings) was successful in reducing relapse rates, reducing symptomology, and increasing compliance with medication regimes. The program focused on providing psychoeducational information to family members about the disorder and assistance in improving communication and problem-solving skills. The researchers have since expanded the program to include adolescents with BP (Miklowitz et al., 2009). In their investigation, they compared family-focused therapy for adolescents (FFT-A) to a brief psychoeducational treatment (enhanced care [EC]). The FFT-A program included assessment and interventions for "expressed emotion" (EE) in parents, a parenting communication style that is characterized by criticism, hostility, or emotional overinvolvement. The 58 adolescents (13–17 years of age) with BP and their parents were randomly assigned to the FFT-A condition (21 sessions over the course of 9 months involving problem solving, communication training, and psychoeducation) or the EC condition, which involved 3 psychoeducation sessions. Evaluators, who were blind to the subject's group affiliation, recorded depressive and manic symptoms every 3 months over the course of 2 years. Results revealed that parents who were rated high on EE reported less family cohesion and adaptability than parents who were low in EE. Adolescents who were from families that were high in EE showed more improvement in symptom reduction (depressive and manic) when enrolled in the FFT-A program compared to the EC program. However, those adolescents whose parents were low in EE did not demonstrate any differences between participation in the two programs. The researchers suggest that parental EE moderated the success of the family intervention program on the reduction of adolescent symptoms of BP and recommend future programs include a screening of parental EE to determine which patients might be benefitted most by the more intense program (FFT-A).

A number of psychosocial treatments also include guidelines for managing sleep disturbance, such as interpersonal therapy (Frank, Swartz, & Kupfer, 2000), family therapy (Milkowitz et al., 2009), and individual (Lam et al., 2003) or group (Patelis-Siotis et al., 2001) CBT. However, to date, there is a lack of empirical support for specific treatments directed toward reducing sleep disturbance, especially in youth with BP. Harvey (2009) suggests a number of areas that future research initiatives should target to assist in developing treatment interventions for sleep disturbance in youth, including functional analysis of the nature and duration of sleep disturbance, antecedents and consequences, and possible motivations for delay of sleep onset (e.g., text and/or Internet messaging of peers), psychoeducation regarding sleep deprivation and potential causes, regulation of the sleep-wake schedule, problem solving to reduce hypersomnia (extended periods of sleep, such as daytime sleepiness), education regarding the need for transitions between waking and sleeping states, and reduction of sleep-onset difficulties due to bedtime worry and rumination.

Post-Case Questions

1. Given the *DSM-IV-TR* diagnostic criteria (see Appendix D), would Jenny's symptoms meet criteria for bipolar disorder (BP), and if so, what symptoms does she exhibit and what type of BP is Jenny most likely to be diagnosed with?

2. Given her age and symptoms, based on current research findings, what other disorders might Jenny be at risk for developing?

3. Compare and contrast symptoms and disorder presentation for BP using the cases of Matthew Morgan and Jenny Sloan.

4. Suggest a treatment plan for Jenny based on current research findings. What are the main components that your treatment program will need to address?

REFERENCES

Altshuler, L. L., Bartzokis, G., Grieder, T., Curran, J., Jimenez, T., Leight, K., et al. (2000). An MRI study of temporal lobe structures in men with bipolar disorder or schizophrenia. *Biological Psychiatry, 48,* 147–162.

American Academy of Child and Adolescent Psychiatry (AACAP). (2007). Practice parameter for the assessment and treatment of children and adolescents with bipolar disorder. *Journal of the American Academy of Child and Adolescent Psychiatry, 46,* 107–125.

Biederman, J., Faraone, S., Wozniak, J., Mick, E., Kwon, A., Cayton, G., et al. (2005). Clinical correlates of bipolar disorder in a large, referred sample of children and adolescents. *Journal of Psychiatric Research, 39*, 611–622.

Biederman, J., Mick, E., Prince, J. Bostic, J. Q., Wilens, T. E., Spencer, T., et al. (1999). Systematic chart review of the pharmacologic treatment of comorbid attention deficit hyperactivity disorder in youth with bipolar disorder. *Journal of Child and Adolescent Psychopharmacology, 9*, 247–256.

Biffin, F., Tahtalian, S., Filia, K., Fitzgerald, P. B., de Castella, A. R., Filia, S., et al. (2009). The impact of age at onset of bipolar I disorder on functioning and clinical presentation. *Acta Neuropsychatrica, 21*, 191–196.

Blumberg, H. P. (2007). Dimensions in the development of bipolar disorder. *Biological Psychiatry, 62*, 104–106.

Blumberg, H. P., Kaufman, J., Martin, A., Whitemen, R., Zhang, J. H., Gore, J. C., et al. (2003). Amygdala and hippocampal volumes in adolescents and adults with bipolar disorder. *Archives of General Psychiatry, 60*, 1201–1208.

Bowden, C. L. (2001). Strategies to reduce misdiagnosis of bipolar depression. *Psychiatric Services, 52*, 51–55.

Bowring, M. A., & Kovacs, M. (1992). Difficulties in diagnosing manic disorders among children and adolescents. *Journal of the American Academy of Child and Adolescent Psychiatry, 31*, 611–614.

Chang, K., Karchemskiy, A., Barnea-Goraly, N., Garrett, A., Simeonova, D. I., & Reiss, A. (2005). Reduced amygdalar gray matter volume in familial pediatric bipolar disorder. *Journal of the American Academy of Child and Adolescent Psychiatry, 44*, 565–573.

DelBello, M., Hanseman, D., Adler, C., Fleck, D., & Strakowski, S. (2007). Twelve-month outcome of adolescents with bipolar disorder following first hospitalization for a manic or mixed episode. *American Journal of Psychiatry, 164*(4), 582–590.

Dickstein, D. P., Milham, M. P., Nugent, A. C., Drevets, W. C., Charney, D. S., Pine, D. S., et al. (2005). Frontotemporal alterations in pediatric bipolar disorder: Results of a voxel-based morphometry study. *Archives of General Psychiatry, 62*, 734–741.

Duffy, A., Alda, M., Crawford, L., Milin, R., & Grof, P. (2007). The early manifestations of bipolar disorder: A longitudinal prospective study of the offspring of bipolar parents. *Bipolar Disorders, 9*, 828–838.

Egeland, J. (2000). Prodromal symptoms present a decade before diagnosis of bipolar disorder. *Journal of the American Academy of Child and Adolescent Psychiatry, 39*, 1245–1252.

Faedda, G. L., Baldessarini, R. J., Glovinsky, I. P., & Austin, N. B. (2004). Pediatric bipolar disorder: Phenomenology and course of illness. *Bipolar Disorders, 6*, 305–313.

Faedda, G. L., & Teicher, M. H. (2005). Objective measures of activity and attention in the differential diagnosis of psychiatric disorders of childhood. *Essential Psychopharmacology, 6*, 239–249.

Findling, R. I., Gracious, B. L., McNamara, N. K., Youngstrom, E. A., Demeter, C., Branicky, L. A., et al. (2001). Rapid, continuous cycling and psychiatric co-morbidity in pediatric bipolar I disorder. *Bipolar Disorder, 3*, 202–210.

Frank, E., Swartz, H. A., & Kupfer, D. J. (2000). Interpersonal and social rhythm therapy: Managing the chaos of bipolar disorder. *Biological Psychiatry, 48*, 593–604.

Frazier, J. A., Meyer, M. C., Biederman, J., Wozniak, J., Wilens, T. E., Spencer, T. J., et al. (1999). Risperidone treatment for juvenile bipolar disorder: A retrospective chart review. *Journal of the American Academy of Child and Adolescent Psychiatry, 38*(8), 960–965.

Geller, B., Fox, L. W., & Clark, K. A. (1994). Rate and predictors of prepubertal bipolarity during follow-up of 6- to 12-year-old depressed children. *Journal of the American Academy of Child and Adolescent Psychiatry, 33*, 461–468.

Geller, B., Sun, K., Zimerman, B., Luby, J., Frazier, J., & Williams, M. (1995). Complex and rapid-cycling in bipolar children and adolescents: A preliminary study. *Journal of Affective Disorders, 34*, 259–268.

Goldstein, B. I., & Levitt, A. J. (2006). Further evidence for a developmental subtype of bipolar disor-der defined by age of onset: Results from the National Epidemiologic Survey on Alcohol and Related Conditions. *American Journal of Psychiatry, 163*, 1633–1636.

Goldstein, T. R., Birmaher, B., Axelson, D., Goldstein, B. I., Gill, M. K., Esposito-Smythers, C., et al. (2009). Psychosocial functioning among bipolar youth. *Journal of Affective Disorders, 114*, 174–183.

Green, E. K., Raybould, R., Macgregor, S., Gordon-Smith, K., Heron, J., Hyde, S., et al. (2005). Operation of the schizophrenia susceptibility gene, neuregulin 1, across traditional diagnostic boundaries to increase risk for bipolar disorder. *Archives of General Psychiatry, 62,* 642–648.

Hammen, C. (1991). Generation of stress in the course of unipolar depression. *Journal of Abnormal Psychology, 100,* 555–561.

Harvey, A. G. (2009). The adverse consequences of sleep disturbance in pediatric bipolar disorder: Implications for intervention. *Child and Adolescent Psychiatry Clinics of North America, 18,* 321–338.

Harvey, A., Talbot, L. S., & Gershon, A. (2009). Sleep disturbance in bipolar disorder across the life-span. *Clinical Psychology: Science and Practice, 16*, 256–277.

Jackson, A., Cavanagh, J., & Scott, J. (2003). A systematic review of manic and depressive prodromes. *Journal of Affective Disorders, 74*, 209–217.

Judd, L., Akiskal, H., Schettler, P., & Endicott, J. (2007). The long-term natural history of the weekly symptomatic status of bipolar disorder. *Archives of General Psychiatry, 59*, 530–537.

Kim, E. Y., Miklowitz, D., Biukians, A., & Mullen, K. (2007). Life stress and the course of early-onset bipolar disorder. *Journal of Affective Disorders, 99*, 37–44.

Kowatch, R. A., Suppes, T., Carmody, T. J., Bucci, J. P., Jume, J. H., Kromelis, M., et al. (2000). Effect size of lithium, divalproex sodium, and carbamazepine in children and adolescents with bipolar dis-order. *Journal of the American Academy of Child and Adolescent Psychiatry, 39*, 713–720.

Kutcher, S. (2005). ADHD/bipolar children and academic outcomes. *Directions in Psychiatry, 25*, 111–117.

Lam, D. H., Burbeck, R., Wright, K., & Pilling, S. (2009). Psychological therapies in bipolar disorder: The effect of illness history on relapse prevention. A systematic review. *Bipolar Disorders, 11*, 474–482.

Lam, D. H., Watkins, E. R., Hayward, P., Bright, J., Wright, K., Kerr, N., et al. (2003). A randomized con-trolled study of cognitive therapy for relapse prevention for bipolar affective disorder: Outcome of the first year. *Archives of General Psychiatry, 60*, 145–152.

Lewinsohn, P. M., Klein, D. N., & Seeley, J. R. (2000). Bipolar disorders during adolescence. *Acta Psychiatric Scandanavia, 418*, 47–50.

Lish, J. D., Dime-Meenan, S., Whybrow, P. C., Price, R. A., & Hirschfeld, R. M. (1994). The National Depressive and Manic-Depressive Association (DSDA) survey of bipolar members. *Journal of Affective Disorders, 31*, 281–294.

Masi, G., Perugi, G., Toni, C., Millepiedi, S., Mucci, M., Bertini, N., et al. (2004). Predictors of treatment nonresponse in bipolar children and adolescents with manic or mixed episodes. *Journal of Child and Adolescent Psychopharmacology, 14*, 395–404.

McClellan, J., McCurry, C., Snell, J., & DuBose, A. (1999). Early onset psychotic disorders: Course and outcome over a two-year period. *Journal of the American Academy of Child and Adolescent Psychiatry, 38*, 1380–1389.

Mehl, R. C., O'Brien, L. M., Jones, J. H., Dreisbach, J. K., Mervis, C. B., & Gozal, D. (2006). Correlates of sleep and pediatric bipolar disorder. *Sleep, 29*, 193–197.

Miklowitz, D. J., George, E. L., Richards, J. A., Simoneau, T. L., & Suddath, R. L. (2003). A randomized study of family-focused psychoeducation and pharmacotherapy in the outpatient management of bipolar disorder. *Archives of General Psychiatry, 60*, 904–910.

Miklowitz, D. J., George, E. L., Taylor, D. O., Schneck, C. D., Sullivan, A. E., Dickinson, L., et al. (2009). Expressed emotion moderates the effects of family-focused treatment for bipolar adolescents. *Journal of the American Academy of Child and Adolescent Psychiatry, 48*, 643–651.

Miklowitz, D. J., Goldstein, M. J., Nuechterlein, K. H., Snyder, K. S., & Mintz, J. (1998). Family factors and the course of bipolar affective disorder. *Archives of General Psychiatry, 45*, 225–231.

Patelis-Siotis, I., Young, L. T., Robb, J. C., Marriott, M., Bieling, P. J., Cox, L. C., et al. (2001). Group cognitive behavioral therapy for bipolar disorder: A feasibility and effectiveness study. *Journal of Affective Disorders, 65*, 145–153.

Pavuluri, M. N., Birmaher, B., & Naylor, M. W. (2005). Pediatric bipolar disorder: A review of the past 10 years. *Journal of the American Academy of Child and Adolescent Psychiatry, 44*, 846–871.

Pavuluri, M. N., Graczyk, P. A., Henry, D. B., Carbray, J. A., Heidenreich, J., & Miklowitz, D. J. (2004). Child- and family-focused cognitive-behavioral therapy for pediatric bipolar disorder: Development and preliminary results. *Journal of the American Academy of Child and Adolescent Psychiatry, 43*, 528–537.

Post, R. M. (2004). The status of the sensitization/kindling hypothesis of bipolar disorder. *Current Psychosis and Therapeutics Reports, 2*(4), 135–141.

Rademacher, J., DelBello, M., Adler, C., Stanford, K., & Strakowski, S. (2007). Health-related quality of life in adolescents with bipolar disorder. *Journal of Child and Adolescent Psychopharmacology, 17*, 97–103.

Rutter, M., Silberg, J., O'Connor, T., & Simonoff, E. (1999). Genetics and child psychiatry II: Empirical research findings. *Journal of Child Psychology and Psychiatry and Allied Disciplines, 40*, 19–55.

Scott, J., & Meyer, T. D. (2007). Prospects for early intervention in bipolar disorders. *Early Intervention in Psychiatry, 1*(1), 111–113.

State, R. C., Frye, M. A., Altshuler, L. L., Strober, M., DeAntonio, M., Hwang, S., et al. (2004). Chart review of the impact of attention-deficit/hyperactivity disorder comorbidity on response to lithium or divalproex sodium in adolescent mania. *Journal of Clinical Psychiatry, 65*, 1057–1063.

Steiner, H. (2000). Evaluation and management of violent behavior in bipolar adolescents. *In program and abstracts from the American Psychiatric Association, 153rd Annual Meeting, Abstract 19D.* Retrieved September 25, 2009, from http://www.medscape.com/viewarticle/420304

Steiner, H., Saxena, K., & Chang, K. (2003). Psychopharmacologic strategies for the treatment of aggression in juveniles. *CNS Spectrums, 8*, 298–308.

Strober, M. (1992). Bipolar disorders: Natural history, genetic studies and follow-up. In M. Shafii & S. L. Shafii (Eds.), *Clinical guide to depression in children and adolescents* (pp. 251–268). Washington, DC: American Psychiatric Press.

Strober, M., Lampert, C., & Burrough, J. (1990). Relapse following discontinuation of lithium maintenance therapy in adolescents with bipolar I illness: A naturalistic study. *American Journal of Psychiatry, 147*, 457–461.

Swann, A. C., Steinberg, J. L., Lijffijt, M., & Moeller, F. G. (2008). Impulsivity: Differential relationship to depression and mania in bipolar disorder. *Journal of Affective Disorders, 106*, 241–248.

Tueth, M. J., Murphy, T. K., & Evans, D. L. (1998). Special considerations: Use of lithium in children, adolescents and elderly populations. *Journal of Clinical Psychiatry, 59*, 66–73.

Wilens, T., Biederman, J., Kwon, A., Ditterline, J., Forkner, P., Chase, R., et al. (2004). Risk for substance use disorders in adolescents with bipolar disorder. *Journal of the American Academy of Child and Adolescent Psychiatry, 43*, 1380–1286.

Youngstrom, E., Meyers, O., Youngstrom, J. K., Calabrese, J. R., & Findling, R. L. (2006). Diagnostic and measurement issues in the assessment of pediatric bipolar disorder: Implications for understanding mood disorder across the life cycle. *Development and Psychopathology, 18*(4), 989–1021.

David Steele

Hopelessness and Despair

David sat at his desk staring off into space. When he glanced back down at the paper in front of him, he realized that he had been drawing boxes for the last half hour. Each box connected to the next. Just like his life. There was no way out and there was no way in. He was boxed into a corner. There was no escape.

David hated school and he hated the kids. They were all a bunch of phonies. No one understood anything that mattered. He could hear them at their lockers, talking and laughing. They were all so ridiculous, so shallow. They were all full of themselves. They didn't see life like he did. They never would. He was sick and tired of the whole damn thing. He had done his thing. He had tried it their way. But they always wanted something from him. There was always a catch. Either they needed to borrow money or they needed a ride somewhere. They always wanted something. He was sick of being used. He hated them anyway. Better this way.

His mother's voice talked at him from the other side of the closed door. She said something about going out for the evening, something about making sure his homework was done, and then he heard the front door close behind her. Good, she was gone. He didn't need her interruptions, either. She was always going out somewhere. No wonder his father left. She was never home. Life was just one big party. She was as shallow as the rest of them. She didn't understand him, either. She said he was just a moody teenager. Laughed at him. Called him "James Dean, tortured teen." The funny thing was, that didn't even upset him anymore. He was beyond upset. Upset needed feelings. He felt nothing. He looked back down at the drawings of the boxes; they were all empty, too. Just sides. Nothing inside. Empty boxes.

It was very quiet now. Just four walls with emptiness inside. Dead air. Death. He thought about death a lot. They put dead people in boxes. Was he dead already? There was no noise. There was no feeling. Ah . . . the betrayal. Thoughts. Dead people don't think. Dead people don't have to listen to the same damned thoughts echoing in their heads over and over and over. What was the noise in his head? Was that a voice talking to him from the grave? A dead person calling to claim him? Or was it just the sound of his own voice, caught in his head and bouncing back and forth in the emptiness? . . . Dead people are better off. If he were dead, would anyone care? Would anyone notice that he wasn't in class? He thought about the philosophical argument about the tree falling in the forest. How did it go? If a tree falls in the forest and no one is there to hear it . . . did it make a noise? If he killed himself, and no one cared . . . did he even exist? David started to write a suicide note but gave up because he couldn't think of anyone who would be interested in his thoughts. He berated himself because he couldn't even make his mind up about this. He was pathetic. He would wait for another day. He didn't even have the energy to figure out how to do it. Maybe just walk into the traffic. But then, what if you screw up with that, too, and only get run over and lose a leg or something. That would be worse. He walked into the living room and poured himself another shot of whiskey. At least he knew one thing, the whiskey would stop the thinking soon, and he would pass out. Passing out worked. You stopped thinking, at least for a while. . . .

David's case is typical of many adolescents who live in a private world of despair. The majority never end up in a psychologist's office or a clinic. Some suffer in silence. Others end their suffering.

ISSUES, TRENDS, AND TREATMENT ALTERNATIVES

Youth with *unipolar* depression do not experience the highs and lows of bipolar disorder; instead, they experience a pervasive sense of sadness, irritability, or loss of pleasure in their lives. While some of the negative feelings may result from situational factors (loss of a friend, break-up of a romance, problems at home or school), emotional pain can also result from biological causes, such as low levels of the neurotransmitter serotonin. Depression can occur as a result of the complex interplay between biopsychosocial and environmental factors (Harrington, Rutter, & Fombonne, 1996), which can add to problems with the regulation of affect in children and youth (Cicchetti & Toth, 1995). Depression can be conceptualized as *depressed mood, depressive syndrome,* or *depressive disorder,* depending on the nature and severity of the mood (Angold, 1988).

Children and youth experience *depressed mood* when temporary symptoms of depression and irritability are due to negative outcomes from some situation (e.g., getting a bad grade on a test, getting into a fight with a friend). A *depressed syndrome* is a cluster of symptoms of depression that occur together and share similar features. The Achenbach behavioral scales (Achenbach & Resorla, 2001) include two depressive syndromes: *anxious/depressed syndrome* (symptoms of depression that are accompanied by anxiety) and the *depressed/withdrawn syndrome* (symptoms of depression that share common features of low positive affect). The *DSM-IV-TR* (APA, 2000) recognizes three primary categories of *depressive disorders,* based on symptom severity and duration: *adjustment disorder with depressed mood, major depressive disorder,* and *dysthymia.* Adjustment disorder with depressed mood is a temporary response to a known stressor that occurs within 3 months of an event and lasts no longer than 6 months (e.g., a child who reacts with irritability and sadness to a relocation because the child has moved away from friends and school). Major depressive disorder (MDD) is a pervasive feeling of sadness, irritability, or loss of pleasure that lasts for at least 2 weeks and is accompanied by at least five of nine other symptom from the following areas: emotional (sadness, guilt, emptiness), motivational (loss of interest), behavioral (insomnia or hypersomnia), cognitive (recurrent thoughts of suicide, death, diminished concentration), and physical (psychomotor retardation/agitation, fatigue, loss of appetite/increased appetite, loss of energy). Dysthymia is a low-grade depression involving fewer symptoms (two instead of five) over a longer duration (2 years for adults; 1 year for children). Children and adolescents may have symptoms similar to adults; however, depressed mood can often appear as "irritable mood," and symptom presentations will vary given different developmental levels. See Appendix D for the *DSM-IV-TR* diagnostic guidelines for MDD and dysthymia.

There has been growing concern about the onset of mood disorders in children and youth and the lifelong impact that this can have (Costello et al., 2002). It is estimated that 20% of all adolescents will experience at least one episode of depression by age 18, and 65% will report less severe, transient symptoms (Lewinsohn, Hops, & Roberts, 1993). Prevalence rates vary according to type of depression (major depression vs. dysthymia) and whether the population sampled is normative or clinical. According to Kovacs and colleagues (Kovacs, Devlin, Pollock, Richards, & Mukerji, 1997), major depression in children and adolescents usually lasts from 7 to 9 months, while the average duration for dysthymia is 4 years. There is increasing evidence that episodes of pediatric depression can be highly recurrent. Emslie, Rush, and Weinberg (1997) found that 72% of their sample had a relapse within 5 years, while Park and Goodyer (2000, p. 148) report that "short-term relapse is common, occurring in 40–60% of children and adolescents within two months of remission" (reduction of symptoms during a specified period of time).

Recently, using a modified *DSM-IV* diagnostic profile (four instead of five symptoms required, and eliminating the need for a stable mood state over 2 weeks), researchers at the Washington University School of Medicine (Luby et al., 2002, 2004, 2006) found that preschoolers evidenced episodes of *hedonic depression* (a reactive form of depression) and *anhedonic depression* (melancholy and loss of pleasure). Characteristics that accompanied depression in preschoolers included delayed milestones (walking, talking), regression in previously acquired milestones, and night terrors or nightmares.

In school-age children, depression can manifest in acting-out behaviors (anger), withdrawal, and low frustration tolerance, which can negatively affect academic achievement and social relationships (Yorbik, Birmaher, Axelson, Williamson, & Ryan, 2004). Depression at this stage of development is most likely related to situational events rather than due to genetic heritability. Children who live in stressful environments and are exposed to more stressful events (family conflict, parenting style, peer rejection) are at increased risk for developing depression (Eley, Deater-Deckard, Fombonne, & Fulker, 1998). Although children may experience symptoms that are similar to adult symptoms (loss of interest, apathy, sadness, self-doubt, feelings of worthlessness, guilt, and despair), young children may also experience feelings of separation anxiety and exhibit a wide variety of physical complaints (Mitchell, McCauley, & Burke, 1988; Ryan, Puig-Antich, & Ambrosini, 1987). Childhood symptoms of depression often include symptoms of irritability, somatic complaints, and social withdrawal. Behavior disorders, ADHD, and anxiety disorders are often comorbid with depression (*DSM-IV-TR*, APA, 2000).

Rates of depression increase dramatically with age, rising from 2% in childhood to between 4% and 7% in adolescence (Costello et al., 2002). In adolescent populations, depression may appear as irritability mixed with features of anxiety or anger (Compass, Connor, & Hinden, 1998), and there is a higher rate of the melancholic (anhedonic) subtype of depression. Depression in children and adolescents may go undiagnosed due to a failure to recognize irritability, anxiety, and physical complaints (headaches, body pains, and stomachaches) as signs of depression. In addition, adolescent "mood swings" may be considered as normal teenage angst by some parents. While there are equal numbers of boys and girls who will experience depression in childhood, by 16 years of age, girls are twice as likely to be depressed as boys (Hankin & Abramson, 2001). Findings from studies that have followed adolescents with MDD suggest that the disorder is continuous, specific (Lewinsohn, Rohde, Klein, & Seeley, 1999), and linked to increased risk for mortality from suicide, parasuicidal behaviors, substance use, negative life events, and poor levels of academic and social functioning (Weissman et al., 1999). Associated features of adolescent depression may include psychomotor retardation; hypersomnia; and delusions, especially auditory hallucinations (*DSM-IV-TR*).

In their sample of youth with depressive disorders, Escher, Romme, Buiks, Delespaul, and van Os (2002) found that hallucinations tended to persist if they were severe and frequent, and associated with anxiety and/or depression. In their review of studies conducted concerning auditory hallucinations in nonpsychotic children, Best and Mertin (2007) conclude that auditory hallucinations seem to be a consistent feature in cases where youth demonstrate high levels of anxiety and/or depression.

Between 40% and 60% (Angold & Costello, 1993; Rohde, Lewinsohn, & Seeley, 1994) of depressed children and youth have at least one other comorbid disorder, the most common of which are anxiety, substance abuse, and disruptive behavior disorders. Twenty percent of youth that experience a depressive episode will develop bipolar disorder. Depression in children and adolescents has been linked to multiple causes, including family history (Kovacs, Obrosky, Gastonis, & Richards, 1997), biological factors (low levels of serotonin, high levels of cortisol), and cognitive factors (negative and maladaptive thought processes). Factors that can increase the risk of depression in children include stress (Lewinsohn, Rogdem, & Seeley, 1998); loss of a parent or loved one (Wells, Deykin, & Kierman, 1985); romantic break-up (Monroe, Rohde, & Seeley, 1999); school problems (Gould, Fisher, Parides, Flory, & Shaffer, 1996); and family problems, including family poverty, conflict with parents (Hammen, 2006), and the stress and challenges of living with a single parent (Garrison, Addy, Jackson, McKeon, & Waller, 1992). Personality factors linked to increased risk for MDD and suicide include high levels of neuroticism, novelty seeking, and low self-esteem (Fergusson, Beautrais, & Horwood, 2003). Protective factors that can buffer youth from depression include family cohesion/connectedness (Borowsky, Ireland, & Resnick, 2001) and positive team sport involvement (Boone & Leadbeater, 2006). Although having friendships is a protective factor for both boys and girls, the nature of the friendship varies by gender. While girls benefit from having a cohesive and interconnected set of friends who are not at odds with each other, a protective factor for boys involves a network of friends who participate in common activities (Bearman & Moody, 2004).

Treatment Alternatives for Depression

The nature of the treatment method used can reflect the therapist's theoretical perspectives: cognitive behavioral, family and parenting, or biological basis of behavior. Kaslow and Thompson (1998) reviewed interventions for depression targeting children and adolescents, the majority of which involved cognitive-behavioral therapy (CBT). Although a number of the programs demonstrated success in alleviating depressive symptoms, none of the studies met with the stringent criteria for well-established treatments. Furthermore, the authors noted that most of the interventions had been adapted from adult treatments and neglected to include modifications related to the child's or adolescent's developmental stage. They found only two child studies and two adolescent studies that met criteria for probably efficacious interventions set forth by the APA Task Force (APA Task Force on Psychological Intervention Guidelines, 1995).

The child studies that met the standard were two studies conducted by Stark and colleagues (Stark, Reynolds, & Kaslow, 1987; Stark, Rouse, & Livingston, 1991) demonstrating the benefits of CBT self-control therapy. Adolescent studies meeting the standard included studies by Lewinsohn and colleagues (Lewinsohn, Clarke, Hops, & Andrews, 1990; Lewinsohn, Clarke, Rhode, Hops, & Seeley, 1996). In the first study (Lewinsohn et al., 1990), adolescents who received a 14-week CBT program or adolescents whose parents conjointly received a 7-week CBT program reduced more symptoms of depression than the wait-list control group. Replication of the study (Lewinsohn et al., 1996) with some modifications revealed similar results with maintenance of reduced depressive symptoms at follow-up, 2 years later. Kaslow and Thompson (1998) concluded their review by emphasizing the need for future studies to recognize developmental differences and incorporate cultural perspectives.

Weisz, Doss, and Hawley (2005) conducted a meta-analysis of empirically supported youth treatment approaches for anxiety, depression, ADHD, and conduct problems. For adolescents, youth-based programs were more common for all disorders compared to family-focused treatments. The most common youth-based treatment program for depression was based on behavioral/learning-based perspectives (78%), with CBT being the most common component in this category (67%). Programs for depression were most often delivered in group (89%), compared to individual (11%) format, with an average of 12 group sessions per program.

In their review of programs aimed at the prevention of depression in children and adolescents, Gladstone and Beardslee (2009) found that several programs have developed their prevention strategies based on cognitive-behavioral and/or interpersonal approaches building on the success of these programs in the treatment of depressive disorders in youth (Kaslow & Thompson, 1998). Gladstone and Beardslee suggest that common features among these approaches include "clearly identified, well-specified targets for preventive interventions that are manual-based, delivered with fidelity, and involve cognitive and social-relationship dimensions" (2009, p. 213). Results of the review (see Gladstone & Beardslee, 2009) produced several promising programs, such as the Penn Resiliency Program (Gillham, Brunwasser, & Freres, 2008), the Interpersonal Psychotherapy Prevention Program for High-Risk Teens (Young, Mufson, & Davis, 2006), and Problem Solving for Life (Spence, Sheffield, & Donovan, 2005).

Medical Management of Depressive Disorders in Children and Youth

Between 30% and 40% of children fail to show a positive response to medication for depression (Emslie et al., 1997). Difficulties with prescribing medications for mood disorders in childhood can be related to the fact that there are very few pediatric trials and, as a result, the majority of medications are prescribed "off label," since they contain no information about pediatric use. Some studies have shown that selective serotonin reuptake inhibitors (SSRIs) have limited success for pediatric populations (March et al., 2004).

Although initial studies concerning medical treatments for adolescent depression revealed contradictory results, these studies involved trials of tricyclic antidepressants. Recently, trials of SSRIs point to more persuasive evidence for the benefits of fluoxetine (Prozac) and paroxetine (Paxil). In controlled studies, fluoxetine was proven effective for children and adolescents (Emslie et al., 1997), while paroxetine has proven successful with adolescents (Keller, Ryan, & Strober, 2001). However, the FDA has recommended that paroxetine not be used with children or adolescents. Currently, fluoxetine is the only FDA-approved medication for use with children 8 years of age or older.

Based on a review of outcomes regarding the use of medications with children and youth, the FDA found statistical evidence for increased suicidal ideation and behaviors among youth taking the antidepressant medications (Newman, 2004). Although one of the most common symptoms of depression is lethargy and loss of energy, antidepressant medications serve to increase the energy level. However, often the energy returns before the mood improves, resulting in an increased risk for suicide (the youth is now mobilized to act on the depression and engage in suicidal impulses). As a result, the FDA issued a *black box warning* (the most serious warning level available) regarding the use of antidepressant medication (SSRIs) for child and adolescent depression. The FDA also cautioned that antidepressants could trigger a manic episode in patients with bipolar disorder.

There is significant controversy regarding the use of medications for children and youth with depressive disorders. Some researchers (Emslie et al., 1997) have found success with fluoxetine; however, potentially serious side effects from the use of the drug also exist. At least one adolescent male (Webb & Cranswick, 2003) was reported to have developed auditory hallucinations telling him to kill his family and himself shortly after taking fluoxetine for the first time. As a result, controversy has resulted as to whether the risks outweigh the benefits; however, there is also evidence to suggest that the use of medications can increase treatment success. The Treatment for Adolescents With Depression Study (TADS) revealed that using CBT with antidepressants was significantly more effective than CBT alone (Apter et al., 2005; March et al., 2004), while other studies have found that the use of antidepressants act to reduce the risk of suicidal behavior (Olfson, Shaffer, Marcus, & Greenburg, 2003; Valuck, Libby, Sills, Giese, & Allen, 2004). Bridge and colleagues (2007) conducted a comprehensive review of all pediatric medication trials in the past 18 years (1988–2006) and concluded that based on the results, the benefits of using antidepressant medications far outweighed any risks.

SUICIDE RISK, TREATMENT, AND PREVENTION

Suicide Risk

Although rare in childhood, current suicide rates for children are 8 times higher than noted in the 1950s (Goldman & Beardslee, 1999), and suicide is now the third leading cause of death among 10- to 19-year-olds (Borowsky et al., 2001). Twice as many females attempt suicide, but males are four times more likely to succeed, due to the more lethal methods used by males. In September 2007, the Centers for Disease Control (CDC) released a report concerning the largest annual increase in suicide rate for youth in the 10- to 14-year bracket, with 94 suicides during 2003–2004 compared to 56 suicides the previous year. Increases were also noted in the 15- to 19-year span for that year as well. Methods also reported a change from using firearms in 1990 to hanging/suffocation in 2004, which accounted for 71% of the deaths reported for females in the 10- to 14-year category, and 49% of deaths among the older girls (15–19). Males continued to use firearms as the most frequent method (CDC, 2007).

The CDC suicide factsheet (CDC, 2009) reports that in 2007, 14.5% of U.S. high school students surveyed (18.7% of females, 10.3% of males) stated that they had seriously considered attempting suicide in the previous 12 months, while 6.9% (9.3% of females, 4.6% of males) reported that they had actually made a suicide attempt in the previous 12 months. Among the 15- to 21-year-old group, suicide is responsible for 12% of all deaths annually.

According to the CDC report on youth suicide, the top three methods used by youth to commit suicide include firearms (46%), suffocation (39%), and poisoning (8%). However, more youth survive than complete suicides, and approximately 149,000 youth between the ages of 10 and 19 were seen in emergency departments across the United States to receive medical support for self-inflicted injuries. The following behaviors were noted as risks for potential suicide in the CDC report:

- History of previous suicide attempts
- Family history of suicide
- History of depression or other mental illness
- Alcohol or drug abuse
- Stressful life event or loss
- Easy access to lethal methods
- Exposure to the suicidal behavior of others
- Incarceration (CDC, 2007)

Although major depression seems to be the most prominent risk factor for suicide in girls (Shaffer et al., 1996), somatic symptoms, peer suicide attempt, and illicit drug use were all found to increase the risk of suicide in females regardless of ethnicity (Borowsky et al., 2001). Having made a previous suicide attempt is the most lethal risk factor for males (Shaffer et al., 1996), along with weapon carrying at school and same-sex romantic attraction (Borowsky et al., 2001). Other risk factors that cut across gender and ethnicity include violence victimization, violence perpetration, alcohol use, marijuana use, and school problems. In their examination of adolescent profiles for more than 13,000 students between 1995 and 1997 (Grades 7–12), Borowsky and colleagues (2001) found that having three protective factors reduced suicide attempts by between 70% and 85%. Protective factors were identified as parent and family connectivity, emotional well-being (girls), and high grade point average (boys). Although acting on suicidal impulse has been linked to serotonin malfunction in adults, this association has not been confirmed in children and adolescents. Children and adolescents who contemplate suicide feel intense emotional distress and choose death as a means of ending severe psychological pain. Kaminski and Fang (2009) found that victimization of youth by peers significantly increased the risk of suicidal ideation. Youth who were victimized by peers (threatened or injured) were more than twice as likely (2.4) to report suicidal thoughts and more than three times as likely (3.3) to report suicidal behavior than peers who were not victimized.

Suicide Treatment Program

A major stumbling block in the treatment of youth with suicidal thoughts is the fact that youth who are experiencing these negative feelings are among the least likely to reach out for help (Carlton & Deane, 2000). Intervention should restrict suicidal youth to a very structured environment where they can be placed on a suicide watch and where a "no harm" contract is employed. Hospitalization in a psychiatric unit may be required in some cases, and monitoring with reevaluation of potential future hospitalizations is crucial at this stage (Rudd & Joiner, 1998). Cognitive therapy can be helpful in reframing thoughts of hopelessness and improving problem-solving skills for increased adaptive functioning.

Multisystem therapy (MST) has been successful in the treatment of youth with a wide variety of serious emotional difficulties (Henggeler, Clingempeel, Brondino, & Pickrel, 2002). MST is an ecologically based and manualized program that incorporates a youth's family and community resources (peers and school system) in the therapeutic process. Huey and colleagues (2004) found that for youth with severe psychiatric illness who were at risk for suicidal behavior, MST proved more effective in reducing future suicide attempts than hospitalization.

The American Association for Child and Adolescent Psychiatry (AACAP) Practice Parameters for Assessment and Treatment of Children with Suicidal Behavior (2001) suggests the following therapeutic approaches for the treatment of suicidal behavior in children and adolescents: cognitive-behavioral therapy (CBT), interpersonal psychotherapy for adolescents (IPT-A), dialectical behavioral therapy (DBT), and psychodynamic and family therapy. Interpersonal therapy for adolescents is a program that consists of weekly meetings (for 12 weeks) with the goal of increasing problem-solving skills. Results suggest that the program successfully reduced depressed symptoms in adolescent participants (Mufson, Weissman, Moreau, & Garfinkel, 1999)

Dialectical behavioral therapy (DBT; Linehan, 1993) has been successful in treating some of the most challenging behaviors, including self-harm, in patients with borderline personality disorder (BPD). DBT is a therapeutic approach that is designed to treat individuals who experience emotional dysregulation, which is an inability to manage emotions, especially negative emotions, due to heightened levels of arousal. The program integrates methods from the cognitive, behavioral, and psychodynamic schools of thought. Goals of the program are to increase the ability to tolerate stress, increase social skills, and provide lessons and opportunities to learn how to respond more effectively to challenging life situations. The therapist's role is to empathize with the clients and validate their needs. Individual therapy is supported by enrollment in skill-building practice sessions (group therapy) to develop the needed skills to relate more effectively to others in a safe environment. The program evolves around three stages:

1. Increase skills in managing behavior, while decreasing behaviors that are suicidal, interfere with therapy, and reduce the quality of life.
2. Increase awareness of stress-related trauma and reduce the distress.
3. Focus on long-range goals such as increased self-esteem and interpersonal success.

The efficacy of DBT has been reviewed extensively (Koerner & Dimeff, 2000; Robins & Chapman, 2004), and although some critics have found fault with methodology in some of the studies, the success of the program in reducing harmful behaviors such as suicide attempts and other acts of self-harm in patients with BPD has resulted in recent applications of the approach to treat adolescents with suicidal ideation (Rathus & Miller, 2002). Preliminary results have been promising.

Suicide Prevention Programs

Prevention programs can focus on one of three audiences: widely based, or *universal,* health promotion programs targeting all children; *selective, or secondary prevention, programs* that target those at risk for suicide (Hayden & Laurer, 2000); and *indicated, or tertiary, prevention programs* for those youth who are having suicidal thoughts or who have attempted suicide previously.

Unfortunately, mass approaches to suicide prevention, such as suicide hot lines (Shaffer, Garland, & Bacon, 1989) and in-school awareness programs (Shaffer, Garland, Vieland, Underwood, & Busner, 1991), have, for the most part, not been successful in preventing suicide, while some programs have actually increased the risk of suicidal ideation in vulnerable youth (iatrogenic effects). However, the majority of these programs have adopted a "stress" model that attributes suicidal behavior to induced stress in healthy people, as opposed to a mental illness model, which views suicide as the outcome of mental illness (CCEP, 2006). At a global level, however, it is possible that routine screens can serve to identify at-risk students for more intensive services (Shaffer & Craft, 1999). Borowsky and colleagues (2001) suggest that targeting protective factors is an important key to developing successful suicide prevention programs. Targeting risk factors such as substance abuse, stress, and lack of social support, and protective factors such as family cohesiveness, academic success, and emotional well-being, may well be important ingredients in future prevention programs for these children of despair.

Increasing rates of suicide in North America have focused attention on urgent need for the development and evaluation of suicide prevention programs. Given the vulnerable nature of the target population, concerns have been voiced about the need to protect against possible iatrogenic effects that might be imbedded in the program (Gould et al., 2005; Shaffer et al., 1991). Schools are an obvious venue for service delivery, since children and youth spend the majority of their time within the school environment. As a result, in the United States, the majority of suicide prevention programs are school based (Kalafat & Elias, 1995). Within this context, programs have been delivered in a number of different formats, including *curriculum based prevention programs, staff in service programs,* and *schoolwide student screening programs* (Eckert, Miller, DuPaul, & Riley-Tillman, 2003).

Curriculum-based programs are usually brief (a few hours) and provide psychoeducational information about symptoms associated with suicidal ideation and offer information about community resources. Although there has been some reported success in the reduction of suicidal ideation, there has been a lack of empirical support (Mazza, 1997) and evidence that the programs may actually have a negative impact on those who are most in need (Shaffer et al., 1991). In one study, participants actually reported an increase in feelings of hopelessness and despair after involvement in the program (Overholser, Hemstreet,

Spirito, & Vyse, 1989). Based on their comprehensive review of curriculum-based suicide prevention programs, Gould and Kramer (2001) have advised caution in launching future programs.

Faculty and staff awareness programs have been widely used despite the fact that there is very little empirical support to attest to the value of this approach; although at least one study has suggested that staff in-service was a successful component in a school-based program (Zenere & Lazarus, 1997). Kalafat and Elias (1995) have suggested that another barrier to the success of school-based programs was reluctance of personnel to participate in the programs based on the incorrect assumption that discussing suicide could actually lead to suicidal behavior.

One of the most successful universal prevention programs that has been launched recently is the *Signs of Suicide (SOS) Prevention Program*. The SOS Program (Aseltine, 2003; Aseltine & DeMartino, 2004) is unique relative to previous programs in its dual emphasis on suicidal ideation as a mental illness (rather than stress induced) and the detrimental effect of alcohol on those who suffer from mental illness. The program has been empirically proven to reduce suicidal behavior and reduce suicide attempts by 40%. SAMHSA's National Registry of Effective Programs has recognized the SOS program, which was adopted by 675 schools as of the 2004–2005 academic year. A randomized clinical trial has also ruled out any possibility of iatrogenic effects resulting from participation in the program.

The focus of SOS is on training adolescents as first responders to recognize the warning signs of suicide in peers and teaching them to understand the importance of treating suicidal ideation as a medical emergency in need of an immediate response. The program uses the acronym *ACT (acknowledge, care, and tell)*:

- ACKNOWLEDGE the signs of suicide that others display and take them seriously.
- Let the person know you CARE about him or her, and that you want to tell.
- Then TELL a responsible adult.

Descriptions of the SOS Program are available from several sources, including Aseltine, 2003; Aseltine, James, Schilling, and Glanovsky, 2007; and Aseltine and DeMartino, 2004. The program includes an educational component with a curriculum designed to increase student awareness of suicidal ideation, including a film, *Friends for Life,* with an accompanying discussion guide to assist in developing appropriate ways to act and respond to someone who is depressed or suicidal. The program also includes a self-screening component (BSAD; Lucas et al., 2001): a self-administered instrument to determine risk based on suicidal ideation and problem drinking. Students are advised to seek help if they score above a given level on the screening survey. The program's emphasis is on suicidal ideation as a product of mental illness, not a normal response to stress or disappointment and, as such, it requires an emergency response, similar to any serious medical illness. A 2-year investigation of the program operating in nine schools with socially, economically, and geographically diverse high school students revealed that the program was effective in reducing the number of suicide attempts and in increasing awareness, as well as adaptive attitudes, about suicide and depression in youth (Aseltine et al., 2007).

Post-Case Questions

1. Given David's depression and suicidal ideation, what risk factors should have alerted family and school personnel to David's condition?

2. If you were a school counselor and David was a participant in the SOS program in your school, what results would you anticipate from his self-report survey and why?

3. If you were aware of David's suicidal ideation, what recommendations would you make to his parents? How should the intervention begin?

4. Suppose that David's mother had become aware of his depressed mood, and the physician was recommending placing David on antidepressant medication. What advice would you give her?

5. What symptoms of depression does David exhibit, and would they meet criteria for a diagnosis of major depressive disorder or dysthymia? Justify your response.

REFERENCES

Achenbach, T. M., & Rescorla, L. A. (2001). *Manual for the ASEBA School-Age Forms & Profiles*. Burlington, VT: University of Vermont, Research Center for Children, Youth & Families.

American Association for Child and Adolescent Psychiatry (AACAP). (2001). Practice parameter for the assessment and treatment of children and adolescents with suicidal behaviors. *Journal of the American Academy of Child and Adolescent Psychiatry, 40*(7), 24S–51S.

American Psychiatric Association (APA). (2000). *Diagnostic and statistical manual of mental disorders* (4th ed., text rev.). Washington, DC: Author.

American Psychological Association (APA) Task Force on Psychological Intervention Guidelines. (1995). *Template for developing guidelines: Interventions for mental disorders and psychosocial aspects of physical disorders*. Washington, DC: American Psychological Association.

Angold, A. (1988). Childhood and adolescent depression: I. Epidemiological and etiological aspects. *British Journal of Psychiatry, 152*, 601–617.

Angold, A., & Costello, E. J. (1993). Depressive comorbidity in children and adolescents: Empirical, theoretical, and methodological issues. *Journal of the American Academy of Child and Adolescent Psychiatry, 150*, 1779–1791.

Apter, A., Kronenberg, S., & Brent, D. (2005). Turning darkness into light: A new landmark study on the treatment of adolescent depression. Comments on the TADS study. *European Child and Adolescent Psychiatry, 14*, 113–116.

Aseltine, R. H. (2003). Evaluation of a school-based suicide prevention program. *Adolescent and Family Health, 3*, 81–88.

Aseltine, R. H., & DeMartino, R. (2004). An outcome evaluation of the SOS suicide prevention program. *American Journal of Public Health, 94*, 446–451.

Aseltine, R. H., James, A., Schilling, E. A., & Glanovsky, J. (2007). Evaluating the SOS suicide prevention program: A replication and extension. *BMC Public Health*. Retrieved August 15, 2007, from http://www.biomedcentral.com/1471-2458/7/161

Bearman, P. S., & Moody, J. (2004). Suicide and friendships among American adolescents. *American Journal of Public Health, 94*, 89–95.

Best, N. T., & Mertin, P. (2007). Correlates of auditory hallucinations in nonpsychotic children. *Clinical Child Psychology and Psychiatry, 12,* 611–623.

Birmaher, B., Ryan, N. D., Williamson, D. E., Brent, D. A., & Kaufman, J. (1996). Childhood and adolescent depression: A review of the past 10 years. Part II. *Journal of the American Academy of Child and Adolescent Psychiatry, 35,* 1575–1583.

Boone, E. M., & Leadbeater, B. J. (2006). Game on: Diminishing risks for depressive symptoms in early adolescence through positive involvement in team sports. *Journal of Research on Adolescence, 16,* 79–90.

Borowsky, I. W., Ireland, M., & Resnick, M. D. (2001). Adolescent suicide attempts: Risks and protectors. *Pediatrics, 107,* 485–502.

Bridge, J. A., Iyengar, S., Salary, C. B., Barbe, R. P., Birmaher, B., Pincus, H. A., et al. (2007). Clinical response and risk for reported suicidal ideation and suicide attempts in pediatric antidepressant treatment: A meta-analysis of randomized controlled trials. *Journal of the American Medical Association, 297,* 1683–1696.

Carlton, P. A., & Deane, F. P. (2000). Impact of attitudes and suicidal ideation on adolescents' intentions to seek professional psychological help. *Journal of Adolescence, 23,* 35–45.

Centers for Disease Control (CDC). (2007). *Youth suicide.* Retrieved September 27, 2009, from http://www.cdc.gov/ncipc/dvp/Suicide/youthsuicide.htm

Centers for Disease Control (CDC). (2009). *Suicide fact sheet: Suicide at a glance.* Retrieved October, 2009, from http://www.cdc.gov/violenceprevention

Cicchetti, D., & Toth, S. L. (1995). Developmental psychopathology and disorders of affect. In D. C. Cohen & D. J. Cohen (Eds.), *Developmental Psychopathology* (Vol. 2, pp. 369–342). Hoboken, NJ: John Wiley.

Compass, B. E., Connor, J. K., & Hinden, B. R. (1998). New perspectives on depression during adolescence. In R. Jessor (Ed.), *New perspectives on adolescent risk behavior.* Cambridge, UK: Cambridge University Press.

Connecticut Center for Effective Practice (CCEP). (2006). *Endangered youth: A report on suicide among adolescents involved with child welfare and juvenile justice systems.* Retrieved September 2009, from http://www.chdi.org

Costello, J., Pine, D., Hammen, C., March, J., Plotsky, P. M., Weissman, M., et al. (2002). Development and natural history of mood disorders. *Biological Psychiatry, 52*(6), 529–542.

Eckert, T. L., Miller, D. N., DuPaul, G., & Riley-Tillman, T. C. (2003). Adolescent suicide prevention: School psychologists' acceptability of school-based programs. *School Psychology Review, 32,* 57–76.

Eley, T. C., Deater-Deckard, K., Fombonne, E., & Fulker, D. W. (1998). An adoption study of depressive symptoms in middle childhood. *Journal of Child Psychology and Psychiatry and Allied Disciplines, 39,* 337–345.

Emslie, G. J., Rush, A. J., & Weinberg, W. A. (1997). A double-blind, randomized, placebo-controlled trial of fluoxetine in children and adolescents with depression. *Archives of General Psychiatry, 54,* 1031–1037.

Escher, S., Romme, M., Buiks, A., Delespaul, P., & van Os, J. (2002). Independent course of childhood auditory hallucinations: A sequential 3-year follow-up study. *British Journal of Psychiatry, 181,* 10–18.

Fergusson, D. M., Beautrias, A. L., & Horwood, L. J. (2003). Vulnerability and resiliency to suicidal behaviors in young people. *Psychological Medicine, 33,* 61–73.

Garrison, C. Z., Addy, C., Jackson, K. L., McKeon, R., & Waller, J. L. (1992). Major depressive disorder and dysthymia in young adolescents. *American Journal of Epidemiology, 135,* 792–802.

Gillham, J., Brunwasser, S. M., & Freres, D. R. (2008). Preventing depression in early adolescence. In J. R. Abela & B. L. Hankin (Eds.), *Handbook of depression in children and adolescence* (pp. 309–322). New York: Guilford.

Gladstone, T. R. G., & Beardslee, W. R. (2009). The prevention of depression in children and adolescents: A review. *Canadian Journal of Psychiatry, 54,* 213–221.

Goldman, S., & Beardslee, W. R. (1999). Suicide in children and adolescents. In D. G. Jacobs (Ed.), *The Harvard Medical School guide to suicide assessment and intervention.* San Francisco: Jossey-Bass.

Gould, M. S., Fisher, P., Parides, M., Flory, M., & Shaffer, D. (1996). Psychosocial risk factors of child and adolescent completed suicide. *Archives of General Psychiatry, 53,* 1155–1162.

Gould, M. S., & Kramer, R. A. (2001). Youth suicide prevention. *Suicide and Life-Threatening Behavior, 31*(Suppl.), 6–31.

Gould, M. S., Marrrocco, F., Kleinman, M., Thomas, J., Mostkoff, K., Cote, J, et al. (2005). Evaluating iatrogenic risk of youth suicide screening programs. *Journal of the American Medical Association, 293,* 1635–1643.

Hammen, C. (2006). Stress generation in depression: Reflections on origins, research and future directions. *Journal of Clinical Psychology, 62,* 1065–1082.

Hankin, B. L., & Abramson, L. Y. (2001). Development of gender differences in depression: An elaborated cognitive vulnerability–transactional stress theory. *Psychological Bulletin, 127,* 773–796.

Harrington, R., Rutter, M., & Fombonne, E. (1996). Developmental pathways in depression: Multiple meanings, antecedents and endpoints. *Development and Psychopathology, 8,* 601–616.

Hayden, D. C., & Lauer, P. (2000). Prevalence of suicide programs in schools and roadblocks to implementation. *Suicide and Life-Threatening Behavior, 30*(3), 239–251.

Henggeler, S., Clingempeel, W. G., Brondino, M. J., & Pickrel, S. G. (2002). Four-year follow up of multisystemic therapy with substance abusing and substance dependent juvenile offenders. *Journal of the American Academy of Child and Adolescent Psychiatry, 41*(7), 868–874.

Huey, S., Henggeler, S. W., Rowland, M., Halliday-Boykins, Cunningham, P. B., Pickrel, S., et al. (2004). Multisystemic therapy effects on attempted suicide by youths presenting psychiatric emergencies. *Journal of the American Academy of Child and Adolescent Psychiatry, 43*(2), 183–190.

Jacobs, J. (1971). *Adolescent suicide.* New York: John Wiley.

Kalafat, J., & Elias, M. J. (1995). Suicide prevention in an educational context: Broad and narrow foci. *Suicide and Life-Threatening Behavior, 25,* 123–133.

Kaminski, J. W., & Fang, X. (2009). Victimization by peers and adolescent suicide in three U.S. samples. *Journal of Pediatrics.* Retrieved October 2009 from http://www.jpeds.com/article/S0022-3476(09)00466-1/abstract

Kaslow, N. J., & Thompson, M. P. (1998). Applying the criteria for empirically supported treatments to studies of psychosocial interventions for child and adolescent depression. *Journal of Clinical Child Psychology, 27,* 146–155.

Keller, M. B., Ryan, N. D., & Strober, M. (2001). Efficacy of paroxetine in the treatment of adolescent major depression: A randomized, controlled trial. *Journal of the American Academy of Child and Adolescent Psychiatry, 40,* 762–772.

Koerner, K., & Dimeff, L. A. (2000). Further data on dialectical behavior therapy. *Clinical Psychology: Science and Practice, 7*(1), 104–112.

Kovaks, M., Devlin, B., Pollock, M., Richards, C., & Mukerji, P. (1997). A controlled family history study of childhood-onset depressive disorder. *Archives of General Psychiatry, 54,* 613–632.

Kovacs, M., Obrosky, D. S., Gastonis, C., & Richards, C. (1997). First-episode major depressive and dysthymic disorder in childhood: Clinical and sociodemographic factors in recovery. *Journal of the American Academy of Child and Adolescent Psychiatry, 36,* 777–784.

Lewinsohn, P. M., Clarke, G. N., Hops, H., & Andrews, J. (1990). Cognitive-behavioral treatment for depressed adolescents. *Behavior Therapy, 21,* 385–401.

Lewinsohn, P. M., Clarke, G. N., Rhode, P., Hops, H., & Seeley, J. (1996). A course in coping: A cognitive-behavioral approach to the treatment of adolescent depression. In D. Hibbs & P. S. Jensen (Eds.),

Psychosocial treatments for child and adolescent disorders: Empirically based strategies for clinical practice (pp. 1109–1135). Washington, DC: American Psychiatric Association.

Lewinsohn, P. M., Hops, H., & Roberts, R. E. (1993). Adolescent psychopathology: Prevalence and incidence of depression and other *DSM III-R* disorders in high school students. *Journal of Abnormal Psychology, 102,* 133–144.

Lewinsohn, P. M., Rogdem, P., & Seeley, J. R. (1998). Major depressive disorder in older adolescents. Prevalence, risk factors, and clinical implications. *Clinical Psychology Review, 18,* 765–794.

Lewinsohn, P. M., Rohde, P., Klein, D. N., & Seeley, J. R. (1999). Natural course of adolescent major depressive disorder 1: Continuity into young adulthood. *Journal of the American Academy of Child and Adolescent Psychiatry, 38,* 56–63.

Linehan, M. M. (1993). *Cognitive behavioral treatment of borderline personality disorder.* New York: Guilford.

Luby, J. L., Heffelfinger, A., Mrakotsky, C., Hessler, M., Brown, K., & Hildebrand, T. (2002). Preschool major depressive disorder: Preliminary validation for developmentally modified *DSM-IV* criteria. *Journal of the American Academy of Child and Adolescent Psychiatry, 41,* 928–937.

Luby, J. L., Mrakotsky, C., Heffelfinger, A., Brown, K., & Spitznagel, E. (2004). Characteristics of depressed preschoolers with and without anhedonia: Evidence for a melancholic depressive subtype in young children. *American Journal of Psychiatry, 161,* 1998–2005.

Luby, J. L., Sullivan, J., Belden, A., Stalets, M., Blankenship, S., & Spitznagel, E. (2006). An observational analysis of behavior in depressed preschoolers: Further validation of early onset depression. *Journal of the American Academy of Child and Adolescent Psychiatry, 45,* 203–212.

Lucas, C. P., Zhang, H., Fisher, P., Shaffer, D., Regier, D. A., Narrow, W. E., et al. (2001). The DISC Predictive Scales (DPS): Efficiently screening for diagnoses. *Journal of the American Academy of Child and Adolescent Psychiatry, 40,* 443–449.

March, J., Silva, S., Petrycki, Curry, J., Wells, K, Fairbaink, J., et al.: TADS Research Team. (2004). Fluoxetine, cognitive-behavioral therapy and their combination for adolescents with depression. *JAMA, 292*(7), 807–820.

Mazza, J. J. (1997). School-based suicide prevention programs: Are they effective? *School Psychology Review, 26,* 382–396.

Mitchell, J., McCauley, E., & Burke, P. M. (1988). Phenomenology of depression in children and adolescents. *Journal of the American Academy of Child and Adolescent Psychiatry, 27,* 12–20.

Monroe, S. M., Rohde, P., & Seeley, J. R. (1999). Life events and depression in adolescence: Relationship loss as a prospective risk factor for first onset of major depressive disorder. *Journal of Abnormal Psychology, 108,* 606–614.

Mufson, L., Weissman, M. M., Moreau, D., & Garfinkel, R. (1999). Efficacy of interpersonal psychotherapy for depressed adolescents. *Archives of General Psychiatry, 56,* 573–579.

Newman, T. (2004). A black-box warning for antidepressants in children? *New England Journal of Medicine, 351*(16), 1595–1598.

Olfson, M., Shaffer, D., Marcus, S. C., & Greenberg, T. (2003). Relationship between antidepressant medication treatment and suicide in adolescents. *Archives of General Psychiatry, 60,* 978–982.

Overholser, J., Hemstreet, A. H., Spirito, A., & Vyse, S. (1989). Suicide awareness programs in the schools: Effects of gender and personal experience. *Journal of the American Academy of Child and Adolescent Psychiatry, 28,* 925–930.

Park, R. J., & Goodyer, I. M. (2000). Clinical guidelines for depressive disorders in childhood and adolescence. *European Child and Adolescent Psychiatry, 9,* 147–161.

Rathus, J. H., & Miller, A. L. (2002). Dialectical behavior therapy adapted for suicidal adolescents. *Suicide and Life Threatening Behavior, 32*(2), 146–157.

Robins, C. J., & Chapman, A. L. (2004). Dialectical behavior therapy: Current status, recent developments, and future directions. *Journal of Personality Disorders, 18*(1), 73–89.

Rohde, P., Lewinsohn, P. M., & Seeley, J. R. (1991). Comorbidity of unipolar depression: II. Comorbidity with other mental disorders in adolescents and adults. *Journal of Abnormal Psychology, 100,* 214–222.

Rohde, P., Lewinsohn, P. M., & Seeley, J. R. (1994). Are adolescents changed by an episode of major depression? *Journal of the American Academy of Child and Adolescent Psychiatry, 33,* 1289–1298.

Rudd, M. D., & Joiner, T. E. (1998). An integrative conceptual framework for assessing and treating suicidal behavior in adolescents. *Journal of Adolescence, 21,* 489–498.

Ryan, N. D., Puig-Antich, J., & Ambrosini, P. (1987). The clinical picture of major depression in children and adolescents. *Archives of General Psychiatry, 44,* 854–861.

Shaffer, D., & Craft, L. (1999). Methods of adolescent suicide prevention. *Journal of Clinical Psychiatry, 60,* 70–74.

Shaffer, D., Garland, A., & Bacon, K. (1989). Prevention issues in youth suicide. In D. Shaffer, I. Philips, & N. Enzer (Eds.), *Prevention of mental disorders, alcohol and drug abuse in children and adolescents* (OSAP Prevention Monograph 2, pp. 373–412). Rockville, MD: Alcohol, Drug Abuse and Mental Health Administration.

Shaffer, D., Garland, A., Vieland, V., Underwood, M., & Busner, C. (1991). The impact of curriculum-based suicide prevention programs for teenagers. *Journal of the American Academy of Child and Adolescent Psychiatry, 30,* 588–596.

Shaffer, D., Gould, M. S., Fisher, P., Trautment, P., Moreau, D., Kleinman, M., et al. (1996). Psychiatric diagnosis in child and adolescent suicide. *Archives of General Psychiatry, 53,* 339–348.

Spence, S. H., Sheffield, J. K., & Donovan, C. L. (2005). Long-term outcome of a school-based, universal approach to prevention of depression in adolescents. *Journal of Consulting and Clinical Psychology, 73,* 160–167.

Stark, K. D., Reynolds, W. M., & Kaslow, N. J. (1987). A comparison of the relative efficacy of self-control therapy and a behavioral problem-solving therapy for depression in children. *Journal of Abnormal Child Psychology, 15,* 91–113.

Stark, K. D., Rouse, L., & Livingston, R. (1991). Treatment of depression during childhood and adolescence: Cognitive-behavioral procedures for the individual and family. In P. Kendall (Ed.), *Child and adolescent therapy* (pp. 165–206). New York: Guilford.

Valuck, R. J., Libby, A. M., Sills, M. R., Giese, A. A., & Allen, R. R. (2004). Antidepressant treatment and risk of suicide attempt by adolescents with major depressive disorder: A propensity-adjusted retrospective cohort study. *CNS Drugs, 18*(15), 119–132.

Webb, A., & Cranswick, N. (2003). Fluoxetine induced auditory hallucinations in an adolescent. *Journal of Paediatric Child Health, 39,* 637–639.

Weissman, M. M., Wolk, S., Golstein, R. B., Moreau, D., Adams, P., Greenwald, S., et al. (1999). Depressed adolescents grow up. *Journal of the American Medical Association, 281,* 1707–1713.

Weisz, J. R., Doss, A. J., & Hawley, K. M. (2005). Youth psychotherapy outcome research: A review and critique of the evidence base. *Annual Review of Psychology, 56,* 337–363.

Wells, V. E., Deykin, E. Y., & Kierman, G. L. (1985). Risk factors for depression in adolescence. *Psychiatric Development, 3,* 83–108.

Yorbik, O., Birmaher, B., Axelson, D., Williamson, D., & Ryan, N. (2004). Clinical characteristics of depressive symptoms in children and adolescents with major depressive disorder. *Journal of Clinical Psychiatry, 65,* 1654–1659.

Young, J. F., Mufson, L., & Davies, M. (2006). Efficacy of interpersonal psychotherapy-adolescent skills training: An indicated preventive intervention for depression. *Journal of Child Psychology and Psychiatry, 47,* 1254–1262.

Zenere, F. J., & Lazarus, P. J. (1997). The decline of youth suicidal behavior in an urban, multicultural public school system following the introduction of a suicide prevention and intervention program. *Suicide and Life-Threatening Behavior, 27*(4), 387–403.

Sarah Burke

Food for Thought

Sarah, a 16-year-old teenager, came to the clinic accompanied by her mother, Ann. Sarah presented as a typical teenager of average height and weight. There was a tension between mother and daughter that was readily recognizable to the clinic staff from the outset. Shouting had accompanied the car ride all the way to the clinic and both Sarah and her mom looked like they had been through an emotional war. Ann was biting her lip as they walked through the door, while Sarah gave a sideways glance that could have knocked her mother over.

Sarah's behavior was escalating out of control.

DEVELOPMENTAL HISTORY/FAMILY BACKGROUND

During the telephone intake interview, Ann reported the following background information. Sarah's birth was natural and unremarkable. Developmental milestones were all within the normal range with the exception of speech/language acquisition, which was delayed. Sarah was a quiet baby with a good appetite, and she had no serious health problems. There was a history of tonsillitis and severe throat infections about twice a year, but surgery has never been done to correct this due to Sarah's reluctance to have the procedure. There is no history of mental illness in the family, although Sarah's father did abuse alcohol and drugs, which Ann believes contributed to his eventual heart disease and untimely death when Sarah was 12 years of age.

Sarah was relatively easy to manage as a toddler and she has always been soothed by music. Ann added that as late as 3 years of age, Sarah's speech was largely still unintelligible due to articulation difficulties. As a result, Sarah tended to be very unwilling to speak, especially if strangers were within hearing range. Ann wondered if some of Sarah's speech delay might have been attributed to the fact that Sarah's father was a boisterous, loud, and verbally abusive man. The marriage was rocky for some time, and when Sarah was 4 years of age, the marriage finally crumbled. The tension in the home was horrible, because they all had to continue living under the same roof until her father found other accommodations. During this time, Ann tried to avoid any interaction with Sarah's father, since every incident turned into another eruption.

Ann feels that Sarah might have been fearful and reticent to speak around her father and this made her nervous about speaking, period. Ann still feels that Sarah continues to have very conflicted feelings about her dad. Arguments in the household were common, and the children seemed to shrink from their father at times. Sarah's older sister, Cindy, coped by literally living at a neighbor's house with her friend, Tammy. Eventually, Sarah's dad moved out. Once her dad left, it seemed that Sarah's behavior took a turn for the worse.

After that time, Sarah began to have temper tantrums when she did not get her own way. She would scream so loud that Ann was sure the neighbors thought she was killing her. These incidents were often precipitated by Ann's denying something Sarah wanted, but sometimes there seemed to be no apparent reason for the outburst. During these times, Ann would plead, make deals, cajole, or threaten punishment if Sarah would not desist. These methods usually failed, and she would eventually give in to Sarah's demands. Sometimes Sarah would stop the tantrum on her own, without any intervention. Given Sarah's difficult behaviors, delayed speech, and late birthday, Ann was very tempted to delay Grade 1 school entrance for a year to allow Sarah more time to mature. Since Ann is a teacher, she even thought about homeschooling, but decided against it. Ann wonders if she did the right thing, since Sarah has always lagged somewhat behind her peers academically and socially.

Sarah and her older sister, Cindy, who is 18 years of age, have never really gotten along. Cindy has always been a very good student and one who has not had to apply herself too arduously in order to make good grades. Ann feels that Sarah resents her sister for this, and Sarah feels that her older sister sometimes makes fun of her and her struggles with academics. The parent adds that Sarah and her older sister, a senior in high school, argue very frequently, and their arguments sometimes become physical. During one episode, Sarah slammed a door on her sister's hand, causing her sister considerable pain.

Although Sarah is a cheerleader and drill team member at school and appears to be popular enough to be voted into these activities, Ann feels that she can be very domineering with her friends. Ann has heard Sarah engage in very intense disagreements with friends on the phone. She has overheard Sarah cursing and shouting at people on the phone, and Sarah sometimes speaks of "fronting" someone, meaning that she confronts them angrily or in a hostile way. Ann also stated that she believes Sarah sometimes feigns illness, giving some vague physical complaint, either in order to get sympathy or to stay home from school.

Sarah is currently enrolled in the 11th grade at Truman High School. Her grades are passing, but presently she has particular problems with math and chemistry. Sarah has always struggled with math, and Ann is concerned that this will negatively affect Sarah's college prospects. Sarah has also verbalized some insecurity about her academic abilities, and she worries about her future in college. However, when Ann tries to help Sarah with her homework, Sarah reacts very belligerently, resulting in arguments and accusations about Ann interfering in her life. On the one hand, Sarah wants her mother out of her life. On the other hand, Sarah can be a very demanding child whose needs have to be met immediately. On these occasions, Sarah expects her mother to "be on call" when Sarah needs something. Ann stated that she is constantly "running here and there" on errands for Sarah, and she wishes that Sarah could take more responsibility for herself.

Ann also revealed several factors that have caused her to be increasingly concerned about Sarah's welfare and motivated her to make contact with the clinic. Recently, many fights between Sarah and her mother have centered on Sarah's boyfriend. When Ann tries to broach the subject of the boyfriend, Sarah can become very defensive and verbally aggressive. She has thrown things and cursed her mother. Sarah accuses her mother of meddling in her affairs and of being unfair and domineering. Ann states that she has legitimate concerns because she knows some of the boyfriend's history, which includes involvement with drugs and rumors of possibly having fathered an illegitimate child. The boyfriend can also be quite thoughtless and mean. He has made comments on more than one occasion about Sarah putting on weight, which has reduced Sarah to tears. As a result, Sarah will go off food for days, until she is literally starving, and then break down and clean out the fridge. Ann has begun to worry about Sarah's eating habits, since she found a bottle of diet pills hidden in Sarah's room. Ann has not confronted Sarah about this, since Sarah would certainly "throw a fit" about her mother sneaking into her room and invading her privacy. Ann is also concerned that Sarah is having sexual relations with the boyfriend, given his past history.

When Sarah's father died of complications due to heart disease, she was 12 years old. Upon the death of her father, Sarah was inconsolable for a time and seemed to withdraw into herself. She was often irritable and moody during this time and had difficulty sleeping. Her weight fluctuated from weight loss to weight gain. Due to the history of divorce and the subsequent death of the father, Ann believes she may have overindulged Sarah's behaviors and minimized some difficulties in order to avoid confrontation with her. Ann wonders why Sarah is not more like her sister; she feels frustrated and unappreciated when Sarah accuses her of meddling.

Ann summed up the telephone interview, outlining her present concerns by saying that she wished Sarah could behave more tactfully with friends in resolving problems and she wished Sarah could understand that what seems like meddling is genuine motherly concern. Ann added that Sarah's academic difficulties worry her as well as Sarah, and this seems to add to the tension between them. While she does not approve of Sarah's present boyfriend, she does not forbid Sarah's seeing him. On the other hand, the mother does not hide her disdain for him, either. She can see the negative influence the boy has on Sarah and how he negatively affects her self-image and confidence. In her final comments, Ann added that she is tired of everyone having to "tiptoe around Sarah" in order to avoid a confrontation with her. Ann added, "I would like to go through just one normal week with Sarah."

Sarah was well dressed for the interview and immediately stated that she was pleased that her mother had to wait outside and wasn't going to be part of the interview. Sarah's speech still reflects some slight articulation difficulties, but her speech is intelligible. Sarah tends to speak rather rapidly, and the examiner had to ask her to repeat herself on occasion. Sarah seemed at ease during the interview and was forthcoming with information. She was somewhat animated but generally appropriate. Sarah admitted to having difficulties with peer relations and said when she gets into fights, she confronts people, and then writes them off: "I just pretend they don't exist! I will sometimes even tell them, 'You're dead to me.'" Sarah was very vocal about her resentment regarding her mother's involvement in her personal matters.

Sarah also seemed to be sensitive about her academic abilities, and added that she never did well in math and that she "hated it." When describing her social contacts, Sarah said that she most admired Ashley, a peer in school, because she was smart, pretty, tanned, and thin. She also wished she could live in Ashley's house because her parents were rich and they had a pool. She spoke at length about her boyfriend, saying that her mother doesn't understand him at all. She added that she thinks her mother is jealous because her mother doesn't have a boyfriend and she does. Sarah admits to being sad sometimes, and she wishes her dad were still alive. She wishes her mom would just "chill" and stay out of her business. When asked about the one thing she would change about herself, Sarah said her appearance. She said she wished she were taller and thinner, like Ashley. She admitted to going on diets to lose weight, and said that she has tried just about every diet in the teen magazines and some of her mother's diets as well. She described her mother as "anorexic" and obsessed with weight, saying she eats a piece of cheese for lunch. Sarah was asked how she felt after she ate a big meal. She said, "I feel disgusting, like a blimp. I get really mad at myself for being so grotesque." She said she makes a bargain with herself that if she doesn't eat any more that week, she will be able to binge again the next weekend. When asked if she ever took pills or vomited to get rid of the food, Sarah flatly denied doing either, then retracted, saying she had tried vomiting once, but didn't like it. The examiner was not convinced that Sarah was being completely honest, especially since her mother had discovered the diet pills. The therapist's instincts were correct. Sarah was taking diet pills on a regular basis and vomiting had become a ritual on the weekends while her mother and sister were at work. Sarah would consume volumes of food over the course of a few hours and would feel horrible afterward. Vomiting made her feel better because that way she could get rid of the food, and it was like it never happened in the first place.

REASON FOR REFERRAL

Ann had finally acted on her instincts to get help for Sarah, since Sarah was becoming very verbally abusive to her mother, somewhat reminiscent of the abuse Ann had sustained from her husband during the course of their failed marriage. Were it not for the abusive situation, Ann might have missed the other cues that suggested Sarah was having many more difficulties than were apparent on the surface. However, it was Ann's feelings of helplessness and fears of confronting Sarah that finally resulted in the referral to the clinic.

ASSESSMENT RESULTS

Information regarding specific instruments and the interpretation of standard scores and T scores can be found in Appendix C.

The examiner noted that Sarah's test behaviors revealed a tendency toward impulsive responding and poor check-back skills (misreading math calculation signs). Frustration tolerance was also low, and Sarah tended to give up easily. These behaviors, however, were considered to be consistent with Sarah's everyday approach to challenging tasks, and results were considered to be a valid index of her current functioning levels.

Sarah's overall score on the Wechsler Intelligence Scale for Children (WISC-IV) revealed a Verbal Comprehension Index (VCI) of 89 (range 83–96) and a Perceptual Reasoning Index (PRI) of 83 (range 76–93). Verbal weaknesses were noted in Comprehension and Similarities. On the PRI, Sarah had significant problems with the Matrix Reasoning task and in reproducing the Block Designs. Given this profile, it would be anticipated that Sarah would encounter academic difficulties, especially in math. Academically, according to the Woodcock Johnson III Achievement Test (WJIII), Sarah was approximately 1 year behind her present grade placement in Broad Reading and Broad Written Expression, but almost 3 years behind across all math areas (calculation, fluency, and reasoning).

Sarah completed the Eating Disorder Inventory-2 (EDI-2), and her profile revealed significant elevations on the Desire for Thinness and the Body Dissatisfaction scales. An elevated Bulimia scale also supported suspicions regarding Binge Eating/Purging Behaviors, and scores for Impulse Regulation were also elevated. In response to interview questions and in her responses to the Child Depression Inventory (CDI), Sarah did not endorse symptoms of depression to any significant degree; however, scores for Ineffectiveness and Interpersonal Problems were in the at-risk level. On the Revised Child Manifest Anxiety Scale (RCMAS-2), scores for Worry/Oversensitivity and Social Concerns were also within the at-risk range. Responses to the Beck Youth Scales noted concerns in areas of an elevated Anger Expression score and lowered scores for Self-Esteem.

Sarah's mother completed the Conners Parent Rating Scale (CPRS:L), which yielded several subscales elevated to the clinically significant level: Oppositional Behavior (T = 74), Anxious-Shy (T = 77), Perfectionism (T = 72), Social Problems (T = 99), Psychosomatic (T = 99), and Emotional Lability (T = 77). Sarah's mother's responses suggest that difficulties are evident in having few friends, feelings of being socially detached, and lack of self-confidence. In view of suspected bulimic activity, there is a cautionary note regarding the significant number of physical complaints endorsed. Overall, the parent's rating of Sarah represents an elevated general profile that might represent global problematic behavior or comorbid functioning.

ISSUES, TRENDS, AND TREATMENT ALTERNATIVES

Contemporary preoccupation with thinness and the "thin ideal" has resulted in many young women developing a sense of body dissatisfaction, which can result in an obsession with weight loss and dieting. Disordered eating patterns can place adolescent females at increased risk for developing eating disorders. Eating disorders have become the third leading cause of chronic illness among young women 15 to 19 years of age (Rosen, 2003). Currently, the *DSM-IV-TR* (APA, 2000) recognizes three major categories of eating disorders: anorexia nervosa (AN), bulimia nervosa (BN), and eating disorder not otherwise specified (EDNOS), which is reserved for those atypical cases that do not meet all criteria for AN or BN, or that have subclinical symptom presentations. Binge-eating disorder (BED) was recommended for evaluation in the most recent revision of the *DSM-IV-TR* for possible inclusion in the *DSM-V.* Currently, BED is classified under the category of EDNOS. The *DSM-IV-TR* diagnostic guidelines for eating disorders are available in Appendix D.

Approximately half of those diagnosed with AN will demonstrate symptoms of the *restricting subtype,* who practice restraint and self-starvation to achieve their goal of maintaining their weight of less than 85% of what would be expected given their height (based on the Metropolitan Life Insurance tables or pediatric growth charts available for projected height/weight ratios). Those with the *binge-eating/purging subtype* of AN may engage in excessive exercise or other means (laxatives, diuretics) to reduce the caloric content of foods ingested. Studies have revealed that those who have the binge-purge subtype of AN report less overall life satisfaction and lower global functioning than their counterparts who have the restricting subtype (Herzog et al., 1999). The restricting subtype can become trapped in an *anorexic cycle* involving repetitive thoughts of fear of obesity and distorted body image, causing anxiety, which drives dieting and starvation, leading to obsessions with food that start the cycle over again. Low body weight often results in the cessation of the menstrual cycle (*amenorrhea*), which is one of the criteria for the diagnosis of AN (*DSM-IV-TR;* APA, 2000). Individuals with AN can suffer from serious medical complications that can place them at increased risk for physical collapse and subsequent hospitalization due to severe dehydration and electrolyte imbalance. Although primarily associated with onset in adolescent girls and young women, it is also possible to diagnose AN in adolescent boys, young men, individuals in later childhood, and older women. The lifetime prevalence rate for AN is approximately 1% of the population, although until recently, the disorder was primarily seen in Western and developed, industrialized societies. One out of 10 with AN who are hospitalized will die, either from physical complications or suicide (*DSM-IV-TR;* APA, 2000, p. 588). Unfortunately, only 10% with the disorder will achieve a complete recovery, while approximately 50% will experience partial recovery (Herzog et al., 1999).

Individuals who suffer from BN have many of the same symptoms of eating disturbance as those with AN; however, they do not present with the same degree of medical problems since they are not successful in maintaining their weight loss and tend to fluctuate between being overweight and being underweight. The *DSM-IV-TR* currently recognizes two subtypes of BN based on their patterns of compensatory behaviors: a *purging subtype* (purging, such as vomiting, enemas, diuretics, follows eating to expel the food from the body) or a *nonpurging subtype* (engaging in excessive exercise or fasting). Individuals with BN who engage in binge-and-purge episodes risk negative physical side effects such as erosion of teeth enamel and deterioration of the esophagus due to damage from stomach acids resulting from repetitive vomiting. In clinical samples, more than 90% of those with BN report self-induced vomiting as the most common form of purging (Reba et al., 2005), while using several types of purging methods (multiple purging) has been associated with greater disorder severity, frequency of bingeing, comorbid depression, impulsivity, anxiety, and personality disorder (Edler, Haedt, & Keel, 2007). In their study of adolescents and young women with eating disorders, Dalle Grave, Calugi, and Marchesini (2009) found that individuals who engaged in vomiting (as opposed to the use of laxatives or diuretics) scored higher on novelty seeking, a temperament trait associated with impulsivity, dramatization, and thrill seeking (Cloninger, Svrakic, Przybeck, & Wetzel, 1994). Dalle Grave and colleagues suggest that the use of vomiting by those with these characteristics might represent the preferred method of purging due to the immediacy of the effect.

Anorexics and bulimics are both subject to faulty cognitions; however, the bulimic's thought processes serve to perpetuate a self-destructive *binge-purge cycle* of anger and guilt. Prebinge thought patterns of anger, guilt, and loss of control are followed by binge eating. Binge eating serves to increase the sense of anger, guilt, and loss of control. Postbinge feelings of depression, disgust, and self-deprecation follow, which can be alleviated only by getting rid of the excess food. Once compensatory measures are taken and the food is expelled, the bulimic once again feels a sense of calm and self-control. The cycle perpetuates behaviors that are inherently self-rewarding and compulsive. Tendencies for bulimics to also exhibit comorbid disorders of depression and anxiety are well documented (Herzog, Keller, Sacks, Yeh, & Lavori, 1992; Johnson, Cohen, Kasen, & Brook, 2002). Stice, Burton, and Shaw (2004) found that substance abuse and depression were related in a bidirectional way for those with BN, such that either disorder increased the risk of also succumbing to the other disorder. Among adolescents with BN, substance use also is related to engaging in other high-risk behaviors, such as suicide attempts, sexual activity, and theft (Conason &

Sher, 2006). It has been suggested that illicit drug use among this population, especially stimulants, amphetamines, or cocaine, may be related to the drugs' tendencies to also suppress the appetite. Lifetime prevalence for BN has been reported to be between 1% and 5% and is significantly higher in females than males: a ratio of 10 to 1 (*DSM-IV-TR,* APA, 2000; Lewinsohn, Striegel-Moore, & Seeley, 2000). Onset is typically in late adolescence or early adulthood; however, many individuals with BN can go undiagnosed, and less than half of those who suffer from BN seek treatment (Hudson, Hiripi, Pope, & Kessler, 2007).

Individuals with AN or BN share common and excessive fears about weight gain, preoccupation with food and thinness, and a distorted sense of body shape linked to tendencies to evaluate their self-worth relative to their body image. Often the eating disorder can surface after a period of intense dieting. Individuals with eating disorders often experience feelings of depression, anxiety, and a desire to be perfect (Thompson-Brenner & Westen, 2005). Having an eating disorder places an individual at increased risk for self-harm, suicide attempts, and substance abuse that can often start with excessive use of diet pills (Levitt, Sansone, & Cohn, 2004; Ruuska, Kaltiala-Heino, Rantanen, & Koivisto, 2005). Personality dynamics of those with the binge-purge subtype type of AN and the purge subtype of BN relative to the other subtypes evidence poorer impulsive control, have greater risk for substance abuse, experience more emotional distress (DaCosta & Halmi, 1992; Garner, Garner, & Rosen, 1993), have elevated rates of suicide attempts (Milos, Spindler, Hepp, & Schnyder, 2004), and exhibit more symptoms of posttraumatic stress disorder (Blinder, Cumella, & Sanathara, 2006). Geist, Davis, and Heinman (1998) found high comorbidity rates (15%) for oppositional defiant disorder in adolescent girls with binge-purge features in their eating-disorder population.

However, despite the similarities, there are also significant differences between AN and BN, especially between the restricting subtype of AN and the binge-purge subtype of BN. For example, the onset for AN can be earlier (range 14–19 years) than the onset for BN (range 15–21 years). There are several other differences between these two disorders, such as the dynamics inherent in personality and family systems and the fact that anorexics maintain a body weight less than 85% of the normative weight, while bulimics are more likely to be of average weight or slightly overweight. Differences in family dynamics are evident between those with AN and BN. Traditionally, while families of those with AN tend to be enmeshed, overprotective, overly rigid, and in denial of conflict (Kog & Vandereycken, 1989), families of those with BN are more likely to have a history of psychopathology, open hostility and confrontation, expressed emotion, parent-child conflict, and relational aggression (Johnson & Connors, 1987). The role of family dynamics in eating disorders has also been investigated in research. In analyzing the responses of mother-father-daughter triads in response to the Structural Analysis of Social Behavior, Humphrey (1989) found that parents communicated very different messages to anorexics and bulimics. Families of anorexics tended to be controlling and allowed little room for their daughters' self-expression. They communicated a mixed message of nurturance but no tolerance for expression of feelings. Families of bulimics, on the other hand, demonstrated more overt signs of emotional conflict and often blamed and berated their daughters.

Etiology of Eating Disorders

Studies of the onset and etiology of eating disorders have found that eating disorders can often begin with patterns of disordered eating that eventually can progress to dysfunction and distress. It has been estimated that between 9% and 11% of youth demonstrate symptoms of AN or BN (Stice, Killen, Hayward, & Taylor, 1998). Eating disorders can result from interactions among many bio-psycho-social variables.

From a biological perspective, etiology of eating disorders can be linked to genetic factors. Research concerning familial linkages to eating disorders has revealed that relatives of anorexics and bulimics have a 7- to 12-times greater risk of having an eating disorder than nonrelatives. In addition, this population also has greater prevalence of other comorbid disorders, such as major depression, obsessive-compulsive disorder, and anxiety disorders (Lilenfeld, Kay, & Greenco, 1998; Strober, Freeman, Lampert, Diamond, & Kaye, 2000). If an identical twin has BN, there is a 23% chance that the other twin will also develop the disorder (Walters & Kendler, 1995). Also, developmentally, at a time when young girls are beginning to be more conscious of their weight, they actually begin to accumulate fat (*adiposity*) in their arms, legs, and trunk to prepare their bodies for puberty (Brandao, Lombardi, Nishida, Hauache, & Vieira, 2003). The increase in physical body mass is highly correlated with reports of increased body dissatisfaction among girls at this time (Stice & Whitenton, 2002) and elevated levels of distress due to a lack of success in attempts at dieting (Nowak, 1998). On the other hand, males tend to develop more muscle mass at this time, which is looked on more positively.

In addition to family links to eating disorders from a genetic basis, there are also connections to eating disorders from a psychosocial perspective. Family dynamics have also been associated with different types of eating disorders. In their classic studies of anorexic families, Minuchin, Rosman, and Baker (1978) found these families to be highly overprotective and enmeshed (intrusive parent), with rigid boundaries, and in denial of any underlying conflict. From a family systems perspective, Minuchin and colleagues (1978) suggest that the dynamics in the family environment set the stage for the adolescent to simultaneously act on her *independence* by refusing to eat, while at the same time triggering the delay or cessation of menstruation that ensures her continued *dependence* on the need for increased parental intervention and control. By contrast, individuals with BN are often impulsive and confrontational, and engage in high-risk behaviors within the context of their family environments that exhibit a lack of control, open conflict, and hostility (Fairburn Welch, Doll, Davies, & O'Conner, 1997).

In their article "The Mass Marketing of Disordered Eating and Eating Disorders," Hesse-Biber, Leavy, Quinn, and Zoino (2006) blame media messages from television, the Internet, movies, and magazines for the "cult of thinness" and for increased body dissatisfaction that has evolved. Although initially thought to be a "white woman's problem" (Botta, 2000), concerns have now crossed ethnic (Goodman, 2002; Walcott, Pratt, & Patel, 2003) and gender boundaries (Walcott, Pratt, & Patel, 2003). However, while females are driven to thinness, males are more inclined to "bulk up" and, as a result, anabolic steroid abuse has become a growing public health concern in the United States, as well as Europe and Australia (Kanayama, Pope, Cohane, & Hudson, 2003; Kindlundh, Isacson, Berglund, & Nyberg, 1999). From a sociocultural perspective, there has been an increased tendency to evaluate the influences of peers, family, and the media (tripartite model; Thompson et al., 1995) on body dissatisfaction in youth, which is occurring at younger and younger ages. Mellin, Irwin, and Scully (1992) found that as many as 80% of 9- and 10-year-old girls reported feeling fat and had engaged in binge-eating and dieting episodes. A 2005 survey of adolescent attitudes and behaviors regarding body dissatisfaction (Youth Risk Behavior Surveillance; CDC, 2005) reported that females engaged in significantly more unhealthy weight-loss methods than males and that the percentage of females trying to lose weight increased with grade level, from 60% in Grade 9 to 64% in Grade 12. Unhealthy weight-loss methods also varied by grade level, with the following most popular method by grade: fasting in Grade 9 (18.4%); vomiting or taking laxatives in Grade 10 (7.2%), and pills or powders in Grade 12.

Pressure from family or peers and lack of a support system can serve to reduce self-concept and increase body dissatisfaction among youth (Wichstrom, 1999), while teasing about weight from peers can increase the risk for engaging in bulimic behaviors (Thompson, Coovert, Richards, Johnson, & Cattarin, 1995). Weight-related teasing from family members, especially fathers, places young females at risk for lower levels of self-esteem; internalization of the thin ideal; and increased rates of social comparison, depression, and engaging in restrictive or bulimic behaviors (Keery, Boutelle, van den Berg, & Thompson, 2005). Gross and Nelson (2000) found that "any" messages related to food or body image risk being "perceived" as negative by vulnerable girls. Criticism from mothers served to reduce self-esteem (Sherwood & Neumark-Sztainer, 2001) and increase disordered eating behaviors (Gross & Nelson, 2000). One study even found that maternal comments that supported their daughter's comments about food or weight also backfired and were interpreted negatively by the sensitive girls (Hanna & Bond, 2006). Although Rodin, Striegel-Moore, and Silberstein (1990) called for increased research concerning protective factors to guard against eating disorders, there continues to be very little information available to this end. However, recent research in the area of dissonance intervention, which will be discussed shortly, is very promising (Seidel, Presnell, & Rosenfield, 2009; Stice, Marti, Spoor, Presnell, & Shaw, 2008).

Treatments, Interventions, and Prevention Programs

Treatment for AN. Treatment for AN often occurs in response to a medical crisis resulting from significant weight loss (Comerci & Greydanus, 1997; Mehler & Andersen, 1999) and can be extremely challenging, since patients have likely been placed into treatment against their will (Patel, Pratt, & Greydanus, 2003). The goal will be to deliver service in the least restrictive environment (Pyle, 1999); the nature of the medical intervention required (feeding tubes, restoring electrolyte balance) will determine where the treatment is delivered.

The initial focus of the treatment is to restore the patient's health and return the nutritional and metabolic state back to normal. Once stable, individual, group, and family psychotherapy; nutritional counseling; and exercise management can be introduced. During this phase of treatment, appropriate behavioral interventions, such as behavior modification, contingency management, and activity management (offering increased access to privileges or tangible rewards, such as access to telephone and television) can be instrumental in supporting a return to normalization and stabilization (Patel et al., 2003). The overall focus of treatment will be on long-term gains, and recovery in the absence of relapse (Comerci & Greydanus, 1997).

Distortions in body perception and obsessions with food constitute part of the maladaptive thinking patterns (perfectionism, negative thinking) in those with AN (King, 2001). Cognitive-behavioral treatment (CBT) programs focus on reframing disordered thought patterns about eating and body image into more positive and realistic appraisals (Robin, Siegel, & Moye, 1995). Robin, Bedway, Diegel, and Gilroy (1996) combined CBT (reframing need for independence and alternative ways of achieving control) with family therapy (including psychoeducational awareness and communication effectiveness) and achieved a 64% success rate (teens reached ideal body weight) after 16 months of treatment, which was maintained by 82% of the participants 1 year later.

Treatment for BN. Compared to those with AN, hospitalization will be required in less than 5% of cases with BN (Phillips, Greydanus, Pratt, & Patel, 2003). Although hospitalization will be rare, the use of medications and the need for medication management are on the increase, as prescriptions for antidepressants become more common in the treatment of BN (Caruso & Klein, 1998; Freeman, 1998). In seeking treatments for bulimia, investigation of potential biological factors has led researchers to suggest a link between eating disorders and low levels of serotonin (Carrasco, Diaz-Marsa, Hollander, Cesar, & Saiz-Ruiz, 2000) or chemicals such as GLP-1 that serve as a natural appetite suppressant (Turton et al., 1996). In support of genetic and biological theories, studies of monozygotic twins with eating disorders have revealed concordance rates as high as 23%, compared with only 9% for fraternal twins (Walters & Kendler, 1995). Antidepressants (SSRIs, such as fluoxetine and Prozac) can assist 25% to 40% of those diagnosed with BN (Mitchell et al., 2002).

CBT is the most widely researched treatment for BN, and long-term success has been reported (Agras & Apple, 1997; Lewandowski, Gebing, Anthony, & O'Brien, 1997; Wilson & Fairburn, 1993). In their review of more than 30 controlled studies, Agras and Apple (1997) found approximately 50% of clients using CBT eliminate bingeing and purging after treatment, and although some of the participants in these studies report a periodic relapse of bingeing and purging, follow-up studies (some as long as 5 years) indicate the success remains stable over time for the majority of participants. Recent efforts to incorporate dissonance-based intervention in CBT programs have demonstrated even more success in the treatment of individuals with BN. Based on theories of cognitive dissonance, dissonance intervention engages females who have a highly internalized sense of the thin-ideal to challenge the ideal and create an alternative set of beliefs, ultimately resulting in feelings of discomfort about the thin-ideal. Results have revealed long-term effects (2- and 3-year follow-up) for significant reduction of body dissatisfaction, negative affect, and bulimic symptoms (Stice et al., 2008).

Other therapeutic programs for BN have included *Interpersonal Psychotherapy (IPT)*, which rather than focusing on the eating disorder, targets the client's interpersonal relationships and focuses on ways to make these more satisfactory (Agras & Apple, 1997; Fairburn et al., 1997). Although *family-focused therapy* is another potential alternative, well-controlled studies of family intervention for BN are lacking and more research is needed in this area. Given the family dynamics, perhaps training in communication style (e.g., focus on reducing expressed emotion) should be explored.

Prevention Programs

To date, for the most part, programs targeting the prevention of disordered eating habits among young females (early to late adolescence) have met with limited success (Striegel-Moore, Jacobson, & Rees, 1997). While primary or universal prevention programs have targeted reducing the risks and increasing the protective factors for developing eating disorders in the population at large, secondary prevention programs have focused on the early identification of symptoms of eating disorders (e.g., body dissatisfaction) with the intent of reducing the risk.

Primary prevention programs have basically focused on one of two goals: psychoeducational awareness (healthy weight management, adverse effects of dieting), or enhancing assertiveness skills (resistance to societal pressures). Although the programs have been successful in enhancing the participants' awareness levels, they have not been successful in changing attitudes toward dieting (Carter, Stewart, Dunn, & Fairburn, 1997; Piran, 1997). Carter and colleagues (1997) also note that although initial results can be encouraging, longer-term results may actually indicate potential harmful effects, which in their study revealed a rebound effect with an increase in dieting behavior (higher than recorded preintervention) 6 months postintervention. Pratt and Woolfenden (2006) reviewed 12 prevention programs matched for strict inclusion criteria (randomization, control group). Similar to other prevention programs targeting youth, the majority of programs (9 out of 12) were school based. Their review yielded only one procedure that was successful in reducing the risk of eating disorders, namely, discussions and critical evaluations of media messages regarding body image (Kusel, 1999; Neumark-Sztainer, Sherwood, Coller, & Hannon, 2000). On a more encouraging note, Stice, Shaw, and Marti (2007) found 9 of 51 prevention programs that not only reduced risk factors, but maintained reduced eating disorder symptoms on follow-up. As noted earlier, dissonance-based intervention holds considerable promise as a component in future prevention programs (Seidel et al., 2009; Stice et al., 2007).

Post-Case Questions

1. Within family systems theories, four characteristics have been observed in "anorexic families": enmeshment, overprotectiveness, rigidity, and denial of family conflict (Minuchin et al., 1978). "Bulimic families," on the other hand, tend to have greater tendencies toward predisorder conflict with parents; greater incidence of family pathology, especially substance abuse or depression; and more perceived intense family conflict (Neuman & Halvorson, 1983).

   Discuss how Sarah's family characteristics support or contrast with this theory.

2. Discuss some reasons why Sarah's sister, Cindy, did not develop an eating disorder, while Sarah did. Support your discussion from the viewpoint of a theorist from each of the following models: biomedical, psychodynamic, behavioral, cognitive, family systems, and attachment/parenting style. How might developmental contexts interact to create greater risk or protective factors for the two sisters?

3. Do Sarah's symptoms meet criteria for an eating disorder according to the *DSM-IV-TR?* Justify your response.

4. Bruch (1991) has developed a theory linking parenting style to eating disorders that combines facets of psychodynamic and cognitive theories. Bruch argues that severe and frequent mother-daughter conflicts result in lack of adequate ego development in the child (poor sense of independence and control) and cognitive distortion regarding eating habits. Developing this line of thought, Bruch suggests that effective parents correctly identify their child's internal state and match comfort needs with appropriate responses. If a child is hungry, food is provided; if a child is emotionally upset, emotional comfort is provided; and if a child is cold, the parent provides a warm blanket or clothing.

However, ineffective parents do not attend appropriately to the child's internal cues and provide inappropriate responses, such as trying to comfort an anxious child with food. Children who grow up in these environments do not learn to recognize their own internal signals and confuse feelings of anxiety, anger, or distress with feelings of hunger. Feeling helpless and out of control, adolescent girls may respond by taking excessive measures to assert their control over their own bodies. Research has provided some support for Bruch's theory. Studies have shown that bulimics often equate anxiety with hunger (Rebert, Stanton, & Schwarz, 1991). In addition, bulimics' desire to please often results in their reliance on others' opinions and views, consequently feeling less sense of control in their own lives (Walters & Kendler, 1995). Describe how Bruch's theory might be used to explain Sarah's eating disorder.

REFERENCES

Agras, W. S., & Apple, R. F. (1997). *Overcoming eating disorders*. San Antonio, TX: Graywind.

American Psychiatric Association (APA). (2000). *Diagnostic and statistical manual of mental disorders* (4th ed., text rev.). Washington, DC: Author.

Blinder, B. J., Cumella, E. J., & Sanathara, V. A. (2006). Psychiatric comorbidities of female inpatients with eating disorders. *Psychosomatic Medicine, 68*, 454–462.

Botta, R. (2000). The mirror of television: A comparison of black and white adolescents' body image. *Journal of Communication*, 144–159.

Brandao, C. M., Lombardi, M. T., Nishida, S. K., Hauache, O. M., & Vieira, J. G. (2003). Serum leptin concentration during puberty in healthy nonobese adolescents. *Brazilian Journal of Medical & Biological Research, 36*, 1293–1296.

Bruch, H. (1991). The sleeping beauty: Escape from change. In S. I. Greenspan & G. H. Pollock (Eds.), *The course of life: Vol. 4. Adolescence*. Madison, CT: International Universities Press.

Carrasco, J. L., Diaz-Marsa, M., Hollander, E., Cesar, J., & Saiz-Ruiz, J. (2000). Decreased platelet monamine oxidase activity in female bulimia nervosa. *European Journal of Neuropsychopharmacology, 10*, 113–117.

Carter, J., Stewart, D., Dunn, V., & Fairburn, C. (1997). Primary prevention of eating disorders: Might it do more harm than good? *International Journal of Eating Disorders, 22*, 167–172.

Caruso, D., & Klein, H. (1998). Diagnosis and treatment of bulimia nervosa. *Seminars in Gastrointestinal Disease, 9*(4), 176–182.

Centers for Disease Control and Prevention (CDC). (2005). Youth risk behavior surveillance. *MMWR 2006, 55*(SS55).

Cloninger, C. R., Svrakic, D. M., Przybeck, T. R., & Wetzel, R. D. (1994). *The temperament and character inventory (TCI): A guide to its development and use*. St. Louis, MO: Center for Psychobiology of Personality.

Comerci, G. D., & Greydanus, D. E. (1997). Eating disorders: Anorexia nervosa and bulimia. In A. D. Hoffmann & D. E. Greydanus (Eds.), *Adolescent medicine* (3rd ed., pp. 683–699). Stamford, CT: Appleton & Lange.

Conason, A. H., & Sher, L. (2006). Alcohol use in adolescents with eating disorders. *International Journal of Adolescent Medicine and Health, 18*, 31–36.

DaCosta, M., & Halmi, K. (1992). Classifications of anorexia nervosa: Question of subtypes. *International Journal of Eating Disorders, 11*, 305–313.

Dalle Grave, R., Calugi, S., & Marchesini, G. (2009). Self-induced vomiting in eating disorders: Associated features and treatment outcome. *Behavior Research and Therapy, 47*, 680–684.

Edler, C., Haedt, A. A., & Keel, P. K. (2007). The use of multiple purging methods as an indicator of eating disorder severity. *International Journal of Eating Disorders, 40,* 515–520.

Fairburn, C. G., Welch, S., Doll, H. A., Davies, B. A., & O'Connor, M. F. (1997). Risk factors for bulimia nervosa: A community-based case-control study. *Archives of General Psychiatry, 54,* 509–517.

Freeman, C. (1998). Drug treatment for bulimia nervosa. *Neuropsychobiology, 37,* 72–79.

Garner, D. M., Garner, M., & Rosen, L. (1993). Anorexia nervosa "restricters" who purge: Implications for subtyping anorexia nervosa. *International Journal of Eating Disorders, 12,* 171–185.

Geist, R., Davis, R., & Heinman, M. (1998). Binge/purge symptoms and comorbidity in adolescents with eating disorders. *Canadian Journal of Psychiatry, 43,* 507–512.

Goodman, R. (2002). Flabless is fabulous: How Latina and Anglo women read and incorporate the excessively thin body ideal into every experience. *Journalism and Mass Communication Quarterly, 79,* 712–727.

Gross, R. M., & Nelson, E. S. (2000). Perceptions of parental messages regarding eating and weight and their impact on disordered eating. *Journal of College Student Psychotherapy, 15,* 57–78.

Hanna, A. C., & Bond, M. (2006). Relationships between family conflict, perceived maternal verbal messages and daughters' disturbed eating symptomatology. *Appetite, 47,* 205–211.

Hesse-Biber, S., Leavy, P., Quinn, C. E., & Zoino, J. (2006). The mass marketing of disordered eating and eating disorders: The social psychology of women, thinness and culture. *Women's Studies International Forum, 29,* 208–224.

Herzog, D., Dorer, D., Keele, P. K., Selwyn, S., Ekeblad, E., Flores, A. T., et al., (1999). Recovery and relapse in anorexia and bulimia nervosa. *Journal of the American Academy of Child and Adolescent Psychiatry, 38,* 829–837.

Herzog, D. B., Keller, M. B., Sacks, N. R., Yeh, C. J., & Lavori, P. W. (1992). Psychiatric comorbidity in treatment-seeking anorexics and bulimics. *Journal of the American Academy of Child and Adolescent Psychiatry, 31,* 810–818.

Hudson, J. I., Hiripi, E., Pope, H. G., & Kessler, R. C. (2007). The prevalence and correlates of eating disorders in the national comorbidity survey replication. *Biological Psychiatry, 61*(3), 348–358.

Humphrey, L. L. (1989). Observed family interactions among subtypes of eating disorders using structural analysis of social behavior. *Journal of Consulting and Clinical Psychology, 57,* 206–214.

Johnson, J. G., Cohen, P., Kasen, S., & Brook, J. S. (2002). Eating disorders during adolescence and the risk for physical and mental disorders during early adulthood. *Archives of General Psychiatry, 59,* 545–552.

Johnson, C., & Connors, M. E. (1987). *The etiology and treatment of bulimia nervosa: A biopsychosocial perspective.* New York: Basic Books.

Kanayama, G., Pope, H. G., Cohane, G., & Hudson, J. I. (2001). "Body image" drugs: A growing psychosomatic problem. *Psychotherapy Psychosomatic, 7,* 61–65.

Keery, H., Boutelle, K., van den Berg, P., & Thompson, J. K. (2005). The impact of appearance-related teasing by family members. *Journal of Adolescent Health, 37,* 120–127.

Kindlundh, A. M., Isacson, D. G., Berglund, L., & Nyberg, F. (1999). Factors associated with adolescent use of doping agents: Anabolic-androgenic steroids. *Addiction, 94,* 543–553.

King, N. (2001). Young adult women: Reflections on recurring themes and a discussion of the treatment process and setting. In B. Kinoy (Ed.), *Eating disorders: New directions in treatment and recovery* (2nd ed., pp. 148–158). New York: Columbia University Press.

Kog, E., & Vandereycken, W. (1989). The speculations: An overview of theories about eating disorder families. In W. Vandereyckm, E. Kog, & J. Vanderlinden (Eds.), *The family approach to eating disorders: Assessment and treatment of anorexia nervosa and bulimia nervosa* (pp. 7–24). New York: PMA.

Kusel, A. B. (1999). Primary prevention of eating disorders through media literacy training of girls. *Dissertation Abstracts International B: The Sciences & Engineering, 60*(4–B), 1859.

Levitt, J. L., Sansone, R. A., & Cohn, L. (Eds.). (2004). *Self-harm and eating disorders: Dynamics, assessment, and treatment*. New York: Brunner Routledge.

Lewandowski, L. M., Gebing, T. A., Anthony, J. L., & O'Brien, W. H. (1997). Meta-analysis of cognitive behavioral treatment studies for bulimia. *Clinical Psychology Review, 17,* 703–718.

Lewinsohn, P. M., Striegel-Moore, R. H., & Seeley, J. R. (2000). Epidemiology and natural course of eating disorders in young women from adolescence to young adulthood. *Journal of the American Academy of Child and Adolescent Psychiatry, 39,* 1284–1292.

Lilenfeld, L. R., Kay, W. H., & Greenco, C. G. (1998). A controlled family study of anorexia nervosa and bulimia nervosa: Psychiatric disorders in first-degree relatives and effects of proband comorbidity. *Archives of General Psychiatry, 32,* 1031–1038.

Mehler, P. S., & Andersen, A. E. (1999). *Eating disorders: A guide to medical care and complications*. Baltimore, MD: Johns Hopkins University Press.

Mellin, L. M., Irwin, C., & Scully, S. (1992). Prevalence of disordered eating in girls: A survey of middle class children. *Journal of the American Dietetic Association, 92,* 851–853.

Milos, G., Spindler, A., Hepp, U., & Schnyder, U. (2004). Suicide attempts and suicidal ideation: Links with psychiatric comorbidity in eating disorder subjects. *General Hospital Psychiatry, 26,* 129–135.

Minuchin, S., Rosman, B. L., & Baker, L. (1978). *Psychosomatic families: Anorexia nervosa in context*. Cambridge, MA: Harvard University Press.

Mitchell, J. E., Halmi, K., Wilson, G. T., Agras, W., Kraemer, H., & Crow, S. (2002). A randomized secondary treatment study of women with bulimia nervosa who fail to respond to CBT. *International Journal of Eating Disorders, 32,* 271–281.

Neuman, P. A., & Halvorson, P. A. (1983). *Anorexia nervosa and bulimia: A handbook for counselors and therapists*. New York: Van Nostrand-Reinhold.

Neumark-Sztainer, D., Sherwood, N., Coller, T., & Hannon, P. (2000). Primary prevention of disordered eating among preadolescent girls: Feasibility and short term effects of a community-based intervention. *Journal of the American Dietetic Association, 100,* 1466–1473.

Nowak, M. (1998). The weight-conscious adolescent: Body image, food intake, and weight related behavior. *Journal of Adolescent Health, 23*(6), 389–398.

Patel, D. R., Pratt, H. D., & Greydanus, D. E. (2003). Treatment of adolescents with anorexia nervosa. *Journal of Adolescent Research, 18,* 244–260.

Phillips, E. L., Greydanus, D. E., Pratt, E. D., & Patel, D. R. (2003). Treatment of bulimia nervosa: Psychological and psychopharmacologic considerations. *Journal of Adolescent Research, 18,* 261–279.

Piran, N. (1997). Prevention of eating disorders. *Psychopharmacology Bulletin, 33,* 419–423.

Pratt, B. M., & Woolfenden, S. R. (2006). *Interventions for preventing eating disorders in children and adolescents [The Cochrane Library* (Issue 1)]. Oxford, UK: Update Software.

Pyle, R. L. (1999). Dynamic psychotherapy. In M. Hersen & A. S. Bellack (Eds.), *Handbook of comparative interventions for adult disorders* (2nd ed.). New York: John Wiley

Reba, L., Thornton, L., Tozzi, F., Klump, K. L., Brandt, H., Crawford, S., et al. (2005). Relationships between features associated with vomiting in purging-type eating disorders. *International Journal of Eating Disorders, 38,* 287–294.

Rebert, W. M., Stanton, A. L., & Schwarz, R. M. (1991). Influence of personality attributes and daily moods on bulimic eating patterns. *Addictive Behaviors, 16,* 497–505.

Robin, A. L., Bedway, M., Diegel, P. T., & Gilroy, M. (1996). Therapy for adolescent anorexia nervosa. Addressing cognitions, feelings and the family's role. In E. D. Hibbs & P. S. Jensen (Eds.), *Psychosocial treatments for child and adolescent disorders: Empirically-based strategies for clinical practice*. Washington, DC: APA.

Robin, A. L., Siegel, P. T., & Moye, A. (1995). Family versus individual therapy for anorexia: Impact on family conflict. Topical Section: Treatment and therapeutic processes. *International Journal of Eating Disorders, 17,* 313–322.

Rodin, J., Striegel-Moore, R. H., & Silberstein, L. R. (1990). Vulnerability and resilience in the age of eating disorders. Risk and protective factors for bulimia nervosa. In J. Rolf, A. S. Masten, D. Cicchetti, K. H. Nuechterlein, & S. Weintraub (Eds.), *Risk and protective factors in the development of psychopathology* (pp. 361–383). Cambridge, MA: Cambridge University Press.

Rosen, D. (2003). Eating disorders in children and young adolescents: Etiology, classification, clinical features, and treatment. *Adolescent Medicine—The Spectrum of Disordered Eating: Anorexia Nervosa, Bulimia Nervosa and Obesity: State of the Art Review, 14*, 49–59.

Ruuska, J., Kaltiala-Heino, R., Rantanen, P., & Koivisto, A. M. (2005). Psycopathological distress predicts suicidal ideation and self-harm in adolescent eating disorder outpatients. *European Child and Adolescent Psychiatry, 14*, 276–281.

Seidel, A., Presnell, K., & Rosenfield, D. (2009). Mediators in the dissonance of eating disorder prevention program. *Behavior Research and Therapy, 47*, 645–653.

Sherwood, N. E., & Neumark-Sztainer, D. (2001). Internalization of the sociocultural ideal: Weight-related attitudes and dieting behaviors among young adolescent girls. *American Journal of Health Promotion, 15*, 228–231.

Stice, E., Burton, E. M., & Shaw, H. (2004). Prospective relations between bulimic pathology, depression and substance abuse: Unpacking comorbidity in adolescent girls. *Journal of Consulting and Clinical Psychology, 72*, 61–72.

Stice, E., Killen, J. D., Hayward, C., & Taylor, C. B. (1998). Age of onset for binge eating and purging during late adolescence: A 4-year survival analysis. *Journal of Abnormal Psychology, 107*, 671–675.

Stice, E., Marti, C. N., Spoor, S., Presnell, K., & Shaw, H. (2008). Dissonance and healthy weight eating disorder prevention programs: Long-term effects from a randomized efficacy trial. *Journal of Consulting and Clinical Psychology, 76*, 329–340.

Stice, E., Shaw, H., & Marti, C. N. (2007). A meta-analytic review of eating disorder prevention programs: Encouraging findings. *Annual Review of Clinical Psychology, 3*, 207–231.

Stice, E., & Whitenton, K. (2002). Risk factors for body dissatisfaction in adolescent girls: A longitudinal investigation. *Developmental Psychology, 38*, 669–678.

Striegel-Moore, R. H., Jacobson, M. S., & Rees, J. M. (1997). Risk factors for eating disorders. *Adolescent nutritional disorders: Prevention and treatment* (pp. 98–109). New York: Academy of Sciences.

Strober, M., Freeman, R., Lampert, C., Diamond, J., & Kaye, W. (2000). Controlled family study of anorexia nervosa and bulimia nervosa. Evidence of shared liability and transmission of partial syndromes. *American Journal of Psychiatry, 157*(3), 393–401.

Thompson, J. K., Coovert, M. D., Richards, K. J., Johnson, S., & Cattarin, J. (1995). Development of body image, eating disturbance, and general psychological functioning in female adolescence: Covariance structure modeling and longitudinal investigations. *International Journal of Eating Disorders, 18*, 221–236.

Thompson-Brenner, H., & Westen, D. (2005). Personality subtypes in eating disorders: Validation of a classification in a naturalistic sample. *British Journal of Psychiatry, 186*, 516–524.

Turton, M. D., O'Shea, D., Gunn, I., Beak, S. A., et al. (1996). A role for glucagon-like peptide-1 in the central regulation of feeding. *Nature, 379*, 69–72.

Walcott, D. D., Pratt, H. D., & Patel, D. R. (2003). Adolescents and eating disorders: Gender, racial, ethnic, sociocultural and socioeconomic issues. *Journal of Adolescent Research, 18*, 223–243.

Walters, E. E., & Kendler, K. S. (1995). Anorexia nervosa and anorexia-like syndromes in a population based female twin sample. *American Journal of Psychiatry, 152*, 64–71.

Wichstrom, L. (1999). The emergence of gender difference in depressed mood during adolescence: The role of intensified gender socialization. *Developmental Psychology, 35*, 232–245.

Wilson, G. T., & Fairburn, C. G. (1993). Cognitive treatments for eating disorders. *Journal of Consulting and Clinical Psychology, 61*, 261–269.

Jason Coleman

Disconnected Connections

Jason was almost 16 years of age when he was brought to the clinic by his social worker, accompanied by his foster mother, Mrs. Belcour.

DEVELOPMENTAL HISTORY/FAMILY BACKGROUND

Little is known of Jason's early history, but according to reports, Jason's parents died when he was 4½ years of age. There were reported stories of a murder-suicide, as both parents were found in a submerged car that had crashed through a bridge. As had happened on other occasions, Jason was not in the car, since he had been left with an aunt while his parents frequented the local bar. Jason's mother was barely a teenager when he was born and had a troubled history of substance abuse and running away from an abusive home situation. Jason's father was also a runaway who had his own history of substance abuse and reckless behavior. Although they never married, they lived together and fought often. There were concerns that Jason's father was abusive physically when he was drinking, which was often, and after his death, it was learned that he was also a registered sex offender.

After his parents' tragic death, Jason was initially cared for by a maternal aunt; apparently the aunt was also physically abusive, and Jason moved in with his maternal grandparents 2 years later. At 6½ years of age, Jason's behavior was becoming more and more difficult to control. Despite his impulsive behaviors, which were often reckless and dangerous, Jason also demonstrated intense fears, such as a fear of the dark and fear of water. He would scream hysterically if the grandparents turned the lights out in his room or even tried to pull his shirt over his face to get dressed or undressed. Often he would wake up in the middle of the night, screaming in terror. Because of his fears of water, he was afraid to go in the bathtub and cleanliness became an ongoing issue. At school, children would call him names and Jason would retaliate by hitting, punching, and kicking. Temper tantrums were frequent at home, and intense. Jason would often throw himself on the floor, arching his back, kicking and screaming. He would also bang his head on the floor or walls or anything he could find. His grandparents were increasingly concerned about safety issues. At

233

one point, Jason was hospitalized for 3 days due to injuries and an apparent concussion sustained when a tantrum resulted in a fall down a flight of stairs. When upset, Jason could not be comforted or consoled. Mood shifts were frequent, and at times Jason seemed to be out of reach and "in a world of his own." On these occasions, he would "zone out" and seem to lose contact with everyone around him. The grandparents eventually went to child protection services to seek help in managing Jason's behavior and to obtain weekend relief. Ultimately, they gave him up altogether when he set a fire in their bedroom.

Jason went through a series of foster placements like a revolving door, breaking down each placement in succession. It was as if he would destroy the placement before the placement could reject him. His life became a self-fulfilling prophecy. During this time, Jason was seen for psychotherapy at a regional treatment center. His behavior was described as "chronically hostile," and play sessions were directed toward assisting Jason to understand his behavior and to relate more positively to those around him. Jason's themes in play therapy were full of violence and destruction. He would smash toy cars together, bury toy dolls in the sand, and put ropes around the stuffed animals and dangle them from clothes hooks. While Jason was receiving treatment, his social worker continued to search for a stable therapeutic foster placement and eventually found such a placement in a city 90 miles away. In order to assist with his transition, Jason was assessed at the center. Intellectual assessment revealed that despite average intelligence, Jason did evidence significant difficulties with short-term memory, attention, concentration, and visual motor functioning. Academically, Jason was below the expected level in the core academic areas. The psychologist who did the assessment also noted that Jason was emotionally distraught, depressed, and fearful about his move so far away. Ritalin was prescribed to assist Jason with attention and concentration in his new school placement.

Jason joined the Belcour family just prior to his 10th birthday. He would be the only child in the home, since the Belcours agreed not to take in any additional foster children at that time. Throughout his history with the Belcour family, behavioral difficulties would be evident whenever Jason felt threatened or insecure. During the initial stages of his placement, the foster parents were trained to recognize that Jason would test his new placement in ways that would test the limits of their patience and endurance. Jason had developed a highly predictable pattern of self-defeating behaviors that were designed to break down the foster placement. However, these behaviors were motivated by his highly anxious fears of abandonment and constant need for reassurance.

Eventually, the behaviors lessened and Jason looked as if he was beginning to settle into the family. Although Jason's behaviors continued to challenge the Belcours, these behaviors began to escalate about 18 months ago. Jason began staying out late, and had been truant from school. When confined to his bedroom, Jason sneaked out the bedroom window and was found wandering the streets with a friend. Despite coming home smelling of cigarettes, Jason denied that he was smoking. Mrs. Belcour sought the assistance of the social worker, and Jason began to take part in weekly counseling sessions in an attempt to get his behavior in check. Ritalin dosage was also increased at that time.

Recently, Jason's behaviors were escalating out of control. He managed to obtain Mrs. Belcour's pin number (looking over her shoulder while she withdrew money from her account), removed her ATM card from her purse, and withdrew $500 from her bank account. The Belcours recently agreed to foster another child, Walt, who they thought might be a stabilizing influence on Jason, since Jason could assume the role of the "older brother."

However, Walt was a child who was of limited intellectual ability and Jason took advantage of his new position of power and Walt's limitations by manipulating Walt. He convinced Walt to assist him in breaking into the house across the street, saying that the boy who lived there had stolen his CD collection. Eventually, it was also learned that alcohol was missing from the Belcours' liquor cabinet, although the bottles were cleverly filled with soda pop to avoid immediate detection. Jason had also recently earned a 3-day suspension from school for being rude to one of his teachers.

Jason, a tall and lean adolescent, 15 years 6 months of age, presented well and was cooperative and congenial throughout the assessment. He offered to carry the testing materials from the car and assisted the psychologist in clearing excess paper from her desk to get ready for the assessment. He was not overly spontaneous in response to open-ended conversation; he responded better to direct questions and then proceeded to elaborate and embellish his responses. In response to questions directed toward areas of interest in school, Jason cited welding, auto work, and woodworking. When asked what he would like to do when he finished school, Jason stated that he would like to become a "pyrotechnician." Jason then asked the psychologist if she knew what a "pyrotechnician" was. The psychologist asked Jason what type of schooling would be required for such a position. Jason stated that this was a job that required a 4-year university degree and that it involved staging "blow-ups" for television and the movies. If this was not a possible career, he said, his next choices were to be a trucker or a race car driver. At this point in the interview, Jason began asking the psychologist about becoming a "shrink" and wondered how long it takes to get such a degree. He said that he figured that this was a profession that probably made lots of money. Conversation then was directed to where a psychologist might live in the city. When this was not responded to directly, Jason said that he lived in a section of town where people lived who had less money than psychologists.

Throughout the assessment, Jason attempted to become more familiar with the examiner and often asked questions that pushed the boundaries of the relationship, but never quite went beyond the bounds of decorum. When asked about his recent episode of being caught for a "break and enter," Jason denied any direct involvement and stated that he was only waiting outside for his friend. He was upset that the police would not believe him.

REASON FOR REFERRAL

Given Jason's escalating behaviors, there were concerns that Jason might act out to the extent that he would have to leave the Belcour home and be placed with juvenile justice. A comprehensive assessment was requested to determine what was causing Jason's recent behaviors and how best to intervene on his behalf.

ASSESSMENT RESULTS

Information regarding specific assessment instruments and guidelines to the interpretation of standard scores and T scores can be found in Appendix C.

Although Jason's responses to the WISC-IV revealed an overall level of intellectual functioning within the average range (full scale IQ range 99–107), this global picture did little to represent the wide range of scatter on his profile. There was a 25-point discrepancy between his Verbal Comprehension Index IQ (VCI = 95) and his Perceptual Reasoning Index (PRI = 120); a discrepancy of that magnitude is rare and seen in less than 1% of the population. The Working Memory Index (WMI) was a significant area of weakness (SS = 75), as was his speed of speed of symbol copying (SS = 7), which resulted in a score that placed the Processing Speed Index (PSI = 86) in the low average range. On the Bender Gestalt test of visual motor integration, Jason's time to complete the symbols was in excess of 15 minutes: a task that should take an average 7-year-old about 7 minutes to complete. Jason's lack of planning ability was evident as he did not leave enough room to place all the designs on one page, and as a result drawings often collided with one another. He had significant problems executing angled designs and substituted lines for dots, all signs that are associated with some form of brain damage.

Jason demonstrated some surprising strengths, given several years of interrupted schooling and lack of consistent exposure to formal education. Scores in areas of general knowledge, abstract reasoning, vocabulary development, and practical reasoning were all within the average range for his age. What was so remarkable was Jason's superior ability that surfaced in areas of perceptual reasoning, evident in excellent attention to visual details (perceptive/observation skills), his ability to quickly obtain solutions to problems involving visual reasoning, and the analysis and synthesis of visual information.

When the academic portion of the assessment was introduced, Jason attempted to delay the task at hand by engaging in a lengthy conversation about who developed the tests and how much money test-makers earn. He asked whether they got paid every time a test was given, like royalties that songwriters make. It was apparent that Jason was feeling uncomfortable about his weak academic skills, so only a brief academic assessment was conducted in order to focus more on isolating strengths and weaknesses in information processing and the assessment of emotional status. Although Jason was currently enrolled in Grade 10, he was functioning at the following levels according to the Wide Range Achievement Test (WRAT-3): Decoding, Grade 8; Spelling, Grade 4; and Math Calculations, at a Grade 6 level. Reading comprehension and speed of reading were at a mid–Grade 6 range.

Jason was intrigued with the memory assessment and was very cooperative during the administration of the Wide Range Assessment of Memory and Learning (WRAML-2). Results were enlightening, and demonstrated that despite excellent visual problem-solving skills (WISC-IV), Jason had a very weak memory for visual sequence (1st percentile), which often is associated with poor spelling. Considering the memory weakness in conjunction with poor copying speed, it became readily apparent why Jason became highly frustrated and resistant when asked to produce written work. Jason also demonstrated weaknesses in attention/concentration on the WRAML-2.

Jason's former teacher and foster mother completed parallel forms of The Behavior Rating Inventory of Executive Functioning (BRIEF). Jason's foster mother and teacher both rated Jason within the clinical range for the Behavioral Regulation Index (executive functions that regulate emotions and behaviors) with significant T scores for problems in areas of *Inhibit* (ability to stop an action or not react to an impulse), *Shift* (ability to move from one task or situation to another), and *Emotional Control* (ability to regulate emotional responses). Significant difficulties were also evident across the academic and home environments in all areas rated, including initiating goal-directed activity, working memory, planning, organization of task materials, and self-monitoring of responses.

Jason and his foster mother completed the Jesness Behavior Checklist. Although Jason presented as a candid and cooperative respondent, there were wide and significant discrepancies between his self-rating scales and ratings completed by his foster mother. The profiles presented a mirror image: According to Jason, all behaviors were within the average to high average positive range; according to his foster mother, the majority of behaviors were well below average, in the very negative range. Mrs. Belcour endorsed the following behaviors below the second percentile: ability to take responsibility for his actions, ability to avoid engaging others in negative interactions, lack of depression/withdrawal, lack of stealing, lack of adherence to rules, weak frustration tolerance/resistance to teasing, and more. According to Mrs. Belcour, only two areas of behavior were within the normative range: independence and sociability.

However, on the Jesness Inventory Revised (JI-R), Jason's scores revealed significant elevations on the Asocial Index (T score = 64), indicating a predisposition to resolve problems in ways that showed a disregard for social customs and rules, and the Social Maladjustment scale (SM; T score = 62), often associated with a negative self-concept and high sensitivity to criticism. Individuals who score high on the SM scale often feel that they are misunderstood, are unhappy, and can be hostile. Jason also scored in the clinically significant range on the DSM-IV scale for Conduct Disorder (CD; T = 62). Individuals who score high on the CD scale show persistent patterns of behavior that can be aggressive, destructive, and deceitful, often entailing violations of rules. Overall, his performance fit the profile for the Pragmatist/Manipulator (MP) subtype on the Jesness Inventory.

In addition to weak agreement between Jason's ratings and his foster mother's ratings on the Jesness Behavior Checklist, ratings on the Depression and Anxiety Scales for Youth (DAYS) revealed self-ratings for depression (16th percentile) and anxiety (50th percentile) to be within normative expectations, compared to his foster mother's clinically significant ratings for Depression (98th percentile) and Anxiety (91st percentile).

ISSUES, TRENDS, AND TREATMENT ALTERNATIVES

While children with oppositional defiant disorder (ODD) demonstrate a persistent pattern of behavior toward authority figures that is negativistic, defiant, disobedient, and hostile, youth with conduct disorder (CD) evidence more serious disruptive behaviors that cause harm to others either by violation of their rights, or by breaching major societal norms or rules (*DSM-IV-TR;* APA, 2000). Although it was once thought that ODD represented an early and milder precursor to CD along a continuum of disruptive behavior disorders, research supports the existence of two separate disorders. Although 90% of youth with CD also had ODD, only 25% of all children with ODD go on to develop CD (Rey, 1993). Furthermore, a meta-factor analytic study by Frick and his colleagues (1993) produced behavior clusters that support two unique disorders: ODD-type behaviors of aggression and opposition that represent more overt and nondestructive forms of behavior; and property and status violations, or covert and destructive behaviors more typical of CD behaviors. The CD category of disruptive behavior disorders includes behaviors such as aggression to people and animals, destruction of property, deceitfulness or theft, and serious rule violations. The complete *DSM-IV-TR* diagnostic criteria for CD is available in Appendix D.

In adolescence, the pituitary gland works overtime as puberty is initiated. This can result in increased release of the hormone cortisol by the adrenal glands, causing the hypothalamus-pituitary-adrenal (HPA) system to activate "fight or flight" signals, especially in those who are vulnerable to increased stress. When faced with stressful events, arousal causes physiological *reactivity* that eventually decreases in a poststress state of *recovery* (Linden, Earle, Gerin, & Christenfeld, 1997). Within the autonomic nervous system, the sympathetic nervous system is responsible for the activation phase, while the parasympathetic nervous system is responsible for recovery (Porges, 2003). Developmentally, individuals become increasingly more able to regulate affect as they refine their ability to self-regulate in conditions that impose increasing challenges. However, for some individuals, having an overly active sympathetic system and a relatively weak parasympathetic system can result in inflated emotional reactions of anger and avoidance. This can be especially true for youth who demonstrate mental health and behavioral difficulties, such as externalizing problems, internalizing problems, and issues of attention or overactivity (Beauchaine, Gatzke-Kopp, & Mead, 2007).

There are a number of risk factors that can contribute to poor ability to regulate emotions, impulsivity, lack of planning ability, and poor social problem solving that can result in disruptive behavior disorders. During the first years of development, a secure attachment relationship can provide the necessary foundation for the growth of an "autonomous self, the acquisition of effective peer relations and successful adaptation to school . . . and the legacy of early attachment relationships may include the enhanced, flexible and positive (or restricted, inflexible and/or maladaptive) social skills that are acquired in the first relationship" (Thompson, 1999, pp. 269–270).

Main and Solomon (1990) found a "disorganized/disoriented" pattern of attachment in infants who displayed fear and anxiety upon reuniting with the parent. This disorganized/disoriented pattern has been associated with family correlates of child maltreatment and/or parent psychopathology (Lyons-Ruth & Jacobvitz, 1999) and has been linked to aggression toward peers and externalizing behaviors emerging in preschool (Troy & Sroufe, 1987) and persisting throughout elementary (Renken, Egeland, Marvinney, Mangelsdorf, & Sroufe, 1989).

Reactive attachment disorder (RAD) was initially included in the third edition of the DSM (*DSM-III;* APA, 1980) and has undergone substantial revision since that time. Terms such as "*failure to thrive, nonorganic failure to thrive, psychosocial dwarfism, maternal deprivation, anaclitic depression, hospitalism, and reactive attachment disorder*" have been used over time to refer to the disorder (Richters & Volkmar, 1994, p. 328). The *DSM-IV-TR* (APA, 2000) described the disorder as a persistent pattern of disturbed and developmentally inappropriate behavior in social relatedness with onset within the first 5 years, and resulting from "pathogenic care." A complete list of the *DSM-IV-TR* criteria for RAD is available in Appendix D. Failure to initiate or respond to social interactions in a developmentally appropriate manner can be demonstrated in two different ways: *inhibited type* of RAD, which evidences excessively "inhibited, hypervigilant, or highly ambivalent and contradictory responses (e.g., mixture of approach, avoidance, and resistance of comforting, or may exhibit frozen watchfulness)"; or *disinhibited type* of RAD, which displays "diffuse attachments" manifested in "indiscriminate sociability with marked inability to exhibit appropriate selective attachments (e.g., excessive familiarity with relative strangers or lack of selectivity in choice of attachment figures)" (*DSM-IV-TR;* APA, 2000, p. 130).

Despite prolific research initiatives in the area of the attachment process, there are relatively few studies of RAD, although findings suggest that this can represent a fairly substantial subset of adoptees. Boris, Zeanah, Larrieu, Scheeringa, and Heller (1998) found that 42% of their adopted population met criteria for an attachment disorder. Follow-up studies of children adopted from institutions in Romania have found evidence of both types of attachment disorders, although the disinhibited type was the most common for those who were adopted out (O'Connor, 2002; Zeanah, 2000), while the inhibited type (emotionally withdrawn behaviors) was most prevalent in children who continued to live in the Romanian institutions (Smyke, Dumitrescu, & Zeanah, 2002). Investigators have also found that the disinhibited/indiscriminate behaviors persisted for years, regardless of whether the children had developed secure attachments to their adoptive caregivers (Chisholm, 1998; O'Conner et al., 2003). On the other hand, Zeanah and colleagues (2004) found that 17% of their sample met criteria for both types of attachment disorders, simultaneously. Although a diagnosis of RAD is usually made in early childhood, it is not surprising to see symptoms carried over into adolescence. Children may become disruptive and disorganized with poor affect control and low frustration tolerance, as well as inattention, impulsivity, and hyperactivity. By the time they reach mid adolescence, it is not uncommon to find numerous comorbid diagnoses (ADHD, PTSD, ODD, mood disorder, or CD), while a diagnosis of RAD may have been missed altogether (Kemph & Voeller, 2008).

Longitudinal studies have found that the impact of early deprivation can be found in increased risk for cognitive and physical delays, as well as later psychopathology (O'Connor & Rutter, 2000). Neuropsychological research has suggested that early deprivation of maternal care can alter neural pathways, causing dysfunction of the HPA system manifested in elevated cortisol levels (Heim et al., 2002), influencing levels of the neurotransmitters dopamine (Insel, 2003) and serotonin (Battaglia et al., 2005).

Given the significant potential for abuse and/or neglect in the history of children and youth with RAD, it is not surprising to find that these children and youth may meet criteria for both RAD and posttraumatic stress disorder (PTSD; Hinshaw-Fuselier, Boris, & Zeanah, 1999). Although relatively recent, since the early 1990s research has increasingly focused on how symptoms of PTSD might be presented at different developmental levels, and the potential biological, psychological, and social outcomes that might result from exposure to extreme psychic trauma and stress in childhood and youth (Pynoos, 1990, 1994). Although PTSD is classified as an anxiety disorder by the *DSM-IV-TR* (APA, 2000), it differs from the other anxiety disorders in one significant way: while other anxiety disorders result from "perceptions of threat" that cause distress although most recognize that the fears are unreasonable, individuals who suffer from PTSD do so because they have been exposed to a catastrophic and traumatic event that results in feelings of "horror or helplessness," which can be displayed as disorganized and agitated behaviors in children and adolescence (*DSM-IV-TR*, APA, 2000, p. 467). A more detailed list of the criteria for PTSD and a description of how the symptoms manifest at different developmental stages can be found in Appendix D. Individuals who suffer from PTSD exhibit symptom clusters that represent reexperiencing of the event, avoidance of stimuli associated with the event, and persistent levels of increased arousal. Symptoms differ across the developmental stages, with increased risk of engaging in risky behaviors in adolescence. In children and youth, a common symptom of PTSD is emotional numbing (Carrion, Weems, Ray, & Reiss, 2002), which can result from emotional exhaustion due to experiencing high levels of arousal over a prolonged period of time (Weems, Saltzman, Reiss, & Carrion, 2003). The onset of PTSD prior to age 14 has been associated with increased interpersonal problems, while later onset has been linked to increased academic problems (Amaya-Jackson & March, 1995). Children and youth are also more likely to suffer from Type II trauma related to repeated exposure to trauma, such as abuse over time, compared to Type I trauma, which relates to a one-time occurrence (Terr, 1991).

Executive functions represent the control system or central processes responsible for managing, organizing, and planning goal-directed activity within our cognitive and emotional world. This neuropsychological system of "regulatory control" plays an enormous role "in the child's cognitive, behavioral and social-emotional development" to the extent that whether the neuropsychological system is "intact or impaired, has substantial implications for everyday social and academic function" (Gioia & Isquith, 2004, p. 136.). Executive functions evolve around four major tasks: defining the problem (representation), developing a plan, following through and executing the plan, and evaluating the outcome. In order to accomplish the four major tasks, children and youth must learn to develop skills in decision making, planning, cognitive flexibility, the ability to inhibit or ignore competing responses, and monitoring and evaluating the outcomes. Although the structural bases of executive function are only starting to be understood, executive functions have been increasingly associated with brain systems involving the frontal and anterior temporal lobes (Levin et al., 1993). Children who exhibit executive functioning deficits often have damage to the prefrontal regions, which cause dysfunction in such areas as planning and cognitive flexibility (Ylvisaker, Szekeres, & Hartwick, 1992), organization, memory, and behavioral inhibition (Scheibel & Levin, 1997). There are many different patterns of executive dysfunction that may be related to different disorder profiles (Gioia, Isquith, Kenworthy, & Barton, 2002), and several potential causes of deficits in executive functioning, including in utero exposure to toxins, low birth weight, birth trauma, traumatic brain injury (TBI), or genetics (Gioia, 2005).

Finally, the last issue in the case of Jason Coleman is the pending termination of foster care. The majority of youth on the brink of termination from foster care face significant challenges. For the majority, termination means disconnecting from supportive adults, services, and socioeconomic supports that could significantly increase their opportunities for becoming successful and self-sustaining adults (Metzger, 2006). In their review of the recent research concerning aging out of foster care, Avery and Freundlich (2009) discuss the repercussions of terminating youth from services at 18 years of age, at a time when they are entering a period of "emerging adulthood," which represents "a developmental transition period between adolescence and adulthood" (p. 248). The authors suggest that at this stage, "independent living" should be reconceptualized as "interdependent living" with the proviso of assigning an adult to act as a committed overseer of the process prior to termination.

Treatment Alternatives

While parent training programs can be an effective way of treating children with ODD (see the case study of Scott Michaels), several concerns have been raised regarding optimum treatments for youth with more serious forms of CD. In the past, few treatments have demonstrated effectiveness with this difficult-to-serve population; furthermore, there is a risk of potential iatrogenic effects when troubled youth are aggregated for treatment (Dishion, McCord, & Poulin, 1999). A continuum of service delivery is available for youth with serious emotional and behavioral disorders, ranging from the least intrusive (outpatient resources) to the most intrusive (residential treatment centers) environments, based on the severity and nature of the problems. Although initial empirical investigations were limited to analogue-type studies (Weisz, Weiss, Han, Granger, & Morton, 1995), more recent investigations of community-based alternatives, such as *multisystem therapy* (MST), have produced promising results.

Frick (2001) suggests that based on our current understanding of the complexity of CD, in order for treatment to be effective, it must attempt to address the vast range of factors within the child (genetic and environmental history) and within the child's developmental contexts (family, school, societal and economic, cultural) that serve to precipitate and maintain the symptoms. In addition, Frick emphasizes the need to tailor the treatment to the various developmental pathways that may be involved. Programs designed to meet individual needs, such as the FAST Track Program (Stormshak, Bierman, McMahon, Lengua, & Conduct Problems Prevention Research Group [CPPRG], 2000) and MST (Borduin, Mann, Cone, & Henggeler, 1995; Henggeler, Schoenwald, Borduin, Rowland, & Cunningham, 1998) have met with increased success.

Increasing emphasis on community-based interventions has generated research initiatives comparing residential treatment with community-based treatment alternatives. Chamberlain and Reid (1991, 1998) found that juveniles assigned to specialized foster care programs were more successful than peers assigned to residential treatment centers or family/relatives' homes. Wilmshurst (2002) found significantly better outcomes for youth with severe emotional and behavioral problems when the youth received interventions provided by family preservation workers in the home (using cognitive-behavioral methods), compared to youth who were removed to a 5-day residential program for treatment (using brief solution-focused therapy). Furthermore, the Wilmshurst study found that while children and youth in the community-based program demonstrated significant improvement in all areas 1 year posttreatment, youth who had attended the residential program revealed poorer outcomes and significant increases in internalizing symptoms (e.g., depression) postintervention. MST is a community treatment alternative that has been proven to be more effective than hospitalization in serving the needs of juvenile offenders (Henggeler & Borduin, 1990; Schoenwald, Brown, & Henggeler, 2000). The success of the MST program has been attributed to the use of cognitive-behavioral methods within an ecologically valid context (Schoenwald, Borduin, & Henggeler, 1998).

Recently, several theorists have turned to attachment theory to assist in understanding the disturbed interpersonal relations of youth with CD and RAD, as well as PTSD. There is an emerging body of literature addressing the relationship of attachment theory to early deprivation of maternal care (see Cassidy & Mohr, 2001, for review), suggesting negative outcomes that may result from perinatal exposure to toxins, poor parenting, and a lack of "goodness of fit" between parent and child temperament (Kemph & Voeller, 2008). Research from a biomedical perspective has suggested that some children may possess a particular genotype (5-HTT short allele of the serotonin transporter polymorphism associated with increased reactivity and arousal of the amygdala and cortisol systems) that may make them more vulnerable to the effects of poor parent-child relationships (Barr et al., 2003; Hariri, 2002), while other researchers have focused on the potential impact of early maternal deprivation on altering the nature and course of brain development in the child (overactivity of the hypothalamic-pituitary-adrenal [HPA] system results in elevated cortisol levels in response to stress). It has been found that infants who are traumatized evidence elevated levels of cortisol when reunited with their caregivers (Spangler & Grossmann, 1999), compared to those who are securely attached, who are comforted by reuniting with the caregiver, resulting in a reduction in cortisol levels (Nachmias, Gunnar, Mangelsdorf, Parritz, & Buss, 1996). Given the complex interrelationships between genotype and neurotransmitter mechanisms that are operating in severe cases of CD, RAD, and PTSD, pharmacological intervention may be a necessary corollary to cognitive and behavioral interventions, especially medications that target increasing serotonin or decreasing dopamine levels.

In addition to underlying neuropsychological dynamics, infants who are exposed to deprivation in care often experience disruptions in the development of normal mother-infant communication, which should pave the way for engaging in shared relationships with others in the future. Lyons-Ruth (2008) has reasoned that infants who experience a lack of reciprocity in affective communication, such as joint attention and social referencing, which typically promotes "affective sharing" in normal infants, fail to develop a sense of self-awareness and other awareness based on shared feelings. As a result, when they are capable of understanding intention (usually around 18 months of age), these young children may respond by a "shunning of sharing" with an unstable caregiver, recognizing that the caregiver is the cause of their distress. Theories such as this could pave the way for interventions directed toward helping young children restructure and rebuild connective networks to enable increased relatedness in the future.

Based on work with children in the foster care system, Steinhauer (1998) suggests that precursors of neglect, abuse, and/or multiple moves, and/or multiple caregivers set the stage for a reactive attachment disorder resulting in attachment-resistant children. According to Steinhauer, it is imperative that treatment for conduct-disordered youth recognize the underlying dynamics of disturbed attachment responsible for creating a self-defeating working model focused on self-concept as worthless/unacceptable, perception of others as unavailable/abusive, and an inability to self-soothe or turn to others for comfort. Although there is minimal empirical support regarding interventions for youth with CD that is based on attachment theory, a program developed by Holland, Moretti, Verlaan, and Peterson (1993) has produced some encouraging results. Kemph and Voeller (2008) note that although changes in cognitive functioning and language and motor development may be successful for children and adolescents with RAD, improving social relatedness, especially in adolescence, may be a more challenging task. The authors reiterate what was stated earlier by Steinhauer (1998), namely that treatment of RAD "requires many repetitions of appropriate thoughts and behaviors over a prolonged period of time to foster the changes necessary to form new neuronal patterns which may enable the adolescent to develop socially acceptable relationships with other people" (Kemph & Voeller, 2008, p. 174).

The American Academy of Child and Adolescent Psychiatry (AACAP, 2005) practice parameters for the assessment and treatment of children and adolescents with RAD suggests a number of possible treatment alternatives, including enlisting the caregiver (if emotionally available) as a cotherapist, encouraging the development of sensitive responsiveness (Hart & Thomas, 2000); or conducting conjoint therapy with the child and primary caregiver together (Lieberman & Zeanah, 1999). The AACAP suggests two established models for dyadic interactive therapy, including infant-parent psychotherapy (Lieberman, Silverman, & Pawl, 2000) or interaction guidance (McDonough, 2000). The former therapy focuses on emotional communication and affective sharing in the dyad, while the latter, with the help of videotaped excerpts, strives to increase awareness of behavioral patterns of interaction with the intent of shaping caregiver responses in a more positive direction. The next stage in the treatment process is to include other family members in the process, while a third stage involves individual therapy with the child. The AACAP (2005) also notes that treatments for aggressive behaviors, such as parent psychoeducation (Brestan & Eyberg, 1998; Webster-Stratton, 1998) or MST (Henggeler et al., 1998) are also appropriate for aggressive responses in children with RAD.

Regarding potential medical intervention for RAD, the AACAP recommends caution, especially in prescribing medications for preschoolers who are in the formative stages of brain development (Greenhill et al., 2003; Jensen et al., 1999), and suggests perhaps pharmacological intervention for comorbid disorders—such as PTSD, anxiety disorders, disruptive behavior disorders, or mood disorders—may be indicated.

Although the AACAP (2005) report acknowledges the need for firm limits and recognizes that physical restraint may be necessary for protective purposes in some cases of extreme aggression, the report does not recommend the use of intrusive treatments, such as forced eye contact, soothing or "holding" of children, or physical restraints, against the child's will that have no empirical support and are likely to trigger responses of fear and humiliation rather than "connection" and "reattachment." The report cites, as examples, the case of a 10-year-old girl who died while undergoing "rebirthing" therapy (Crowder, 2000) and the death of a 4-year-old resulting from an "attachment based" treatment where the child was restrained while being forced to drink excessive amounts of water (Adams, 2002).

In his discussion of interventions for deficits in executive function, Gioia (2005) emphasizes the need to pinpoint specific domains where deficits exist relative to task demands. Once developmentally appropriate expectations for executive functions can be established, then the focus is to teach children the process of goal-directed problem solving as it applies to everyday functioning and meaningful routines (Goal-Plan-Do-Review). Within such a context, children will begin to internalize the process and become better able to monitor what worked and what didn't work and why (Ylvisaker, Szekeres, & Feeney, 1998).

Post-Case Questions

1. Jason demonstrates symptoms of several possible comorbid disorders. Using the *DSM-IV-TR* (APA, 2000) as a guide, what disorders would Jason meet criteria for and what symptoms does he demonstrate that match these criteria?

2. The following is an excerpt from the psychologist's written report concerning Jason:

   Jason's responses to the Jesness Inventory suggest that he may utilize his strong visual perceptive skills in ways which may be highly effective in a manipulative and controlling manner. Jason's profile suggests a tendency to perceive the world in terms of power and control, both in very subtle ways and in ways which may be more directive in their controlling influence. At the extreme, manipulation may be used to satisfy his own needs and may, in this manner, become satisfying in and of itself. To this end, misbehavior may be evident in "conning," or deception, which is often a means of self-gratification in its ability to "outsmart" others. Unfortunately, given Jason's intellectual capacity, his strong skills may be misdirected toward influencing others who may not be his intellectual equal. Jason's Jesness Profile also suggests strong tendencies toward denial of responsibility for actions/consequences of his behaviors.

Discuss the above with reference to how the following models would interpret Jason's underlying processes: biomedical, psychodynamic, family systems, cognitive, behavioral, and theories of attachment and parenting. Include references to how these processes would interact with various developmental contexts: individual, family and school, social and economic, and cultural.

3. The psychologist felt that history would predict that in times of perceived change or uncertainty, Jason would act out in a misdemeanor roughly equivalent in intensity to the amount of anxiety he was feeling. Furthermore, since thefts involved large amounts of money taken from the foster household, it was important to look at what changes or perceived changes were happening in that environment: the introduction of a new foster child, a pending move farther out into the country, the impact of turning 16 as a potential threat to loss of his foster placement. Discuss how these factors might be explained in driving Jason's self-defeating behaviors.

4. Develop case formulations for Jason from three different perspectives. How might you integrate community resources in your treatment planning for Jason?

REFERENCES

Adams, B. (2002, September 29). Families struggle to bond with kids. *Salt Lake Tribune.*

Amaya-Jackson, L., & March, J. (1995). Posttraumatic stress disorder in adolescents: Risk factors, diagnosis and intervention. *Adolescent Medicine, 6,* 251–269.

American Academy of Child and Adolescent Psychiatry (AACAP). (2005). Practice parameter for the assessment and treatment of children and adolescents with reactive attachment disorder of infancy and early childhood. *Journal of the American Academy of Child and Adolescent Psychiatry, 44,* 1206–1219.

American Psychiatric Association (APA). (1980). *Diagnostic and statistical manual of mental disorders* (3rd ed.). Washington, DC: Author.

American Psychiatric Association (APA). (2000). *Diagnostic and statistical manual of mental disorders* (4th ed., text rev.). Washington, DC: Author.

Avery, R. J., & Freundlich, M. (2009). You're all grown up now: Termination of foster care support at age 18. *Journal of Adolescence, 32,* 247–257.

Barr, C. S., Newman, T. K., Shannon, C., Parker, C., Dvoskin, R. L., & Becker, M. L. (2003). Rearing condition and rh5-HTTLPR interact to influence limbic–hypothalamic–pituitary–adrenal axis response to stress in infant macaques. *Biological Psychiatry, 55,* 733–738.

Battaglia, M., Ogliari, A., Zanoni, A., Citterio, A., Pozzoli, U., Giorda, R., et al. (2005). Influence of the serotonin transporter promoter gene and shyness on children's cerebral responses to facial expressions. *Archives of General Psychiatry, 62,* 85–94.

Beauchaine, T. P., Gatzke-Kopp, L., & Mead, H. K. (2007). Polyvagal theory and developmental psychopathology: Emotion dysregulation and conduct problems from preschool to adolescence. *Biological Psychology, 74,* 174–184.

Borduin, C. M., Mann, B. J., Cone, L. T., & Henggeler, S. W. (1995). *Family therapy and beyond: A multisystemic approach to treating the behavior problems of children and adolescents.* Pacific Grove, CA: Brooks/Cole.

Boris, N. W., Zeanah, C. H., Larrieu, J. A., Scheeringa, M., & Heller, S. S. (1998). Attachment disorders in infancy and early childhood: A preliminary study of diagnostic criteria. *American Journal of Psychiatry, 155,* 295–297.

Brestan, E. V., & Eyberg, S. M. (1998). Effective psychosocial treatments of conduct-disordered children and adolescents: 29 years, 82 studies and 5,272 kids. *Journal of Clinical Child Psychology, 27,* 180–189.

Carrion, V. G., Weems, C. F., Ray, R., & Reiss, A. L. (2002). Toward an empirical definition of pediatric PTSD: The phenomenology of PTSD symptoms in youth. *Journal of the American Academy of Child & Adolescent Psychiatry, 41,* 166–173.

Cassidy, J., & Mohr, J. J. (2001). Unresolved fear, trauma and psychopathology: Theory, research and clinical considerations related to disorganized attachment across the life span. *Clinical Psychology Science Practice, 8,* 275–298.

Chamberlain, P., & Reid, J. (1991). Using a specialized foster care community treatment model for children and adolescents leaving the state mental hospital. *Journal of Community Psychology, 19,* 266–276.

Chamberlain, P., & Reid, J. (1998). Comparison of two community alternatives to incarceration for chronic juvenile offenders. *Journal of Consulting and Clinical Psychology, 66,* 624–633.

Chisholm, K. (1998). A three-year follow-up of attachment and indiscriminate friendliness in children adopted from Romanian orphanages. *Child Development, 69,* 1092–1106.

Crowder, C. (2000, July 29). Prosecutors add charges for rebirthing therapist. *Denver Rocky Mountain News.*

Dishion, T. J., McCord, J., & Poulin, F. (1999). When interventions harm: Peer groups and problem behavior. *American Psychologist, 54,* 755–764.

Frick, P. J. (2001). Effective interventions for children and adolescents with conduct disorder. *Canadian Journal of Psychiatry, 46,* 597–608.

Frick, P. J., Lahey, B. B., Loeber, R., Tannenbaum, L., Van Horn, Y., Christ, M. A., et al. (1993). Oppositional defiant disorder and conduct disorder: A meta-analytic review of factor analyses and cross-validation in a clinic sample. *Clinical Psychology Review, 13,* 319–340.

Gioia, G. A. (2005, November). *Executive functions in the schools: Concepts, assessment & intervention.* Paper presented at the Florida Association of School Psychologists, Annual Conference, Hollywood, Florida.

Gioia, G. A., & Isquith, P. K. (2004). Ecological assessment of executive function in traumatic brain injury. *Developmental Neuropsychology, 25,* 135–158.

Gioia, G. A., Isquith, P. K., Kenworthy, L., & Barton R. M. (2002). Profiles of everyday executive function in acquired and developmental disorders. *Child Neuropsychology, 8,* 121–137.

Greenhill, L., Jensen, P., Abikoff, H., Blumer, J., DeVaugh-Geiss, J., Fisher, C., et al. (2003). Optimizing strategies for developing and implementing psychopharmacological studies in preschool children. *Journal of the American Academy of Child and Adolescent Psychiatry, 42,* 406–414.

Hariri, A. (2002). Serotonin transporter genetic variation and the response of the human amygdala. *Science, 297,* 400–403.

Hart, A., & Thomas, H. (2000). Controversial attachments: The indirect treatment of fostered and adopted children via parent co-therapy. *Attachment and Human Development, 2,* 306–327.

Heim, C., Newport, D. J., Heit, S., Graham, Y. P., Wilcox, M., Bonsall, R., et al. (2000). Pituitary-adrenal and autonomic responses to stress in women after sexual and physical abuse in childhood. *American Medical Association, 284,* 592–597.

Henggeler, S. W., & Borduin, C. M. (1990). *Family therapy and beyond: A multisystemic approach to treating the behavior problems of children and adolescents.* Pacific Grove, CA: Brooks/Cole.

Henggeler, S. W., Schoenwald, S. K., Borduin, C. M., Rowland, M. D., & Cunningham, R. B. (1998). *Multisystemic treatment of antisocial behavior in children and adolescents.* New York: Guilford.

Hinshaw-Fuselier, S., Boris, N. W., & Zeanah, C. H. (1999). Reactive attachment disorder in maltreated twins. *Infant Mental Health Journal, 20,* 42–59, 1999.

Holland, R., Moretti, M. M., Verlaan, V., & Peterson, S. (1993). Attachment and conduct disorder: The response program. *Canadian Journal of Psychiatry, 38,* 420–431.

Insel, T. R. (2003). Is social attachment an addictive disorder? *Physiologial Behavior, 79,* 351–357.

Jensen, P. S., Bhatara, V. S., Vitiello, B., Hoagwood, K., Feil, M., & Burke, L. B. (1999). Psychoactive prescribing practices for U.S. children: Gaps between research and clinical practice. *Journal of the American Academy of Child and Adolescent Psychiatry, 38,* 557–565.

Kemph, J. P., & Voeller, K. K. S. (2008). Reactive attachment disorder in adolescence. *The Annals of the American Society for Adolescent Psychiatry, 30,* 159–178.

Levin, H. D., Culhane, K. A., Mendelsohn, E., Lilly, M. A., Bruce, D., Fletcher, J., et al. (1993). Cognition in relation to magnetic resonance imaging in head-injured children and adolescents. *Archives of Neurology, 50,* 897–905.

Lieberman A. F., Silverman, R., & Pawl, J. (2000). Infant-parent psychotherapy. In C. H. Zeanah (Ed.), *Handbook of infant mental health* (2nd ed., pp. 472–484). New York: Guilford.

Lieberman, A. F., & Zeanah, C. H. (1999). Contributions of attachment theory to infant-parent psychotherapy and other interventions with infants and young children. In J. Cassidy & P. Shaver (Eds.), *Handbook of attachment* (pp. 555–574). New York: Guilford.

Linden, W., Earle, T. L., Gerin, W., & Christenfeld, N. (1997). Physiological stress reactivity and recovery: Conceptual siblings separated at birth? *Journal of Psychosomatic Research, 42,* 117–135.

Lyons-Ruth, K. (2008). Contributions of the mother-infant relationship to dissociative, borderline, and conduct symptoms in young adulthood. *Infant Mental Health Journal, 29,* 203–218.

Lyons-Ruth, K., & Jacobvitz, D. (1999). Attachment disorganization: Unresolved loss, relational violence and lapses in behavioral and attentional strategies. In J. Cassidy & P. R. Shaver (Eds.), *Handbook of attachment: Theory, research, and clinical applications* (pp. 520–554). New York: Guilford.

Main, M., & Solomon, J. (1990). Procedures for identifying infants as disorganized/disoriented during the Ainsworth Strange Situation. In M. T. Greenberg, D. Cicchetti, & E. M. Cummings (Eds.), *Attachment in the preschool years* (pp. 121–160). Chicago: University of Chicago Press.

McDonough, S. (2000). Interaction guidance: An approach for difficult-to-engage families. In C. H. Zeanah (Ed.), *Handbook of infant mental health* (2nd ed., pp. 485–493). New York: Guilford.

Metzger, S. (2006). *Permanency for teens: New York City's emerging policy* [Voices for America's Children, Casey Family Services issue brief]. Retrieved January 11, 2007, from http://www.casey familyservices.org/pdfs/casey_teens.pdf

Nachmias, M., Gunnar, M., Mangelsdorf, S., Parritz, R., & Buss, K. (1996). Behavioral inhibition and stress reactivity: The moderating role of attachment security. *Child Development, 67,* 508–522.

O'Connor, T. G. (2002). Attachment disorders of infancy and childhood. In M. Rutter & E. Taylor (Eds.), *Child and adolescent psychiatry: Modern approaches* (4th ed., pp. 776–792). London: Blackwell.

O'Connor, T. G., Marvin, R. S., Rutter, M., Olrick, J. T., Britner, P. A., & The English and Romanian Adoptees Study Team. (2003). Child-parent attachment following early institutional deprivation. *Development and Psychopathology, 15,* 19–38.

O'Connor, T. G., Rutter, M., & English & Romanian Adoptees Study. (2000). Attachment disorder behavior following early severe deprivation: Extension and longitudinal follow-up. *Journal of the American Academy of Child & Adolescent Psychiatry, 39*(6), 703–712.

Porges, S. W. (2003). Social engagement and attachment: A phylogenic perspective. *Roots of Mental Illness in Children, 1008,* 31–47.

Pynoos, R. S. (1990). Post-traumatic stress disorder in children and adolescents. In B. Grafinkel, G. Carlson, & E. Weller (Eds.), *Psychiatric disorders in children and adolescents* (pp. 48–63). Philadelphia: W. B. Saunders.

Pynoos, R. S. (1994). Traumatic stress and developmental psychopathology in children and adolescents. In R. S. Pynoos (Ed.), *Posttraumatic stress disorder: A clinical review* (pp. 64–98). Lutherville, MD: Sidran Press.

Renken, B., Egeland, B., Marvinney, D., Mangelsdorf, S., & Sroufe, L. A. (1989). Early childhood antecedents of aggression and passive-withdrawal in early elementary school. *Journal of Personality, 5,* 257–281.

Rey, J. M. (1993). Oppositional defiant disorder. *American Journal of Psychiatry, 150,* 1769–1777.

Richters, M. M., & Volmar, F. R. (1994). Reactive attachment disorder of infancy or early childhood. *Journal of the American Academy of Child and Adolescent Psychiatry, 33*(3), 328–332.

Scheibel, R. S., & Levin, H. S. (1997). Frontal lobe dysfunction following closed head injury in children: Findings from duropsycholgy and brain injury. In N. A. Krashegor, G. R. Lyon, & P. S. Goldman-Rakie (Eds.), *Development of the prefrontal cortex: Evolution, neurobiology and behavior.* Baltimore: Brookes.

Schoenwald, S., Borduin, C. H., & Henggeler, S. W. (1998). Multisystemic therapy: Changing the natural and service ecologies of adolescents and families. In M. Epstein, K. Kutash, & A. Duchnowski (Eds.), *Outcomes for children and youth with emotional and behavioral disorders and their families: Programs and evaluation best practices* (pp. 485–511). Austin, TX: PRO-ED.

Schoenwald, S. K., Brown, T. L., & Henggeler, S. (2000). Inside multisystemic therapy: Therapist, supervisory, and program practices. *Journal of Emotional and Behavioral Disorders, 8,* 113–127.

Smyke, A. T., Dumitrescu, A., & Zeanah, C. H. (2002). Disturbances of attachment in young children: I. The continuum of caretaking casualty. *Journal of the American Academy of Child and Adolescent Psychiatry, 41,* 972–982.

Spangler, G., & Grossmann, K. (1999). Individual and physiological correlates of attachment disorganization in infancy. In J. Solomon & C. George (Eds.), *Attachment disorganization* (pp. 95–126). New York: Guilford.

Steinhauer, P. D. (1996). The diagnosis, prevention and management of attachment disorders in children. *P.R.I.S.M.E., 6,* 604–617. (Original in French)

Steinhauer, P. D. (1998). *Separation and attachment: Treatment issues.* Paper presented to The Children's Aid Society of the County of Perth, Stratford, Ontario.

Stormshak, E. A., Bierman, K. L., McMahon, R. J., Lengua, L., & The Conduct Problems Prevention Research Group. (2000). Parenting practice and child disruptive behavior problems in early elementary school. *Journal of Clinical Child Psychology, 19,* 17–29.

Terr, L. C. (1991). Childhood traumas: An outline and review. *American Journal of Psychiatry, 148,* 10–20.

Thompson, R. A. (1999). Early attachment and later development. In J. Cassidy & P. Shaver (Eds.), *Handbook of attachment* (pp. 265–286). New York: Guilford.

Troy, M., & Sroufe, L. A. (1987). Victimization among preschoolers: Role of attachment relationship history. *Journal of the American Academy of Child and Adolescent Psychiatry, 26,* 166–172.

Webster-Stratton, C. (1998). Preventing conduct problems in Head Start children: Strengthening parenting competencies. *Journal of Consulting & Clinical Psychology, 66,* 715–730.

Weems, C. F., Saltzman, K. M., Reiss, A., & Carrion, V. G. (2003). A prospective test of the association between hyperarousal and emotional numbing in youth with a history of traumatic stress. *Journal of Clinical Child and Adolescent Psychology, 32,* 166–171.

Weisz, J. R., Weiss, B. B., Han, S. S., Granger, D. A., & Morton, E. (1995). Effects of psychotherapy with children and adolescents revisited: A meta-analysis of treatment outcome studies. *Psychological Bulletin, 117,* 450–468.

Wilmshurst, L. (2002). Treatment programs for youth with emotional and behavioral disorders: An outcome study of two alternate approaches. *Mental Health Services Research, 4*(2), 85–96.

Ylvisaker, M., Szekeres, S., & Feeney, T. (1998). Cognitive rehabilitation: Executive functions. In M. Ylvisaker (Ed.), *Traumatic brain injury rehabilitation: Children and adolescents* (2nd ed., pp. 234–254). Boston: Butterworth-Heinemann.

Ylvisaker, M., Szekeres, S., & Hartwick, P. (1992). Cognitive rehabilitation following traumatic brain injury in children. In M. G. Tramontana & S. R. Hooper (Eds.), *Advances in child neuropsychology* (pp. 168–218). New York: Springer.

Zeanah, C. H. (2000). Disturbances of attachment in young children adopted from institutions. *Journal of Developmental and Behavioral Pediatrics, 21,* 230–236.

Zeanah, C. H., Scheeringa, M., Boris, N. W., Heller, S. S., Smyke, A. T., & Trapani, J. (2004). Reactive attachment disorder in maltreated toddlers. *Child Abuse and Neglect, 28,* 877–888.

Tori Benson

Skin Deep; Cutting Through the Pain

Tori was dropped off for her first appointment by her father, who appeared very uncomfortable and as though he was not sure whether he should stay or go. Tori, who just turned 16 years of age 2 weeks ago, had quit school on her birthday. She seemed sullen and had a look of disgust on her face. Her father wanted assurance from her that she would not bolt, once he had left, and she gave him a sideways glance, saying, "Yeah, whatever." He made arrangements to pick her up in an hour and then left. That was the first time the psychologist had met Tori, although she initially interviewed the parents about their concerns a week earlier. Parents were at a loss as to how to manage Tori, whose behaviors had clearly escalated out of control. Tori agreed to accompany the psychologist to her office, saying, "Yeah, Shrink, let's go to your shrink room." When Tori had quit school on her birthday, 2 weeks ago, she had also left town and took a Greyhound bus to visit an older friend who was living on her own in another city. Tori had just been reunited with her parents a few days ago. Before she returned home, the parents, realizing that their daughter would land on their doorstep within the next few days and feeling totally unable to relate to her, had contacted the psychologist to ask for help for Tori, when she returned.

DEVELOPMENTAL HISTORY/FAMILY BACKGROUND

When George and Andrea Benson contacted the psychologist, they had just been informed that their wayward daughter had been found in a city several miles away. They had been frantic for days, not knowing what had happened to her; they were hoping for the best, yet fearing the worst. Although they contacted the police immediately, there was a delay of several hours between when Tori boarded the bus and when her parents actually knew that she was missing. It had been a typical morning, with Tori leaving for school at the same time that her parents left for work. It wasn't until her mother checked for messages later that day that she realized her daughter did not attend school at all that day. Andrea's first reaction was one of anger, thinking that Tori had lied to them and skipped school again. Andrea called George, who told her to calm down, saying that Tori was probably using her birthday as an excuse to treat herself with time off and a shopping trip with her friends. When the phone was not answered at home, they just thought that Tori was avoiding a confrontation. They had confiscated her cell phone, so they did not have another way to contact her. Not that she would have answered her cell phone, if she were avoiding her parents. Andrea was even more upset because it was Tori's birthday and she and George had planned a quiet meal at her favorite restaurant for the three of them to celebrate her "sweet sixteen."

Tori lives with her parents, Andrea and George Benson, who are 38 and 40 years of age. There is another child, a sister, Cindy, who is 10 years old. Tori and Cindy do not get along and can be quite competitive with each other for their parents' attention. When asked about Tori's milestones, parents seemed to have little recollection of when important events occurred and actually provided more information about Cindy's development than Tori's. Andrea explained that although the pregnancy and birth were uneventful, she was quite depressed after Tori was born and, as a result, she really does not have very good recollection of Tori's early life at all. This was a dark time in their lives, when George had an alcohol problem that often resulted in blackouts, when he could not remember what he had done for an entire day. Andrea was seriously depressed, but medication did not agree with her, so she also indulged in alcohol to help her forget and sleep. There were financial problems, and Andrea said that she does not know how they all came through that time without any serious problems. As for Tori, she spent most of her time in day care during the day, and with a neighborhood boy who was several years older, who took Tori under his wing. Even though he was 12 and Tori was 4, he was like a big brother to her and they spent a lot of time together, which was a good thing for Andrea, because at least she felt that Tori was safe and had a companion. This relationship with the boy lasted until Tori was 6 years old, when the boy and his parents left town unexpectedly. As a result, Tori was crushed, having lost her "big brother," and was very lonely and sad, not having developed any friendships with children her own age. In addition, at that time, Andrea also realized she was pregnant again, and Tori became very jealous that there would be another child in the house.

When asked about any family history of mental illness, the Bensons were quite reluctant to offer any information initially; however, they eventually reported problems on both sides of the family. There is a family history of alcoholism, on the father's side, with George's father reportedly an alcoholic. George's nephew, who is about 3 years older than Tori, has been arrested several times for possession of drugs, and is currently serving a sentence in the correctional facility. George's mother was a very eccentric woman who claimed to be the descendent of Danish royalty, and forever complained about her lot in life. According to George, she was a very dramatic woman who would have done well as an actress on the stage. Andrea's family members were less flamboyant by description; however, the difficulties that were reported shared a common theme relating to problems with impulse control. Andrea's brother is currently incarcerated for theft, DUI, and an incident of road rage, while her sister has been arrested repeatedly for shoplifting, which has been attributed to kleptomania.

Tori was just beginning to make friends at school when her father was transferred to another city about 200 miles from where they had been living. At this time, Tori was 8 years of age and in Grade 3. Her parents recalled that Tori was very upset about the move and had a very difficult time adjusting to her new school and classmates. Often, during this period,

Tori would beg to stay home from school, and cry, complaining of stomachaches and pains. She became increasingly resentful of her little sister, who was 2 years of age and could stay home with her mother, while Tori had to go to school. Her parents tried to arrange visits with her previous friends by inviting them to come over, or arranging for Tori to visit them, but these were not as frequent as Tori would have liked. They did say, however, that a few years ago, Tori met a girl on one of her bus trips to the other city, and that Tori developed an immediate friendship with and really looked up to the girl. The girl, Josie, was older (they guessed about 19–20 years of age) and had been on her own for some time. When Tori ran away on her birthday, she went to visit Josie, who took her in for the week. Andrea and George were very concerned because they knew very little about Josie and were fearful that she might be a bad influence on Tori. To this date, they have very little information about Josie or what she does for a living.

Tori has disliked attending school since the third grade when the family moved to another city and school. Academically, although she has never been assessed for special education services, she has had mediocre grades, barely passing each year. When Tori is unhappy with her school, parents have responded by transferring her to another school. As a result, Tori has attended six schools in the past 8 years. Last year, she was successful in obtaining only one credit in the Grade 10 program.

REASON FOR REFERRAL

When Tori's parents initially approached the psychologist, they were looking for an immediate solution to their problems with Tori. However, given Tori's age and the surrounding circumstances, in the initial part of the interview with the parents, the psychologist focused on enlightening them about the ethical problems and difficulties inherent in working with adolescents. The psychologist's first step was to engage the parents in allowing her to work with Tori in an environment that encouraged disclosure, without Tori fearing that everything she told the psychologist would be relayed back to her parents. It was explained that unless the adolescent is assured that disclosures will be treated confidentially, nothing will be disclosed. Furthermore, it was emphasized that the long-term goal would be to encourage Tori to discuss these issues with her parents, through the help of the psychologist at her side as a mediator. The psychologist also discussed that Tori would be informed in the first session that there are three conditions under which the psychologist would have a duty to report information to the authorities: information regarding (1) any intent to self-harm, (2) any intent to harm others, or (3) reporting being the victim of prior abuse (sexual, physical). Once parental support was obtained, the psychologist agreed to meet with Tori, given that Tori was agreeable. The psychologist also mentioned that if Tori was not in agreement (they were not able to convince her to seek help) and they were concerned about her welfare, they should, with the agreement of a mental health professional, seek an involuntary commitment order to ensure her safety.

Tori, a tall, thin, adolescent, presented with numerous complaints during the psychologist's initial contact with her. Tori made it clear during the first meeting, that the counseling sessions were her parents' idea to fix up how they had "f—— up her life." When asked how her life had been derailed by her parents, Tori recounted her school history in a life-less list of facts devoid of emotion. When asked to recall a time when she was happy at school, Tori stated that she could not remember anything positive about school. Instead, she seemed to hang on to bitter memories of every situation that went wrong for her. She said that she never rebounded after her parents moved when she was in Grade 3. She said that the kids in this town are horrible and that she was unable to fit in because they were snobs. Although Tori talked about "fitting in," the way she dressed and her outward flamboyance suggested that fitting in was the last thing on her mind. For the first meeting, she was dressed in a pair of distressed jeans, which were more "holes" than denim, barely hanging together by a thread. She wore a dangling earring made out of a fishing lure and carried a purse that was covered in feathers that were glued to the bag. She was also wearing dark black lipstick that matched her nail polish.

During the first session, several attempts were made to elicit from Tori what her plans were for the future, in terms of possibly returning to school, and what plans she might have if the situation at home deteriorated again. Tori mentioned a number of alternatives, which revealed that she had given it some thought, although it was questionable how much thought had gone into the process. Tori rattled off a number of possible living arrangements, including moving in with her boyfriend, doing telemarketing and living off student welfare, finding accommodations in a group home, or turning herself in to the psychiatric hospital. Each alternative was delivered in a matter-of-fact tone, with very little accompanying emotion. When asked if she was depressed or had been depressed in the past, Tori said that she had been on Prozac and Paxil previously, but that her mother made her get off the Paxil because she thought that it was related to Tori doing other "drugs." Tori agreed, maybe the Paxil did have something to do with other drugs she was doing at the time. When asked about a future career, Tori said that maybe she would be a fashion designer. At that point, attention was drawn to her unique way of dress, and Tori seemed quite proud of her look, which she said could start a fashion trend.

When Tori arrived for her next session, it was readily apparent that she had spent a great deal of time getting ready for the session in her selection of clothing, accessories, and grooming. However, Tori also was bare sleeved and sported a number of very obvious cuts to her arm. When questioned about the cuts, Tori admitted to cutting herself with a razor when she is distressed. She was very open about the cutting, saying that she had a big fight with her boyfriend and that often she feels most like cutting when she is emotionally distressed or depressed. She was interested in learning about ways to curb the tendencies to cut (e.g., worry beads, playing the guitar, etc.). There were no additional cuts in the following two sessions.

During the next session, Tori began to open up a bit more and talked about family matters, focusing on her sister, Cindy, and the fights that Tori and Cindy had been having. Tori recalled a recent incident where Cindy embarrassed her at a family gathering, in front of her grandmother and aunt. She asked if the psychologist would call her parents and explain to them that she was trying, but that Cindy was making it difficult for her to improve. She complained of problems sleeping, and said she did not feel like eating. She announced that she had been wearing a heart monitor the past week, and that she is now down to 87 pounds. Her thoughts seemed to run into each other and made it difficult at times for the psychologist to separate what was reality from fantasy, or bids for increased attention. The weight was discussed, and Tori was told that if her eating did not improve, the psychologist would be obligated to transfer her case to someone who specialized in eating disorders. Tori missed her next appointment, and when this was followed up, her father reported that Tori was visiting friends for the week in the city.

When Tori arrived at her next appointment, she appeared very nervous. Her hair was blue in color, and she was now wearing a nose ring and lip ring. When asked why she seemed edgy, Tori said, "It's been a while," and then seemed to settle down a bit. At that point, she revealed several fresh cuts to her arms, wrist, and ankle that she had done the night before. She admitted to feeling very depressed and said at times that she just wanted to leave this place and go back to the city. She was especially distraught about her boyfriend, who she said was a "skinhead." She said that he could be very mean to her and she didn't want to see him anymore. She said that when she cut, she felt nothing; there was no pain. She said she wanted to know if she still could feel anything. All she felt was emptiness. She also added that she had gained weight and was now 103 pounds. When asked what she thought about that made her sad, she said that most kids were going back to school now, and that she didn't want to do that, but didn't have any other plans either. When asked if she would complete some questionnaires to help the psychologist better understand her, Tori agreed.

ASSESSMENT RESULTS

Tori completed the Child Depression Index (CDI) and Revised Child Manifest Anxiety Scale (RCMAS-2). Both scales have a limited number of items and can usually be completed within about 15–20 minutes. However, Tori required almost 45 minutes to answer the questionnaires. She seemed to have significant problems making up her mind as to which answer was appropriate and seemed to need to read the items several times before responding. Given her test behavior, it is possible that she is having significant problems concentrating due to depression/anxiety or that she may have an underlying learning disability that is interfering with her ability to be a fluid reader. In either case, it was a glimpse concerning why she might have been experiencing such academic difficulties all these years. Due to time constraints, Tori was given the Youth Self Report (YSR) to be completed at home and brought back with her to the next session.

Responses to the CDI and RCMAS-2 revealed the following information. Tori's responses to the CDI placed overall depression at a T score of 87, which is three standard deviations above the norm for her age. She scored in the clinically significant range in areas of negative mood due to feelings of "ineffectiveness." Other areas of difficulty were noted in interpersonal problems, anhedonia, and negative self-esteem. Anxiety ratings overall were just below the level of clinical significance, although significant elevations were found on scales indicating worry/sensitivity and anxiety resulting from social expectations (social anxiety). Tori also completed the Youth Self Report scale (YSR), and results indicated significant clinical elevations on several scales, including withdrawn, anxious/depressed, thought problems, delinquent behavior, internalizing behavior, and the total problem scale.

Psychologist's Summary and Impressions

Tori is a 16-year-old high-risk adolescent who presents with numerous symptoms of depression and social anxiety and significant problems with impulse control and emotion regulation (cutting). Throughout the sessions, Tori often presented with a confused sense of time and orientation, making it difficult to chart the course of her history and particular events in her life. Toward the end of the sessions, it was becoming increasingly apparent that Tori was without a sense of direction at a time when most adolescents are planning a return to school. Her feelings of depression and sense of ineffectiveness may have a direct bearing on her sense of being lost and without a future. Given her short-sighted sense of perspective, Tori has ruled out most of her school options based on social acquaintances who attend the schools and with whom Tori does not get along. However, it is also important to understand that her only reason for attending school at this point would be to maintain social contacts, rather than accomplish any educational goals. In our sessions, there has been a push/pull dynamic based on Tori's need for increased attention/nurturing and her persistent fears of abandonment and rejection. There are many gaps in her history that are unaccounted for, and it is unknown whether there may have been an early history of sexual abuse (childhood friend who was an older male), although mother did disclose an early history of maternal depression, being emotionally unavailable for Tori, and a lack of monitoring and supervision were evident in Tori's early life between the ages of birth and 6 years of age.

In her last counseling session, Tori requested a referral to a female adolescent group home where she had been placed on a temporary basis a year ago. She recalled a female counselor there who she said made her feel "safe." Tori was accepted at the group home and, at last contact, was doing relatively well, saying she wanted to go back to school and become a counselor for kids in trouble.

ISSUES, TRENDS, AND TREATMENT ALTERNATIVES

Self-injurious behavior (SIB) has been described as "deliberate, repetitive self-harming actions like cutting, burning, poisoning, strangulation, etc." (Ohmann et al., 2008, p. 226), and has increasingly been identified in female adolescent psychiatric populations (De Leo & Heller, 2004; Wood, Trainor, Rothwell, Moore, & Harrington, 2001). Onset of SIB has often been associated with family or peer problems, disciplinary problems, crises, or bouts of low self-esteem (Beautrais, Joyce, & Mulder, 1997; Hawton, Cole, O'Grady, & Osborn, 1982; Ystgaard, Reinholdt, Husby, & Mehlum, 2003). Childhood trauma (Yates, 2004; Ystgaard et al., 2003), depression (Kumar, Pepe, & Steer, 2004), anxiety (Burgess, Hawton, & Loveday, 1998), personality disorders (Clery, 2000), eating disorders (Favaro & Santonastaso, 1998), and posttraumatic stress disorder (Kisiel & Lyons, 2001) have all been found to increase the likelihood of SIB.

From a neurobiological perspective, self-regulatory behaviors have been associated with the frontal cortex and the limbic system, including the anterior cingulate, hippocampus, and amygdala (Davidson, Pizzagalli, Nitschke, & Putnam, 2002). More specifically, the right side of the prefrontal cortex is responsible for behavioral inhibition (Ohmann et al., 2008). Deficits in executive functions have been related to problems with behavior and emotion regulation in individuals with a wide variety of emotional and behavioral problems, including posttraumatic stress disorder (PTSD), borderline personality disorder (BPD), depression, ADHD, obsessive-compulsive disorder, and the disruptive behavior disorders (Barkley, Edwards, Laneri, Fletcher, & Metevia, 2001; Coolidge, Segal, Stewart, & Ellett, 2000). In their samples of adolescent females, feelings of low self-esteem in the face of inadequate coping strategies were significantly related to deliberate SIB (Ohmann et al., 2008; Ystgaard et al., 2003). In their study of almost 100 female adolescent patients with SIB, and controls (77 patients), Ohmann and colleagues (2008) found that the patients with SIB most often had diagnoses of BPD and PTSD compared to controls, and that child trauma and depression were most predictive of SIB. The most common form of SIB in their sample was cutting. The researchers suggest that their findings provide support for theories of "SIB as a *'learned'* behavior independent of underlying neuropsychological problems. According to this model, traumatic experiences and parental pathology predispose to SIB and depression" (p. 230). In this context, SIB is initially used as a means to reduce psychic pain, and then later becomes a learned response, based on the self-rewarding mechanism of SIB as a pain reliever.

Studies have found that individuals who demonstrate symptoms of disorders of impulse control, such as BPD or antisocial personality disorder, share a common predisposition to react to stressful circumstances in a dysregulated and destructive manner. While vulnerable males tend to develop antisocial personality disorder, females are more prone to develop BPD and to direct damaging behaviors inwardly in ways that are self-destructive. Heightened activation of the amygdala and cortical systems (Barr et al., 2003; Hairiri, 2002) can render individuals with BPD vulnerable to suicide attempts or other self-destructive behaviors during stressful times (Stanley, Molcho, & Stanley, 2000). Individuals who inherit the short form of the 5HTT (serotonin transporter allele) are at twice the risk of developing borderline or antisocial symptoms, while those who inherit two of the short alleles are four times more likely to develop impulse disorders. These odds occurred independent of early rearing conditions or depressed symptoms (Lyons-Ruth et al., 2007).

Crawford, Cohen, Chen, Anglin, and Ehrensaft (2009) studied the impact of extended maternal separations, prior to age 5, on the potential risk for developing BPD and found that early separations predicted increased symptoms of BPD from early adolescence to middle adulthood. Although these separations were documented as "physical," it is also possible that mothers who are not emotionally available may have a similar impact on their children, since childhood history of neglect, abuse, and insecure attachment have all been associated with increased risk for BPD (Zanarini et al., 2002).

There has been a reluctance to diagnose personality disorders in adolescents due to the widely held belief among mental health practitioners that identity formation is not complete until early adulthood. This belief is supported by the *DSM-IV-TR* (APA, 2000), which states that "although personality disorder categories may be applied to children or adolescence," it is only "in those relatively unusual instances in which the individual's particular maladaptive personality traits appear to be pervasive, persistent and unlikely to be limited to a particular developmental stage, or an episode of an Axis I disorder" (p. 687). Furthermore, the

DSM adds that diagnoses in someone under 18 years of age would require that symptoms be exhibited for at least a year, with the exception being antisocial personality disorder, which, by definition, requires that the individual be at least 18 years of age. However, in their chapter concerning bipolar disorder in adolescents, Miller, Neft, and Golombeck (2008) state that in their clinical experience, "many multi-problem adolescents meet criteria for a personality disorder but are diagnosed and treated only for Axis I disorders." Furthermore, the authors emphasize that "when Axis II criteria are ignored, many adolescents may not receive specific treatment for their dysfunctional behaviors, or worse, receive inappropriate treatments" (p. 87). As a result of inappropriate or no treatment, these adolescents could experience more serious outcomes, such as delinquency, social isolation, suicidal ideation, substance abuse, and academic failure (Kernberg, Weiner, & Bardenstein, 2000). Although it is possible to diagnose BPD in adolescence, if symptoms are of a long-standing nature (1 year), the *DSM* does not provide guidelines as to how symptoms of the disorder may present differently in adolescents and adults.

In adults, BPD can include symptoms of dissociative or paranoid thoughts, an unstable sense of self, mood swings that can be extreme and uncontrollable, lack of impulse control, a tendency toward self-harm, and fears of abandonment that often result in highly turbulent relationships (*DSM-IV-TR,* APA, 2000). Pervasive and high levels of psychic pain and desperation often accompany suicide attempts or other SIB (Westen, Shedler, Durrett, Glass, & Martens, 2003). Al-Alem and Omar (2008) suggest that since the *DSM-IV-TR* (APA, 2000) diagnosis of BPD is based on the presence of five out of a possible nine symptoms, the classification leads to a vast heterogeneity of diagnosis, whether in adolescents or adults that can mimic symptoms of other disorders (e.g., anxiety disorders, bipolar disorder), which may result in BPD remaining undiagnosed (p. 401).

In their study of "Children in the Community," Bernstein and colleagues (1993) reported that early adolescent BPD was predictive of a number of negative outcomes, including grade retention, school dropout, and social problems. Adolescent females who demonstrated symptoms of BPD reported more break-ups in intimate relationships, abuse, and stress during the high school years (Daley, Burge, & Hammen, 2000). In their longitudinal study of adolescents with BPD, Winograd, Cohen, and Chen (2008) found that for individuals who demonstrated higher levels of borderline symptoms in early adolescence, negative outcomes continued even into their twenties and thirties, suggesting that borderline symptoms during adolescence represent a lifelong concern, rather than a temporary developmental phase (Bradley, Conklin, & Westen, 2005). Results from Winograd and colleagues (2008) support earlier findings of Paris (2005) that BPD symptoms in adolescence are associated with worse prognosis in adulthood, and that the *DSM-IV-TR* (APA, 2000) criteria can be used to effectively diagnose the disorder in adolescence.

Treatment

Miller and colleagues (2008) outline several challenges that clinicians must face working with adolescents who have symptoms of BPD, including controversies regarding diagnosis, fears of abandonment, complex relationship issues at home and at school, and suicidal or self-harm behaviors. The disorder often results in impaired relationships, resulting in feelings of emptiness and despair, which adversely impact cognitive functioning and academic performance. Parents and teachers often criticize the teens for "not caring," which causes increased emotional dysregulation and continuation of the negative cycle, leading to increased incidences of self-harm, dysfunction, and emotion dysregulation. According to Miller and colleagues (2008), treatment problems exist because "teenagers diagnosed with BPD who often have numerous coexisting problems, including suicidal and self-injurious behaviors, and whose families are also crisis-driven, are particularly difficult to engage and sustain in treatment" (p. 93). Due to the impulsivity inherent in this population, approximately two thirds of those with BPD will drop out of treatment within a few months (Linehan, 1993). Dropouts among adolescent populations range from 33% to 77% (Armbruster & Fallon, 1994; Dierker, Nargiso, Wiseman, & Hoff, 2001).

Another challenge to therapy for adolescents with BPD is that they often come from families where emotional problems are common. Growing up in an unstable family environment that is low in warmth and has a history of parental psychopathology, as well as potentially abusive conditions, increases the likelihood of BPD in adolescents (Bradley, Jenei, & Westen, 2005). In such family constellations, therapists often are faced with dilemmas involving treating the adolescent, and other family members who themselves are in need of treatment, as well as addressing invalidating communication styles that often can undermine therapeutic progress (Miller et al., 2008).

Although the "best" method of treatment is still being investigated, one of the most promising treatments with adults is dialectical behavioral therapy (DBT). Recently, researchers have found that cognitive analytic therapy (CAT) can also be effective in reducing psychopathology in adolescents with BPD and serve as an early intervention program. The following description will review both therapeutic treatments.

Dialectical Behavioral Therapy (DBT). DBT was developed by Marsha Linehan (1993a) to address the underlying emotional dysregulation that results in a reduced capacity for individuals to deal with negative emotions, such as anxiety, depression, and anger. DBT is a cognitive-behavioral therapy that targets affective instability and impulsivity. There are four stages to the treatment. In the first stage, the therapist strives to address issues of suicidal and self-injurious behaviors, reduce self-destructive behaviors, and increase coping skills. In the second stage, the therapist would help the client to experience emotions without shutting down, avoiding, or dissociating from them, and to work through past issues of trauma or abuse and symptoms of PTSD. In the third stage, the focus is on self-sustaining and long-term goals, such as increased independence and self-worth, and the development and monitoring of goals for self-improvement, whether these involve career, education, or interpersonal relationships. In the fourth and final stage (which was added later by Linehan), individuals with BPD face their feelings of "emptiness" and attempt to reconnect with those in their environment. The DBT model combines psychotherapy and cognitive-behavioral skills training and is focused on acceptance and change. Linehan's DBT model was developed to address the underlying dynamics of BPD, which develop in a childhood environment that chronically invalidates an individual's feelings and selfhood. As a result, individuals with BPD seek out proof of or validation for their feelings in other people in their environment (Skodol et al., 2002). Patients who attend DBT agree to a contract for 1 year of attending weekly group sessions for 2 ½ hours and individual sessions for 1 hour. The contract can be renewed if progress is evident (Al-Alem & Omar, 2008).

In individual sessions, the therapist provides an environment that validates the individual's attempts at balancing self-acceptance and developing improved skills for coping with emotional situations. A trusting relationship between the therapist and individual with BPD is essential to provide assurance that borderline symptoms will not be punished while at the same time providing guidance regarding the harmful effects of self-destructive behaviors, such as drug abuse, promiscuity, or other behaviors (Linehan, 1993a). Behavioral groups provide an opportunity to develop and practice behavioral skills in a safe environment.

Miller and colleagues (2008) suggest that for adolescents with BPD, enlisting the family in treatment is important in improving compliance and effectiveness of the treatment. In this case, family therapy sessions will serve to mobilize support for all family members and provide an opportunity to increase the "range of behavioral skills, and solve family problems," while at the same time providing the adolescent with the necessary skills and training (p. 93). Miller, Rathus, and Linehan (2007) have outlined the areas of dysfunction in BPD that correspond to BPD symptoms (*DSM-IV-TR,* 2000) that have been realigned to correspond to skill modules in the DBT program:

Problem Areas Skills Modules

1)	Self-dysregulation	Core mindfulness skills
2)	Interpersonal dysregulation	Interpersonal effectiveness skills
3)	Behavioral and cognitive dysregulation	Distress tolerance skills
4)	Emotional dysregulation	Emotion-regulation skills
5)	Adolescent-family dilemmas	Walking the middle path

While the first four skill sets are parts of the original program (Linehan, 1993b), the fifth module, "walking the middle path," addresses the lack of balance between thoughts and behaviors within the family environment. According to Miller and colleagues (2007), families and adolescents with BPD need to achieve a balance and stop vacillating between polarized responses in three important areas:

1. parenting practices that go from leniency to authoritarian control,
2. conceptualizing normal behaviors as pathological and pathological behaviors as normal, and
3. fostering dependency versus independence and autonomy. (p. 94)

Early Intervention. Chanen and colleagues (2008) investigated the potential success of early intervention for BPD using cognitive analytic therapy (CAT) versus individuals with BPD who were provided with good clinical care (GCC). This was a randomized controlled study of 86 adolescent patients, 78 of which were available for follow-up data collection.

Study inclusion required evidence of at least two symptoms of BPD and one other comorbid disorder. CAT is described as a "time-limited, integrative psychotherapy." It combines "elements of psychoanalytic object relations theory and cognitive psychology" (Chanen et al., 2008, p. 479). The program, which was developed by Ryle and Kerr (2002), has been used increasingly in Europe to treat BPD (Ryle, 1997, 2004). Results revealed that early intervention individuals in both groups showed significant positive outcomes, although CAT achieved clinical goals more rapidly than GCC. The researchers state that the study is the first published randomized controlled study to demonstrate that early intervention for BPD can be a successful endeavor without incurring risks of possible iatrogenic effects of early diagnosis and treatment.

Post-Case Questions

1. If Tori refused to meet with the psychologist, what recourse would her parents have, given her age?

2. The diagnosis of BPD in adolescents is controversial. What are some of the arguments for and against diagnosis of BPD in adolescents?

3. Does Tori meet the *DSM-IV-TR* (APA, 2000) criteria for BPD? If so, how? If not, why not? What suggestions do you have for how symptom criteria might be altered for individuals in adolescence, or should they be altered?

4. Individuals with BPD often have other comorbid disorders. Does Tori meet criteria for any of the other *DSM-IV-TR* diagnoses? If so, which diagnoses are possible?

5. Based on your knowledge of BPD, what family characteristics are evident that may have increased her risk for developing BPD?

6. Discuss Tori's symptoms from the following theoretical perspectives: biological, psychodynamic, cognitive-behavioral, and attachment/parenting.

REFERENCES

Al-Alem, L., & Omar, H. A. (2008). Borderline personality disorder: An overview of history, diagnosis and treatment in adolescents. *International Journal of Adolescent Medical Health, 20,* 495–504.

American Psychiatric Association (APA). (2000). *Diagnostic and statistical manual of mental disorders* (4th ed., text revision). Washington, DC: Author.

Armbruster, P., & Fallon, T. (1994). Clinical, sociodemographic, and systems risk factors for attrition in a children's mental health clinic. *American Journal of Orthopsychiatry, 64,* 577–585.

Barkley, R. A., Edwards, G., Laneri, M., Fletcher, K., & Metevia, L. (2001). Executive functioning, temporal discounting, and sense of time in adolescents with attention deficit hyperactivity disorder (ADHD), and oppositional defiant disorder (ODD). *Journal of Abnormal Child Psychology, 29,* 541–556.

Barr, C. S., Newman, T. K., Shannon, C., Parker, C., Dvoskin, R. L., & Becker, M. L. (2003). Rearing condition and rh5-HTTLPR interact to influence limbic-hypothalamic-pituitary-adrenal axis response to stress in infant macaques. *Biological Psychiatry, 55,* 733–738.

Beautrais, A. L., Joyce, P. R., & Mulder, R. T. (1997). Precipitating factors and life events in serious suicide attempts among youths aged 13 through 24 years. *Journal of the American Academy of Child and Adolescent Psychiatry, 37,* 504–511.

Bernstein, D. P., Cohen, P., Velez, C. N., Schwab-Stone, M., Siever, L. J., & Shinsato, L. (1993). Prevalence and stability of the *DSM-III-R* personality disorders in a community-based survey of adolescents. *American Journal of Psychiatry, 150,* 1237–1243.

Bradley, R., Conklin, C. Z., & Westen, D. (2005). The borderline personality diagnosis in adolescents: Gender differences and subtypes. *Journal of Child Psychology and Psychiatry, 46,* 1006–1019.

Burgess, S., Hawton, K., & Loveday, G. (1998). Adolescents who take overdoses: outcome in terms of changes in psychopathology and the adolescents' attitudes to their care and their overdoses. *Journal of Adolescence, 21,* 209–218.

Chanen, A. M., Jackson, H. I., McCutcheon, L. K., Jovev, M., Dudgeon, P., Pan Yuen, H., et al. (2008). Early intervention for adolescents with borderline personality disorder using cognitive analytic therapy: Randomized controlled trial. *British Journal of Psychiatry, 193,* 477–484.

Clery, C. (2000). Self-directed violence in adolescence: A psychotherapeutic perspective. In G. Boswell (Ed.), *Violent children and adolescents: Asking the question, why* (pp. 91–103). London: Whurr.

Coolidge, F. L., Segal, D. L., Stewart, S., & Ellett, J. A. (2000). Neuropsychological dysfunction in children with borderline personality disorder features: A preliminary investigation. *Journal of Research and Personality, 34,* 554–561.

Crawford, T. N., Cohen, P. R., Chen, H., Anglin, D. M., & Ehrensaft, M. (2009). Early maternal separation and the trajectory of borderline personality disorder symptoms. *Development and Psychopathology, 21,* 1013–1030.

Daley, S. E., Burge, D., & Hammen, C. (2000). Borderline personality disorder symptoms as predictors of four-year romantic relationship dysfunction in young women: Addressing issues of specificity. *Journal of Abnormal Psychology, 109,* 451–460.

Davidson, R. J., Pizzagalli, D., Nitschke, J. B., & Putnam, K. (2002). Depression: Perspectives from affective neuroscience. *Annual Review of Psychology, 53,* 545–574.

De Leo, D., & Heller, T. S. (2004). Who are the kids who self-harm? An Australian self-report school survey. *Medical Journal of Australia, 181,* 140–144.

Dierker, L., Nargiso, J., Wiseman, R., & Hoff, D. (2001). Factors predicting attrition within a community initiated system of care. *Journal of Child and Family Studies, 10,* 367–383.

Hairiri, A. (2002). Serotonin transporter genetic variation and the response of the human amygdala. *Science, 297,* 400–403.

Kernberg, P. F., Weiner, A. S., & Bardenstein, K. K. (2000). *Personality disorders in children and adolescents.* New York: Basic Books.

Kisiel, C. L., & Lyons, J. S. (2001). Dissociation as mediator of psychopathology among sexually abused children and adolescents. *American Journal of Psychiatry, 158,* 1034–1039.

Kumar, G., Pepe, D., & Steer, R. A. (2004). Adolescent psychiatric inpatients' self-reported reasons for cutting themselves. *Journal of Nervous and Mental Disease, 192,* 830–835.

Linehan, M. M. (1993a). *Cognitive-behavioral treatment of borderline personality disorder.* New York: Guilford.

Linehan, M. M. (1993b). *Skills training manual for treating borderline personality disorder.* New York: Guilford.

Lyons-Ruth, K., Holmes, B., Sasvari-Szekely, M., Ronai, Z., Nemoda, Z., & Pauls, D. (2007). Serotonin transporter polymorphism and borderline or antisocial traits among low- income young adults. *Psychiatric Genetics, 17,* 339–343.

Miller, A. L., Neft, D., & Golombeck N. (2008). Borderline personality disorder and adolescence. In P. D. Hoffman & P. Steiner-Grossman (Eds.), *Borderline personality disorder: Meeting the challenges to successful treatment* (pp. 85–98). Hawthorne, NJ: Hawthorn Press.

Miller, A. L., Rathus, J. H., & Linehan, M. M. (2007). *Dialectical behavior therapy with suicidal adolescents.* New York: Guilford.

Ohmann, S., Schuch, B., Konig, M., Blaas, S., Fliri, C., & Popow, C. (2008). Self-injurious behavior in adolescent girls: Association with psychopathology and neuropsychological functions. *Psychopathology, 41,* 226–235.

Paris, J. (2005). The development of impulsivity and suicidality in borderline personality disorder. *Development and Psychopathology, 17,* 1091–1104.

Pavaro, A., & Santonastaso, P. (1998). Impulsive and compulsive self-injurious behavior in bulimia nervosa: Prevalence and psychological correlates. *Journal of Nervous and Mental Disease, 186,* 157–165.

Ryle, A. (1997). *Cognitive analytic therapy of borderline personality disorder: The model and the method.* Chichester, UK: John Wiley.

Ryle, A. (2004). The contribution of cognitive analytic therapy to the treatment of borderline personality disorder. *Journal of Personality Disorders, 18,* 3–35.

Ryle, A., & Kerr, I. B. (2002). *Introducing cognitive analytic therapy.* Chichester, UK: John Wiley.

Skodol, A. E., Siever, L. J., Livesley, W. J., Gunderson, J. G., Pfohl, B., & Widiger, T. A. (2002). The borderline diagnosis II: Biology, genetics and clinical course. *Biological Psychiatry, 51,* 951–963.

Stanley, B., Molcho, A., & Stanley, M. (2000). Association of aggressive behavior with altered serotonergic function in patients who are not suicidal. *American Journal of Psychiatry, 157,* 609–614.

Westen, D., Shedler, J., Durrett, C., Glass, S., & Martens, A. (2003). Personality diagnoses in adolescence: *DSM-IV* Axis II diagnoses and an empirically derived alternative. *American Journal of Psychiatry, 160,* 952–966.

Winograd, G., Cohen, P., & Chen, H. (2008). Adolescent borderline symptoms in the community: Prognosis for functioning over 20 years. *Child Psychology and Psychiatry, 49,* 933–941.

Wood, A., Trainor, G., Rothwell, J., Moore, A., & Harrington, R. (2001). Randomized trial of group therapy for repeated deliberate self-harm in adolescents. *Journal of the American Academy of Child and Adolescent Psychiatry, 140,* 1246–1253.

Yates, T. M. (2004). The developmental psychopathology of self-injurious behavior: Compensatory regulation in posttraumatic adaptation. *Clinical Psychology Review, 24,* 35–74.

Ystgaard, M., Reinholdt, N. P., Husby, J., & Mehlum, L. (2003). Deliberate self-harm in adolescents. *Tidsskr Nor Laegeforen, 123,* 2241–2245.

Zanarini, M. C., Yong, L., Frankenburg, F. R., Hennen, J., Reich, D. B., Marino, M. F., et al. (2002). Severity of reported childhood sexual abuse and its relationship to severity of borderline psychopathology and psychosocial impairment among borderline inpatients. *Journal of Nervous and Mental Disease, 190,* 381–387.

Juan Hernendez

The Crash

Juan is a Hispanic adolescent who recently turned 16 years of age. Juan had returned to school a month ago after a fatal car crash. Juan had been off school for a week due to minor physical injuries sustained in the accident; however, he asked to be discharged early from the hospital to attend the funeral of his best friend, Rico. He agreed to see the school psychologist at the urging of the school guidance counselor. The counselor had been approached by several of Juan's teachers, who were concerned about his slipping grades and uncharacteristic flat demeanor.

BACKGROUND INFORMATION:
AN INTERVIEW WITH THE SCHOOL PSYCHOLOGIST

When the school psychologist met Juan for the first time, she was impressed with his manners and soft-spoken demeanor. Often, when she met adolescent males for the first time, their discomfort in seeing the "school psychologist" was evident in a defensive and guarded façade that required considerable effort to break through. But Juan was different; he seemed "approachable." The following is a sample summary of some of the most important excerpts from two interviews that occurred over the following 2 weeks (one session per week):

Session One

Psychologist: Juan, it is very nice to meet you, and I want to thank you for agreeing to see me.

Juan: Yes, Ma'am.

Psychologist: Juan, please have a seat. It is always important for me to know why you think you have been asked to see me. I want to know what you have been told about this meeting and what you believe it's all about.

Juan: Well, Ma'am, I think my teachers are concerned because I am not doing so well in classes and I think that they think that I have problems learning. You know, like special ed. kids need help. Well, because they're not as smart or maybe something like that.

Psychologist: Okay. You are having problems keeping up with your work and your grades are slipping. Is that correct?

Juan: Well, I guess. Yes, sort of. Yes.

Psychologist: And you think that your grades are not good because you might not be so smart?

Juan: Well, yes . . . no. I mean, I don't know. Like why would I be having no problems in school before and now I'm having problems. I mean I don't get it. I'm confused. I feel bad, because my teachers are good but I don't know why it's not working. I just can't concentrate. I sit in class and "space out." I don't know what has happened when I tune back in. I don't know what is going on.

Psychologist: Okay. Let's just go back a bit and try to think of when your problems concentrating started.

Juan: I don't know . . . I'm confused. Since, well since I came back, it's like different.

Psychologist: Back from what . . . like back from the accident?

Juan: Yeah . . . I guess, sort of. Yeah, from then.

Psychologist: Juan, when did the accident happen?

Juan: At night.

Psychologist: How long ago was the accident?

Juan: I'm not sure, like maybe 6 weeks.

Psychologist: Do you want to tell me about it?

Juan: Can we talk about something else? I don't want to talk about it right now.

Psychologist: Sure, what would you like to talk about?

Juan: I don't know.

Psychologist: Let's talk about the courses you are taking now, and which ones are causing you the most problems. Is that okay?

Juan: Sure. Social Studies. I was doing well in that class because the teacher is really cool and the stuff is pretty interesting. But when I was away, they talked about important stuff that she keeps referring to and I have no idea what she is talking about. And the textbook is hard to read. I mean, I start reading a page and by the time I get to the end of the page, I don't know what I read. It's like the words don't mean anything.

Psychologist: Sounds like you are having problems concentrating on what you are reading.

Juan: Yes, I guess so. I guess my mind is somewhere else. It's not on the book.

Psychologist:	Okay, I have a few suggestions. First of all, I suggest you talk to the Social Studies teacher and ask if you can meet with her so that she can fill you in on what you missed while you were away. That way, when she refers to stuff that you weren't there for, you will have a better chance of understanding what she is talking about. Does that sound right to you?
Juan:	Yes, that sounds like a good idea. I will do that today.
Psychologist:	When you are reading the text, after you read one paragraph, stop and ask yourself what you just read. Does you textbook have questions on the sidebars, or headings for each section?
Juan:	There are no questions, but there are headings.
Psychologist:	Okay. When you go to read a section, turn the heading into a question. Do you have your Social Studies book with you? Great. See here where the heading says, "The Lewis and Clark Expedition." Change that heading into a question before you read the paragraph. For example, using the heading, ask yourself, Why is the Lewis and Clark Expedition important? Then read the paragraph to find the answer. That way you will be thinking about the question while you read and it will help you concentrate better, looking for the answer. Does that make sense?
Juan:	Yes, great. That is very helpful.
Psychologist:	Okay. One more thing I would like you to do for me today. I have some questionnaires that I would like you to fill out. They are not hard. The questionnaires are about your thoughts and feelings about a number of different things, and they will help me understand how I can be most helpful to you.
Juan:	Sure, no problem.
Psychologist:	Great. Would you like to meet with me again next week?
Juan:	Okay. Yes, that's fine.
Psychologist:	All right, then, is this time still good for you?
Juan:	Yes, I have a spare period, so I won't be missing class.
Psychologist:	Okay. Let's meet here again next week and we can go over your responses to the questionnaires.

Session Two

Psychologist:	Hello, Juan. How did your week go?
Juan:	All right, I guess.
Psychologist:	Were you able to meet with your Social Studies teacher? And how did that go?
Juan:	Yes, she was very good about it and filled me in on what I missed and explained why it is important to what we are studying now. So it helped out.

Psychologist: Did you try my suggestion for reading the text, but turning headings into questions?

Juan: I did and it worked a bit, but I am still having problems reading parts where there are no headings, because I forget what the question was.

Psychologist: Are you having problems concentrating in classes, as well?

Juan: Yes. My mind just keeps wandering and then I go blank and I don't know what has gone on or where I have been. Sometimes it's a little scary. It's like I am losing whole blocks of time.

Psychologist: Okay, Juan, let's talk about the questionnaires you filled out for me. I am going to explain the results by showing you this graph. See, here is where most people's scores would fall, if they were not experiencing difficulties. See, at this level, you have scores for things like being aggressive or breaking rules. Which shows that you don't have any problems with controlling your anger, or obeying rules, because you scored in the average range in those areas. As the scores increase, it means that you answered more questions in that area, suggesting that you are experiencing more problems. Okay, let's look at how you answered questions about depression. There were a number of questions about depression on a number of the different questionnaires you filled out. And all the depression scales were high. According to what you have answered, it seems like you have a lot of feelings of sadness, not liking yourself, feeling guilty and feeling bad like things are always happening to you. You say that you have thought about killing yourself, but you would not do it. Is that how you really feel?

Juan: Yeah, it's pretty bad. I wouldn't kill myself because that would be very bad for my parents and I wouldn't do that to them. This was bad enough.

Psychologist: You also say that you don't have any friends. I thought you were part of a group?

Juan: That was before the accident; now they all blame me. No one talks to me anymore and they all say it was me who killed Rico. I walk in a room and they all stop talking and just stare at me. It's like I am not even there. Like a ghost. You know, a couple of nights ago, I had this dream and Rico was in it and he was in my house drinking milk out of the milk carton in the fridge. He would always do that and it would make my mom so mad, but this time we were all laughing about it. He looks so real it was like he was still alive. I miss him so much; we were like brothers; we went everywhere together. I spent more time at his house than I did at my own. And now his family won't speak to me either, because they say I killed their son. My parents and Rico's parents used to be good friends and now no one is talking to no one. I can hear the crash in my head. I can see Rico's face just before the truck hit us. I tried to swerve but the road was wet and we skidded right into the truck. I turned the wheel. That's why Rico is dead. If I didn't turn the wheel, he would be alive. It should have been me who was killed.

Psychologist: Juan, it was not your fault, it was an accident.

Juan: Yeah, tell that to the police. The police are still going over the evidence, but they say I was speeding, which caused the car to go out of control. I still might get arrested for manslaughter and maybe have to go to jail.

Psychologist:	Juan, do you have a lawyer?
Juan:	I don't know; my dad was going to see what he can do. We don't have much money.
Psychologist:	Juan, would you like me to speak to the school social worker for you? She does a lot of work with the Juvenile Detention Center. Maybe she could find out some information for you.
Juan:	Yes, that would be great because it's like I have no future. I can't plan for a future because I don't know if I will be here or in jail.
Psychologist:	I will contact her as soon as we are done today. Were you hurt in the accident?
Juan:	I just had a cracked rib. I left the hospital early because I wanted to go to the funeral. It was so horrible; they were all crying. He was so dead, and I was not. And I didn't even look like I was hurt.
Psychologist:	Tell me what you do when you go home from school. Do you have problems sleeping? Are you involved in any activities?
Juan:	No, I don't sleep well. I feel tired but I'm all edgy too, and so if I fall asleep, I wake up a lot. I don't know what I do. I go home and turn on the TV, but I don't even know what I am watching half the time. I don't go out with friends because they just remind me of Rico and so I just stay here. Sometimes I feel like a zombie, you know, like I am going through the motions but nobody is home. It's like nothing is real, it is all a dream. Like I am going away in my mind, but I am still here. It doesn't make sense to me. It's like my mind has gone blank.
Psychologist:	Juan, what you are describing are a lot of symptoms of posttraumatic stress disorder (PTSD) and a dissociative state that sometimes accompanies it. That is the sense of feeling that things are "surreal," or a kind of emotional numbing that often takes place. I am going to recommend a number of things for you, including a visit to your family physician to discuss your problems sleeping. With your permission and that of your parents, I would also like to write a report summarizing our talks and the results of your responses to the questionnaires and send a copy to your physician to see if he can arrange a referral for you to get counseling for issues related to grief and PTSD, since we are going into summer break and my services will not be available over the summer. How do you feel about that?
Juan:	Yes, that would be good.
Psychologist:	And I will get in touch with the social worker now and ask her to find out what the status is of the police report on the accident, and if she can meet with us next week, if she is available. How does that sound?
Juan:	Thank you, that would be very good.

ASSESSMENT RESULTS

Information regarding specific assessment instruments and guidelines for the interpretation of T scores are available in Appendix C.

Juan responded to several rating scales provided by the school psychologist, including Youth Self Report (YSR), the Child Depression Inventory (CDI), the Revised Children's Manifest Anxiety Scale (RCMAS-2), and the Trauma Symptom Checklist for Children (TSCC-A). Responses indicated significant elevation on scales for depression on the CDI, including Overall Depression (T = 80), Negative Mood (T = 78), Ineffectiveness (T = 80), Anhedonia (T = 72), and Negative Self-Esteem (T = 70). On RCMAS-2, Juan has significant elevations on the scales for Physiological Anxiety (T = 85) and Worry (T = 70). Scores on the YSR were clinically significant for anxious/depressed (T= 74), withdrawn/depressed (T = 72), thought problems (T = 68), and attention problems (T = 68). In addition to elevated scores for anxiety and depression on the TSCC-A, Juan also revealed clinically significant ratings for posttraumatic stress (PTS) and dissociation (DIS). On the PTS scale, Juan endorsed such items as having "bad dreams or nightmares" and "remembering scary things," while on the DIS scale he responded that he experienced "feeling like I am not in my body," "feeling dizzy," "feeling like things aren't real," "going away in my mind," "forgetting things," "my mind going blank," and "daydreaming," all occurring on a frequent basis.

ISSUES, TRENDS, AND TREATMENT ALTERNATIVES

PTSD was initially introduced as a formal diagnosis in the *DSM-III* (APA, 1980). In the following revision (*DSM-III-R;* APA, 1987), the diagnosis of PTSD was extended to apply to children and youth. There is controversy in the field regarding how the disorder should be diagnosed in children and youth, since the *DSM* has largely adhered to adult criteria. The *DSM-III-R* included only two minor alterations to account for child patterns, including adding "repetitive play" as a possible cluster-B criterion of *reexperiencing,* and "loss of acquired developmental skills" as a symptom under cluster-C *avoidance and numbing.* Since that time, "loss of acquired developmental skills" has been removed as a criterion, and the *DSM-IV* has added one additional child criterion for cluster A, suggesting that responses to the trauma of intense fear, horror, and helplessness that occurs in adults may appear as "disorganized or agitated behavior" in children and youth, and added two criteria to cluster B (reexperiencing) to include "frightening dreams" and "trauma-specific reenactment" in children. The current version, the *DSM-IV-TR* (APA, 2000), has retained the above criteria, but nothing more has been added.

The *DSM-IV-TR* currently requires six symptoms in addition to the experience of a traumatic event, which many clinicians feel is excessive, especially since many of the symptoms require verbal descriptions, which may be beyond a child's capacity. Scheeringa, Zeanah, Drell, and Larrieu (1995) have suggested a new cluster of symptoms that may be more developmentally appropriate called "new fear and aggression," of which only one symptom is necessary. The symptoms that fall within this cluster would include new aggression, new separation anxiety, fear of toilet training alone, fear of the dark, and any new fears of events or things not directly related to the trauma. Scheeringa and colleagues (1995) also are in favor of removing the need for required impairment in social or occupational functioning. According to the system suggested by Scheeringa and colleagues (1995), only four symptoms would be required, in addition to trauma, two less than would be required by the *DSM.* While some are in agreement, others feel that this system may be too lenient, resulting in a number of false positives (Perrin, Smith, & Yule, 2004). In the interim, Perrin and colleagues (2004) suggest that the *International Classification of Diseases (ICD-10;* WHO, 1992) might provide a better clinical description of PTSD for children and youth with its emphasis on characteristic symptoms of "repetitive and intrusive memories" and "conspicuous emotional detachment, numbing of feeling, and avoidance of stimuli that might arouse recollections of the trauma are often present but are not essential for the diagnosis" (WHO, 1992, p. 148).

There is debate about whether unique criteria should be established for children and youth to reflect developmental differences in how reactions to traumatic events or posttraumatic stress symptoms (PSS) may be perceived, interpreted, recalled, and expressed (Scheeringa, Zeanah, Myers, & Putman, 2003). Although a number of PSS might be generic across the life span, such as general reactions to distress, nightmares, and fears (Silverman & La Greca, 2002), there are PSS that have been found to be more typical for children and youth, such as repetitive trauma play, dreams of monsters or rescue, regressive behavior, separation anxiety, somatic problems (headaches and stomachaches), and declines in academic performance (AACAP, 1998; Drake, Bush, & van Gorp, 2001; *DSM-IV-TR,* APA, 2000). In addition, following Terr's (1991) model, there is still debate on how to assess the relative exposure to trauma in children who have been exposed to a single traumatic event (Type I), versus exposure to a series of traumatic events or a stressor that is ongoing over a long period of time (Type II). In addition, little is known about how PTSD might be expressed by youth from different ethnic backgrounds, since different cultures have different ways of responding to emotionally charged events and expressing emotions (Cooley & Boyce, 2004). Although there have been increasing attempts to develop measures for assessing PTSD and PSS in children and youth, there is less consensus on how these measures either increase our understanding of the disorder in children or how they can inform treatment (Lonigan, Phillips, & Richey, 2003). Although most evaluations of children involve a test battery composed of a variety of assessments and involving multiple informants, in cases of PTSD there is evidence of low agreement between parent and child reports of PSS (Jensen et al., 1999), and that child self-reports may actually be more accurate (Korol, Green, & Gleser, 1999) and provide more reliable information regarding their emotional and physiological arousal levels (internal states) than other informants who rely on their observations of the child (Vogel & Vernberg, 1993). Hawkins and Radcliffe (2006) reviewed 65 articles to identify current methods of identifying PTSD and PSS in children and youth. They reported finding seven measures, including clinician-administered interviews and self-report questionnaires, which they were able to further categorize into eight trauma domains. However, Hawkins and Radcliffe (2006) found little consensus regarding the measures used within each trauma domain.

Estimates of prevalence rates vary due to the wide variety of different measures used to evaluate the nature of youth reactions to possible traumatic stressors and depending on whether populations sampled are clinical or community samples. Studies have established that youth can develop PTSD symptoms to a wide variety of traumatic stressors (Brown, Madan-Swain, & Lambert, 2003), with severity of symptoms related to the intensity of exposure (Cooley-Quille, Boyd, Frantz, & Walsh, 2001); physical proximity to the event (Pynoos, 1994); or vicarious exposure (Horowitz, Weine, & Jekel, 1995), such as observing traumatic events on television (Huesmann, Moise-Titus & Podolski 2003) or living in a war zone (Laor, Wolmer, & Cohen, 2001). In addition to location and type, the number of exposures can also influence the severity of PTSD (Allwood, Bell-Dolan, & Husain, 2002). Elklit (2002) reports a lifetime prevalence of PTSD in nonclinical samples of youth to be between 5% and 10%, with girls reporting more episodes of traumatic events than boys, and with between 25% and 87% of all youth reporting exposure to at least one traumatic event prior to 20 years of age.

Posttraumatic stress disorder (PTSD) can occur with mild to severe symptoms of dissociation. In their study of children with PTSD due to sexual abuse, Kaplow, Hall, Koenen, Dodge, and

Amaya-Jackson (2008) found that children who were sexually abused earlier in life had higher levels of PTSD symptoms when the abuse was disclosed. However, they also found that symptoms of dissociation were predictive of later attention problems in this population. It is possible that that the strong links between attention problems and PTSD that have been found in adults (e.g., Bremner, Krystal, Southwick, & Charney, 1995) and children (Merry & Andrews, 1994; Saigh, Mroueh, & Bremner, 1997) may be mediated by dissociative symptoms. Dissociation has been found to interfere directly with children's perception of their environment and their integration and processing of incoming information, resulting in problems with attention and concentration (Putnam, 1997). The main center for connectivity between the two hemispheres of the brain is located in the corpus collosum, which is responsible for facilitating and integrating information between the two hemispheres (Ramaekers & Njiokiktjien, 1991). Individuals who experience dissociative symptoms reveal lower levels of "connectivity" in the corpus collosum (De Bellis, 2001), which may result in fragmented information processing and increased attention problems. As a result of their findings, Kaplow and colleagues (2008) suggest that as far as PTSD and attention problems are concerned, it may be the accompanying dissociative symptoms, which are so often comorbid with PTSD, that actually are responsible for this relationship.

Studies have found that increased levels of distress post trauma are associated with increased severity of later PTSD (DiGallo, Barton & Parry-Jones, 1997). Increased risk for more severe PTSD has also been associated with symptoms of mental confusion, negative self-appraisal of symptoms, avoidance, and dissociation (Ehlers, Mayou, & Bryant, 2003). Having a parent who has a tendency toward avoidant behaviors has been associated with increased PTSD reactions in children involved in motor vehicle accidents (Ehlers et al., 2001).

Treatment Alternatives

The cognitive-behavioral explanation of PTSD considers that the thoughts and behaviors that result from exposure to the traumatic event are normal responses to catastrophic and life-threatening circumstances; however, the persistence of these responses after the fact and their generalization to nonthreatening events become maladaptive. Theoretically, within the context of a classical conditioning paradigm, the unconditional responses to the trauma (unconditional stimuli), such as increased autonomic arousal (fight-or-flight responses), startle response, fear, and numbing, begin to be elicited by previously neutral stimuli in the environment that have been conditioned by association to the traumatic event. As a result, numerous stimuli in the environment now can act as triggers to memories and feelings associated with the trauma (reexperiencing and increased arousal). Attempts to avoid exposure to the conditioned stimuli result in avoidance and escape responses, which become negatively reinforced because they remove the individual from the stressor (numbing and avoidance).

Empirical support for the effectiveness of cognitive-behavioral therapy (CBT) with adults has been well documented (Olasov-Rothbaum, Meadows, Resick, & Foy, 2000). Studies of CBT with sexually abused children have found group CBT to be superior to traditional group therapy (Deblinger, Steer, & Lippman, 1999) while Cohen and Mannarino (1997) found that CBT was superior to nondirective therapy.

Geonjian and colleagues (1997) found treatment with CBT to be superior to no treatment for children exposed to an earthquake in Armenia, while March, Amaya-Jackson, Murray, and Schulte (1998) found an 18-week group-administered CBT program to be effective for the majority of children and youth treated for a single-incident trauma.

Feeny, Foa, Treadwell, and March (2004) conducted a meta-analysis concerning treatment programs for children and youth with PTSD and PSS, and found a number of programs that employed cognitive-behavioral methods (CBT) using a variety of different techniques, including exposure treatments, eye-movement desensitization and reprocessing (EMDR), anxiety-management training (AMT), and group treatments.

Exposure Treatments. Applying exposure treatment programs to fears that accompany PTSD can be a very successful method of alleviating fears and anxiety in adults (Olasov-Rothbaum et al., 2000). Perrin and colleagues (2004) describe several methods for adapting exposure techniques for children and youth. Each of the programs evolves around a three-step program originally called *systematic desensitization.* The following example will illustrate how systematic desensitization could be used to treat a fear of dogs, after a child was bitten on the hand by the neighbor's pet:

1. The creation of a fear hierarchy (rating the level of anxiety associated with the fear, in this case the dog) and training in the use of the *SUDS scale* (subjective units of distress), which involves levels of anxiety or distress (from calm to very nervous and scared, e.g., scale of 1–10)
2. Training in relaxation techniques
3. Pairing of relaxation with fear response at each step in the fear hierarchy

Applying systematic desensitization to a fear of dogs would involve establishing a fear hierarchy. With the help of the SUDs scale, the therapist and child construct a fear hierarchy involving a number of steps. For example, if seven steps are selected, and the therapist and child identify "petting a dog" as the SUD that causes an absolute 10 on a scale of 1–10, then the therapist will place "petting a dog" as the highest step in the hierarchy and work down from there. Based on a number of dog-related items reviewed with the child, the therapist comes up with the following fear hierarchy:

1. Story about a dog
2. Stuffed toy dog
3. Picture of a dog
4. Film of a dog
5. Proximity to dog in a cage
6. Proximity to dog in the room
7. Petting the dog

As the therapist proceeds through each level on the hierarchy, she will ask the child to describe the SUD level and apply the relaxation techniques until the SUD is close to zero. At that point, the therapist can go to the next step, repeating the process until eventually the child reaches the final level and is no longer fearful or anxious about petting a dog.

The procedure as outlined can occur in two different ways: *imaginal exposure* or *in vivo exposure.*

Imaginal procedures are those that are indirect, with the child imagining the situation without actually going through it in real life. In vivo exposure would be going through each step as it actually occurs in real life. Although some situations lend themselves better to imaginal procedures, in vivo exposure techniques are more effective.

Eye-Movement Desensitization and Reprocessing (EMDR). Because this technique is similar to flooding and exposure techniques, it can also be grouped under CBT types of interventions. The technique (Shapiro, 1995) is controversial and involves engaging the client in rapid eye movements (tracking a back-and-forth target, e.g., the therapist's hand or fingers moving rapidly back and forth) while thinking about a traumatic memory. Although empirical support is limited, at least one study has demonstrated success for children exposed to a hurricane (Chemtob, Nakashima, & Carlson, 2002).

Anxiety-Management Training (AMT). AMT (Meichenbaum, 2007) is a program that uses reframing or cognitive restructuring (CR) to replace negative thought patterns with more positive alternatives. Farrell, Hains, & Davies (1997) found AMT was a successful component in their program for sexually abused children, while Perrin and colleagues (2004) suggest that CR can be an effective technique for dealing with responsibility (the accident was my fault), guilt (especially survivor guilt), and shame resulting from exposure to traumatic events. Perrin and colleagues also suggest that CR can assist in addressing magical thinking or omen formation (I just knew it would happen) and heightened sense of arousal and danger associated with the event (fear of going into a car after a crash).

Post-Case Questions

1. Would Juan qualify for a diagnosis of PTSD according to the *DSM-IV-TR?* If so, what symptoms does he have that would meet the *DSM* criteria? What symptoms does he not exhibit that you would expect to see? How might you explain the lack of symptoms?

2. Culturally, do you think that Juan's Hispanic background makes his situation better or worse than if he were from a different culture? What does the research say about culture and emotional expression?

3. Based on Juan's symptoms, develop a CBT program using cognitive restructuring (CR) to assist him in reducing his feelings of self-blame and survivor guilt. If Juan were fearful of getting behind the wheel and driving again, develop a systematic desensitization program that would help him regain his confidence about driving again.

REFERENCES

AACAP Official Action: Practice Parameters. (1998). Practice parameters for the assessment and treatment of children and adolescents with posttraumatic stress disorder. *Journal of the American Academy of Child and Adolescent Psychiatry, 37,* 4S–26S.

Allwood, M. A., Bell-Dolan, D., & Husain, S. A. (2002). Children's trauma and adjustment reactions to violent and nonviolent war experiences. *Journal of the American Academy of Child and Adolescent Psychiatry, 41,* 450–457.

American Psychiatric Association (APA). (1980). *Diagnostic and statistical manual of mental disorders* (3rd ed.) Washington, DC: Author.

American Psychiatric Association (APA). (1987). *Diagnostic and statistical manual of mental disorders* (3rd ed., rev.). Washington, DC: Author.

American Psychiatric Association (APA). (2000). *Diagnostic and statistical manual of mental disorders* (4th ed., text revision). Washington, DC: Author.

Bremner, J. D., Krystal, J. H., Southwick, S. M., & Charney, D. S. (1995). Functional neuroanatomical correlates of the effects of stress on memory. *Journal of Traumatic Stress, 8,* 527–553.

Brown, R. T., Madan-Swain, A., & Lambert, R. (2003). Posttraumatic stress symptoms in adolescent survivors of childhood cancer and their mothers. *Journal of Traumatic Stress, 16,* 309–318.

Chemtob, C. M., Nakashima, J., & Carlson, J. (2002). Brief treatment for elementary school children with disaster-related posttraumatic stress disorder: A field study. *Journal of Clinical Psychology, 58*(1), 99–112.

Cohen, J. A., & Mannarino, A. P. (1997). A treatment study for sexually abused children: Outcome during a one-year follow-up. *Journal of the American Academy of Child and Adolescent Psychiatry, 36,* 1228–1235.

Cooley, M. R., & Boyce, C. A. (2004). An introduction to assessing anxiety in child and adolescent multiethnic populations: Challenges and opportunities for enhancing knowledge and practice. *Journal of Clinical Child and Adolescent Psychology, 33,* 210–215.

Cooley-Quille, M., Boyd, R. C., Frantz, E., & Walsh, J. (2001). Emotional and behavioral impact of exposure to community violence in inner-city adolescents. *Journal of Clinical Child Psychology, 30,* 199–206.

De Bellis, M. D. (2001). Developmental traumatology: The psychobiological development of maltreated children and its implications for research, treatment, and policy. *Development and Psychopathology, 13,* 539–564.

Deblinger, E., Steer, R. A., & Lippmann, J. (1999). Two-year follow-up study of cognitive behavioral therapy for sexually abused children suffering post-traumatic stress symptoms. *Child Abuse and Neglect, 23,* 1371–1378.

DiGallo, A., Barton, J. M, & Parry-Jones, G. (1997). Road traffic accidents: Early psychological consequences in children and adolescents. *British Journal of Psychiatry, 170,* 358–362.

Drake, E. B., Bush, S. F., & van Gorp, W. G. (2001). Evaluation and assessment of PTSD in children and adolescents. In E. Spencer (Ed.), *PTSD in children and adolescents* (pp. 1–31). Washington, DC: American Psychiatric Publishing.

Ehlers, A., Mayou, R. A., & Bryant, B. (2003). Cognitive predictors of posttraumatic stress disorder in children: Results of a prospective longitudinal study. *Behaviour Research and Therapy, 1,* 1–11.

Elklit, A. (2002). Victimization and PTSD in a Danish national youth probability sample. *Journal of the American Academy of Child and Adolescent Psychiatry, 41,* 174–181.

Farrell, S., Hains, A., & Davies, W. (1998). Cognitive behavioral interventions for sexually abused children. *Behavior Therapy, 29,* 241–256.

Feeny, N., Foa, E. B., Treadwell, K. R. H., & March, J. (2004). Posttraumatic stress disorder in youth: A critical review of the cognitive and behavioral treatment outcome literature. *Professional Psychology: Research and Practice, 35,* 466–476.

Goenjian, A. K., Karayan, I., Pynoos, R., Steinberg, A., Najarian, I., Asarnow, J., et al. (1997). Outcome of psychotherapy among early adolescents after trauma. *American Journal of Psychiatry, 154,* 536–542.

Hawkins, S. S., & Radcliffe, J. (2006). Current measures of PTSD for children and adolescents. *Journal of Pediatric Psychology, 31*(4), 420–430.

Horowitz, K., Weine, S., & Jekel. J. (1995). PTSD symptoms in urban adolescent girls: Compounded community trauma. *Journal of the American Academy of Child and Adolescent Psychiatry, 34,* 1353–1361.

Huesmann, L. R., Moise-Titus, J., & Podolski, C. (2003). Longitudinal relations between children's exposure to TV violence and their aggressive and violent behavior in young adulthood: 1977–1992. *Developmental Psychology, 39*(2), 201–221.

Jensen, P. S., Rubio-Stipec, M., Canino, G., Bird, H. R., Dulcan, M. K., Schwab-Stone, M. E., et al. (1999). Parent and child contributions to diagnosis of mental disorder: Are both informants always necessary? *Journal of the American Academy of Child and Adolescent Psychiatry, 38,* 1569–1579.

Kaplow, J. B., Hall, E., Koenen, K. C., Dodge, K. A., & Amaya-Jackson, L. (2008). Dissociation predicts later attention problems in sexually abused children. *Child Abuse and Neglect, 32*(2), 261–275.

Korol, M., Green, B. L., & Gleser, G. C. (1999). Children's responses to a nuclear waste disaster: PTSD symptoms and outcome prediction. *Journal of the American Academy of Child and Adolescent Psychiatry, 38,* 368–375.

Laor, N., Wolmer, L., & Cohen, D. (2001). Mothers' functioning and children's symptoms 5 years after a SCUD missile attack. *American Journal of Psychiatry, 158*(7), 1020–1026.

Lonigan, C. J., Phillips, B. M., & Richey, J. A. (2003). Posttraumatic stress disorder in children: Diagnosis, assessment, and associated features. *Child and Adolescent Psychiatric Clinics of North America, 12,* 171–194.

March, J. S., Amaya-Jackson, L., Murray, M. C., & Schulte, A. (1998). Cognitive-behavioral psychotherapy for children and adolescents with posttraumatic stress disorder after a single-incident stressor. *Journal of the American Academy of Child and Adolescent Psychiatry, 37,* 585–593.

Meichenbaum, D. H. (2007). Stress inoculation training: A 20-year update. In P. M. Lehrer, R. L. Woolfolk, & W. E. Sime (Eds.), *Principles and practice of stress management* (3rd ed., pp. 497–516). New York: Guilford.

Merry, S. N., & Andrews, L. K. (1994). Psychiatric status of sexually abused children 12 months after disclosure of abuse. *Journal of the American Academy of Child and Adolescent Psychiatry, 33*(7), 939–944.

Olasov-Rothbaum, B., Meadows, E. A., Resick, P., & Foy, D. W. (2000). Cognitive-behavioral therapy. In E. Foa, T. Keane, & M. Friedman (Eds.), *Effective treatments for PTSD: Practice guidelines from the International Society for Traumatic Stress Studies* (pp. 60–83). New York: Guilford.

Perrin, S., Smith, P., & Yule, W. (2004). Treatment of PTSD in children and adolescents. In P. M. Barrett & T. H. Ollendick (Eds), *Handbook of interventions that work with children and adolescents* (pp. 217–242). Chichester, UK: John Wiley.

Putnam, F. W. (1997). *Dissociation in children and adolescents: A developmental perspective.* New York: Guilford.

Pynoos, R. S. (1994). Traumatic stress and developmental psychopathology in children and adolescents. In R. S. Pynoos (Ed.), *Posttraumatic stress disorder: A clinical review* (pp. 64–98). Lutherville, MD: Sidran Press.

Ramaekers, G., & Njiokiktjien, C. (1991). *The child's corpus callosum.* Amsterdam: Suyi Publications.

Saigh, P. A., Mroueh, M. N., & Bremner, J. D. (1997). Scholastic impairments among traumatized adolescents. *Behaviour Research and Therapy, 35*(5), 429–436.

Scheeringa, M. S., Zeanah, C. H., Drell, M. J., & Larrieu, J. A. (1995). Two approaches to diagnosing posttraumataic stress disorder in infancy and early childhood. *Journal of the American Academy of Child and Adolescent Psychiatry, 34,* 191–200.

Scheeringa, M. S., Zeanah, C. H., Myers, L., & Putman, F. W. (2003). New findings on alternative criteria for PTSD in preschool children. *Journal of the American Academy of Child and Adolescent Psychiatry, 42,* 561–570.

Shapiro, F. (1995). *Eye movement desensitization and reprocessing: Basic principles, protocols, and procedures.* New York: Guilford.

Silverman, W. K., & La Greca, A. M. (2002). Children experiencing disasters: Definitions, reactions, and predictors of outcomes. In A. M. La Greca, W. K. Silverman, E. M. Vernberg, & M. C. Roberts (Eds.), *Helping children cope with disasters and terrorism* (pp. 11–33). Washington, DC: American Psychological Association.

Terr, L. (1991). Childhood traumas: An outline and overview. *American Journal of Psychiatry, 148,* 10–20.

Vogel, J. M., & Vernberg, E. M. (1993). Children's psychological responses to disasters. *Journal of Clinical Child Psychology, 22,* 464–484.

WHO. (1992). *International classification of diseases* (10th rev. ed.). Geneva: World Health Organization.

Tyrone Wilson

The Gang's All Here

Tyrone Wilson, 15 years of age, is an African American youth who is the older brother of Neesha Wilson (see Case of Neesha Wilson). Although the two siblings were brought up under somewhat similar circumstances, there was a significant difference in the outcomes for the two children. While Neesha's story is one of resilience, Tyrone suffered through significant challenges that have escalated out of control since his father left the family 3 years ago.

DEVELOPMENTAL HISTORY/FAMILY BACKGROUND

Tyrone lives with his 10-year-old sister, Neesha, and their mother in a two-bedroom apartment. The apartment is small but very well kept. Tyrone sleeps on the couch, which folds out into a bed. Tyrone's mother is currently working two jobs: cleaning offices and working as a hairstylist. Mrs. Wilson graduated from hairstylist classes last year. Although her career as a hairstylist has a lot of potential, she is only beginning to develop clientele. She also works part time cleaning offices. Despite the lack of financial resources, the children are clean and adequately fed. Mother admits to drinking more than she should have when she was pregnant with Tyrone. She said,

> You know you read about it a lot now, but when I was growing up, I mean I was 19 when I got pregnant with Tyrone, I just became legal drinking age, and it was time to party. I was done with high school and I was taking some community college courses and working part time at the deli. Their dad was a mechanic and he worked hard and long hours. When we were done with working, like we just were ready to let loose.

When asked how much she drank during her pregnancy, Mrs. Wilson said there wasn't a night that she didn't drink probably one or two beers, plus a couple of glasses of wine. She stated that she did not do any drugs whatsoever during her pregnancy. When she conceived Neesha, she was more mature and had heard more about drinking and pregnancy, so she did not drink while pregnant with Neesha. Tanya stated that although there are some nights that she is not home because she may be working, she is not too concerned about the children since she has family nearby. She can send the children to her sister's place a few blocks away, or if they do not want to go, they can stay home, since she also has a cousin who lives in the apartment complex, who can drop by if the children need something. Also, Tyrone is old enough to babysit his sister; however, given his behavior problems, she prefers to have an adult nearby.

When asked about Tyrone's developmental milestones, Tanya said that he seemed to start out on the wrong foot. She said that she and her husband were not great parents, because they were so young and immature and Tyrone was a difficult child to manage. Tanya said that Tyrone was an agitated infant and did not eat or sleep well. He was a late talker but was walking by 14 months. He was a difficult child to potty train since it seemed to take forever for him to make the connection. He was also an impulsive child, and still is, which can get him into trouble, since he often acts without thinking. He also does not seem to learn from past mistakes and will do the same thing over again, even if he was punished for it previously.

He managed to have some academic success when enrolled in special education, but he continually would get into trouble for not obeying the rules. His mother feels that part of his disability is that he cannot understand rules, but the school did not agree. Tanya felt that punishments at school for rule violations (in-school suspensions, after-school detentions, being kept in at recess, etc.) resulted in Tyrone becoming more resentful and anxious about school. Social skills were also poor, and Tyrone experienced problems being accepted by the other children and was often isolated as a result. She said that she began to feel guilty because Tyrone was having so many problems, so after trying a few different schools, she decided to try homeschooling, which would also allow her to stay home with Neesha, who was then 4 years of age, and she would not have to pay for day care. But eventually, Neesha was ready for school and Tanya felt it was unfair to Neesha to hold her back from a normal school experience, so they enrolled Tyrone back into the school system. At this time, Tyrone was almost 11 years of age and the school recommended an updated assessment, since Tyrone had not had an evaluation since he was 6 years of age. Results of the assessment at that time revealed intellectual functioning in the below average range (full scale IQ was 84, range 80–89), with scores for the Perceptual Reasoning Index in the average range (PRI = 93, range 87–100) and much higher than Verbal Comprehension (VCI = 80, range 74–89). The Similarities subtest, which measures abstract reasoning, was very challenging for Tyrone. A severe problem was noted in speed of processing, likely due to poor eye-hand coordination and deficits in short-term visual memory. Academically, Tyrone was functioning at approximately a mid–Grade 4 level in reading and written expression (approximately 1 ½ years below the expected level) and almost 2 ½ years below the expected level in mathematics. Problem solving was especially weak, and Tyrone did not know which numbers were relevant to the questions and which were not needed to solve the problem. Based on his assessment results, it was recommended that Tyrone receive special education assistance to assist in meeting his educational goals.

Initially, Tyrone seemed to improve his academic skills with the resource room help. However, after his father left, Tyrone became very unsettled and started to experience more problems socially and academically. He was suspended for fighting, and when the suspension was lifted, he immediately got into another fight and was placed in an alternative school program for students with severe behavioral problems.

At home, Tyrone was getting more and more difficult to control. When his mother worked nights, he would stay out until 3:00 or 4:00 a.m. and leave his sister Neesha alone. On these occasions, he would threaten to make Neesha's life miserable if she told her mom that he was not home. On the nights that Tanya was not working, she would often go to bed early. She said that she was fatigued and just needed to sleep a lot. This also gave Tyrone more freedom to come and go at all hours of the night. One night, when Tyrone eventually arrived home, he was very badly beaten. He would not tell his mother, but this was the night he was "beaten down" as part of his initiation into the gang. That was the night that he was "jumped in," which is the term used for the rite of passage for new male gang members who gain entry into the gang by being beaten up by their brothers. It wasn't so bad, Tyrone thought, since afterward, all the gang members hugged him. This was his new family. For Tyrone, joining the gang would give him protection on the streets and the respect he was looking for. However, it also opened the door to drugs and crime. Tyrone started hanging out on the streets and getting involved in petty theft (stealing bikes for parts), and by 14 he was regularly smoking marijuana and drinking beer on a daily basis.

REASON FOR REFERRAL

Currently, Tyrone is in detention following his recent arrest for robbery and assault with a weapon. He and two of his gang members were arrested as they confronted and threatened two youth with knives, as they were waiting for a bus. Tyrone was especially belligerent and aggressive during the incident, wielding his knife in the air and shouting lyrics from "gangsta" rap music.

The detention center is a short-term, secure facility, sometimes called a *youth jail,* where a youth may be held "during the processing and disposition of the youth's legal case for the purposes of evaluation or placement if a secure environment is deemed necessary" (AACAP, 2004, p. 2). The judge had ordered an assessment to determine the nature of Tyrone's difficulties and to assist in determining an appropriate placement (e.g., juvenile correctional facility, community-based or other residential treatment program, etc.).

ASSESSMENT RESULTS

Forensic Assessments Versus More Traditional Psychological Assessments

Forensic assessments differ from the more conventional psychological assessments that have been discussed in this book in several ways. Traditional psychological assessments are conducted for a variety of reasons (e.g., to evaluate educational or occupational aptitudes or investigate mental health concerns) and may include assessments of intelligence (learning capacity), achievement (academic performance), cognitive or neuropsychological functioning (information processing, brain-based functioning, executive functions), personality assessment (traits and personal style), and emotional or behavioral status (mood disorders, anxiety, etc.). However, forensic assessments are more likely to be conducted to address questions of *competency* on two levels:

1. Is the individual competent to stand trial (Is the individual competent at the *time of the trial*)?

2. Was the individual competent at the *time of the crime* (which addresses issues of criminal responsibility)?

In the former situation, three areas of competency are considered to determine whether the individual is mentally competent to stand trial: does the defendant understand the charges; does the defendant understand the seriousness of the potential outcomes of the trial; and is the defendant capable of assisting in his or her own defense? Regarding whether the individual was competent at the time of the crime, experts would be called in to provide opinions as to whether the defendant was suffering from diminished capacity because of a mental or emotional disorder that interfered with the ability to distinguish right from wrong.

Forensic assessments may also investigate whether an individual is *malingering,* or pretending to be more incapacitated (competency or mental illness), in order to obtain a lesser penalty. Other questions that forensic assessments may address include determining the risk of recidivism (repeat offending), or providing information about the psychological factors that may be contributing to the maladaptive and criminal behavior.

In addition to differences in the types of assessment instruments that may be used and the general goals of the assessment, forensic assessment also differs in the nature of the psychologist (mental health practitioner)/client relationship. While most children and adolescents are referred for assessment by concerned parents and teachers, forensic assessments are conducted to answer forensic questions and, as a result, clients are often mandated to participate in the process by the authorities. Therefore, rather than developing a therapeutic relationship, the psychologist is required to remain neutral.

Assessment Findings

Information regarding specific assessment instruments and guidance in the interpretation of standard scores and T scores can be found in Appendix C.

The forensic psychologist reviewed Tyrone's file and noted his developmental history, especially the information regarding his mother's drinking habits during the pregnancy. The psychologist also reviewed the intellectual assessment information noting intellectual delays in language functions, relative to average scores for perceptual reasoning. The need for special education assistance was also noted, especially for significant difficulties with mathematics. There were indications that behavior problems have been ongoing, with poor ability to profit from prior experiences, and weak social skills, making him vulnerable to gang recruitment and involvement in crime and drug usage.

In order to answer a number of forensic questions, the psychologist administered a battery of tests, including the Structured Assessment of Violence Risk in Youth (SAVRY), the

Jesness Inventory Revised (JI-R), the Vineland Adaptive Behavior Scales, and the Behavior Rating Inventory of Executive Function (BRIEF). A summary of *historical risk factors* from the SAVRY included history of nonviolent offending and poor school achievement. *Social contextual risk factors* were significant with many items endorsed, including peer delinquency, peer rejection, stress and poor coping, poor parental management, lack of personal/social support, and community disorganization. Individual risk factors on this instrument were highly significant, as Tyrone matched many of the high-risk items, including negative attitudes, risk taking/impulsivity, substance-use difficulties, anger-management problems, low empathy/remorse, attention-deficit/hyperactivity difficulties, poor compliance/commitment to school. Unfortunately, significant problems indicated by personal risk factors were not offset by any protective factors that could buffer the harmful effects posed by the risk factors.

On the JI-R, the *DSM-IV* subscales of Conduct Disorder and Oppositional Defiant Disorder were both clinically significant. In addition, Tyrone had high clinical loadings on the Personality scales for social maladjustment, immaturity, alienation, asocial index, manifest aggression, and withdrawal. He also endorsed significant items on scales measuring depression, social anxiety, and denial. On the subtype scales, Tyrone's responses placed him in the clinical range for the following subscales: aggressive/undersocialized and conformist/immature. The Vineland Adaptive Behavior Scales were completed by Tyrone's mother, and according to her responses, Tyrone obtained the following standard scores: Communication Skills, 80; Daily Living Skills, 80; and Socialization Skills, 75. Therefore, adaptive behavior was below the norm for all areas assessed, and especially poor in the area of social competence.

On the BRIEF, the subscales of the Metacognitive Index (MI) were significant for deficits in areas of working memory, self-monitoring, and organization/planning ability. On the Behavioral Regulation Index (BRI), significant problems were evident in his ability to inhibit responses, in his ability to shift attention between tasks, and in the area of emotional control.

The psychologist noted that although Tyrone did not have any of the physical features often associated with fetal alcohol syndrome (FAS), such as dysmorphic facial features or microcephaly, he did exhibit a number of abnormalities often associated with fetal alcohol effects (FAE), including small stature, delays in motor and speech performance, poor coordination, and impulsive/hyperactive behaviors. Also, his poor social skills and inability to consider the consequences of his behaviors are characteristics that often can make youth with FAE vulnerable to gang recruitment and having eventual problems with the law.

ISSUES, TRENDS, AND TREATMENT ALTERNATIVES

Fetal Alcohol Spectrum Disorders (FASD)

There are several issues that have been raised concerning how to best define and diagnose FAS and other variations that exist among those with fetal alcohol spectrum disorders (FASD). Currently, the term FASD is used to refer to "the spectrum of structural anomalies and behavioral and neurocognitive disabilities" evident in individuals who have been exposed to alcohol prenatally (Hoyme et al., 2005, p. 39). Individuals with FAS present with cardinal diagnostic features, in various degrees of severity: facial anomalies, central nervous system damage/dysfunction, and exposure to alcohol in utero (Hoyme et al., 2005). Although individuals who have the more severe and physically recognizable form of FAS may be more readily diagnosed, many cases of FAS often are undetected and undiagnosed (Little, Snell, Rosenfeld, Gilstrap, & Gant, 1990), while those with more subtle forms of FASD are at even higher risk for going undetected (Astley & Clarren, 2000). Controversy has also surrounded the term fetal alcohol effects (FAE), since the term has been used to refer to such a wide variety of symptoms that it is often of little diagnostic value (Anase, Jones, & Clarren, 1995). In 1996, a study group of the Institute of Medicine (IOM) developed five diagnostic categories under the label of FASD:

1. FAS with confirmed maternal alcohol exposure
2. FAS without any confirmed maternal alcohol exposure
3. Partial FAS with confirmed maternal alcohol exposure
4. ARBD: alcohol-related neurodevelopmental disorder
5. ARND: alcohol-related birth defects (Stratton, Howe, & Battaglia, 1996)

Children and youth with ARBD and ARND have normal faces, growth, and development, but those with ARBD have specific structural malformations, while those with ARND demonstrate characteristics and behavioral patterns typically associated with fetal alcohol exposure (Hoyme et al., 2005). One of the characteristic problems facing children and youth with ARND is marked impairment in executive functioning (EF) associated with poor judgment and failure to consider the consequences of their behaviors. EF is used to describe cognitive abilities that are required to adequately perform complex tasks, including cognitive flexibility, planning, organization, sequencing, response inhibition, and self-regulatory behaviors (Eslinger, 1996). Connor, Sampson, Bookstein, Barr, and Streissguth (2000) studied EF in individuals diagnosed with FAS or FAE and controls. Results revealed that the mean IQ scores were higher for those with FAE (SS mean = 90) than those with FAS (SS mean = 79) and that subjects with FAS and FAE performed poorer on tasks of executive functions than would have been predicted by IQ alone. The researchers noted deficits in EF related to "shifting or changing strategies, especially when there is uncertainty about which rules to employ" and problems in interpersonal relationships due to an inability to detect subtle cues resulting in feeling isolated or from being "prone to inappropriate behaviors that could get them into trouble both socially and legally" (Conner et al., 2000, p. 351). Hoyme and colleagues (2005) list a number of characteristics commonly found in the behavioral profile of children with FASD, including

> problems with communication and speech (talking too fast or interrupting others), difficulties in personal manner (clumsiness, disorganization, and losing or misplacing things), emotional lability (rapid mood swings, overreacting), motor dysfunction (difficulty playing sports), poor academic performance (poor attention

span and completing tasks), deficient social interactions (lack of awareness of the consequences of behavior and poor judgment) and unusual physiologic responses (hyperactivity and sleep disturbances). (p. 45)

In their study of 415 patients with FAS and FAE, Streissguth and colleagues (2004) found that 42% reported placement in special education, 66% had received resource room assistance, and 65% had received remedial help for reading and arithmetic. Adaptive scores from the Vineland Adaptive Behavior Scales and performance on arithmetic were two of the greatest areas of deficit for both groups. Adverse life outcomes were evaluated for five different areas: inappropriate sexual behaviors (ISB), disrupted school experiences (DSE), trouble with the law (TWL), confinement (CNF), and alcohol and drug problems (ADP). Of the study sample, 53% of adolescents had been suspended from school, 29% had been expelled, and 25% had dropped out. The most common areas of school difficulty included problems with attention, incomplete work, problems getting along with peers, and being disruptive in class. Sixty percent of adolescents and adults reported TWL, with crimes against persons (45%), shoplifting/theft (36%), and assault (17%), the three most common areas of criminal activity. Sixty-seven percent of adolescents had been charged, arrested, or convicted, while 35% were actually incarcerated for a crime. Twenty-nine percent of adolescents admitted to ADP. The authors found that one of the strongest correlates for adverse outcomes was age of diagnosis, with the odds increasing from twice to four times the risk, if age of diagnosis was after 12 years of age. A significant finding from the study was that patients with FAE had higher rates of adverse outcomes in all five areas than those with FAS, and double the odds of TWL and ADP than those with FAS. Streissguth and colleagues (2004) suggest that those with FAE, who do not have the physical features associated with FAS, nevertheless are significantly impaired in academic and adaptive behavior.

Gang Involvement

The number of youth who are members of gangs has increased over the past number of years, with estimates of more than 650,000 youth who are gang members in the United States (Howell, 1998). Joining a gang can increase the risk of participating in antisocial activities, which can result in incarceration, injury, and even death (Hammond & Yung, 1993). There are two primary theories that have been developed to explain why some youth join gangs: *selection theory,* which suggests that aggressive youth are drawn to gang activity (Staub, 1996); or *socialization theory,* which suggests that youth who join gangs become aggressive as they model gang behaviors (Winfree, Backstrom, & Mays, 1994). In their longitudinal study of predictors for gang membership, Lahey, Gordon, Loeber, Stouthamer-Loeber, and Farrington (1999) found some support for selection theory, as youth who were already on an aggressive pathway were more likely to become gang members. In their study, increased risk for gang membership was also predicted by having friends who engaged in delinquent behaviors, and less parental supervision in early adolescence. In their study, 23.8% of African American boys joined antisocial gangs prior to 19 years of age, compared to 3.9% of non-Hispanic white males.

Race is a strong predictor of poverty and the problematic behaviors that may result, such as delinquency, violence, and substance use (Dryfoos, 1990; McLoyd, 1998). However, individual differences exist in that not all African American male youth experience the problematic behaviors associated with poverty and race (Mincy, 1994). Taylor and colleagues (2003) examined characteristics of African American adolescent males who were involved in gangs (GI) participating in criminal behaviors (drug use, violence) relative to African American adolescent males who were involved in community groups (CG). Researchers found very different attitudes and attributes among the two groups. Youth in CG were more likely to describe their parents as supportive, as having rules, and as settling disagreements peacefully. As for drugs, while the CG sample reported having as many friends who got high as did not, the GI youth were significantly more likely to associate with friends who get high. Attitudes toward school were also highly discrepant, with the GI sample attending school to socialize or to meet parent demands, while those from the CG sample attended school to get a better job or go to college. With respect to role models, youth in the GI group were more likely to have a "rapper" as a role model, and those in the CG sample were more likely to seek advice from a role model.

Brown (1998) interviewed African American gang members and their caregivers and concluded that there was a pervasive sense of loss of hope and feelings that youth have no chance of making it outside of the gang. Campbell (1992) found that many of the African American youth who joined gangs shared similar backgrounds, such as living in poverty-stricken areas and coming from single-parent households, and often joined a gang based on peer pressure, inability to find a job, and the need to belong. In his research on the parents of gang members, Knox (1994) suggests that youth who have a low level of self-esteem, which is not nurtured by parents, may be able to recover if the self-esteem is nurtured by some other agency of socialization, such as school or other faith-based organizations. However, if this does not happen, then the youth will be socialized by the gang. According to Vigil (2002), minority youth are subjected to multiple marginality, "living and working in marginal situations and conditions," where there is a breakdown of social control, and are socialized by the street and assume the street or "gang" identity (p. 8), as the gang replaces the family and becomes the family.

Treatment/Prevention

FASD. Of course, the best prevention for FASD is to increase awareness of the dangers of females drinking during pregnancy. As there has been no safe amount of alcohol determined, abstinence is the best method. Prevention programs can be launched on several levels, including primary/universal prevention (targeting all pregnant females), secondary/selective prevention (targeting pregnant women who are at risk for drinking), and tertiary/indicated prevention (targeting women who drink who become pregnant).

There is an increased risk for individuals with FASD to become involved in the juvenile justice system (Streissguth et al., 2004; Streissguth & Kanter, 1997), due to problems in the areas of intellectual disabilities, learning disabilities, hyperactivity, attention deficits, and poor social skills, which can increase their chances of breaking the law. In their fact sheet on FASD and the juvenile justice system, the Substance Abuse and Mental Health Services Administration (SAMHSA, 2007) suggests that youth with FASD can be impulsive and not consider the consequences of their actions. Furthermore, their poor sense of personal boundaries, susceptibility to peer pressure, and tendency to be easily led can all contribute to their vulnerability for criminal and gang-related behaviors. SAMHSA (2007) emphasizes many ways that youth with FASD pose a "challenge" to the judicial system, including their inability to understand the process and communication problems. As a result, it is recommended that youth should be screened for FASD at all entry points into the juvenile justice system to ensure that if the condition exists, it can be detected. The resource also encourages attorneys to become aware of FASD and the consequences that this can have in order to appropriately advocate for their client, in areas of

- Competency (understand the charges and participate in their defense)
- Diminished capacity (ability to distinguish right from wrong)
- Decisions to decline/remand/waive (juvenile rather than adult facility)
- Sentencing (FASD as a mitigating factor)
- Treatment (appropriate court-ordered interventions)

The SAMHSA (2007) report also cautions that incarceration may increase the risk of reoffending, due to the iatrogenic effects of deviancy training from other youth in detention. It is also recommended that probation or aftercare include a supervised and structured living situation, where life skills can be monitored and supported.

Given their cognitive limitations, it is unlikely that insight-oriented therapy would be beneficial; however, training in ways to improve executive functions can assist in developing better skills to enable individuals to be more successful in their relationships with others and in following through on task demands. Involvement in community groups can also foster increased socialization with more normative peers and counteract gang involvement.

Gang Involvement. Most gang members showcase their involvement by a form of dress, behaviors, hand signals, and tattoos (Gaustad, 1990). Potential gang members are typically recruited when they reach the teen years, when developmentally, adolescents are seeking a sense of belonging to a group and identity formation. The gang can provide both (Reiboldt, 2001). While Latino members join gangs for a sense of "macho," African American youth join gangs to be "cool" (Hunt & Laider, 2001). In their study of gang member characteristics, Esbensen, Winfree, He, and Taylor (2001) found these youth to be more impetuous and violent, engage in more high-risk behaviors, and report less feelings of guilt.

There are a number of prevention programs that have been launched to reduce the successful recruitment of new gang members. Vigil (2002) suggests that unless the policymakers understand why gangs formed from a cultural and economic perspective, then intervention and prevention will not be possible. Further, he states that a proactive approach is necessary and must begin in early childhood, in low-income areas, with secondary prevention programs aimed at those children most at risk. Interventions must also focus on the critical preteen years (9–12), when youth are at the optimum age for gang recruitment. Finally, tertiary intervention should focus on those youth who have already joined a gang to recruit them back into society, not through punitive means (incarceration), but by offering mentoring, tutoring, and counseling for them, as well as their families.

Post-Case Questions

1. The concepts of *equifinality* (several possible pathways can lead to the same outcome) and *multifinality* (being raised in similar circumstances can result in different outcomes) have been suggested to assist our understanding of the nature of different developmental trajectories (Cicchetti & Rogosch, 1996). Although Neesha and Tyrone were siblings who were raised in the same household, Neesha's story is one of resilience, while Tyrone's path has led to gang membership and the juvenile justice system. What are some of the factors that have contributed to the negative outcomes that Tyrone has experienced?

2. There are many issues and different definitions for the fetal alcohol spectrum disorders (FASD). Which type of FASD is most likely to apply to Tyrone, and what characteristics are most common in this form of FASD?

3. What are some reasons that gang membership was so attractive to Tyrone, and how is this complicated by FASD?

4. Name several ways in which a forensic assessment differs from a more conventional psychological assessment.

5. Why are so many individuals with FASD involved with the juvenile justice system, and what are the challenges that the juvenile justice system must face in dealing with these cases?

REFERENCES

American Academy of Child and Adolescent Psychiatry (AACAP). (2004). *Practice parameter for the assessment and treatment of youth in juvenile detention and correction facilities.* Retrieved December 5, 2009, from http://www.aacap.org

Anase, J. M., Jones, K. L., & Clarren, S. K. (1995). Do we need the term "FAE"? *Pediatrics, 95,* 428–430.

Astley, S. J., & Clarren, S. K. (2000). Diagnosing the full spectrum of fetal alcohol exposed individuals: Introducing the 4-digit diagnostic code. *Alcohol, 35,* 400–410.

Brown, W. B. (1998). The fight for survival: African-American gang members and their families in a segregated society. *Juvenile and Family Court Journal, 49,* 1–14.

Campbell, A. (1992). Black single female headed households and their children's involvement in gangs. Unpublished, California State University, Long Beach, CA. As cited in Carlie, M. (2002), *Into the abyss: A personal journey into the world of street gangs.* Retrieved December 19, 2009, from http://faculty.missouristate.edu/m/MichaelCarlie/Preface/preface.htm

Cicchetti, D., & Rogosh, F. A. (1996). Editorial: Equifinality and multifinality in developmental psychopathology. *Development and Psychopathology, 8,* 597–600.

Connor, P. D., Sampson, P. D., Bookstein, F. L., Barr, H. M., & Streissguth, A. P. (2000). Direct and indirect effects of prenatal alcohol damage on executive function. *Developmental Neuropsychology, 18,* 331–354.

Dryfoos, J. G. (1990). *Adolescents at risk: Prevalence and prevention.* New York: Oxford University Press.

Esbensen, F., Winfree, L., He, N., & Taylor, T. (2001). Youth gangs and definitional issues: When is a gang a gang, and why does it matter? *Crime & Delinquency, 47,* 105–130.

Eslinger, P. J. (1996). Conceptualizing, describing and measuring components of executive function: A summary. In G. T. Lyon & N. A. Krasnegor (Eds.), *Attention, memory and executive function* (pp. 367–395). Baltimore: Brookes.

Gaustad, J. (2000). *Gangs.* ERIC Document Reproduction Service No. ED321419.

Hammond, R. W., & Yung, B. (1993). Psychology's role in the public health response to assaultive violence among young African American men. American *Psychologist, 48,* 142–154.

Howell, J. C. (1998). *Youth gangs in the United States: An overview.* Washington, DC: Office of Juvenile Justice and Delinquency Prevention.

Hoyme, H. E., May, P. A., Kalberg, W. O., Kodituwakku, P., Gossage, P., & Trujillo, P. (2005). A practical clinical approach to diagnosis of fetal alcohol spectrum disorders: Clarification of the 1996 Institute of Medicine criteria. *Pediatrics, 115,* 39–47.

Hunt, G., & Laider, K. (2001). Alcohol and violence in the lives of gang members. *Alcohol, Research and Health, 25,* 66–71.

Knox, G. W. (1994). *An introduction to gangs.* Bristol, IN: Wyndham Hall Press.

Lahey, B. B., Gordon, R. A., Loeber, R., Stouthamer-Loeber, M., & Farrington, D. P. (1999). Boys who join gangs: A prospective study of predictors of first gang entry. *Journal of Abnormal Child Psychology, 27,* 261–276.

Little, B. B., Snell, L. M., Rosenfeld, C. R., Gilstrap, L. C., & Gant, N. F. (1990). Failure to recognize fetal alcohol syndrome in newborn infants. *American Journal of Disabilities in Children, 144,* 1142–1146.

McLoyd, V. C. (1998). Children in poverty: Development, public policy, and practice. In W. Damon (Ed.), I. E. Sigel, & K. A. Renninger (Vol. Eds.), *Handbook of psychology: Vol. 4. Child psychology in practice* (5th ed., pp. 135–208). New York: John Wiley.

Mincy, R. B. (1994). Conclusions and implications. In R. B. Mincy (Ed.), *Nurturing young black males: Challenges to agencies, programs, and social policy* (pp. 187–203). Washington, DC: Urban Institute Press.

Reiboldt, W. (2001). Adolescent interactions with gangs, family and neighborhoods: An ethnographic investigation. *Journal of Family Issues, 22,* 211–242.

Staub, E. (1996). Cultural-societal roots of violence: The examples of genocidal violence and of contemporary youth violence in the United States. *American Psychologist, 51,* 117–132.

Stratton, K. R., Howe, C. J., & Battaglia, F. C. (Eds.). (1996). *Fetal alcohol syndrome: Diagnosis, epidemiology, prevention, and treatment.* Washington, DC: National Academy Press.

Streissguth, A. P., Bookstein, F. L., Barr, H. M., Sampson, P. D., O'Malley, K., & Young, J. K. (2004). Risk factors for adverse life outcomes in fetal alcohol syndrome and fetal alcohol effects. *Developmental and Behavioral Pediatrics, 25,* 226–238.

Streissguth, A. P., & Kantor, J. (Eds.). (1997). *The challenge of fetal alcohol syndrome: Overcoming secondary disabilities.* Seattle: University of Washington Press.

Substance Abuse and Mental Health Services Administration (SAMHSA). (2007). *Fetal alcohol spectrum disorders and juvenile justice: How professionals can make a difference.* Retrieved December 18, 2009, from http://www.fasdcenter.samhsa.gov/documents/WYNK_JuvJust_Profs.pdf

Taylor, C. S., Lerner, R. M., von Eye, A., Bobek, D., Balsano, A. B., Dowling, E., et al. (2003). Positive individual and social behavior among gang and nongang African American male adolescents. *Journal of Adolescent Research, 18,* 496–522.

Vigil, J. D. (2002). *A rainbow of gangs.* Austin: University of Texas Press.

Winfree, T. L., Backstrom, T. V., & Mays, G. L. (1994). Social learning theory, self reported delinquency, and youth gangs: A new twist on a general theory of crime and delinquency. *Youth and Society, 26,* 147–177.

Supplemental Case Information

CASE OF COLBY TYLER: RESULTS FROM PSYCHOLOGICAL TESTING

Results of the multimodal assessment battery are presented in the following pages in the form of standard scores, T scores, and/or percentiles. Interns will be expected to evaluate, interpret, and integrate findings to formulate a more refined diagnostic impression. Anecdotal comments from the clinic psychologist (e.g., comments on test behaviors, etc.) are presented whenever these comments might aid in interpretation of the findings. In addition, a list of endorsed items is provided for any scales (checklists and rating scales) elevated to clinical levels to facilitate interpretation of behavioral patterns within and across sources of information.

Results are presented in their entirety rather than in summarized form to provide the intern with maximum opportunity to develop independent skills in the analysis and synthesis of information from multiple sources.

General Cognitive (WISC-IV) and Academic (WRAT-IV) Results

Wechsler Intelligence Scale for Children, Fourth Edition (WISC-IV)

Index and Scales	Standard Score (Range 95% confidence level)	Percentile
Verbal Comprehension Similarities (19) Vocabulary (19) Comprehension (19)	155 (Range 145–158) Superior Range	99.9
Perceptual Reasoning Block Design (19) Matrix Reasoning (17) Picture Concepts (18)	149 (Range 137–153) Superior Range	99.9
Working Memory Digit Span (14) Letter–Number Sequence (16)	129 (Range 119–134) High Average to Superior Range	97
Processing Speed Symbol Search (11) Coding (10)	103 (Range 94–112) Average Range	58
Full Scale IQ	147 (Range 141–151)	99.9

Administrator Comments: Excellent speed and dexterity on block design; intuitive holistic learner. Excellent effort and good sense of humor. Very articulate. Frustration evident on lower-scored tasks.

Wide Range Achievement Test (WRAT-IV)

Subject	Standard Score	Percentile	Grade Level
Word Reading	134	99	Post High School
Sentence Comprehension	145	99	Post High School
Reading Composite	140	99	Post High School
Spelling	131	98	Post High School
Math Computation	122	93	High School

Administrator Comments: Fluent decoder, handwriting very difficult to read, awkward pencil grip. Math questions required extra paper to compute; used unusual strategies but got the correct answers.

Checklists and Rating Scales

Assessment results are presented for Colby's responses to three assessment instruments that measure social, emotional, and behavioral functioning: Achenbach System of Empirically Based Assessment (ASEBA; Achenbach & Rescorla, 2000), The Conners Rating Scales, Revised (Conners, 1997), Conners-Wells Self-Report Scale for Adolescents (Conners & Wells, 1997), and the Beck Youth Inventories of Emotional and Social Impairment, 2nd ed. (Beck, Beck, & Jolly, 2005).

ASEBA

The following scores are from the multi-informant assessment using the Child Behavior Checklist (CBCL, completed by Colby's mother), the Teacher Report Form (TRF; completed by Colby's teacher) and the Youth Self Report (YSR; completed by Colby).

If the previous scores were plotted on a profile, it would be possible to compare scores between raters, graphically. Figure AA.1 provides an example of what Colby's ASEBA profile would look like based on parent and teacher ratings.

The Revised Conners Rating Scales

The Conners rating scales allow for multiple informants to provide information concerning common attention problems and symptoms of attention-deficit/hyperactivity based on criteria from the *DSM-IV-TR* (APA, 2000). There are long and short versions of the rating scales available. In this case, the Conners Parent Rating Scale (CRRS-R:L), Conners Teacher Rating Scale (CTRS-R:L), and Conners-Wells Adolescent Self-Report Scale: Long (CASS:L) were completed by Colby's mother, teacher, and himself.

Achenbach System of Empirically Based Assessment (ASEBA) Scales

SYNDROMES	CBCL (T Score)	TRF (T Score)	YSR (T Score)
INTERNALIZNG PROBLEMS			
Anxious/Depressed	**70** Need to be perfect, Fearful others out to get him, Worthless, Self-conscious, Worries	62	63
Withdrawn/Depressed	**65**	62	64
Somatic Complaints	**72** Tired, Aches, Headaches, Eye, Skin, Stomach	59	**72** Dizzy, Tired, Aches, Headaches, Nausea, Eye, Skin, Stomach
Total Internalizing	**73**	63	**68**
Other Problems			
Social Problems	50	54	50
Thought Problems	**67** Mind wanders off, Repeats things, Stares	58	61
Attention Problems	**70** Problems with concentration, Restless, Confused, Daydreams, Poor schoolwork, Stares	63	59
EXTERNALIZING PROBLEMS			
Rule Breaking	50	53	50
Aggressive Behavior	**65**	62	61
Total Externalizing	60	60	56
TOTAL PROBLEMS	61	63	63

Other Problems: Accident prone, Sleeps less than most, Stores stuff, Trouble sleeping.

Anecdotal Comments (Teacher): Additional effort is needed, achievement below ability, weak study skills, inconsistent effort, assignments not completed, frequently late in the morning. Good natured, well liked.

Note: Bold-faced numbers indicate scales in the significant range (93rd percentile and above). Individual items endorsed by the respondent are listed for each of the significant scales.

Figure AA.1   A Comparison of Parent and Teacher Ratings for Colby on the ASEBA

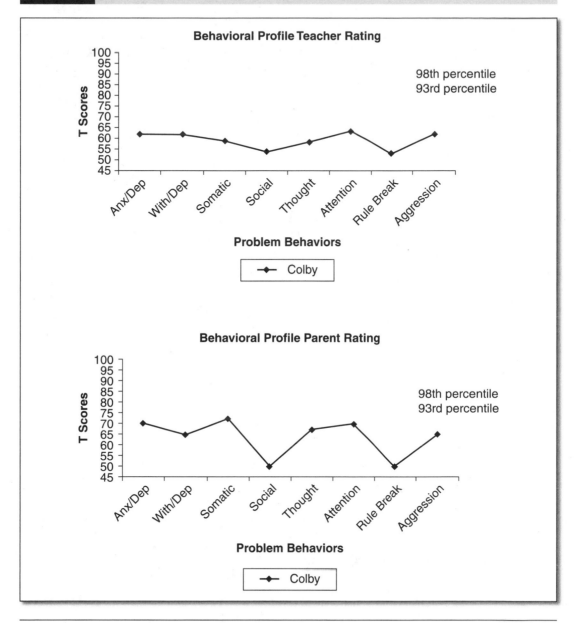

Normal: T score range = 40–60
Borderline Clinical: T score range = 65–69 (93rd percentile)
Clinically Significant   T score 70+ (98th percentile)

Revised Conners Rating Scales

Behaviors	Rating Scales		
	Parent (CPRS-R:L) (T Scores)	Teacher (CTRS-R:L) (T Scores)	Youth (CASS:L) (T Scores)
Oppositional	58	57	
Cognitive Problems/ Inattention	62	**72** Avoids/reluctant to engage in tasks of sustained mental effort; Fails to finish	60
Hyperactivity	54	57	52
Anxious/Shy	44	**67**	
Perfectionism	48	46	
Social Problems	45	48	
Psychosomatic	**72** Stomachaches, pains		
Conners ADHD Index	57	**68**	63
Conners Global Index: Restless/Impulsive Emotional Lability	**65** **67**	64 **79** Easily frustrated, mood swings, temper	
Global Index Total	**67**	**68**	
DSM-IV: Inattentive	60	**70**	**72**
DSM-IV: Hyp/Impulsive	54	59	47
DSM-IV: Total	58	**67**	61
CASS Scale Only:			
Family Problems			52
Emotional Problems			58
Conduct Problems			50
Anger Control Problems			61

Note: Shaded areas for items not on the rater's scale.

Teacher (CTRS-R:L) and Colby (CASS:L) agreed on the same six items of inattention:

- Careless errors, misses details
- Avoids sustained mental effort
- Difficulty organizing
- Loses necessary items
- Poor follow-through
- Easily distracted

Beck Youth Inventories of Emotional and Social Impairment (2nd Edition)

This self-report scale has twenty questions for each area assessed. Youth respond to a Likert-type response format to indicate the degree to which an item is like or unlike them: Never = 0; Sometimes = 1; Often = 2; Always = 3.

Beck Youth Inventories

Area Assessed	T Score	Percentile
Self-Concept Inventory Items endorsed for negative self-concept (0, 1) Feel strong; Like myself; Do things well; Happy to be me; Proud of myself; Good at remembering	44	35
Depression Inventory for Youth Items rated as 2 or 3: Think life is bad; Trouble sleeping (3); Feel sorry for myself; Feel like crying; Feel sad	63	93
Anxiety Inventory for Youth Items rated as 2 or 3: Worry about school, Get nervous, Worry I will get bad grades (3), Worry about the future (3), Worry others will get mad, Worry I might lose control (3), I always worry (3), Problems sleeping (3), My heart pounds (3), Fear I might get sick (3)	**67**	95
Anger Inventory for Youth	50	62
Disruptive Behavior Inventory for Youth	44	31

COLBY: CASE FORMULATION AND DISCUSSION

Assessment Report for Colby Tyler

Reason for Referral. Colby was referred for assessment due to presenting complaints of "poor school outcomes" and "temper outbursts."

Assessment Instruments

> Wechsler Intelligence Scale for Children (WISC-IV)
>
> Wide Range Achievement Test (WRAT-4)
>
> Child Behavior Checklist (CBCL)
>
> Teacher Report Form (TRF)
>
> Youth Self-Report (YSR)
>
> Conners Parent Rating Scale (CPRS-R:L)
>
> Conners Teacher Rating Scale (CTRS-R:L)
>
> Conners-Wells Self-Report Scale (CAAS:L)
>
> Beck Youth Inventories
>
> Child Depression Inventory
>
> Clinical Interviews

Background Information. Colby was a full-term baby who weighed 6 lb. 2 oz. Labor was lengthy (12 hours) and forceps were used for delivery. Mother stated that she was under much stress during pregnancy due to marital conflict, and admitted to smoking as well as having an occasional drink.

Colby was difficult to manage as an infant due to eating problems (often hungry, sensitive stomach, vomiting) and sleeping problems (difficulties falling asleep and staying asleep). However, he was a good-natured and inquisitive toddler. Developmental milestones were within the norm, with the exception that Colby spontaneously began to read words at 2 years of age, a skill that continued to develop and progress at a rapid rate. Colby's health has been good, with the exception of a severe outbreak of hives at 5 years of age shortly after he entered kindergarten. The cause remained undiagnosed and there has not been a recurrence. Hearing and vision have been assessed, and results indicate that hearing is normal. Colby wears glasses for distance vision. There is a family history of mood disorders, anxiety disorders (maternal grandmother), family violence, and aggressive impulses, likely related to alcohol abuse (maternal grandfather).

Colby's parents have recently separated (6 months ago); however, marital conflict has been ongoing throughout the 15-year marriage. There was a previous brief separation 7 years ago. Colby and his sister Susy (7 years of age) are living with their mother and visit their father every Wednesday and every second weekend. Colby gets along well with his mother, but the relationship with his father is often strained and conflicted. Colby has stated that his father is often critical of what he does and will often make sarcastic remarks about him in front of his friends. Colby feels that he cannot please his father. Colby often appears very agitated on Wednesday evenings and after returning from weekend visits with his father. Colby's young sister, Susy, is also having transition problems.

Colby gained entrance to the gifted program in the fourth grade as a result of a districtwide screening program. Colby scored in the very superior range (full scale IQ 151) on the intellectual assessment conducted at that time. The gifted program was offered for students from Grades 4–8, one day a week at a regional school that served the needs of gifted students from all district schools. Colby was very successful in the program, which offered extensive computer access and various activities emphasizing higher-order functioning (e.g., mind-bender logic games). However, school reports concerning regular school programming were very disappointing, noting problems in areas of inconsistent effort, incomplete assignments, tardiness, not bringing required materials to class, and poor work habits. Colby's most recent report card for his first high school term was extremely disappointing with one A, four C's, and one D (Chemistry). Colby has also been late many times for classes, since he is having difficulty getting up in the mornings due to staying up very late in the evenings.

Present Assessment Results and Interpretation

Colby was seen for two assessment sessions. Rapport was readily established and effort was good throughout. Therefore, results are considered to be a valid estimate of current functioning levels. Test behavior was notable in the following ways. Colby was able to complete puzzles and block designs very quickly with an intuitive holistic learning style. Some frustration was noted on paper-and-pencil tasks, and on these exercises Colby was much slower to respond and used an awkward pencil grasp. Colby seemed to fatigue when required to complete a series of three rating scales. Colby stopped halfway through the exercise to start a spontaneous conversation, unrelated to the forms he was completing. Colby was also easily distracted by extraneous noises in the room, which was relatively quiet by normal standards. When he would return his attention to the questionnaires, he had some difficulty with reorienting to task and finding his place in the booklet.

Colby scored in the Superior range on the WISC-IV (full scale IQ range 141–154) at the 99th percentile relative to similar-age peers. Although overall score for the Verbal Comprehension Index of 155 (range 145–158) was better than scores on the Perceptual Reasoning Index, 149 (range 137–153), the difference was not significant. Colby's score on the Coding subtest was significantly lower than the mean of all other subtests. A difference of this magnitude would be seen in less than 5% of the population. Colby's score on the Working Memory Index of 129 (range 119–134) was significantly lower than Colby's score on the Verbal Comprehension Index (range 145–158), while his score for Processing Speed 103 (range 94–112) was significantly lower than all other indices. The Working Memory Index, which comprises the Digit Span and Letter–Number Sequence tasks, can provide a measure of working memory involving processes of attention, concentration, sequential processing, and short-term memory. The Processing Speed Index includes a symbol search task, which taps mental speed, and a coding task, which taps psychomotor speed and is considered to measure visual-motor coordination, visual memory, and planning ability.

Academically, according to the WRAT-IV, Colby's reading composite and spelling scores were commensurate with his intellectual ability and indicated functioning at or above the

99th percentile. Colby scored at the 93rd percentile for arithmetic computation, which is slightly below the expected level. Colby used unusual strategies to assist in recalling multiplication tables (e.g., for 7×8, Colby added eight 7s together to get 56); however, he was able to obtain correct answers using these methods. Colby was a fluent decoder and was able to successfully read all words presented. Colby used an awkward pencil grasp for paper-and-pencil tasks, and handwriting was difficult to decipher due to poor number and letter formations. Although there was no formal test of written expression, Colby was asked to write a short story about any topic of his choice. Colby experienced much difficulty getting started and after a few false starts (writing and erasing sentences) Colby began a story about "The First Man on the Moon." However, he abandoned this effort after about 10 minutes and changed the topic to "My Perfect Vacation." His final product was a brief, but well-written, account of a fantasy vacation to Mars.

Information concerning behavioral and emotional functioning was obtained from clinical interviews and from responses to Rating Scales and Checklists completed by Colby (YSR, CAAS, Beck Inventories), his mother (CBCL, CPRS), and homeroom teacher (TRF, CTRS). Colby's mother rated Total Internalizing (CBCL) within the clinically significant range (T = 73), while Colby's self-rating (YSR) placed Total Internalizing within the borderline clinical range (T = 68). Colby (T = 72) and his mother (T = 72) both endorsed significant levels of Somatic Complaints, while Colby's mother also noted clinically significant levels for Anxious/Depressed (T = 70) behaviors (*Feeling worthless, Self-conscious, Fearful, Worried*), and Attention Problems (T = 70), noted in problems with concentration, restlessness, daydreaming, poor school progress, and weak impulse control. Although Colby's teacher did not indicate any syndromes to be within the clinical or borderline clinical ranges, further analysis revealed that Inattention on the Attention Problems subscale was at the 95th percentile, indicating problems with concentration, failure to finish tasks, daydreaming, lack of motivation, underachievement, and poor schoolwork. Anecdotal comments from the teacher revealed that Colby was late for classes 18 times in the first term and that effort was very inconsistent. Although his teacher also noted overall Adaptive Functioning was within the borderline clinical range (T = 39), this was mainly due to low scores for effort and performance. Ratings also noted strengths in areas of behavior (TRF), social competence (CBCL, YSR), and participation in nonacademic activities (sports, hobbies, part-time job).

Parent responses to the Conners Rating Scale (CPRS) revealed a significant elevation on the Psychosomatic Subscale (T = 72), noting problems with stomachaches, aches and pains, and frequent before-school complaints. Therefore, parent responses were consistent in endorsing somatic or psychosomatic complaints across both the CBCL and the CPRS. Colby's mother also noted significant problems in emotional responsiveness on the Emotional Lability subscale (T = 67), evident in temper outbursts and abrupt mood changes. In addition, parent responses to the Conners Global Index Total (T = 67) endorsed the following behaviors occurring much of the time: excitable and impulsive, failure to finish tasks, inattentive, easily distracted, temper outbursts, fidgeting, easily frustrated, and abrupt mood swings.

Teacher ratings on the Conners scales (CTRS) noted significant elevations for Cognitive Problems/Inattention (T = 72), noted in behaviors of avoidance/reluctance to engage in tasks requiring sustained mental effort, failure to finish tasks, and lacks interest in schoolwork. Teacher ratings for the *DSM-IV* Inattentive Scale (T = 70) were also indicative of significant problems: careless errors/misses details, avoids sustained mental effort, difficulty organizing information, loses necessary items, poor follow-through, and ease of distractibility.

Emotional Lability (quick temper, ease of frustration, quick mood swings) was also noted to be within the clinically significant range (T = 79) by Colby's teacher. Colby also rated himself as having significant problems on the DSM-IV Inattentive scale (T = 72) of the CASS and endorsed "forgetful in daily activities" in addition to all items that his teacher had indicated for the same scale.

Colby's responses to the Beck Youth Inventories revealed that Anxiety (T = 67) and Depression (T = 63) were moderately elevated, while Self-Concept (T = 44) was lower than average, at the 25th percentile. Colby admitted to having many worries about school, getting bad grades, and his future.

He also endorsed fears of becoming ill and admitted to having fears about losing control. Trouble falling asleep and staying asleep were also noted as problematic, often resulting in being late for school in the mornings. Although there were no indications of suicidal ideation, the Child Depression Inventory (CDI) was also administered to obtain additional information concerning possible depressive features. Colby's overall level of Depression on the CDI (T = 47) was within normal limits with no significant findings for any of the subscales. The most elevated scale on the CDI was predictably on the Ineffectiveness scale (T = 59), although this was not out of the normal range.

SUMMARY AND DIAGNOSTIC IMPRESSIONS

Colby is a 14-year-old teenager who was referred for assessment by his mother due to concerns regarding poor school outcomes and temper outbursts. Colby is currently enrolled in the Grade 9 program, and reports received at the end of his first term suggest that he is underachieving significantly based on his intellectual ability, which is within the very superior range. In the past 6 months, in addition to a transition to high school from elementary school, Colby has also had to deal with the recent split-up of his parents. These stressors have likely caused preexisting problems to escalate, evident in increased levels of anxiety, depression, and emotional reactivity (frustration, temper tantrums).

Although it is possible that Colby's current reactions might be interpreted as an adjustment reaction to current life stressors (transition to high school, parents' separation), given the current assessment findings, family history, and chronic nature of Colby's academic difficulties, a diagnosis of attention-deficit/hyperactivity disorder—predominantly inattentive type—is suggested. According to *DSM-IV-TR* (APA, 2000) criteria, Colby presents with at least six of the behaviors required to warrant such a diagnosis, noted in behaviors of inattention, distractibility, problems with completing assignments, poor organizational skills, avoidance of activities requiring sustained mental effort, and forgetfulness in daily activities. These behaviors have appeared at home and at school and have been evident since Colby enrolled in formal education. Lack of diagnosis to date, however, can likely be attributed to Colby's extremely high level of intelligence, which has allowed him to cope in the earlier grades and served to mask the severity of his problem. However, with increased emphasis on written and independent work, Colby's inability to engage in planned, meaningful, and goal-directed behavior, and his reluctance to sustain effort in tasks that are long, arduous, and often group oriented, has resulted in increasingly poor school performance.

Given the disparity between Colby's intellectual ability and his poor performance, and in view of continued family conflict, it is not surprising that Colby would also present with symptoms of anxiety, depression, and lowered self-concept. Assessment results also reveal that Colby has a high level of emotional reactivity to stressors that is primarily internalized and likely to find expression in somatic complaints (sleep problems, digestive complaints, headaches). However, when frustration tolerance is especially low, Colby may also be prone to externalize feelings of frustration in outbursts of anger. When Colby expresses his feelings in an angry outburst, however, venting of feelings is often only temporary and often results in negative feelings of loss of control and erosion of his self-concept.

Based on the diagnostic impressions, the following recommendations are suggested:

- The importance of considering stimulant medication to assist with enhancing school performance was thoroughly discussed with Colby and his mother.
- It is essential that Colby's father also attend a session to receive feedback concerning this assessment to ensure understanding of Colby's difficulties.
- Colby should receive supportive psychotherapy to provide an outside venue to express his feelings regarding his ADHD and family problems and to receive relaxation training to assist in reducing anxiety levels and difficulties falling asleep.
- The family should be engaged as a whole (father, mother, and son) or as two dyads (father-son, mother-son) in a training program to develop problem-solving skills to address key areas of conflict, such as responsibilities, boundaries (rights), and curfews. A program similar to that developed by Robin and Foster (Robin, 1990) is suggested to develop consistent problem-solving approaches that will focus on using behavioral techniques to reduce the potential for engaging in emotionally reactive patterns.
- Results of the assessment should also be discussed with school officials to provide greater understanding of how the school might address Colby's needs for support in several areas. Organizational aids (e.g., day planner or agenda, school mentor) should be provided to help Colby remain on task and to provide guidelines for breaking tasks down into smaller segments to assist with sustaining goal-directed behavior, and to assist Colby in monitoring his performance. Greater use of home and school communication would also be helpful. Colby would also benefit from being given additional time to complete tests, due to slow writing and processing skills.
- Remediation in handwriting skills and/or keyboarding skills would assist in improved speed of written expression. If obtaining one is possible, the use of a laptop would likely greatly enhance performance. Provide extra time during test-taking activities.

Case Discussion and Differential Diagnosis

Evidence in support of a diagnosis of ADHD, primarily inattentive type:

1. Symptom Criteria
   Colby demonstrated at least six of the required diagnostic criteria of the *DSM-IV-TR* (APA, 2000) for attention-deficit/hyperactivity disorder—predominantly inattentive type, evident

since at least 7 years of age and across at least two settings (home, school): *difficulty sustaining attention, fails to finish, difficulty organizing tasks, avoids tasks with sustained mental attention, loses necessary items, easily distracted,* and *often forgetful.*

2. Associated Features Often Linked With ADHD

These features noted in the *DSM-IV-TR* as associated with ADHD were also evident: low frustration tolerance, temper outbursts, mood lability, poor self-esteem, and dysphoria.

Negative parent-child interactions (especially with the father) and academic deficits and school problems often associated with ADHD-inattentive were also noted in the presenting problems (*DSM-IV-TR,* APA, 2000, pp. 87–88).

Poor handwriting and slow speed of writing: More than half of children with ADHD will also exhibit *dysgraphia* (Mayes, Calhoun, Chase, Mink, & Stagg, 2009). Dysgraphia is a specific type of learning disability or disorder of written expression that may manifest in spelling errors, poor letter formations, spacing, handwriting, and excessive time required to complete written tasks (*DSM-IV-TR;* APA, 2000, p. 54). In their study of youth with ADHD and controls, Adi-Japha and colleagues (2007) found that relative to controls, children with ADHD exhibited poor quality of handwriting and spent more time writing long (but not short) words. Furthermore, they produced letters and words that were inconsistent and disproportionate in size, resulting in inefficient and illegible written production, and an inability to stay within limits for writing and copying in the schoolroom. Results indicated that for children with ADHD who had normal reading skills, handwriting problems were related to impaired motor processes.

In order to gain better control when writing, Schoemaker, Ketelaars, Van Zonneveld, Minderaa, and Mulder (2005) found that children with ADHD increased the mean pen pressure. Although the resulting product is still disproportionate, and this does not impact fluency, it may explain why many children and youth with ADHD complain that their hands are stiff and that writing is a tiresome task.

3. Other Behavioral Risks Linked to ADHD

   a. *sleep difficulties,* such as falling asleep, frequent waking, tiredness due to sleep-wake schedule (Barkley, 1991), difficulty getting up in the morning (Barkley, 1998), and initial and middle insomnia (Chervin et al., 2002); and

   b. *increased rates of academic failure and depression reported at adolescence* due to demands for greater independent work in light of the ADHD, and failure to compete assignments based on poor organization skills and work habits (Barkley, 1998; Cantwell, 1996).

4. Cognitive Associations Linked to ADHD

Colby's scores on the WISC-IV were extremely high overall (very superior range); however, his *weakest scores were on the Coding and Symbol Search* subtests, which compose the *Processing Speed Index (PSI),* which in this case was significantly lower than all other indices. The next lowest subtest was the *Digit Span,* with the Working Memory Index (WMI) significantly lower than Verbal Comprehension Index.

Processing Speed Index (PSI). The PSI comprises the Coding and Symbol Search subtests. Both tests have a 2-minute time limit and are scored for speed and accuracy. While Coding requires psychomotor speed (copy symbols to match with the correct numbers), Symbol Search is a visual scanning task that requires the child to determine if the target symbol is represented in a given group of symbols. The PSI is a measure of psychomotor speed and coordination, short-term visual memory, attention, and cognitive flexibility (Sattler & Dumont, 2004).

Studies have shown that children with neurological disorders (ADHD, high-functioning autism, learning disability) perform less well on the PSI and the Working Memory Index (WMI) than children without these disorders (Calhoun & Mayes, 2005; Sattler & Dumont, 2004). In their study of subtypes of ADHD (ADHD-combined [ADHD-C] and ADHD-inattentive [ADHD-I]), Mayes, Calhoun, Bixler, and colleagues (2009) found that children in the ADHD-I groups (ADHD with anxious-depressed symptoms and ADHD alone) were significantly slower on the PSI than the ADHD-C groups.

Results from studies by Calhoun and Mayes (2005) and Mayes, Calhoun, Chase, and colleagues (2009) provide support for significant processing speed differences in subtypes of ADHD, with the inattentive type showing the greatest deficit in processing speed, due not only to attention difficulties, but to "sluggish cognitive tempo, under-arousal, low energy and lethargy (hypoactivity)" that can be associated with the predominantly inattentive type (Calhoun & Mayes, 2005). Colby's scores on the PSI (103) were significantly lower than all other indexes and similar to most with ADHD-inattentive type; coding was the lowest scale score of all (10).

Working Memory Index (WMI) or Freedom From Distractibility Index (FDI). The WMI (WISC-IV) consists of a digit-repetition task (forward and backward) and a letter–number sequence task (mixed presentations of numbers and letters are recalled with the numbers first in numerical order, followed by the letters in alphabetical order). Previously, the WISC-III contained a Freedom From Distractibility Index (FDI) composed of the digit span task and a mental arithmetic task. The current WMI removes the possibility of performance being compromised by weak math skills. The WMI and the previous FDI both measure attention and working memory (Sattler & Dumont, 2004). There is much conflicting evidence as to whether the WMI/FDI can successfully discriminate between children with ADHD and other populations (learning disabled, normal). While there is consensus that the WMI/FDI should not be used as an exclusive marker for ADHD (Kaufman, 1994; Kaufman & Lichtenberger, 2000), Schwean and Saklofske (1998) found that the WMI/FDI was the lowest index score for children with ADHD across three separate studies (Anastopoulos, Spisto, & Maher, 1994; Prifitera & Dersh, 1993; Schwean, Saklofske, Yackulic, & Quinn, 1993). Calhoun and Mayes (2005) found that 87% of children with ADHD-inattentive type and 82% of children with ADHD-combined type experienced significantly lower scores on WMI/FDI relative to their Verbal Comprehension Index (VCI) and Perceptual Reasoning Index (PRI). Colby's score on the WMI (129) was significantly below scores for VCI (155) and PRI (149).

5. Risks Factors From the Developmental History

Prenatal influences/birth history

Difficult delivery by forceps

Early eating and sleeping difficulties

Differential Diagnoses

Rationale in Ruling Out Other Comorbid or Competing Diagnoses

1. *ADHD-Combined Type.* ADHD-combined type was ruled out, since Colby did not present with sufficient symptoms (six) of impulsivity and hyperactivity.

2. *ADHD + Depressive Disorder (Major Depressive Disorder, Dysthymia, or Bipolar Disorder).* Since depressed patients also note diminished concentration and sleep difficulties, and bipolar patients can elicit irritability, poor control, physical hyperactivity, distractibility, and excessive talking when in a manic state, there is a need to rule out the possibility of comorbid mood disorders.

   Mood disorders and ADHD co-occur in approximately 20% to 30% of the population. Since ADHD without hyperactivity is associated with higher levels of internalizing symptoms, including depression (Schmidt, Stark, Carlson, & Anthony, 1998), investigating the possibility of a mood disorder is essential in the current evaluation. In this case, *major depressive disorder, dysthymia,* and *bipolar disorder* were ruled out because symptoms of sleep problems, concentration problems, and low self-esteem were better accounted for by associated features of ADHD and related to lack of academic progress or positive feedback regarding academics. Test results support this assumption.

3. *ADHD-Anxiety Disorder.* ADHD and anxiety have been found to overlap or co-occur in 25% to 40% of the population. Anxiety is thought to positively moderate for more impulsive behaviors through mechanisms of behavioral inhibition (Wenar & Kerig, 2000). Anxiety in childhood can take the form of *separation anxiety (SAD), phobias, panic attacks, obsessive-compulsive disorder (OCD), general anxiety disorder (GAD), acute stress disorder,* or *posttraumatic stress disorder (PTSD).* In this case, although Colby did not present with symptoms of any of the anxiety disorders, he shared many of the symptoms suggestive of GAD (restless, fatigued, irritable, difficulty concentrating, sleep disturbance). However, GAD was ruled out because the focus of the anxiety was confined to performance anxiety associated with ADHD.

   Given Colby's tendencies to internalize, however, there is a possibility that Colby might develop more pronounced symptoms of anxiety and/or depression or a *somatoform* disorder in the future, if the ADHD cannot be managed more successfully.

4. *ADHD-LD.* Colby presents with significant underachievement relative to his intellectual potential. Handwriting is immature, and he takes excessive time to complete written material. However, if keyboarding skills were applied, it would be likely that Colby would be able to produce increased amounts of written information. It is the current proposition that a diagnosis of a specific *learning disorder (LD),* such as a disorder of written expression, should be placed on hold at this time until keyboarding is introduced. It is the current belief that Colby's difficulties with written expression are primarily due to problems with organizing information due to ADHD. However, it is important to monitor progress in this area very closely.

5. *Developmental Coordination Disorder.* Although handwriting was poor, due to poor pencil grip, Colby was well coordinated in all other activities, was good in sports, and achieved developmental milestones within the norm.

REFERENCES

Adi-Japha, E., Landau, Y. E., Frenkel, L., Teicher, M., Gross-Tsur, V., & Shalev, R. S. (2007). ADHD and dysgraphia: Underlying mechanisms. *Cortex, 43,* 700–709.

American Psychiatric Association (APA). (2000). *Diagnostic and statistical manual of mental disorders* (4th ed., TR). Washington, DC: Author.

Anastopoulos, A. D., Spisto, M. A., & Maher, M. C. (1994). The WISC-III freedom from distractibility factor: Its utility in identifying children with attention deficit hyperactivity disorder. *Psychological Assessment, 6,* 368–371.

Barkley, R. A. (1991). The ecological validity of laboratory and analogue assessment methods of ADHD symptoms. *Journal of Abnormal Child Psychology, 19,* 149–178.

Barkley, R. A. (1998). *Attention deficit hyperactivity disorder: A handbook for diagnosis and treatment* (2nd ed.). New York: Guilford.

Calhoun, S. L., & Mayes, S. D. (2005). Processing speed in children with clinical disorders. *Psychology in the Schools, 42,* 333–342.

Cantwell, D. P. (1996). Attention deficit disorder: A review of the past 10 years. *Journal of the American Academy of Child and Adolescent Psychiatry, 35,* 978–987.

Chervin, R. D., Archbold, K. H., Dillon, J. E., Panahi, P., Pituch, K. J., Dahl, R. E., et al. (2002). Inattention, hyperactivity, and symptoms of sleep-disordered breathing. *Pediatrics, 109,* 449–456.

Kaufman, A. S. (1994). *Intelligent testing with the WISC-III.* New York: John Wiley.

Kaufman, A. S., & Lichtenberger, E. O. (2000). *Essentials of WISC-III and WPPSI-R assessment.* New York: John Wiley.

Mayes, S. D., Calhoun, S. L., Bixler, E. O., Vgontzas, A. N., Mahr, F., Hallwig-Garcia, J., et al. (2009). ADHD subtypes and comorbid anxiety, depression and oppositional-defiant disorder: Differences in sleep problems. *Journal of Pediatric Psychology, 34,* 328–337.

Mayes, S. D., Calhoun, S. L., Chase, G. A., Mink, D. M., & Stagg, R. E. (2009). ADHD subtypes and co-occurring anxiety, depression, and oppositional defiant disorder: Differences in Gordon diagnostic system and Wechsler working memory and processing speed index scores. *Journal of Attention Disorders, 12,* 540–550.

Prifitera, A., & Dersh, J. (1993). Base rates of WISC-III diagnostic subtest patterns among normal, learning-disabled and ADHD samples. *Journal of Psychoeducational Assessment,* 43–55.

Robin, A. R. (1990). Training families with ADHD adolescents. In R. A. Barkley (Ed.), *Attention-deficit hyperactivity disorder: A handbook for diagnosis and treatment* (pp. 462–497). New York: Guilford.

Sattler, J. M., & Dumont, R. (2004). *Assessment of children WISC-IV and WPPSI-III supplement.* San Diego, CA: Jerome M. Sattler.

Schmidt, K. L., Stark, K. D., Carlson, C. D., & Anthony, B. J. (1998). Cognitive factors differentiating attention deficit-hyperactivity disorder with and without a comorbid mood disorder. *Journal of Consulting and Clinical Psychology, 66,* 673–679.

Schoemaker, M. M., Ketelaars, C. E., Van Zonneveld, M., Minderaa, R. B., & Mulder, T. (2005). Deficits in motor control processes involved in production of graphic movements of children with attention-deficit-hyperactivity disorder. *Developmental Medicine and Child Neurology, 47,* 390–395.

Schwean, V. L., & Saklofske, D. H. (1998). WISC-III assessment of children with attention deficit hyperactivity disorder. In A. Prifitera & D. Saklofske (Eds.), *WISC-III: Clinical use and interpretation* (pp. 91–118). San Diego, CA: Academic Press.

Schwean, V. L., Saklofske, D. H., Yackulic, R. A., & Quinn, D. (1993). WISC-III performance of ADHD children. *Journal of Psychoeducational Assessment,* 56–70.

Wenar, C., & Kerig, P. (2000). *Developmental psychopathology: From infancy through adolescence* (4th ed.). New York: McGraw-Hill.

CASE OF SCOTT MICHAELS: RESULTS FROM PSYCHOLOGICAL TESTING

Results of the multimodal assessment battery are presented in the form of standard scores, T scores, and/or percentiles. Anecdotal comments from the clinic psychologist (e.g., comments on test behaviors, etc.) are presented whenever these comments might aid in interpretation of the findings. In addition, a list of endorsed items is provided for any scales (checklists and rating scales) elevated to clinical levels to facilitate interpretation of behavioral patterns within and across sources of information.

Results are presented in their entirety rather than in summarized form to provide the intern with maximum opportunity to develop independent skills in the analysis and synthesis of information from multiple sources.

General Cognitive (WISC-IV, WJIII Cog) and Academic (WJIII Ach) Results

Wechsler Intelligence Scale for Children, Fourth Edition (WISC-IV)

Index and Scales	Standard Score (Range 95% confidence level)	Percentile
Verbal Comprehension Similarities (7) Vocabulary (8) Comprehension (6)	83 (Range 77–91) Borderline to Average Range	13
Perceptual Reasoning Block Design (8) Matrix Reasoning (9) Picture Concepts (10)	93 (Range 85–100) Low Average to Average Range	30
Working Memory Digit Span (7) Letter–Number Sequence (6)	80 (Range 74–89) Borderline to Low Average	9
Processing Speed Symbol Search (10) Coding (7)	90 (Range 82–100) Low Average to Average Range	26
Full Scale IQ	88 (Range 83–93)	21

Administrator Comments: Requested many repetitions of more complex verbal information, such as comprehension questions. Extreme difficulty with letter–number sequence task: could not understand that numbers were to be cited first in numerical order, followed by letters in alphabetical order. Could not remember the instructions from trial to trial; word finding problems on similarities task. Vocabulary limited. As comprehension questions became more involved, he got more confused and required prompting to expand verbal responses. Often off-target or peripheral in responses; missed the main point. Responded to "lost" as if responding to "found" in comprehension question and exchanged meanings for interrogatives (e.g., responded to a *what* question with a *when* response). Slow to respond to visual tasks. Scott did not earn any bonus points on block design. He did better on visual nontimed tasks. Poor attention to details: missed a symbol on Coding, which made five incorrect symbols in a row and had to go back and erase and restart, which cost him time.

Wide Range Achievement Test (WRAT-IV)

Subject	Standard Score	Percentile	Grade Level
Word Reading	95	37	3
Sentence Comprehension	80	10	2
Reading Composite	86	18	2
Spelling	86	18	2
Math Computation	103	58	4

Administrator Comments: Visual whole-word speller; poor phonetic speller and sound substitutions (correct = qurecht; circle = curcal). Sentence comprehension revealed poor sequencing of information, which altered the meaning.

Woodcock Johnson Achievement Test (WJIII-Ach)

Subject	Standard Score	Percentile	Grade Level
Basic Reading Skills	91	26	4
Reading Comprehension	79	8	1.5
Math Calculation	100	50	4
Math Reasoning	82	11	2
Written Expression	83	13	2

Administrator Comments: Sequencing and processing problems lowered scores in math reasoning (word problems), reading comprehension (could not retain sequence of information to assist with comprehension), and written expression. Could not follow directions for written expression and answers did not match the oral prompt that was given.

Woodcock Johnson Cognitive Test (WJIII Cog)		
Cluster/Area	*Standard Score*	*Percentile*
Overall Comprehension/Knowledge	86 (82–90)	17
Verbal Comprehension	83 (78–88)	13
General Information	89 (89–94)	23
Overall Processing Speed	76 (74–79)	6
Visual Matching	75 (72–79)	5
Decision Speed	83 (79–87)	13
Overall Cognitive Fluency	67 (65–69)	1
Retrieval Fluency	74 (67–82)	4
Rapid Picture Naming	70 (68–71)	2

Administrator Comments: Seemed to have considerable difficulty with retrieving words when asked (name as many animals as you can, etc.), and also took significantly longer than expected to label pictures of common objects. Became very frustrated on retrieval tasks and said that it wasn't fair because he wasn't given enough time.

Checklists and Rating Scales

Assessment results are presented for Scott's responses to three assessment instruments that measure social, emotional, and behavioral functioning: Achenbach System of Empirically Based Assessment (ASEBA; Achenbach & Rescorla, 2000); The Conners Rating Scales-Revised (Conners, 1997); and the Beck Youth Inventories of Emotional and Social Impairment, 2nd ed. (Beck, Beck, & Jolly, 2005).

ASEBA

The scores below are from the multi-informant assessment using the Child Behavior Checklist (CBCL; completed by Scott's mother) and the Teacher Report Form (TRF; completed by Scott's teacher).

Anecdotal Comments (Teacher): Starting to get more argumentative. Can be bossy at times, especially with younger children. Academics are starting to slide. Good sense of humor but can also be sarcastic. Good when he is doing what he wants to do. Can be stubborn and immature.

The Revised Conners Rating Scales

The Conners rating scales allow for multiple informants to provide information concerning common attention problems, and symptoms of attention-deficit/hyperactivity based on

Achenbach System of Empirically Based Assessment (ASEBA) Scales

SYNDROMES	CBCL (T Score)	TRF (T Score)
INTERNALIZING PROBLEMS		
Anxious/Depressed	**65**	61
Withdrawn/Depressed	**67 Borderline**	64
Somatic Complaints	56	57
Total Internalizing	**68 Borderline Clinical**	**62**
Other Problems		
Social Problems	**65**	**70 Clinical** Doesn't get along, Jealous, Not liked, Prefers younger kids
Thought Problems	**65**	58
Attention Problems	**70** Acts young, Fails to finish, Can't sit still, Stares, Confused	**70** Acts young, Fails to finish, Daydreams, Impulsive, Problems with directions, Poor schoolwork, Messy, Inattentive, Doesn't listen
EXTERNALIZING PROBLEMS		
Rule Breaking	**65**	56
Aggressive Behavior	**73** Argues, Brags, Mean, Demands attention, Destroys own stuff, Disobeys, Jealous, Fights, Attacks, Screams, Shows off, Stubborn, Mood changes, Temper, Loud play	63
Total Externalizing	**71**	62
TOTAL PROBLEMS	**65**	**67**
Teacher Attention Problems Subscale	**Inattention 95th percentile**	**Hyperactive/Impulsive 95th percentile**

Note: Bold-faced numbers indicate scales in the significant range. Individual items endorsed by the respondent are listed for each of the significant scales.

criteria from the *DSM-IV-TR* (APA, 2000). There are long and short versions of the rating scales available. In this case, the Conners Parent Rating Scale (CRRS-R:L) and Conners Teacher Rating Scale (CTRS-R:L) were completed by Scott's mother and teacher.

Achenbach System of Empirically Based Assessment (ASEBA) Scales

Behaviors	Rating Scales	
	Parent (CPRS-R:L) (T Scores)	*Teacher (CTRS-R:L)(T Scores)*
Oppositional	**71** Argues, Loses temper, Irritable, Defies, Touchy/annoyed, Blames others, Annoys others	65
Cognitive Problems/ Inattention	60	**70** Forgets what he has learned, Careless mistakes, Avoids tasks of sustained effort, Doesn't listen, Problems with organization, Loses things, Poor follow-through
Hyperactivity	**66** Problems with quiet play, Restless	**70** Excitable impulsive, Restless/overactive, Difficulty waiting his turn, Fidgeting, Difficulty quiet play, Blurts out answers, Interrupts others
Anxious/Shy	50	60
Perfectionism	52	49
Social Problems	53	**68** Poor social skills, Does not know how to make friends, Unaccepted by group, One of last to be picked for games
Psychosomatic	42	
Conners ADHD Index	60	**68**
Conners Global Index: Restless/Impulsive	54	**67**
Emotional Lability	**72** Cries often & easily, Rapid mood shifts	65
Global Index Total	62	**66**
DSM-IV: Inattentive	59	**72** Forgets what already learned, Poor attention to details, Avoids tasks of sustained attention, Does not seem to listen, Difficulty organizing, Loses things necessary for tasks, Fails to follow-through
DSM-IV: Hyp/Impulsive (Continued)	**68** Fidgets, Squirms, Problems with quiet play, Problems remaining seated	**70** On the go, Leaves seat, Problems waiting turn, Problems remaining seated, Fidgets, Interrupts, Incessant talking, Always on the go
DSM-IV: Total	**66**	**70**

Note: Shaded areas for items not on the rater's scale.

Beck Youth Inventories of Emotional and Social Impairment (2nd Edition)

This self-report scale has 20 questions for each area assessed. Youth respond to a Likert-type response format to indicate the degree to which an item is like or unlike them: Never = 0, Sometimes = 1, Often = 2, Always = 3.

Beck Youth Inventories

Area Assessed	T Score	Percentile
Self-Concept Inventory Items endorsed for negative self-concept (0, 1) Feel strong; Like myself; Just as good as others; Normal; Good person; Do things well; Happy to be me; Proud of self	57	75
Depression Inventory for Youth Items rated as 2 or 3: Feel like bad things happen to me; I want to be alone	39	11
Anxiety Inventory for Youth Items rated as 2 or 3: My dreams scare me, I'm afraid I might get hurt, Afraid something bad might happen to me	40	15
Anger Inventory for Youth Items rated as 2 or 3: People try to cheat me; I feel like screaming; People are unfair; People try to hurt me; Life is unfair; People bully me; People make me mad, bother me, try to control me, put me down, are against me; I get angry; When I get mad, I stay mad and have trouble getting over it	**86**	99
Disruptive Behavior Inventory for Youth Items rated as 2 or 3: Others get me into trouble, I fight with others, I like getting people mad, I hate listening to others, I argue with adults, I like it when others are scared of me, I like to trick people, I break things when angry, I swear at adults	**68**	94

CASE OF ARTHUR WATSON: RESULTS FROM PSYCHOLOGICAL TESTING

Results of the multimodal assessment battery are presented in the form of standard scores, T scores, and/or percentiles. Interns will be expected to evaluate, interpret, and integrate findings to formulate a more refined diagnostic impression. Anecdotal comments from the clinic psychologist (e.g., comments on test behaviors, etc.) are presented whenever these comments might aid in interpretation of the findings. In addition, a list of endorsed items is provided for any scales (checklists and rating scales) elevated to clinical levels to facilitate interpretation of behavioral patterns within and across sources of information.

Results are presented in their entirety rather than in summarized form to provide the intern with maximum opportunity to develop independent skills in the analysis and synthesis of information from multiple sources.

General Cognitive (WISC-IV) and Academic (WRAT-IV) Results

Wechsler Intelligence Scale for Children, Fourth Edition (WISC-IV)		
Index and Scales	*Standard Score (Range 95% confidence level)*	*Percentile*
Verbal Comprehension Similarities (1) Vocabulary (1) Comprehension (3)	55 (Range 51–62) Mentally Deficient Range	0.1
Perceptual Reasoning Block Design (4) Matrix Reasoning (4) Picture Concepts (7)	69 (Range 65–76) Mentally Deficient to Borderline Range	2
Working Memory Digit Span (1) Letter Number Sequence (2)	55 (Range 51–62) Mentally Deficient Range	0.1
Processing Speed Symbol Search (2) Coding (2)	54 (Range 49–61) Mentally Deficient Range	0.1
Full Scale IQ	57 (Range 53–64) Mentally Deficient Range	0.2

Administrator Comments: Arthur is left-handed. He asked for numerous repetitions of comprehension questions. He experienced problems understanding verbal instructions without any visual aids. Better able to process visual information. Enjoyed picture concepts, until it became more complex and then got frustrated, and engaged in random responding. Block design was an all-or-nothing approach (he either got it right or did not get it at all).

Wide Range Achievement Test (WRAT-IV)

Subject	Standard Score	Percentile	Grade Level
Word Reading	52	0.1	1.5
Sentence Comprehension	50	0.1	1.3
Reading Composite	50	0.1	1.3
Spelling	57	0.2	1.5
Math Computation	Below 45	<0.1	1.2

Administrator Comments: Very frustrated. Said he knew it but forgot because it is summer. Upset with math computations, used his fingers for counting, and said the test was not fair because he didn't take that type of math yet. Number and letter formations were very large and immature. Responded well to a calm approach and confirmation that he did his best and that was most important.

ASEBA

The scores below are from the multi-informant assessment using the Child Behavior Checklist (CBCL; completed by Arthur's parents). The Teacher Report Form (TRF) was not available, since Arthur is currently not attending school, and it was not possible to obtain the Youth Self Report (YSR) due to comprehension/attention problems.

Achenbach System of Empirically Based Assessment (ASEBA) Scales

SYNDROMES	CBCL (T Score)
INTERNALIZING PROBLEMS	
Anxious/Depressed	**70 Clinical Range** Lonely, Feels others are out to get him, Worthless, Nervous, Sad, Worries
Withdrawn/Depressed	**65**
Somatic Complaints	**68 Borderline** Complains of headaches, Tired, Aches
Total Internalizing	**71 Clinical Range**
Other Problems	
Social Problems	**70 Clinical Range** Acts young, Not get along, Not liked, Clumsy
Thought Problems	**65**
Attention Problems	**85 Clinical Range** Acts young, Fails to finish, Can't concentrate, Problems sitting still, Confused, Impulsive, Poor schoolwork, Inattentive, Stares

EXTERNALIZING PROBLEMS	
Rule Breaking	55
Aggressive Behavior	**75** Demanding attention, Attacking others, Temper outbursts, Teasing, Threatening, Argues, Jealous, Mood changes, Loud
Total Externalizing	**68**
TOTAL PROBLEMS	**72**
Other Problems: Speech Problems, Sleep problems, Bites nails	

Note: Bold-faced numbers indicate scales in the significant range. Individual items endorsed by the respondent are listed for each of the significant scales.

Anecdotal Comments: Interview revealed that parents believe that attention problems are result of ADHD, and do not consider that these symptoms may be an indication that Arthur is frustrated, and unable to attend, finish tasks, and achieve in school and is confused due to his inability to comprehend tasks.

Measures of Adaptive Functioning

Vineland Adaptive Behavior Scales

These scales were completed by the caregiver and provide an index of adaptive functioning in three areas: Communication, Daily Living, and Socialization.

Vineland Adaptive Behavior Scales

Domains	Raw Score	Standard Score	Age Equivalent
Communication Domain			
Receptive			
Expressive			
Written			
Total Communication	125	83	12 years 6 months
Daily Living Skills Domain			
Personal			
Domestic			
Community			
Total Daily Living Skills	161	99	15 years 3 months
Socialization Domain			
Interpersonal Skills			
Play and Leisure Skills			
Coping Skills			
Total Socialization Skills	117	96	14 years 9 months

Anecdotal Comments: Arthur's chronological age is 15 years 5 months. Parent believes that Arthur is functioning at his appropriate age level in the majority of areas. Communication is in the low average range.

American Association of Mental Retardation (AAMR) Adaptive Behavior Scale: ABS-S:2

PART I: Domain Scores	Standard Score (0 to 20)	Percentile	Age Score
Independent Functioning	17	99	16+
Physical Development	10	50	16+
Economic Activity	11	63	16+
Language Development	7	16	8 years 6 months
Numbers & Time	11	63	16+
Prevocation/Vocational	10	50	16+
Self-direction	20	37	16+
Responsibility	11	63	16+
Socialization	9	37	16+

American Association of Mental Retardation (AAMR) Adaptive Behavior Scale: ABS-S:2 (higher standard scores indicate higher adjustment)

PART II: Domain Scores	Standard Score (0 to 20)	Percentile
Social Behavior	9	37
Conformity	10	50
Trustworthiness	14	91
Stereotyped & Hyperactive	8	25
Self-Abusive Behavior	63	11
Social Engagement	10	50
Disturbing Interpersonal Behavior	7	16

Anecdotal Comments: Consistent with ratings on the Vineland scales, Arthur's mother rates his functioning on Part I domains (adaptive functioning) to be above his age level in all areas, except Language Development. Ratings for Part II domains (social and emotional maturity) reveal problems in disturbing interpersonal behaviors, and stereotyped and hyperactive behaviors.

CASE OF SHIRLEY YONG: RESULTS FROM PSYCHOLOGICAL TESTING

Results of the multimodal assessment battery are presented in the form of standard scores, T scores, and/or percentiles. Interns will be expected to evaluate, interpret, and integrate findings to formulate a more refined diagnostic impression. Anecdotal comments from the clinic psychologist (e.g., comments on test behaviors, etc.) are presented whenever these comments might aid in interpretation of the findings. In addition, a list of endorsed items is provided for any scales (checklists and rating scales) elevated to clinical levels to facilitate interpretation of behavioral patterns within and across sources of information.

Results are presented in their entirety rather than in summarized form to provide the intern with maximum opportunity to develop independent skills in the analysis and synthesis of information from multiple sources.

General Cognitive (WISC-IV) and Academic (WRAT-IV) Results

Wechsler Intelligence Scale for Children, Fourth Edition (WISC-IV)

Index and Scales	Standard Score (Range 95% confidence level)	Percentile
Verbal Comprehension Similarities (9) Vocabulary (11) Comprehension (11)	100 (Range 93–107) Average Range	50
Perceptual Reasoning Block Design (7) Matrix Reasoning (8) Picture Concepts (8)	84 (Range 79–93) Low Average Range	14
Working Memory Digit Span (8) Letter–Number Sequence (6)	83 (Range 77–92) Low Average Range	13
Processing Speed Symbol Search (11) Coding (10)	83 (Range76–94) Low Average Range	13
Full Scale IQ	86 (Range 81–91) Low Average Range	18

Administrator Comments: Methodical approach to completing the block design task, and she did not earn any bonus points due to the time taken. Very perfectionistic, lining up edges on blocks so they matched perfectly. Although picture concepts and matrix reasoning are not timed, Shirley spent excessive time agonizing over her selections, and changed her responses often, throughout. Multiple responses to verbal questions, as if unsure of her responses, and elaborated extensively, often resulting in responses digressing from the original point. Frequent requests for feedback regarding her responses, e.g., "Is that right?"

Wide Range Achievement Test (WRAT-IV)

Subject	Standard Score	Percentile	Grade Level
Word Reading	92	30	Grade 5
Sentence Comprehension	95	37	Grade 5
Reading Composite	93	32	Grade 5
Spelling	106	66	Grade 6
Math Computation	90	25	Grade 4

Administrator Comments: Word decoding was not fluid. Often stopped to check for feedback. Read very slowly. Math questions noted several erasures and changed answers. Used tally marks in the margins to check on accuracy of multiplication tables. Shirley counted on her fingers to check addition. Did not attempt many math items, and left them blank. Spelling also took additional time due to perfectionistic tendencies, and careful attention to letter formations. Did not use cursive writing, because she said that printing was neater.

Checklists and Rating Scales

Assessment results are presented for Shirley's responses to four assessment instruments that measure social, emotional, and behavioral functioning: Achenbach System of Empirically Based Assessment (ASEBA; Achenbach & Rescorla, 2000), the Conners Rating Scales-Revised (Conners, 1997), the Beck Youth Inventories of Emotional and Social Impairment, 2nd ed. (Beck, Beck, & Jolly, 2005), the Child Depression Inventory (CDI; Kovacs, 1992), and the Revised Children's Manifest Anxiety Scale (RCMAS-2; Reynolds & Richmond, 2008).

ASEBA

The scores below are from the multi-informant assessment using the Child Behavior Checklist (CBCL; completed by Shirley's mother), the Teacher Report Form (TRF; completed by Shirley's teacher), and the Youth Self Report (YSR; completed by Shirley).

Achenbach System of Empirically Based Assessment (ASEBA) Scales

SYNDROMES	CBCL (T Score)	TRF (T Score)	YSR (T Score)
INTERNALZING PROBLEMS			
Anxious/Depressed	**73** Fearful, Self-conscious	**72** Fear of mistakes, Very conforming	**72** Cries, Feels guilty, Self-conscious
Withdrawn/Depressed	**68** Secretive, Underactive	**66**	**69** Secretive, Shy, Underactive, Withdrawn
Somatic Complaints	**74** Tired, Aches, Nausea	**66**	**69** Tired, Aches, Headaches, Stomach Problems
Total Internalizing	**75 Clinical Range**	**72 Clinical Range**	**77 Clinical Range**
Other Problems			
Social Problems	57	**63**	**70** Not get along, Teased, Not liked, Withdrawn
Thought Problems	**73** Obsessions, Repeats acts	**70** Obsessions, Repeats acts	**70** Obsessions, Repeats acts, Collects stuff, Strange behavior
Attention Problems	**70** Concentration, Confused, Nervous	60	**67** Concentration, Confused, Daydreams, Nervous, Poor schoolwork
EXTERNALIZING PROBLEMS			
Rule Breaking	50	50	50
Aggressive Behavior	50	50	50
Total Externalizing	44	42	27
TOTAL PROBLEMS	*58*	*58*	*52*
Other Problems	Fears, Nail biting, Nightmares, Sleeps less		Fears, Fears school, Gets hurt a lot, Bites nails, Nightmares, Eats too much, Overweight, Sleeps less, Sleep problems (wakes up in middle of night)

Note: Bold-faced numbers indicate scales in the significant range. Individual items endorsed by the respondent are listed for each of the significant scales.

Anecdotal Comments: On the Anxious/Depressed scale, all three raters endorsed perfectionistic, nervous, worries.

The Revised Conners Rating Scales

The Conners rating scales allow for multiple informants to provide information concerning common attention problems, and symptoms of attention-deficit/hyperactivity based on criteria from the *DSM-IV-TR* (APA, 2000). There are long and short versions of the rating scales available. In this case, the long version of the Conners Parent Rating Scale (CRRS-R:L) and Conners Teacher Rating Scale (CTRS-R:L) were completed by Shirley's mother and teacher.

Revised Conners Rating Scales

Behaviors	*Rating Scales*	
	Parent (CPRS-R:L) *(T Scores)*	*Teacher (CTRS-R:L)* *(T Scores)*
Oppositional	62	46
Cognitive Problems/ Inattention	**70** Difficulty with homework, Sustained mental effort, Fails to complete work, Trouble concentrating, Needs supervision	**69** Forgets what learned, Fails to finish, Not reading as expected, Poor in math
Hyperactivity	44	46
Anxious/Shy	**85** Timid, Afraid of people, Afraid of new situations, Lots of fears, Shy/withdrawn, Clings to adults	**78** Feelings easily hurt, Timid, Easily frightened, Sensitive to criticism, Shy/withdrawn
Perfectionism	**88** Everything must be just so, Keeps checking and rechecking, Fusses about cleanliness, Must be done same way, Rigid, Has rituals, Sets high goals for self, Upset if things are rearranged	**85** Perfectionistic, Everything must be just so, Keeps checking and rechecking, Overfocused on details, Likes neat and clean, Things done same way every time, Rigid
Social Problems	**84** Loses friends quickly, doesn't know how to make friends, Feels inferior to others	**90** Unaccepted by group, Last to be picked, No friends, Doesn't know how to make friends, Poor social skills
Psychosomatic	**90** Stomachaches, Aches and pains, Aches before school, Complaints without cause, Headaches, Tired/fatigued	

Behaviors	Rating Scales	
Conners ADHD Index	**67** Problems with sustained mental effort, Concentration problems, Fails to finish, Inattentive	62
Conners Global Index: Restless/Impulsive Emotional Lability Global Index Total	 62 60 62	 46 58 54
DSM-IV : Inattentive	62	**66**
DSM-IV: Hyperactive/Impulsive	43	45
DSM-IV: Total	54	58

Note: Shaded areas for item not on the rater's scale.

Beck Youth Inventories of Emotional and Social Impairment (2nd Edition)

This self report scale has 20 questions for each area assessed. Youth respond to a Likert-type response format that indicates the degree to which an item is like or unlike them: Never = 0; Sometimes = 1; Often = 2; Always = 3.

Beck Youth Inventories

Area Assessed	T Score	Percentile
Self-Concept Inventory Items endorsed for negative self-concept (0, 1) Just as good as other kids, Good at jokes, People think I am good at things, Like my body	28	4.5
Depression Inventory for Youth Items rated as 2 or 3: Trouble sleeping, Feel no one loves me, Stomach hurts, Feel bad things will happen, Feel stupid, Do things badly, Feel bad about what I do, Feel like crying, Feel sad	**70**	95
Anxiety Inventory for Youth Items rated as 2 or 3: Worry might be hurt at home, Scary dreams, Worry at school, Think of scary things, Worry about being teased, Afraid of making mistakes, Get nervous, Afraid of being hurt, Worry people might get mad at me, I worry a lot, Problems sleeping, Heart pounds, Afraid bad things will happen to me, Afraid might get sick	**79**	98.5

(Continued)

Beck Youth Inventories (Continued)

Area Assessed	T Score	Percentile
Anger Inventory for Youth Items rated as 2 or 3: Think people are unfair, Think others try to hurt me, Life is unfair, People bully me, People try to put me down	57	82
Disruptive Behavior Inventory for Youth (No ratings 2 or higher)	47	47

Anecdotal comments: For the Anxiety inventory, Shirley responded with a rating of often or always for 80% of the items on the scale (16 out of 20 items).

Further Assessment of Anxiety and Depression

Revised Children's Manifest Anxiety Scale, 2nd ed. (RCMAS-2)

The RCMAS-2 is a children's self-report scale used to assess anxiety levels in children and youth. This recently revised scale can be used with children 6 to 19 years of age and contains five scales, including a scale that provides a measure of validity of the child's responses (consistency index).

RCMAS-2

Scale	T Score	Percentile
Physiological Anxiety	**68**	96
Defensiveness	50	51
Worry	**73**	99
Social Anxiety	**70**	98
Inconsistent Responding Index	45	30

Anecdotal Comments: Physiological symptoms included feel sick to my stomach, hands feel sweaty, and have trouble getting my breath. Endorsed majority of items for worry and feeling anxious around other people (social anxiety).

Child Depression Inventory: CDI

This self-report instrument has 27 items that are arranged in a hierarchy from little to moderate and severe problems (e.g., *I can do most work. I can do some work. I can't do any work.*). Children select which response from the three alternatives is most like them.

Child Depression Inventory

Scale	T Score	Percentile
Total CDI Score	**74**	*99*
Negative Mood Sad many times, Worry bad things will happen to me, Things bother me many times	64	92
Interpersonal Problems Do not like being with people many times, Get into fights with others often	**67**	94
Ineffectiveness Do many things wrong, Have to push myself to do schoolwork, Schoolwork is not as good as before, Can never be as good as other kids	**70**	98
Anhedonia I have trouble sleeping every night, Tired all the time, Many days I do not feel like eating, Worry about aches and pains, Feel alone many times	**69**	97
Negative Self-Esteem Not sure if things will work out for me, Do not like myself, Think about killing myself, but would not do it, Look ugly, Not sure if anybody loves me	**73**	99

Hopeless Scale: Kazdin (1986)

True-and-false scale to assess degree of hopelessness. Endorsed the following items as FALSE: Want to grow up because . . . things will get better; Can imagine my life 10 years from now; I will get more good things in life than most other kids. Endorsed the following items as TRUE: Things just don't work out the way I want them to; Tomorrow seems unclear and confusing to me. Total Score = 5, which is just below the threshold for High Hopelessness.

Systems of Classification

Given the complexity of issues involved in child and adolescent psychopathology, it is not surprising that clinicians may reveal wide variations in how they conceptualize maladjustment in childhood. In the introduction, the case of Terry Hogan provided a living example of the myriad explanations that could be presented to explain the emotional and behavioral concerns that were evident, based on the assumptions inherent in different theoretical perspectives. This disparity is evident in how terms are defined, how processes are conceptualized, and the relative weight certain factors are assigned in the overall design.

Although most clinicians would agree that a major goal of child assessment is to determine where the child's presenting behavior fits within the realm of adaptive and maladaptive behaviors, there are several issues regarding how to categorize or classify the behavior within the broad scheme of other mental disorders or maladaptive behaviors.

There are at least three major clinical approaches to organizing and classifying information concerning child and adolescent disorders or problem behaviors: categorical classification (*DSM*), empirical or dimensional classification (e.g., behavioral rating scales: ASEBA: Achenbach & Rescorla, 2001; BASC- 2: Reynolds & Kamphus, 2004), and comparing behaviors to normative expectations or developmental psychopathology. It is assumed that information regarding these classification systems will be well documented in any number of other clinically relevant courses, and it is not the intention of this text to provide additional coverage in these areas.

However, a major intent of the text is to provide the student with information that will assist in understanding the complexity of the child's environment and to assist in the application of that understanding to contextually relevant materials.

To this end, presentation of information on educational classification is considered to be highly relevant to practice in the real world and an area that is likely to have minimal coverage in other clinical courses. Questions at the end of each case study will reinforce the presentation by addressing some of the variations between the clinical and educational systems of classification regarding the classification of four primary disorders: mental retardation/intellectual and developmental disabilities learning disabilities, serious emotional disturbance, and attention-deficit/hyperactivity disorder.

A CLINICIAN'S GUIDE TO EDUCATIONAL CLASSIFICATION

Historical Background and Theoretical Information

Education and the Law

Given the nature and impact of the child's environment on issues of assessment and treatment, the importance of having a working knowledge of legislation affecting the rights of the disabled child within the educational system cannot be understated. Three laws are of particular importance in this regard: the Americans with Disabilities Act Amendments Act of 2008 (ADAAA), which was passed by Congress in December 2008; Section 504 of the Rehabilitation Act of 1973; and Individuals with Disabilities Education Improvement Act (IDEA, 2004), which was signed into law December 2004 and became effective as of July 1, 2005. From a perspective of governance, the U.S. Department of Education (DOE) is responsible for overseeing public school compliance with laws pertaining to issues of civil liberties (ADAAA, Section 504) and educational rights (IDEA, 2004).

ADAAA and Section 504

Very briefly, the ADAAA and Section 504 are civil rights laws that prohibit discrimination against individuals with disabilities. The ADAAA prohibits discrimination on the basis of disability in employment, public services, and accommodation to perform major life activities, such as caring for oneself, performing manual tasks, seeing, hearing, speaking, breathing, learning, and working. In the new version, ADAAA has added eating, sleeping, walking, standing, lifting, bending, reading, concentrating, thinking, and communicating to "major life activities" for which reasonable accommodations are required for individuals with disabilities to enable them to perform essential job functions. Some examples of reasonable accommodations include removing transportation barriers, redesigning equipment, assigning aides, and providing communication in various formats. ADAAA also covers accommodations to students who may be involved in community job placements.

Section 504 is a federal law that protects the rights of individuals with disabilities enrolled in programs and activities that are federally funded and receiving financial assistance from the U.S. Department of Education. Under Section 504, school districts are required to provide a "free appropriate public education" (FAPE) to each qualified student with a disability in the school district's jurisdiction, regardless of the nature or severity of the disability. Services may be provided in regular or special education programs; however, they must be designed to meet the student's individual educational needs as adequately as the needs of nondisabled students are met. Under Section 504, if a physical or mental impairment substantially restricts one or more major life activities, then individuals are eligible for services. Children who do not meet criteria for special services under IDEA may obtain accommodations to support their learning, behavioral, or emotional needs under Section 504. Often, children with attention-deficit/hyperactivity disorder (ADHD) who do not require more specialized programming, such as is available under IDEA, or who do not qualify under IDEA, can receive accommodations under Section 504. It is important to note that any student who qualifies for special education services would also be eligible under Section 504, but the reverse is not necessarily true (i.e., a student eligible under Section 504 is not necessarily eligible under IDEA).

Safeguards for parents and guardians under Section 504 include prerequisite permission for assessments and informed notice of any significant placement changes. The local education agencies (e.g., school districts) are required to provide due process hearings if parents disagree with the identification, evaluation, or placement decisions.

Critique. Both civil rights laws provide vague descriptions of who may qualify as disabled. Under each law, any individual with a disability who (a) has a physical or mental impairment that substantially limits one or more life activities, or (b) has a record of such impairment, or (c) is regarded as having such an impairment, qualifies. The federal government does not provide direct funding to implement either of the civil rights laws. There are limited tax credits available to remove architectural barriers, and federal agencies provide grants to public and private institutions supporting training and technical assistance. Section 504 is also the fiscal responsibility of the state. Funds from IDEA may not be used to service children who are eligible solely under Section 504, although, as of 2005, in the spirit of "early intervention" for school-age children, IDEA has determined that districts can use up to 15% of the funding available for students enrolled in regular education for students who are at risk of needing special education services in the future. These funds can be used to provide direct services or teacher training.

IDEA 2004

The Individuals with Disabilities Education Improvement Act (IDEA, 2004) is a revision of IDEA that was reauthorized in 1997. The IDEA is an education act that provides federal funding assistance to state and local education agencies to guarantee that special education services (individualized educational programs, or IEPs) and related services (e.g., speech and language pathology, physical and occupational therapy) are available for children up to 21 years of age who are deemed disabled. Under IDEA, there are 13 possible categories of eligibility for disabilities: autism; deaf-blindness; deafness; emotional disturbance; hearing impairment; mental retardation; multiple disabilities; orthopedic impairment; other health impairment; specific learning disability; speech or language impairment; traumatic brain injury; and visual impairment, including blindness. Several changes were included in IDEA 2004, including increased state and school district accountability, educational accountability, educational requirements (accommodations, and alternate assessments for children with disabilities), efficiency (paperwork reduction, meetings), student conduct (alternative setting placements changed from 45 calendar to 45 school days, and positive behavioral interventions), and provision of discretionary funds for early intervention. One of the major changes in the law concerns criteria surrounding specific learning disabilities, which will be discussed shortly.

Critique. There have been several criticisms regarding IDEA that have been directed toward (a) problems of definition or classification of disabilities and (b) issues of inconsistencies in interpretation or compliance with federal guidelines at the state and local levels. Three of the 13 categories of disabilities eligible for funding under IDEA have been especially problematic and have generated significant research and controversy: mental retardation (educable mentally retarded [EMR]) or mild mental retardation [MMR]/intellectual disabilities), learning disabilities, and emotional and behavioral disturbance/serious emotional disturbance (EBD/SED).

MacMillan and Reschly (1998) have referred to these three categories as the "judgmental categories" because classification reliability for these three categorical groups is considerably less than that for the more biologically based and well-defined disabilities (e.g., disabilities of physical or sensory impairment). Issues in the classification/identification of ADHD will be addressed shortly.

APPLICATIONS, LIMITATIONS, AND SPECIAL TOPICS IN CLASSIFICATION

Intellectual Disabilities (ID)

As has been noted previously, the term mental retardation has recently been changed to intellectual and developmental disabilities (IDD) by the American Association on Intellectual and Developmental Disabilities (AAIID, 2007), which has replaced the American Association on Mental Retardation (AAMR). With the development of intelligence tests in the early 1900s, increasing emphasis was placed on using IQ scores as the single defining feature of for intellectual disability (ID). By the mid-1900s, this practice was receiving increasing criticism for two important reasons: (a) concentration on IQ scores placed minimal emphasis on the role of social adaptation in defining ID populations, and (b) the growing belief that IQ scores were biased with respect to psychosocial and cultural influences. Proponents of including social adaptive factors in the definition of ID cited cases of the "6-hour retardates" who might encounter significant cognitive problems during their 6-hour schoolday, but whose social adaptive skills allowed them to function successfully outside the school system. In 1959, the AAMR officially stated that determination of mental retardation should include consideration of deficits in adaptive behavior as well as subnormal intellectual functioning. Despite AAMR's attempts to lobby in favor of deemphasizing IQ scores as the sole determinants of mental retardation, the practice continued for several years.

During the 1960s and 1970s, disproportionate numbers of minority students in special education programs increased concerns regarding the efficacy of IQ tests for minority populations, resulting in several lawsuits during this period. One such class action suit, *Larry P. v. Riles,* resulted in significant restrictions on the use of intellectual assessments for placing African American children in special education programs in California. In 1975, the passing of PL 94-142 (the Education for All Handicapped Children Act) provided the necessary support for the rights of the disabled and reaffirmed the need to incorporate both adaptive and intellectual features in the definition of mental retardation.

Today there are still concerns regarding the identification of disproportionate numbers of ethnic minorities who are placed in special education. Using data from 4,902 school districts sampled in the 1992 School Civil Right Compliance Report survey, Oswald, Coutinho, Best, and Nguyen (2001) found that African American students were nearly 2½ times as likely to be identified as having MMR and about 1½ times as likely to be identified as seriously emotionally disturbed (SED) compared to their non–African American peers. The study also revealed that poverty had a significant relation to this skewed representation; however, the direction of effects differed by condition for African American children. While African American children living in poverty were more likely to be identified as MMR, African American children in more affluent areas were more likely to be identified as SED.

Currently there are three systems of classification regarding intellectual disabilities (mental retardation): *DSM-IV-TR* (APA, 2000); AAIDD, 2007; and IDEA, 2004.

DSM-IV-TR (APA, 2000). There are three criteria necessary for a diagnosis of mental retardation according to the *DSM-IV-TR:* significantly subaverage intellectual functioning (below an IQ of approximately 70, approximately two standard deviations below the mean), concurrent deficits or limitations in adaptive functioning in at least two areas, and onset before the age of 18 years. The *DSM-IV-TR* further codes the degree of retardation according to level of intellectual functioning: mild (IQ 50–55 to 70), moderate (IQ level 35–40 to 50–55), severe (IQ level 20–25 to 35–40), and profound (IQ below 20–25). More detailed information regarding diagnostic criteria can be found in Appendix D.

AAIDD. The classification system of the AAIDD includes the same three criteria as the *DSM-IV-TR* with respect to IQ cutoff, adaptive functioning, and age of onset. However, the two systems differ in subsequent specifications. While the *DSM-IV-TR* codes MR relative to degrees of severity, the most recent classification of the AAIDD (2009a) profiles types of ID based on the degree of support services required: intermittent, limited, extensive, or pervasive (AAMR, 2002). The AAIDD system is based on the belief that proper supports will effectively enhance the functioning and quality of life for individuals with ID:

> While intellectual functioning, adaptive behavior, and age of onset remain the criteria for evaluating intellectual disability, supports remain the cornerstone of the AAIDD Definition System. AAIDD believes that once a diagnosis of intellectual disability is made, planning and providing supports is the key to reduce the mismatch between a person's capabilities and the skills, and what is required to successfully participate in all aspects of daily life. (AAIDD, 2009b)

Furthermore, while the *DSM-IV-TR* suggests that it is possible to diagnose MR in individuals whose IQ is between 71 and 75 (measurement error of ± 5 points) if they have sufficient adaptive behavior deficits, the AAIDD has been lobbying to raise the IQ cutoff from 70 to 75.

Education. Although the educational system also recognizes the need to include social and adaptive features of ID, most state education codes allocate funds for special education to children with disabilities, such as ID and the learning disabled (LD), based on IQ score cutoffs to determine eligibility for services. Initially, children who had an IQ between 55 and 80 were classified as educable mentally retarded (EMR), sometimes also referred to as educable mentally handicapped (EMH), while children who had an IQ between 25 and 55 were considered trainable mentally retarded (TMR), or trainable mentally handicapped (TMH). Currently, there is variation across states, with most states accepting an IQ cutoff between 70 and 75 to designate ID, although some states, like Iowa, have retained higher cutoff levels

(IQ 85; MacMillan & Forness, 1998). Within education, there has been continued controversy regarding how students are to be identified as ID; how these students are best serviced, once identified; and more recently, in the wave of AAIDD (2007), how these students should best be labeled.

Investigation of classification procedures or how students are identified has revealed both inconsistencies in the application of classification procedures and concerns regarding the impact of minority status and poverty levels on the decision-making process. Regarding classification, MacMillan and Forness (1998) found that of the 150 students (Grades 2, 3, and 4) referred to the student study teams (SST) from five school districts in California, only 6 of the 43 children who scored below 75 on the WISC-III (and met diagnostic criteria for MR) were classified/identified as MMR, while 19 were classified as LD—despite the fact that the mean academic levels were approximately 2½ standard deviations (SDs) below the mean. The authors suggest that comorbid externalizing problems in the 6 children identified as MR likely influenced placement decisions. Using this same subject sample of 150 students, MacMillan, Gresham, and Bocian (1998) also investigated outcomes for borderline students (IQ 71–85) and found that almost half (48%) of children referred to the SST were within the borderline range. Of this number, 27, or 41%, were ultimately categorized as LD. Of the 19 students who were within an acceptable limit for MR designation (71–75), only 1 was identified as MR.

Results from these and other studies have led MacMillan and colleagues to question the direction of special education, which has become increasingly insistent on assigning children to specific categories to meet compliance issues. With the recent changes to IDEA 2004, it is likely that increased use of response to intervention will result in either reducing the need for specific categories, or resulting in increased need to classify. Time will tell.

IDEA requires that student eligibility for special education be linked to only one disability category. As a consequence, children are assigned to only one category of disability, despite the fact that high rates of comorbidity exist between categories. Problems are most pronounced in what MacMillan and Reschly (1998) have called the "judgmental categories"—mild mental retardation (MMR), learning disabilities (LD), and emotionally and behaviorally disordered (EBD).

Learning Disabilities

The definition of LD, also referred to as specific learning disabilities (SLD), has remained a highly controversial area of debate. Currently there are several conflicting sources available for purposes of classification:

DSM-IV-TR: Learning Disorders and Communication Disorders. The *DSM-IV-TR* refers to learning disabilities as learning disorders (formerly called academic skills disorders), which can be evident in three primary areas: reading disorder, mathematics disorder, and disorders of written expression. A fourth category of learning disorder, NOS (not otherwise specified), might be diagnosed when significant impairment is evident but criteria are not met for the individual disorders. A learning disorder is diagnosed when measures of achievement (standardized assessments) are substantially below (discrepancy of more than two standard deviations between achievement and IQ) what is expected based on age, schooling, and level of intelligence. However, the discrepancy criteria are somewhat flexible (between 1 and 2 SDs) if other factors (cognitive, comorbid mental disorder, ethnic or cultural background) compromise IQ scores. The diagnostic guidelines from the *DSM-IV-TR* are available in Appendix D.

In keeping with other diagnostic features of the *DSM-IV-TR*, level of impairment is a key determining factor in defining learning disorders, and the impairment must significantly interfere with academic achievement or with functions of daily living. The definition is also exclusionary in that if sensory deficits are present, they must be ruled out as the primary cause of the learning difficulties. According to the *DSM-IV-TR*, it is expected that 5% of children in the public school system might be identified as having a learning disorder.

Although disorders of reading and mathematics are somewhat self-explanatory, it is important to note that disorders of spelling or of handwriting alone are excluded from a diagnosis of disorders of written expression. The key defining feature between learning disorders and ID is that for most cases with ID, achievement is commensurate with IQ, while for those with learning disorders as defined by the discrepancy criterion used in the *DSM-IV-TR*, there is a significant discrepancy existing between their IQ and their achievement.

The *DSM-IV-TR* also defines communication disorders, which consist of disorders of expressive language, mixed expressive-receptive disorder, phonological disorder (developmental articulation disorder), and stuttering.

Education: Specific Learning Disabilities (SLD). The federal definition of a learning disability appears in the Individuals with Disabilities Education Improvement Act (IDEA, 2004). (The document is available online at http://idea.ed.gov.)

IDEA 2004: Specific Learning Disability (SLD) Definition and Criteria

Definition

IDEA (2004) did not change the definition for SLD from the 1997 version. IDEA defines an SLD by the following criteria:

Specific learning disability

(i) means a disorder in one or more of the basic psychological processes involved in understanding or in using language, spoken or written, that may manifest itself in the imperfect ability to listen, think, speak, read, write, spell or to do mathematical calculations, including conditions such as perceptual disabilities, brain injury, minimal brain dysfunction, dyslexia, and developmental aphasia.

(ii) Disorders not included: Specific learning disability does not include learning problems that are primarily the result of visual, hearing or motor disabilities, of mental retardation, of emotional disturbance, or of environmental, cultural, or economic disadvantage. (Federal Register, 2006:300.8 (10), p. 46757)

Concerns exist with the wording of the definition, which was not changed despite several issues, including the use of vague terms such as *basic psychological processes* and *imperfect ability*.

Identification Procedures and Criteria

Despite maintaining the same definition, IDEA 2004 did make significant changes regarding *identification procedures and criteria* surrounding the use of the discrepancy criteria.

According to IDEA, 2004, policy and procedures to determine whether a child has an SLD are now at the discretion of the state, and

1. *Must not require* the use of a severe discrepancy between intellectual ability and achievement for determining whether a child has a specific learning disability;
2. *Must permit the use* of a process based on the child's response to scientific, research-based intervention;
3. *May permit the use* of other alternative research-based procedures for determining whether a child has a specific learning disability. (Federal Register, 300.307 (a), p. 46786)

This determination is made by the child's educational team, which includes a child's parents, a team of qualified professionals (child's teacher or teacher qualified to teach students of the child's age), and at least one professional who is qualified to conduct diagnostic examinations (school psychologist, speech pathologist, remedial reading teacher). Furthermore, the team must rule out that lack of achievement is not primarily due to a disability (visual, motor, hearing), mental retardation, emotional disturbance, cultural factors, economic disadvantage, limited English proficiency, or inappropriate instruction.

To ensure that underachievement is not due to inadequate teaching, documentation (data) of appropriate instruction (observations, and repeated assessments) and monitoring of progress during instruction are required. Ultimately, children who do not make adequate progress and continue to demonstrate a need for special education and related services will require parental permission for further (comprehensive) evaluation. IDEA considers evidence of SLD in eight possible areas of performance:

1. Oral expression
2. Listening comprehension
3. Written expression
4. Basic reading skill
5. Reading fluency skill
6. Reading comprehension
7. Mathematics calculation
8. Mathematics problem solving

Procedures acceptable, under IDEA, to determine SLD:

1. *Response to Intervention (RTI):* Evidence that the child does not improve in the identified academic areas when using a process (*a series of interventions*) based on the child's response to scientific, research-based intervention; or

2. *Pattern of Strengths and Weaknesses:* The child exhibits a pattern of strengths and weaknesses in performance, achievement or both relative to age (using grade level standards or intellectual information). This profile analysis (intra-individual differences in standard achievement scores or intellectual functioning [IQ]) often results in a comparison of response profiles within and between assessment instruments (academic achievement). This procedure has typically been used to determine a discrepancy between IQ and achievement in the past, and could still be used in this capacity.

National Joint Committee on Learning Disabilities (NJCLD). The NJCLD defines *learning disabilities* (LD) as a general term referring to heterogeneous groups of disorders manifested by significant difficulties in the acquisition and use of listening, speaking, reading, writing, reasoning, or mathematical abilities.

These disorders are intrinsic to the individual, presumed to be due to central nervous dysfunction, and may occur across the life span. Problems in self-regulatory behaviors, social perception, and social interaction may co-occur, but themselves do not constitute an LD. Although LD may occur with other handicapping conditions (e.g., sensory deficits, emotional disturbance, mental retardation, or cultural differences), they are not the result of those conditions or influences (NJCLD, 1987).

Learning Disabilities Generically and Specifically Defined. Byron Rourke has conducted numerous studies concerning subtypes of LD based on discrepancy response patterns evident on intelligence tests. As a result of his work, Rourke suggests a generic definition of LD is most appropriate. Although this "generic" definition supports the NJCLD definition in general, a major point of difference is evident in Rourke's view that "the term LD is also appropriately applied to instances where persons exhibit significant difficulties in mastering social and other adaptive skills and abilities" (Rourke, 1989, p. 215). Furthermore, according to Rourke, it is possible that emotional disturbances and other adaptive deficiencies may arise from the same patterns of central processing assets and deficits that generate the manifestations of academic and social LD (Rourke, 2000).

ISSUES IN THE DEFINITION AND CLASSIFICATION OF CHILDREN AND ADOLESCENTS WITH LEARNING DISABILITIES

Definitions of learning disabilities have been criticized on several fronts. The *DSM-IV-TR* definition has been faulted for being too narrow and considering only disorders of reading, mathematics, and written expression (excluding spelling) as true academic disorders. The definition has also been criticized theoretically in defining LD by exclusion (ruling out other disorders), thereby implying that coexisting disorders cannot occur. The NJCLD definition improves on the *DSM-IV-TR* by ruling in the possibility of co-occurring disorders and by introducing the heterogeneity of learning disorders; however, it fails to provide any operable guidelines for how to measure "significant difficulties in the acquisition" of academic skills. Although Rourke's generic definition also remains vague with respect to measurement of "significant difficulties in mastery" of academic skills, his definition improves on other definitions in the recognition of the existence of LD in areas of social and adaptive functioning. The federal definition (IDEA) has also been criticized for usage of vague terms such as *basic psychological process* and lack of guidance regarding measurement of the "manifestation of an imperfect ability." In addition, definition by exclusion also implies that disorders cannot coexist with LD. The *DSM-IV-TR* is the only definition that provides an objective measurement to define a significant discrepancy between IQ and achievement, and suggests a 2 standard deviations (SDs) rule be applied as a general guideline, although this criterion can be reduced to between 1 and 2 SDs if other factors compromise IQ level. However, as will be discussed shortly, there are several differences of opinion regarding the use and measurement of a discrepancy-based model.

Considering the differences evident in the four definitions presented, it is not difficult to understand why the concept of learning disabilities has met with such controversy. According to Kavale (2005), "The present SLD definition is too broad to be wrong and too vague to be complete" (Kavale, 2005). Furthermore, Kavale contends that "changes to the operational definition (RTI) without changes to the formal definition" are "indefensible" and result in a "disconnect between the formal definition and the operational definition" (p. 553). In support of this argument, Mather and Gregg (2006) agree for the need to achieve consensus on both the conceptual definition for SLD and the operational diagnostic criteria that will be used for the identification of SLD.

Some clinicians define the discrepancy between achievement and age expectations by comparing current grade level to current functioning level. A 2-year rule has been used in several instances; for example, a child in Grade 4 is functioning at least 2 years behind his or her current grade placement. However, using a fixed criterion may penalize students in the early grades while being too lenient for students in the later grades. Sattler (2002) states that some definitions attempt to address this issue by using a gradient of discrepancy based on grade level: 1 year for Grades 1 and 2, 1.5 years for Grades 3 and 4, 2 years for Grades 5 through 8, and 3 years for secondary school performance levels.

However, Sattler cautions against comparing achievement grade scores with actual grade scores since the practice is not sound statistically and is likely to lead to invalid conclusions.

Another method of defining discrepancy is to compare standard scores obtained on IQ tests with standard scores available from achievement tests. A common criterion applied to this method is to use discrepancies between 15 and 22 points (1.5 to 2 SDs) as significant. However, this method has also been criticized at the upper and lower levels. Comparisons at the upper levels may note a significant discrepancy, yet it is arguable whether this discrepancy would define a disability (e.g., IQ 145; achievement 125). At lower IQ levels, students who tend to score lower on IQ tests (low SES) may not reveal significant discrepancy in the other direction (e.g., IQ 85; achievement 75).

Furthermore, according to Sattler (2002), processing difficulties that affect achievement (e.g., vocabulary, comprehension, factual information) may also serve to reduce scores for intellectual functioning that requires the same processing abilities. Another difficulty arises when a significant discrepancy exists between IQ components, for example,

Verbal IQ (IQ = 85) and Performance IQ (IQ = 115). Under these conditions, the full scale IQ is rendered meaningless, since it represents only a numeric average of discrepant scores (Kaufman & Lichtenberger, 2000). Some clinicians would select the higher of the two IQs (in this case, Performance IQ), arguing that this score is the most representative of the child's true ability; others might select the Verbal IQ, stating Verbal IQ correlates better with academic performance. Despite these limitations and other statistical problems inherent in making comparisons between different test instruments (Sattler, 2002), Sattler's conclusion is in agreement with that suggested by Kavale, Forness, and MacMillan (1998), which supports the need to retain a discrepancy model as a necessary determining eligibility for LD. However, more research is needed to determine how best to employ this model (Sattler, 2002). Kavale, Holdnack, Mostert, and Schmied (2003) voice concern about throwing the baby out with the bathwater, and argue for more rigorous methods in implementing the discrepancy approach rather than adopting a new model.

Despite criticisms of the discrepancy model, many have failed to embrace the RTI approach as an alternative since the model is vague, especially concerning the potential role of teachers and diagnosticians; and how SLD will be differentiated from other disabilities: "if RTI cannot discriminate, how can it classify" (Mastropieri and Scruggs, 2005, p. 528).

Yet others prefer to take the middle ground and suggest a combination of the two approaches. Kavale et al. (2003) suggest using RTI as an initial step, or a "pre-referral writ large" that could enhance quality control in the regular classroom, but that is, in isolation, insufficient as an identification system for SLD. Similarly, Semrud-Clikeman (2005) suggests that RTI needs to integrate neuropsychology into the process, then screenings could focus on *predictor variables* (e.g., *working memory, attention, and executive functions*) that would not only allow for monitoring of progress in these crucial areas, but also provide access to those students who are at higher risk in these areas.

Emotional Disturbance

Educational: IDEA. Although the IDEA provides guidelines and definitions for categories of disabilities, there continues to be wide variation at the state level concerning how categories are defined. In addition, many of the disabilities that fall under IDEA are defined in educational terms, which can be at odds with more clinical definitions of childhood disorders. One such area is the category of emotional disturbance (previously called seriously emotionally disturbed). Children who are classified in this category will have a wide variety of emotional problems and/or behavioral concerns. Within IDEA, children who are considered to be emotionally or behaviorally disturbed are defined as having a long-lasting condition causing significant educational impairment that manifests in one of the following five areas:

1. Learning difficulties not explained by intellectual, sensory, or health factors
2. Difficulties developing or maintaining satisfactory interpersonal relationships with peers and teachers
3. Age-inappropriate behaviors or feelings in response to normal circumstances

4. Pervasive mood of unhappiness or depression

5. Tendencies to develop physical symptoms in response to personal problems or problems at school

Although the category of emotional disturbance includes schizophrenia, children who are socially maladjusted are excluded from this category, unless it can be determined that they have an emotional disturbance.

Center for Mental Health Services (CMHS). The CMHS is a federal agency that provides mental health services for children under 18 years of age. According to CMHS, service is provided to children and youth who present with a diagnosable mental, behavioral, or emotional disorder meeting criteria set out in the *DSM-IV-TR.* The disorder must also meet criteria of duration and functional impairment as defined in the *DSM-IV-TR.*

Social Security Administration (SSA). The federal guidelines of the SSA define a mental condition as one that can be medically proven and that results in marked and severe functional limitations of substantial duration.

DSM-IV-TR. Given descriptions in the IDEA, it is possible that children who qualify under the category of emotional disturbance may be found in the *DSM-IV-TR* disorders represented by internalizing disorders, such as mood disorders, anxiety disorders, or somatic disorders; or by externalizing disorders, such as oppositional defiant disorder or conduct disorder. Although schizophrenia is a category recognized by the *DSM-IV-TR,* it is very rare in children. Diagnostic criteria for some of the more common types of emotional disturbance in children and youth can be found in Appendix D.

Council for Exceptional Children. The Council for Exceptional Children has lobbied for a new and improved definition that changes the label from emotional disturbance to emotional or behavioral disorder (EBD) and defines the disorder as a condition in which behavioral or emotional response is so different from the generally accepted, age-appropriate, ethnic, or cultural norms as to adversely affect self-care, social relationships, personal adjustments, academic progress, classroom behavior, or work adjustment. Despite strong support, the definition has not been incorporated into the latest revisions of IDEA.

National Mental Health and Special Education Coalition. The coalition has also actively lobbied for changes in the federal definition of emotional disturbance. The National Association of School Psychologists has adopted and endorsed the definition put forth by this group (NASP, 2005). This definition adopts the label of emotional or behavioral disorder (EBD) for responses that are so different from expectations (age, cultural, or ethnic norms) that they adversely compromise educational performance. The responses are demonstrated in more than one setting (at least one of which is school related) and are unresponsive to direct intervention in a general educational setting. EBD can coexist with other disabilities. The category may include schizophrenia, affective disorders, anxiety disorders, or other sustained disturbances of conduct or adjustment.

ISSUES IN THE DEFINITION AND CLASSIFICATION OF CHILDREN AND ADOLESCENTS WITH EMOTIONAL DISTURBANCE

The IDEA definition of emotional disturbance is highly controversial and is problematic for several reasons. First, although the category of emotional disturbance would apply to children who have evidence of internalizing disorders, such as anxiety, depression, or withdrawal (sometimes referred to as a behavior deficit), the definition also applies to an extent to those children who experience externalizing disorders (such as problems of aggression, defiance, and conduct, sometimes referred to as a behavioral excess).

However, because IDEA does not consider children who exhibit socially maladaptive behaviors as part of this category, this definition has led some states to exclude children with conduct disorder from identification within this category, since they interpret behaviors directed toward the violation of the rights of others to be an example of socially maladaptive behavior, while other states consider these behaviors as part of the category (Gonzalez, 1991). The problem is intensified by the fact that children with conduct disorder represent one of the largest diagnostic groups. Wide variations in rates of reporting children within the category of emotional disturbance or serious emotional disturbance (Connecticut reported 2.06% with SED in 1996, and Arkansas reported 0.09%) suggest different qualification criteria as well as the severity of children included (MacMillan, 1998).

Second, terms used to define duration (long period of time) and intensity (marked degree) are not operationally defined and provide no guidelines for measurement. Third, although states must designate criteria that do not conflict with the federal guidelines of IDEA, there is wide interpretive leeway in how emotional disturbance is defined by various states (McInerney, Kane, & Pelavin, 1992). In addition, some states have adopted labels other than emotional disturbance for this category, and labels of behavior disordered (BD) or emotionally and behaviorally disordered (EBD) have been frequently substituted.

Fourth, studies have demonstrated that children with labels of serious emotional disturbance (SED) are not a homogenous population (Rosenblatt & Furlong, 1998; Walrath, Nickerson, Crowel, & Leaf, 1998), and investigators have questioned the usefulness of labels such as SED and EBD with respect to defining treatments (Kershaw & Sonuga-Barke, 1998). One study by Duncan, Forness, and Harsough (1995) suggests that the LD label may be the preferred starting point for intervention and often the first label of choice regardless of the nature of the problem. In their investigation, they found that the majority of children labeled as SED were initially classified as LD, until the requirement for more intensive service resulted in reclassification.

Attention-Deficit/Hyperactivity Disorder

Educational Definition of ADHD. The most recent revision of IDEA has added "attention deficit disorder" and "attention deficit hyperactivity disorder (ADHD)" to the list of disabilities. Prior to this change in regulations, children with ADHD were able to receive special education assistance under Section 504 of the Rehabilitation Act of 1973, a broader piece of antidiscrimination legislation. Children with ADHD can now be deemed disabled under the category of Other Health Impairments, which are defined as "having limited strength, vitality or alertness, including a heightened alertness to environment stimuli, that results in limited alertness with respect to the educational environment" (IDEA, 2004). Other disabilities in the same category include acute health problems such as asthma, diabetes, epilepsy, a heart condition, hemophilia, lead poisoning, leukemia, and rheumatic fever. A diagnosis of ADHD alone does not guarantee services under IDEA. The ADHD must adversely affect education to warrant special education.

Issues in the Definition and Classification of Children and Adolescents With ADHD. Children with ADHD often have comorbid features of emotional or behavioral disturbance and learning disabilities. Children with ADHD may also qualify under other IDEA categories, such as LD or EBD. At early developmental levels, ADHD features may overlap and share symptom features of developmental delay, a noncategorical option of IDEA available for children 3 to 9 years of age. Problems exist concerning how to assess children with ADHD, and high rates of overlap in symptoms between ADHD and other disorders/conditions (anxiety, abuse, posttraumatic stress disorder, etc.).

REFERENCES

Achenbach, T. M., & Rescorla, L. A. (2001). *Manual for the ASEBA School-Age Forms & Profiles.* Burlington, VT: ASEBA.

American Association on Intellectual and Developmental Disabilities. (2009a). *Intellectual disability: Definition, classification and systems of support* (11th ed.). Washington, DC: Author.

American Association on Intellectual and Developmental Disabilities. (2009b). Intellectual disability. Retrieved December 20, 2009, from http://www.aaidd.org/intellectualdisabilitybook/content_2348.cfm?navID = 267

Duncan, B. B., Forness, S. R., & Harsough, C. (1995). Students identified as seriously emotionally disturbed in day treatment: Cognitive, psychiatric and special education characteristics. *Behavioral Disorders, 20,* 238–252.

Gonzalez, P. (1991). *A comparison of state policy of the federal definition and a proposed definition of "serious emotional disturbance."* Washington, DC: National Association of State Directors of Special Education.

Kaufman, A. S., & Lichtenberger, E. O. (2000). *Essentials of WISC-III and WPPSI-R assessment.* New York: John Wiley.

Kavale, K. A. (2005). Identifying specific learning disability: Is response to intervention the answer? *Journal of Learning Disabilities, 38,* 553–562.

Kavale, K., Forness, S., & MacMillan, D. L. (1998). The politics of learning disabilities: A rejoinder. *Learning Disability Quarterly, 21,* 306–317.

Kavale, K. A., Holdnack, J., Mostert, M. P., & Schmied, C. M. (2003, December). *The feasibility of a responsiveness to intervention approach for the identification of specific learning disability: A psychometric alternative.* Paper presented at the National Research Center on Learning Disabilities Responsiveness-to-Intervention Symposium, Kansas City, MO.

Kershaw, P., & Sonuga-Barke, E. (1998). Emotional and behavioral difficulties: Is this a useful category? The implications of clustering and comorbidity, the relevance of a taxonomic approach. *Educational and Child Psychology, 15,* 45–55.

MacMillan, D. L., & Forness, S. R. (1998). The role of IQ in special education placement decisions: Primary and determinative or peripheral and inconsequential. *Remedial and Special Education, 19,* 239–253.

MacMillan, D. L., Gresham, F. M., & Bocian, K. M. (1998). Current plight of borderline students: Where do they belong? *Education and Training in Mental Retardation and Developmental Disabilities, 33,* 83–95.

MacMillan, D. L., & Reschly, D. J. (1998). Over-representation of minority students: The case for greater specificity or reconsideration of the variables examined. *Journal of Special Education, 19,* 239–253.

MacMillan, R. C. (1998). A longitudinal study of the cost effectiveness of educating students with emotional or behavioral disorders in a public school setting. *Behavioral Disorders, 25,* 65–75.

Mastropieri, M. A., & Scruggs, T. E. (2005). Feasibility and consequences of response to intervention: Examination of the issues and scientific evidence as a model for the identification of individuals with learning disabilities. *Journal of Learning Disabilities, 38,* 525–531.

Mather, N., & Gregg, N. (2006). Specific learning disabilities: Clarifying, not eliminating a construct. *Professional Psychology: Research and Practice, 37,* 99–106.

McInerney, M., Kane, M., & Pelavin, S. (1992). *Services to children with serious emotional disturbance.* Washington, DC: Pelavin Associates.

National Association of School Psychologists (NASP). (2005). *Position statement on students with emotional and behavioral disorders.* Retrieved December 20, 2009, from http://www.nasponline.org/about_nasp/pospaper_sebd.aspx).

National Joint Committee on Learning Disabilities. (1987). Learning disabilities: Issues on definition. *Journal of Learning Disabilities, 20,* 107–108.

Oswald, D. P., Coutinho, M. J., Best, A. M., & Nguyen, N. (2001). The impact of socio-demographic characteristics on the identification rates of minority students as mentally retarded. *Mental Retardation, 39,* 351–367.

Reynolds, C. R., & Kamphaus, R. W. (2004). *BASC2: Behavior Assessment System for Children manual.* Circle Pines, MN: American Guidance Service.

Rosenblatt, J. A., & Furlong, M. J. (1998). Outcomes in a system of care for youth with emotional and behavioral disorders: An examination of differential change across clinical profile. *Journal of Child and Family Studies, 7,* 1217–1232.

Rourke, B. P. (1989). *Nonverbal learning disabilities: The syndrome and the model.* New York: Guilford.

Rourke, B. P. (2000). Neuropsychological and psycho-social subtyping: A review of investigations within the University of Windsor laboratory. *Canadian Psychology, 41,* 34–51.

Sattler, J. (2002). *Assessment of children: Behavioral and clinical applications* (4th ed.). San Diego, CA: Author.

Semrud-Clikeman, M. (2005). Neuropsychological aspects for evaluating learning disabilities. *Journal of Learning Disabilities, 38,* 563–568.

Walrath, C., Nickerson, K., Crowel, R., & Leaf, P. (1998). Serving children with serious emotional disturbance in a system of care. Do mental health and non–mental health agency referrals look the same? *Journal of Emotional and Behavioral Disorders, 6,* 205–213.

Guidelines to the Interpretation of Test Scores and Assessment Information

INTERPRETING STANDARD SCORES

Scores for most intelligence tests, like the Wechsler Intelligence Scale for Children (WISC-IV) and the Differential Abilities Scale (DAS-2); standardized academic assessments, such as the Woodcock Johnston Academic Assessment (WJACIII) and Wide Range Achievement Test (WRAT-IV); and measures of adaptive functioning (Vineland Adaptive Behavior Scales) are based on standard scores derived from the standard normal distribution. The standard normal distribution has an average score of 100 and a standard deviation of 15. On these assessment instruments, approximately 68% of the population will score within one standard deviation of the mean (scores ranging between 85 and 115). The normal curve is a bell-shaped distribution with the most intense concentration of individuals in the middle of the curve, and progressively less population represented under the curve toward the end points. The normal curve, standard deviations, and standard scores are presented in Figure AC.1.

Intelligence and Standard Scores

The average IQ score is 100, and approximately 68% of the population will obtain an IQ score between 85 and 115. Scores that range from 80–89 are considered to be within the "low average" of intelligence, while scores above 115 but below 125 are considered to be in the "high average" range.

As we progress to the left of center, individuals who score two standard deviations below the mean would obtain an IQ of 70, which is the cutoff point for a diagnosis of mental retardation. Individuals who score at this level are in the bottom 2% of the population.

Figure AC.1 Standard Normal Distribution IQ Scores and T Scores

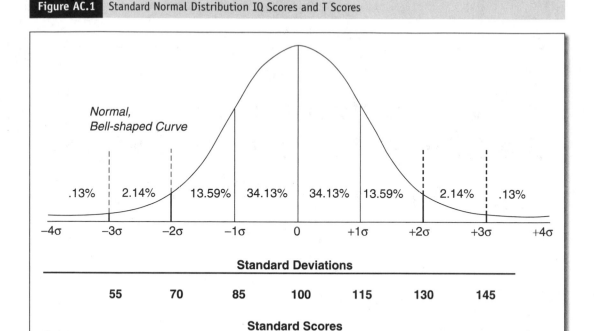

Approximately 2% of the population will obtain an IQ between 55 and 70, which would be considered in the mild range of mental retardation, intellectually. Individuals who score below an IQ of 55 (less than .13%) would be at the threshold of more severe levels of mental retardation (moderate retardation IQ 35–40 to 50–55; severe retardation 20–25 to 35–40; and profound mental retardation, below IQ of 20–25). In order to be diagnosed with mental retardation, the *DSM-IV-TR* (APA, 2000) requires an IQ of approximately 70 (+ or – 5, for standard error of measure), impairments in at least two areas of adaptive functioning (e.g., work, leisure, communication skills, self-care, health and safety, etc.), and onset before the age of 18.

As we progress to the right of center, individuals who score two standard deviations above the mean would obtain an IQ score of 130, which is usually the cut point for "gifted" status for most gifted programs and is at the 98th percentile. Mensa is a society for gifted individuals that has been in existence since 1946. The word *mensa* comes from the Latin word for *table* and was chosen to stand for a round-table society whose only criteria for acceptance was to achieve a score at or above the 98th percentile on a standard test of intelligence (retrieved August 9, 2009, from http://www.mensa.org/index0.php?page=10). Individuals who score at an IQ of 140 are at the top .13% of the population.

Assessments of Adaptive Functioning and Standard Scores

According to the *DSM-IV-TR* (APA, 2000), *adaptive functioning* "refers to how effectively individuals cope with common life demands and how well they meet the standards of personal independence expected of someone in their particular age group, sociocultural background and community setting" (p. 42). For a diagnosis of mental retardation, in addition to deficits in IQ noted previously, the child must also demonstrate impaired adaptive functioning in at least two of the following areas: communication, self-care, home living, social/interpersonal skills, use of community resources, self-direction, functional academic skills, work, leisure, and health and safety. Adaptive scales, such as the Vineland Adaptive Behavior Scales and the AAMR Adaptive Behavior Scale-School (ABS-S:2), provide standard scores for adaptive behaviors in a number of different domains, such as communication, daily living, and socialization. As well as standard scores, the scales also provide scale scores ranging from 0 to 18, with the average scores being 10, which is at the 50th percentile. The assessment results for Arthur in Appendix B provide examples of test scores for adaptive functioning.

Academic Assessments and Standard Scores

There are several methods of assessing academic functioning, including *curriculum-based assessments, or CBA* (comparing a student's current level of functioning relative to where they should be, given curricula for their current grade placement), and *standardized academic assessments* (comparing student performance relative to norms established for other students of the same age group based on national samples). Similar to intelligence scores, the vast majority of the population (68%) would be expected to score within one standard deviation of the norm (100), which would be represented by a range of standard scores from 85 to 115.

Through the use of standard scores, it is possible to compare intelligence scores (IQ) to academic scores based on the same standard unit of measure (standard scores). In this way, it can be determined whether students are achieving academically at the same levels that would be predicted given their IQ score. For example, if a student achieved an IQ score of 100, then it would be anticipated that academic scores should be within the range of 85 to 115 (within one standard deviation of the norm). If, on the other hand, a student with an IQ of 125 produces an academic score in a given subject area (e.g., reading, written expression, or mathematics) well below this level (e.g., reading standard score is 85), then we know there is a significant difference between these two scores.

Discrepancy Criterion: In the discussion of learning disorders, the *DSM-IV-TR* (APA, 2000) suggests that a discrepancy between IQ and achievement scores is considered to be significant if it is "*substantially below*" and it "is usually defined as a discrepancy of more than 2 standard deviations between achievement and IQ" (p. 49). In our previous example, if an individual obtained an IQ of 125, then a significant discrepancy would exist if achievement scores were below 95 (125 – 30). The discrepancy criterion has been used historically to determine if children qualified for assistance as learning disabled; however, as will be discussed at greater length in Appendix D, the latest revision of the Individuals with Disabilities Education Improvement Act (IDEA, 2005) has made it possible for an alternative criteria, known as *Response to Intervention (RTI)*, to be used by school districts to identify children with learning disabilities.

INTERPRETING T SCORES

Scores for most behavioral rating scales (Achenbach ASEBA Scales; BASC-2; Conners Scales), response inventories (Beck Inventory, Childhood Depression Scale), and personality inventories are based on T scores derived from the T score normal distribution. The T score distribution has an average score of 50 and a standard deviation of 10. On these assessment instruments, the majority of the population will score within one standard deviation of the mean (scores ranging between 40 and 60). Scores at or above a T score of 65 represent functioning at the 95th percentile and these individuals are often seen to be at risk of developing more serious difficulties and in need of monitoring. Individuals scoring at or above a T score of 70 are considered to be in the clinically significant range and in need of immediate intervention. The T score distribution is also available in Figure AC.1.

Description of Individual Assessment Instruments and Resources

Achenbach, T. M., & Rescorla, L. A. (2001). *Manual for the Achenbach System of Empirically Based Assessment: ASEBA School-Age Forms and Profiles.* Burlington, VT: University of Vermont Research Center for Children, Youth, & Families.

Comment: Revised and re-normed in 2001, this scale has parent, teacher, and youth self-report versions (for youth 11 years and older). The ASEBA rating scales measure behaviors on eight syndrome scales: Anxious/Depressed, Withdrawn/Depressed, Somatic Complaints, Social Problems, Thought Problems, Attention Problems, Rule-Breaking Behavior, and Aggressive Behavior. Composite scores are also available for Total Internalizing, Total Externalizing, and Total Problems. The revised version also contains six *DSM*-oriented scales, including Affective Problems, Anxiety Problems, Somatic Complaints, Attention Deficit/Hyperactivity Problems, Oppositional Defiant Problems, and Conduct Problems.

Barkley, R. A. (1987). *Defiant children: Parent-teacher assignments.* New York: Guilford.

Barkley, R. A. (1997). *Defiant children: A clinician's manual for assessment and parent training* (2nd ed.). New York: Guilford.

Comment: Contains many excellent resources and handouts for parents, as well as scales and parent and teacher questionnaires.

Beck, A., Beck, J., & Jolly, J. (2005). *The Beck Youth Inventories of Emotional and Social Impairment (BYI).* San Antonio, TX: Psychological Corporation.

Comment: Five brief (20-item) self-report scales measuring Self-Concept, Depression, Anxiety, Anger, and Disruptive Behavior, in children and youth, from 7 years of age.

Borum, R., Bartel, P., & Forth, A. E. (2002). *Manual for the Structured Assessment of Violence Risk in Youth: SAVRY. Consultation version.* Tampa: University of South Florida, Florida Mental Health Institute.

Comment: The SAVRY is intended for youth 12 to 18 years of age and comprises 24 items representing three risk domains (Historical Risk Factors, Social/Contextual Risk Factors, and Individual/Clinical Factors). Each risk item has a three-level rating structure with specific rating guidelines (low, moderate, or high). In addition to the 24 risk factors, the SAVRY also includes six Protective Factor items that are rated as either *present* or *absent.*

Conners, C. K. (1998). *Conners Rating Scales-revised technical manual.* North Tonawanda, NY: Multi-Health Systems.

Comment: Contains long and short versions of parent and teacher rating forms for attentional and behavioral problems. Manual also provides information about the Conners-Wells Self Report Scale for Adolescents (C. K. Conners & K. Wells, 1997). Scales provide T score ratings for the type of ADHD (Inattentive, Hyperactive-Impulsive), as well as many behaviors often associated with the disorder, including oppositional, cognitive, anxious-shy, perfectionistic, emotional lability, and social problems.

Conners, C. K. (2008). *Conners 3rd edition (Conners 3).* North Tonawanda, NY: Multi-Health Systems.

Comment: This updated version has added new items and scales to the parent, teacher, and child self-report forms, including empirical scales for executive functioning, learning problems, aggression, peer relations, and family relations. Items for oppositional defiant disorder (ODD) and conduct disorder (CD) have been added to the *DSM-IV-TR* symptom scales, in addition to a number of validity scales.

Dunn, L. M., & Dunn, L. M. (1997). *Peabody Picture Vocabulary Test—third edition.* Circle Pines, MN: American Guidance Service.

Elliott, C. D. (2007). *Differential Ability Scales, second edition (DAS II).* San Antonio, TX: Psychological Corporation.

Comment: Two versions of the scale are available: preschool-age level (2 years 6 months to 5 years 11 months) and school-age level (6 years to 17 years 11 months). Scores are provided for Verbal Ability, Nonverbal Ability, Spatial Ability, and General Conceptual Ability (GCA). The Early Years Form allows for the tabulation of a Special Nonverbal Composite for children whose verbal skills would significantly lower their overall conceptual score.

Gardner, D. M. (1991). *The Eating Disorder Inventory-2.* Odessa, FL: Psychological Assessment Resources.

Comment: A 91-item self-report scale measuring traits associated with eating disorders; it yields eight scales, such as Body Dissatisfaction, Drive for Thinness, and Perfectionism.

Gilliam, J. E. (1995). *Gilliam Autism Rating Scale: GARS.* Austin, TX: Pro-Ed.

Comment: Autism quotient derived from ratings on four scales: Stereotyped Behaviors, Communication, Social Interaction, and Developmental.

Gioia, G. A., Isquith, P. K., Guy, S. C., & Kenworthy, L. (2000). *The Behavior Rating Inventory of Executive Function: BRIEF professional manual.* Odessa, FL: Psychological Assessment Resources.

Comment: The BRIEF is a rating scale completed by parents and teachers that provides information about executive functions in two broad areas: Behavior Rating Index (impulse control, shifting between tasks, and modulation of emotional responses), and Metacognitive Index (task initiation, working memory, planning/organization, organizing materials, and self-monitoring). A Global Executive Composite can be derived from scores obtained on the two broad scales. In addition to the clinical scales, there are also scales to calculate inconsistency and negativity.

Goodman, W., Rasmussen, S., & Price, L. (1988). *The Children's Yale Brown Obsessive Compulsive Scale (CY-BOCS).* New Haven, CT: Connecticut Mental Health Center, Clinical Neuroscience Research Unit.

Guy, S. C., Isquith, P. K., & Gioia, G. A. (2004). *BRIEF self-report professional manual: Brief-SRl.* Odessa, FL: Psychological Assessment Resources.

Comment: This self-report scale comprises 80 items that measure behaviors and cognitive functioning in areas similar to those measured by the BRIEF. It is suitable for individuals from 11 to 18 years of age.

Jesness, C. F. (1988). *JBC: Jesness Behavior Checklist.* North Tonawanda, NY: Multi-Health Systems.

Comment: A multiple rating scale for youth (13 to 20 years) at risk for antisocial behavior. Self-Report and Observer Rating Scale measures behavior across 14 scales, including Social Control, Anger Control, and Conformity.

Jesness, C. F. (2003). *Jesness Inventory-Revised (JI-R).* North Tonawanda, NY: Multi-Health Systems.

Comment: Self-report scale for youth measuring 11 personality traits (e.g., social maladjustment, immaturity, alienation, withdrawal-depression, denial) and 9 subtype scales (e.g., undersocialized aggressive, conformist/immature, pragmatist/manipulator, introspective/neurotic). In addition, there are two *DSM-IV* scales providing ratings for conduct disorder (CD) and oppositional defiant disorder (ODD).

Kazdin, A. E., Rodgers, A., & Colbus, D. (1986). The Hopelessness Scale for Children: Psychometric characteristics and concurrent validity. *Journal of Consulting and Clinical Psychology, 54,* 241–245.

Comment: A 17-item true/false questionnaire measuring hopelessness based on future expectations. Research supports hopelessness as a correlate of depression and suicide.

Kovacs, M. (1992). *Child Depression Inventory.* North Tonawanda, NY: Multi-Health Systems.

Comment: Self-report measure for children and youth 7 to 17 years of age. In addition to a Total Depression score, the scale rates depressive symptoms in five areas: Negative Mood, Interpersonal Problems, Ineffectiveness, Anhedonia, and Negative Self-Esteem.

Lachar, D., & Gruber, C. P. (1995). *Personality Inventory for Youth (PIY) manual.* Los Angeles: Western Psychological Services.

Comment: Objective, multidimensional, self-report measure for children and youth 9 to 18 years of age. Assesses emotional and behavioral adjustment, family and school impressions, and academic adjustment. Includes validity and consistency scales.

Lambert, N., Nihira, K., & Leland, H. (1993). *ABS-S:2: The Adaptive Behavior Scale–School* (2nd ed.). Austin, TX: Pro-Ed.

Comment: Rating scale to assess adaptive functioning and maladaptive behaviors in children and youth.

Myles, B. S., Bock, S. J., & Simpson, R. L. (2001). *ASDS: Asperger Syndrome Diagnostic Scale examiner's manual*. Austin, TX: Pro-Ed.

Comment: Asperger's quotient derived from ratings on five scales: Language, Social, Maladaptive, Cognitive, and Sensorimotor.

Naglieri, J. A., LeBuffe, P. A., & Pfeiffer, S. I. (1994). *The Devereaux Scales of Mental Disorders: DSMD manual*. San Antonio, TX: The Psychological Corporation.

Comment: The DSMD measures functioning in six areas, which represent three composite scales: Externalizing (conduct, attention), Internalizing (anxiety, depression), and Critical Pathology (autism, acute problems). In addition, there is a Total DSMD score for total functioning.

Newcomer, P. L., et al. (1994). *DAYS: Depression and Anxiety in Youth Scale*. Austin, TX: Pro-Ed.

Comment: Parent, teacher, and child self-report scale with 22 items (true/false format) suitable for children and youth 6 to 19 years old.

Reich, W., Welner, Z., Herjanic, B., & MHS Staff. (1997). *Diagnostic Interview for Children and Adolescents computer program (DICA-IV)*. North Tonawanda, NY: Multi-Health System.

Reynolds, C. R., & Kamphaus, R. W. (2004). *Behavior Assessment System for Children: BASC-2 manual*. Circle Pines, MN: American Guidance Service.

Comment: Multiple informant (parent, teacher, child) rating scales for adaptive and maladaptive behaviors, from 2 years to adolescence. Includes validity indexes to screen for excessive positive or negative response profiles. Composite scales include Adaptive Skills, Behavioral Symptoms Index, Externalizing, Internalizing, and School Problems. The composite scores are calculated from numerous *Primary* (depression, learning, withdrawal, anxiety) and *Content* scales (anger control, resiliency, etc.).

Reynolds, C. R., & Richmond, B. O. (2008). *Revised Child Manifest Anxiety Scale-2*. Los Angeles: Western Psychological Services.

Comment: This 49-item scale can be administered to children 6 to 19 years of age and measures anxiety in four different areas: Physiological Anxiety, Worry, Social Anxiety, and Defensiveness. The scale also includes an inconsistent responding index.

Sattler, J. M. (2001). *Assessment of Children: Cognitive Applications* (4th ed.). La Mesa, CA: Jerome M. Sattler.

Sattler, J. M. (2002). *Assessment of Children: Behavioral and Clinical Applications* (4th ed.). La Mesa, CA: Jerome M. Sattler.

Sparrow, S. S., Balla, D. A., & Cicchetti, D. V. (1984). *Vineland Adaptive Behavior Scales*. Circle Pines, MN: American Guidance Service.

Comment: Interview format. Measures adaptive behavior in four areas: Communication, daily living skills, socialization, and motor skills.

Wechsler, D. (2002). *Manual for the Wechsler Intelligence Scale for Children–WISC-IV.* San Antonio, TX: Psychological Corporation.

Comment: The Wechsler Intelligence Scale for Children (WISC-IV) is in its fourth revision. Currently, the WISC-IV has four major scales: Verbal Comprehension, Perceptual Reasoning, Working Memory, and Processing Speed. The Verbal Comprehension score reflects one's ability to think in the abstract, vocabulary development, and social judgment. Perceptual Reasoning requires visual conceptual skills, the analysis and synthesis of visual information (block designs), and reasoning with abstract visual designs. Working Memory measures the ability to concentrate without distraction while mentally manipulating information. Processing Speed predicts how quickly one can complete paper-and-pencil tasks.

Wilkinson, G. S., & Robertson, G. J. (2006). *The Wide Range Achievement Test: WRAT 4, administration manual.* Wilmington, DE: Wide Range.

Comment: This test provides standard scores, percentiles, and grade levels for academic performance in areas of word reading, sentence comprehension, reading composite, spelling, and math computation.

Woodcock, R. W., McGrew, K. S., & Mather, N. (2001). *Woodcock-Johnson III, Tests of Achievement.* New York: Riverside.

Comment: The WJIII Ach provides scores for academic performance in 22 different areas, from letter-word identification, to punctuation and capitalization. Scores can be calculated in a variety of ways to provide composite academic information. For example, Broad Reading is calculated based on scores for letter-word identification, reading fluency, and passage comprehension; Broad Math includes scores for calculation, math fluency, and applied problems.

Woodcock, R. W., McGrew, K. S., & Mather, N. (2001). *Woodcock-Johnson III, Tests of Cognitive Function.* New York: Riverside.

Comment: The WJIII Cog consists of 20 tests that measure processing in areas of verbal comprehension, visual/auditory learning, and auditory working memory.

The *DSM-IV-TR* (APA, 2000) Diagnostic Guidelines

CONTENTS

Anxiety Disorders (DSM-IV-TR; APA, 2000)

Type of Anxiety	Symptom Criteria		
Adjustment Disorder With Anxiety (p. 683)			
Temporary response to identified stressor.	[] Nervousness [] Worry	[] Fears of separation from caregivers	
Specific Phobias (pp. 449–450)			
Persistent, irrational fear of object or event: animals, environmental (heights, storms), situational (airplanes, school), injection/blood.	[] Exposure to event causes anxiety (possible panic attack) [] Children may not recognize fear is irrational [] Situation/event is avoided to prevent intense anxiety response [] Lasting at least 6 months		
Separation Anxiety Disorder (p. 125)			
Intense avoidance and fear of separation from home or caregiver, plus 3 from following 8 symptoms, lasting at least 4 weeks.	[] Separation causes intense distress [] Fear harm will come to caregiver	[] Worry over future separations [] School refusal [] Fear of being alone	[] Fear of sleeping alone [] Nightmares about separation [] Physical complaints
General Anxiety Disorder (p. 476)			
Intense worries about family, friends, school, etc., lasting at least 6 months. Anxiety & worry associated with at least 3 symptoms, only 1 in children.	[] Overly restless, on edge	[] Problems sleeping [] Tension in muscles [] Irritable	[] Problems with concentration [] Tires easily, fatigued
Obsessive Compulsive Disorder (OCD; pp. 462–463)			
Persistent thoughts (obsessions) drive repetitive behaviors (compulsions) and preoccupations in a number of possible areas (at least 1 hour a day).	[] Fear of contamination [] Excessive cleanliness [] Excess washing, teeth brushing	[] Order, symmetry [] Obsessive neatness [] Safety (check doors, locks) [] Repetitive rituals	[] Hoarding, collecting useless objects [] Compulsive list making

Type of Anxiety	Symptom Criteria		
Social Phobia (p. 456)			
Pervasive fear of embarrassment in social or performance situation. Children must show appropriate with familiar peers and adults, for at least 6 months (if under 18 years).	[] Avoids social situations [] Exposure increases anxiety (tantrums)	[] Avoidance interferes with normal routines [] Exposure may cause panic attacks	[] Fear may result in tremors, blushing [] Discomfort in social situations
Panic Attacks (p. 432)			
Intense feeling of fear, panic; arises suddenly and peaks within 10 minutes. Accompanies many disorders. Four or more symptoms.	[] Palpitations [] Sweating [] Trembling [] Choking	[] Dizziness [] Urge to escape [] Loss of control [] Depersonalization	[] Breathing problems [] Chest pain [] Numbing [] Chills
Posttraumatic Stress Disorder (PTSD; pp. 467–468)			
Response to experiencing or witnessing traumatic event; **and** feelings of fear, helplessness, or horror; children may appear disorganized and agitated. With at least 1 symptom of reexperiencing, 3 symptoms of avoidance and numbing, 2 symptoms of increased arousal. Lasting at least 1 month.	Reexperiencing: [] Repetitive trauma play [] Dreams of monsters, or rescue [] Distress to triggers of event [] Flashbacks	Avoidance and Numbing: [] Detachment [] Diminished interest [] Flat affect [] Belief foresee future [] Can't recall event [] Avoid activities associated with event	Increased Arousal: [] Sleep problems [] Irritable/angry outbursts [] Hypervigilance [] Concentration problems [] Startle response

Attention-Deficit/Hyperactivity Disorder: ADHD (*DSM-IV-TR*; APA, 2000, pp. 92–93)

Three Types

1. Predominantly Inattentive (6 symptoms)

2. Predominantly Hyperactive-Impulsive (6 symptoms)

3. Combined Type (12 symptoms; meet criteria for both 1 & 2)

Six Symptoms From Inattention	*Six Symptoms From Hyperactivity-Impulsivity*	
Inattention	**Hyperactivity**	**Impulsivity**
[] Poor attention to details (misses key parts of information)	[] Fidgets, squirmy	[] Problems waiting turn
[] Problems sustaining attention in boring/repetitive tasks	[] Problems remaining seated when required to sit	[] Blurting out answers
[] High level of distractibility; distractions interfere with task completion	[] Runs, climbs, excessively (or restlessness if a teenager)	[] Intrusive, interrupts others
[] Insufficient attention to details and organizational framework	[] Loud play and problems playing quietly	
[] Doesn't "seem" to listen	[] Always on the go, driven like a motor	
[] Problems organizing information	[] Excessive talking	
[] Avoids and dislikes tasks requiring sustained mental effort		
[] Forgetfulness		
[] Loss of tools required to accomplish tasks (misplaces notes, pens, pencils, books, etc.)		
Additional Criteria [] Some symptoms present before age 7 [] Symptoms evident in more than one setting		
Other Possible Symptoms [] Problems with sleep [] Anxious [] Irritable [] Accident prone	[] Depression [] Physical complaints [] Oppositional defiant [] Poor sense of time	[] Aggression [] Social skills [] Learning problems [] Sluggish tempo

Autism and Asperger's Disorder: Pervasive Developmental Disorders (*DSM-IV-TR*; APA, 2000, pp. 75, 84)

Autism Only Qualitative Impairment in Communication At least 2 symptoms	Autism & Asperger's Disorder Qualitative Impairment in Social Interaction At least 1 symptom	Autism & Asperger's Disorder Restrictive, Repetitive, or Stereotyped Behaviors At least 1 symptom
[] Delay or lack of speech — lack of speech-related gestures	[] Lack of nonverbal behavior — lack of social gestures — lack of eye contact — flat facial expression	[] Preoccupation with interests with intense focus — interest in dates, numbers — intense interest in one area (maps, dinosaurs, bottle caps)
[] Lack of initiating/sustaining speech — failure to maintain conversation — responds to questions inappropriately	[] Lack of appropriate peer relationships — remains aloof, standoffish — lacks understanding of social rules	[] Preoccupation with nonfunctional routines or rituals — lining up objects — using the same route every day
[] Stereotyped or repetitive speech — repeats or echoes words or phrases — odd monotone (robotlike) — uses "I" inappropriately — refers to self in third person	[] Does not engage in social referencing — does not spontaneously share — does not point or share interest in objects, activities — does not include others in activities	[] Repetitive and stereotyped mannerisms — hand flapping — twirling — clapping — rocking — swaying
[] Lack of typical play — lack of imitative play — lack of imaginative play — lack of make-believe play — lack of spontaneous play	[] Lack of social or emotional reciprocity — does not share feelings — does not share a smile — does not return a social gesture — prefers solitary activities — includes others only as mechanical aid — unaware of others' feelings or distress	[] Preoccupation with parts of objects — spinning a wheel on a car, or propeller on an airplane — buttons — opening and closing doors — attached to an inanimate object (button, rubberband)
Autism: Total of 6 symptoms from above, in all [] Onset prior to 3 years of age [] Abnormal functioning in at least one of three areas: (1) social interaction, (2) social communication, and 3) symbolic or imaginative play		*Asperger's Disorder: at least 3 symptoms from above* [] No significant delay in language [] No significant delay in cognitive or adaptive behavior [] Normally curious child
Other Possible Symptoms [] Stares blankly [] Walks on tiptoes [] Resists physical contact	[] Laughs or giggles inappropriately [] Highly resistant to any change in routine [] Tantrums when upset	[] Does not understand jokes [] Unreasonably fearful [] Easily frustrated [] Makes odd sounds

Behavior Problems and Disruptive Behavior Disorders (*DSM-IV-TR*; APA, 2000)

Type of Behavior Problem	*Symptom Examples/Criteria*		
Aggressive Behavior	[] Argues [] Gets into fights [] Talks back [] Overly critical of others [] Spreads rumors	[] Mean [] Demands attention [] Bullies/threatens [] Loses temper often [] Teases [] Not liked by others	[] Disobedient [] Disturbs others [] Easily excitable [] Loud [] Defiant
Oppositional Defiant Disorder: ODD (p. 102)	[] *Persistent, hostile, defiant, disobedient, and negative pattern of behaviors against authority figures* *Plus 4 from the following 8 symptoms*		
Lasting at least 6 months	[] Loss of temper [] Argumentative with adults [] Defiant, noncompliant	[] Deliberately annoying [] Blames others for mistakes or problems [] Touchy, easily irritated	[] Angry, resentful [] Spiteful, vindictive
Conduct Disorder: CD (pp. 98–99)	[] *Persistent pattern of violation of social norms or the rights of others,* *Plus 3 from the following 15 criteria*		
Childhood Onset Type: *At least one symptom is evident prior to 10 years of age* *Adolescent Onset Type:* *No symptoms evident prior to 10 years of age*	*Aggression* [] Bullies/threatens [] Initiates fights [] Use of weapon [] Cruelty others [] Cruelty animals [] Forced theft (mugging) [] Forced sex	*Deceit or Theft* [] Break-in (house, car) [] Cons others [] Theft (shoplifting) *Property Destruction* [] Fire setting [] Vandalism	*Rule Violations* [] Stayed out all night * [] Run away [] Frequent truancy * * *Evidence of occurrence prior to 13 years of age*

Intellectual Disabilities (formerly mental retardation; see note) (*DSM-IV-TR;* APA, 2000, p. 49)

	Symptom Criteria
	• Significant subaverage intellectual functioning (IQ of approximately 70) • Impairment in at least two areas of adaptive functioning: communication, self-care, home living, social/interpersonal skills, community resource use, self-direction, functional academics, work, leisure, health and safety • Onset prior to 18 years of age
Level of Severity: IQ Range	*Percentage of the IDD Population; Expectations*
Mild (IQ 50–55 to about 70)	85% of all IDD are in the mild range. Social, communication, and sensorimotor skills minimally impaired in preschool years. Start to show greater discrepancies from norm with age. Can master academics up to approximately Grade 6 level. Can master vocational skills with proper support and supervision.
Moderate (IQ 35–40 to 50–55)	10% of all IDD are in the moderate range. Most develop communication skills in early years. Can acquire academics up to approximately a Grade 2 level. Adolescents likely to experience problems socially. Unskilled or semiskilled work under supervision, or sheltered workshops.
Severe (IQ 20–25 to 35–40)	3% to 4% of all IDD are in the severe range. Little or no early communication skills. May develop language during school period. Academically, can learn to read some basic survival vocabulary. Close supervision, simple tasks, and likely live in group home.
Profound (IQ below 20 or 25)	1% to 2% of all IDD are in the profound range. Most have other neurological conditions. Impairments in early sensorimotor skills. May develop self-care, communication, and motor skills with intense supports and supervision.

Note: In the *DSM-IV-TR* (APA, 2000), the diagnostic category is mental retardation; however, the name has been changed to intellectual and developmental disabilities (IDD) by the American Association on Intellectual and Developmental Disabilities (AAIDD, 2007) from the American Association on Mental Retardation (AAMR). Further discussion of how the different systems classify IDD can be found in Appendix B.

Learning Disorders (*DSM-IV-TR*; APA, 2000)

General Definition	*General Criteria (see Note)*
Refers to learning problems detected by achievement on individually administered, standardized tests in reading, mathematics, or written expression	• Achievement is *substantially below* expectations, for age, schooling, and intelligence • Substantially below refers to discrepancy of more than 2 standard deviations between IQ and achievement (lesser discrepancy if clinical judgment of IQ score is somehow compromised) • Disorder significantly interferes with academic achievement or daily living • If sensory deficit exists (e.g., vision, hearing), learning disorder must be beyond what would be expected given deficit
Types of Learning Disorders	*Specific Criteria*
Reading Disorder (Dyslexia; p. 53): reading accuracy, speed, comprehension	• Achievement in reading is *substantially below* expectations for age, schooling, and intelligence • Disorder significantly interferes with academic achievement or daily living • If sensory deficit exists, reading problems are in excess of the expected
Mathematics Disorder (Discalculia; p. 54): math calculation, reasoning, understanding mathematical terms, operational signs, counting, learning mathematical steps or multiplication tables	• Achievement in math is *substantially below* expectations for age, schooling, and intelligence • Disorder significantly interferes with academic achievement or daily living • If sensory deficit exists, reading problems are in excess of the expected
Written Expression (Disgraphia; p. 56): punctuation, grammar, organization, multiple spelling errors, very poor handwriting; however, if only spelling or poor handwriting, diagnosis usually not applied	• Achievement in written expression is *substantially below* expectations, for age, schooling, and intelligence (since there are few standardized measures of written expression, may require a functional assessment) • Disorder significantly interferes with academic achievement or daily living • If sensory deficit exists, reading problems are in excess of the expected

Note: In the *DSM-IV-TR* (APA, 2000), the diagnostic category for learning disorders differs now from the educational classification for learning disability (LD), which no longer requires evidence of a significant discrepancy between IQ and achievement. Further discussion of how the different systems classify LD can be found in Appendix B.

Mood Disorders (*DSM-IV-TR*; APA, 2000)

Type of Mood Disorder	Symptom Criteria		
Adjustment Disorder With Depressed Mood (p. 683)			
Temporary reaction to identified stressor (6 months or less)	[] Tearfulness [] Irritability	[] Depressed mood [] Hopelessness	
Dysthymic Disorder: DD *Lasting at least 2 years (1 year in children; pp. 380–381)* Major Depressive Disorder: MDD *Lasting at least 2 weeks (p. 375)*	[] *Pervasive "irritable" mood (depressed mood state)* *or* [] *Loss of interest or pleasure*		
Dysthymic Disorder (DD) *Requires one of the above and at least 2 symptoms from list of 7* Major Depressive Disorder (MDD) *Requires one of the above and at least 4 symptoms from the list of 7*	[] Failure to meet expected weight/ height ratios; poor appetite [] Insomnia or hypersomnia	[] Excessive thoughts of worthlessness/ guilt; low self-esteem [] Poor concentration, attention, indecisive	[] Psychomotor agitation or lethargy [] Fatigue, loss of energy [] Suicidal thoughts/ feelings of hopelessness
Bipolar Disorder (p. 362)	[] *Abnormally elevated, expansive, or irritable mood* *Plus 3 from the following 7 symptoms*		
Meet criteria for MDD (see above) plus at least 3 or more manic symptoms for at least 1 week	[] Heightened self-esteem, grandiosity [] Decreased need for sleep	[] Flight of ideas [] Distractibility [] Increased goal-directed activity	[] Excessive need to talk, pressured speech [] Excessive high-risk activities (theft, spending)
Other Characteristics of Bipolar Disorder in Children	[] Aggression [] Goofy [] Explosive	[] Giddy [] Loss of temper	[] Mad/cranky [] Loss emotional control

Other Disorders Of Childhood (*DSM-IV- TR;* APA, 2000, pp. 127, 130)

Selective Mutism	
Description	*Criteria*
Failure to speak in specific social situations (e.g., in school, on playground), despite ability to speak in selected situations	• Failure to speak in specific situations • Disorder interferes with daily living, education, social interactions • Disorder has been in existence for more than 1 month, not counting the first month of school • Failure to speak is not related to speech problems, or understanding spoken language • Not due to a communication disorder (e.g., articulation, stuttering), pervasive developmental disorder, or psychotic disorder

Reactive Attachment Disorder of Infancy or Early Childhood	
Criteria	
A. Marked disturbance in social relatedness beginning before 5 years of age and associated with pathological care (abuse, neglect, etc.). Extreme neglect increases the risk. Disturbance is in form of either of the following types of behavioral responses:	
Inhibited Type: Failure to initiate and respond to social interactions in a developmentally appropriate way, evident in inhibited, hypervigilant, or highly ambivalent or contradictory (approach/avoidance, resistance to being comforted, freezing and staring).	Disinhibited Type: Indiscriminate social responsiveness/lack of selectivity of attachment figures: excessive familiarity with relative strangers, lack of selectivity in choosing attachment figures.
B. Above behaviors not the cause of developmental delay or part of pervasive developmental disorder.	
C. Pathogenic care evident in at least one of the following areas: • Chronic disregard for child's emotional needs (comfort, stimulation, affection) • Persistent failure to meet basic physical needs • Repeated changes in caregivers (e.g., repeated changes in foster care placements)	
D. Disturbance is the result of pathogenic care as stated in C.	

Index

Supporting researchers for more than 40 years

Research methods have always been at the core of SAGE's publishing program. Founder Sara Miller McCune published SAGE's first methods book, *Public Policy Evaluation*, in 1970. Soon after, she launched the *Quantitative Applications in the Social Sciences* series—affectionately known as the "little green books."

Always at the forefront of developing and supporting new approaches in methods, SAGE published early groundbreaking texts and journals in the fields of qualitative methods and evaluation.

Today, more than 40 years and two million little green books later, SAGE continues to push the boundaries with a growing list of more than 1,200 research methods books, journals, and reference works across the social, behavioral, and health sciences. Its imprints—Pine Forge Press, home of innovative textbooks in sociology, and Corwin, publisher of PreK–12 resources for teachers and administrators—broaden SAGE's range of offerings in methods. SAGE further extended its impact in 2008 when it acquired CQ Press and its best-selling and highly respected political science research methods list.

From qualitative, quantitative, and mixed methods to evaluation, SAGE is the essential resource for academics and practitioners looking for the latest methods by leading scholars.

For more information, visit **www.sagepub.com**.